SOCIOLOGY and American Social Issues

SOCIOLOGY and American Social Issues

Leonard Gordon
ARIZONA STATE UNIVERSITY

with

Patricia Atchison Harvey
COLORADO STATE UNIVERSITY

HOUGHTON MIFFLIN COMPANY/BOSTON

Dallas

Geneva, Illinois

Hopewell, New Jersey

Palo Alto

London

Copyright © 1978 by Houghton Mifflin Company

All rights reserved. No part of this work may be reproduced or transmitted in any form or by any means, electronic or mechanical, including photocopying and recording, or by any information storage or retrieval system, without permission in writing from the publisher.

Printed in the U.S.A.

Library of Congress Catalogue Card Number: 77-78577
ISBN: 0-395-25369-1

to R.J.F.G.

CONTENTS

Preface   xv

PART 1/Basic Sociological Concepts and Methods   1

CHAPTER 1/The Sociological Perspective   3
FOR WHOM THE BELL TOLLS   3
HOW SOCIOLOGISTS FEEL ABOUT SOCIAL PROBLEMS   4
The Applied Orientation   5
SOCIOLOGICAL CONSIDERATION OF SOCIAL PROBLEMS   5
Functions and Dysfunctions   5
Normalcy as Change   6
COMMON SENSE AND NONSENSE   7
THE NATURE OF SOCIOLOGY   8
Modern Beginnings of Sociology   8
Twentieth Century Developments   9
EMPLOYMENT OPPORTUNITIES IN SOCIOLOGY   11
THE QUESTION OF SOCIAL BEHAVIOR   12
Rural–Urban Migration   12
Pluralistic Society   13
SOCIAL POLICY AND SOCIOLOGY   14
Public and Private Social Policy   14
Sociology and Government   15
Sociology and Objective Analysis   16

SUMMARY   16
QUESTIONS FOR DISCUSSION   17
REFERENCES   17

CHAPTER 2/Basic Concepts: Culture, Socialization, and Social Organization   19

THE MAJOR CHARACTERISTICS OF SOCIETY   19
THE CONCEPT OF CULTURE   19
Values and Norms   20
Major American Value Themes   20
The Pervasive Influence of Culture   21
TWO CULTURALLY DIVERSE ADAPTATIONS TO THE ENVIRONMENT   22
A Study of Cultural Diversity   22
Cultural Diversity in the Gold Coast and the Chicago Slums   23
Ethnocentrism, Cultural Relativity, and Pluralism   27
Cultural Relativism and Cultural Pluralism   31
SOCIALIZATION   31
Development of the Social Self   31
Social Status   37
Role-Playing   40
SOCIAL ORGANIZATION TO MEET FUNCTIONAL NEEDS   43
The Social Fabric of Society   43
Types of Social Organization   44
The Functional Division of Labor   47
Territorially Based Groups   50
Groups With a Purpose   51
SUMMARY   52
Culture   52
Socialization into the Culture   52
Social Organization   53
QUESTIONS FOR DISCUSSION   53
REFERENCES   54

CHAPTER 3/The Basic Institutions of the Society   57

FUNCTIONS, DYSFUNCTIONS, AND INSTITUTIONS   57
FIVE UNIVERSAL INSTITUTIONS   58
Institutions as the Broadest Organized Social Structures   58
The Cultural Imperative for Effective Institutions   60
THE FAMILY   60
Universality of the Family   60
Functions of the Family   60
Structural Forms of the Family   65
Social Change and the Family   66
RELIGION   67
Universality of Religion   67
Functions of Religion   67
Structural Forms of Religion   69
Social Change and Religion   72
EDUCATION   72
Universality of Educational Institutions   72
Functions of Education   73
Structural Forms of Education   75
Social Change and Education   76
GOVERNMENT   80
Universality of Government   80
Functions of Government   80
Structural Forms of Government   80
Social Change and Government   83
THE ECONOMY   84
Universality of Economic Institutions   84
Functions of the Economy   85
Structural Forms of the Economy   86
Social Change and the Economy   90
SUMMARY   91
QUESTIONS FOR DISCUSSION   92
REFERENCES   93

CHAPTER 4/Methods of Inquiry: The Emphasis on Accuracy 99

THE NEED FOR ACCURACY 99
The Importance of Empiricism 99
Sociology and Other Research Disciplines 100
Verifying Assertions About Social Behavior 101
DISTINGUISHING FACT FROM OPINION 101
Detecting Biased Reporting 101
Checking Eyewitness Accounts 103
BACKGROUNDS TO SYSTEMATIC RESEARCH 104
Testing Simple Propositions 104
Descriptive and Analytic Research 105
Hypotheses and Experimental Research 105
Experimental and Control Groups 106
TOOLS OF THE TRADE 107
Observation 107
Interviews 108
Sampling 116
SAMPLING: MANY PATHS TO ONE GOAL 116
Nonprobability Samples 117
Probability Samples 117
The Use of Statistical Measures 118
Use of Available Data 121
Content Analysis 122
A Final Note on Tools of the Trade 124
SUMMARY 125
QUESTIONS FOR DISCUSSION 125
REFERENCES 126

PART 2/Issues Facing American Individuals 129

CHAPTER 5/Adolescence and the Life Cycle 131

ADOLESCENTS AND SOCIETY 131
THE PLACE OF ADOLESCENCE IN THE LIFE CYCLE 132
Characteristics of the Family Life Cycle 132
Adolescence as a Problem Period 133
Past Parental Experiences and Current Adolescent Realities 134
DEVELOPMENTAL TASKS OF THE ADOLESCENT YEARS 135
Lack of Clear Rites of Passage 135
Achieving a Sense of Self-Identity 136
Adolescent Rebelliousness 139
Adolescence as a Transitional Stage and as a Subculture 140
Contraculture and the Hippie Movement 141
Adolescent–Adult Attitude Differences 143
Dependence vs. Independence 146
ADOLESCENTS' RESPONSES TO THEIR POSITION IN SOCIETY 147
Rule-Breaking 147
Individual Deviance 148
Deviant Acts as Collective Behavior 149
Social Movements to Challenge the Status Quo 150
Legitimacy of Legal Protests 152
SOCIETAL ACCOMMODATION TO ADOLESCENT PROBLEMS 154
Historical Acceptance of Dissenting Views 154
Resistance vs. Acceptance 154
SUMMARY 155
QUESTIONS FOR DISCUSSION 156
REFERENCES 156

CHAPTER 6/Social Class and Poverty 161

SOCIAL CLASS AND SOCIAL OPPORTUNITY 161
Social Class as a Basis for Analyzing Society 162
Broadening the Meaning of Class 163
THE CHANGING STRUCTURE OF SOCIAL CLASS 166
Criteria for Social Class Status 166
Degrees of Social Acclaim and Prestige 167
DETERMINING SOCIAL CLASS RANKINGS 168
Changing Class Status 171
UPWARD AND DOWNWARD MOBILITY 171
Open and Closed Systems 172
The Nature of Class Boundaries 173
Vertical Mobility 174
AUTOMATION AND CYBERNATION 175
Mass Production and a Mass Work Force 175
The Frontier and the Open Class System 175
Class Effects of the Cybernetic Revolution 176
Class Status Rewards and Penalties 178
THE RACIAL FACTOR 178
Current Consequences of a Former Caste System 178
The Neglected Ethnics 180
THE QUALITY AND INEQUALITY OF LIFE 183
Criteria Used to Measure Poverty 183
Social Recognition of Poverty 184
The Urban Setting and Relative Deprivation 184
PROPOSALS TO END POVERTY 187
Poverty Is Being Poor 190
Poverty Is Being Despised 192
Poverty Is Being Incompetent 195
Poverty Is Being Powerless 196
SUMMARY 197
QUESTIONS FOR DISCUSSION 198
REFERENCES 199

CHAPTER 7/Anomie and the Elderly 205

THE ELDERLY AND SOCIETY 205
Social Gerontology 205
From Social Respect to Social Isolation 207
The Future of the Elderly 209
Values and Life Styles 209
THE PHYSIOLOGICAL FACTOR IN AGING 209
Cross-Cultural Effects of Aging 210
THE ELDERLY AS A MINORITY GROUP 211
The Roleless Image of the Elderly 211
Ageism 212
Stereotypes 212
DISENGAGEMENT AND THE AGING PROCESS 215
Challenges to the Assumptions of Contrasting Theories 216
Objective and Subjective Forms of Deprivation 217
SOCIETAL ACCOMMODATIONS TO THE PROBLEMS OF THE ELDERLY 219
Limitations of Reform Legislation 219
Fighting Human Obsolescence in and out of Frustrations 221
SUMMARY 222
QUESTIONS FOR DISCUSSION 223
REFERENCES 223

PART 3/Issues Facing American Groups 227

CHAPTER 8/Collective Conflict and Intergroup Relations 229
MINORITY GROUPS IN SOCIETY 229
History of Minority Problems 229
Analyzing Intergroup Relations 230
THE MEANING OF MINORITY STATUS 230
Minority Group Characteristics 231
Minority Acceptance of Egalitarian Ideology 232
HISTORICAL INTERGROUP CONFLICT 232
From Interreligious Conflict to Accommodation 234
From Interethnic Conflict to Accommodation 236
From Interracial Conflict to Continuing Attempts at Accommodation 238
THE AMERICAN RACIAL DILEMMA 240
Prejudice and Discrimination 240
The Moral Dilemma 242
The Continuing Dilemma 244
BLACK-LED CHALLENGES TO THE STATUS QUO 245
The Late Fifties and Early Sixties: Hope for Change 245
The Middle and Late 1960s: Despair and Challenge 250
The Women's Movement and Other Organizing Minorities 252
SIGNS OF INTERGROUP ACCOMMODATION 257
Objective Indicators of Accommodation 257
Subjective Indicators of Accommodation 259
SUMMARY 261
QUESTIONS FOR DISCUSSION 262
REFERENCES 262

CHAPTER 9/Community Organization and Disaster 267
DISASTER AND SOCIETY 267
DIMENSIONS OF DISASTER 268
Natural and Manmade Disasters 269
Community Response 270
Reorganizing in Extreme Circumstances 270
Some Popular Misconceptions About Disasters 272
Distortion by Dramatic Media Coverage 273
SHOCK AND RESPONSE 275
Stages of Response 275
The Informal Sporadic Period 275
The Emergent Adaptive Stage 276
RECOVERY AND RECONSTRUCTION 281
Voluntary Associations 283
Disaster Preparation 284
WARNING SYSTEMS 286
Communicating Danger Signs 286
Sequential Effects 288
Hypersensitivity 289
SUMMARY 290
QUESTIONS FOR DISCUSSION 291
REFERENCES 292

CHAPTER 10/Human Ecology and the Crisis of the Cities 297
THE MODERN URBAN CONDITION 297
Cities and Suburbs 298
THE URBAN TRANSFORMATION 299
Rural and Urban Distinctions 299
The Push-Pull Complex 299
Specialization and Technology 301
Rural and Urban Defined 304
Ecological Cities 304

IMAGES OF THE CITY   304
The Rural Heritage   306
Myth and Reality on the Frontier   308
The Popularity of Small Towns   308
Adjusting to Urban Living   310
THEORIES OF ECOLOGICAL CONCENTRATION   311
The Concentric Zone Theory   312
The Sector Theory   314
The Multiple Nuclei Theory   315
Social Area Analysis   315
POWER IN THE URBAN SETTING   316
The Impact of the Movement to the Suburbs   316
Community Power   317
URBAN PLANNING   322
Slum Clearance and Housing Projects   323
Megalopolis as a Focus of Planning   324
Urban Renewal: Problems and Prospects   326
SUMMARY   330
QUESTIONS FOR DISCUSSION   331
REFERENCES   331

Part 4/Issues Facing Americans on a Global Scale   335

CHAPTER 11/Demography and the Population Explosion   337

DEMOGRAPHY AS A FIELD OF STUDY   337
The Population Explosion   339
POPULATION GROWTH AND DEMOGRAPHIC ANALYSIS   341
Demographers' Assessments   342
Population Composition   343
THE CONTROLLING TRIAD: MIGRATION, FERTILITY, AND MORTALITY   345
Migration   346
Fertility   348
Mortality   351

POPULATION AND THE AMERICAN FUTURE   353
The American Demographic Transition and Its Limitations   354
Zero-Population Growth   354
Effects of Population Distribution and Its Limitations   354
Birth Control and Religion   356
Birth Control and Race   358
Pressures to Control Population Growth   358
The Commission on Population and the American Future   360
MALTHUSIAN GLOOM REVISITED   362
Malthus and Contemporary Society   362
A GLOBAL POPULATION STRATEGY   364
Population Projections   364
The Global Perspective   366
SUMMARY   369
QUESTIONS FOR DISCUSSION   370
REFERENCES   370

CHAPTER 12/Social Cohesion in Cold and Hot Wars   373

THE UNITED STATES AS A MILITARY POWER   373
Recent Emergence of a Large Standing Military   374
Technological Militarism and the Costs of Deterrence   374
THE MILITARY-INDUSTRIAL COMPLEX   380
Evidence of the Military-Industrial Complex   382
Potential Consequences of the Military-Industrial Complex   384
DEHUMANIZATION AND DESTRUCTION   386
Legitimizing Bureaucratic Authority   386
Dehumanizing the Opposition   388

COHESION AND MORALE   391
Fear and Retreatism   391
Disaffection from the Government   394
REFLECTIONS ON DOMESTIC AND INTERNATIONAL STABILITY   395
Adjusting to the Reality of Global Conflict   396
SUMMARY   397
QUESTIONS FOR DISCUSSION   398
REFERENCES   399

PART 5/Social Change and the Future   403

CHAPTER 13/The Sociological Imagination   405
IMAGINATION AND SCIENCE   405
Critical Consciousness   405
The Probing Nature of Sociology   407
SOCIOLOGY AS A FORM OF CONSCIOUSNESS   407
Four Sociological Motifs   407
THEORETICAL PERSPECTIVES AND THE DEFINITION OF PROBLEMS   412
Social Pathology Theory   413
Social Disorganization Theory   414
Value Conflict Theory   414
Deviance and Functional Theory   416
Labeling Theory   416
BEHIND THE SOCIAL FAÇADE   418
Presidential Study Commissions   418
National Advisory Commission on Civil Disorders   419
National Commission on the Causes and Prevention of Violence   421
National Commission on Obscenity and Pornography   422
Resistance to the Commissions' Reports   424

PRIVATE TROUBLES AND PUBLIC ISSUES   424
The Humanistic Strain in Sociology   425
ADJUSTING TO RAPID SOCIAL CHANGE   426
Coping with Day-to-Day Life   426
SOCIETY-WIDE POLICIES   429
Tension Management Theory   430
Systems Theory   431
SUMMARY   433
QUESTIONS FOR DISCUSSION   433
REFERENCES   434

CHAPTER 14/Fears for the Future   439
THE BASIS OF FEARFUL PERSPECTIVES   439
Textbook Warnings of Social Pathology   439
The Decline of the Family   442
THE SOCIOLOGY OF THE ABSURD   443
Inner-Directed Stability and Other-Directed Alienation   443
THE LITERATURE OF DESPAIR   445
Uncertainty and Alienation   445
Visions of Dictatorial Controls   448
THE PROSPECT OF CHANGING OR PERISHING   453
Victims of Groupthink   453
Gloomy Projections About Rights and Resources   456
The Imperative for Directed Change   457
SUMMARY   459
QUESTIONS FOR DISCUSSION   459
REFERENCES   460

CHAPTER 15/Hopes for the Future   463
THE CAUSE FOR HOPE   463
Some Encouraging Social Realities   463
Increasingly Flexible American Attitudes   464
Reasons for Hope   472

SOCIOLOGY AND THE STUDY OF THE FUTURE 473
Common Values 474
SURVIVING THE TWENTIETH CENTURY 475
The Need for an Informed Public and Enlightened Leadership 476
Old and New Values 477
Future Shock and Present Imperatives 479
BEYOND SURVIVAL 480
Exponential Growth 481
Microdecisions and Macrodecisions 483
SUMMARY 484
QUESTIONS FOR DISCUSSION 485
REFERENCES 485
APPENDIX A/Capsule View of the History of Sociological Analysis 489
APPENDIX B/Sociological Research Use of the Scientific Method 494
GLOSSARY 509
NAME INDEX 517
SUBJECT INDEX 528

PREFACE

This is an issues-oriented introduction to sociology. It is designed for one semester courses (although it could be adapted to a quarter term) and for students who may or may not go on to take further sociological courses. No previous academic knowledge of the subject is assumed. Each of the five parts and fifteen chapters has been designed to stimulate inquiry and clear thinking about social behavior. In addition to basic introductory concepts, eight major issues are considered, about half the total in most social problems texts and two or three times the total included in most introductory texts. The subjects were selected with an eye toward those that will likely be most important to a student ten, twenty, and thirty years from now when he or she will have more influence and responsibility in our complex and changing society. While taking up a number of social problems issues, the primary focus throughout the book is upon basic sociological analysis. If successful, this book will provide grounding in such basic sociological concepts as "socialization," "social organization," and "social stratification." These and related concepts are basic tools that help one to understand such fundamental processes as how conflict develops and how social cohesion can be attained in the American democratic social system.

Part One introduces the history and nature of sociology, both *what* social behavior is studied and *how* it is studied by means of universal scientific methods. In this part the student is provided with the prerequisite tools—basic concepts and objective methods of inquiry—for clear thinking about social behavior and social issues.

Part Two focuses on problems facing the millions of individuals who are adolescent, elderly, or poor. Part Three involves intergroup relations, organized responses to disasters, and the range of problems in big cities that affect, informally and formally, organized groups in the society. The issues in Part Four, population pressures and international conflict tensions, are global in scope but have a great impact on American society.

Part Two, Three, and Four provide analytic concepts within which to examine substantive social issues. For example, in Chapter 8 intergroup racial and ethnic relations are discussed within the context of social conflict and accommodation on the one hand and collective behavior and social movements on the other. The essential point here is to familiarize the reader with analyzing social behavior by applying to it research-tested sociological concepts. This provides a handle to understand some complicated but manageable social issues.

Social change and the future is the topic of Part Five. We are living in an historical period of enormous changes. Virtually everything is changing from the kinds of jobs to be available in our advanced technological economy to the social positions and roles of blacks, women, the young and the old. No one knows for sure what the future holds. However, the analytic tools presented in the first four parts are aimed in Part Five at employing the "sociological imagination" in considering realistic possibilities for resolving vital social issues in the near and distant future.

This book provides no simple answers or panaceas. Rather, it presents the student with some visions of what the future may hold for our society, based upon realistic assessments of the social situation of the past and present. Some visions are fearful, most are hopeful. The book's aim is the understanding of sociological principles and facts from which policy opinions and convictions can intelligently be formed.

At the end of each chapter are discussion questions and a list of terms and concepts to be reviewed. To further stimulate thought, quotes of great writers and philosophers are often presented before and in context of chapters to help introduce subject matter. Cartoons and other visual aids are liberally used to illustrate concepts that may appear dry and lifeless in definition alone. The charts and diagrams in the text have been selected for their clarity and relevance. Available for use with the text is a study guide, written by Patricia Harvey. The purpose of employing these learning aid techniques is to try and ensure that a lively subject is presented in a lively fashion.

Primary acknowledgment goes to Patricia Harvey. Professor Harvey made many contributions to polishing the final manuscript, in addition to employing her considerable talents to the development of the text's Study Guide and Instructor's Manual. Second, the suggestions of Consulting Editor Norman Storer, particularly in the early stages of the manuscript's development, were most valuable. I also appreciate the suggestions and encouragement of the many people who took the time to review the manuscript. They are James F. Coty, Charles Stewart Mott Community College; Frances R. Cousens, University of Michigan at Dearborn; Ernest J. Green and Constance Verdi, Prince George's Community College; Michael Horton, Pensacola Junior College; John E. Johnson, Brunswick Junior College; Henry W. Peddle, Elgin Community College; Clinton R. Sanders, University of Connecticut; Joseph F. Scott, Jersey City State College; Joann Vanek, Queens College of the City University of New York; and Andrew M. Weber, Catonsville Community College.

PREFACE xvii

Many colleagues and students at Arizona State University have also materially helped in the development of this text. To list them all would extend the length of the book many pages, but the time and effort taken by some was so extensive that notation is called for. The insights of Arizona State colleagues William Anderson and Thomas Ford Hoult were particularly helpful, as were those of David Altheide, José Cobas, Bernard Farber, Ronald Hardert, Lura Henze, John Hudson, John Johnson, Albert Mayer, John Owen, and Erdwin Pfuhl. These research and teaching colleagues have offered an excellent example of fruitful efforts and much encouragement. The same qualities are attributable to Morris Axelrod and Fred Lindstrom from whom I borrowed research reference materials. Graduate students who were particularly helpful were Steve Housker, Patricia Johnson, Philip Kock, Gail McMullen, and Claudia Tautfest. The preparation of the manuscript in its early stages by Peggy Cowan, Norma Fisher, and Randi Dorn of the Arizona State Sociology Department secretarial staff is greatly appreciated. The Houghton Mifflin Company staff assigned to this book has my sincere thanks for the high quality of their professional assistance in seeing this manuscript through to publication. Three young adults by the names of Susan, Matthew, and Melissa were encouraging and helpful on the home front. Rena, my wife, employed her insights as a cultural geographer in proofing the manuscript as well as providing much support along the way, and it is to her that I dedicate this book.

L. G.

SOCIOLOGY and American Social Issues

Part 1

BASIC SOCIOLOGICAL CONCEPTS AND METHODS

To see in order to foresee, to foresee in order to control.

Auguste Comte

Chapter 1

THE SOCIOLOGICAL PERSPECTIVE

No man is an island . . . every man is a piece of the continent, a part of the main. . .

John Donne

FOR WHOM THE BELL TOLLS

In saying that no man is an island, John Donne, poet and churchman, tells us symbolically that each of us is a part of society. Whether we are female or male, black or white, rich or poor, we are all born into a world in which our lives are inescapably influenced by others, just as we influence their lives. Their problems become our problems. When the bell tolls, it tolls for thee, and me.

We ask ourselves what we want and don't want. As a nation, we value education, occupational success, personal and social happiness, and well-being. We value stability. We abhor criminal activities. We have high hopes for our youth.

But with these goals in mind, consider the following social facts about Americans today, reported by the United States Census and other standard sources of information about this country:

One of every two high school seniors does not continue on to college.

Only half of those students who enter college receive a degree after four years.

Half of all American families have annual incomes of less than $13,000, and one in ten lives on less than $5,000 per year.

Three of every ten Americans arrested for crimes are under twenty-one years of age.

One person in ten develops a mental illness requiring professional treatment.

One of every four Americans changes his or her residence every year.

Unless current trends are altered, it is likely that more than one of these statements will describe the reader of this book before many years have passed. If only in terms of self-interest, then, the reader should be interested in the social forces that produce these facts, many of which we define as symptoms or results of *social problems*. It is clear that such problems as crime, mental illness, poverty, and strong intergroup tensions have a marked effect on the quality of life.

The continuation of the oldest practicing democracy in the world depends on how successfully we meet and deal with the many social problems we confront. Our society and this generation are being tested, and the final verdict is not yet in.

HOW SOCIOLOGISTS FEEL ABOUT SOCIAL PROBLEMS

Sociologists view themselves more as researchers than as practitioners. Generally, their position can be compared to that of physicists whose research concepts are applied to practical problems by engineers and others. Social workers and members of such practical social assistance professions as law and medicine hold the same professional relationship to sociologists that engineers do to physicists.

Does this emphasis on research exclude sociologists who have a deep concern with pressing social issues? Most sociologists believe that one of the primary purposes of sociological analysis is to relate sociological knowledge to the practical concerns of society. Table 1-1 shows that while sociologists do not generally see themselves as social physicians, they believe that their role is to be critics of society, to strive to increase the effectiveness of social institutions, and to contribute to the welfare of the society by providing an understanding of social processes. That many sociologists deny any conflict between basic research and analysis of social problems is shown by their strong support for the statement that "some of the most powerful theories in sociology have emerged from the study of social problems." (See Appendix A.)

Table 1-1   Sociologists Look at Themselves

Statement	%* Agree	% Uncertain	% Disagree
Some of the most powerful theories in sociology have emerged from the study of social problems.	75.6	12.5	11.9
One part of the sociologist's role is to be a critic of contemporary society.	70.6	10.0	19.4
One of the social functions of sociology is to strive to increase the effectiveness of social institutions.	56.1	17.1	26.8
The sociologist contributes to the welfare of society mainly by providing an understanding of social processes, not through ideas for changing these.	52.3	9.4	38.3
The sociologist has an obligation to help society in something of the same way in which the doctor is obliged to help his patients.	38.6	11.2	50.2

* The percentages are based upon a national sample of 3,440 sociologists.

SOURCE: Alvin Gouldner and J. Timothy Sprehe, "Sociologists Look at Themselves." Published by permission of Transaction, Inc., from TRANSACTION, vol 2, no. 3. © 1965 by Transaction, Inc.

THE APPLIED ORIENTATION Note that a substantial number of sociologists believe that they have an obligation to help society in something of the same way in which the doctor is obligated to help his patients. This text suggests a number of ways to alleviate social problems such as poverty and intergroup tensions, and so favors the *applied orientation*. Many sociologists and others who share similar concerns use *sociological analysis* in attempting to resolve social issues.

SOCIOLOGICAL CONSIDERATION OF SOCIAL PROBLEMS

Tying basic sociological concepts to the analysis of particular social issues has an advantage. It helps avoid the quick and highly emotional answers people often advance either to maintain the status quo or to solve specific problems. Without an understanding of the roots of a social problem, actions taken to solve it frequently fail entirely and may create new problems as well.

Some questions about oversimplified responses to specific problems will illustrate the point: Why did voters in San Francisco reject a freeway system after city authorities had initiated freeway construction that cost tens of millions of tax dollars? Why did stiff penalties for selling drugs in New York State fail to reduce rates of drug use? Why was the 1965 Moynihan report, citing the alleged pathology of black families as the main cause of black underachievement, discredited by most professional students of interracial relations as well as by the vast majority of black leaders (Rainwater and Yancy, 1967)?

FUNCTIONS AND DYSFUNCTIONS Each of these proposed actions led to unexpected and unintended results. Social life is so complex that it is common for the *manifest*, or intended, aims of people's actions to lead to *latent*, or unintended and unforeseen, consequences. In the case of San Francisco, for example, one *manifest function*[*1] of city government is to satisfy the collective needs of its citizens; in this case, the need was for efficient transportation. A *latent dysfunction** of freeway construction, however, is that it often destroys the cohesion of many established neighborhoods.

In the case of New York State, the principal manifest function of stiffer penalties for drug sellers was to reduce the amount of drug use by its citizens. But a latent dysfunction of these penalties was that they tended to result in more desperate, often violently criminal, efforts by drug users to secure ever scarcer drugs.

Those reacting to the Moynihan report expressed concern not only for what they saw as distortions of fact but also for its impact on programs designed to serve blacks. In general, the report placed the responsibility for black problems on the black family, thus allowing other groups to ignore or disclaim responsibility for assisting those in need. While the report had a manifest fact-finding function, its conclusions were assumed by many to be potentially dysfunctional for a significant part of the population. We must look not only at both functional and dysfunctional consequences of social behavior but also at the causes of such behavior. For example, Robert Merton illustrates through his analysis of political machines that important functions for subsections of American society are fulfilled in ways which, although they are visible to an outside observer, are in fact unintended and unrecognized by participants. Suspending our moral judgments of the machine, we can evaluate the functions it serves. The manifest functions of political machines obviously include

---

[1] All items italicized and asterisked throughout the text are defined in the Glossary.

SOURCE: © 1972 United Features Syndicates, Inc.

pursuing activities that bring wealth and power to members of the machine. However, Merton suggests for us a number of *latent functions* served.

MANIFEST AND LATENT FUNCTIONS: MERTON'S MACHINE

From: Robert K. Merton, *On Theoretical Sociology* (New York: The Free Press, 1967), pp. 126–135, paraphrased with permission. Copyright 1967 by Robert K. Merton. Copyright 1957 by The Free Press, a Corporation. Copyright 1949 by The Free Press.

Robert King Merton, a spokesman for the theoretical school called *structural functionalism*,* has defined for us two analytical types of functions. Manifest functions are those objective consequences contributing to the adjustment or adaptation of the system which are intended and recognized by participants in the system. Latent functions are neither intended nor recognized (Merton, 1967:105).

1. The political machine provides, through a centralized power structure, alternative (unofficial) structure to fulfill existing needs of citizens not being met by legal government operating with dispersed power.

2. It humanizes and personalizes assistance to those in need in a bureaucratic, impersonal society. It provides friendship.

3. It provides aid to those who feel degraded by procedures for asking aid from other organizations. It offers help rather than abstractions like law and justice.

4. It controls competition, stabilizing business activity and allowing favored business interests to maximize profits.

5. The machine provides alternative channels of social mobility for those otherwise excluded from more conventional routes to personal advancement.

6. The machine provides goods and services for which there is an economic demand, but which are unavailable through legitimate channels.

Merton explains why so many reform efforts to turn the rascals out do not succeed:

Any attempt to eliminate an existing social structure without providing adequate alternative structures for fulfilling the functions previously fulfilled by the abolished organization is doomed to failure.... To seek social change without due recognition of the manifest and latent functions performed by the social organization undergoing change, is to indulge in social ritual rather than social engineering... [T]hese concepts are not "merely theoretical" (in the abusive sense of the term), but are eminently practical. In the deliberate enactment of social change, they can be ignored only at the price of considerably heightening the risk of failure.

NORMALCY AS CHANGE Consider the recent assassinations and attempted assassinations of major political and religious leaders, the resignation of a United States president under political fire, riots in our major cities, student uprisings to protest war. The series of protest movements of the 1960s and 1970s has affected relationships between blacks and whites, men and women, young and old. Forces producing such events must be understood. Some argue that all this is temporary and that we will return to normalcy. Others argue that we are in a continuing social revolution that began with the Declaration of Independence in 1776 and shows no signs of stopping. There is evidence for both views.

This text provides no neat, catchall answers. Rather, it is geared to stimulate inquiry — questioning and analysis. Psychologists have demonstrated that students at every age are capable of critical thinking and learn more when they use it (Bruner, 1960). One need not wait until entering graduate school or the job market to begin critical analysis. There is much basic information in this text, but the emphasis is on advancing the use of sociological concepts and effective thinking, not on information for its own sake.

COMMON SENSE AND NONSENSE

Our social world is extremely complex, and popular opinions about it are often based on the oversimplified view that because we are alive and are social beings, we know about social reality without any need for study or objective consideration. Sociologists have conducted numerous surveys to find out what people generally believe (see Lazarsfeld, 1949; Marwell, 1966). One such study is summarized below. Note your own and other people's reactions to these statements (adapted from Lazarsfeld, 1949, pp. 379–380).

1. Better educated people show more psychoneurotic symptoms than do those with less education. (The mental instability of the intellectual as compared to the more impassive psychology of the person of average intelligence has often been commented upon.)

2. People from rural backgrounds are usually in better spirits when away from home, as in college or military service, than are people from cities. (After all, they are more accustomed to difficulty and hardship than are urban dwellers.)

3. White southerners score higher on IQ tests than do northern blacks. (It is common knowledge that, whether owing to heredity or social environment, blacks score lower than whites on IQ tests.)

4. At work, most women experience difficulties in personal relations with men. (The women's liberation movement has made it clear that women feel oppressed by men in our culture, with the result that they cannot relate well to men in professional situations.)

5. Soldiers are more eager to be returned to the States while there is a fighting war going on than after the ending of hostilities. (People cannot be blamed for not wanting to be killed.)

These are all popular *beliefs;* most people agree with them. When sociologists observe and record (through techniques described in Chapter 4) actual behavior with respect to such statements, they provide the basic social information to be studied. Why not take all this for granted and save time and energy? Because *every one of these statements is the direct opposite of what researchers actually found to be true.* The classic study *The American Soldier in World War II* (Stouffer, vols. 1 and 2, 1949) shows that:

1. The higher the average educational level of people, the *less likely* they were to have psychoneurotic symptoms (vol. 2, pp. 420–428).

2. People from urban backgrounds *displayed generally higher spirits* away from home than did people from rural backgrounds (vol. 1, pp. 333–336).

3. Blacks from the North *averaged higher IQ scores* than did whites from the South (vol. 1, p. 491).

4. Most women experienced *few difficulties* in personal relations with their male peers in the armed forces (vol. 1, pp. 44–46).

5. During World War II, most soldiers wanted to stay in the service as long as the fighting was continuing (vol. 1, p. 335).

Auguste Comte (1798–1857), a French social philosopher who gave sociology its name, stressed the need for empirical research to unify social theories. SOURCE: Brown Brothers.

The reader, given the actual results of the investigation to begin with, might well think, "Of course, that's obvious." But is it? The popular beliefs listed earlier do not jibe with the facts. Since every kind of human reaction is conceivable, it is of great importance to know which actually occur most frequently and under what conditions. Only then can common sense be separated from nonsense about human behavior. As Henry David Thoreau said, "Why level downward to our dullest perception always and praise that as common sense? The commonest sense is the sense of men asleep, which they express by snoring." It is here that sociological research can make one of its contributions.

THE NATURE OF SOCIOLOGY

While sociology is considered a science, it developed from philosophy, literature, and other humanistic disciplines. Questions that we now think of as sociological have been raised throughout history in the works of Socrates, Galileo, Shakespeare, George Sand, Bertrand Russell, and others. These have included propositions about the nature of companionship, power, war and peace, family structure, and nearly every other aspect of human behavior and social relations.

MODERN BEGINNINGS OF SOCIOLOGY The writer and philosopher Auguste Comte is called a founding father of sociology because he gave the field its name. Like many philosophers, Comte advanced his own interpretation of human society. Calling himself a *positivist* (1858), one who believes that sensory experience is the only valid basis of knowledge, Comte suggested that humankind has progressed through three universal stages: the *theological* (religiously based), the *metaphysical* (a transition period), and a *positive* or *scientific* stage. After the catastrophic wars and totalitarian upheavals of the twentieth century, few people today fully accept Comte's belief in universal progress through these stages. Instead, he is best remembered for his insistence that sociology, the most important of all the sciences in his view, be firmly based on facts rather than upon speculation and ideology.

Most early sociological contributions were made by Europeans. Two of the most influential thinkers were Emile Durkheim of France and Max Weber (pronounced *Vāber*) of Germany. Both men were fundamentally concerned with the sources of stability and instability in society. In his study of suicide (1897), Durkheim demonstrated the great influence upon individual behavior of varying forms and degrees of social integration. Shortly after the turn of the century, Weber produced penetrating analyses of the nature of bureaucracy, of the relationship between religious beliefs and economic behavior, and of the philosophical foundations of scientific sociology (Weber, 1947 trans.).

TWENTIETH CENTURY DEVELOPMENTS In the twentieth century, sociological research has been dominated by Americans. In a series of lectures at Columbia University, the British sociologist John Madge outlined the origins of scientific sociology, concentrating on a dozen American research efforts (Madge, 1962). He described investigations of such questions about American life as: How did immigrants to the United States adjust to their new surroundings? What is racial prejudice and how does it operate? How do soldiers react during military combat? What is life like in small-town America now that most people are moving to larger cities and suburbs? Of course, no science can or should belong to a single nation; contributions to sociology now flow from every nation of the world.

Since Comte's day, sociologists have been testing ideas about human behavior. Because sociology demands *empirical research*,* evidence gained through systematic observation and experiment, it is classed as a science; sociologists are represented in the prestigious National Academy of Sciences. (See Chapter 4, on methods of sociological inquiry.)[2]

The tradition of research in American sociology can be traced to the founding of the first department of sociology at the University of Chicago in 1896. Ernest W. Burgess and Robert E. Park viewed Chicago as a social laboratory, and in the early 1900s, they and other Chicago sociologists collected detailed information on different sections of that city. They developed a documented profile of Chicago, showing similarities and differences in quality of housing, income levels, suicide rates, marriages, divorces, and many other aspects of city life.

THE CHICAGO SCHOOL Until the 1930s, the Chicago School was a major source of trained sociologists in the United States, and from the work of Park and Burgess and their students came many theories about the growth of cities, about social organization, and about the dynamics of other forms of urban behavior. Because of the durability of their insights, many of their research efforts survive as classic studies.

From Comte in the mid-nineteenth century, through the Chicago School in the early twentieth century, to the establishment of strong departments of sociology in universities throughout the country today, a sociological tradition has emerged. This tradition is twofold. On the one hand, there is a continuation of the older philosophic practice of posing questions about social behavior. On the other, there is the increasingly sophisticated practice of gathering empirical information relevant to these questions and testing various answers to them. Out of such research come further questions

---

[2] Note additional material on research methods relevant to the sociological use of the scientific method in Appendix B.

Ernest W. Burgess (1886–1966) and Robert E. Park (1864–1944) were two prominent members of the Chicago School, which viewed the city as a "social laboratory" that documented various aspects of urban social life. SOURCE: University of Chicago Library.

to be answered, and so the cycle continues. The combination of questions about human behavior and intensive research adds up to a rounded scientific effort.

SPECIALIZATION IN THE FIELD Like all research disciplines, sociology has developed a large number of specialties. The American Sociological Association's *Guide to Graduate Departments of Sociology* (1975:224–239) lists over three dozen. These include such general topics as history of social thought, theory, and social change. Other specialties focus on social institutions: marriage and the family, industrial sociology, and the sociology of education. There are specializations in various methods of research, including mathematical sociology and methodology (both qualitative and quantitative approaches). Finally, the issue-oriented specialties (a major focus of this text), include collective behavior and social movements, deviant behavior and social disorganization, and racial and ethnic relations.

Sociologists continually work at providing knowledge of and insights into matters which are of direct interest to citizens: What factors encourage our high divorce rate? Which features of one's occupation promote or diminish job satisfaction? What are the social effects of widespread unemployment on a population? What does it mean to grow old in a youth-oriented society? Does equal justice under the law exist?

The American Sociological Association has over fourteen thousand members; there are more than enough questions about society — and techniques through which they may be answered — to keep all of them occupied.

EMPLOYMENT OPPORTUNITIES IN SOCIOLOGY

Sociology is a field of study that by its nature provides varied occupational opportunities. Sociological training is useful in securing work in a number of occupations in which insights into social behavior are important. There are numerous jobs available for those who have studied the causes of deviant behavior — alcoholism, illegal prostitution, drug abuse, juvenile delinquency. Many students seek fuller training in more specialized aspects of deviance by selecting additional coursework, where such programs are available, in social work and criminal justice.

Those interested in urban and other community problems can find work in government agencies that provide assistance to communities experiencing deterioration and its attendant problems. In fact, agencies for investigating and rehabilitating delinquents are often found in urban areas, sponsored by county, state, or federal sources. Some universities have departments of urban studies in which sociology students may receive specialized training.

With the increasing interest of government and private groups in providing marriage and family counseling, jobs are available for those who have experience in family studies. As in other areas of specialization, the student should consider electives in other programs offered by the college or university that will enrich training in the specialty. For example, some universities have departments of family studies and child development.

Perhaps your interest is in politics. Sociology will not necessarily help you get elected to office, but if you are trained in interviewing, taking polls, analyzing statistics, or other skills of interest to those seeking office, you may become a member of a politician's staff. Some officials employ research staffs to obtain and verify information of interest in the development of legislation.

Other specialties that provide job opportunities include medical sociology, social gerontology (problems of the elderly), educational sociology (techniques and problems of teaching), and many others.

There are jobs in public agencies, such as county mental health clinics, and in private business, for example market research firms. If you are skilled in research statistics, and computer technology, the possibilities for work, even in nonsociological fields, increase. The federal government employs many statisticians, for example, in a variety of bureaus.

With additional education, say a teaching certificate, one might teach high school sociology along with other courses. A master's degree opens up positions that require advanced training, such as director of a counseling agency or urban renewal office. People with undergraduate sociology degrees sometimes take advanced degrees in social work for more practical training in specific programs such as rehabilitating alcoholics.

Though a Ph.D. degree is now considered a necessity for teaching in most colleges and universities, the direction in sociology is currently away from training only for replacements for professors. Instead, universities are training highly qualified people to take active places throughout the occupational structure, using their insights into theories of social behavior to bring scientific sense to the problems which face us now and will face us in the future.

THE QUESTION OF SOCIAL BEHAVIOR

If there is one constant in modern American society, it is that most people will experience major changes within their lifetime. This fact poses a number of fundamental questions for sociologists: What social changes are occurring? How do they happen? Why? What are their consequences? How can people adapt effectively to change?

Answering these questions requires documented empirical research. Sociologists generally recognize that comprehensive analysis of society must draw upon other related social sciences, including economics and history as well as anthropology (which studies social groups in other, usually nonliterate societies) and psychology (which studies the mental processes and emotional behavior of individuals).

To respond to these questions, one must focus on the basic structure of social group behavior in the context of modern industrial society. The following case illustrates how research-based sociological analysis, with assistance from related social sciences, can help us better understand a particular social situation.

RURAL - URBAN MIGRATION Let us consider a typical black family that has moved from rural Mississippi to Detroit. The United States *Census**, which counts the American population every ten years, has documented the movement of blacks and whites since 1790. Using census figures along with geographic, historical, and economic data, we know that since early in this century, blacks have been moving in increasing numbers from the rural South into major cities across the nation (Report on National Growth, 1972:12–14). These families face not only a change from their former rural existence but adjustment to a pattern of urban life which is itself continually changing.

Such a black family is likely to settle first among other blacks in the city. Their neighbors are generally not kin; they come from different parts of the rural South. The grandparents have limited savings, if any, and their careers as tenant farmers or agricultural laborers do not qualify them for social security assistance. They are dependent on welfare from the government and on their children's incomes.

Their children also have a series of adjustments to make. If the husband has learned a trade (perhaps in the Army), he may be able to get a blue-collar job in a factory. While he is unemployed, his family may not qualify for welfare assistance. Some states put general restrictions on welfare when there is an able-bodied man in the household (tenBroek, *et al.*, 1966). In addition, he may discover that his wife finds work more easily than he does (Farley and Hermalin, 1972:353–367). There may be considerable new pressure on the stability of the nuclear family (husband–wife–child[ren]) in addition to the history of discrimination extending back to segregation and slavery in the Old South.

As the family's income rises, they may move toward the edge of the city and eventually into the suburbs. Earlier newcomers to the city, such as the Italians, Greeks, Jews, and other ethnic groups, followed the same pattern of movement. The women in this black family, one generation removed from rural tradition, maintain the home. The children attend schools within or on the margins of the city that are more crowded and have fewer resources than those in more prosperous suburbs. These schools supposedly teach the children how to live in urban society.

Table 1-2 shows the pattern of the rural-to-urban movement of which this family is a part. When the grandparents of our example were born at the turn of the century, most Americans lived in small towns. Industrial expansion in the Roaring Twenties, coupled with an agricultural recession, drew millions to the cities. At the same time, other millions from Europe and elsewhere had moved into cities looking for a better life.

Table 1-2 Urban and Rural Composition of the United States, 1790-1970

Year	Percent urban	Percent rural
1790	5.1	94.9
1800	6.1	93.9
1810	7.3	92.7
1820	7.2	92.8
1830	8.8	91.2
1840	10.8	89.2
1850	15.3	84.7
1860	19.8	80.2
1870	25.7	74.3
1880	28.2	71.8
1890	35.1	64.9
1900	39.7	60.3
1910	45.7	54.3
1920	51.2	48.8
1930	56.2	43.8
1940	56.5	43.5
1950	64.0	36.0
1960	69.9	30.1
1970	73.4	26.6

SOURCE: *Statistical Abstract of the United States* (Washington, D.C.: U.S. Department of Commerce, 1971), p. 24.

Since the founding of the republic, living patterns in the United States have shifted from rural areas and small towns to cities and suburbs. Since 1920, the population has been mostly urban, and the city is the scene of most contemporary American social issues. This mass population shift has continuing consequences on the attempts of individuals and social groups to adjust to life in the society.

American blacks for the most part remained in farming while most other Americans were shifting from a rural to an urban setting. The Great Depression of the 1930s slowed the general urban movement for a time (see Table 1-2), but expanding job opportunities since World War II have given it new impetus. The pattern of limited economic opportunity on the farms and greater opportunity in cities has influenced many blacks in recent years.

PLURALISTIC SOCIETY Our black family now lives in a mixed neighborhood. It may look much as it did ten, twenty, or even thirty years ago. The old residents may resent the new and different families. The ones who are better off are planning to move to the suburbs.

The black family lives in a *pluralistic** social setting, with more ethnic and religious groups than they ever saw or knew of in their former farm community. They must learn how to get along well in a community where their closest kin no longer live within walking or commuting distance. Even though their new community offers better prospects for jobs and a potentially higher standard of living, they must wonder about its stability. As suburbs grow, the city family finds itself in a community with declining tax revenues for such basic services as schools, police, and fire protection.

We have drawn upon facts and interpretations from history, geography, economics, psychology, and anthropology as well as statistical materials to develop this case of a typical black family newly arrived in the city. The sociologist not only records such social facts but also determines how they came to be and how they advance or retard social stability. Why do more young adults and older family members live apart from each other than in the past? Why are there continuing tensions between racial minorities and other groups? Why do more retired people live in cities and young workers in the suburbs? It is as important to know *why* as to know *what* is going on.

SOCIAL POLICY AND SOCIOLOGY

To the basic questions, *What is going on in society?* and *Why is it going on?* we add a third, which touches on the applications of sociology: *Knowledge for what?* In other words, what is the relationship between sociology and social policy? This question was asked many years ago by Robert Lynd (1939).

Social policy is the development of a course of organized social actions selected from among alternatives. The very process by which sociological analysis points to alternative responses to practical issues may affect the way social policy is developed. As Constantina Safilios-Rothschild observes (1974:12):

The existence of many options will in most cases require a new model of socialization that teaches people how to cope with a multiplicity of options.[3] People will need to learn to perceive, evaluate, and choose among different alternatives.

Not everyone will want new options; not all will want to choose among those available. But the increasing use of sociological research will point out the range of available options for those who wish to consider them.

PUBLIC AND PRIVATE SOCIAL POLICY Specific social policies are usually set by the government. Government policy determines, for example, that all American citizens have the right to vote at age eighteen. Social policy may also involve private interests, such as the decision of a corporation to hire racial minorities and women. It may also involve individual decisions, such as encouraging a neighborhood association to develop a Little League. In each case, decision-makers must consult alternative policies. Increasingly, sociology is being asked for guidance in the formulation of social policy. This text acknowledges the growing interest in applied sociology by introducing many basic sociological concepts in the context of social issues. Yet it is necessary to keep sociology in realistic

A leading theoretician in sociology, Robert K. Merton represents a wedding of basic and applied policy-oriented research in sociology.

---

[3] *Socialization** is developed in Chapter 2.

perspective. Sociology is growing, but it is still limited in its ability to offer specific policy guidance. As Robert Merton, one of the most influential theorists in sociology, observed (1967:49): "The urgency or immensity of a practical social problem does not ensure its immediate solution. At any given moment, men of science are close to the solutions of some problems and remote from others."

SOCIOLOGY AND GOVERNMENT For all their acknowledged limitations, sociology and the related social sciences do not have the luxury of waiting until their theories are as exact as those of medicine or the physical sciences before applying them to problems. Consider the United States Supreme Court ruling in the famous *Brown* case of 1954, which held that racial segregation in public schools was unconstitutional. The Court specifically cited social research to refute the argument of *separate but equal* put forth by representatives of segregated school districts (*Brown* v. *Topeka Board of Education*, 1954). Again, when racial disorders struck dozens of cities in the 1960s, the President's National Advisory Commission on Civil Disorders (*Report of the National Advisory Commission on Civil Disorders*, 1968) engaged teams of sociologists to document what happened and to present analyses upon which to base new social policies.

When and how sociological analysis is used in the formulation of a social policy depends on the state of knowledge in that area and on the willingness of people to use that knowledge. Let us look at two contrasting examples.

Sociological research contributed toward formulating the point system used to muster out men and women from the armed forces at the end of World War II. The system was developed after a representative cross-section of American military personnel throughout the world was interviewed. Their responses suggested that highest preference should be given to those who had been on the front lines and those who had served longest. Given the enormous task of discharging over 10 million people in a way that would not overly disrupt the armed forces or the civilian population, there were some built-in problems. Private citizens and members of Congress urged that the priority list be changed so that those over age thirty, those with children, or some other groups be released from service first. Yet, research found the system that the soldiers themselves thought most equitable. The result was that (Stouffer, Volume 2:530)

[i]n spite of skepticism about Army promises, the reaction of soldiers to the fairness of the point system was decidedly favorable. Seldom in the entire experience of the Research Branch had such a vote of confidence been given to any Army policy.

A case in which policy-makers ignored social research occurred in the recommendations of the President's National Commission on Obscenity and Pornography. After reviewing past findings and conducting extensive research on the effects of erotica in books and films, the Commission concluded in its official report (1970:32):

Research designed to clarify the question has found no evidence to date that exposure to explicit sexual materials plays a significant role in the causation of delinquent or criminal behavior among youth or adults. The Commission cannot conclude that exposure to erotic materials is a factor in the causation of delinquent or criminal behavior among youth or adults. The Commission cannot conclude that exposure to erotic materials is a factor in the causation of sex crimes or sex delinquency.

Clearly the implication of this conclusion was that censorship of books and movies alleged to be obscene ought to be reduced or ended. Yet, the administration and the Congress generally ignored the Commission's report and recommendations. Then the Supreme Court, in a series of five decisions in 1973, expanded the legal basis for banning obscenity and pornography by holding that community standards could determine what could be read in books or seen in movies (New York *Times*, June 22, 1973:1). Thus state and local authorities were legally empowered to challenge nationally distributed publications and films, though research found no evidence that pornography causes major forms of deviant-delinquent behavior.

SOCIOLOGY AND OBJECTIVE ANALYSES This text pursues the sociological goal of shedding light on the nature of society and some of the basic issues that affect the quality of American life. To succeed in this effort, one must maintain an attitude of objectivity — to see things as they are whether we like them or not. Social issues touch most people's lives. Emotions can run high on questions that involve conventional wisdom, such as school desegregation and the legal availability of obscene materials. This wisdom may be backed by long-held general beliefs based on social awareness and a concern for the general interest, or it may be based only on prejudice, which distorts awareness and leads to a defense of special interests. Or it may simply be based on long-established ways of doing things.

Answers to questions of social policy, of what to do about social reality, vary between Democrats and Republicans, business leaders and labor leaders, and with most other opposing social groups. But all must ultimately deal with what really exists if effective policies are to be developed by individuals, private groups, industries, and government. One use of sociological analysis is to point out the social costs of different decisions. How likely are schools to increase their general quality for all if one set of policies is pursued rather than another? Given one policy, or another, or none, how likely is domestic tranquillity to be maintained in the big cities? This book takes the approach suggested by Merton (1967:50):

The most useful orientation toward the relationship of current sociology and practical problems of society is . . . a developmental orientation, rather than one that relies on sudden mutations of one sociologist that suddenly bring solutions to major social problems or to a single encompassing theory. Though this orientation makes no marvelously dramatic claims, it offers a reasonably realistic assessment of the current condition of sociology and the ways in which it actually develops.

SUMMARY

This chapter introduces the content of *sociology* and *sociological analysis*. Sociology examines human interaction and the possible consequences on the individual's life of various kinds of social interaction. Some problems in sociology call for an issues-oriented approach, others for a research-based approach. We have distinguished between *manifest* and *latent* consequences of people's actions and have seen how the sociological perspective moves beyond common sense notions of social awareness that are often misleading or wrong.

In the nineteenth century, philosophical views about the social nature of human beings combined with methods of scientific research to produce sociology as an independent discipline. From such beginnings, the field has grown to include over three dozen areas of specialization in theory, methods, and substantive aspects of social life. Whatever the area of specialization, all sociologists study human interaction scientifically. The questions constantly asked by sociologists are *What is going on?* and *Why is it going on?* The description of the social forces affecting the life of a black family moving from rural Mississippi to urban Detroit demonstrates the objective, research-based, interdisciplinary nature of the field.

To the questions *What is going on?* and *Why is it going on?* we add a third question: *Knowledge for what?* Sociologists, we have seen, use sociological analysis to formulate *social policy*. Social policy is the development of alternative courses of organized action to maintain or to achieve a particular social condition. It is here that sociology turns to *applied research** (that with immediate practical implications), rather than pure or *basic research** on the nature of society or of a given social situation. Sociology is a young science, and consequently should not be expected to point out the full range of possibilities and costs of social policies. Only with this reservation can the policy implications of sociological analysis be used most effectively.

QUESTIONS FOR DISCUSSION

1. Select an international and a national news item from the daily press which you believe may have an important effect on your life. Explain how and why you believe that you and others will be affected by this event. What if anything might you do about it?

2. Describe for classmates an action you or others took in which you recognized the *manifest functions* but only later realized the *latent functions* (or *dysfunctions*). Was there any way in which you could have anticipated these *latent (dys)functions* (consequences)? Which type of function turned out to have the most important consequences?

3. Review the common sense beliefs listed by Paul Lazarsfeld, all of which proved to be wrong. Select one such belief and suggest a social policy based (1) upon the false common sense belief and (2) upon the research-based reality.

4. The early Chicago School emphasized empirical, verifiable research on how people interact in society. How does this approach differ from the positivist approach of Auguste Comte? The common sense approach?

5. Review your understanding of the following terms and concepts:

manifest functions

latent (dys)functions

common sense

empirical research

Chicago as a social laboratory

the Chicago School

social policy

basic versus applied research

REFERENCES

Brown v. Board of Education
    1954   Volume 347 of United States Reports (official reports of the Supreme Court). Washington, D.C.: Government Printing Office. 483.

Bruner, Jerome
    1960   The Process of Education. Cambridge: Harvard University Press.

Comte, Auguste
    1858   The Positive Philosophy of Auguste Comte. Harriet Martineau (trans.). New York: Blanchard.

Durkheim, Emile
    1951   Suicide (1897). J. Spaulding and G. Simpson (trans.). New York: The Free Press.

Farley, Reynolds and Albert Hermalin
    1972   "The 1960s: decade of progress for blacks?" Demography, 9 (August).

Gouldner, Alvin and J. Timothy Sprehe
    1965   "How sociologists look at themselves." Trans-Action 2 (May/June): 42–44.

1975   Guide to Graduate Departments of Sociology. Washington, D.C.: The American Sociological Association.

1972   Inquiries in Sociology. Prepared by Sociological Resources for the Social Studies. Sponsored by the American Sociological Association and Supported by the National Science Foundation. Boston: Allyn and Bacon.

Lazarsfeld, Paul
1949   "The American soldier — an expository review." The Public Opinion Quarterly, 13:378–380.

Lynd, Robert
1939   Knowledge for What? Princeton, N.J.: Princeton University Press.

Madge, John
1962   The Origins of Scientific Sociology. New York: The Free Press.

Marwell, Gerald
1966   Introducing Introductory Sociology: The Social Awareness Test. The American Sociologist, 1:253–254.

Merton, Robert
1967   On Theoretical Sociology. New York: The Free Press.

Moynihan, Daniel
1965   The Negro Family: The Case for National Action. Washington, D.C.: United States Department of Labor.

1972   The NAS [National Academy of Science] and sociology. The American Sociologist, 7:1.

Park, Robert
1949   Race and Culture. New York: The Free Press of Glencoe.

Rainwater, Lee and William Yancy.
1967   The Moynihan Report and the Politics of Controversy. Cambridge, Mass.: The M.I.T. Press.

1968   Report of the National Advisory Commission on Civil Disorders. Washington, D.C.: Government Printing Office.

1970   Report of the National Commission on Obscenity and Pornography. New York: Bantam Books.

1972   Report on National Growth. Washington, D.C.: Government Printing Office.

Safilios-Rothschild, Constantina
1974   Women and Social Policy. Englewood Cliffs, N.J.: Prentice-Hall.

Stoddard, Ellwyn
1972   The normative presentation of scientific sociology: a professional anathema. Summation, 3:1–15.

Stouffer, Samuel
1949   The American Soldier, vols. 1 and 2. Princeton, N.J.: Princeton University Press.

tenBroek, Jacobus and Editors of the California Law Review
1966   The Law of the Poor. San Francisco: Chandler.

Weber, Max
1947   The Theory of Social and Economic Organization. A. M. Henderson and T. Parsons (trans.). New York: Oxford University Press.

Chapter 2

BASIC CONCEPTS: CULTURE, SOCIALIZATION, AND SOCIAL ORGANIZATION

Some people eat with a knife and fork, others with chopsticks, and still others use their fingers. . . . To each of us, of course, our way of doing things is the right way. This would not matter so much if it were not for the complications of the "missionary syndrome," which leads us to try to persuade other people to abandon their ways and take up ours.

Marston Bates[1]

---

[1] From: Marston Bates, "Vive la Difference." *Ants, Indians, and Little Dinosaurs.* (New York: Scribners, 1975), p. 367.

THE MAJOR CHARACTERISTICS OF SOCIETY

We may define a *society** as the network of social relationships that unite people who occupy a particular area and who have been more or less united for several generations. Thus we speak of American society or German society or Cherokee society.

All societies share certain basic characteristics. In this chapter we shall discuss three of the most important of these characteristics: *culture**, *socialization**, and *social organization**. A people's culture is its common heritage of traditions, values, and way of life. Socialization is the process through which society's new members (primarily but not exclusively those who are born into it) are made part of society by developing a concept of self and learning the roles they are to play in their society. Social organization is the complex of informal and formal groups through which society's members satisfy their individual and collective needs.

THE CONCEPT OF CULTURE

You may have heard the phrase, she or he is a "highly cultured person." Perhaps you picture someone who supports opera, ballet, Shakespeare. In this case, the sociological use of a word differs from its use in everyday living. From an anthropological and sociological point of view, the common use of the word is misleading, for the social scientist would say that *every* member of a society is highly cultured. As the Harvard anthropologist Clyde Kluckhohn once said, "A humble cooking pot is as much a cultural product as a Beethoven sonata" (1949:17).

VALUES AND NORMS Culture is so all-encompassing that it is a good basic concept to begin with in analyzing social behavior. It embraces everything related to the "distinctive way of life of a group of people, their complete design for living" (Kluckhohn, 1951:86). The nineteenth-century British anthropologist Edward B. Tyler defined culture as "that complex whole which includes knowledge, belief, art, morals, law, custom, and any other capabilities acquired by man as a member of society" (Tyler, 1924:1). A culture is thus a complete set of prescriptions for how life is to be lived in a given society. These prescriptions are based on a set of *values** the implementation of which is guided by *norms**.

We can think of values as generalized conceptions of the desirable, meaning that they describe what members of society prefer to something else. For example, in America, the inhabitants of a riverside city prefer to build dams against floods than wait passively and fatalistically for the next flood. This situation demonstrates the American value that Robin Williams describes as *active mastery*. Every culture has a large number of values, usually organized in order of relative importance, and for the most part logically consistent with each other.

Norms are specific rules of behavior and are ultimately related to achievement of values. They may apply to only a few members of society or to everyone; they may be detailed or general; and they may exist over many generations or be faddish and short-lived. The duties of the president, for example, pertain to only one individual at a time; although they are described in the Constitution and have the character of law, they are formalized norms that have lasted for two hundred years.

Informal norms also affect behavior of the individual who occupies the office of president. In 1972, a presidential candidate was hampered as a contender by widespread publicity that he cried in public, thus violating a norm that dictates how men, particularly men seeking high office, should behave. The Watergate scandal was reported not only in terms of legal violations but also of personal characteristics of the offenders, which were viewed as inappropriate to persons occupying high office. The 1976 sex scandals in the United States House of Representatives further eroded people's faith in public officials as supporters of the moral values and norms of their constituents. We do not all condemn men who show emotion publicly or presidents who protect executive privilege or elected officials who have private sexual affairs. Too much actual behavior belies that. Rather, our *mores** require us to restrict such behavior if it interferes with the performance of public duty.

Informal norms, although they lack the force of law, can be quite binding on individuals; or they may amount to nothing more than matters of personal preference. The everyday obligation to be polite to strangers is an informal norm that, though not a legal requirement, has persisted for centuries and applies to all. Current norms regarding hair length and style are by contrast probably passing fancies that will soon be replaced by different norms.

MAJOR AMERICAN VALUE THEMES Major value themes supported by Americans are noted by Robin Williams in his book *American Society*. While Williams admits there are exceptions and alternatives in our complex nation of many diverse groups, he has drawn for us a picture of most likely value orientations for this particular culture as a whole (1970:501–502).

1. American culture is organized around the attempt at *active mastery* rather than *passive acceptance*. Into this dimension falls the low tolerance of frustration; the refusal to accept ascetic renunciation;

the positive encouragement of desire; the stress of power; the approval of ego-assertion, and so on.

2. It tends to be interested in the *external world* of things and events, of the palpable and immediate, rather than in the inner experience of meaning and affect. Its genius is manipulative rather than contemplative.

3. Its world-view tends to be *open* rather than closed: It emphasizes change, flux, movement; its central personality types are adaptive, accessible, outgoing, and assimilative.

4. In wide historical and comparative perspective, the culture places its primary faith in *rationalism* as opposed to *traditionalism;* it deemphasizes the past, orients strongly to the future, does not accept things just because they have been done before.

5. Closely related to the above is the dimension of *orderliness* rather than unsystematic *ad hoc* acceptance of transitory experience. (This emphasis is most marked in the urban middle classes.)

6. With conspicuous deviations, a main theme is a *universalistic* rather than a *particularistic* ethic.

7. In interpersonal relations, the weight of the value system is on the side of "horizontal" rather than "vertical" emphases: peer relations, not superordinate-subordinate relations: equality rather than hierarchy.

8. Subject to increased strains and modification, the ... culture emphasizes *individual personality* rather than group identity and responsibility.

THE PERVASIVE INFLUENCE OF CULTURE How powerful is the effect of culture on a person's daily life? Very powerful. This does not mean that individuals cannot or do not accept or reject part or even all of their cultural heritage. Yet the influence of culture is so great that individual deviations from it are not easy, particularly if the changes are major. One anthropologist expressed it in these terms (Hilmer, 1924:247):

A child born and raised among the Hottentots will acquire the habits, the attitudes, the morals of the Hottentots.... Furthermore it does not make much difference whether the child is of the same stock as the people among whom he is raised or not; he will become one of them just the same.

Through the process of interaction with others, people learn the values and norms of those whose opinion matters. Through this learning process, which is more fully discussed in the section on socialization, one takes in or *internalizes* culture; one makes it one's own. Others reward you for learning what is from their point of view the right thing and punish you for wrong choices. Those who have power to force or persuade through these positive and negative *sanctions*[2], or enforcements, are the definers of culture. Over time, we may not remember where all the rules, beliefs, and practices that we share with others came from, but because we have internalized them, we are seen as acceptable members of our culture.

Clyde Kluckhohn gives two classic examples of how influential culture is in conditioning individuals (1949:19):

Some years ago I met in New York City a young man who did not speak a word of English and was obviously bewildered by American ways. By "blood" he was as American as you or I, for his parents had gone from Indiana to China as missionaries. Orphaned in infancy,

---

[2] Not all sanctions are equally strong, nor are all individuals equally subject to sanctions. If a child steals a cookie, the punishment is probably less severe than if he or she stole money. An adult thief probably pays a higher penalty for stealing money than does the child who steals money.

he was reared by a Chinese family in a remote village. All who met him found him more Chinese than American. The facts of his blue eyes and light hair were less impressive than a Chinese style of gait, Chinese arm and hand movements, Chinese facial expression, and Chinese modes of thought. The biological heritage was American, but the cultural training had been Chinese. He returned to China. Another example of another kind: I once knew a trader's wife in Arizona who took a somewhat devilish interest in producing a cultural reaction. Guests who came her way were often served delicious sandwiches filled with a meat that seemed to be neither chicken nor tuna fish yet was reminiscent of both. To queries she gave no reply until each had eaten his fill. She then explained that what they had eaten was not chicken, not tuna fish, but the rich, white flesh of freshly killed rattlesnakes. The response was instantaneous — vomiting, often violent vomiting. A biological process is caught in a cultural web.

The latter example illustrates how strongly we are bound by our cultural patterns and tastes. To us, our competitive and materialistic culture seems more civilized than others, no matter how spirited they may be. The fact that other cultures are unlike ours reflects historical experience and differences in physical setting. Since there are usually several different ways to get along in the same physical surroundings, it is often the case that a group's history carries more weight in shaping its culture than do its immediate physical circumstances.

TWO CULTURALLY DIVERSE ADAPTATIONS TO THE ENVIRONMENT

Every human being has three major environments to contend with: humanity's *biological inheritance*, with all its potentials and limitations; the group's *physical setting*, including climate and geography; and the *social environment*, including values and traditions. A group's culture enables the group to adapt to this environment.

Biological and physical environments may vary considerably in such characteristics as proneness to disease and even height and strength, and of temperature range and the kinds and amounts of food that can be produced. Yet the manmade social environments vary the most. Even when different cultural groups with the same biological inheritance reside in the same physical setting, their adaptations to that setting are often markedly different.

Let us consider how various cultural groups in American society have come to terms with their environments. These groups illustrate *cultural pluralism** in two contrasting settings, New Mexico in the arid Southwest, and the bustling metropolis of Chicago. In both, different cultural groups live in the same community but respond to the environment in culturally diverse ways.

A STUDY OF CULTURAL DIVERSITY In the mid 1950s, thirty scientists undertook a study of the region south of Gallup, New Mexico, where communities with five different cultural traditions lived: Zuni and Navajo Indians, Mormons, Catholic Spanish-Americans, and Protestant homesteaders from Texas (Vogt and Roberts, 1956:25–30). The five thousand people in this region had to contend with the same high-altitude, semiarid physical environment, where the problems of living are formidable. Rainfall averages only twelve to fifteen inches a year, and the growing season is short and changeable, as is typical of the American Southwest at an altitude of seven thousand feet above sea level. The small Zuni River, a tributary of the Little Colorado, cannot fully water the potentially fertile and productive soil.

Thus in making a living, each culture was faced with similar environmental problems. There was some interaction among the groups, and with the development of roads, telephones, mass media, and overlapping working and living patterns, there is likely to be more. Still the powerful influence of each culture is evident as each group worked out its own solution to the problem of survival (Vogt and Roberts, 1956:26).

The Zunis, oldest of the peoples in the region, conduct a long-established irrigation agriculture supplemented by stock raising and by crafts, notably the making of silver jewelry. The Navajos were originally roving hunters and gatherers and came into the region only a century ago; they have become dry farmers and sheepherders with wage work providing an increasing percentage of their income as contact with our American culture becomes more extensive. Livestock ranching and wage work provide the principal income for the three Spanish–American villages, which were settled about 75 years ago. The Mormons — who favor the values of cooperation — also established in this region since the 1880s, have been conspicuously successful at irrigation farming; they also engage in livestock ranching and wage work. The Texans — who stress individualistic social relations — staked out the last Homestead Act lands in the regions during the 1930s, as refugees from the dust bowl to the east; they raise cattle and carry on a commercial and largely mechanized dry-land farming, with pinto beans as their principal crop.

THE INFLUENCE OF HISTORY AND TRADITION The responses of these five groups to the difficulties of living in the arid Southwest are clearly influenced by their respective history and traditions. Within this cultural differentiation, researchers noted varying *patterns* of responses (social scientists are always looking for patterns) to special difficulties such as drought. The Zuni and Navajos performed ceremonies, including rain dances. The Spanish–Americans tended to be fatalistic. All three of these patterned responses reflect in varying degrees the belief that humans lack control over the forces of nature. In contrast, the Mormons, through tight-knit communal organizations, and the Texans, through individual initiative, used technological approaches such as cloud-seeding and reducing crop acreages. These two patterned responses reflect the belief that the forces of nature can be controlled or manipulated by human effort.

While the cultural traditions of each group influenced its responses, we must remember that many social forces operate in any given situation. They must be taken into account in order to assess accurately any people's reactions and their consequences. What we see as irrational or rational behavior depends on our *subjective* feelings about the *objective* actions taken. The concepts of rationality and irrationality are defined by language and thought which are in turn affected by culture. Most urban Americans, used to material comforts, would identify with the Mormon and Texan responses, though these approaches are not entirely rational. For example, technology used to solve problems often creates others in the form of air and water pollution. The apparently nonrational approaches of the Indians and Spanish–Americans may, in the long run, have some beneficial ecological effects.

FACTORS IN CULTURAL ADAPTABILITY Response to environmental situations is related not only to history and tradition but also to the capacity of a culture for *discovery* (developing new information which permits a new response), *innovation* (recombining existing information in a new way), and *diffusion* (the willingness to accept ideas and materials from other cultures). Ralph Linton gives an excellent example of cultural diffusion in his description of the "100 Percent American" (see Chapter 13).

CULTURAL DIVERSITY IN THE GOLD COAST AND THE CHICAGO SLUMS The variety of cultural adaptations to environments is not confined to such sparsely populated areas as the great Southwest. It is equally evident in the American city. While many westward movements have created pluralistic cultural groups such as that found south of

BASIC SOCIOLOGICAL CONCEPTS AND METHODS

Gallup, even larger groups have migrated to the cities, attracted by the promise of a high standard of living.

DIFFERENT CULTURES IN ONE URBAN SETTING In the late 1920s, Harvey Zorbaugh and a research team made a classic study of multiple cultural groups in an urban community. One of the University of Chicago School studies in that city, it was entitled *The Gold Coast and the Slum* (1929). Zorbaugh analyzed a section of central Chicago known as the Near North Side. Among the ninety thousand people living in this section were several groups demonstrating highly contrasting cultural responses to life in the city. In the area known as the Gold Coast, many upper-class, largely white Protestant families lived, and still do. To the west, there was an area of low-cost furnished rooms. Few families lived there; over half the adult population was unmarried. Still further west was Little Italy, a

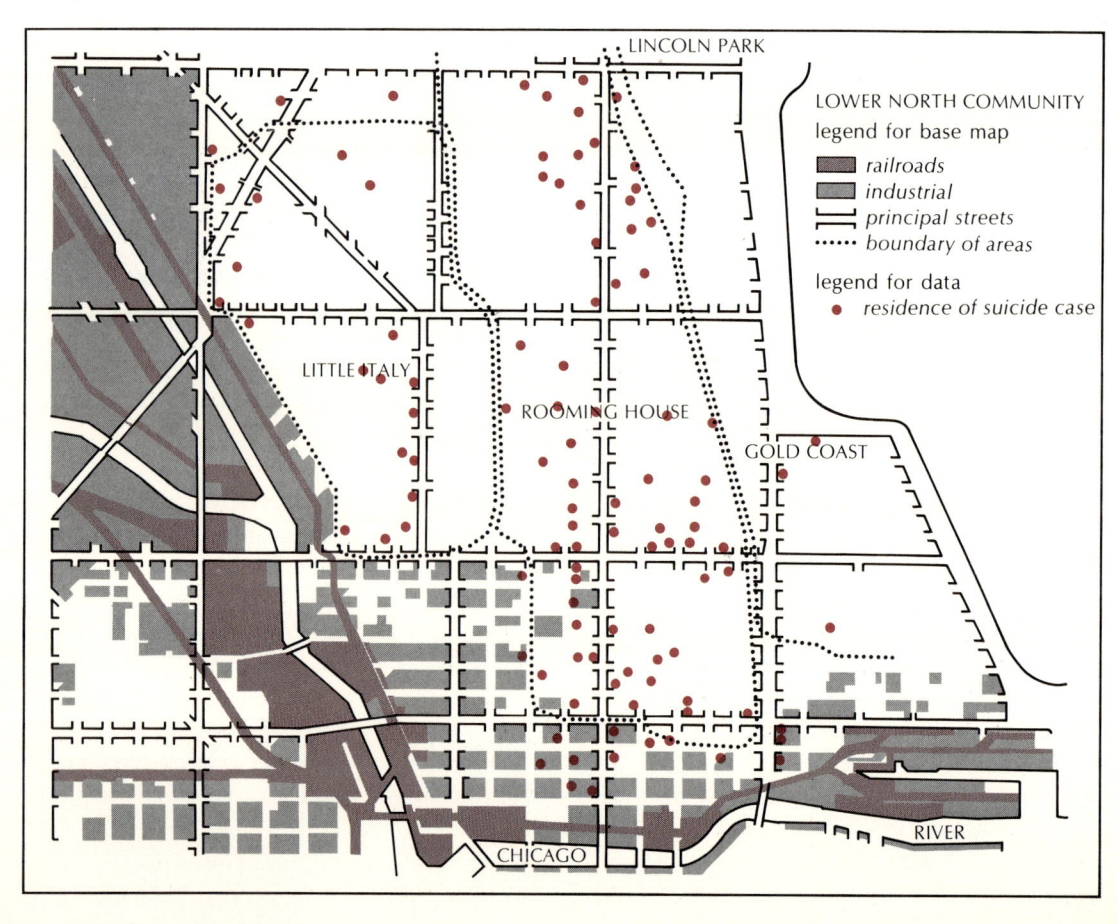

Figure 2-1 This map of the Near North Side in Chicago shows how incidences of suicide varied according to the social life experiences of the cultural groups in the area. Note that the fewest suicides occurred along the Gold Coast where the people of highest status and greatest wealth lived, while the highest incidence occurred in the Rooming House section where most people were poor. SOURCE: *The Gold Coast and the Slum* by Harvey Zorbaugh (University of Chicago Press).

neighborhood of distinct ethnic groups including Italians, Swedes, Irish, blacks, Jews, Chinese, and others. All these were recent immigrants to the city, including the blacks who had migrated from the rural South.

Each of these groups was distinct in that its cultural experiences influenced its attempts to live in the city. The upper-class Gold Coasters were established residents, socially influential and economically stable. They operated a tight-knit social system and had a printed social register. In sharp contrast, the rooming-house residents, while also mostly native-born white Protestants, had relatively little social organization. Their unemployment rate was high, and they were transient, moving in and out of the area after a few months or a year or two. There was a high incidence of suicide in this area, which harbored many lost souls afflicted by *anomie** (see Chapter 7), a sense of alienation and *normlessness*.

ANOMIC ROOTLESSNESS IN THE CITY   This sense of anomie also afflicted the immigrant groups that had moved into the area. These people had been uprooted from life in Europe and were not yet integrated into the social life of Chicago. Many of them lacked clear norms and values to govern their lives. They were in a no man's land between their European background, often rural, and the flexible, secular, urban values of the American city.

This problem was evident in and near Little Italy. Here were twenty-eight distinct nationality groups. As John F. Kennedy pointed out in *A Nation of Immigrants* (1964), all of us except American Indians had relatives who came to this land of promise. Therefore, we can learn something about ourselves by noting how these immigrants adjusted to life in Chicago and how their children began to take the difficult step of becoming members of a new society while retaining some ethnic identity. This transition is described by Zorbaugh (154):

The immigrant generation, feeling little other pressure than the necessity of learning the minimum of the English language required to get along economically, shuts itself off in a Little Sicily or a ghetto and lives to itself. The American-born generation, however, is not able to live to itself. The law requires it to attend American schools; and in many other ways it is precipitated into American cultural life. It finds itself living in two social worlds, social worlds which define the same situation in very different ways. At once cultural conflicts arise; perhaps merely vague bewilderment and unrest, but often definite problems of personal behavior. In the normal native community the family and the community meet these problems for the child. But the foreign family and community are not able to do this completely or successfully.

This situation breeds teenage gangs, in which young people look to each other for peer guidance. Often, open conflict breaks out between gangs of different ethnic backgrounds.

PROBLEMS IN ESTABLISHING A SENSE OF COMMUNITY   Among the distinct cultural groups of the Near North Side, a common pattern was found in that all groups, except the secure Gold Coast families, experienced great difficulty in maintaining or reconstructing a sense of community. In small towns such as those south of Gallup, the church, the school, and town meetings or political organizations exist as community institutions and function with community support. In contrast what happened in the populous Near North Side in Chicago was that (Zorbaugh, pp. 182, 214)

the church has ceased to bear any vital relationship to local life; the school, while still in the "community," is part of a great system of schools, centrally directed, and little interested in local problems; and the "town meeting" has become a ward club, where "the boys" and political job holders gather to take orders from the ward boss, and perhaps to "sit in" on a few hands of poker... in the city black and white, rich and poor, Protestant and Catholic, cannot be gotten to rub elbows and be neighbors as people do in small towns. The city just isn't like that.

For all this loosening of old institutional ties and occasional conflict between ethnic youth gangs, the various groups did generally adjust to each other. Among the poorer groups, there was a distinct cosmopolitanism, and the people seemed genuinely tolerant of each other. The two exceptions were the Gold Coast and the Sicilian communities. The people of the Gold Coast viewed themselves as the established social elite and stood aloof from the affairs of the neighborhood outside their own circle. Their participation was impersonal, limited for the most part to contributions to social welfare services. Of the recently settled ethnic groups in the 1920s, the Sicilian community was the least open to interaction with people from other cultures.

The Sicilians continued most of the values and traditions of the villages in Sicily from which they had come. They adhered to a set of *mores*, which

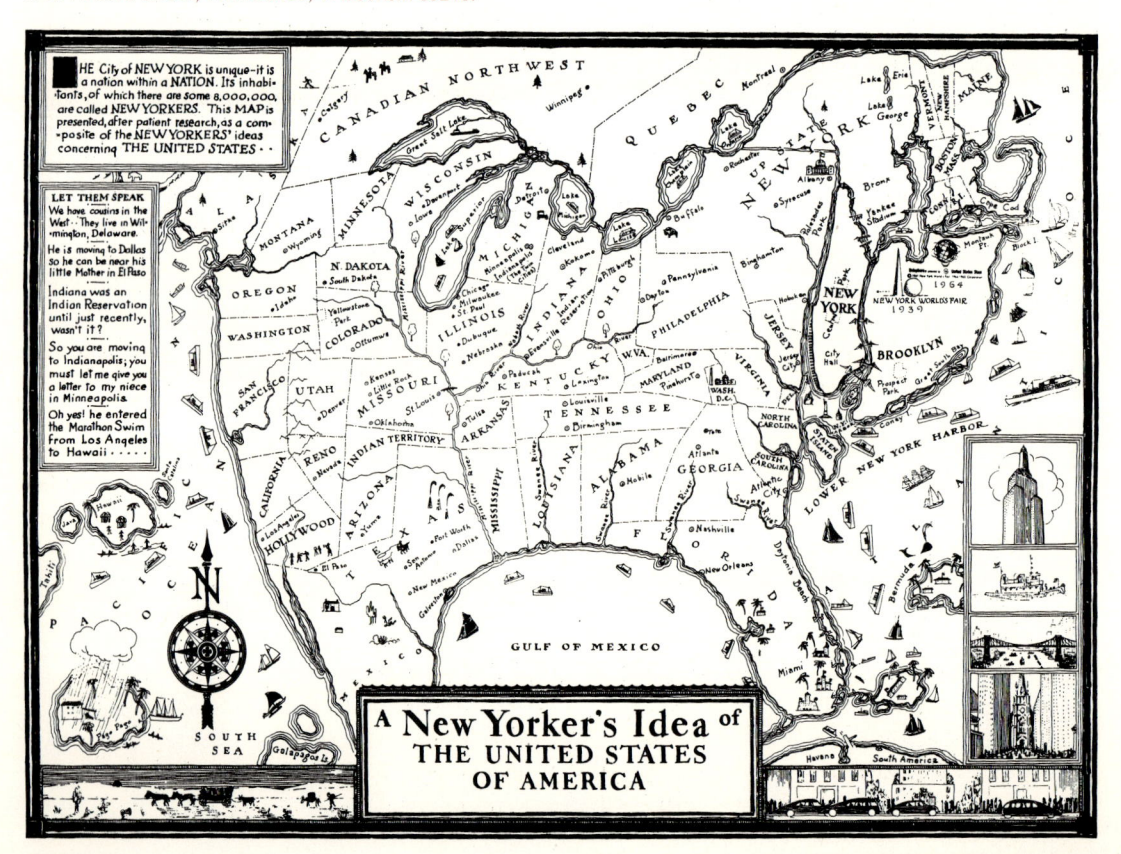

Figure 2-2 In this ethnocentric view of how the United States appears to some New Yorkers, it is comforting to see that most states are recognized even if they are somewhat smaller than Brooklyn. It would be interesting to see how New York City might be depicted by a native Iowan. SOURCE: F. V. Theirfeldt, 3766 N. 53rd Street, Milwaukee, Wisconsin 53216.

involved deeply felt values and traditions, in contrast to more lightly held *customs** and *folkways**. The Sicilians' mores, including absolute loyalty to family and to their own cultural community, were considered essential to their welfare and continued existence. Thus, when a small minority became engaged in crime during the Prohibition era of the 1920s, they favored organized crime, while other ethnic groups whose crime rate was as high were not as tightly organized. As the Sicilians and other ethnic groups became more integrated into the social life of the broader American community, their general crime rate, organized or unorganized, declined. Even so, popular themes like those of *The Godfather* perpetuate the criminal image of people of Sicilian origin.

The cosmopolitan aspect of life in a major American city differs in many ways from life in a small American community, where there are both fewer people and fewer groups. Yet in both settings the cultural heritage and experience of each group powerfully influence their behavior. These cultural influences persist, though change has come to both the community south of Gallup and to the Near North Side. Near Gallup, the population is growing rapidly and suburbs are developing. In Chicago, as in other major cities, the exodus to the suburbs has increased the physical as well as the social distance among cultural groups. These trends and their significance will be discussed in Part 2. They are important in understanding how the many cultural groups in American society are adapting to their physical and social environments.

ETHNOCENTRISM, CULTURAL RELATIVITY, AND PLURALISM Within a particular society there can exist many distinct cultures, even though there is a tendency for them to adapt to each other, to borrow cultural items such as words, forms of dress, norms, and even values from one another, and eventually to become less and less distinct from each other. At the same time, however, as a particular culture is passed along to a new generation, it acquires a kind of rightness or *legitimacy* based on tradition. And it is generally true that people who share a particular culture believe it to be better than any other.

ETHNOCENTRIC MISCONCEPTIONS ABOUT OTHERS One aspect of this tendency was observed by Walter Lippmann while serving as a member of President Wilson's diplomatic team at the Versailles Peace Conference following World War I. Mr. Lippmann described the significant misconceptions that representatives of the various Allied nations held about each other's cultures. He called these misconceptions *stereotypes** (see Chapter 8), or overgeneralized pictures that we have in our heads of other people and other places (Lippmann, 1946:70). He found that the diplomats tended to exaggerate both their own generally positive cultural characteristics and the generally negative ones of others to such an extent that reality escaped them. Thus they displayed cultural *ethnocentrism**, by which one's own culture is invariably judged to be better than any other. Ethnocentrism, which results from strongly supported cultural values, may serve the useful function of increasing one's appreciation of and commitment to one's own cultural group. Carried to an extreme, it often produces misconceptions.

Daniel Wallingford's cartoon illustrates a classic example of provincial ethnocentrism. Note that the borough of Brooklyn is larger than the rest of the city, which is in turn larger than the state of New York — or Texas; and Hollywood (presumably New Yorkers see quite a few movies) is larger than the rest of California. All this suggests that many New Yorkers never venture west of the Hudson River, or that if they do, they wear social blinders.

Ethnocentrism causes many of the intergroup problems our society faces by creating the feeling that one's own culture is superior and others are inferior. The members of one's own cultural group are known as *in-group** members, designated by such identifying terms as *we, us,* and *our.* In contrast are *out-group** members, referred to by such terms as *they, them,* and *their.*

SOME CONSEQUENCES OF ETHNOCENTRISM
Our history offers many examples of behavior that contradicts the American democratic creed. Consider the rationale used to defend the discriminatory restrictive immigration law of 1924, which was not removed from the books until 1965. The law held that only 2 percent of the total number of any foreign nationality who were United States citizens in 1890 — which was before most mass immigration had occurred from southern and eastern Europe — would be allowed to enter the United States in any given year (Bernard, 1952:685–690). That quota system effectively kept out most potential immigrants from Italy, Poland, Greece, Russia, and other southern and eastern European countries as well as from Asia. At the same time, immigration from Great Britain and northern Europe was kept open. Note the ethnocentrism reflected in the law, and consider its probable effect on those whose ancestors came from one of the restricted nations.

This kind of reasoning has been a large factor in the waves of racial intolerance that have periodically marked our history. During World War II, the government rounded up thousands of Japanese-American citizens, confiscated their property, and held them in detention camps for the duration of the war (Bloom and Riemar, 1949:202–204). Yet not one of these people was ever found to have been disloyal to the United States. Their sons formed a combat unit that fought in the European theater; it became one of the most decorated units in the American Army during the war. More recently, a political minority, those who were active protestors against United States involvement in Vietnam, feared that political dissidents might be similarly imprisoned in detention camps. Although their fears were unfounded, they cited the case of the Japanese-Americans as a reason for their concern.

These Japanese-Americans were victimized by the prejudice that has held racial minorities to be inferior and untrustworthy. How did white Americans come to think this way in a culture that espouses the belief that all men are created equal and endowed by their creator with certain inalienable rights? Those words were drafted into the Declaration of Independence, but others were drawn up for inclusion in the Constitution.

Enslavement of blacks ended in the nineteenth century, but the original language of the Constitution (Article 1, Section 2) states that "representatives and direct taxes shall be apportioned among the several states . . . by adding to the whole

Cross-cultural references can help put our own cultural assumptions in perspective. SOURCE: Copyright © 1971 *The Chicago Sun Times.* Reproduced by courtesy of Wil-Jo Associates, Inc. and Bill Mauldin.

"WHO'LL VOLUNTEER FOR MISSIONARY WORK AMONG THE WARRING TRIBES OF NORTHERN IRELAND?"

number of free persons . . . and . . . three-fifths of all other persons" (that is, of black slaves).³ This provision was a compromise with the slave states of the South, whose leaders wanted the representation and political power to which their full population, black and white, entitled them without giving up slavery and its economic benefits (Beard, 1960:41-42, 131). The result was only partial citizenship for black slaves and, by implication, only partial humanity.

It is now more than a century since the Fourteenth Amendment nullified the three-fifths provision of the Constitution. Yet, white ethnocentricity is still a powerful influence. One test of this is *social distance**, the degree to which one group is willing to associate with another. Most white Americans place themselves apart from Americans of a different color or cultural heritage. Whites tend to value whiteness above blackness, and we use such expressions as "that's mighty white of you," "I'm free, white, and twenty-one," or "he's the black sheep of the family." The sources of these values are complex and involve the historical residue of slavery, the economic and political status of blacks, and other factors.

SOCIAL DISTANCE MEASURES   Still, in our culture the result of this widely held value is measurable. One such measure is the *Social Distance Quotient** (SDQ) devised by Emory Bogardus to measure social distance (1959).⁴ Bogardus formulated a list of statements representing varying degrees of social intimacy or distance. He asked selected Americans, mostly white Protestants of British or northern European ethnic heritage, to check off those classifications to which they would willingly admit members of a given group. The Social Distance Quotient was based on the average of the following seven ratings:

to close kinship by marriage (1 point)

to my club as personal chums (2 points)

to my street as neighbor (3 points)

to employment in my occupation (4 points)

to citizenship in my country (5 points)

as visitors to my country (6 points)

would exclude from my country (7 points)

Thirty ethnic, religious, and racial groups were listed in Bogardus's first sampling in 1926. Good information on trends in social distance is available because samples were again drawn in later years. The results of the 1926, 1946, and 1966 samples are provided in Table 2-1. Note that while the total social distance white Americans place between themselves and others has narrowed, the rank remains similar, with blacks and other racial minority groups at the bottom.

The impact of cultural norms, in this case ethnocentric ones, is made clear by Bogardus. He notes that racial and ethnic minority group members, such as blacks and Jews, have preferences similar to those of the majority group with one

---

³ While the word "persons" refers to blacks who were slaves, the constitutional provisions on Indians provided that Indians were to be excluded. As such these native Americans were viewed as members of foreign (tribal) nations. Relations with them were centered in the Department of War. It was not until the twentieth century, in 1924, that Indians were allowed to become American citizens. In some states, citizenship rights came even later. For example, in Arizona, Indians did not have voting rights until 1948. Some Indians today regard their rights as questionable.

⁴ The Social Distance Quotient (SDQ) was originally called a Racial Distance Quotient (RDQ). However, since it measures the social distance between religious and nationality groups as well as racial groups it has increasingly been referred to as SDQ rather than RDQ.

Table 2-1   Changes in Social Distance Measurements

1926 Sample of 1,726 throughout U.S.		1946 Sample of 2,053 throughout U.S.		1966 Sample of 2,605 throughout U.S.		
Cultural group	SDQ*	Cultural group	SDQ	Cultural group	SDQ	
1. English	1.06	1. Americans (U.S. white)	1.08	1. Americans (U.S. white)	1.07	
2. American (U.S. white)	1.10	2. Canadians	1.16	2. English	1.14	
3. Canadians	1.13	3. English	1.23	3. Canadians	1.15	Primarily
4. Scots	1.13	4. French	1.47	4. French	1.36	British
5. Irish	1.30	5. Irish	1.56	5. Irish	1.40	and
6. French	1.32	6. Swedish	1.57	6. Swedish	1.42	Northern
7. Germans	1.46	7. Scots	1.60	7. Norwegians	1.50	European
8. Swedish	1.54	8. Germans	1.61	8. Italians	1.51	
9. Hollanders	1.56	9. Hollanders	1.63	9. Scots	1.53	
10. Norwegians	1.59	10. Norwegians	1.66	10. Germans	1.54	
11. Spanish	1.72	11. Finns	1.80	11. Hollanders	1.54	
12. Finns	1.83	12. Italians	1.89	12. Finns	1.67	
13. Russians	1.88	13. Poles	2.07	13. Greeks	1.82	Primarily
14. Italians	1.94	14. Spanish	2.08	14. Spanish	1.93	Southern
15. Poles	2.01	15. Greeks	2.09	15. Jews	1.97	and
16. Armenians	2.06	16. Jews	2.15	16. Poles	1.98	Eastern
17. Czechs	2.08	17. Czechs	2.22	17. Czechs	2.02	European
18. Indians (Amer.)	2.38	18. Armenians	2.33	18. Indians (Amer.)	2.12	
19. Jews	2.39	19. Japanese-Amer.	2.34	19. Japanese-Amer.	2.14	
20. Greeks	2.47	20. Indians (Amer.)	2.35	20. Armenians	2.18	
21. Mexicans	2.69	21. Filipinos	2.46	21. Filipinos	2.31	
22. Mexican-Amer.	—	22. Mexican-Amer.	2.51	22. Chinese	2.34	
23. Japanese	2.80	23. Turks	2.52	23. Mexican-Amer.	2.37	Primarily
24. Japanese-Amer.	—	24. Russians	2.56	24. Russians	2.38	non-white
25. Filipinos	3.00	25. Chinese	2.68	25. Japanese	2.41	racial
26. Negroes	3.28	26. Japanese	2.70	26. Turks	2.48	groups
27. Turks	3.30	27. Negroes	2.74	27. Koreans	2.51	
28. Chinese	3.36	28. Mexicans	2.79	28. Mexicans	2.56	
29. Koreans	3.60	29. Indians (from India)	2.80	29. Negroes	2.58	
30. Indians (from India)	3.91	30. Koreans	2.83	30. Indians (from India)	2.62	

SOURCE: Emory S. Bogardus, "Comparing Racial Distance in Ethiopia, South Africa and the United States, *Sociology and Social Research* 52 (University of Southern California, 1968), p. 152.

major exception: *each tends to place his own group members near the top of the scale.* Ethnocentrism is not confined to any one group.

CULTURAL RELATIVISM AND CULTURAL PLURALISM
An alternative perspective to ethnocentrism is *cultural relativism**, which holds that no single universal standard should be used to judge any culture's way of life. Ethnocentrism holds to the *culturally absolute* value that the beliefs and behavior of one's own culture are the only acceptable ones.

VALUE CONFLICTS   In American society, we believe in cultural relativism and also in the contradictory value. In our modern urban society, where masses of people live close to each other, the former appears to be the stronger feeling and practice for most. It is unlikely that these two opposing cultural values can coexist indefinitely.

The American social environment is heavily influenced by the Puritan belief in individual redemption and hard work. At the same time, a degree of *cultural pluralism** characterizes American society, where a variety of national, racial, and religious groups live together and influence each other's values. Even in the early colonial period, there were religious *subcultures* (groups that are not dominant in numbers or power, whose designs for living differ from mainstream culture) besides the Puritans, including Catholics, Episcopalians, Jews, and Quakers. Blacks and Indians were also included in colonial society, although their social situation was problematic. In the nineteenth century, immigration brought in thousands of southern and eastern Europeans, some Orientals, and a large Mexican population in the Southwest after the Mexican War of the 1840s. Figure 2-3 shows main ethnic streams across this continent in our agrarian-dominant period. The direction of these streams still influences patterns of settlement.

All these groups produced considerable cultural disagreement about certain values. For example, many religions have food taboos (bans or prohibitions), but on different foods. Orthodox Jews do not eat pork; until recently, Catholics were not permitted to eat meat or fowl on Fridays. Some values touch fundamental questions about family life. Most Catholics oppose divorce; early Mormons practiced polygyny (a form of polygamy in which one man marries two or more wives), while most others in the culture practiced monogamy (one husband, one wife).

While there are few universally accepted values and behaviors within American society or throughout the world, they do exist. As Kluckhohn observed, "No culture tolerates indiscriminate lying, stealing, or violence within the in-group" (1962:294). Beyond this, acceptable practices vary enormously even within the same community.

Our cultural values, norms, beliefs, and practices find their bases and perpetuation in the socialization process, to which we now turn.

SOCIALIZATION

DEVELOPMENT OF THE SOCIAL SELF
From their teens on, most people ask themselves what kind of person they are, what they want to do with their lives, and what they believe about various social issues: Do I think well of myself, or am I highly self-critical? Do I want a college degree or some other kind of training? Shall I vote for Democrats or Republicans? What do I want to do for a living? The answers to these and other questions are related to the processes through which we learn to fit into society. This process is called *socialization**.

THE ROLE OF LANGUAGE AND OTHER FORMS OF COMMUNICATION   Socialization is the process by which we develop our identity as Americans, Catholics, Californians, men or women, or as members of any other groups with which we iden-

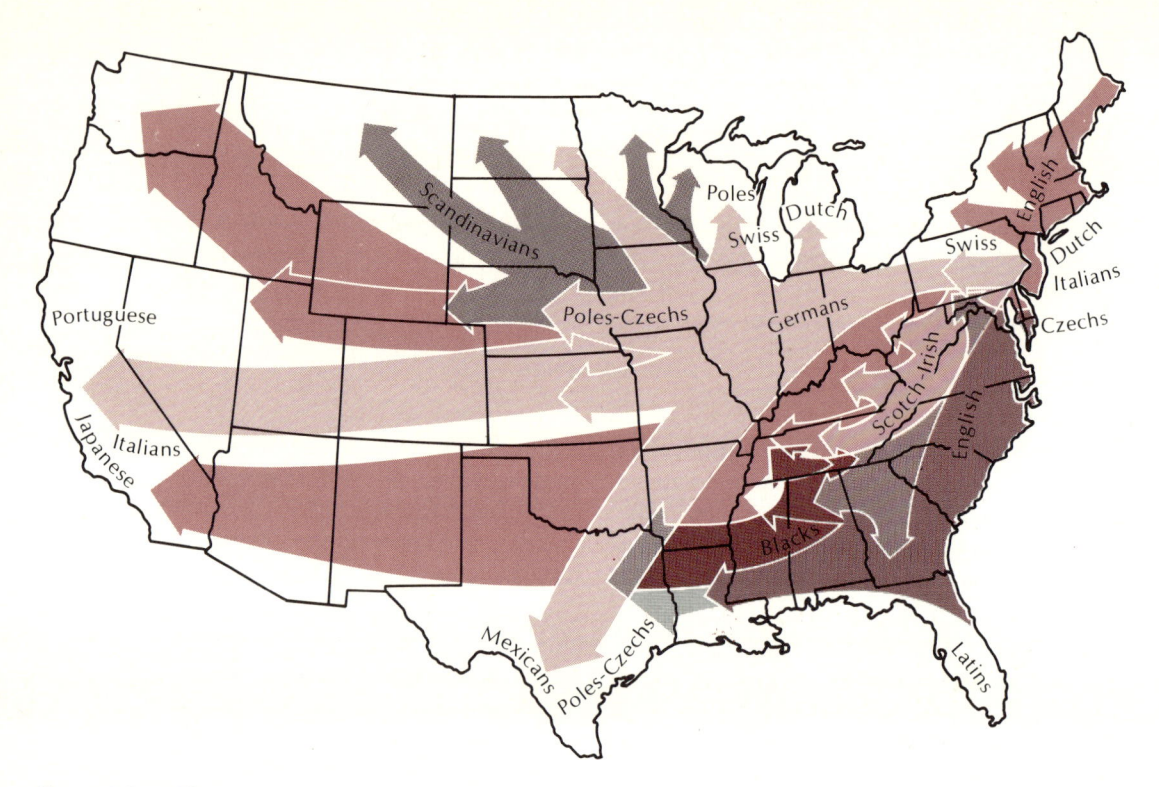

Figure 2-3 The arrows in the map show major migrations of ethnic groups in America's agrarian dominant period. Other nationalities fewer in number are indicated in type. These settlement patterns continue to affect demographic characteristics in the United States today. SOURCE: Map by Bob Kean for *Farm Journal: The Business Magazine of American Agriculture*. February, 1976, pp. 24–25.

tify or are identified by others. The socialization process begins in infancy in the family, where a child learns to relate to other people. The symbols he or she learns, both verbal and nonverbal, are crucial to the process. While spoken language soon becomes the child's most important means of interacting with others, such forms of communication as gestures and tone of voice can be just as important. As psychologist Alberta E. Siegel points out about this process of *symbolic interactionism**:

Speech and language are the hallmark of the human condition, but they play very little role in the life of the infant. Human infants, like other primates, are more attuned to nonverbal communication than to verbal. They derive meaning not from the words people say; but from their gestures, postures, and facial expressions, and from the tone of voice and melody of their speech. It is only toward the end of the first year of life that they begin to understand a few of the words spoken in their presence, and in the second year to speak a few words themselves. The term "infant" means "without speech," but we are not misled into thinking that infants are without communicative skills. They have them, but they are the communicative skills of all primates rather than the distinctively human skills: the infant's communicative alertness centers on how others move and on the emotional tone of their vocalizations rather than on language narrowly defined.

Furthermore, young children do not lose their receptivity to nonverbal communication as speech develops. Young children remain visually dominated. They can understand us better by watching us than by listening to our verbal flow. And they can tell us how they feel more fluently through their drawings than through words.

THE LOOKING GLASS SELF AND SIGNIFICANT OTHERS   Charles Horton Cooley identified the development of what he called the *looking-glass self** (1922:184) to explain the early stage of learning how to become a social being. As George Herbert Mead observed (1934:154), while we may change our self-images as we grow up, we are heavily influenced by our identification with such *significant other** persons as our parents, brothers and sisters, and others with whom we are close. When they react to us, these significant others serve as mirrors, or looking glasses, in which we view ourselves. Later our *peers**, those of approximately our own age and social status, may further influence our self-perceptions. In a complex urban society, there are additional significant others in the socialization process beyond family and friends; they include teachers, employers, ministers, and even people we see on television and learn of in the other mass media. One study, based on Scandinavian research, of children's identification with television figures suggests that older children — about age twelve — seek clear moral norms when they watch television (Feilitzen and Linne, 1975:54).

The looking-glass self is involved in most early social interactions. Whether the people with whom we identify like or dislike us, whether they think us bright or stupid, attractive or ugly, we are influenced by them in our views of ourselves. Until we begin to develop independent views of ourselves, this early mirror image may affect the way we react to different situations. These influences on self-concept, whether or not they are based on reality, can develop in time into a *self-fulfilling prophecy*. Sometimes called the *Thomas theorem**, the self-fulfilling prophecy can be seen in numerous situations in daily life (Thomas, 1931:189).[5]

THE SELF-FULFILLING PROPHECY   In a study published in 1968, called *Pygmalion in the Classroom*, Rosenthal and Jacobson described the prophecy in action. Teachers were told that, according to a test supposed to predict children's potential, certain children were likely to do well in class. In fact, the test had no such predictive powers, but because teachers believed the predictions, the children were treated according to their supposed abilities. Many showed remarkable improvement in classwork. In addition, the authors found that prejudice had an effect on the prophecy. Gains of minority children were more grudgingly acknowledged, sometimes offset by low ratings in other areas of competence such as intellectual curiosity and ability to show affection.

Charles Silberman summarized the self-fulfilling prophecy when he observed (Silberman, 1970:83):

A teacher's *expectation* can and does quite literally affect a student's *performance*. The teacher who assumes that her students cannot learn is likely to discover that she has a class of children who are indeed unable to learn; yet another teacher, working with the same class but without the same expectation, may discover that she has a class of interested learners. The same obtains with respect to behavior: the teacher who assumes that her students will be disruptive is likely to have a disruptive class on her hands.

---

[5] In discussing his study of Polish immigrants in Chicago at the turn of the century, W. I. Thomas noted that one of the major reasons why Polish youngsters often performed poorly in school was that they were socialized into believing that they were less bright than other children. On this observation, Thomas coined the concept of "self-fulfilling prophecy." W. I. Thomas, *The Child in America: Problems and Programs.* (New York: Knopf, 1928).

It should be remembered that the prophecy works not only because of the belief of another but also because one accepts a false definition of oneself from which real consequences emerge.

THE CULTURAL PERSONALITY   The socialization of the individual in the family and in other social units mirrors a larger cultural pattern. Each family, each school, each business reflects the culture of which it is a part. For all the individual differences within a culture, commonalities in socialization exist. Some scholars describe the product of these common values and norms as a *cultural personality*. Most American boys, and increasingly girls (see the selection "Sex Role Socialization in Children's Picture Books" on this point), are socialized to believe it natural to compete to win, whether in taking tests, playing sports, or earning a living. This has been particularly true for boys. An exaggerated form of this personality disposition is the masculine *machismo** orientation of some men who exhibit highly aggressive virility and an exploitative attitude toward women.

SEX-ROLE SOCIALIZATION IN CHILDREN'S PICTURE BOOKS

From: Lenore Weitzman with Deborah Eifler, Elizabeth Hokada, and Catherine Ross, "Sex-Role Socialization in Picture Books for Preschool Children," *American Journal of Sociology 77* (Chicago: University of Chicago Press, 1972), pp. 1131–1139. © 1972 by the University of Chicago. All rights reserved.

The researchers drew upon a representative sample of preschool books that won prizes such as the Caldecott Medal, which is presented by the Children's Service Committee of the American Library Association. The research results indicated that these widely used children's books presented a sharply differential role treatment for boys and for girls.

We can summarize our first findings about differences in the activities of boys and girls by noting that in the world of picture books boys are active and girls are passive. Not only are boys presented in more exciting and adventuresome roles, but they engage in more varied pursuits and demand more independence. The more riotous activity is reserved for the boys. Mickey, the hero of *In the Night Kitchen* (Sendak, 1970), is tossed through the air and skips from bread to dough, punching and pounding. Then he makes an airplane and flies out into the night and dives, swims and slides until he is home again. Similarly, Archie and Peter race, climb, and hide in the story of *Coggles* (Keats, 1969). Obadiah travels to the wharf in the cold of Massachusetts winter, and Sylvester searches for rocks in the woods.

In contrast, most of the girls in the picture books are passive and immobile. Some of them are restricted by their clothing — skirts and dresses are soiled easily and prohibit more adventuresome activities. In *The Fool of the World and the Flying Ship* (Ronsome, 1963), the hero, the Fool, is dressed in a sensible manner, one which does not inhibit his movement in the tasks he has to accomplish. The princess, however, for whom all the exploits are waged, remains no more than her long gown allows her to be: a prize, an unrealistic passive creature symbolizing the reward for male adventuresomeness.

A second difference between the activities of boys and girls is that the girls are more often found indoors. This places another limitation on the activities and potential adventures of girls. Even Sam, in *Sam, Bangs, and Moonshine* (Ness, 1967), stays inside as she directs the activity of the books. Sam constructs a fantasy world and sends Thomas, a little boy, on wild goose chases to play out her fantasies. It is Thomas who rides the bicycle and climbs the trees and rocks in response to Sam's fantasy. Sam, however, waits for Thomas at home, looking out the windows or sitting on the steps.... Similarly, in the *Fool of the World* (Ransome, 1968), the princess remains peering out the window of her castle, watching all the activities on her behalf. While boys play in the real world outdoors, girls sit and watch them — cut off from that world by the window, porch, or fence around their homes. This distinction parallels Erik Erikson's (1964) conception of the masculine outer space and the feminine inner space.

Our third observation deals with the service activities performed by the girls who remain at home. Even the youngest girls in the stories play traditional feminine roles, directed toward pleasing and helping their brothers and fathers. Obadiah's sisters cook in the kitchen as he sits at the table sipping hot chocolate after his adventures. In *The Emperor and the Kite* (Yolen, 1967), the emperor's daughters bring food to the emperor's table, but their brothers rule the kingdom.

While girls serve, boys lead. Drummer Hoff, although only a boy, plays the crucial role in the final firing of the cannon. Lupin, the Indian boy in *The Angry Moon* (Sleator, 1970), directs the escape from the moon god.... He leads Lapowinsa, a girl exactly his size and age, every step of the way. Even at the end of the story, after the danger of the Angry Moon is past, Lupin goes down the ladder first "so that he could catch Lapowinsa if she should slip."

Training for a dependent passive role may inhibit a girl's chances for intellectual or creative success. It is likely that the excessive dependency encouraged in girls contributes to the decline in their achievement which becomes apparent as they grow older. Maccoby (1966, p. 35) has found that "for both sexes, there is a tendency for more passive-dependent children to perform poorly on a variety of intellectual tasks, and for independent children to excel."

The rescues featured in many stores require independence and self-confidence. Once again, this is almost exclusively a male activity. Little boys rescue girls or helpless animals. Lupin saves a crying Lapowinsa from the flames. Obadiah saves the seagull from a rusty fishhook, and Alexander saves Willie, the windup mouse, from the fate of becoming a "tossed-out toy." In *Frederick*, Frederick's creativeness helps to spare his companions from the worst conditions of winter. In *Sam, Bangs, and Moonshine* (Ness, 1967), Sam does not play the role of the rescuer although she is the central character. Rather, her father must step in and rescue Thomas and Bangs from drowning. In the end, Sam herself "must be" saved from the potential consequences of her fantasy.

Finally, we want to note the sense of camaraderie that is encouraged among boys through their adventures. For example, *The Fool of the World* depends upon the help and talents of his male companions.... In *Goggles* (Keats, 1969), the two male companions together outwit a gang of older boys. Similarly, the bonds of masculine friendship are stressed by Alexander, Frederick, and Frog and Toad.

In contrast, one rarely sees only girls working or playing together. Although in reality women spend much of their time with other women, picture books imply that women cannot exist without men. The role of most of the girls is defined primarily in relation to that of the boys and men in their lives. It is interesting to note that Sam turns to a boy, not a girl, to accomplish all of the activity of her fantasies. Her dreams would have no reality without Thomas....

It is easy to see why many little girls prefer to identify with the male role (Hartup, 1962; Brown, 1956). The little girl who does find the male role more attractive is faced with a dilemma. If she follows her desires and behaves like a tomboy, she may be criticized by her parents and teachers. On the other hand, if she gives up her yearnings and identifies with the traditional feminine role, she will feel stifled. Girls who wish to be more than placid and pretty are left without an acceptable role alternative. They must choose between alienation from their own sex of assignment, and alienation from their real behavioral and temperamental preferences.

The rigidity of sex-role stereotypes is not harmful only to little girls. Little boys may feel equally constrained by the necessity to be fearless, brave, and clever at all times. While girls are allowed a great deal of emotional expression, a boy who cries or expresses fear is unacceptable. Just as the only girls who are heroines in picture books have boys' names or are foreign princesses, the only boys who cry in picture books are animals — frogs and toads and donkeys.

The price of the standardization and rigidity of sex roles is paid by children of both sexes. Eleanor Maccoby (1966, p. 35) has reported that analytic thinking, creativity, and general intelligence are associated with cross-sex typing. Thus, rigid sex-role definitions not only foster unhappiness in children but they also hamper the child's fullest intellectual and social development.

SEX-ROLE SOCIALIZATION IN CHILDREN'S LITERATURE REVISITED: GREAT HERA! IT'S WONDER WOMAN!

From "Wonder Woman: An Introduction by Gloria Steinem" in *Wonder Woman*, a *Ms.* Book (New York: Holt, Rinehart and Winston, 1972). © Ms. Magazine Corp. Reprinted with permission.

The comic book heroine Wonder Woman was created in 1941 by William Moulton Marston, an American psychologist who wrote under the pseudonym Charles Moulton. She was a brave, patriotic person capable of great accomplishments. Gloria Steinem tells us what she meant to young girls seeking a role model.

Her creator had ... seen straight into my heart and understood the secret fears of violence hidden there. No longer did I have to pretend to like the "Pow!" and "Crunch!" style of Captain Marvel or the Green Hornet. No longer did I have nightmares after reading ghoulish comics filled with torture and mayhem. Comics made all the more horrifying by their real-life setting in World War II. (It was a time when leather-clad Nazis were marching in the newsreels and in the comics, and the blood on the pages seemed frighteningly real.) Here was a heroic person who might conquer with force, but only a force that was tempered by love and justice. She converted her enemies more often than not. And if they were destroyed, they did it to themselves, usually in some unbloody accident.

She was beautiful, brave, and explicitly out to change "A world torn by the hatred and wars of men."

She was Wonder Woman.

Looking back now at these Wonder Woman stories from the 40's, I am amazed by the strength of their feminist message. One typical story centers on Prudence, a young pioneer in the days of the American Frontier. (Wonder Woman is transported there by her invisible plane, of course, which also served as a time machine.) Rescued by Wonder Woman, Prudence realized her own worth and worth of all women. "I've learned my lesson," she says proudly in the final scene. "From now on, I'll rely on myself, not on a man." In yet another episode, Wonder Woman herself says, "I can never love a dominant man who is stronger than I am." And throughout the strips, it is only the destructive, criminal woman — the woman who has bought the whole idea that male means aggression and female means submitting — who says "Girls want superior men to boss them around."

Many of the plots revolve around evil men who treat women as inferior beings. In the end, all are brought to their knees and made to recognize women's strength and value. Some of the stories focus on weak women who are destructive and confused. These misled females are converted to self-reliance and self-respect through the example of Wonder Woman. The message of the strips is sometimes inconsistent and always oversimplified (these are, after all, comics), but is still a passable version of the truisms that women are rediscovering today: that women are full human beings; that we cannot love others until we love ourselves; that love and respect can only exist between equals.

Wonder Woman's family of Amazons on Paradise Island, her band of college girls in America, and her efforts to save individual women are all welcome examples of women working together and caring about each other's welfare. The idea of such cooperation may not seem particularly revolutionary to the male reader: men are routinely depicted as working well together, but women know how rare and therefore exhilarating the idea of sisterhood really is.

Wonder Woman's mother, Queen Hippolyte, offers yet another welcome example to young girls in search of a strong identity. Queen Hippolyte founds nations, wages war to protect Paradise Island, and sends her daughter off to fight the forces of evil in the world. Perhaps most impressive in an age fraught with Freudian shibboleths, she also marshals her queenly strength to protect her daughter in bad times. How many girl children grew to adulthood with no experience of a courageous and worldly mother, except in these slender stories? How many adult women disdain the birth of a female child, believe it is "better" to bear male children, and fear the competition and jealousy they have been conditioned to believe is "natural" to a mother and daughter? Feminism is just beginning to uncover the sense of anger and loss in girls whose mothers had no power to protect them in the world, and so trained them to be victims, or left them to identify with their fathers if they had any ambitions outside the traditional female role.

Wonder Woman symbolizes many of the values of the woman's culture that feminists are now trying to introduce into the mainstream; strength and self-reliance for women; sisterhood and mutual support among women; peacefulness and esteem for human life; a diminishment both of "masculine" aggression and of the belief that violence is the only way of solving conflicts.

Like many cultural characteristics, the competitive orientation is not universal. For example, the cooperative and friendly Arapesh of New Guinea are socialized quite differently (Mead, 1950:15–19). When American soldiers organized a race with a group of Arapesh children and offered a prize for the winner, something happened that was, from the American point of view, inexplicable. The Arapesh children made sure that nobody took the lead or fell behind. They all ended the race in a tie. The children had been socialized to cooperate in whatever they did.

SOCIAL STATUS   In our mass society, the socialization of people into cooperative, competitive, or other behavior is considerably more complex than in village life like that of the Arapesh. How cooperative or competitive a person is, how much confidence she or he develops, and other personality characteristics are influenced by such factors as whether the individual is female or male, black or white, rich or poor. Each of these categories carries with it an identity that makes up one's *social status** and a pattern of behavior associated with the social *role** one plays while occupying a given status.

The terms *status* and *role* deserve special attention. Some sociologists use the two terms interchangeably to denote the relevant characteristics of individuals who are expected to behave in a certain way because they have a particular kind of relationship to given others (Hoult, 1969:316). It is more useful to consider status and role as interrelated but separate concepts.

FILLING SOCIETY'S POSITIONS   Social status generally refers to a position an individual occupies in society, such as housewife, pedestrian, congresswoman, or electrician. Each status carries with it a distinctive array of rights and obligations in relation to other statuses (Merton, 1967:41). Status also carries the connotation of prestige, although we must remember that while *high status* properly indicates a status with relatively high prestige (for example a judge or an all-star quarterback), it is incorrect to say that someone has *more* status than another. (See the selection "The Concept of Social Status" for a more extensive definition of status characteristics.)

Norms, characteristic of all statuses, are rules of behavior that pertain to the occupants of social statuses rather than to the individuals themselves. What one ought to do while occupying the status of college student may be quite different from what

Athletic events reflect some American cultural orientations, including the emphasis on leisure activity and a competitive spirit. SOURCE: Stephen J. Potter/Stock Boston.

one ought to do while working as a part-time checker in a supermarket, even though an individual may occupy both statuses at different times. Some norms cut across statuses, but high social status may lessen the impact of universal norms. A poor shoplifter may be sent to jail while her or his wealthy counterpart may be treated courteously by the shop and police and quietly allowed to work out a financial settlement.

THE CONCEPT OF SOCIAL STATUS

From: Norman Storer, *Focus on Society* (Reading, Mass.: Addison-Wesley, 1973), pp. 25–27.

Let us assume that a Martian spends a month observing different earthlings. As soon as he looks over his notes, he begins to see that there is a good deal of similarity in what different people do when they are in similar situations. This seems to be the case regardless of physical appearance or the psychological habits that show up when these individuals are alone. Most of them kiss their wives goodbye in the morning, give money to the busdriver or the conductor on the train, and follow the suggestions of one or more people where they work.

He has discovered, in short, that he can predict different types of behavior — of interaction — better by knowing something about the nature of the situation (where, when, and who else is involved) than he can by knowing something about the individual's psychological makeup. He has found that the young man and the old man, the grouchy man and the friendly man, all go through roughly the same patterns of interaction when they are saying goodbye to their wives, buying a newspaper, answering the telephone, being introduced to a stranger, and so on. To be sure, there are subtle differences in how they do these things, but these would become apparent only after the Martian had become quite familiar with the general pattern in each case.

(Rather than wait for him to become completely familiar with our earthly customs, we can assume at this point that our Martian has served his didactic purposes and can be sent home. From here on, we're by ourselves again.)

Next comes the question of how it is that a person knows how to interact with a particular person. What is it about the other person that tells him what he should do, and what the other person is likely to do?

It turns out that he uses a number of different clues to tell him what sort of behavior is appropriate — what the other person, and still others as well, will welcome or at least tolerate as behavior on his part. The sex of the other person, the particular situation they are in, the time of day, the other person's clothing — all these provide a good deal of guidance in the matter.

For instance, you assume that the person standing behind the counter in a bakery during the daytime and wearing a white garment, whether male or female, is a salesclerk. On the basis of these three clues alone, you have a pretty good idea of what to expect of this person, and what he expects of you. He or she is there to take your money and see that you get the cake or bread you want. There will be little difficulty for the two of you in carrying out an efficient and satisfactory pattern of interaction here.

Similarly, the man in the blue uniform, standing at the intersection, is undoubtedly a policeman. You know what to expect of him, and what he expects of you. Place and clothing have given you all the information you need.

It should be noted that we have summed up this information by giving the person in question a name: *salesclerk, policeman*. But there are many occasions when observable clues will not be enough to tell us how to interact with someone. So we must ask him what to expect — and we do this by asking the name of his social position rather than his personal name. When a stranger knocks on our door, we ask, "Who is it?" — but we mean, "What is your social position?" rather than "What is your name?"

The stranger knows what we mean by "Who is it?" and will answer, "Gasman," or "Paperboy," or "Special delivery." It would be foolish for him to reply, "My name is William Jones," for this would not be appropriate; it would tell us nothing about what to expect of him or what he expects of us. Sometimes he must even make up a position, as in the answer, "I'm a stranger — my car has broken down in front of your house."

In each of these cases, once we have figured out or have been told the name of the person's social position, we know generally how to interact with him. This sociological concept uses the idea of social position, or *status*. We noted earlier, for instance, that the Martian sociologist's subject changed his behavior as he moved from the home to the bus to the office — and we can say now that he changed his status as he entered each new situation. At first he was a husband, and also a father; then he was a passenger (a special kind of customer); and finally he assumed the status of employee.

A status, then, is in effect the name of a social position. It is not something we can touch; rather it serves to identify a bundle of rights and obligations that go together and can be associated with an individual in a particular situation. As the sociologist uses the term, incidentally, status doesn't imply anything in the way of good or bad, high or low. "Howard Smith, *Shoeshine boy*," is a status, just as "*Governor* Howard Smith" is, and neither involves (or has) any *more* status, than the other — even though the governor clearly occupies a *higher* status than the shoe-shine boy.

We should recall at this point... the sociologist's tendency to use common words in special ways, or with more precision than they are used in everyday language. While *status* usually carries the connotation of relative prestige or importance, in sociology the term means simply a "social position" that exists as a particular combination of rights and duties.

We should note also that a status may be more or less formal. A well-formalized status would be one like that of "bank president": it is widely recognized, and we are aware of the position even when it is not occupied. An informal status, on the other hand, would be something like that of "class clown" in a high school; here, no one feels that the position should be filled if there is no one who fits it naturally.

The concept of social status is central to sociology, for patterns of social behavior ordinarily develop in connection with statuses. If people's expectations for others concerning rights and obligations become routine, it is because they are able to associate these expectations with statuses. No matter who stands and lectures to a roomful of college students, the students' expectations of this person are based on his or her status as professor rather than on his or her personal characteristics. Should your English professor begin to do rope tricks or perform a belly dance, it would probably be more difficult for you to accept that person as a serious scholar, an attribute expected of professors. Since we often respond more to the status than the person, it is common for us to be surprised when we find someone we know only in one status, let's say our professor, occupying another role, say charity volunteer or disco dancer.

ROLE-PLAYING Shakespeare's famous lines, "All the world's a stage, and all the men and women merely players," make a good point about the many statuses each of us occupies. Think for a moment of the many different social situations you are in on a given day. At times you may be acting the part associated with the status of daughter or son, brother or sister, student, friend, teammate, or employee. The behavior expected of someone in each of these statuses is that person's *role** (Gross, 1958:18). Note that a role may consist of many behaviors. Think how many different performances a mother gives each day.

How you play a role is subject to interpretation by the beholder. He may come to view your actions as in keeping with your unique personality ("she's always a little weird"), or as responses typical of the role called for by the status you occupy ("a big sister should help a kid out"). Unfortunately, those who are at a great social distance from you may see your role behavior as a stereotype ("that's how those people act"). So much of social behavior can be understood in terms of the roles related to their various statuses that it is useful to consider the concept of role separately.

ROLE AS AN INTERACTION CONCEPT Roles associated with any status involve expected behavior within a social relationship with one or more persons occupying other statuses. The status of daughter assumes a parent; the status of student assumes a teacher. These and other roles develop to meet people's needs. For example, students are expected to be literate, and English teachers are expected to use their knowledge and skills to help students become literate. These roles are formally set; however, we often instruct or learn from others in informal ways ("Hey, show me your guitar. Could you teach me to play something? I'll show you how to do macramé if you will"). In a general sense, each of us sometimes has the status of student and sometimes of teacher.

People take on the different roles associated with these and other statuses in order to accomplish a variety of tasks required by a society. The organization of these and other roles becomes a *division of labor** needed for the efficient functioning of society. The division of labor in society involves much more than behavior in an economic context. It includes interaction in all forms of social organizations — occupational roles, or husband–wife, student–teacher, or priest–worshiper relationships.

ROLES BASED UPON ASCRIBED AND ACHIEVED STATUS Some roles are related to *ascribed** status and some to *achieved** status.[6] Ascribed status

---

[6] Even in societies that rely on ascribed statuses, there is evidence of movement toward greater emphasis on achieved statuses. A classic case is the decline of the age-old *caste* system in India. Until the mid-twentieth century, in India all statuses were ascribed at birth. Marriage was forbidden between members of different castes, and all occupational roles were determined at birth, including an *untouchable* and unemployable caste. Since India's independence from British colonial rule in 1947, the caste system has been officially ended. Some practices remain, though. In American society, the racial caste system of the South (Davis, Gardner, and Gardner, 1941) was significantly challenged in the 1950s and 1960s (see Chapter 6, Social Class and Poverty, and Chapter 8, Collective Conflict and Intergroup Relations).

involves little personal choice. Age, sex, race, and family background all confer ascribed statuses. One does not choose to be female or male, fifteen or fifty, black or white. Yet each of these personal characteristics carries with it expectations of behavior. Females in our culture have been expected to fulfill the roles of wife, mother, and helpmate. Blacks have been expected to fill society's need for cheap labor. Fifteen-year-olds have been expected to be students cooperating in the process of being socialized into the larger culture. Ordinarily one has no freedom to select one's age, ethnicity, or sex, even though it is possible to lie or even to undergo a sex-change operation.

When people with ascribed characteristics do not fulfill role and status expectations, conflict frequently occurs, sometimes producing social change. The ascribed characteristics of age, race, and sex are being increasingly rejected as people's values change in favor of achieved status as a basis for prescribed role behaviors.

A CASE OF FAILED ASCRIBED EXPECTATIONS AND RESULTING SANCTIONS   In 1931, e. e. cummings, a major poet of this century, published this poem, which expresses his value against war and his awareness of the sanctions, sometimes brutal, against one whose ascribed status deviates from prevailing views:[7]

OLAF GLAD AND BIG
e. e. cummings

i sing of Olaf glad and big
whose warmest heart recoiled at war:
a conscientious object-or

his wellbelovéd colonel(trig
westpointer most succinctly bred)
took erring Olaf soon in hand;

but—though an host of overjoyed
noncoms(first knocking on the head
him)do through icy waters roll
that helplessness which others stroke
with brushes recently employed
anent this muddy toiletbowl,
while kindred intellects evoke
allegiance per blunt instruments—
Olaf(being to all intents
a corpse and wanting any rag
upon what God unto him gave)
responds,without getting annoyed
"I will not kiss your fucking flag"

straightway the silver bird looked grave
(departing hurriedly to shave)

but—through all kinds of officers
(a yearning nation's blueeyed pride)
their passive prey did kick and curse
until for wear their clarion
voices and boots were much the worse,
and egged the firstclassprivates on
his rectum wickedly to tease
by means of skilfully applied
bayonets roasted hot with heat—
Olaf(upon what were once knees)
does almost ceaselessly repeat
"there is some shit I will not eat"

our president,being of which
assertions duly notified
threw the yellowsonofabitch
into a dungeon, where he died

Christ(of His mercy infinite)
i pray to see;and Olaf,too

preponderatingly because
unless statistics lie he was
more brave than me:more blond than you.

---

[7] (Copyright 1931, 1959 by e. e. cummings. Reprinted from his volume, *Complete Poems 1913-1962*, by permission of Harcourt Brace Jovanovich, Inc.)

An achieved status also carries with it certain rights and obligations, but it is ordinarily a matter of individual choice. One has a certain amount of freedom, for instance, in choosing an occupation, deciding whether or not to marry, joining a political party, or selecting a major in college. One thus achieves the statuses of accountant, wife, Republican, union representative, or premed student and accepts the normative expectations that accompany each one.

It is more frequently the case that a particular status, once achieved, becomes ascribed. A person may choose voluntarily to hold up a bank but, after serving time for this crime, finds that the label ex-con will influence others' expectations of him or her, no matter how much he or she wants to be free of this status. Less damaging, certainly, but still annoying is being stuck with the status of former basketball star or beauty queen. One's ascribed status may influence one's choices of achieved statuses. The military history of the United States records few high-ranking women officers, and no black candidate has emerged as a serious contender for the presidency. While the distinction between ascribed and achieved statuses is generally useful, these examples show that it is by no means entirely rigid.

STATUS CONFLICT AND ROLE STRAIN *Status conflict** occurs when an individual has difficulty deciding which of two or more statuses to occupy. The conflict may be due to indecision on the individual's part or to opposing pressures imposed by others, but it is always uncomfortable. If you are taking a test in school, for example, and a friend whispers, "What's the answer to number five?" you must choose between obeying the norms that pertain to the status of student (be honest and don't help someone else cheat) and those that apply to the status of friend (a friend should help a buddy in trouble).

Growing pains among teenagers often arise from the conflict generated when one tries to do things that will establish an adult status (such as getting a job) while still wanting to play a less demanding adolescent role, such as dragging Main Street every night.

It is probably a sign of a healthy society when status conflict is kept at a low level. A society in which status conflicts are common would be weakened as its members frequently found themselves unable to live up to each other's expectations. Social order can tolerate only limited unpredictability. On the other hand, through questions and challenges to existing statuses and roles, social change for both good and ill emerges.

Even when there is no doubt as to which status a person occupies at a given time, he or she may still face occasional *role strain**. Strain is experienced when one's roles in relation to two or more statuses seem to require mutually exclusive courses of behavior. A dating partner may want you to develop a permanent relationship, while your parents expect you to be more committed to work or study than to romantic involvement. Or friends may demand that you support different stands on a particular issue, such as drug use or abortion.

Status conflict may be resolved by ordering one's values, asking, "Which status is it more important for me to occupy now?" It may also be resolved by separating in time and/or space the occasions when two potentially conflicting statuses are occupied. Taking the dating example, one may marry secretly, hoping to satisfy both parents, who continue to believe their child is uncommitted (single status), and the spouse who sought the commitment (married status). Role strain, because it is related to status, is handled through similar techniques. In the same example, role strain is based on being unable to pursue mutually exclusive courses of behavior (marrying, not marrying) which are related to statuses (single, married). By removing the pressures to accept contradictory statuses and roles, both conflict and strain disappear.

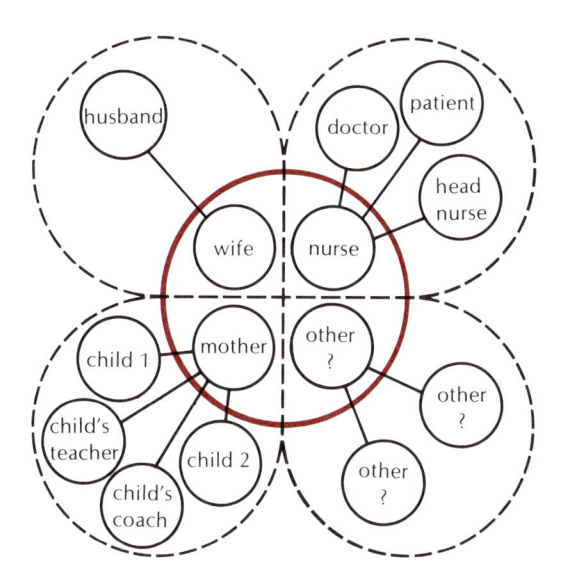

Figure 2-4 The many statuses an individual may occupy make up the *status set*, seen in the central circle. The wings bounded by broken lines show the four separate *role sets* that accompany each of the statuses. Social interaction based on role-playing occurs in these role sets.

More often, we are forced to make choices. We may have to give up statuses or seek compromises when we are asked to do contradictory things. The desire to avoid conflict and role strain does not guarantee success. When choices must be made, we may well wonder about the road not taken.

ROLE SETS AND STATUS SETS The complexity of roles and statuses is such that each can be viewed in terms of *sets*. The many statuses that a person occupies make up that person's *status set**, and since there is usually a number of roles one may play while occupying a particular status, we say that each status has a *role set** (Merton, 1968:423).

The status of nurse, for example, involves a series of relationships with various other statuses: doctor, head nurse, patient, and so on. Since different rights and obligations are involved in each relationship, we speak of each relationship as a different role, and of all these roles together as the nurse's role set. Within the family, similarly, the status of mother includes role relationships with each child, the children's teachers and friends, and perhaps with Little League coaches or Four H Club sponsor. The same individual may occupy the status of wife, which indicates a role relationship with a husband. However, there is no *direct* role relationship between mother and husband although the same two people are involved. For the woman of our example, the statuses of nurse, wife, and mother are all included in the status set.

We don't often consciously think about our status sets and role sets unless problems emerge in role-playing, yet our social life is spent in establishing, maintaining, and sometimes altering these social placements. It should be noted that for many years the trend in American society has been to emphasize achieved over ascribed status. In particular, the civil rights movement has aimed at eliminating the disadvantages associated with ethnic, racial, and sexual statuses, all of them ascribed. In other words, the scripts according to which we play our roles upon the world stage are continually being rewritten, usually with the purpose of putting society's changing values into practice.

Social statuses and the roles that link them form the basic units of *social organization**. Whether they make up family groups or economic enterprises, religious congregations or political parties, they form the structures through which society meets its many needs.

SOCIAL ORGANIZATION TO MEET FUNCTIONAL NEEDS

THE SOCIAL FABRIC OF SOCIETY The *social fabric* that holds a society together consists of its diverse social structures. As Daniel Webster pointed out, "There are many objects of great value to man which cannot be attained by unconnected individuals, but must be attained if at all by association." Socialization trains and motivates people to occupy the social statuses that make up social structures. The social status (not the individual, who can occupy many statuses) forms the basic unit of any organized social structure such as the family, a small neighborhood group, a business firm, or a government agency. Each of these recognizable social structures is a part of society's social organization. Only through patterns of social relationships do members of society manage to provide most of the necessities for physical and social survival. These necessities are called *functional imperatives**, for without them, basic human and societal needs could not be met (Parsons, 1956:68).

Underlying the many forms of social organization that we find in different societies, every society must in one way or another develop structures of interrelated statuses that satisfy these essential needs. Such structures are generally known as *social institutions**. The principal institutions are those of the family, religion, education, government, and economy, and each is characterized by a number of statuses and the roles that link them together, as well as by a distinctive combination of cultural values and norms. So important are these universal institutions that the next chapter is devoted entirely to them.

MULTIPLE REASONS PROPELLING PEOPLE TO ORGANIZE As we have noted, social organizations exist to serve essential individual and collective needs. They arise because of *propinquity*, or physical closeness; individuals living together must develop regular social relationships with each other, if only to avoid continual conflict over use of space and natural resources. And social structures are organized in order to accomplish specific human purposes such as operating railroads, electing candidates to political office, caring for the ill, and training accountants and physicists.

It should be noted that there are some forms of social behavior that do not fit our definition of social organization. *Collective behavior** in the form of a fad, riot, or panic may appear to be totally unorganized and to lack the stability and predictability we associate with established social units. Yet in fact, there are patterns in such behavior, and these will be considered later in connection with social problems. As Broom and Selznick observe, "Social organization consists also of relations that isolate people or groups and that foster disharmony and conflict" (1973:19). Just as sociological theory has been developed to explain stable and predictable structures and events (called *structural functionalism*), so too have efforts been made to explain tensions and instability through the development of *conflict theory*.

Each of the fundamental characteristics of social organization will be taken up in the four parts of this section. First, we shall consider different types of social organization, looking particularly at differences between small and large groups. Next we shall examine the functional division of labor that exists within nearly all social structures. Third is a look at territorial groups, such as communities and states. Last, we shall focus upon purposeful groups, which include all kinds of businesses, labor unions, civil rights groups, and other goal-oriented formal organizations.

TYPES OF SOCIAL ORGANIZATION We develop our sense of self through social interaction with others, internalizing culture and identifying with significant others. Whether someone is viewed as a mother, father, student, lover, teammate, or salesclerk, she or he usually behaves in accordance with the roles established for her or his social position. The roles associated with each status naturally involve interaction with others occupying other statuses. Almost by definition, these role relationships involve recurring, patterned behavior, and on the basis of the kinds of interaction that occur, we identify different kinds of *social groups**.

An important way to characterize social groups is to distinguish between those in which relationships are intimate and informal and those where interaction is formal and relatively impersonal. The former are called *primary groups**, and the latter *secondary groups**. A family, a friendship group, and a small rock band are primary groups, while a salesclerk and her customer or a university professor and his class of four hundred are secondary groups.

Ferdinand Tonnies noted that whole societies were of two main types, the *Gemeinschaft** or agrarian type and the *Gesellschaft** or urban type, based largely on whether the characteristics of primary or secondary group life predominated (1940).

THE SHIFT FROM A GEMEINSCHAFT TO A GESELLSCHAFT SOCIETY   Until the beginning of the nineteenth century, the United States, being primarily a rural and small-town society, had mostly primary-group relations. It was thus largely a *Gemeinschaft,* or communal type of society. But no society, including nineteenth-century America, fits Tonnies's categories exactly, for these are *ideal types** useful as analytical instruments to describe any society (Weber, 1949:106). Such ideal types provide a basis for evaluating the major organizational features of a society or a group within it and show approximately where on a continuum, a straight line of continuous development between end points, the society fits.

The consequences for people living in a predominately *Gemeinschaft* or *Gesellschaft* society are quite different. Primary groups and *Gemeinschaft* societies, whether in agrarian India, arid North Africa, or poverty-stricken pockets of the Appalachian mountains in Pennsylvania and West Virginia, offer warmth and close interpersonal relations but have economic limitations and low standards of living. On the other hand, secondary groups and *Gesellschaft* societies, as in Japan, the nations of western Europe, and most parts of the United States, offer individuals technical efficiency and higher standards of living. At the same time, they offer impersonality and social isolation. Thus the two types create a profound human dilemma expressed in this poem by Edward Field.[8]

A BILL TO MY FATHER
Edward Field

I am typing up bills for a firm to be sent to their
    clients.
It occurs to me that firms are sending bills to my
    father
Who has that way an identity I do not often realize.
He is a person who buys, owes, and pays,
Not papa like he is to me.
His creditors reproach him for not paying on time
With a bill marked "Please Remit."
I reproach him for never having shown his love for me
But only his disapproval.
He has a debt to me too
Although I have long since ceased asking him to come
    across;
He does not know how and so I do without it.
But in this impersonal world of business
He can be communicated with:
With absolute assurance of being paid
The boss writes, "Send me my money"
And my father sends it.

GEMEINSCHAFT VALUES IN A GESELLSCHAFT SETTING   The practical results of this dilemma are quite evident. Of the five groups near Gallup, New Mexico, described earlier, three were primarily *Gemeinschaft* in nature: the Zuni and Navajo Indians and the Spanish–Americans. These groups' members maintained warm and close ties but responded

---

[8] From Edward Field, "A Bill to My Father," in *Stand Up Friend with Me* (New York: Grove Press, 1963). Reprinted by permission of Grove Press, Inc. Copyright © 1963 by Edward Field.

Table 2-2 Ideal Types of Groups and Cultures

	Groups[c]		Cultures[d]	
	Continuum		Continuum	
	Primary[a]	Secondary[b]	Gemeinschaft-folk[a]	Gesellschaft-urban[b]

Nature of groups	Informal as:
	nuclear family
	extended kinship
	peers, friends,
	cliques
		Formal as:
		educational
		religious
		economic
		  trade union
		  business
		  association
		  professional
		  association
			Ascribed, hereditary roles
			Relationships generally of a primary nature
				Achieved, earned roles
				Relationships generally of a secondary nature

Characteristics of group life	Internal constraints Intimate relationships Generalized functions not delimited to specific tasks Long duration and open-ended Small number of members	External constraints Impersonal relationships Specialized functions to achieve particular ends Duration of a goal oriented delimited duration Large number of members	Tradition oriented, resistant to change with maintenance of traditional values and practices Social controls through folkways and mores Limited range of alternative patterns of life styles Ethnocentric tendencies and correlative suspicion of "outsiders" Social relationships long-lasting, intimate and personal	Future oriented, open to rapid change with breakdown of traditional values and practices Social controls through legal norms supplementing unwritten codes Complex organizations and bureaucracies featured Wide range of alternative patterns of life style available Universalistic tendencies with cosmopolitan openness to newcomers Social relations often transitory and impersonal

to drought in the least rational and technically adaptive manner and so lessened their opportunities for material success. The value of the warm, interpersonal social groups of the Native American and Chicano cultures becomes evident when impersonal urbanized cultures run into difficulty. In the Depression years of the 1930s, millions of Germans felt the need for a common identity and a renewed sense of traditional kinship. Adolph Hitler and his Nazi party offered a rebirth of this concept *(Volksgemeinschaft)* based upon a community of blood and soil. The appeal was so great that the highly civilized German people abandoned their democratic Weimar Republic (Shirer, 1960:80–113).

Americans, even in the depths of the Great Depression and through hot and cold wars, have never abandoned their long-established democratic and humanistic values. Yet, as Robert Nisbet notes, the traditional American symbolic vocabulary of *individual, progress, reason,* and *freedom* now includes such additional problematic terms as *disorganization, insecurity, breakdown,* and *instability* (1953:7).

Clearly, it is not likely that we shall return to a small-town, *Gemeinschaft* America. But the survival of democratic values depends on our ability to sustain the primary group qualities of an earlier era in a modern, technically efficient mass society with its emphasis on secondary groupings and complex bureaucratic organizations.

[a]Note the overlapping similarities between the characteristics of primary groups and Gemeinschaft cultures.

[b]Note the overlapping similarities between the characteristics of secondary groups and Gesellschaft cultures. Keep in mind that these are ideal types and no culture is entirely primary- or secondary-group oriented, or Gemeinshaft or Gesellschaft, but rather tend to be primarily one or the other.

[c]SOURCE: Adapted from Kingsley Davis, *Human Society* (New York: Macmillan, 1949), p. 306. Copyright 1948, 1949 by The Macmillan Company.

[d]SOURCE: Adapted from Harold M. Hodges, Jr., *Conflict and Consensus,* 2nd edition (New York: Harper & Row), pp. 152–153. Copyright © 1971, 1974 by Harold M. Hodges, Jr. Reprinted by permission of Harper & Row, Publishers, Inc.

THE FUNCTIONAL DIVISION OF LABOR A basic feature of the social organization of any society is the division of labor, which is necessary to meet such functional needs as rearing children, producing food, distributing goods and services, and maintaining physical security. This is true whether a society is *Gemeinschaft* or *Gesellschaft,* but there is an important difference. Preliterate societies have a basic division of labor based on age and sex. Men generally control the economy, hunt, or otherwise secure the food supply; women rear children; and children are socialized by sex into one pattern or the other. In contrast, modern society has a more complex series of specialized tasks that are not as clearly assigned according to age, sex, or any other ascriptive social category. In American society, for example, women increasingly earn a significant part of the family income, and men often help rear young children.

Here is a good example of division of labor in society. Even in the Sistine Chapel, Michelangelo's famous endeavors were part of a larger set of organized activities that kept the chapel functioning. SOURCE: Reproduced by permission of Ed Fischer.

"Excuse me, Michelangelo, but I've got to get at the pipes."

SPECIALIZATION IN MODERN SOCIETY Our modern economic structure calls for a high degree of *specialization*, the social differentiation of statuses and associated role tasks. For example, it is one thing to be a small farmer who grows, prepares, and consumes his own food and sells or barters only small amounts of it. It is quite another thing when the farmer must have more land, more farmhands,

Emile Durkheim (1858–1917) made major contributions to our understanding of how society functions. SOURCE: The Bettmann Archive.

and more equipment to grow enough food to meet the needs of many people in a distant city. This process entails more work than one farmer can accomplish. He thus finds that he is only a small part of the total production process. Transportation, preparation, and delivery of food, whether grains, vegetables, or meat, requires a high degree of specialized social interaction and interdependence. Sometimes in our frustration over the cost of food, we mutter about middlemen, showing a general awareness that there are many steps and many people between the farmer and our tables.

Many such organized processes are at work in the urban industrial economy. Early in this century, Henry Ford learned that automobiles could be produced far more efficiently by converting workers from generalized assemblers to specialized technicians on an assembly line. One set of workers may turn bolts on fenders while another works only on windows and still another on parts of the engine. While this process increases production of a standardized, mass-produced product, it may also have the latent function of fragmenting human relationships in the world of work, as depicted in Charlie Chaplin's classic movie *Modern Times* (1935).

The division of labor concept applies to more than the economic sector of society. In every social institution, there is some division of labor which may have little to do with getting paid but which is necessary for the continued functioning of the unit. Mothers are not paid to bandage scraped knees. Workers are not paid for taking their turn at getting coffee.

FUNCTIONAL INTERDEPENDENCE To meet the needs of society, tasks are highly specialized. In the process of specialization, people become *functionally interdependent* on each other in the performance of desired or needed tasks. The roles of student and teacher could not exist independent of each other. Similarly, customers desire and buy products businesspeople offer for sale, while no business can operate without customers.

We have mentioned the concept of *functions**. Functions are those observed consequences that make for the adaptation or adjustment of a given system (Merton, 1967:105). The term *system* here can refer to a small or large group, a basic institution such as the economy, or to society as a whole. The division of labor in any system can serve to advance its adaptation and adjustment. The division of labor is part of what cultural anthropologist Ruth Benedict identified as the process of *synergy** (Maslow and Honigman, 1970:320–333), a concept drawn from medicine, in which the combined action of chemicals and cells produces a result greater than the sum of their separate actions. When the division of labor in family units, government structures, economic organizations, and other social settings meets both individual needs of participants and collective needs of the social system, the results tend to be synergistically favorable. When division of labor fails to meet these needs, problems are likely to occur.

INCREASING BUREAUCRATIZATION   While some division of labor exists in all societies, it is in societies of the urban *Gesellschaft* type that the process is most complex. A trend today in the organized social life beyond the family is increasing *bureaucratization**. The large numbers of people and multiple statuses in churches, schools, businesses, and government units require an administrative technique to coordinate their activities. This administering and coordinating process has been incorporated into the organizational structure called *bureaucracy*.

Max Weber identified these rational characteristics of bureaucracy (1946a translation: 329–341):

Ruth Benedict (1887–1948) contributed a number of cross-cultural studies that provided insight into universal principles of social behavior. SOURCE: American Anthropological Association.

1. There is a division of labor among the staff and a narrowing of responsibilities into smaller units generally called offices or bureaus. The responsibility of each office is delineated, and task or job descriptions are planned in advance.

2. Lines of authority are clear and are organized in a hierarchy with each official responsible to a

superior on the next level. The aim is to fix responsibility in order to coordinate activities in the implementation of one or more broad policies or goal-seeking efforts.

3. People fill positions according to their technical or professional qualifications and technical skills. Educational and other qualifications, like the tasks of separate offices, are delineated before a position is filled.

4. Rules and regulations govern the way officials and others perform their tasks. Responsibility is fixed so that who gives orders to whom and who takes orders from whom is determined before a position is filled. Rules and regulations also provide a basis for instituting change in the organization such as changes in policies or goals or for personnel promotion and retirement.

Bureaucracies do not always work the way they are supposed to. The red tape, the frequent buck-passing, and other faults of bureaucracies and bureaucrats tend to obscure their usefulness. Yet for all the frustrations of registering for college courses, mailing an important letter across the country, or paying income taxes, we owe the fact that the system works at all to the existence of a bureaucracy.

Weber was far from an absolutist about the virtues of bureaucracy. While arguing that bureaucratization was an irreversible trend in modern society, he was keenly aware of the possible inefficiencies and of the damaging impact the process can have on individuality and the very humanity of the people in the system. Indeed, Weber warned of the need to cushion the impact of bureaucratization.

MAKING THE SYSTEM WORK Weber's work and other modern analyses of complex bureaucratized organizations (Blau, 1956; Etzioni, 1964; Bennis, 1966) examine how to maintain bureaucratic efficiency while providing maximum flexibility of individuals within and without the bureaucratic system. One way in which people influence the organization within bureaucracies is through the *informal organization,* in which communication may cut across various formal lines of authority. Examples are office or assembly area friendship groups, which do not follow formal lines of authority and communication, and the grapevine as a means of informal communication.

Movements to check unbridled and unresponsive bureaucracies include citizens' groups of the early 1970s, such as Ralph Nader's consumer-oriented Center for Responsive Law and John Gardner's Common Cause, an organization designed as a watchdog of ethics and efficiency in government. It is ironic but perhaps inevitable that these and other groups formed to make bureaucracies meet the needs of the people have themselves become bureaucratized as the amount of material they must process increases.

TERRITORIALLY BASED GROUPS The boundaries of any social structure are usually defined in terms of social interaction, not of geography, though for certain kinds of social organization, the boundaries include the physical setting. The patterned relationships in a *neighborhood* imply a physical location within a community. A *community,* in turn, is a collection of people who interact within a limited territory. On a larger scale, one essential characteristic of a nation is its geographic boundaries, within which the society's government has legal sovereignty.

Human ecology* (see Chapter 10) is the study of social organization based on territoriality. Students of human ecology learn how people adapt to their physical environment. The size of and the number of people within a territory can influence the kinds of social organization that exist in the area. Thus, a small town of several thousand is likely to develop a high degree of *Gemeinschaft,* or close interpersonal relations. A large city with a population of one million or more is likely to produce a high degree of *Gesellschaft,* or of secondary interpersonal relations.

The patterning of social relations within territorial boundaries can be seen most clearly in new community settlements. In contemporary society, this generally means suburban communities, most of which have developed since World War II, rather than older established small towns or large cities. In new suburban communities, spontaneous social organization develops among people previously unrelated to each other.

William H. Whyte, Jr., provided a perceptive analysis of the impact of the territorially based setting of social organization in the new suburb of Park Forest outside Chicago (1956:330–361). Park Forest was laid out in over one hundred neighborhood courts. Each court included about forty houses separated from other courts by roadways, schools, or other physical divisions. People living within a court affected each other's behavior tremendously. If one court happened to have a high proportion of community leaders, the likelihood of a new family being caught up in community improvement projects was high. If a court had a concentration of bridge-players or churchgoers, then the social life in that neighborhood, as well as the degree of social conformity expected, was clearly affected. Whyte even observed that the placement of driveways had an effect on social closeness. If two driveways adjoined each other, friendly relationships between their owners were more likely to develop than if they were separated by a house.

We have already considered the importance of culture in determining how people adapt to their physical environment. Here is the other side of the coin: whatever a group's cultural orientation, some of the social organization that develops in it is influenced by the space its members occupy and how this space is used.

GROUPS WITH A PURPOSE People in *Gesellschaft* society organize and join many various kinds of *limited-purpose* organizations designed to accomplish particular goals. In a mass society, where most relationships are secondary, it is often necessary to join with others one does not know in order to meet various social needs. No longer, as in rural society generally or in small-town America of an earlier period, can individuals depend primarily on family, kin, and lifelong friends to assist them in satisfying all their personal and collective needs.

Consequently, there is a proliferation of formal organizations with a variety of specific goals. By *formal,* we mean any organization that has a charter, constitution, or by-laws, elected or appointed officers, and procedures by which to accomplish goals. Purposeful organizations, often bureaucratized, can be voluntary associations such as the civil rights group, the National Association for the Advancement of Colored People (NAACP); labor unions such as the United Auto Workers (UAW), the prime function of which is to gain advantageous contracts with corporations; and companies such as General Motors, designed to run a business and produce profits. Most institutional activities, in fact, are carried out by purposeful groups. Unlike some territorially based groups such as neighborhoods, which may not have specific goals, purposeful groups always have specific goals. This is true whether they are territorially based (for example, the UAW is concentrated in and around Detroit) or have no specific locale, like the NAACP, which has chapters throughout the nation and takes up civil rights issues wherever they appear.

Americans have organized and joined so many kinds of purposeful groups that most adults belong to one or more of them (CBS News Almanac, 1976:878–883). The American Red Cross, organized to provide emergency medical assistance in times of natural disaster, has 36 million members. The American Federation of Labor–Congress of Industrial Organizations (AFL–CIO), which seeks continuing wage and job security, has over 13 million members. The National Education Association (NEA), which seeks greater public support for public education, has over one million. The National Grange, an organization of farmers, has over a half million members. What these and the thousands of other associations have in common is specific goals. Such wide-ranging purposeful groups are a permanent and growing feature of American and other modern societies.

Finally, it should be noted that there are two important aspects of social organization which have not been discussed in this chapter, since each requires special and detailed treatment. These are the basic institutions of society, which we take up in Chapter 3, and social stratification, which is discussed in Chapter 6 in connection with problems of wealth and poverty.

SUMMARY

Culture*, *socialization**, and *social organization** are three basic sociological concepts used to describe and analyze the nature of society. They are fundamental to an understanding of any aspect of social behavior.

CULTURE *Culture** is a prescriptive blueprint for the distinctive way of life of a group of people, their complete design for living. Every culture embodies *values**, which are expressed in specific rules of behavior called *norms**. These can be grouped into patterns or major cultural themes. We exert powerful *sanctions** to ensure that people internalize acceptable culture patterns.

A common characteristic of culture is *ethnocentrism**, in which one's own culture is invariably judged to be better than others. Ethnocentrism in its more intense forms produces stereotyping of others and leads to racial and cultural conflicts within society. Social distance measurements since the 1920s have provided evidence that ethnocentrism is declining in American society.

The doctrine of *cultural relativity* may also develop in the value system of a society. This holds that no single cultural standard should be used to judge the worth of another culture.

Cultural pluralism is a condition in which different cultural groups live harmoniously within the same society. American society, with its many different cultural groups, is a particularly interesting example of this phenomenon.

Culture has a powerful influence on human behavior. We described the way different cultural groups with widely varying *mores**, *customs**, and *folkways** adapt differently to the same physical environment.

SOCIALIZATION INTO THE CULTURE Beginning at birth, human beings begin the *socialization** process, the means by which we learn to become part of our society. In childhood, we develop a looking-glass concept of self; we form ideas about ourselves and our value system through interaction with *significant others** around us, such as our immediate family, neighbors, and peers.

As we grow, we acquire an increasing number of *statuses** beyond the family. With each new status, social relationships with others widen and become more complex.

Some of our statuses are *ascribed**, involving little choice and based on inherited characteristics such as age and sex. Many statuses are *achieved**, and have characteristics over which the individual has some control and can change, such as occupation or marital status.

Each status carries with it several *roles**, which guide the behavior expected of the person occupying it when he or she is interacting with others in other statuses.

Each individual has a *status set*, and for each of these statuses there is a corresponding *role set*.

Interaction with others may result in *status conflict* and *role strain.*

Status positions are the basic units of all *social organization.*

SOCIAL ORGANIZATION *Social organization** is the social fabric by which the society is held together. It is through the social organization of society that people pattern their individual and group relations to provide the necessities of life for physical and social survival, or to satisfy society's *functional imperatives**.

Three underlying bases of social organization are *propinquity,* or nearness, which makes it possible to interact regularly; *function,* by which basic societal needs are met; and *purpose,* by which certain goals become the basis for a given form of social organization.

Social organizations have been classified as *primary** or *secondary groups** and as *Gemeinschaft** or *Gesellschaft** societies. Primary groups are intimate and informal, and because of this must be relatively small. Secondary groups are more often formal and impersonal, and tend to be larger. When a whole society is characterized mainly by primary group relations, it is considered a *Gemeinschaft*-type society. When a whole society is characterized primarily by secondary group relations, it is considered a *Gesellschaft*-type society. These are ideal types, however, and no society is entirely one or the other.

Division of labor* to meet different functional needs is a basic feature of all social organization. Some division of labor characterizes virtually all forms of organized social life. In complex modern society, most purposeful organizations coordinate and administer their members' actions to achieve desired goals through the process of bureaucratization.

Territoriality is another basis of social organization. A neighborhood, a community, and a state all have a territorial delimitation of their boundaries.

In modern mass *Gesellschaft* society, most people belong to purposeful associations designed to accomplish particular goals.

QUESTIONS FOR DISCUSSION

1. Why are culture and social behavior interdependent?

2. If culture and social behavior are interdependent, then why do many people in the same society behave differently?

3. Name some significant others in your life. How alike or different are they in terms of their values and points of view?

4. Describe some things about yourself and your peers which illustrate ascribed and achieved status characteristics. Are some characteristics a combination of both?

5. Are the concepts of ethnocentrism and cultural pluralism opposites, or can they operate side by side without conflict in the same society?

6. How are the statuses and roles people take on altered as they move from rural to urban areas?

7. What problems can you foresee if there were no division of labor in an organization in which you have worked or would like to work?

8. To what purposeful groups do you or other members of your family belong? What role(s) must be played by members in order to accomplish your goals? How are these roles related to division of labor?

9. Review your understanding of the following terms and concepts:

culture

socialization

social organization

mores

bureaucratization

Thomas theorem (self-fulfilling prophecy)

looking-glass self

status conflict

role strain

role set

REFERENCES

Beard, Charles with Mary Beard and William Beard
1960   New Basic History of the United States. New York: Doubleday.

Benedict, Ruth (see also Maslow)
1946   Patterns of Culture. New York: Pelican.

Bennis, Warren
1966   Changing Organizations. New York: McGraw-Hill.

Bernard, William
1952   "The quota system in operation." R. Leopold and A. Link (eds.), Problems in American History. Englewood Cliffs, New Jersey: Prentice-Hall: 685–690.

Blau, Peter
1956   Bureaucracy in Modern Society. New York: Random House.

Bloom, Leonard and Ruth Riemer
1949   Removal and Return. Berkeley: The University of California Press.

Bogardus, Emory
1959   Social Distance. Yellow Springs, Ohio: Antioch Press.
1968   "Comparing racial distance in Ethiopia, South Africa and the United States." Sociology and Social Research 52: 149–156.

Broom, Leonard and Philip Selznick
1973   Sociology (fifth edition). New York: Harper and Row.

Columbia Broadcasting System
1976   CBS News Almanac. Maplewood, N.J.: Hammond Almanac.

Cooley, Charles Horton
1922   Human Nature and the Social Order. New York: Scribners.

cummings, e. e.
1959   100 Selected Poems. New York: Grove Press: 37–38.

Davis, Allison, Burleigh Gardner and Mary Gardner
1941   Deep South. Chicago: University of Chicago Press.

Davis, Kingsley
1949   Human Society. New York: Macmillan.

Durkheim, Emile
1947   The Division of Labor. G. Simpson (trans.). Glencoe, Ill.: The Free Press.

Etzioni, Amitai
1964   Modern Organizations. Englewood Cliffs, New Jersey: Prentice-Hall.

Feilitzen, Cecilia v, and Olga Linné
1975   "Identifying with television characters." Journal of Communication: 25:4:51–55.

Gross, Neal with Ward Mason and Alexander McEachern
1958   Explorations in Role Analysis. New York: John Wiley & Sons.

Hilmer, Herman
1924   "The outlook for civilization." The Pedagogical Seminary (September): 247.

Hodges, Harold
 1974 Conflict and Consensus. New York: Harper & Row.

Homans, George
 1967 "Fundamental social processes." N. Smelser, Sociology. New York: John Wiley and Sons: 29–78.

Hoult, Thomas Ford
 1969 Dictionary of Modern Sociology. Totowa, New Jersey: Littlefield, Adams.

Kennedy, John F.
 1964 A Nation of Immigrants. New York: Harper and Row.

Kluckhohn, Clyde
 1949 Mirror for Man. New York: McGraw-Hill.
 1951 "The study of culture." D. Lerner and H. Lasswell (eds.), The Policy Sciences: Stanford, California: Stanford University Press: 86.
 1962 Culture and Behavior. New York: The Free Press.

Lewis, Sinclair
 1921 Main Street. New York: Harcourt, Brace.

Lippmann, Walter
 1946 Public Opinion. New York: Penguin.

Maslow, Abraham and John J. Honigman
 1970 "Synergy: some notes on Ruth Benedict." American Anthropologist 72:320–333.

Mayer, J.P.
 1943 Max Weber and German Politics. London: Faber.

Mead, George Herbert
 1934 Mind, Self and Society. Chicago: University of Chicago Press.

Mead, Margaret
 1950 Sex and Temperament in Three Primitive Societies. New York: New American Library.

Merton, Robert
 1957 "The role-set: problem in sociological theory." The British Journal of Sociology 8:106–120.
 1967 On Theoretical Sociology. New York: The Free Press.
 1968 Social Theory and Social Structure. New York: The Free Press.

Nisbet, Robert
 1953 The Quest for Community. New York: Oxford University Press.

 1972 Official Associated Press Almanac 1973. New York: Almanac Publishing Company.

Parsons, Talcott
 1956 Economy and Society. Glencoe, Ill.: The Free Press.
 1961 "General theory in sociology." R. Merton, L. Broom and L. Cottrell (eds.), Sociology Today. New York: Basic Books: 3–37.

Rosenthal, Robert and Lenore Jacobson
 1968 Pygmalion in the Classroom. New York: Holt, Rinehart and Winston.

Shirer, William
 1960 The Rise and Fall of the Third Reich. New York: Simon and Schuster.

Siegal, Alberta E.
 1975 "Communicating with the next generation." Journal of Communication, 25:4: 14–24.

Silberman, Charles E.
 1970 Crisis In the Classroom: The Remaking of American Education. New York: Vintage.

Storer, Norman
1973   Focus on Society. Reading, Massachusetts: Addison-Wesley.

Thomas, W.I.
1931   "The relation of research to the social process." Essays on Research in the Social Sciences. Washington, D.C.: The Brookings Institution: 189.

Tonnies, Ferdinand
1940   Gemeinschaft and Gesellschaft (first edition, 1887). Charles P. Loomis (trans. and ed.). Fundamental Concepts of Sociology. New York: American Book Company.

Tyler, Edward
1924   Primitive Culture (seventh edition). New York: Brentano's.

Vander Zanden, James
1966   American Minority Relations. New York: The Ronald Press.

Vogt, Evon and John Roberts
1956   "A study of values." Scientific American 5: 25-30.

Weber, Max
1949   The Methodology of the Social Sciences. E.A. Shils and Finch (trans. and eds.). Glencoe, Illinois: The Free Press.
1946a   From Max Weber: Essays in Sociology. H.H. Gerth and C. Wright Mills (trans. and eds.). New York: Oxford University Press.
1946b   The Theory of Social and Economic Organization. New York: Oxford University Press.

Weitzman, Lenore, Deborah Eifler, Elizabeth Hokada, and Catherine Ross
1972   "Sex-role socialization in picture books for preschool children." American Journal of Sociology 77(May):1125-1150.

Whyte, William H., Jr.
1956   The Organization Man. New York: Simon and Schuster.

Williams, Robin
1970   American Society: A Sociological Interpretation. New York: Knopf. Reprinted with permission.

Zorbaugh, Harvey
1929   The Gold Coast and the Slum. Chicago: University of Chicago Press.

Chapter 3

THE BASIC INSTITUTIONS OF THE SOCIETY

The primary purpose of mankind has always been to survive in a natural world which has not invariably been friendly to us. In our written, remembered, and sensed history, there has always been more work to do than we could do. Our needs were greater than their possible fulfillment. Our dreams were so improbable that we moved their reality to the heavens. . . . We have the things and we have not had time to develop a way of thinking about them. . . . [W]e have not had time to learn inside ourselves the things that have happened to us.

John Steinbeck[1]

---

[1] From John Steinbeck, *America and Americans* (New York: Viking Press, 1966), pp. 174–175.

FUNCTIONS, DYSFUNCTIONS, AND INSTITUTIONS

The *functions** of a unit of social organization are its consequences for society. The major social *institutions** — the family, religion, education, government, and the economy — are those parts of society that have developed to meet functional needs. *Functional analysis**, a theoretical framework used by many sociologists, examines social groups and activities in terms of what George Homans called rewarding, or *functional* consequences and their punishing, or *dysfunctional* consequences (1962: 33–34). Analysis of social organization in general, and of institutions in particular, deals with both functional and dysfunctional consequences of the organized procedures of institutions (Bierstedt, 1963: 341).

Organized units within social institutions can also have both functional and dysfunctional consequences. The automobile industry, for example, is part of the economic institution. Cars serve the needs of millions of Americans as transportation to work, school, stores, places of recreation, and so on. Widespread use of automobiles also produces air pollution, which is damaging to health and injurious to units of the economic institution such as the tourist industry. A *manifest* aim of the auto industry and of car buyers is transportation; but air pollution, which was unanticipated and unintended, is a *latent (dys)function* of using automobiles.

Not all latent consequences of institutional practices are dysfunctional. The rain dances of the

Navajo and Zuni Indians had the manifest aim of producing rain. While the rain dance was less likely to produce rain than the cloud-seeding used by the Texans and Mormons, the dances did have a latent function: they increased the social solidarity of the tribe and gave them a psychological defense against fear and the sense of powerlessness (Yinger, 1957:46).

This case illustrates a limitation of functional analysis as some sociologists view it: what is considered functional by one cultural group may not be by another, a problem especially evident in a pluralistic society such as ours. As Alvin Gouldner and Richard Peterson warn, "Functionalism ... rests upon a ... dubious assumption of system interdependence which ignores the question of the different influences of system elements" (1962:8).

In our urbanized technological society, there does appear to be functional interdependence among groups, to the degree that general social stability is maintained. This is true whether the groups are Native Americans on reservations, rural white Protestants, urban blacks, or other culturally identifiable groups. Still, Gouldner's and Peterson's warning is a useful one.

FIVE UNIVERSAL INSTITUTIONS

Whatever its cultural orientation, every group organizes the essential tasks of social living through certain established *institutions**. The five generally recognized are: the family, religion, education, government, and the economy. Within these institutions, we develop our values and become socialized into our culture. Even as this process is taking place, the institutions themselves are changing. While there are great variations in the nature of these institutions from one society to another, all societies have them in some form; they are necessary for social survival.

One may ask how we know that the United States and all other societies share certain institutions. The answer is to be found in the cross-cultural analysis made by cultural anthropologists and synthesized by the Human Relations Area File (HRAF). The HRAF systematizes references to hundreds of analyses of different cultures around the world. They show that, for all the cultural variation among the world's peoples, there are certain universal responses to societal needs. As we saw in the last chapter, all societies have some form of *division of labor**. As the division of labor becomes *institutionalized** — as procedures become organized, systematized, and stable — then societies develop *social structures**, "the relatively stable [patterned] interrelationships ... among the aspects of the system" (Hoult, 1969:304).

INSTITUTIONS AS THE BROADEST ORGANIZED SOCIAL STRUCTURES The basic institutions of the society form the broadest organized social structures. In addition to the familial, religious, educational, governmental, and economic structures, some anthropologists and sociologists also consider the military and organized sports and games to be universal social institutions, though these are often treated as part of another basic institution, such as government or the economy. Additionally, some cultural institutions, such as science and literature, are not universal but exist only in technological and literate societies. (Their functions in American society are discussed in later chapters in relation to various social issues.)

PROPOSED LIST OF BASIC SOCIETAL STRUCTURES: DEFINED IN TERMS OF ASSOCIATED BASIC SOCIETAL FUNCTIONS AND CORE RELATIONSHIPS AND PRESENTED WITH INFERRED INDIVIDUAL-ORIENTED FUNCTIONS

From: Robert F. Winch, *The Modern Family* (New York: Holt, Rinehart, and Winston, 1971), pp. 16–17.

I. Familial
   A. Core functions
      1. society-oriented: to provide replacements for dying members
      2. individual-oriented: to provide a sense of "immortality," or temporal continuity, with ongoing society
   B. Core relationship: father–mother–child
   (An alternate and more restricted view is that the one "essential" enduring core relationship is the mother–child.)

II. Economic
   A. Core functions
      1. society-oriented: to produce and distribute the goods and services required for the maintenance of the members
      2. individual-oriented: to provide the material means of maintenance and pleasure and perhaps of status-improvement
   B. Core relationships
      1. with respect to production: worker–manager
      2. with respect to distribution: producer–consumer

III. Political
   A. Core functions
      1. society-oriented: to accommodate conflicting interests and to maintain internal and external order
      2. individual-oriented: to provide protection and to resolve conflicting claims without recourse to violence
   B. Core relationship: official–constituent

IV. Socializing-educational[a]
   A. Core functions
      1. society-oriented: to train replacements for social roles and social positions
      2. individual-oriented: to provide the individual with the skills required for participation in society
   B. Core relationship: teacher–pupil

V. Religious
   A. Core functions
      1. society-oriented: to achieve and to maintain solidarity and consensus about general goals, values, and norms and to prevent a state of normlessness; to maintain a state of purposefulness
      2. individual-oriented: to provide procedures for meeting crises and explanations for otherwise unexplainable occurrences and thus to assuage anxiety; to prevent feelings of alienation
   B. Core relationship: priest–parishioner

[a] It is customary to depict the process whereby an infant becomes an adult as consisting of two aspects: *socialization* and *education*. There is precedent for using the term *socialization** to refer to the process of personality development and for using *education* to refer to the acquisition of values and of skills, both intellectual and motor. But sometimes *socialization* is used with the connotation of education (as when we speak of XYZ Corporation socializing college graduates into organization men), and sometimes *socialization* is used in a broader sense to include both personality development and education.

The broad sense is intended here. To communicate this as clearly as possible the hyphenated form *socialization–education* is introduced. The adjectival form is *socializing–educational*. At times one or the other of these pairs may be dropped when there is occasion to emphasize the connotation of the remaining term.

Socialization–education is not to be confused with emotional gratification. To be sure, emotional gratification enters into learning, but so does food. Our conceptual formulation draws a distinction with the result that we shall regard socialization-education as referring both to a basic societal structure and its core function, while we shall think of emotional gratification as a function fulfilled largely through primary relationships, including those in the nuclear family.

It is mainly through these universal institutions that the essential tasks of social life are organized and accomplished. As we consider procreation and the socialization of children and the ways in which standards of right and wrong are learned, goods and services are distributed, and the public health and safety are protected, we shall consider functions of the family, the economy, or some other of the five basic institutions. If a society's institutions function well, it is possible for some individuals or groups to stop participating in them without destroying the whole system. Keep in mind that statuses and how they are filled, rather than the acts of specific individuals, determine whether an institution is functioning well. For example, though some people divorce, the institution of the family persists. Penn Central may go bankrupt, but the economic system continues to function. And so with individuals in government. After the assassination of President Kennedy, New York *Times* columnist James Reston commented, in an article entitled "Nobody Can Assassinate a Government" (1963:12):

This is not a bad time to remember that the Government of the United States has a life of its own. It is a permanent institution. It cannot be assassinated by anything less than the destruction of the nation.

Should the major institutions such as government fail to adapt to destructive and disruptive developments or to new conditions, then they could become *dysfunctional*, which would lead to consequences that lessen the adaptation or adjustment of the system (Merton, 1967:105).

THE CULTURAL IMPERATIVE FOR EFFECTIVE INSTITUTIONS Should we be unable to adapt institutions to our needs, then the very existence of the society would be endangered. In American society, institutions have demonstrated great adaptability. They have faced and are facing a number of challenges by disruptive developments. This will be evident as we consider each of the basic institutions in respect to four characteristics: (1) the universality of the institution, (2) the functions it fulfills, (3) its structural forms, and (4) its response to social change.

THE FAMILY

In any discussion of basic institutions, a good place to begin is with family structure. The family is a universal institution that meets certain functional needs of people, has a wide range of structural forms, and is undergoing changes to adapt to new conditions.

UNIVERSALITY OF THE FAMILY The Human Relations Area Files make it clear that there is no known society without some form of family unit. Whatever this form, it is sanctioned by *marriage*. As defined by David Mace, marriage in our culture is "a close, intimate interpersonal relationship between husband and wife in which the concept of personal fulfillment and the expression of need through close intimacy is the goal deliberately sought" (Mace, 1962:2). The functions served by the family and its structural forms have undergone major changes in the twentieth century in America and in most other societies.

FUNCTIONS OF THE FAMILY Both the current normative *nuclear family** of husband, wife, and their children and the historical *extended kinship family**, have long met a number of functional needs in the society.[2]

CHANGING STATUSES AND ROLES WITHIN FAMILIES The institution was characterized in earlier times by a clear division of labor as an economic organization, often on a farm or in a small business. In the modern urban setting, most of the goods and services required by individuals and the family are produced not by the family itself but in the larger economic sector of the society.

In these changed circumstances, children no longer have economically essential tasks to perform. One consequence is that children now tend to be an economic liability rather than an asset. At the same time, the status and role of women have undergone fundamental changes. With increased recognition of their individual rights, more education, less time at home with their children, who attend school longer than in the past, and an occupational structure increasingly open to them, women have begun to pursue interests outside the home. The response to these changes has been a decline in the number of children born into most families (see Figure 3-1).

The family continues to function as the chief source of primary interpersonal relations. While people are having fewer children, they are likely to want them for other than economic reasons. In a society in which traditional close relations with extended kin have been weakened, the family provides for most people blood-related allies in an indifferent world.

CONTINUED PROCREATIONAL AND SOCIALIZATION FUNCTIONS The normative family of husband, wife, and children continues to function in

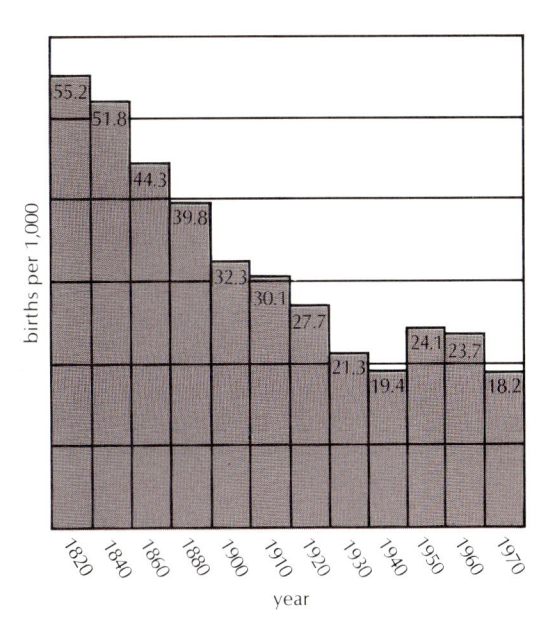

Figure 3-1   Birth rates per 1,000 females (ages 15–44) for the United States, 1820–1970.

society in traditional ways — reproduction, protection and care of children, and the socialization of children into the larger society.[3] Since these functions are fundamentally related to procreation, the family has always had a major role in regulating sexual expression. The changing social status of women outside the family, the availability of effective contraceptives, and the declining need for large numbers of children are three factors in the emergence of a freer sexual ethic in American and other modern societies. These developments have enabled most people to make a distinction between

---

[2] Some anthropologists reject the presence of the child's father as universal to the definition of nuclear family, citing numerous cases in which the basic family unit is mother–child (Fox, 1967: 37, 39–40).

[3] Although the family in most cultures is the initial socializing unit for children, there are exceptions. An example is the Israeli *kibbutz* (ki-boots). The *kibbutz* often assigns the care of small children to a communal nursery except for a few hours each day which children spend with their parents. When children leave the nursery, they remain with age-mates in a communal setting rather than with their families. See Edwin Samuel, *The Structure of Society in Israel* (New York: Random House, 1969).

recreational sex and procreational sex (see Hunt, 1974). The family plays a crucial role in socializing adolescents into the perception and practice of combining procreational sex with marriage.

Whatever the functions of other institutions such as religion and education in socializing children, it is still the family that plays the initial role in placing children in the social structure. Indeed, the family usually decides whether the children should attend a particular church or school. The functions of the family and of other institutions are both interrelated and interdependent as recorded by Robert Winch (see Contrasts in Family Function). For example, inadequate health care in a family can reduce the ability of young persons to respond to the socialization process in school (Gussow, 1970:205–208). Conversely, a dilapidated, overcrowded school in a deteriorating neighborhood can keep families from caring for many of their children's needs.

CONTRASTS IN FAMILY FUNCTION

From: Robert F. Winch, *The Modern Family* (New York: Holt, Rinehart, and Winston, 1971), pp. 67–70.

In the excerpted material below, Robert F. Winch, a sociologist who specializes in family studies, compares and contrasts functions attributed to three types of family structure: those found in traditional China among the peasantry, on the *kibbutzim* of Israel, referred to in the text, and in the American family unit.

We have examined a maximally functional family — that of the peasantry in traditional China — and a minimally functional family — from the Israeli kibbutz... whose pseudonym is Kiryat Yedidim. For each of our five basic societal functions let us note how these two societies anchor the dimension of familial functionality, and we may note in passing where between these termini the middle-class American urban (or suburban) family seems to lie. [See Proposed List of Basic Societal Structures for the functions cited.]

With respect to the *economic* function, the Chinese family was the unit both of production and of consumption. In the kibbutz, the unit of production is (not the family but) the community, and the unit of consumption is (not the family but) the individual. With respect to the economic function, then, the ends of our dimension are well represented by these two societies. For the most part, in America the corporation and not the family is the unit of economic production, but the family is a widely recognized unit of consumption.

The Chinese family served as a unit of *political* function in that it contained order within the family and assumed at least part of the responsibility for protecting its members from the aggression and depradation of outsiders. The adjudication of disputes, both within the family and between family members and outsiders was a responsibility for the elders. No such arrangement prevails in the kibbutz, where the kibbutz as a whole enforces sanctions and provides for... protection.... In America we have known of families functioning as political units — e.g. the feuding Hatfields and McCoys of Kentucky — but we are generally much closer to the kibbutz in placing political functioning in extra-familial institutions.

The entire socializing-educational process for a peasant child was performed within the Chinese family.... In sharp contrast, the kibbutz baby is taken from the mother at the age of four days and is reared to adulthood by the community. All responsibility for instruction resides with the teachers. With the development in America of kindergartens, prekindergartens, and nursery schools there has been an increasing disposition to turn over children to the schools at younger age levels. Since the average age at which children leave school has been increasing, moreover, the family has been relinquishing and the school absorbing more and more of the total responsibility for socializing and educating American children.

For the Chinese, the *religious* function of integrating goals was performed in past at least, by the formal religions (Taoism and Buddhism), the expression and reinforcement of the group's solidarity — another aspect of the religious function — was centered in ancestor worship, a family ritual that was a kind of religious observance. For the members of the anticlerical and antitheological kibbutz the integration of goals was addressed largely through a sociopoliticoeconomic utopianism. Probably the central arena for the interpretation, implementation, and reinforcement of this ideology was the general assembly (or town meeting). All members participated in parties and ceremonies (e.g., secularized versions of Passover and Hannukah), which were the principal way of expressing the solidarity of the group. Once again the kibbutz family was not a relevant unit. In America it seems that the integration of goals is carried out mostly by the four extrafamilial institutions. Such economic organizations as corporations, trade associations, advertising media, and occupational groups define goals. Occasionally the national government assumes leadership, especially in times of crisis, such as war or depression. The school and the church are quite self-conscious in trying to define the "good" and moral life and to specify a way to achieve it. It does not appear that the American family is involved systematically in goal integration although it is clear that individual parents are very active in this area. In America solidarity is expressed in a variety of ways and settings. With respect to the family, it occurs in the celebration of birthdays, anniversaries, and holidays. The church does it too, especially through ceremonies at *rites de passage* — christenings, confirmations, weddings, and funerals. But there are many other settings — school rallies, fraternity meetings, service clubs, baseball games, and national elections, to cite only a few. Again, in America the family is not as inconsequential as is conceivable, nor is it as influential as it can be.

Although we have not sought to address formally the matter of the derived functions . . . in the Chinese or the kibbutz family, we shall comment on them briefly. . . . For the Chinese peasant, *position-conferring* was carried out almost entirely by the family. To be sure, there was some social mobility. A man might obtain an appointment in the civil service, rise in the hierarchy, and achieve a social status above that of his family, but this would be exceptional. In the Kiryat Yedidim of 1951 we have noted Spiro's assertion that status differentials were absent. . . . The critical position-conferring was that of granting or withholding membership in the kibbutz, and this was done by a vote of the members. In America the family provides the child with an initial ascribed social status, and the occupational system provides him with an opportunity to alter that ascribed status either upward or downward.

The *parental functions of nurturance and control* are, of course, carried out within the Chinese family. In the kibbutz a good deal of the "parentifying," especially with respect to control, is carried out in the children's residences by nurses and teachers. Parents of the kibbutz tend to be indulgently nurturant but not controlling. In America parental functioning is graded with the age of the child. Until he enters the school system, the parental function is typically discharged by the family. Thereafter the family shares it with the school and gradually with other social structures. For the young child, then, the exercise of the parental function by the American family resembles that of the Chinese family, but as the child ages, extrafamilial structures become more important, and the situation becomes more like that in the kibbutz.

In the matter of *emotional gratification* it appears that intrafamilial relationships were seen as important sources of affection and gratification in China. Although the marital relationship was not expected to be highly gratifying nor was that between father and son, intimacy and affection were regarded as usual in the relations between brothers, between father and daughter, and between mother and son.[a] Spiro reports that in the kibbutz of Kiryat Yedidim the marital relationship is based on love and that parents and children usually treat each other with a considerable show of affection.

Now let us note how familial function can affect the role of love in mate-selection. We have noted that in the maximally functional Chinese family love is regarded as irrelevant to mate-selection. The incoming bride should represent a liaison with an important family; she should possess skills relevant to her role, and she should show industry in carrying out that role. In middle-class America there is a cultural expectation that mates should select each other on the basis of mutual love. Occasionally third parties express snide doubts about the sincerity (or mutuality) of that love. It appears that such doubts are especially likely if the bride is the daughter of the groom's boss or if a poor girl is marrying a rich man, i.e., if one party appears to be improving his or her situation appreciably through the marriage. This can be translated into our functional language to the effect that the degree of doubt about the sincerity of the love underlying a person's marriage seems positively correlated with the degree to which that person will get a higher level of consumption (economic function) and/or a higher social status (position-conferring function).

Note that our description of Kiryat Yedidim renders it improbable that a person could select a mate for any of the reasons just enumerated because the kibbutz family carries out none of these functions. If the level of one's consumption is set on a principle of equality by the collective, there is no way of marrying to improve one's level of consumption. If there are no status differentials (or if they exist but are unrelated to the family organization), there is no way to marry upward. If there is no private property, there is nothing to inherit. It seems to follow then that the fewer and less important the functions that are carried out by the family, the less incentive there is to select a mate on any other basis than compatibility and congeniality, affection and love. Or to phrase it more baldly, the less important the family becomes, the more probable are love-marriages.[b]

This same principle can be observed in the case of parent-child relationships. In the Chinese family the father-son relationship had great functional strength. In their mutual core relationships the man served as foreman, teacher, priest, and so on, to the boy's roles of worker, pupil, parishioner, and so on. In the kibbutz on the other hand it would be sheer coincidence if the boy's father should also be his foreman or his teacher or be related to him in any other extrafamilial functional capacity. The Chinese boy's perception of his father was typically one of awe and respect; his behavior toward the father was typically avoidant and deferent. The boy of the kibbutz relates to his father with easy but demanding camaraderie. It appears that although functional activities are likely to have individual-oriented payoffs, they are also likely to eventuate in frustration and feelings of hostility, especially on the part of the person in the subordinate role. Consistent with the latter part of this observation is Levy's report that the Chinese did not expect such highly functional relationships as that between father and son to be affectionate; rather, they "were accustomed to find emotional warmth and affectionate response of a high degree of intensity in precisely those relationships of weakest strength in the kinship structure."[c] Moreover, it seems as though the founders of Kiryat Yedidim had come to somewhat the same conclusion, had lamented the intrafamilial hostility of the shtetl — especially that directed toward the father — and accordingly designed a new type of family in which the level of hostility would be lower because of the absence of functions.

From these observations it follows that functions constitute bonds that tie family members to each other, irrespective of the feelings they may have for each other. For this reason the highly functional family tends to be a highly stable family. The absence of function (in the relatively functionless family) leaves feelings as the basis for interpersonal relationships. Thus the cohesiveness of the relatively nonfunctional family depends on mutual love. For this reason the relatively nonfunctional family tends to be an unstable family. We shall return to this thesis later in the book.

Last and certainly not least is the observation that these two polar types of family are receding from their extremities of function and structure and are moving toward an intermediate position, i.e., they are becoming more like each other and more like the middle-class family of urban and suburban America.

[a] Marion J. Levy, Jr., *The Family Revolution in Modern China* (Cambridge, Mass.: Harvard University Press, 1949).

[b] Further discussion of some of these points appears in Robert F. Winch, *Mate-Selection: A Study of Complementary Needs* (New York: Harper and Row, 1958), chs. 1–4, 14, 15.

[c] Levy, p. 196. See also Shu-ching Lee, "China's Traditional Family, Its Characteristics and Disintegration," *American Sociological Review*, 18: 272–280 (1953), p. 275.

STRUCTURAL FORMS OF THE FAMILY While marriage is central to family structure, this structure can and does take many forms. The normative practice in America is *monogamy**, one husband and one wife living in a nuclear household with their children. A growing number of people are choosing to bear no more than two children, preferring to adopt any additional children they may desire (Fullerton, 1972:132). This pattern of nuclear, monogamous households seems natural to us, but a comparison with other cultures and with our past suggests that the current American pattern is atypical. Some years ago, working with the Human Relations Area Files, George Murdock analyzed marriage and family forms in 238 societies. In only forty-three did strict monogamy prevail. Over 80 percent (195) practiced some form of *polygamy**, two or more husbands or, more typically, two or more wives (1949:24).

VARIATION IN AMERICAN FAMILY FORMS With some exceptions, the American pattern has historically been monogamous but not nuclear (Parsons, 1965). Until the 1920s, the normative unit was an extended kinship network in a small town. The average family had more than twice the number of children than at present. It was common to find grandparents, aunts, uncles, and other relatives, and sometimes two or more nuclear families in the same household or nearby. The present city- or suburban-based family with a few children, living away from close kin, is a mid-twentieth-century phenomenon for most.

While for most Americans, the monogamous, sexually exclusive marital unit has remained the ideal sanctioned by law, there have been and are experimental structures. Two well documented examples are the polygamous practices of the Mormons, led by Brigham Young, in Utah in the nineteenth century, and the multiple-partner relationships in the community of Oneida, New York in the late nineteenth century, under the leadership of the Protestant minister John Humphry Noyes (see Kephart on "Experimental Family Organization," 1972:154–190). Today there are a variety of experiments. Some, such as *open marriage* (O'Neill and O'Neill, 1972), are an extension of monogamy in which the range of sexual partners is expanded with no implication of sharing economic and child-raising responsibilities. Others try similar multiple-partner arrangements in which separate nuclear families share economic and child-rearing responsibilities, forming a sort of extended family (Constantine and Constantine, 1973). In the 1960s and 1970s, various polygamous communal group arrangements emerged, but they generally last less than a year, broken by the need for job mobility and societal pressures against so radical a departure from the norm (Kanter, 1972).

These alternative forms of marriage and family life represent well under 10 percent of the total. Yet, given the high divorce rate (see Fig. 3-2) and other signs of strain on the normative family, these new forms seem to be symptomatic of major efforts at adjustment. Furthermore, the number of stable alternatives that have emerged suggest that American society may be evolving toward multiple family forms.

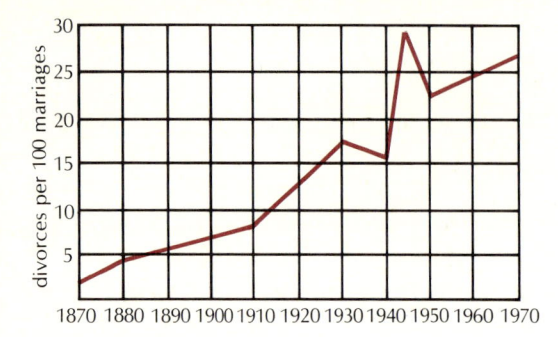

Figure 3-2 Divorces per 100 marriages for the United States, 1820–1970.

SOCIAL CHANGE AND THE FAMILY How effectively has the institution of the family adjusted to modern society? Specific matters related to social change will be considered in Chapter 5, on adolescence, and Chapter 7, on the elderly. Here we shall discuss some general developments. We have seen that one adjustment has been to scale down the size of the family, both in number of children and by limiting close regular ties with extended kin. This smaller size increases the obligations on each family member.

The nuclear family structure is undergoing considerable strain. It is often ill-equipped to help its members adjust to the pressures of the larger society. One measure of the breakdown of family units is the divorce rate, which has increased substantially in the past century. In the last quarter century, there have been about twenty-five divorces for every hundred marriages. Perhaps even more revealing of strain is a study of those who stay married. John Cuber and Peggy Harroff surveyed a sample of upper-middle-class Americans, those relatively well educated and affluent if not rich, a group within which one could expect a relatively high degree of contentment. Yet, Cuber and Harroff concluded, "The overriding generalization of this study is that marriage is often continued out of habit, tradition, practical convenience, or austere social sanctions, and that what the mental hygienist might call a good man–woman relationship in marriage is the exception rather than the rule" (Cuber and Harroff, 1973:110).

The cultural preoccupation with romantic love as a basis for marriage aggravates our frustrations. In other cultures, romantic love as a basis for selecting a mate is relatively rare. Factors such as economic or genealogical concerns are the important considerations in many cultures. Our emphasis on the pursuit of individual happiness and finding one other person who will be all things to us forever puts strong demands on marriage partners. Judith Katz, in her article on "How Do You Love Me? Let Me Count the Ways," offers the following view of the romantic love ideal (1976:17):

... Romantic love in fact is antithetical to universalistic love. It requires the lover love one person to the exclusion of loving others. If you acted the same toward all people, no matter how loving that behavior, you would not appear to love any one person in the way the romantic definition demands.

The difficulties evident in the American family structure are one consequence of the interdependence of the family and other basic institutions, all of which are undergoing rapid change. The changing legal rights and roles of women in the larger society have shifted authority from the husband to equal shares for husband and wife. Precisely where the American family is heading is not clear. Bernard Farber, the family and kinship analyst, identifies the powerful pressures emerging (1973:158):

Future legislation and judicial interpretation may regulate marital selection (for eugenic [mating of the genetically sound] reasons), fertility (for population control), childrearing practices (for mental and physical health, tenure [duration] in marriage (for the welfare of the household), and domestic privacy (for the general welfare of the community). Add to these the modifications induced by technological and economic development, the capriciousness of history and the drifts in population composition and dynamics, and you have the nuances of future domestic life. What will the child of the eventual ... family ... be like?

Is it possible that the government will control who you can marry? It does so now. Laws restrict who can marry: licenses must be obtained. We are really speaking of *expanded* control. Is it possible that we will have marriage contracts that specify financial obligations? We do now. Think about nonsupport suits, alimony, and child support. These legal concerns are based on breaches of contract, for marriage is a legal contract as well as a religious union. Will the specification be more full and precise? The new is often an extension of the old.

RELIGION

The trends that affect the family also influence religion. While religious institutions are less important than in the past (Hoult, 1958:141–171), they continue to play a major role in our lives. Furthermore, there is evidence of awakened cultural interest in new and non-Western religions.

UNIVERSALITY OF RELIGION Can religion be considered a universal cultural phenomenon? China, Russia, and other communist societies, with over one-third of the world's population, officially adhere to the view of Marx and Lenin that religion is the opiate of the masses. Communism is generally discussed in political and economic terms, but it has certain qualities of organized religion (see *Christian Century*, 1952:1215). Counterparts of the Christian Church exist in communism in its inspired revealers of truth, its dogma, heresy trials, excommunications, saints and martyrs, its hierarchy, missionaries, and so on. In fact, all cultures exhibit some features of what Emile Durkheim described as religion: "a unified system of beliefs and practices relative to sacred things, uniting into a single moral community all those who adhere to those beliefs and practices" (Durkheim, 1947 trans.: 47).

FUNCTIONS OF RELIGION Religious beliefs may serve a *legitimizing* function for other institutions. For example, the childbearing and childrearing functions of the family are sanctioned in all major religions, and the criminal laws often reflect religious admonitions such as "Thou shalt not bear false witness" and "Thou shalt not kill." Religious practitioners often aid us in times of personal and social crisis, and religious beliefs and rituals offer clear and specific ways of managing deep emotions and psychological loss.

All these and other functions of religion were characterized by Emile Durkheim as promoting social cohesion (1974 trans.: 427):

There can be no society which does not feel the need of upholding and reaffirming at regular intervals the collective ideas which make its unity its personality ... What essential difference is there between an assembly of Christians celebrating the principal dates of the life of Christ, or of Jews remembering the exodus from Egypt or ... a reunion of citizens commemorating ... some great event in the national life?

Historical evidence suggests a modification of this analysis. Religion may be functional as Durkheim suggests, but it may also be dysfunctional. The sociological question is, under what conditions is religion one or the other?

COHESIVE AND DIVISIVE TENDENCIES Durkheim's definition appears reasonable under two sets of conditions: when everyone adheres willingly to one religion or when, within the same culture, different religious groups tolerate and respect each other. What happens when religious groups are intolerant and hostile? The result may be dysfunctional for an entire society or a significant part of it. Consider the role of religious dissent in the American colonists' break with the official Anglican Church, or the bitterness and loss of life surrounding the prolonged strife in Northern Ireland, both religiously and politically motivated. Each side clings to its point of view, rejecting any possi-

'YOU SEE, ME BOY, IT'S A SIN IF IT'S COMIN' THISAWAY, BUT IT'S A BLESSING IF IT'S GOIN' THATAWAY!'

SOURCE: Reprinted by permission of the *Denver Post*.

ble value in the other. Thus tension continues, as suggested in the Keefe cartoon.

Religious teaching about *out-groups** has frequently been a factor in excluding people from social clubs and other social interaction, as for example the exclusionary policies against Jews practiced by some clubs. An example of sanctified racial hatred is the missionary Baptist Association of Texas's resolution of 1954 (the year of the Supreme Court school desegregation decision), which states (*Southern School News*, 1954:15):

We publish to the world that we protest the attempts being made to desegregate the races, because we believe such would inevitably lead into a hybrid monstrosity that would defy the word and will of God.

Large religious denominations in the United States give formal support to the American creed that all men are created equal. Insofar as religious groups adhere to this creed in practice, they advance Durkheim's functional analysis of social cohesion.

RELIGIOUS AND ECONOMIC VALUES Religion may also have *latent*, unintended, *functional consequences*. Max Weber felt that the Protestant theological perspective sparks an entrepreneurial spirit (eagerness to pursue business ventures) and consequently gave rise to capitalism and economic development in Western society (Weber, 1930). He believed that Lutheran and Calvinistic doctrine turned Christians toward salvation through this world rather than awaiting salvation in the hereafter. Material prosperity was an outward sign of salvation, and hard work and thrift were the means by which to gain such rewards.

What evidence is there that Weber's thesis has any validity for contemporary American society? In his contemporary classic, *The Religious Factor*, Gerhard Lenski tested this *Protestant ethic* by evaluating the economic behavior of different socioreligious groups in a large city. He found that Jews and Protestants ranked first and second on the economic scale and Catholics third, suggesting that both Judaism and Protestantism encourage individualistic, competitive patterns (Lenski, 1963:101).

Lenski's conclusions appear generally valid, though the worldly success of specific groups raises questions about just how influential the religious factor is. While it is true that some Protestant groups and Jews are at the top of the economic scale, other Protestant groups are at the bottom. Furthermore, analysis of the Jewish community shows that over a third earn less than the average family income (Demerath, 1965:2). And what about Catholics, who presumably do not share the Protestant ethic's value structure? Lenski associated them with the collectivistic, security-oriented working-class patterns of thought and action, as opposed to the Protestant ethic and its associated spirit of capitalism and economic growth. Yet Catholics as a whole have above-average family incomes. This does not negate the thesis of the Protestant ethic, but it may indicate that many American Catholics now follow this ethic in their economic behavior.

Albert Mayer and Harry Sharp, in reviewing this mixture of religion and economic achievement, concluded that religion has less influence on economic achievement in contemporary American society than do other cultural factors (1962). Thus, rural Baptists typically earn less than urban Catholics, since income is generally higher in urban areas.

Even with these qualifications, Lenski's observation on the consequences of the religious factor appears reasonable (1963:320):

Depending upon the socioreligious group to which a person belongs, the probabilities are increased or decreased that he will enjoy his occupation, indulge in installment buying, save to achieve objectives far in the future, believe in the American Dream [that one can go from rags to riches], vote Republican, favor the welfare state, take a liberal view on the issue of freedom of speech, oppose racial integration in the schools, migrate to another community, maintain close ties with his family, have a large family, complete a given unit of education or rise in the class system. These are only a few of the consequences we have observed to be associated with differences in socioreligious group membership, and the position of individuals in these groups.

STRUCTURAL FORMS OF RELIGION The two major types of religious bodies are *sects** and *churches*, or *denominations** (Ernst Troeltsch, 1931:47). Denominational groups often start as sects. Sects are small groups that aspire after personal inward perfection and aim at a direct personal fellowship between the members of each group (Troeltsch, 1931:331). As such, sects often attract the middle classes — particularly the young — who are unhappy with their affluent secular life style (Pope, 1942:122–124). The hippie phenomenon of recent years exemplified the disaffection of the young. Many turned not only to drugs but also (or in place of drugs) to spiritual commitment. In this period, there was a resurgence of interest in the occult. Sects have characteristics similar to those of *cults**. Cults, which are often found among rootless urban groups, are more loosely organized and transitory than sects.

Most Americans adhere to the second of Troeltsch's religious types, a *church* or *denomination*. Where there is a dominant church, like the Anglican Church in England, the Catholic Church in the

DO-ER'S PROFILES
(Pronounced "Jesuit")

WITH PERMISSION OF DEWAR'S "WHITE LABEL SCOTCH"

THE JESUIT

HOME: The world

AGE: 18 plus

PROFESSION: Whatever is for the greater glory of God

HOBBIES: Religion and politics

READING: The Bible and today's newspaper

LAST MOVIE IN: "The Exorcist"

QUOTE: "Man is created to praise, reverence, and serve God, our Lord, and by this means to save his soul... our one desire and choice should be what is more conducive to the end for which we are created."

PROFILE: A priest, a brother, a counselor, a missionary. A teacher, theologian, doctor, lawyer, politician, social activist... human being.

For further information, contact:

California Province / CA, NV, UT, AZ / Rev. John I. Geiszel, S.J. / 7101 W. 80th St. / Los Angeles, CA 90045 / (213) 776-0400

Chicago Province / IL, IN, KY, OH (Cinn. area) / Rev. Patrick T. Darcy, S.J. / 509 N. Oak Park Ave. / Oak Park, IL 60302 / (312) 626-7934

Detroit Province / MI, OH (excluding Cinn.) / Rev. Robert Voglewede, S.J. / 2599 Harvard Rd. / Berkley, MI 48072 / (313) 399-8132

Maryland Province / PA, DE, DC, MD, VA, WV, NJ (lower) / Rev. Eugene P. McCreesh, S.J. / St. Joseph's College / Philadelphia, PA 19131 / (215) 879-1000

Missouri Province / MO, KS, OK, CO, WY, IL (southern) / Rev. Joseph E. Damhorst, S.J. / 5225 Troost Avenue / Kansas City, MO 64110 / (816) 363-4010

New Orleans Province / Southern States, TX, NM / Rev. Kenneth A. Buddendorff, S.J. / 6363 St. Charles Ave. / New Orleans, LA 70118 / (504) 866-5471

New York Province / NY, NJ (north of Trenton), PR / Rev. Daniel J. Mulhauser, S.J. / 501 E. Fordham Rd. / Bronx, NY 10458 / (212) 933-2990

New England Province / Northeastern States / Rev. Jerome Lannan, S.J. / 393 Commonwealth Ave. / Boston, MA 02115 / (617) 266-7233

Oregon Province / OR, WA, ID, MT, AK / Rev. Patrick J. Kenny, S.J. / 420 W. Pine St. / Missoula, MT 59801 / (406) 542-0321

Wisconsin Province / WI, MN, IA, NB, SD, ND / Rev. Gary T. Brophy, S.J. / 1437 Woodland Ave. / Des Moines, IA 50309 / (515) 282-4839

Jesuits are men with a tradition of being contemporary, with zeal and style, unknown and famous, in the world, yet mysteriously not of it, daring to be different. ***Do-ers always vary.***

This takeoff on a popular liquor advertisement is designed to appeal to potential candidates for the priesthood. This is one way in which religious institutions are adjusting to the secular demands of modern society. SOURCE: Courtesy of the New York Province Society of Jesus.

Holy Roman Empire, and the Jewish Sanhedrin in ancient Israel, this denomination becomes an *ecclesia**, with the church exercising political power. No *ecclesia* exists in American society, where the tradition of religious liberty is written into the First Amendment to the Constitution: "Congress shall make no law respecting an establishment of religion, or prohibiting the free exercise thereof..."[4]

Most Americans belong to a large church or denomination. As a reflection of our traditions of religious liberty and separation of church and state, no group is dominant, and small sects (most of which are included in the category Other Protestants in Table 3-1) still abound in our society. Though the United States was settled predominantly by Protestants, the larger Judaeo–Christian heritage is evident in the large numbers of Catholics and Jews in the population. Other religious traditions include those of the indigenous Native American tribes and eastern religions such as Islam and Hinduism (grouped as Other religions in Table 3-1). Given the urban, secular nature of contemporary American society, it is significant that less than 3 percent of the population espouses no religion.

The tradition of religious liberty has produced a number of denominational groupings, particularly among Protestants, who constitute a majority of Americans. The Protestant, Catholic, Jewish, and other large denominational groupings have all been characterized by bureaucratization, with highly educated fulltime ministries and varied physical structures. Tolerance of religious liberty has also encouraged the development of various alternative religions, such as the Satanist Church and other sects and cults.

Table 3-1 Religious Composition of the Population of the United States, Eighteen Years of Age or Older, 1972

Religion	Number (in millions)	Percent
Protestants	81	64
Baptists	25	20
Methodists	18	14
Lutherans	11	9
Presbyterians	6	5
Episcopalians	2.5	2
Other Protestants	18	14
Roman Catholics	33	26
Jews	4	3
Other religions	2.5	2
No religion	4	3
Religion not reported	2.5	2
Total adult U.S. population eighteen and over (1970 Census)	126.2	100
Sample size = 1613		

SOURCE: National Data Program for the Social Sciences (based upon the General Social Survey in the spring of 1972 with a national sample). Chicago: National Opinion Research Center, 1972 Codebook.

How can one explain the social fact that religion is at the same time universal and yet vastly different from one culture to another and even within a given society? Ruth Benedict provides this answer (Maslow and Honigman, 1970:332):

To the comparative student... religion is not an institution whose common characteristic is a striving for ethical values. Rather, it is a sensitive plate upon which peoples have inscribed their emotions and, in so doing, whether these are warm and affiliative feelings or whether they are hostile and malevolent ones, have given them a force of their own that heightens and carries further the love or the hostility with which their social order is charged.

---

[4] Of course there is an occasional lapse from the ideal into a less spiritual reality. The Mormon religion supports polygamy, but Mormons are not allowed its practice by the secular state. Children of Christian Scientists or others whose beliefs forbid certain medical practices may be subjected to treatment over parental objections by means of a court order.

SOCIAL CHANGE AND RELIGION What is the place of religion likely to be in the future? Gallup and Harris polls in the 1960s and 1970s found that fewer than half of American adults attend religious services in a typical week. Yet, the religious institutional structure appears to have an important continuing influence. In 1967, when Detroit experienced the most damaging race riot in American history, spokesmen for religious institutions attempted to relax racial tensions. Their efforts were evaluated (Gordon, 1971; 1973), and two major conclusions were drawn: first, that religious spokesmen had little impact on the behavior of either blacks or whites in open interracial tensions; second, that religious spokesmen were nonetheless able to bring influential black and white community leaders who had previously not interacted with each other into direct communication in order to plan community redevelopment.

This example, and the research of Lenski, Hoult, and others suggests that, though religion is no longer a dominant factor in the behavior of most Americans, it does *influence* their values and hold their respect. Perhaps more important, the institution of religion continues to provide solace for millions at difficult times.

A number of people involved in the Watergate scandal that toppled the Nixon administration turned to religion for comfort in facing the problems brought on by their altered positions in society. People who hope to overcome self-destructive behavior patterns may become zealous converts, as religion protects them from themselves. Adams and Fox, studying "Jesus People" in Southern California, found most to be young whites from middle-class backgrounds who fall into two distinct groups: teenagers who are attracted by the message of free rock music concerts to "turn on" to Jesus, and young adults in their twenties who have dropped out of the drug culture, or are former peace movement activists seeking a means of reentering the system (Adams and Fox, 1973:300-301). For drug culture dropouts, religion may become the new "trip"; for others it combines something new with values supported by the culture as a whole in a predominantly Christian society.

EDUCATION

UNIVERSALITY OF EDUCATIONAL INSTITUTIONS Education is more nearly universal in its processes and functions than in its structural forms. All societies must socialize each new generation in order to preserve and continue their culture. In America today, much of this task is borne by schools, though until recently their role was far less extensive. Indeed, it was not until the 1950s that a majority of Americans completed high school (*Historical Statistics,* 1951:205). In many rural societies, formal schools generally do not exist.

HISTORICAL IMPETUS TOWARD MASS PUBLIC EDUCATION In the colonial and early Federal periods, the family trained young people to participate in the larger culture. Much education beyond the family took place in the churches, and the curriculum in the schools was predominantly religious (Edwards and Richey, 1963:9). The modern public school system began to develop early in the nineteenth century, partly in response to the eighteenth-century liberal and humanitarian movements of which the American Revolution was a part. Another impetus was industrialization and urbanization, and the expanding middle and laboring classes demanded more education because of the opportunities it brought their children (Edwards and Richey, 1963:295-298).

Additionally, as Michael Katz documents, education in the nineteenth century tried to mold students, particularly the urban poor, to fit the developing industrial, bureaucratic society (Katz, 1975:31-32):

As might be expected from their image of the urban poor, school reformers held that "the primary object" in removing the child from the influence of the parent to the influence of the school was "not so much ... intellectual culture, as the regulation of the feelings and dispositions.... Schools existed to serve society by tending the characters of otherwise neglected children."

That task assumed special importance in relation to industrial society. The values to be instilled by the schools were precisely those required for the conduct of a complex urban society — for example the importance of time.... One writer, to make that concern explicit, pointed to the parallel behavior required of the schoolboy and the working man. For both, "precision" had become a necessary habit; "regularity and economy of time" had come to mark "our community, as appears in the running 'on time' of long trains on our great network of railroads; the strict regulation of all large manufacturing establishments; as well as the daily arrangements of our school duties." The connection was unmistakable; schools were training grounds for commerce. What had been "instilled in the mind of the pupil" became "thoroughly recognized by the man as of the first importance in the transaction of business."

It is important to take note of this bias that certain homes and family influences are less desirable than others, a view which continues to affect both schools and family assistance programs.

FUNCTIONS OF EDUCATION The tasks performed by the extensive contemporary school structure are universal: they existed before the structure was developed. In simpler times and places, the educational process was performed mostly by family and religious institutions. The complex nature of modern society has forced educational institutions to take on a major role in bringing young people into the larger culture.

Think how different jobs are today compared to jobs a generation ago and how different life is in a large metropolitan area than it was in earlier rural life or even in cities before World War II, when suburbs were a minor phenomenon. Such large cultural developments have made it difficult for families to assume complete responsibility for socializing the young.

PRACTICAL AND IDEALISTIC AIMS OF SCHOOLS To accomplish this process of socialization, the schools have two prime functional tasks, one *idealistic* and the other *pragmatic*. The idealistic task is to transmit the values and norms of the society, the pragmatic to train people to fit into the occupational structure and in other practical ways of getting along in society. American schools have attempted to combine these approaches. The American philosopher John Dewey founded the influential *pragmatist school* early in the century. Dewey and his followers rejected the notion that education could separate the examination of values from vocational training (Dewey, 1916).

The views of Dewey and the pragmatists have greatly influenced the training of teachers by raising questions about fundamental issues: Should the emphasis in the early grades be on the practical — reading, writing, and arithmetic — or on developing the whole personality and an inquiring mind? At the upper levels, should the emphasis be on general education or professional and vocational specialization? Should these approaches be combined by studying broad concepts in connection with practical disciplines? A student training to be a tax accountant may also ask whether equality of opportunity exists in the society so as to enable people to earn incomes large enough to require the services of an accountant. Indeed, any practical course has broad implications, and any philosophical, literary, or other value-laden course has practical implications.

In transmitting the ideals of the culture and training the young for practical pursuits, the

Table 3-2 Public Elementary and Secondary School Revenue Receipts from Federal, State, and Local Sources: United States, 1919-20 to 1969-70 School Year

School year	Percent	Total amount[a]	Federal[b]	State[b]	Local[b]
1919-20	100	$ 970,000	0.3	16.5	83.2
1929-30	100	2,100,000	0.4	16.5	82.7
1939-40	100	2,260,000	1.8	30.3	68.0
1949-50	100	5,400,000	2.9	39.8	57.3
1959-60	100	14,700,000	4.4	39.1	56.5
1969-70	100	39,100,000	7.9	38.9	53.2

[a] Amount in millions of dollars, rounded.
[b] Source in percent.
SOURCE: Digest of Educational Statistics (Washington, D.C.: Government Printing Office, 1971), p. 54.

schools both *preserve* and *change* the culture. Ideals that support individual liberty and opportunity are a help to young people in adjusting to a culture in which life styles and opportunities are changing rapidly. Likewise, the vast American economic structure is constantly expanding and developing new products and services, so that new kinds of training are required from one generation to the next.

To preserve traditional American culture, then, is to ensure that changes will occur within it. The question is whether the changes are desirable and are institutionalized into the culture in a manageable way.

SOME UNINTENDED FUNCTIONS OF SCHOOLS
Beyond the manifest consequences of education in American society, there are some latent functions and dysfunctions. James Vander Zanden discusses the custodial function (1970:532) of schools. Children are kept confined and accounted for while society pursues other business. Elementary schools provide child-care service, freeing women for jobs outside the home. Schooling prepares young people for skilled jobs and professions while also keeping them out of the job market, where they would compete with an adult work force which is living and working longer than ever before.

Another latent function of some poor schools is that they maintain a high level of ignorance. Table 3-2 shows that most public school funds come from local communities; since some school districts are rich and others poor, there are great differences in the quality of schools.[5] The increase in the proportionate tax funding on the part of state and federal sources has broadened the sources of influences on the kinds of schools to be developed. A major issue is whether the institutionalization of this expanded base of influence on local schools is primarily positive or negative in its effect as the schools attempt to carry on their idealistic and pragmatic socializing functions. Thus, from a certain narrow point of view, it can be argued that institutionalized ignorance helps maintain the superior position of some

---

[5] A typical example of unequal support was brought out in the 1972 case of *Serrano* v. *Priest* in California. In this case it was reported that the expenditure per pupil in the upper-middle-class district of Beverly Hills was $1,516 per pupil, while in the nearby Baldwin Park district, with many poor blacks and Mexican Americans, it was $691. The California Supreme Court held such unequal expenditures to be discriminatory and illegal, setting the stage for major alterations in school funding procedures.

groups (Moore and Tumin, 1949:787-795). Moreover, it also helps to maintain prejudice and to impose dominant group demands on the deprived and underprivileged. In any broad view, of course, maintaining ignorance is dysfunctional, not functional. Yet, given the varied quality of American schools, these functions are part of the social reality, and it is necessary to realize that they do exist in order to understand how the educational system operates. The competency chart in Table 3-3 is compiled using APL competency levels (Adult Performance Levels) based on a study by Dr. Norvell Northcutt and his research team at the University of Texas. The five general areas of knowledge (listed first on the chart) require primary skills (reading, problem-solving, computational skills, writing), also listed on the chart. The study emphasizes ability to function competently at necessary cultural tasks rather than evaluating only one dimension, literacy, as has been done in the past. It assesses individuals' *practical* capacities. Persons are placed into three different APL categories. APL 1s function with difficulty — that is, they have poverty-level incomes or less; inadequate education (eight years or less), and are unemployed or hold low-status jobs. APL 2s are functional but little more. Their incomes are above poverty level, but there is no income margin; educational level is nine to eleven years, and they work at menial jobs or in positions of similar status. APL 3s are proficient in skills and knowledge required by this society. They have high incomes, with room for discretionary use of it, high school educations or more, and high job levels.

STRUCTURAL FORMS OF EDUCATION On an average day one out of four Americans (over 50 million people) is in an educational institution as a student, teacher, or administrator (*Digest,* 1971:5, 7, 25, and 62). We shall examine the complex structure of our educational system by looking at the organizational structure of schooling, the public, parochial, or private nature of schools, and the community sources of support for schools.

THE STRUCTURE OF SCHOOLING Schools in this country are organized on a formal bureaucratic pattern. In a large metropolis such as New York or Los Angeles, in a smaller city such as Albuquerque or Tallahassee, and in a rural community like Gila Bend, Arizona, or Three Rivers, Michigan, their basic structure is the one noted in Figure 3-3. The quality of the schools may differ, as may the social class levels and racial background of the students, and the proportion of students who go beyond high school. In all these communities, there are elementary schools, secondary schools, and nearby if not in the community itself, colleges. Also, the systems are operated by bureaucracies similarly composed. There is always the same general division of labor and functional relationship among Board of Education or Regents, administrators, teachers, and students.

PUBLIC, PAROCHIAL, OR PRIVATE SCHOOLS The three major types of schools in America — public, parochial, and private — use similar grade struc-

Table 3-3 Functional Incompetence in the United States (Adult Competency Levels)

Areas	APL competency levels		
	1	2	3
Occupational knowledge	19.1%	31.9%	49.0%
Consumer economics	29.4	33.0	37.6
Government and law	25.8	26.2	48.0
Health	21.3	30.3	48.3
Community resources	22.6	26.0	51.4
Reading	21.7	32.2	46.1
Problem solving	28.0	23.4	48.5
Computation	32.9	26.3	40.8
Writing	16.4	25.5	58.1
Overall competency levels	19.7	33.9	46.3

SOURCE: Art Branscombe, Denver *Post,* Nov. 16, 1975. p. 20.

tures. These schools are differentiated by their base of financial support and the influences affecting their operation. Public schools are supported by taxes paid by all the people. Parochial and private nonsectarian schools get their primary support from churches or individual sources.

By the nature of their support structure, all schools are subject to different pressures. Public schools receive the broadest pressures. According to a study of organized pressures on public school superintendents (Gross, 1958:50), parents, PTA's, school board members, and teachers are the most active pressure groups. Our culture defines these people as the ones most appropriately interested in education. Note that the group does not include students. Of course in recent years, students have begun to organize to press for specific demands. Nonetheless, it cannot now be said that students as a group exert influence to the degree that others do.

Some pressures may check each other. For example, while PTA's may want more taxes for the local schools, the Chamber of Commerce may be working to lower taxes. Parochial and private schools are subject to fewer but more intense directional pressures.

COMMUNITY SOURCES OF SUPPORT FOR SCHOOLS Over 85 percent of the country's 40 million elementary and secondary school students are in public schools. Of those who are not, most are in Roman Catholic parochial schools or in private nonsectarian schools (Sexton, 1967:23). Since most students attend public schools, the nature of their financial support has a major influence on the quality of schooling in the society.

The major source of funding for public schools is the local property tax. The federal government has no constitutional responsibility for education. In recent years, a variety of social forces has greatly increased the cost of mass education, often beyond the financial resources of local communities. Increasingly more students are going to school longer and being taught by more and better paid teachers in facilities needing more expensive equipment. The result is that many communities have become unable to maintain their schools.

The trend noted in Table 3-2 demonstrates an inverse relationship. As the total cost of public schooling rose from less than $1 billion in 1919-1920 to over $39 billion in 1969-1970, the proportion of local school district support dropped from 83 percent to 53 percent. Increasingly the state and federal governments, with their broader taxing powers, have taken on the burden of supporting public schools. An indication that most people support this trend is that, while more total taxes are being spent on public schools, more local property tax bills are being defeated. Until the early 1960s, three-quarters or more of all local school bond elections passed. But by 1969-1970 only about half passed (*Digest*, 1971:54), a trend which continues. Formal education in America has now grown so large and is so expensive to maintain that the trend toward more state and federal support is likely to persist.

SOCIAL CHANGE AND EDUCATION In the early nineteenth century, Horace Mann of Massachusetts and other leading educators successfully argued for the establishment of a broad-based public school system (Williams, 1937). The United States was then a rural society, and the school year reflected that fact: the length of the school year was set at nine months, enabling young people to work on the farms during the summer growing season.

As we head toward the twenty-first century, are the schools functioning effectively? Or do they show what William F. Ogburn called *cultural lag** (1950:1), the failure to adapt to change as other social institutions have done? The answer is a paradox. The Carnegie Foundation commissioned Charles Silberman to direct a project to evaluate American education. After reviewing the findings, Silberman wrote (1970:12, 14):

Figure 3-3 This basic educational structure is found in communities throughout America. Most Americans now advance beyond the high school diploma. This is an outgrowth of a long trend in which schools have increasingly taken on the process of socializing young people into the culture. SOURCE: *Digest of Educational Statistics, 1971* (Washington, D.C.: Government Printing Office, 1972), Figure 1, p. xiv.

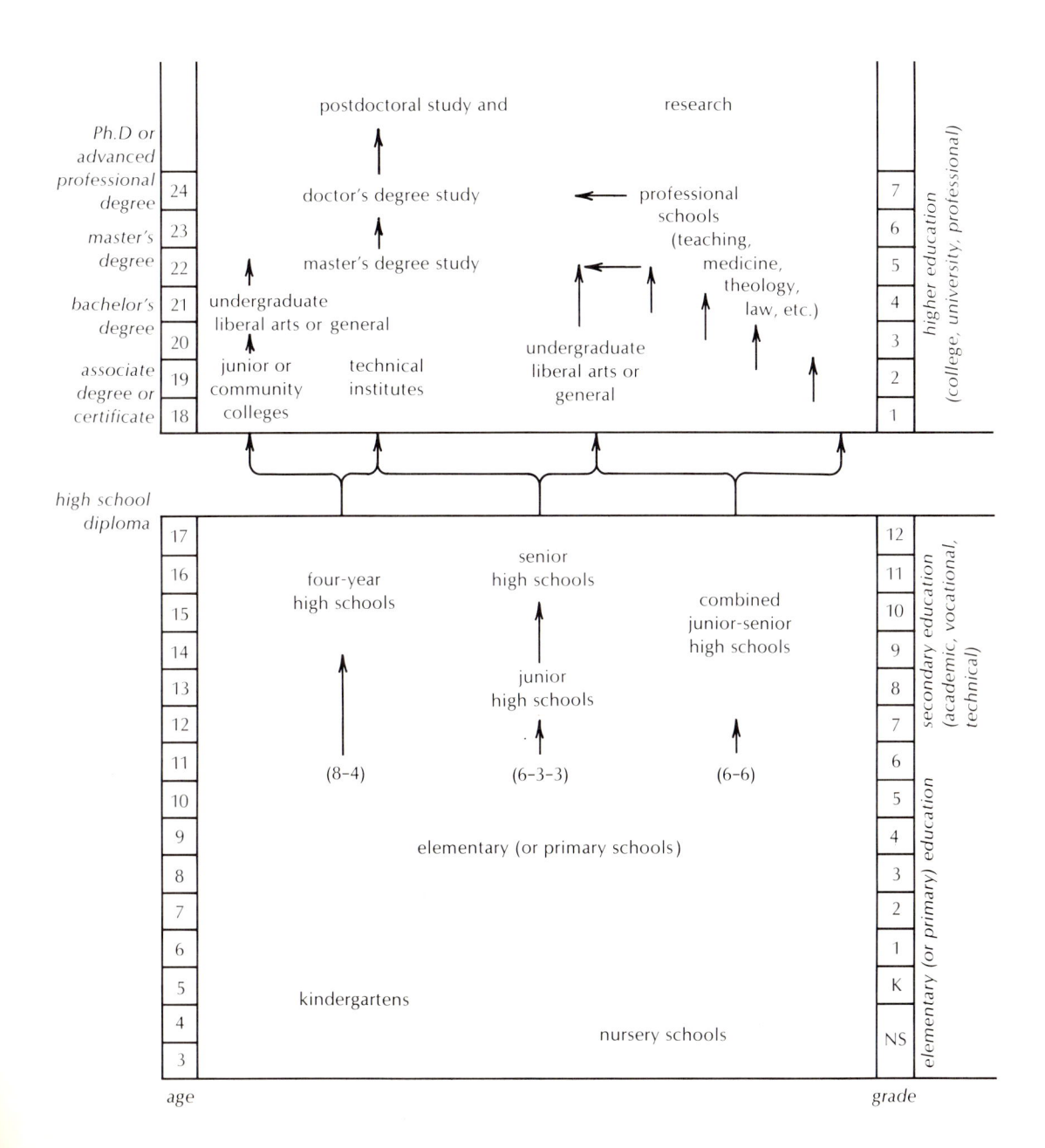

On the one hand ... the United States educational system appears to be superbly successful — on almost any measure, performing better than it did ... fifty, or a hundred years ago ... at the elementary and secondary school levels ... the vast expansion and democratization of higher education in the 1950s and 1960s is an extraordinary achievement ... College attendance, once the almost exclusive prerogative of those with wealth, social position, or extraordinary talent and ambition, is coming to be viewed as the right of every American youth, and social mobility from generation to generation increasingly takes the form of providing one's children with more education than the parents received.

At the same time ... the system would appear to be in grave trouble ... In most large cities and a good many smaller ones ... the public schools are in disarray, torn apart by conflicts over integration, desegregation, decentralization, and community control.

On the larger societal level, the schools are supposed to give all young people a good formal education. Silberman and others show that this is not being done. One of these others is James Coleman, whose national study (1966) focused on the issue of equal educational opportunity. Coleman presented extensive evidence that children of poor families, particularly among racial minorities, do not receive as good an education as do others. Federal courts, influenced by his findings, began to order busing of some students under the equal protection of the law provisions of the Constitution, with the aim of achieving racial desegregation of schools. The ultimate goal was equal educational opportunity for all. This issue is controversial and has not been resolved.

THE EFFECTS OF MASS ROUTINIZATION   Silberman and his associates observed that the large school systems in the nation had become so bureaucratic, formal, and routinized that they did little to stimulate students to learn and to enjoy the process. The preoccupation with order and control seems to have resulted in formal readings and lectures to the exclusion of discussions and working at one's own pace (Silberman, 1970:207-208).

In his popular book *Working,* Studs Terkel interviews a public schoolteacher, a strong supporter of order in the classroom. She tells us (Terkel, 1974:488):

The younger teachers have a more — what is their word — relaxed attitude. It's noisy and it's freedom, where they walk around and do everything. I never learned to teach under conditions like that. The first rule of education for me was discipline. Discipline is the keynote to learning. Discipline has been the great factor in my life. I discipline myself to do everything — getting up in the morning, walking, dancing, exercise. If you won't have discipline, you won't have a nation. We can't have permissiveness. When someone comes in and says, "Oh, your room is so quiet," I know I've been successful.

There is one little girl who stands out in my mind in all the years I've been teaching. She has become tall and lovely. Pam. She was not too bright, but she was sweet. She was never any trouble. She was special. I see her every once in a while. She's a checker at Treasure Island. [A supermarket in the community.] She gives no trouble today, either. She has the same smile for everyone.

ADAPTABILITY THROUGH RESEARCH AND DEVELOPMENT   Patricia Sexton suggests that research and development (R & D) be applied to the schools to counter such old-fashioned attitudes (1967:108-119). R & D is standard in industry and government when new arrangements are tested for their effectiveness or new public programs are developed. Silberman, Coleman, Sexton, and others note the need to experiment — with team teaching, informal individual assignments, interdisciplinary education, and such new electives as computer technology, psychology, and of course sociology. One

The popular public television program "Sesame Street" represents an innovative educational approach that has demonstrated the ability to improve basic skills among young children, especially those from low-income families. SOURCE: Children's Television Workshop.

innovative technique that shows promise is the use of television to reach preschool youngsters. Disadvantaged children from poor families who regularly watch the popular animated play-and-learn format of *Sesame Street* show significant improvement in language and numerical skills (Ball and Bogatz, 1970 and 1971). These and other programs may enable the educational institution to adjust and accommodate to the complexities of modern life.

Ivan Illich has a radical proposal for deschooling society, which calls for placing people who want to learn in contact with those from whom they want to learn. He suggests four approaches for gaining access to information: *reference services using educational objects* in many locations (museums, theaters, factories); *skill exchanges*, which list people interested in serving as models; *peer matching*, whereby individuals may find people with similar interests so they may develop skills together; *reference services to educators-at-large*, so that educators can seek the services of professionals and paraprofessionals whom they trust as teachers and counselors (Illich: 1971). These concepts move the student away from the formality, authoritarianism, and narrowness of typical classrooms, at the same time placing responsibility for learning on the learner. While such proposals are unlikely to be generally adopted, they may help modify the educational system as it now functions.

GOVERNMENT

UNIVERSALITY OF GOVERNMENT In all societies, there is some ultimate authority for the enforcement of those norms of behavior considered essential to the culture. Yet the institutionalization of government through political processes is a phenomenon of modern mass society. As the cultural anthropologist George Murdock noted (1950: 716):

> ... for 99 percent of the approximately one million years that man has inhabited this earth, he lived, thrived, and developed without any true government whatsoever, and, as late as 100 years ago half the peoples of the world ... ordered their lives exclusively through informal controls without benefit of political institutions.

While it may be true that formal, institutionalized government as we know it is recent, the interest in what government does goes back a long way. Over two thousands years ago, Aristotle observed, "Man is by nature a political animal" (1941 trans.: 1129).

FUNCTIONS OF GOVERNMENT In government lies the ultimate authority and power for enforcing broad norms in the society. Government sets the limits of acceptable lawful behavior. In American society and in democracies generally, laws tell people less about what they should do than what they should not do.

LEGAL NORM ENFORCEMENT Given the ultimate power of constituted government, what is the function of punishment for breaking legal norms? It is not mainly to prevent convicted persons from repeating their crimes. The penal system may be intended to work that way, but in fact it does not. Most people serving time in American prisons are repeaters, which reflects on the nonrehabilitative nature of these institutions (Caldwell, 1965:544). Punishment by authorities for serious violations of legal norms, whether rehabilitative or not, does serve a larger social function. As Durkheim suggests: "Punishment ... is ... justified ... to the extent that it is necessary to make disapproval of the act utterly unequivocal" (1961 translation). Punishment helps to *maintain boundaries* as to how far people can express certain forms of behavior without experiencing sanctions. The execution of a convicted murderer in Mississippi would be designed to serve the same boundary-maintaining function as would a life sentence with a chance of parole for the same act in Michigan, which has abolished capital punishment.

PROBLEMS OF CONFLICTING NORMS In a mass society such as ours, with so many ethnic, racial, and religious groups, this norm-enforcing function of government can be a complicated process. It is one thing to enforce norms about which there is wide consensus, such as the rejection of violent bodily assault. It is another thing when an act is acceptable to some cultural groups and not others. Different groups have different moral evaluations of such acts as abortion, consumption of alcohol or cocaine, interracial marriage, and extramarital sexual relations. The legal norms for these acts have been in constant revision because there is no consensus on whether they should be prohibited or restricted; likewise there is disagreement about victimless crimes — homosexuality and prostitution for example — in which both participants seek the encounter.

Whether in accommodating to such value conflicts or in responding to crises such as war, depression, or natural disaster, government is ultimately responsible for maintaining the stability, or *social equilibrium* (see Talcott Parsons, 1951:272–277) of the system.

STRUCTURAL FORMS OF GOVERNMENT The exercise of power is so basic that, before considering structural forms of government, we shall first consider various types of governmental authority. As we have seen, legal boundaries of acceptable behavior in a society are established and enforced through government. The policeman on a beat, the legislator in a congress, or a judge in a court of law all hold status in which they can exercise power and authority over others.

Power and authority in government are made *legitimate* and acceptable to most people by several means. Max Weber identified three types of governmental authority (1947 trans.: 324–362): *traditional* authority, *charismatic* authority, and *rational–legal* authority. In both representative and nonrepresentative government, these legitimating sources of authority play a role in maintaining the system of government.

TRADITIONAL AUTHORITY   Traditional authority is based on practices sanctioned by custom. An example is the hereditary monarchy. The power kings once had was based largely on biological relationship to a former king. Sometimes the people cease to recognize this basis of authority, as in the American, French, and Russian revolutions, when the position of king (or czar) was repudiated. Although government may limit the power of a tradition-based system of authority, this kind of authority is not generally subject to controls by the governed. Tradition-based authority thus has an arbitrary quality.

CHARISMATIC AUTHORITY   Charismatic authority in government springs from the strong appeal of an individual with governing power. As Weber noted, *charisma* is "a certain quality of an individual personality by virtue of which he is set apart from ordinary men and treated as endowed with supernatural, superhuman, or at least exceptional powers or qualities" (1947 trans.: 358). Charismatic leaders tend to arise in times of stress and crisis. Modern examples are Franklin D. Roosevelt, Winston Churchill, Joseph Stalin, and Adolph Hitler. Note that charisma refers simply to the ability to appeal to others, regardless of the leader's character. These leaders, using modern mass media and other techniques, were able to generate charismatic authority in very different kinds of political structures.

In recent years, the importance of radio, television, and the press has been widely observed. In the 1976 presidential election campaign, many candidates bought considerable television time. One candidate actually took voice and drama lessons during the primaries to increase his charismatic appeal. Unfortunately for the candidate, his scheme did not work.

RATIONAL-LEGAL AUTHORITY   Weber's third ideal type of authority is the basis of most governing authority in modern society. The complex division of labor in government, and the bureaucratization inherent in this division, has shifted much authority to an *office* rather than the individual who fills it. As such it is the status of an official that provides the primary basis of authority rather than inheritance or charisma. Governing powers are defined by the rules of office, not by the individual who happens to fill the office. In American society, the emphasis upon rational–legal authority was demonstrated when the highest governing official, the president, was forced to resign in 1974 after transgressing the defined powers of the office. A safeguard of the rational–legal model is its concern for procedures for orderly transfer of power.

Of course, elements of any or all of these three forms of authority can be found in all types of government.

DEMOCRATIC AND TOTALITARIAN PROTOTYPES   Two major structural prototypes in modern government are *democratic* and *totalitarian*. (A third, called *laissez-faire,* involving minimal government participation in people's affairs, is not widely practiced.) No actual society is wholly one type or the other, but each is predominantly one or the other. Democratic governments such as the American and the British tend to maximize individual freedom and minimize state control of individuals in comparison with totalitarian governments such as those of Nazi Germany and the Soviet Union, which maximize state control. Totalitarian societies concentrate power in one political party, empowered to destroy all possible groups which could someday challenge their authority (de Gré, 1946: 535). Such governments may influence other social institutions in a variety of ways. They may support communist economic ideology and take over the private economy, as in the Soviet Union and the People's Republic of China, or they may maintain private capitalism, as in Nazi Germany and Fascist Spain. In all these, power and decision-making are in the hands of an arbitrary authority.

Democracy supplies regular institutional opportunities for changing the governing officials, and a social mechanism which permits the largest possible participation of the population to influence major decisions by choosing among contenders for political office (Lipset, 1963:27). Democratic systems are politically more complex than totalitarian systems. Given the voluntary opportunities to support or oppose government, there is invariably more than one political party. The two major types are the *pluralist,* in which there are usually two major political parties, as in the United States and Great Britain, and the *multipartite,* in which a number of parties compete for power, as in France and Italy.

THE QUESTION OF STABILITY   A fundamental question for all governments is: What structure is most conducive to stability? The best measure of stability in a government is its ability to maintain itself in periods of great stress. The Great Depression of the 1930s was worldwide and gives useful insights into this question.

At the start of the Depression in the early 1930s, three prominent nations with different government structures were confronted by mass unemployment, economic deprivation, and a challenge to their stability. These were the German Weimar Republic, with a multipartite governmental base; the Soviet Union, with one-party rule; and the United States, with a two-party system. Of the three, the two that weathered both the Depression and the world war that followed were the American pluralistic democracy and the Russian totalitarian system.

The structure that broke under the strains was the democratic multipartite system of the Weimar Republic. As the economic crisis deepened between 1928 and 1933, the seven major political parties split the votes so that no party could gain a majority or even enough strength to govern. The stage was set for the spectacular rise of the totalitarian Nazi Fascist party (NSDAP), which started with less than 3 percent of the vote and grew to command almost 44 percent, with enough confidence to destroy the democratic process and set up a totalitarian government along the lines of that in the Soviet Union.

It is always important not to overgeneralize, even from such examples as these. Indeed, it is clear that other factors were operating besides the political structure in each case. The United States has a long history of flexible government institutions extending back to the colonial period. The Soviet Union has a long tradition of repressive control reaching back before the regime of Czar Peter in the seventeenth century. And Germany had a history of Prussian authoritarianism. The Weimar Republic was set up on the heels of Germany's defeat in World War I.

From all this information, cross-cultural evidence still suggests that the multipartite system of the Weimar Republic was the weakest. De Gré concludes that multipartite systems tend to fragment society into a multitude of small, competing groups with a low degree of social stability (1946:535). We have recently seen evidence of this instability in France, Italy, and Portugal.

BUREAUCRACY AND DEMOCRACY What other factors affect stability in democratic systems, the main concern of American culture? Early in this century, both Max Weber and Robert Michels noted that modern mass society cannot function without large *bureaucracies* in which governmental, economic, and other institutional organizations set up pyramids of order based on division of function and authority (Weber, 1947; Michels, 1949). Weber and Michels were concerned with the effect of these bureaucracies in either advancing or undermining democratic values in the society.

Both Weber and Michels saw that a large bureaucracy, while an integrative force, could also produce corporate, labor, and political party machines that could undermine the democratic goals of the society. Subsequent research has shown that it is possible for large organizations to respect the rights of individuals in the organization. For example, Seymour Lipset pointed out the high level of democracy in the skilled International Typographical Union (1956). At least as important as protection of individual rights in complex organizations is the existence of different interest groups that can check and counter one another's power in the following manner (de Gré, 1946:535):

The power of the state is limited by the power of organized public opinion and large special interest groups; the pressure exercised by business interests is counterbalanced by the forces of organized labor; both management and labor must take into account the interests of an integrated consumers' movement and other public agencies; no one religious group possesses a monopoly of spiritual values, and the various religious groups learn to accommodate themselves to one another; religious thought is denied absolute sovereignty over ideas by the presence of independent secular thought maintained by a free press, free universities, free literary research. In the sphere of production, a pluralistic society might allow for the operation of more than one form of economic organization.

The stability given to American democracy by organized interest groups is increased by what Joseph Gusfield called multiple sources of loyalty. Gusfield holds that Americans tend not to be absolutists, partly because they are not polarized into rigidly opposing groups (1962:29). For instance, the lower, middle, and upper socioeconomic classes all include Catholics, Jews, and Protestants.

Such mixing of loyalties based on religion, class, and special interests tends to advance the interests of individuals and to protect them from an all-powerful government. In totalitarian societies, such autonomous interest groups and loyalties are repressed.

All this does not mean that America has developed a democratic Utopia. There are many, particularly in racial minorities, who have met stiff opposition in their organized efforts to develop influential interest groups. Their opportunities to work within the system, and the problems they face, will be considered in Chapter 8 on collective conflict and intergroup relations.

SOCIAL CHANGE AND GOVERNMENT The American system of government has been confronted with rapid and enormous culture-wide changes. In this century, the society has moved from a predominantly rural to a mass urban one. The worldwide depression and military conflicts in this century have demonstrated that American interests are deeply affected by events in other societies.

Consequently, the government has taken on more and more tasks to stabilize and protect society. Disagreement exists over such programs as social security, minimum wage laws, and a large defense establishment — not as to whether we need them but about how much we should spend on them. Big government has grown to meet big needs.

THE ISSUE OF BIG GOVERNMENT Is there a danger for democracy in this move toward bigness in government? In 1956, C. Wright Mills foresaw an emerging *power elite:* "The top of modern American society is increasingly unified, and often seems willfully co-ordinated: at the top there has emerged an elite of power" (1956:324). Dwight Eisenhower warned the nation in his farewell address as president of a military–industrial complex operating to protect its own profitable interests even at the cost of the legitimate needs of society.[6] Yet, it appears that in American culture, the power of the state is checked by the public's watchfulness and the coalitions of special interest groups. This view is expressed as *power pluralism* (see Kornhauser in Bendix and Lipset, 1966:210–218), or manipulation of power by veto groups. Big government has characterized the federal system since the Depression of the 1930s. Such concentrated power bears constant monitoring. Opinions vary on whether federal, state, or local units are in the best position to stimulate economic development, provide good education for all, and meet other public needs. For example, the need for continued government support of national defense has seemed clear to most people since World War II. Seymour Lipset expressed a need for domestic programs to improve conditions and opportunities for a larger part of the population in his award-winning *Political Man* (1963:451):

There is considerable evidence to suggest that higher education, greater economic security, and higher standards of living strengthen the level of culture and democratic freedom.

The continuing problem for America and other modern democracies is how to secure these goals without using means that undermine them. The credibility of government remains an issue not just in election campaigns but in our day-to-day decision-making.

We are concerned about contradictions between what is said and what is done. Strong government with wide popular support must provide satisfactory solutions to the problem of credibility.

THE ECONOMY

UNIVERSALITY OF ECONOMIC INSTITUTIONS

As biological creatures, human beings must ensure survival. This task necessarily involves us in economic activity, to develop the goods and services necessary to sustain life. As the economist Paul Samuelson has observed, all societies must resolve three fundamental economic problems: *What* commodities will be produced and in what quantities? *How* will goods be produced? *For whom* are goods to be produced? (1973:17–18).

These basic questions, common to all societies, are solved quite differently by different economic systems. Samuelson describes some approaches (1973:17–18):

In a primitive civilization, custom may rule every facet of behavior. *What, How* and *For Whom* may be decided by reference to traditional ways of doing things. To members of another culture, the practices followed may seem bizarre and unreasonable; the members of the tribe or clan may themselves be so familiar with existing practices as to be surprised, and perhaps offended, if asked the reason for their behavior. Thus, the Kwakiutl Indians consider it desirable not to accumulate wealth but to give it away in the *potlatch* — a roisterous celebration. . . . In the bee colony, all such [economic] problems, even those involving an extraordinarily elaborate cooperative division of labor, are solved automatically by means of so-called "biological instincts" . . . . At the other extreme we can imagine an omnipotent, benevolent or malevolent dictator who by arbitrary decree and fiat decides What, How and For Whom. Or we might imagine economic organization by decree, but with decrees drawn up by democratic vote, or by delegated legislative authorities.

---

[6] This point is discussed in Chapter 12, Social Cohesion in Cold and Hot Wars.

One does not have to imagine these different systems: they exist. The most influential forms are considered below.

FUNCTIONS OF THE ECONOMY The basic function of any economic system is to ensure the physical survival and stability of the culture. For the American culture, as Samuelson points out (Samuelson, 1973:884):

...[O]bjective analysis of things as they are shows there remain many features of economic life which the concerned younger generation finds ethically troublesome: What matters it to them that monopoly be less prevalent in 1975 than in 1900 — if it still is too much prevalent, and if no great diminution has taken place since 1945? What to them that the poor are less numerous and less poor than they used to be — if still there persist stubborn inequalities of income since 1945? In their eyes, how can a system be deemed satisfactory which still countenances discrimination by race, sex, religion, and ethnic affiliation? True, our modern economic world is better in many ways than the past. But more is now expected of it.

Americans take their economy seriously in a variety of ways. Not only does the system provide the essentials of life and political stability, but also social status is related to income. Thorstein Veblen observed the emphasis in American society on *conspicuous consumption* (Veblen, 1912), keeping up with the Joneses, or more accurately, being able to show up the Joneses with a display of what you have bought. (How many other cultures produce new models of cars and fashions in clothing every year?) The even larger meaning of the economy in American culture is summarized by Robin Williams (1970:150):

American economic institutions often seem the most conspicuous feature of the social structure: America is said to be above all a "business civilization," impressive in its productivity.... The United States is the land of mass production; the Assembly Line is its symbol to the world ... the economic system has acquired such independence from other areas of life that it often gives the appearance of being self-generating and self-perpetuating.

ECONOMIC TROUBLESPOTS Some troublespots have appeared in the American economic system. There are dysfunctions in our emphasis on a rapidly expanding and efficient economy. Don Martindale notes that to keep the economy expanding, advertising manipulates consumers' tastes (1972:39–48). This is true even when the products are clearly harmful, like cigarettes and polluting vehicles. We become socialized to learned needs, the fulfillment of which stimulates the economy, providing jobs and profits. As we absorb cultural values, we learn to support the belief that capitalism and the entrepreneureal spirit are good.

Furthermore, some analysts feel that the mass production aspect of the economy is not entirely beneficial to the generally well-paid production-line workers. William Serrin views the life of America's auto workers as "dull, brutish, weary, stuporous." He observes that it is ironic that this is so, "for the automobile worker is the beneficiary of the best that America has to offer ... nothing less than the American Dream" [of success for anyone who tries hard enough]. (Serrin, 1971: 62–63. Copyright © 1971 by William Serrin. Reprinted from *The Company and the Union*, by William Serrin, by permission of Alfred A. Knopf):

The line, the goddamn line. Fifty-five cars an hour, 440 cars a shift ... two shifts a day, 4400 cars a week ... 44 assembly plants, 9 million cars a year ... lights, machinery, noise ... hundreds of hustling workers, arms moving, legs moving ... tightening bolts, fastening cables ... using big electric wrenches and drills, the hoses stretched out behind them ... and the colors, the brilliant goddamn colors ... aqua, grabber lime, pewter, pinto red, sassy grass green, rosewood, ascot blue, Nevada silver, cottonwood green, in-violet, curious yellow, burgundy fire, glacial blue,

Tor-Red, amber sherwood, formal black, sunflower, sandalwood, cranberry, Sno White, Bahama yellow, true blue, ralley red, yellow gold... The Workers, 700,000 of them across the country, 200,000 of them in the Detroit area... men and women, whites and blacks... big blacks with Afros and young dudes with processes, paunchy whites, paunchy blacks, rednecks, fathers, husbands, suburbanites... women, tight-skinned, almost never pretty, with hair teased in the fashion of ten years ago... 8 hours a day, not counting a half hour off for lunch... 46 minutes of relief time, when a fellow can sit down or use the toilet or have a smoke or get a Coke or a Mallo-Cup... workers sanding gray metal and rough spots on painted metal after the cars have come from the bake oven... taking windshields from a pile, slopping glue on and attaching a rubber sleeve... a worker attaching the windshield to a hydraulic lift with suction cups and swinging it onto the line... workers swinging the engine onto the line... workers swinging the rear axle in and laying the rear springs on the line... the body now automatically dropped over the rear axle, the springs, the drive shaft... tires inflated by machine and workers taking them off conveyors and putting them on the wheels... workers bolting the tires down... workers in the pits underneath the assembly line, like slit trenches, standing all day at Ford or GM, sitting at Chrysler... installing wires, fastening bolts, 8 hours a day, their arms over their heads... workers beating on latches with rubber mallets to make the hoods fit... 8 hours a day, 48 weeks a year, $9000 or so a year, $130 to $150 a week in take-home pay... THE LINE, THE FINEST PRODUCT OF AMERICAN INVENTIVENESS... 350 models to choose from... fascinating, absolutely fascinating, how the engines, tires, fenders, hoods are fed onto the line at the right time, a 429 CID V-8 or a 200 CID Six, the right-size tires, the right-color fenders and hood, the system run by teletype and computer... A WONDER OF THE WORLD...

For many there is a great problem in earning enough money to purchase consumer goods. (In Chapter 6 on poverty and in Chapter 8 on minority relations we present documentation of the great income spread by educational level, race, and sex.) With automation and cybernation (computerization), mass production has become so efficient that the demand for unskilled labor is declining. Since unskilled workers live in rural areas or predominantly black city ghettoes, where economic opportunities for adults and educational opportunities for young people are poor, their future does not look promising.

The economist John Kenneth Galbraith has noted that the advanced American economic structure has created *insular poverty* that locks people into certain poor areas (1969:284–288). It is useful to note that insular poverty creates other problems beyond economic deprivation. Many Americans identify with their work (see the discussion of the Protestant Ethic) and when they are unemployed, they have individual and family problems that are not economic.

STRUCTURAL FORMS OF THE ECONOMY   We again call upon Nobel prizewinning economist Paul Samuelson, this time to delineate the major characteristics of modern economic societies. Samuelson notes that industrial technology has three main features. The first is *capital*, consisting of machinery and other equipment, factories, stores, and stocks of finished and unfinished materials. The American economy is referred to as *capitalist* because this capital is primarily private property; its owners are called capitalists.[7] All modern economies have capital. When capital is owned by the government, the system is socialist or communist (the important differences between these two systems will be noted later in this section). The terms *socialism* and *communism* suggest that the property is publicly, that is socially or communally, owned. A second feature of modern economies is the high degree of *specialization* and *division of labor* necessary

---

[7] Recall Weber's theory on the relationship of Protestant values to capitalism, the acquisition of personal wealth.

to mass produce goods. A third feature is the extensive use of *money* as a means of exchange for goods and services (Samuelson, 1973:49–55).

Older economic systems are of minor and declining importance. The *barter* system, exchanging one product or service for another, common in nomadic and some agrarian societies, is cumbersome and has low economic yield. As the cultural anthropologist Margaret Mead has shown, societies using this system tend to abandon it when given an alternative (1955).

Another old system was *mercantilism,* in which a country depended on colonies as a source of wealth. The British, French, Spanish, and other European powers secured raw materials from their colonial holdings, developed products to sell back to the colonies, and encouraged exports but discouraged imports in their colonies in order to build up their own profits.

The mercantilist system was important in a negative way in the development of the American economic structure. Under this system, there was extensive royal control of the colonial economy (remember "No taxation without representation" and the Boston Tea Party?). The British economist Adam Smith reflected much colonial sentiment about a fair and healthy economic system in his classic *Wealth of Nations,* published the year of the Declaration of Independence, 1776. Smith unsuccessfully recommended free trade with the American colonies (Hockett, 1947:245) and attacked government regulations and other interference with free competition under the mercantilist system. He believed that a *laissez-faire* system (free competition) would enable people to get the goods and services they wanted at the least cost.

COMPETITION AND THE INDUSTRIAL REVOLUTION The establishment of an open competitive system in nineteenth-century America stimulated the Industrial Revolution. Such an expansion of American industry resulted that by the early twentieth century, the United States was the leading industrial society in the world. Large corporations in such basic industries as railroads, oil, and steel came to be dominated by a few individual men and corporations. One of the men was Andrew Carnegie, owner of the U.S. Steel Corporation, a major proponent of industrial capitalism. In 1889, Carnegie wrote in defense of a *laissez-faire* system without strong government controls (1889:654):

Under the law of competition, the employer of thousands is forced into the strictest economics, among which the rates paid to labor figure prominently, and often there is friction between the employer and the employed, between capital and labor, between rich and poor. . . . The price which society pays for the law of competition . . . is . . . great, but the advantages of this law are . . . greater . . . for it is to this law that we owe our wonderful material development, which brings improved conditions in its train.

This was a viewpoint which social scientists such as the British Herbert Spencer (1877) and the American William Graham Sumner (1906) called *Social Darwinism.* Social Darwinism held that the *laissez-faire* law of competition ensured the survival of the fittest in economic matters as Charles Darwin held that among living species, the fittest survive in the struggle for existence.

PRESSURES TO MODIFY THE "LAW OF COMPETITION" Problems with the economic law of competition and its practice led to a modification of the free enterprise system as it now operates. One problem was the rise of *monopolies,* in which some corporations hold exclusive control of commodities and services in their industries. Monopolies prevent open and free competition. A congressional committee, investigating the *money trusts* of the largest corporations such as Standard Oil and United States Steel, found that these corporations so dominated their industries that they (Carman and Syrett, 1952:137–138):

... strike at the very vitals of potential competition in every industry that is under their protection, a condition which if permitted to continue, will render impossible all attempts to restore normal competitive conditions in the industrial world.

One result was the passage of the Clayton Anti-Trust Act of 1914 and a continued monitoring of corporations by government to prevent unfair competition. Recently there have been legal conflicts between large conglomerates such as ITT and others and the legal forces of both government and consumer organizations.

Another problem with the *laissez-faire* system was the condition of industrial labor. As workers left the farms, where incomes were declining, and masses of immigrants came to seek jobs in the factories, they found few laws or organizations to protect them. Little or no help was available to workers injured on the job, wages were kept low, and there were no restrictions on hours worked or the employment of women and children. For an average week of more than six days, the yearly earnings of city factory workers in 1904 were $566 for men, $307 for women, and $186 for children (Hourwich, 1912:298).

THE CURRENT ECONOMIC MIX The final result was the formation of labor unions as part of the American economic structure. By 1935, the National Labor Relations Act was passed, assuring labor unions such as the American Federation of Labor the right to organize and bargain collectively (Carman and Syrett, 1952:518). Other modifications of the free enterprise system included social security payments for the elderly and welfare for the poor and indigent. What we now have is a mixed economy, meaning that some elements of many economic systems appear in our own.

The most prominent other systems in our time are *socialism*, which exists in democratic political societies such as Great Britain and Sweden and *communism*, which exists in totalitarian societies such as the Soviet Union and the People's Republic of China. Socialism and communism have three features in common: (1) government ownership of productive resources, (2) government planning for economic development, and (3) government redistribution of income. They differ from each other in the means by which they achieve these goals. In socialist societies, the means are democratic and can be reversed by the will of the people. In communist societies, the means are achieved by dictatorial fiat without any institutionalized means for people to express opposition.

The American economic system has some features of a socialist economy: the graduated income tax, by which the wealthy are required to pay taxes on a higher proportion of income than are others; the social security system; and such government-sponsored projects as the Tennessee Valley Authority (TVA), which develops electric power. Since most economic enterprises remain in private hands, the economy, while mixed, is still based in capitalism. For a defense of this system see the selection on The Politics of Economics, the Virtues of Profit.

THE POLITICS OF ECONOMICS, THE VIRTUES OF PROFITS

From: Reprinted by permission from TIME, The Weekly Newsmagazine; Copyright Time Inc. 1975.

The following material contrasts socialist and free-enterprise systems, giving the advantages and disadvantages of each. The author concludes that although the capitalist system may be bad, the alternative is worse.

One of the capitalist market system's enduring strengths is precisely its reliance on the profit motive which, like it or not, is a powerful human drive. To many idealists the primacy of the profit motive has long seemed to be a sanctification of selfishness that produces a brutalizing, beggar-thy-neighbor society. Victorian Moralist John Ruskin denounced "the deliberate blasphemy of Adam Smith: Thou shalt hate the Lord thy God, damn His laws, and covet thy neighbor's goods."

But capitalism has the overwhelmingly powerful defense of simple realism. There *is* just enough of a "Scotchman" in most people to make them work harder for their own advancement than for the good of their fellows — a fact that regularly embarrasses socialist regimes. The Soviet Union permits collective farmers to cultivate small private plots in their spare time and sell the produce for their own profit. Those plots account for a mere 4% of the land under cultivation in the U.S.S.R. — yet, by value, they produce a fourth of the country's food.

Profits and other incentives are indispensable to any economic progress. A product or service that is sold for exactly the cost of producing it yields no margin to raise wages, buy new machinery or pursue research leading to new products. Only profits can finance that — whether in a capitalist or a socialist society.

The argument between capitalism and authoritarian economic systems comes down to two questions: Which system can make the most efficient use of manpower, materials and money to create the greatest opportunities for free choice, personal development and material well-being for the greatest number of people? And which system is more just and satisfying in human terms?

An authoritarian economy appeals to many human instincts. It offers stability and security at the expense of freedom and a greater degree of economic (though not political) equality than capitalism. It can provide full employment by creating a surfeit of make-work, low-productivity (and thus low-paying) jobs. It keeps prices stable by fixing them almost invariably at high levels in terms of real income. Yet even the meanness of living standards in such a system may have a certain attraction for millions of people outside those countries who are repelled or surfeited by commercial values. Distrust of money lies deep in the West's history, from St. Francis of Assisi and the Anabaptists to the modern romantics. Authoritarian economies are as materialistic as capitalism, if not more so, but they are often perceived differently. And the ability of the command economy to centralize power has an irresistible appeal for otherwise shaky leaders of developing nations. As Moynihan observes, many of the developing nations have an "interest in deprecating the economic achievements of capitalism, since none of their own managed economies are doing well."

On the historical record, capitalism clearly is more enriching — in every major way. Capitalism, says Eckstein, "is the only engine that has been developed so far that encourages people to be highly innovative, to develop new products and processes." Profit-seeking capitalists have developed all the vital machines of "post-industrial" society. In contrast, centrally managed economies have rarely done well at developing civilian high-technology industry — largely because inventors lack incentive. In socialist economies the same lack has led to appalling shoddiness in many of the services that provide life's amenities.

Capitalists also have produced a far greater quantity and variety of consumer goods and services than socialist central planners. The reason: for all its weaknesses, the market functions as a superbly adaptive super-computer that continuously monitors consumer tastes. Says Walter Heller, "The private market makes trillions of decisions without any central regulation. It is a fantastic cybernetic device that processes huge amounts of information in the form of the consumer voting with his dollars, the retailer telegraphing back to the wholesaler, the wholesaler to the producer."

Communist nations have paid the market the ultimate compliment by trying to introduce elements of market pricing into their own economies, so far with meager success. The trademarks of Communist economies remain indelible: low productivity, shortages of goods, lengthy queues in stores, years-long waits for apartments. In order to spur initiative, most Communist countries also have huge and growing differences in real income (and perquisites) between commissar and collective farmer. Nikita Khrushchev once replied to a charge that the Soviet Union was going capitalist:

"Call it what you will, incentives are the only way to make people work harder."

More important, capitalism's superior productivity is not solely a matter of electric toothbrushes and throwaway soft-drink bottles; the system also does better at filling basic human needs like food. Farmers in the capitalist U.S., Canada and Australia grow enough not only to feed their own peoples but also to export huge surpluses. In contrast, the Soviet Union — although 30% of its workers labor on its vast farmlands — has to import food. So does India, which permits private farming but insists out of socialist principle that the produce be sold at unrealistically low prices.

The freedom of capitalist society at its best must be prized above all. True, some dictatorships are capitalist because most of the economy is privately owned. Still, the major capitalist nations all have popularly elected governments that guard the right of free speech and assembly. Capitalism demands, by definition, that the individual be free within broad limits to spend and invest his money any way he pleases, to own private property and to enter any business or profession that attracts him. The state that grants those significant freedoms demonstrates a reluctance to interfere in the citizen's daily life.

In sharp contrast, the managed economies exist mostly in one-party states or under completely totalitarian regimes. Any government that tries to dictate almost every decision on production, prices and wages assumes an arbitrary power that would be impossible to reconcile with political freedom. In most managed economies, for example, a strike by workers is a crime against the state; it can hardly be prohibited without suppressing the right to advocate such a strike.

In sum, there is no alternative to capitalism that credibly promises both wealth and liberty. Despite its transitory woes and weaknesses, capitalism in the foreseeable future will not only survive but also stands to prosper and spread. Perhaps the most balanced judgment of Adam Smith's wondrous system is Winston Churchill's famous conclusion about democracy. It is the worst system — except for all those other systems that have been tried and failed.

SOCIAL CHANGE AND THE ECONOMY Whether it functions well, as it does for most, or poorly, as for some, the American economic structure is one of the most rapidly changing features of the society. With the significant exception of our pockets of poverty, we are, in Galbraith's words, an affluent society. It is in part this very success that has generated many of the changes in the system.

In this age of the forty-hour work week (thirty-five for some), the economy has afforded the standard of living and the time for most people to engage in leisure activities, which brings new pressures to bear on the economy. For the most part, the economy has simply expanded into such new leisure-time activities as travel and sports. Other pressures push for more significant change. The pressures to clean up air and water pollution stemming from industrial production and products continue, pitting those who believe we can sacrifice some productivity to quality of life and still have what we need against others who believe that the tradeoff will harm us. Still others believe that technological solutions will enable us to have it all.

THE INFLUENCE OF AFFLUENCE American affluence has generated leisure time and resources to allow changes in life styles that in turn affect the economy. Nathan Glazer summarized these changes before the influential American Association of Advertising Agencies. Glazer, a contributing author of *The Lonely Crowd*, a study of increasing conformity in America in the 1940s and 1950s (Reisman, 1950), noted that there are not likely to be national mass markets as in the past. The reason, Glazer stated, is that the very success of the national mass economy has helped create the conditions for more individual choice of life patterns and created a greater variety of life styles. Glazer notes that the culture is seeing less uniformity of dress and thinking than heretofore (1972).

Given a stable economy and continuing education, the findings of Glazer, Samuelson, Galbraith, and others point to an ongoing diversification of the economic structure. This reflects changes stimulated by the economy itself and changes in the economy caused by differing individual and group views. While some major democratic values are advanced in the process, such diversity means that "We will have some hard work to do to maintain the minimal common values and common effort that are needed in a modern complex society" (Glazer, 1972:8).

SUMMARY

We have examined the five basic institutions of the society: the family, religion, education, government, and the economy.

Any unit of social organization may produce *functional* or rewarding, and *dysfunctional* or punishing consequences for society. As the largest functional units of social organization, the major institutions produce the most consequences.

These institutions are social structures in which there are relatively stable patterned interrelationships among the aspects of the system. As such, the operation of each institution affects and is affected by the operation of others.

In addition to the five institutions shown by the Human Relations Area File, some social scientists include as basic institutions the military, organized sports and games, and the cultural institutions of science and literature.

We evaluated each of the five universal institutions in terms of four characteristics: universality, functions, structural form, and social changes affecting the institution.

The major characteristics of the *family** as an institution are that it has always been sanctioned by *marriage**, a formal and durable sexual union of one or more men with one or more women within a set of designated rights and duties. The family farm or family business once gave families an important economic function. There is now greater stress on the family to be the main source of primary, close interpersonal relations in a modern *Gesellschaft** society. Certain traditional functions remain, including reproduction, protection and care of children, and the placing of children in the social structure.

The normative American family structure is *monogamous** — there is one husband and one wife — and *nuclear**, in that the family unit consists of husband, wife, and their children. Other structural forms of the family are evident. In the past, the normative American structural form included *extended kin* living together or close by. Some societies have some form of *polygamy** (three or more spouses). The combination of a high divorce rate and experimental family forms suggests that the American family structure is evolving into one in which the traditional monogamous pattern may be joined by sanctioned multiple family forms.

Religion* now has less impact than in the past, though even in modern societies avowedly anti- or nonreligious institutional forms persist in faith-engendering ritualistic practices that are found in all societies. Religion performs a number of major functions for social cohesion, one being to bring solace in periods of crisis, and another to legitimate cultural values and norms of behavior. The functional consequences of religion affect other aspects of social life, including economic behavior, as Max Weber noted in his analysis of Protestantism. The two major types of religious bodies in American society are *sects** and *denominations**; smaller *cults** are less influential, and the American religious structure does not include *ecclesiastic** religious bodies, which have significant political power. While existing in a predominantly secular society, the religious institution continues to hold the respect and attention of most Americans and to serve functional needs in times of social or personal crisis.

Education is a universal institution because it is the only means of socializing children into the general culture even when no formal school system exists. The complex nature of modern society has extended education to include the major *idealistic* and *pragmatic* functions of inducting young people into the value system of the culture and developing skills practical and useful to the individual and the society. To accomplish their functional tasks, American schools are organized in a formal bureaucratic pattern which includes (mostly public) elementary and secondary schools and colleges. The financing of American education is shifting from the reliance on local school district support to tax support from state and federal sources. Recent in-depth analyses of American education suggest that it is not operating at maximum effectiveness and that it will not do so without significant changes.

In all societies, some ultimate governing authority enforces norms of behavior considered essential to the culture. The power vested in government to punish individuals in the society serves *to maintain boundaries* between acceptable and unacceptable behavior. The boundary-maintaining function of government becomes complex when, as in America, different cultural groups hold differing values about proper and improper behavior. Three major types of *legitimating** government authority are *traditional authority**, *charismatic authority**, and *rational–legal authority**. In modern societies, two prominent types of government are the *democratic** and the *totalitarian** systems. The increasingly complex nature of modern society and the growing interdependence of nations have expanded the role of government in society.

All societies must somehow meet the three fundamental problems of *what* will be produced, *how* goods will be produced, and *for whom* they are to be produced. The most basic economic function is to ensure the physical survival of a society. The seriousness with which Americans take their economy is indicated by the close association between social class and income. The problem of satisfactory distribution of wealth is a continuing one in American as in other societies. The structure of modern industrial economy rests upon *capital,* a high degree of *specialization** and the extensive use of *money* as a medium of exchange. Three prototypes of economic systems are the *laissez-faire** (free enterprise) system of private competitive ownership, the *socialist** system of government ownership and control of economic activity, and the *mixed** economy. The American economy has evolved into a mixed form, but the emphasis is still on free enterprise. The continuing specialization of the American economy is creating changes in other institutions, including the educational system which is expanding at the secondary and college levels in response to changing requirements of the economic system. Should the American economy continue to generate an increasingly affluent society, the effects on the American *work ethic** of a new leisure orientation and changes in general life styles will be considerable.

QUESTIONS FOR DISCUSSION

1. Beyond examples noted in the chapter, how may the operation of an institution produce both functional and dysfunctional consequences for society? Select any specific institution for your discussion. How might its function be affected by another institution?

2. How does the nature of work in American society influence family life?

3. How do you account for the increase in sectarian and cult activity in the United States? How might other institutional changes affect support for minority religions?

4. It has been suggested that we are moving toward multiple marriage in our society. What changes do you see as likely to emerge and why? How might these changes affect divorce rates?

5. To meet the educational needs of more people, young and old, what experiments in new educational forms would you suggest and support?

6. It has been noted that government sets the limits of acceptable behavior. How reasonable or unreasonable do current limits appear to be? Give specific examples.

7. For one particular economic enterprise, give several examples of specialization and the division of labor. Is this situation likely to change in the near future? Why or why not?

8. Review the following terms and concepts:

institutions

(dys)functional consequences

marriage

denominations, sects, and cults

ecclesia

Human Relations Area Files

nuclear family, extended family

kibbutz

Protestant ethic

functional incompetence

charisma

multi-partite

pragmatist school

three fundamental economic problems

conspicuous consumption

REFERENCES

Adams, Robert Lynn and Robert John Fox
  1973 "Mainlining Jesus: the new trip." Judson Landis (ed.), Current Perspectives on Social Problems. Belmont, California: Wadsworth: 300–312.

  1966 Americans at Mid-Decade, Series P. 23, No. 16. Washington, D.C.: Government Printing Office.

Aristotle
  1941 The Basic Works of Aristotle. B. Jowett (trans.). New York: Macmillan.

Ball, Samuel and Gerry Ann Bogatz
  1970 "A summary of the major findings in 'the first year of Sesame Street: an evaluation.'" Princeton, N.J.: Educational Testing Service (October).

  1971 "A summary of the major findings in 'the second year of Sesame Street: an evaluation.'" Princeton, N.J.: Educational Testing Service (November).

Benedict, Ruth (see Maslow)
  1970 "Synergy: some notes of Ruth Benedict" (post-mortem selection by A. Maslow and J. Honigman). American Anthropologist 72: 320–333.

Bierstedt, Robert
  1963 The Social Order. New York: McGraw-Hill.

Branscombe, Art
  1975 "Functional incompetence in the United States." Denver *Post* (November 16): 20.

Bureau of the Census
  1957 Historical Statistics of the United States, Colonial Times to 1957. Washington, D.C.: Government Printing Office.

Caldwell, Robert
  1965 Criminology. New York: The Ronald Press.

Carman, Harry and Harold Syrett
  1952 A History of the American People, II. New York: Knopf.

Carnegie, Andrew
  1889 "The gospel of wealth." North American Review CXVII: 653–657.

Coleman, James et al.
  1966 Equality of Educational Opportunity. Washington, D.C.: Government Printing Office.

Constantine, Larry and Joan Constantine
  1973 Group Marriage. New York: Macmillan.

Cuber, John and Peggy Harroff
  1973 "The more total view: relationships among men and women of the upper middle class." D. Schultz and R. Wilson (eds.), Readings on the Changing Family. Englewood Cliffs, N.J.: Prentice-Hall: 103–110.

  1972 Digest of Educational Statistics, 1971. Washington, D.C.: Government Printing Office.

de Gré, Gerard
  1946 "Freedom and social structure." American Sociological Review 11: 529–536.

Demerath, N. J.
  1965 Social Class in American Protestantism. Chicago: Rand McNally.

Dewey, John
  1916 Democracy and Education. New York: Macmillan.

Durkheim, Emile
  1947 The Elementary Forms of Religious Life. S. Fox (trans.). New York: The Free Press of Glencoe.

  1961 Moral Education. E. Wilson and H. Schnurer (trans.). New York: The Free Press of Glencoe.

Edwards, Newton and Herman Richey
  1963 The Schools in the American Social Order. Boston: Houghton Mifflin.

Farber, Bernard
  1973 Family and Kinship in Modern Society. Glenview, Ill.: Scott-Foresman.

Fox, Robin
  1967 Kinship and Marriage. Harmondworth, England: Penguin.

Fullerton, Gail Putney
  1972 Survival in Marriage: Introduction to Family Interaction, Conflicts, and Alternatives. New York: Holt, Rinehart and Winston.

Galbraith, John
  1969 The Affluent Society. Boston: Houghton Mifflin.

Glazer, Nathan
  1972 "Is there an American character? — a perspective for the '70's." Paper delivered at the 1972 Annual Meeting of the American Association of Advertising Agencies, Boca Raton, Florida (March 17): 8 pp.

Gordon, Leonard
  1971 "Attempts to bridge the racial gap: the religious establishment." L. Gordon (ed.), A City in Racial Crisis. Dubuque, Iowa: Wm. C. Brown: 18–28.
  1973 "Religious institutional spokesmen as catalytic social agents in attempts to alleviate urban racial tensions." Research and Special Programs. Tempe, Arizona: Arizona State University Press.

Gouldner, Alvin and Richard Peterson
- 1962 Notes on Technology and the Moral Order. Indianapolis, Indiana: Bobbs-Merrill.

Gross, Neal
- 1958 Who Runs Our Schools? New York: John Wiley and Sons.

Gusfield, Joseph
- 1962 "Mass society and extremist politics." American Sociological Review 27: 19-30.

Gussow, Joan Dye
- 1970 "Bodies, brains and poverty: poor children and the schools." IRCD Bulletin 6: 3-12.

Hockett, Homer
- 1947 Political and Social Growth of the American People, 1492-1865. New York: Macmillan.

Homans, George
- 1962 Sentiments and Activities. New York: The Free Press of Glencoe.

Hoult, Thomas Ford
- 1958 The Sociology of Religion. New York: The Dryden Press.
- 1969 Dictionary of Sociology. Totawa, N.J.: Littlefield, Adams.

Hourwich, Isaac
- 1912 Immigration and Labor. New York: G. P. Putnam's Sons.

Hunt, Morton
- 1974 Sexual Behavior in the 1970's. Chicago: Playboy Press.

Illich, Ivan
- 1971 Learning Webs in Deschooling Society. New York: Harper and Row.

Kanter, Rosabeth Moss
- 1972 Commitment and Community: Communes and Utopias in Sociological Perspective. Cambridge, Mass.: Harvard University Press.

Katz, Michael B.
- 1975 Class, Bureaucracy, and Schools: The Illusion of Educational Change in America. New York: Praeger.

Katz, Judith Milstein
- 1976 "How do you love me? let me count the ways (the phenomenology of being loved)." Sociological Inquiry 46: 17-22.

Kephart, William
- 1972 The Family, Society and the Individual. Boston: Houghton Mifflin.

Kornhauser, William
- 1966 "'Power Elite' or 'Veto Groups.'" R. Bendix and S. M. Lipset (eds.), Class, Status, and Power. New York: The Free Press: 210-218.

Lenski, Gerhard
- 1963 The Religious Factor. Garden City, N.Y.: Anchor.

Lipset, Seymour
- 1956 Union Democracy. Glencoe, Ill.: The Free Press.
- 1963 Political Man: The Social Bases of Politics. New York: Doubleday.

Mace, David R.
- 1962 "Some reflections on the American family." Marriage and Family Living 22: 258-262.

Martindale, Don
- 1972 American Society. New York: Robert E. Kriegler.

Maslow, Abraham and John J. Honigman
- 1970 "Synergy: some notes on Ruth Benedict." American Anthropologist 72: 320-323.

Mayer, Albert and Harry Sharp
- 1962 "Religious preference and worldly success." American Sociological Review 27: 218-227.

McCary, James
1973   Human Sexuality. New York: Van Nostrand Reinhold.

Mead, Margaret
1955   Cultural Patterns and Technical Change. New York: Mentor Books.

Merton, Robert
1967   On Theoretical Sociology. New York: The Free Press.

Michels, Robert
1949   Political Parties. Glencoe, Ill.: The Free Press.

Mills, C. Wright
1956   The Power Elite. New York: Oxford University Press.

Moore, Wilbert and Melvin Tumin
1949   "Some social functions of ignorance." American Sociological Review 14: 787–795.

Murdock, George
1949   Social Structure. New York: Macmillan.
1950   "Feasibility and implementation of comparative community research." American Sociological Review 15: 713–720.

Ogburn, William
1950   Social Change. New York: Viking.

O'Neill, Nena and George O'Neill
1972   Open Marriage: A New Life Style for Couples. New York: Evans.

Parsons, Talcott
1951   The Social System. Glencoe, Ill.: The Free Press.
1965   "The normal American family." S. Farber, P. Mustacchi, and R. Wilson (eds.), Man and Civilization: The Family's Search for Survival. New York: McGraw-Hill: 31–50.

Pope, Liston
1942   Millhands and Preachers. New Haven: Yale University Press.

Reisman, David, et al.
1950   The Lonely Crowd. New Haven: Yale University Press.

Reston, James
1963   "Nobody can assassinate a government." The New York Times (November 26): 12.

Samuel, Edwin
1969   The Structure of Society in Israel. New York: Random House.

Samuelson, Paul
1973   Economics. New York: McGraw-Hill.

Schur, Edwin
1965   Crimes Without Victims. Englewood Cliffs, N.J.: Prentice-Hall.

Serrin, William
1971   "The assembly line." The Atlantic Monthly (October): 62–63.

Sexton, Patricia
1967   The American School. Englewood Cliffs, N.J.: Prentice-Hall.

Silberman, Charles
1970   Crisis in the Classroom: The Remaking of American Education. New York: Random House.

1954   Southern School News, 1: 15.

Spencer, Herbert
1877   Principles of Sociology. New York: Appleton-Century-Crofts.

1952   "Stalinist scripture." Christian Century 69: 1215.

Sumner, William Graham
1906   Folkways. Boston: Ginn.

Terkel, Studs
1974   Working. New York: Pantheon.

Troeltsch, Ernst
    1931   The Social Teaching of the Christian Churches, 2 vols. O. Wyon (trans.). New York: Macmillan.

Vander Zanden, James
    1970   Sociology. New York: The Ronald Press.

Veblen, Thorstein
    1912   The Theory of the Leisure Class. New York: Macmillan.

Weber, Max
    1930   The Protestant Ethic and the Rise of Capitalism. New York: Charles Scribner's Sons.
    1947   The Theory of Social and Economic Organization. A. Henderson and T. Parsons (trans.). New York: Oxford University Press.

Williams, E. I. F.
    1937   Horace Mann, Educational Statesman. New York: Macmillan.

Williams, Robin
    1970   American Society. New York: Knopf.

Wright, Carol
    1889   A Report on Marriage and Divorce in the United States. Washington, D.C.: Government Printing Office.

Winch, Robert F.
    1971   The Modern Family. New York: Holt, Rinehart, and Winston.

Yinger, Milton
    1957   Religion, Society and the Individual. New York: Macmillan.

Chapter 4

METHODS OF INQUIRY: THE EMPHASIS ON ACCURACY

Most institutions demand unqualified faith; but the institution of science makes scepticism a virtue.

Robert Merton

THE NEED FOR ACCURACY

We have seen that sociology is the study of human interaction in a variety of social settings. Now we turn to the ways in which information on human interaction is collected and verified. The development and substantiation of reliable information about what Herbert Blumer (1972) calls *social situations* constitutes the science of sociology. Early sociologists, such as Auguste Comte and Lester Ward, stressed *social statics,* or the objective study of social systems as they exist at any given time, and *social dynamics,* or the objective study of social change.

THE IMPORTANCE OF EMPIRICISM Whether in the study of social continuity or of social change, *empiricism*,* or the use of various objective methods of observation, has been central. Comte held in his positivist philosophy that stable, democratic society was advancing through a rational historical process, but he also held that objective empirical research should constantly question and test this and all other propositions about society. This questioning and testing of ideas is as appropriate for particular aspects of the society as it is for Comtean propositions about the whole of the social system.

If people believe that Republicans are more business-oriented than Democrats, that women are as career-oriented as men, or that blacks identify with the fate of newly independent African nations, then the task of the empirical sociologist is to question each of these propositions and determine the extent to which it is true. Almost the only absolute in science is absolutely never to accept any proposition as final. Sociologists, like all scientists, must ask themselves the question: What objective evidence, if any, is there to confirm a proposition or series of propositions?

SOCIOLOGY AND OTHER RESEARCH DISCIPLINES Literature, philosophy, and theology all deal with human interaction. As disciplines, their emphasis is generally on ideas about what *ought to be*, based on various aesthetic, ethical, philosophical, political, religious, or other perspectives that do not derive from facts. In contrast, as a scientific discipline, sociology emphasizes in its research process what *is* without labeling it as good, bad, or any other value-laden quality. This does not mean that sociologists do not have values, nor does it mean that values play no part in sociological research. Indeed, sociologists may be led into research fields such as the nature of poverty, racial conflict, or community responses to natural disasters because of their values. The motive for engaging in such research may well be a desire to see an end to poverty or interracial conflict, or a reduction of catastrophic injury in natural disasters. Regardless of a researcher's motives, the social phenomenon he or she is studying must be one that can be verified.

In its empiricism and objectivity, sociology is akin to economics, political science, and psychology, all of which use comparable methods of research. Like sociology, these disciplines have often been called *policy sciences,* in that policymakers often look to them before developing and pursuing economic, political, or other policies. As with these related disciplines, in sociology, scientifically verified social knowledge is a prerequisite for effective guides to action.

The need to control one's personal values in research is perhaps most clearly recognized in the physical sciences. Einstein's formula ($E=mc^2$) was recognized as a basic insight into physical phenomena and ultimately brought nuclear energy to democratic America, Fascist Germany, and communist Russia in spite of their widely differing value systems.

This principle operates similarly in the social sciences. As a Democrat and a liberal Jew, one may be appalled by the fact that about one-third of the Jewish vote in 1972 went to the conservative Republican Richard Nixon. As a conservative Republican and a Protestant, one may be delighted that Mr. Nixon increased his vote among Jews threefold between 1960 and 1972. In either case the *fact* of the vote can be independently verified and agreed upon. On a more abstract level, an economic capitalist may be concerned about inflation or recession in America because of the strain such problems place on the economic system. A socialist may welcome such developments as proof of the inadequacy of an economic system. Differing perspectives may lead to different prescriptions for the social system. Nevertheless, both the capitalist and the socialist can agree on the *reality* of inflation and recession when they occur and can then frame more realistic policies for pursuing their goals. Of course, interest groups may disagree about what constitutes a recession or period of inflation, although such groups may accept certain facts. For example, a 10 percent national unemployment rate may be more than adequate for a labor union to declare that a recession is in progress. It may not be high enough for members of an incumbent political party who fear that a recession would reduce their chances for re-election.

VERIFYING ASSERTIONS ABOUT SOCIAL BEHAVIOR Verifying facts about any assertion regarding social behavior is no simple task. It is important that students be familiar with at least some of the basic procedures used to gather social information. In their widely used text on research methods in social relations, Claire Selltiz and her associates offer this useful perspective (1959: 6):

Even if one does not expect to make specific use of research findings in his job, in our scientific age all of us are in many ways "consumers" of research results. To use them intelligently, we need to be able to judge the adequacy of the methods by which they have been obtained. As a student, for example, you will find that many of the "facts" presented in your courses rest on the results of research. But you may discover that the "facts" reported by one study are quite different from those produced by another study on the same point. One investigator, for example, may report that children who are weaned early grow up to be more independent and better adjusted than those who are nursed for a longer time; another investigator turns up with just the opposite finding. Or several studies may conclude that when Negroes and whites live near each other, each group is likely to become more favorably inclined toward the other; but other studies may conclude that interracial hostility is likely to be especially intense in neighborhoods where Negroes and whites live in close proximity.

Recently the RAND Corporation startled and outraged groups that provide help for alcoholics by suggesting that it is possible for some former alcoholics to drink socially in moderation (RAND Corporation, 1976). The long history of Alcoholics Anonymous in treating cases has led that group to reject any technique for rehabilitation other than total abstinence from drinking. Who is right? In order to judge the adequacy of any given research and to help explain such varied findings as these, you should ask: How were the facts gathered? To what extent have prior opinions affected the reporting process? What kinds of documentation techniques were employed? Could different conditions in two or more studies explain the difference in the findings? This chapter presents some of the criteria we use to judge research.

DISTINGUISHING FACT FROM OPINION

Will Rogers once said, "All I know is what I read in the newspapers." Like him, most of us get much of our information about what is happening in society from the newspapers or other mass media. Rogers was well known for taking what he read with a grain of salt. For one thing, reporters cannot always check facts in the short time available before news deadlines. For another, a conservative, liberal, or other editorial bias may affect how news is reported.

DETECTING BIASED REPORTING A history instructor at the University of Michigan once cautioned his students about citing news media in research papers. He advised using a source such as the New York *Times*, which prints in full and without comment such documents as Supreme Court decisions and presidential addresses and reports daily events without letting the bias of the publishers affect the reporting. He also advised steering clear of newspapers that distort news stories along the lines of their editorial bias.

An example of editorialized news reporting that distorted essential facts was analyzed by Milton Mayer in 1949. An article on the front page of the November 14, 1948, Chicago *Tribune* purported to be a straight news report about a commission on freedom of the press. Members of the commission included Henry R. Luce, publisher of the rival *Time* magazine, University of Chicago Chancellor Robert Hutchins (more recently head of the Center for the Study of Democratic Institutions), and advertising executive William Benton, a former member of

Franklin D. Roosevelt's administration. The *Tribune* had attacked these men editorially on a number of occasions. To illustrate the distorting influence of these editorial views, Mayer reprinted the story as it had appeared but added corrective footnotes. The headline, subheadline, opening paragraph, and Mayer's footnoted and research-based additions are shown in the following manner (Reprinted by permission of Harold Ober Associates Incorporated. Copyright © 1949 by Harper's magazine.):

Headline: NAME ANGELS OF MOVE TO CURB PRESS
Sub-headline: Foundation Aids Hutchins Group[1]
Article's first paragraph:

Multimillion dollar, tax exempt foundations[2] which have given cash grants to Communists or to the publication of communist propaganda[3] are also financing attempts to tamper with freedom of the press[4] in the United States.

---

[1] No foundation in any way contributed to the support, financial or other, of the Commission on Freedom of the Press. The report of the Commission (*A Free and Responsible Press*, Chicago: University of Chicago Press, 1947) states that "the inquiry was financed by grants of $200,000 from Time, Inc., and $15,000 from Encyclopedia Britannica, Inc." These business institutions, like the Tribune Company, are incorporated for profit and operated for profit. They are not foundations. (The financial supporters of the Commission were named by Chairman Robert M. Hutchins in a press release accompanying publication of the report on March 27, 1947.)

[2] See above.

[3] No attempt is made to support this statement in the body of the article.

[4] If "freedom of the press" is defined as unlimited it is already "tampered with" by laws of libel, misbranding, obscenity, sedition, and treason. A cursory examination of the report would reveal repeated denunciations of government ownership, control, or regulation of the press as steps which "might cure the ills of freedom of the press, but only at the risk of killing the freedom in the process" (p. 2). The Commission would even protect the right of newspapers, if they cared to exercise it, to be liars, venalists, and scoundrels: "Many a lying, venal, and scoundrelly public expression must continue to find shelter under a 'freedom of the press' built for widely different purposes, for to impair the legal right even when the moral right is gone may easily be a cure worse than the disease."

There is more, but the point is clear. If you read only the headlines and opening paragraph of the *Tribune* article, what conclusion would you be likely to draw about the commission? After reading the footnotes, what would you think? You may ask to know still more before reaching a conclusion. Yet if we wanted to know whether the commission favored or opposed freedom of the press, as the documentation in the footnotes shows, we would be unlikely to get an accurate picture from the *Tribune* story. As is often the case, this article calls for some analysis to determine the facts.

Occasionally, the reporting of news yields to pressures other than the opinions of those who publish it; for example, deadlines. After the 1976 presidential primary election in Wisconsin, a newspaper reported a close victory for Representative Morris K. Udall; Udall made a victory speech, only to be embarrassed by late returns that showed Jimmy Carter to be the winner.

In our mass society we will continue to rely for much of our information on reports in the mass media. We must be as sure as possible that the radio or television station from which we get the news, the newspaper we read, or even this text present information that is collected properly and is likely to be accurate. Sometimes there is internal evidence of unreliable reporting; for example, Mayer pointed out that the *Tribune* article's opening assertion about grants to communists was never supported in the body of the piece. Sometimes it is necessary to check other sources, as Mayer did in citing from the commission's own published report. Even checking other sources may not be sufficient at all times. In the case of Udall's embarrassing loss to Carter, two television networks had projected Udall as the winner on the basis of sample returns.

CHECKING EYEWITNESS ACCOUNTS What happens when the news media, texts, and other sources of information do report accurately what people say? Does that mean that we know the facts? Not necessarily. In addition to self-evident distortions or contradictions in eyewitness accounts of an event, there remains the problem of verification. The difference between the objective facts of a situation and reports from those on the scene is often great. Samuel Clemens, an experienced newspaper reporter better known as Mark Twain, showed us the difficulty of sorting out truth from evidence, even in court (1951: 110–114, viz. 1907):

> I reported this trial simply for my own amusement ... but I have seen the facts in the case so distorted and misrepresented in the daily papers that I feel it my duty to come forward and do what I can to set the plaintiff and defendant right before the public. This can best be done by submitting the plain, unembellished statements of the witnesses as given under oath before his honor Judge Sheperd, in the San Francisco Police Court....
>
> The case of Smith Vs. Jones being called, each of the parties gave the court a particular circumstantial account of how the whole thing occurred, and then sat down.
>
> The two narratives differed from each other. In reality, I was half persuaded that these men were talking about two separate and distinct affairs altogether, inasmuch as no single circumstance mentioned by one was even remotely hinted at by the other.

In the continuation of the narrative, Mark Twain tells us of the testimony of additional witnesses:

Witness Sowerby tells us that while he was in the saloon, Smith came up to Jones and, without provocation, "busted him in the snoot."

Witness McWilliamson is then called. He recounts the event somewhat differently: "Jones — he sidled up and drawed his revolver and tried to shoot the top of Smith's head off, and Smith run...." The account is confused by the fact that the pistol supposedly fired seven or eight times was a derringer, a type of gun capable of firing only once. Furthermore, the witness decides under examination that the shot(s) was (were) aimed at Smith's body or legs rather than at his head. On crossexamination, McWilliamson declares the weapon to be a bowie knife and the attack an attempted scalping.

Washington Billings is called and sworn. It turns out from his testimony that the fight took place in the street between two men moving toward each other in a drunken stupor. Although they tried to avoid each other, they collided, reaching for cobblestones and falling on each other. "After that, neither of 'em could get up any more, and so they just laid there in the slush and clawed mud and cussed each other."

Witness Jeremiah Driscoll gives another version: "I saw the fight, your Honor, and it wasn't in a saloon nor in the street. I was up in the Square, and they fought with a pine bench and a cane...."

Other witnesses are called who agree on only one point — the motive for the fight was $2.40, but disagreement rages about who was creditor and who was debtor.

The author tells us at this point that he will leave the accused and accuser "before the bar of the world," where "the decision will be a holy and just one."

Was it difficult to keep all the facts straight? Perhaps a little exercise in accounting for the important information would be helpful (see Table 4-1). Mark Twain's "Evidence in the Case" is shown here in tabular form to illustrate a procedure for classification of information commonly used in research. Although the evidence provides no facts, we can at least keep our sources clearly separate, enabling us to see at once the discrepancies that dictate which questions we must research.

Table 4-1   Sorting the Evidence

Witness	Location of assault	Type of injury	Injured	Weapon	Provocation (who started it)	Motive
Sowerby	saloon	hit in nose	Jones	fist	Smith	
McWilliamson	saloon	shot at head/legs attempted scalping	Smith	gun or bowie knife	Jones	
Billings	street	falling, fighting, no serious injury	both or neither	cobblestone	neither	
Driscoll	square			pine bench, cane		
Other witnesses						$2.40 debt

In Mark Twain's fictitious case, we are little concerned with the verdict, but in real life accuracy of information is a serious matter indeed. Each day juries hear evidence, frequently conflicting in content. In some cases, expert witnesses are called, including sociologists. The credibility of their expertise in distinguishing fact from fiction is based upon their rigorous scientific training, which allows them to discard what seems impossible or highly unlikely. Their criteria go beyond common sense. In making your own decisions, training yourself to look at evidence critically will help you make the right choices.

BACKGROUNDS TO SYSTEMATIC RESEARCH

In sociology, the process of verifying facts requires a focused statement or series of statements about social behavior. An example of a statement subject to research is: Rich people have fewer children on the average than do other people. This is a verifiable statement; it can be tested empirically for factual accuracy.

TESTING SIMPLE PROPOSITIONS The development of statements, or *propositions,* for empirical checking is a necessary step in research. This procedure is part of the *scientific method*,* which is discussed at length in Appendix B. Let us consider here some important aspects of sociological research.

Consider the statement: *Rich people have fewer children on the average than do other people.* You may agree with this statement based on *an educated guess.* While the proposition might seem reasonable, empirical checking will confirm the idea. Census data support the statement. Table 4-2 supports it but also places some restrictions on the data we are using. It includes neither unmarried women who bear children nor near-menopausal women who are still able to bear children. Nor can we take this as a table related to social status in a complete way, for there are indicators of status other than income. Also, income may temporarily depress status, as among those unemployed during part of the year. Always check to see what is being included and excluded in a table. Your conclusion may be correct, but it is possible that the reasons upon which you based it were invalid.

Table 4-2 Number of Children Ever Born per 1,000 Married Women 15 to 44 Years Old, by Family Income, 1976

Family income	White	Black
$4,000 to $7,499	3,517	4,287
$7,500 to $9,999	3,377	4,353
$10,000 to $14,999	3,006	3,396
$15,000 and over	2,887	3,117

SOURCE: *Fertility of American Women.* Washington, D.C.: U.S. Department of Commerce Current Population Reports, 1977. Series P-20, No. 308, pages 57–58.

DESCRIPTIVE AND ANALYTIC RESEARCH A second preliminary step in systematic research is to consider how statements are treated. There is a distinction between *descriptive research** and *analytic research**. In the example given in Table 4-2, the collection of *data**, or information, and its presentation is descriptive research in which the distribution of population characteristics is reported. The characteristics are described or set forth without providing an extension into *analytic research,* which attempts to determine and explain why this relationship exists. Such analysis might involve comparing the census data with data from other decennial census tables to determine, for example, that a change has occurred which makes the birthrate more sensitive to family income. One could then hypothesize about what will happen in the future (an increase in the proportion of blacks to whites) or suggest an explanation for a lowering of birth rates across income groups (greater availability of birth control information and devices for all income groups).

HYPOTHESES AND EXPERIMENTAL RESEARCH The term *hypothesis** refers to a statement of assumption(s) about the relationship between two or more phenomena. Hypotheses are essential in *experimental research**, a form of scientific inquiry using controlled observation which permits accurate assessment of the relationship between phenomena. Hypotheses may also be used in nonexperimental research, but they are subject to the most rigorous tests when used in conjunction with experimental techniques. Sociologists often study groups differing only in one relevant respect (Thomlinson, 1965: 34). We use the terms *constant* for a phenomenon that does not vary, for example sex, and *variable* to describe a phenomenon that changes, for example social status. Thus, we might hypothesize that social status rises with increased education. Here we are expressing a *direct relationship* (as one variable increases, so does the other). We might state the same idea another way by saying that social status increases (rises) as ignorance decreases. Here we have stated an *inverse relationship* (the variables move in opposite directions). In reading research findings, always make sure you have understood the directions in which variables change. (Hypotheses, experimental designs, and research are further discussed in Appendix B.)

AN ETHICAL ISSUE It is not generally possible for sociologists to conduct controlled experiments in a laboratory setting as physical and biological scientists often do. The practical and ethical problems of manipulating people preclude most sociological laboratory experimentation. Consider the practical problem of experimenting to determine how people respond to someone yelling "fire" in a crowded room. There is an ethical question, too. What if people were hurt or killed in the experiment? Consequently, sociologists must often rely upon after-the-fact accounts of behavior.

For some research questions, it is possible to test hypotheses in classic experimental form. To do so, one must be able to hold constant all those factors that might be involved in producing the effects of a particular relationship we have hypothesized. Suppose we want to see if aggressive behavior is encouraged by presentation of aggressive visual stimuli. We take three groups that have been matched on characteristics to be held constant. Let's say we have selected males, all aged eighteen, with high school diplomas but no further education. All are from homes with both mother and father present; all are elder children with one brother. All are of the same racial and ethnic background. We could go on, describing ways in which all the subjects are selected to be the same. You can see how difficult it would be to select such a group.

EXPERIMENTAL AND CONTROL GROUPS

Assume we have a group that is well matched. We experiment by exposing one-third of the total group to a stimulus that shows the relationship we suspect, say, a violent television show. A second group the same size will hear a specially prepared radio version of the same show, identical in its content of violent material. These two groups are our *experimental* groups. A third group, our *control* group, will receive no stimulus but will simply wait without knowledge of the experiment being performed with the other groups.

We are testing to see whether the visual stimulus has the greatest impact. If the relationship is not supported, there will be no significant differences in the ways the groups react. If it is supported, the group of television-watchers should be most aggressive after seeing the show. There are other possibilities. Both the visual and nonvisual stimuli may encourage equal amounts of aggression, while the unstimulated control group shows none at all. Or the waiting group might be more aggressive than either of the other two. When such a finding as the latter occurs, the researcher checks his experimental design to see if he has failed to account for something important. Perhaps boredom during a prolonged period of waiting produces more aggression than do the violent stimuli. Perhaps the experiment will be run again with magazines, carefully screened to avoid violent stimuli, made available to the waiting group.

It may even be that an unanticipated consequence will be discovered, such as the discovery that many in both the control and experimental group need eyeglasses. Such an unexpected finding is called *serendipity*; a good researcher is able to see it and sets to work to explain it.

How do we know that aggression has resulted from the stimulus? Typically, a pretest and posttest of some kind are given to the groups in order to measure effects. The groups might be asked to respond to questions that measure aggression both before and after. However, the risk exists that answering the same question twice might make a difference in the respondents' attitudes. Perhaps participants will be asked to write a short story before and another after in which actions of two people are described. These stories may then be *content analyzed* (a topic to be discussed later) to determine whether there are more aggressive images created after than before the experiment. Pretest and posttest results of our hypothetical experiment are shown in Table 4-3. In our hypothetical experiment, we can make ourselves lucky. Our data show the relationships just as we expected them to be. Researchers aren't always so happy with their results. What would you, as a researcher, do if, for example, Group 2 showed high aggression, Group 3 moderate aggression, and Group 1 low aggression at Time 2? (Remember we can control who will participate in the experiment by allowing only those showing low aggression at Time 1 to continue.) At the very least, such empirical findings would suggest that aggression may be related to factors other than visual stimuli.

Because of the difficulty of finding experimental subjects and making the necessary manipulations in the laboratory, sociologists often turn to a modification of this procedure, called *quasi-experimental*, when they cannot ethically or practically control an element of an experiment.

Table 4-3 Possible Results of Classical Experimentation Procedure for Determining Sources of Aggression

Group	Time 1 (pretest)	Stimulus	Time 2 (posttest)
Group 1	low aggression	television, visual violence	high aggression
Group 2	low aggression	radio, auditory violence	moderate aggression
Group 3	low aggression	no stimulus	low aggression

TOOLS OF THE TRADE

An important part of the research process is the detection of false reporting of human behavior. A certain skepticism about the nature of reporting is essential but, like doctors, sociologists ought to get the facts straight in the first place.

Five standard research techniques, or tools of the trade, are: observation, interviews, sampling, using available data, and content analysis. In each of these techniques, tried and tested procedures are used to get accurate information. Sometimes, sociologists use more than one technique at a time so as to get the widest possible perspective and to have a cross-check on information. In studying a street-corner gang, a researcher might ask the leader questions, observe his behavior and take notes, and ask gang members questions about the leader. These techniques are so complex that there are textbooks discussing each of them. Even so, it is useful to consider briefly how they are used to analyze the concepts and social issues with which sociology deals.

OBSERVATION Observation is the most common technique, for it involves simply making a record of behavior as it occurs. It leaves us with a written description of whatever social phenomenon we have chosen to study. Everyday observation is a step toward, but is not in and of itself, a social scientific technique.

Two useful methods have been developed to provide systematic and objective information from observation. One is called *unstructured observation** and the other *structured observation**. Both use carefully kept records, but unstructured observations are less formalized. General guidelines are used rather than specific criteria for observation. In unstructured observations, the observer is often but not always a *participant observer**, taking on, to some extent, the role of a member of the group. Cultural anthropologists often use this technique when they live with a community and informally but systematically observe the life pattern. They generally stay for as long as possible, wanting to observe cultural patterns in all seasons, and recording the social responses to such events in the life cycle as birth, puberty, marriage, and death. (Of course if one wishes to observe death rites in a physically healthy community, it may take some maneuvering to be able to stay until someone actually dies. This is what happened to one cultural anthropologist who lived in a Chinese village community in Taiwan where nobody died during the time he originally allotted for his project; in the end, he had to arrange for several additional months of residency [Gallin, 1961].)

Some of the most productive sociological research has come from unstructured participant observation. As a young Harvard graduate student in the 1930s, William Foote Whyte joined an Italian youth gang and wrote a classic book on the nature of *Streetcorner Society* (1955). While his observations were informal and unstructured, Whyte systematically wrote them down, making a major contribution to the understanding of the effects of primary-group support and status within informal groups. His system has been fruitfully applied more recently in *Talley's Corner* (1967), Elliot Liebow's study of young black street-corner groups in Washington, D. C.

While open-ended by their nature, unstructured observations by social scientists are often based on a checklist in order to avoid overlooking observations that might be important for understanding a social situation (Selltiz, 1959: 208-210; Johnson, 1975). Such a list used by Whyte, Liebow, and others includes: the participants — who they are, how they are related to one another, and background characteristics such as their age, sex, and race; the setting — what kind, whether formal or informal, whether it encourages or discourages certain kinds of behavior; the purpose — why the participants have been brought together, whether by chance, informally, or for an official function or goal; the social behavior — what actually occurs and who does what with whom; and frequency and duration — when the situation occurred, how long it lasted, and whether it is unique or recurring.

It might be useful for you to think of unstructured observations being at one end of a continuum and structured observations at the other. Structured observations, like unstructured, sometimes employ a participant observer, but the observer has a more specifically detailed idea of what information is being sought. For example, a researcher who wants to know the effect of different teaching methods on student participation in class would observe classrooms where different procedures were in use, such as formal lectures, discussion groups, or demonstrations using models or visual aids. One might investigate by sitting in the class either appearing to take a student role (participant observation) or sitting apart from students taking notes (direct observation) or even in a position not visible to students and teacher (indirect observation).

This example suggests the need for other techniques besides observation. If one wants to know why certain students speak up and others do not, it would be useful to ask them (the interview technique).

INTERVIEWS An interview is an act of communication in which one person requests information and another supplies it. In research, the interview has the additional characteristic of being initiated for a specific purpose, and focused on some specific content area (Kahn and Cannell, 1961: 16).

It is not easy to gain accurate information from interviews. It is necessary to formulate questions clearly and then train interviewers to refrain from influencing people's responses and to record responses accurately.

The two basic techniques by which interview information is collected are by *questionnaires* filled out by the respondents themselves and by *interview schedules* recorded by interviewers rather than by the respondents. Each has benefits and weaknesses. Questionnaires more often contain structured or closed questions; interview schedules are more likely to include unstructured or open-ended questions. The former are easier to tabulate but may fail to get information not tapped by the closed questions. The latter have greater depth and can give a more complete account of a respondent's meaning, but the interviewer must be careful not to give clues to the answer sought. Robert Kahn and Charles Cannell (1961) describe an interview with a recently discharged psychiatric patient. A patient responding to a questionnaire may be asked, "Are you confident about going back to your job and being successful at it?" to which he can answer simply *yes*, *no*, or *not sure*.

In an actual interview schedule process reported by Kahn and Cannell (p. 329) the interviewer (I) asked the question in an open-ended manner and received a longer and fuller response:

I: I wanted to have a chance to talk with you a little while today before you did leave town, to get some ideas of your plans following discharge, and also we are sort of interested in how you feel about leaving the hospital. I guess you have been here for a while. If you have, it isn't easy always to just take off and start in working again, particularly with the responsibilities at home.

R: Well, I do think that, uh, having been here for some time, within the shelter of the hospital, uh, it was a certain amount of reluctance, about going, but I feel it is quite natural. As I say, from having enjoyed the shelter of the hospital, uh, presently I feel confident that I can do it, whereas a few months ago I had much more qualms of conscience about it, actually a matter of a few weeks ago, but uh, I have become quite confident that no matter how difficult it may be, that I can overcome it. I think it especially important that I return to work immediately, and uh, for that reason I have made arrangements, I have contacted my employer, and I will be going to work Monday morning.

The respondent answered in such a way that his response, "I feel confident," was considerably qualified. He twice mentioned "the shelter of the hospital," indicating a certain unsureness about his fitness for work. Consequently, while this respondent probably would have checked *yes* on a questionnaire he filled out himself, the interviewer could note an element of unsureness.

Naturally such ambiguities are frustrating to the researcher. In a recent study by Patricia Harvey (1975), both structured and open-ended questions were asked. One woman replied to a structured question that she was very satisfied with her job; but when asked about sources of tension at her job, she offered twelve rather extensive complaints. Finding facts is not as simple as it seems. Perhaps finding things to complain about is a source of satisfaction to the woman.

THE CENSUS AS A SOURCE OF INFORMATION The United States Census is a good example of social information gathered by a combination of questionnaire and interview schedule techniques. By provision of Article 1, Section 2 of the Constitution, the government must take a census of the American population every ten years.

They have been doing so since 1790. The detailed census questionnaire is designed to be filled out by a representative sample of respondents, but if there are language or other communication problems, then a census-taker uses the questionnaire as an interview schedule.

The first set of twelve questions on the 1970 U.S. Census is shown in Figure 4-1. Two of the basic requirements for questionnaires or interview schedules are that all questions be objective and accurate about the population being interviewed. Concerning internal objectivity, note that under Question 4, Color or Race, there is the category Negro or Black. The term *black* was not employed on census forms before 1970. It was used that year because, in the 1960s, a large proportion of this group rejected the term *Negro* and described themselves as *blacks*. Is color or race an appropriate question? Some critics feel that since the Census does not ask for religious preference or national origin, it should be color blind as well. Others hold that accurate information on the educational and economic levels and other *demographic* characteristics of blacks and whites is necessary if we are to judge objectively how equal opportunities are in the society.

Let us assume that questions on race are appropriate. How do we know that the Census provides accurate information as a whole about blacks or whites or any other groups within the population? In this nation of well over 200 million, getting information about everyone is a large task. Certain groups are not easy to locate. Such poor people as migrant laborers, ghetto blacks, and many of the elderly tend not to own their homes and are often on the move, so that when the Census is taken, they sometimes cannot be reached by mail or by interviewers. Consequently, poor young and old people and racial minorities are likely to be undercounted (Chaiklin and Lewis, 1964: 43-47). The lack of

1. WHAT IS THE NAME OF EACH PERSON

who was living here on Wednesday, April 1, 1970 or who was staying or visiting here and had no other home?

Print names in this order:
- Head of the household
- Wife of head
- Unmarried children, oldest first
- Married children and their families
- Other relatives of the head
- Persons not related to the head

2. HOW IS EACH PERSON RELATED TO THE HEAD OF THIS HOUSEHOLD?

Fill one circle.

If "Other relative of head," *also* give exact relationship, for example, mother-in-law, brother, niece, grandson, etc.

If "Other not related to head," *also* give exact relationship, for example, partner, maid, etc.

DO NOT MARK THIS COLUMN

For each of 8 lines (numbered 1–8):
- Last name / First name / Middle initial
- ○ Head of household
- ○ Wife of head
- ○ Son or daughter of head
- ○ Other relative of head— *Print exact relationship* →
- ○ Roomer, boarder, lodger
- ○ Patient or inmate
- ○ Other not related to head— *Print exact relationship* →

9. If you used all 8 lines —Are there any other persons in this household?
○ Yes   ○ No

Do not list the others; we will call to get the information.

10. Did you leave anyone out of Question 1 because you were not sure if he should be listed—for example, a new baby still in the hospital, or a lodger who also has another home?
○ Yes   ○ No

On back page, give name(s) and reason left out.

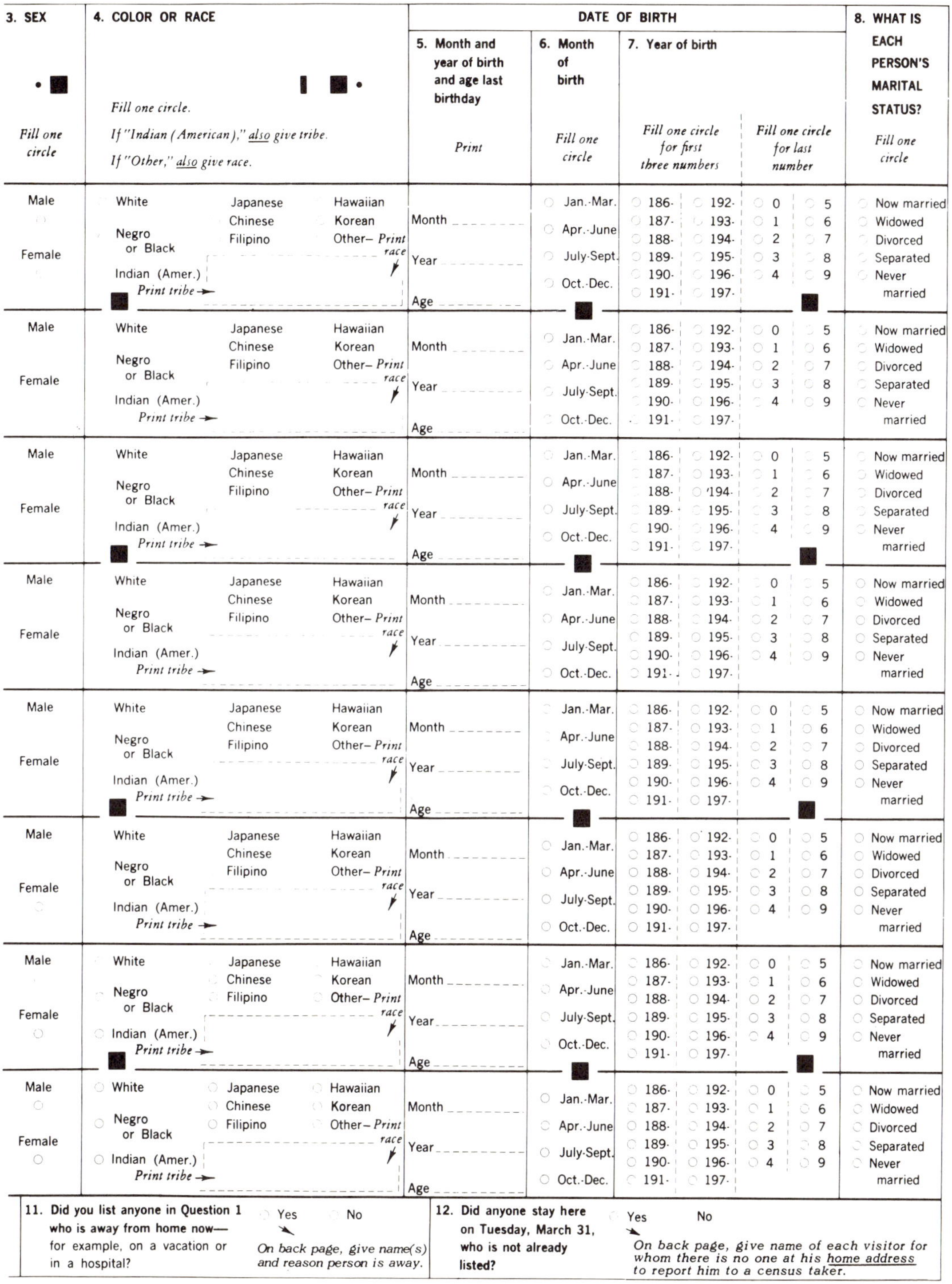

Figure 4-1 United States Census questionnaire, 1970 excerpts.

accurate accounting can affect these people negatively in a variety of ways, including the apportionment of political representation and the provision of such services as schools and welfare assistance. It can also lead to a highly inaccurate estimate of economic and educational achievement among these groups.

USING SCALES BASED ON INTERVIEW DATA
Questionnaires and interview schedules often make use of *scales**. Types of scales frequently found in sociological research are described in the selection Scales: Techniques of Rating. Scales are in vogue more at some times than at others but are never absent as a technique for placing respondents in comparative positions to each other in data analysis. As an example, there are popular tests in magazines: Do You Have a Successful Marriage? What Is Your Anger Quotient? If you haven't taken one, you have surely seen them. These tests are *self-tests*. Many tests in social research collect data using the same questions for each respondent. The data are then evaluated so that scores of respondents can be evaluated in a comparative manner across the spectrum of possible answers.

Scales are generally based on closed questions. The respondent makes a *forced choice* among available alternatives: strongly agree, strongly disagree. Even in self-tests, the score results from comparison of answers. It is useful to note that in these mass popular quiz formats, the respondent is in the position of being asked to make a self-definition from a very limited selection not always well-prepared. These popular materials should be taken with caution. A poor marriage score, for example, may mean merely that your marriage is based on an unconventional life style, not that your marriage is a failure.

SCALES: TECHNIQUES OF RATING

From: Hubert M. Blalock, Jr., *An Introduction to Social Research* (Englewood Cliffs, New Jersey: Prentice-Hall) © 1970, pp. 36–40. Reprinted by permission.

In sociological research, scales are based on data treated in one of several ways. Let us look first at how data are treated and then at several frequently used scale types.

On the crudest and simplest level, classification may be thought of as measurement. If one can classify individuals into mutually exclusive and exhaustive categories, then it becomes possible to count cases and to see the degree to which one category predicts to another. For example, if adults can be classified as "Protestants," "Catholics," "Jews," and "Others," and also as "Republicans," "Democrats," "Independents," and "Others," they can then be cross-tabulated [by religion and by political affiliation.]. . . .

There is no ordering necessarily implied in such classifications. . . . These simple classifications are often referred to as *nominal scales*, deriving from the fact that we have simply given a *name* to the category without implying anything else. . . .

People are often relatively easy to categorize, and in fact they place each other into categories all the time. Mr. Jones may be an accountant, married, a Presbyterian, a Moose, a grandfather, may live on a farm, and so forth. These are manifest characteristics, so to speak. A much more difficult task, however, is that of finding useful ways of *ordering* these classes according to meaningful criteria. For example, most Americans freely admit that occupations can be roughly ranked according to their prestige, though there may be minor disagreements and certain kinds of occupations (e.g., farming) that are difficult to place. Therefore a person may be given an occupational prestige score that places him on a continuum from high to low (or good to bad, skilled to unskilled and so forth). If this is possible, we refer to the resulting scale as an *ordinal scale*.

The defining characteristic of an ordinal scale lies in what is called its transitive property: if A is greater than B (written A > B), and B greater than C, then A must be greater than C. If this does not hold for all individuals, then we do not have a legitimate ordinal scale....

In many instances social scientists must settle for rather crude ordinal scales in which there are numerous ties.... Whenever such ties occur, there is always the question of whether they are really ties or whether these ties merely reflect the crudity of the measuring instrument. Usually it is the latter. Few sociologists hold to the position that one can find a fixed number of distinct social classes composed of completely homogeneous (or tied) individuals. They recognize that there is a continuous gradation of statuses and that they have arbitrarily decided to use six rather than some other number of classes....

At times it is possible to utilize a standard unit of measure, such as the pound, foot, second, or dollar, thus making it possible to speak about the numerical sizes of the differences among scores. These kinds of measures are most common in the physical sciences, but there are some available to the social scientist as well. An obvious one is the monetary unit.... When such objective units exist, it becomes possible to compare differences. For example, if A's income is $20,000, if B's is $14,000 and C's is $8,000, we can say that B's income is halfway between A's and C's, or equivalently that if there were another person with the same income as B's, then his income plus B's would exactly equal the sum of A's and C's. Such an operation would be inappropriate in the case of prestige. One cannot add the prestige of A to that of C in any meaningful sense. Whenever it is possible to compare differences in scores because of the existence of such a standardized unit, we refer to the scale as an *interval scale*.

If, in addition, there is a nonarbitrary zero point, it then becomes possible to compare the ratio of two scores, and we have what is termed a "ratio scale." In practice, whenever we have a definite unit of measurement, such as the dollar or inch, we will in fact have a meaningful zero point (no income or no length). In these cases we may also compare ratios and make meaningful statements such as that one person's income is twice that of another.

Of course the aim of all scientists is to improve measurement as much as possible and to utilize as many interval or ratio scales as is feasible, given limitations of knowledge and cost. But it is often extremely difficult in the social sciences to obtain true interval or ratio scales, though ordinal scales are much more frequent. One of the most challenging tasks confronting the social scientist is that of improving his measurement....

FREQUENTLY USED SCALES

LIKERT SCALE Although there are many scales used by sociologists, in fact many of them made up for use in only the one study for which they were developed, there are general types of scales which continue to be used, regardless of the specific content of items contained. The popular scales cited in the text often employ a *Likert scale*. Likert scales allow treatment of data in ordinal form. Statements are responded to as follows:

Statement: Men are more likely to take charge of the situation in a crisis than are women.

Alternatives: Strongly Agree (5), Agree (4), Uncertain (3), Disagree (2), Strongly Disagree (1)

Statements are grouped in some cases to establish scores for variables under study by averaging the scores for all related questions. If, for example, the respondent "strongly agrees" with the above statement and "agrees" with three others (4 x 3) of like kind, the score would be $12+5=17 \div 4=4.25$. Values have assigned meanings, so that this value of 4.25 for, let us say, our scale of sex role stereotypes means that our respondent has scored "above average" in use of stereotypes, (or from the point of view of liberationists, as an above average chauvinist).

Likert scales may be very short, like our four-item scale above, or may include groups of questions on several subjects or variables. They are often used to measure attitudes, but can be used for other purposes.

THURSTONE SCALE Another type of scale, which is more complicated to construct and requires a forced choice of categories, is the *Thurstone scale*, described as follows:

From: Jacqueline P. Wiseman and Marcia S. Aron, *Field Projects For Sociology Students* (Cambridge, Massachusetts: Schenkman Publishing Company, 1970), pp. 209–211.

The *Thurstone scale*, an eleven-point interval scale, is developed in the following way:

1. The investigator writes a number of positive and negative statements of varying intensity (sometimes as many as 50 to 100) pertaining to the phenomenon he wishes to measure.

2. He then asks people (often 50 to 100) to act as judges, and sort the statements into eleven piles — five degrees of favorable, one neutral, five degrees of unfavorable to the subject. (It is important to note that the investigator does not want the judges' personal opinions of the phenomenon, but rather their opinions concerning the *strength and direction* of the statements about the phenomenon — i.e., is the statement strongly or weakly positive or negative?) The major purpose is to find eleven statements that a majority of judges agree vary in intensity from unfavorable to neutral to favorable. (Theoretically, if enough written statements were available, equivalent scales could be created with different sets of statements.)

Suppose the phenomenon to be tested concerns attitudes toward student demonstrators on college campuses. Some possible statements for the judges to rate as to positive and negative intensity might be:

Student demonstrators should be suspended from college.

Student demonstrators are trying to save this country from ruin.

Student demonstrators are doing and saying what older people in this country would like to do and say but dare not.

Student demonstrators ought to be sent to jail. [And so on. . . .]

3. The investigator records the results of each judge's assessment of the strength of each statement. That is, he keeps track of where each statement is sorted by each judge. He then finds the *median* score for each statement. (The median of any distribution of numbers is found by putting them in rank order and counting from the top or bottom to the *midpoint* of the numbers.) [Note: the median is a descriptive statistic, as are the *mean*, or numerical average of all scores divided by number of cases, and the *mode*, or most often-appearing number.] The median is used in this case to avoid any distortion caused by averaging. This would indicate the approximate point on an eleven-point scale that each statement represents, so far as the judges were concerned.

Another criterion to use in selecting statements is the *range* of judges' scores. [Note: the range or amount of spread between highest and lowest numbers is another descriptive statistic.] Any statement with a large spread of scores would be viewed as unreliable because so much disagreement existed concerning its intensity. Those statements that were consistently sorted into scores very close to each other would be judged reliable indicators of that position on the eleven-point scale.

In the brief illustration that follows, the median among five ratings for three statements is located by finding the halfway point scores placed in order on a continuum. We assume here that there are but five judges. (The more judges, the longer the distribution, but the median is still the midpoint.)

Statement 1	Statement 2	Statement 3
9	2	2
10	3	3
Median 10	Median 3	Median 9
11	3	10
11	4	11

The investigator would assign statement one to position 10 and statement two to position 3, but he would discard statement three as unreliable because of the wide spread in ratings it received from the judges. He will eventually need eleven statements in all.

4. The eleven statements selected (each representative of one point in the scale) would then compose the eleven-point scale, presumably varying in intensity of feeling on a given topic in increments.

5. The scale is now ready to administer to a subject in the research project. Administration consists of asking the person to check the one statement he *most agrees with*. (The items are not presented to the subject in order, but randomly. The assumption is that he also agrees with those of lesser intensity than his selected time, while disagreeing with any stronger statements.

GUTTMAN SCALE A third type of scale which combines features of the Likert and Thurstone is the *Guttman scale*, also called *scalogram* analysis.

From: Norman H. Nie, C. Hadlai Hull, Jean G. Jenkins, Karin Steinbrenner, and Dale H. Bent, *SPSS: Statistical Package for the Social Sciences* (New York: McGraw-Hill, 1975), pp. 529–531.

Guttman scale analysis is a means of analyzing the underlying operating characteristics of three or more items in order to determine if their interrelationships meet several special properties which define a Guttman scale. Guttman scales must first be unidimensional, that is, the component items must all measure movement towards or away from the same single underlying object....

Second, Guttman scales must be cumulative, and it is this property which differentiates Guttman scales from almost all other types of scales and indexes. Operationally, a cumulative scale implies that the component items can be ordered by degree of difficulty and that respondents who reply positively to a difficult item will always respond positively to less difficult items and vice versa.... The Social Distance Scale is an example of this type of scale.

Using the general logic of Guttman scale analysis, one would expect the responses to items to form the pattern illustrated in the following table [where agreement with a statement = 1, disagreement = 0].

Scale Type	A	B	C	D	E
5	1	1	1	1	1
4	0	1	1	1	1
3	0	0	1	1	1
2	0	0	0	1	1
1	0	0	0	0	1
0	0	0	0	0	0

If the five items under analysis formed a perfect Guttman scale, all the responses would conform to the ideal pattern above. That is, all respondents who passed only one item would pass Item E and no others. Respondents passing two items would always pass items D and E and not items A, B, or C. The passing of a more difficult item would never be associated with rejecting a less difficult one.

But data rarely, if ever, perfectly fit the expectations of the researcher. And the test of scalability of the items in the Guttman procedure is the degree to which the data indeed fit the model....

Scales are typically subjected to statistical procedures to determine their *validity* **(Do they measure real differences among those studied on the characteristic studied?) and their** *reliability* **(Would the instrument used, i.e. the scale, consistently measure these differences if used again and again?). Standard scales often report figures on validity and reliability based on experiences with their use.**

SAMPLING A technique for securing accurate information about large populations is *sampling**. In its simplest form, a sample is any part of a large group. Only a relatively small number of people are interviewed in sampling. It is a widely used technique, since it is cheap and efficient in terms of time and energy. Thus, if one wants to know how certain population groups in a given community — men, women, teenagers, blue-collar workers, or any other designated grouping — feel about certain issues, a limited number of the people in the selected population category, or *cohort**, can be sampled. If there are a thousand teenagers in a high school, one may then sample one hundred to find out their views on the legalization of marijuana, career goals, or any other question of interest.

What about the accuracy of samples? If you asked ten of your friends their opinions about a current issue, how accurately will they reflect a larger group of similar age? From such a sample it would be quite risky to project much beyond this friendship web. In sampling any population, there is a chance of what statisticians call *sampling error*. Consequently, sociologists employ statistical devices to reduce the likelihood of error in getting information from a sample. The aim is to get information that truly represents the larger group being sampled. That is why sociologists use not just sampling but *random sampling**.

THE ESSENTIAL QUALITY OF A RANDOM SAMPLE *Random* in this sense means that every person in a larger group has an equal chance of being selected for the sample. A group of ten friends is not random and not representative of the student population as a whole. The very fact that they are all your friends makes it likely that they hold values similar to your own, which may not be typical of the student body as a whole. In generalizing from this sample, you might be making the same classic error the *Literary Digest* made when, based on its 1936 telephone sample (who could afford telephones?), it concluded that Alfred Landon was going to defeat Franklin D. Roosevelt for president in a landslide; in fact, Landon was severely trounced by Roosevelt.

Random selection is used to avoid this kind of built-in bias. If there are one thousand students as in the example above, then if one hundred are selected, their names should be picked from the general mix. We might think of the best process for sampling a stew. One should not sip from the top but mix the stew so that all its ingredients are represented in one spoonful. Since population mixes vary greatly, a variety of random sampling techniques have been developed. Furthermore, computers now make it fairly easy to mix names in any selected population.

SAMPLING: MANY PATHS TO ONE GOAL

The goal of researchers in sampling is to be able to collect from part of a population of interest data that will adequately represent the population so that conclusions of general applicability can be drawn. Samples are taken where the population as a whole cannot participate in the study, as when, for example, one wishes to study phenomena concerning New York City or the United States. A researcher may not be able to afford to study an entire population, even a small one, if there is little money for staff. Another possible problem is lack of time. For a number of good reasons, the researcher chooses to sample, or to select only part, to represent the whole. Here are typical methods of sampling.

NONPROBABILITY SAMPLES In nonprobability sampling, the researcher does not know to what degree of probability the selected sample fairly represents the characteristics of the whole population. Although such a sample can be drawn quickly, and sometimes cheaply, it is considered weaker than probability sampling and is therefore less desirable. Two common types of nonprobability samples are quota samples and availability samples.

A *quota sample* is taken by setting quotas of persons to be included on the basis of characteristics of interest, for example, so many males, so many females, so many blacks, so many whites. A danger of this type of sampling is that those sent out to interview participants will choose people nearest at hand or least resistant to being interviewed. Since many who should be included in order to represent the population are not captured by this system, the quota method may produce a highly biased sample from which biased results are necessarily produced.

Availability samples are gathered, quite simply, from those who are available, until the researcher is satisfied that the collection is sufficiently large. A friend tells a story of a student in her class who remarked that he was sure of a proposition because he had randomly selected people likely to know the facts from among his coworkers on his shift. The facts to which he referred involved the question of whether hippies deserve equal protection under the law. Obviously he had not randomly selected people. They were his friends, they were the people available to him at the convenient time for data gathering, and they were likely to be somewhat biased by their typical interaction pattern with hippies. They were all police officers, and they dealt primarily with those suspected of crimes. It should be easy to see that these available people were not likely to represent fully the population of the city.

PROBABILITY SAMPLES Probability sampling offers an advantage over nonprobability sampling because the researcher can specify through statistical manipulations the probability of any person's inclusion in the sample. Only when this is done can there be an adequate assessment of how representative the sample is. There are several types of probability samples.

Simple *random sampling* means that any person in the population has an equal chance of being selected for the sample. It also makes any combination of cases, or people, equally possible. However, if the sample is drawn without replacement of cases, that is, if once you are chosen you can't be chosen again, it can be said that the assumption that the chances are equal for being chosen for all members of the population is no longer true.

Stratified random samples are more complicated. The researcher may require enough cases from at least two categories — Jews and Catholics, males and females, Native Americans and blacks — that each category is treated separately, although those chosen from *within* each category are randomly drawn. These categories consititute subsamples. When placed together, they make up the sample. The researcher tries to represent adequately specific groups within the population but does not claim to have constructed an accurate miniature of the population. For purposes of study, one might want enough cases to show how Jews feel about a particular subject. Although Jews may represent only 3 percent of the general population of the area being studied, the number selected in the sample might be more than 3 percent of the total of cases studied. Analysis reports this variability among strata; it is accounted for.

Interval samples are drawn from lists. Starting from a randomly chosen point on a list (such as a city directory), the sample takes every tenth name, every twenty-fifth name, or whatever interval meets the needs of sample size. There is a drawback to the procedure; if there is a large ethnic population in a community, one might oversample that population because of the frequency of appearance of some common ethnic names on the list.

Cluster sampling is based on a first sample selected from larger units or *clusters*, which are selected on the basis of random sampling. For example, one may randomly select states from the fifty United States. Within these states, a random selection of cities is made, and from the cluster of cities, a random sample is drawn of whatever unit is required by study. This technique of drawing wheels within wheels, so to speak, is far more efficient in time, money, and labor power of research staff than drawing a simple random sample from the large area from which representative selections must be made.

There are other types of samples, but this brief list introduces the major types and some of their strengths and limitations.

THE USE OF STATISTICAL MEASURES Assume that a random sample has been selected for interviewing. How confident can we be that the results from the sample accurately reflect the larger population? Here again we can tell how much confidence to place in a sample by the use of statistical measures. Without getting into the technical formulas, Figure 4-2 shows the basic idea of the *normal*

Figure 4-2 Normal curve measure of significance.

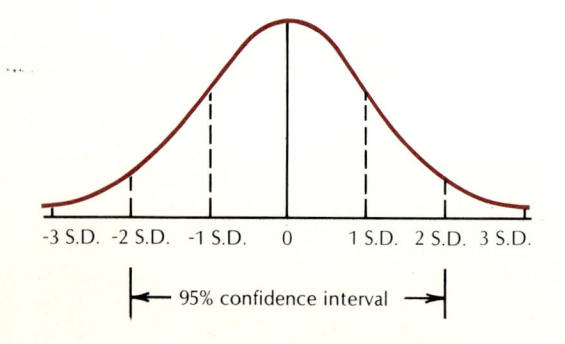

-3 S.D. -2 S.D. -1 S.D. 0 1 S.D. 2 S.D. 3 S.D.

95% confidence interval

curve, which is the distribution range of a group's measured characteristics. The characteristics could be average height, test scores, baseball batting averages, political preferences, or any other measurable behavior. An example of how observations in an actual research project can be plotted on a normal curve to determine significant differences can be seen in Figure 4-3. Any differences between observations outside 2 S.D., or two standard deviations, means that the chances are at least 95 out of 100 that this difference is the result of more than chance. The difference would then be considered *significant.* Possible subjects of comparison could be the comparative earnings of men and women, the different levels of attendance at sports events by people in different communities, or any other social phenomenon (see Figure 4-3).

The term *S.D.* or *standard deviation* is used in Figure 4-3 because one sample finding is used. If the mean were based upon a number of samples, the term used would be *S.E.M.,* or *standard error of mean.* Both the S.D. and S.E.M. are used to determine the range and degree of confidence as to whether the differences observed are statistically significant.

Since statistical measures such as normal curves always allow for variation between the sampled and the total population — technically the standard deviation or standard error of mean — some allowance is always made on samples. When they are used to predict behavior, as in the case of the Gallup or Harris political polls, the sample results may be considered too close to call with confidence if only a percentage or two separates two candidates, as when Richard Nixon beat Hubert Humphrey in the 1968 presidential election. When the choice is as widely separated as in Figure 4-3, indicating that white children are selected over black children as playmates by a 60 percent margin, then the results are easier, even if unacceptable to one's sense of

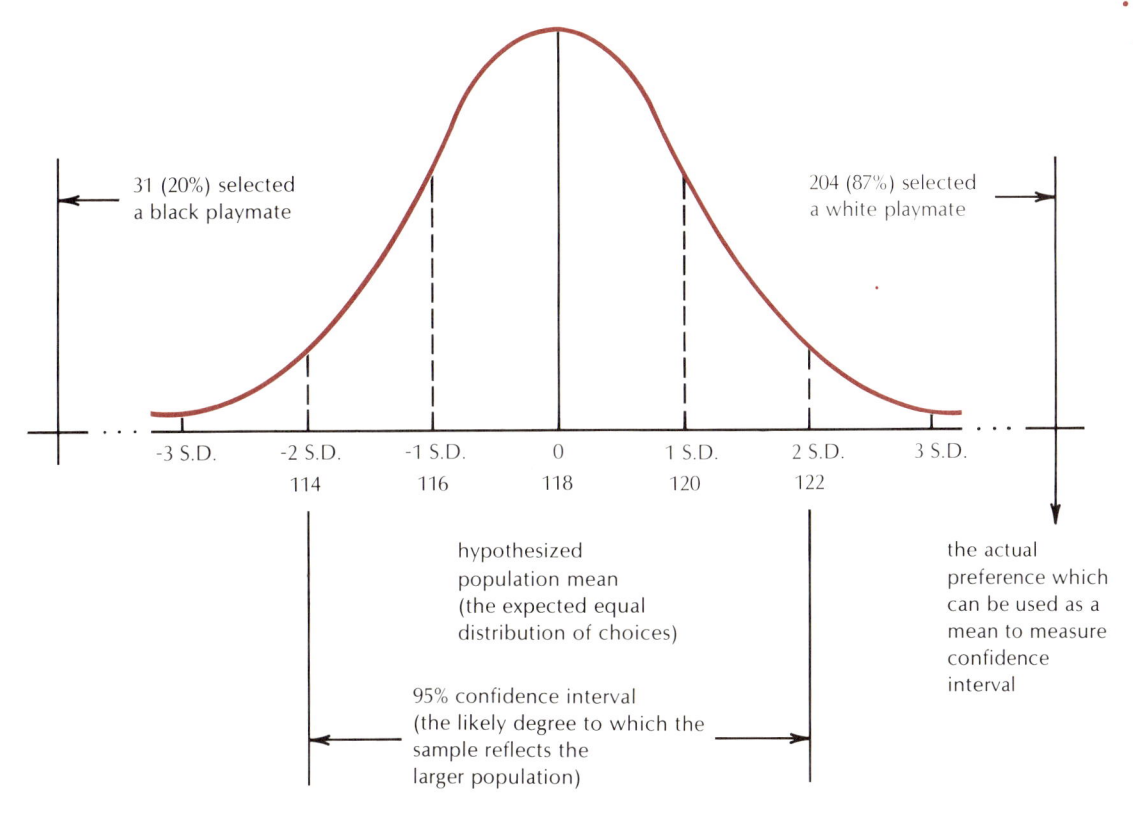

```
                          31 (20%) selected                              204 (87%) selected
                          a black playmate                               a white playmate


        -3 S.D.    -2 S.D.   -1 S.D.    0      1 S.D.   2 S.D.    3 S.D.
                    114       116      118      120      122

                              hypothesized                    the actual
                              population mean                 preference which
                              (the expected equal             can be used as a
                              distribution of choices)        mean to measure
                                                              confidence
                                                              interval
                              95% confidence interval
                              (the likely degree to which the
                              sample reflects the
                              larger population)
```

Figure 4-3 Example of normal curve measure of significance (black and white playmate selections by 235 white first, second, and third graders). SOURCE: Adapted from data presented in Alice Miel, *The Shortchanged Children of Suburbia* (New York: The Institute of Human Relations Press, 1971), p. 17.

values, to predict. Treating the data in Figure 4-3 as part of a normal curve distribution serves as one of many procedures to check the likely validity of the result of a population sample. This particular technique indicates the degree of confidence — usually 95 percent — with which it can be stated that the sample reflects a larger population, in this case early elementary-grade white children in a suburban community. Another finding of this tabulation is that there is in fact a high degree of color consciousness among white preadolescents. Note in the figure that a chance distribution might have resulted in as many as 122, or 51.5 percent, white playmate selections but not 204, or 87 percent, which actually occurred. There are standard statistical formulas that establish the high probability that these selections are significantly different from the hypothesized mean of 118, or 50 percent, and not by chance. The statistical procedures involved are beyond the scope of this book but can be found in any standard statistics text.

The efficiency of random sampling is so great, and the measures of sampling error and other statistical devices so refined, that the U.S. Census now engages in sampling for a proportion of questions. As can be seen in Figure 4-4 there are both 5 percent sample and 15 percent subsample forms. These forms secure more information than is available from the general census forms, with a

Name of person on line (1) of page 2

Last name ______ First name ______ Initial ______

15 and 5 percent

13a. Where was this person born? *If born in hospital, give State or country where mother lived. If born outside U.S., see instruction sheet; distinguish Northern Ireland from Ireland (Eire).*

○ This State
OR
______ *(Name of State or foreign country; or Puerto Rico, Guam, etc.)*

5 percent

b. Is this person's origin or descent— *(Fill one circle)*

○ Mexican ○ Central or South American
○ Puerto Rican ○ Other Spanish
○ Cuban ○ No, none of these

15 percent

14. What country was his father born in?

○ United States
OR
______ *(Name of foreign country; or Puerto Rico, Guam, etc.)*

15. What country was his mother born in?

○ United States
OR
______ *(Name of foreign country; or Puerto Rico, Guam, etc.)*

5 percent

16. *For persons born in a foreign country—*
a. Is this person naturalized?

○ Yes, naturalized
○ No, alien
○ Born abroad of American parents

b. When did he come to the United States to stay?

○ 1965 to 70 ○ 1950 to 54 ○ 1925 to 34
○ 1960 to 64 ○ 1945 to 49 ○ 1915 to 24
○ 1955 to 59 ○ 1935 to 44 ○ Before 1915

15 percent

17. What language, other than English, was spoken in this person's home when he was a child? *Fill one circle.*

○ Spanish ○ Other— *Specify* ______
○ French
○ German ○ None, English only

18. When did this person move into this house (or apartment)? *Fill circle for date of last move.*

○ 1969 or 70 ○ 1965 or 66 ○ 1949 or earlier
○ 1968 ○ 1960 to 64 ○ Always lived in this house or apartment
○ 1967 ○ 1950 to 59

19a. Did he live in this house on April 1, 1965? *If in college or Armed Forces in April 1965, report place of residence there.*

○ Born April 1965 or later } *Skip to 20*
○ Yes, this house .... }
○ No, different house

b. Where did he live on April 1, 1965?

(1) State, foreign country, U.S. possession, etc. ______

(2) County ______

(3) Inside the limits of a city, town, village, etc.?
○ Yes ○ No

(4) *If "Yes,"* name of city, town, village, etc. ______

15 percent

20. Since February 1, 1970, has this person attended regular school or college at any time? *Count nursery school, kindergarten, and schooling which leads to an elementary school certificate, high school diploma, or college degree.*

○ No
○ Yes, public
○ Yes, parochial
○ Yes, other private

15 and 5 percent

21. What is the highest grade (or year) of regular school he has ever attended?
Fill one circle. If now attending, mark grade he is in.

○ Never attended school— *Skip to 23*
○ Nursery school
○ Kindergarten

Elementary through high school (grade or year)
1 2 3 4 5 6 7 8 9 10 11 12
○ ○ ○ ○ ○ ○ ○ ○ ○ ○ ○ ○

College (academic year)
1 2 3 4 5 6 or more
○ ○ ○ ○ ○ ○

22. Did he finish the highest grade (or year) he attended?

○ Now attending this grade (or year)
○ Finished this grade (or year)
○ Did not finish this grade (or year)

23. When was this person born?

○ Born before April 1956— *Please go on with questions 24 through 41.*
○ Born April 1956 or later— *Please omit questions 24 through 41 and go to the next page for the next person.*

5 percent

24. *If this person has ever been married—*
a. Has this person been married more than once?

○ Once ○ More than once

b. When did he get married? ______ Month ______ Year
When did he get married for the first time? ______ Month ______ Year

c. *If married more than once—* **Did the first marriage end because of the death of the husband (or wife)?**

○ Yes ○ No

15 and 5 percent

25. *If this is a girl or a woman—*
How many babies has she ever had, not counting stillbirths?
Do not count her stepchildren or children she has adopted.

1 2 3 4 5 6 7 8
○ ○ ○ ○ ○ ○ ○ ○
9 10 11 12 or more None
○ ○ ○ ○ ○

15 percent

26. *If this is a man—*
a. Has he ever served in the Army, Navy, or other Armed Forces of the United States?

○ Yes
○ No

b. Was it during— *(Fill the circle for each period of service.)*

Vietnam Conflict *(Since Aug. 1964)* .... ○
Korean War *(June 1950 to Jan. 1955)* .... ○
World War II *(Sept. 1940 to July 1947)* .... ○
World War I *(April 1917 to Nov. 1918)* .... ○
Any other time .... ○

Figure 4-4 The 5 percent and 15 percent sample forms for the United States Census questionnaire, 1970.

saving in time, money, and effort from that required to ask all questions of everyone. The 5 percent sampling and 15 percent subsampling forms contain the additional questions designated on the side of this figure, some questions here are asked of the general 5 percent sample and some of 15 percent more extensively interviewed within that same 5 percent of the total population. Completed forms of such a sample randomly selected are easier to collect than are questionnaire responses from the total population. The result often provides needed information on highly mobile groups, for example, many of the elderly and many racial minorities.

THE ROLE OF SURVEY RESEARCH CENTERS Increasingly sociology, like the other social and physical sciences, is developing its own data. In this process, sampling is such an efficient technique that *survey research centers* (SRC's) have been set up at Columbia University, the University of Michigan, the University of California at Berkeley, and other leading academic institutions — including the National Opinion Research Center (NORC), sponsored by the University of Chicago and Northwestern University, that is often quoted in the press. These centers are generally near metropolitan areas where the population is so large that sampling is the most practical way of finding out about a population's characteristics.

Such centers can gather more varied data more often than is provided by the decennial Census. Interviewers, computer programmers, and other technical personnel are available at all times; information gathered in earlier studies can be brought forth to show trends over time. Furthermore, such research centers can provide emergency research when behaviors sociologists want to study suddenly emerge, as in the case of the Los Angeles earthquake of February 9, 1971. The UCLA Survey Research Center immediately turned to data collection as people responded to the catastrophe.

Random sampling techniques with the assistance of computers are generally efficient and accurate. However, it is always sobering for the researcher to be reminded that even the best sampling procedures of large populations involve the risk of error (see the cartoon on p. 123).

USE OF AVAILABLE DATA Sociologists often employ for their own purposes information on human behavior gathered initially without regard for specifically sociological questions. The richest source of such material is the Census and other data collected by such government agencies as the Departments of Labor and Health, Education and Welfare. The government collects and tabulates information to establish political representation or to determine the number of skilled laborers or college graduates in the society. Sociological research can make additional uses of these data.

A prominent example is the use Emile Durkheim made (1897) of statistics on suicide rates among different social groupings in several European societies at the turn of the century (Simpson, 1951 translation). By using available data, Durkheim found wide variations in suicide rates among different groups. There were higher rates for military personnel than for civilians. Within the military, the most common form of suicide fit a category he called *altruistic suicide,* so named because the suicide placed values of the group to which he belonged above his own. For example, a man who felt he had disgraced himself before his fellow officers might, for the good of the group, as he saw it, take his life.

Durkheim also looked at the variable of religion and found that suicide rates were higher for Protestants than for Catholics. The dominant type of suicide among Protestants he called *egoistic suicide,* based on a relatively weak attachment to one's social group. The social organization as well as religious values of Catholics kept members of the faith more closely tied to each other than was the case among Protestant denominations. Protestants, feeling less a part of their groups, more individualistic, were more likely to commit suicide.

"I DON'T CARE WHAT YOUR COMPUTER SAYS; I AM NOT A TYPICAL DELAWARE FATHER."

SOURCE: Copyright 1970 by permission of *Saturday Review* and John Ruge.

He also found higher rates of suicide for groups experiencing rapid change in economic status, either upward or downward. Here the dominant form of suicide he called *anomic* (see Chapter 7); the individual felt a sense of *anomie**, or loss of the capacity to see clearly what norms and values should be called into play to regulate behavior and interpersonal relations. As one's status was altered, there was, in a sense, a lag between the change of status and the ability to take on the appropriate roles. Such individuals, feeling lost in society, may take their own lives.

While members of any of the groups noted could commit suicide for any of the reasons given, dominant types emerged to match given charac- teristics. By this use of available data, Durkheim helped to establish the usefulness of sociological research in understanding the influence of social organization and group identity on behavior.

CONTENT ANALYSIS Mass communications and popular literature are further rich sources of infor- mation. A technique used to examine this material is known as *content analysis,* which is particularly useful in determining the values and beliefs operating in a society, for example, are all villains dark and menacing and all heroines blonde and blue-eyed? Content analysis has been defined as a research technique "for the objective, systematic, and quantitative description of the . . . content of communication" (Selltiz, 1959: 335). This technique involves some of the same considerations found in survey research. Random samples of newspapers, magazines, novels, and other written sources are drawn on to evaluate various attitudes and interests.

An example of content analysis is Albert Ellis's *The Folklore of Sex* (1961). Ellis analyzed American cultural attitudes about sex as represented in the literature of the decade 1950 to 1960. Using samples from widely read magazines and novels in 1950, and then again in 1960, Ellis presented summary excerpts about such topics as fornication, promiscuity, prostitution, and other references to sexual attitudes or behavior. He used two ways of analyzing written sources: direct quotation and tabulating various kinds of references. An example of the former technique is drawn from Ellis's chapter on obscenity, in which he presented negative and restrictive values about the use of obscenity as seen in the literature of the year 1950 (p. 135):

American fiction ... contains a good many anti-"obscenity" attitudes. In the novel, *Earth Abides*, the hero becomes quite incensed at another character telling indelicate stories. In *Abe Lincoln of Pigeon Creek* much is made of honest Abe's refusing to tell certain anecdotes because "there's ladies present." In a story in *Private Detective* a girl allows herself to be blackmailed rather than to have a "slightly off-color record" that she has made become generally known. In *The Man with the Golden Arm* one character is sent to jail "for unbecoming words to a lady," and another, a night-club chorine, apologizes and blushes to her paramour when she explains some of the gestures she employs in the course of her nightly routine.

The changing attitudes toward obscenity in the mass media was then illustrated by Ellis's summary of 1960 sources (p. 141):

... in many contemporary novels "obscene" words are freely employed by the characters; and in some instances such as Hersey's *The War Lover*, the books are literally full of this kind of language. A typical passage (one of many) from the Hersey novel reads: "Soupie actually put in to be shifted to another ground crew because he said it was a f____ing bore to take care of *The Body*, it was like being a f____ing gas-pump winder at a service station; but the powers-that-be wouldn't transfer him. 'What a way to fight a God-damned war,' Soupie said one day. 'In my opinion I avoid all pigs that there's no risk of the clap if you put it to 'em. Life's short. S____! You got to gamble.' "

If the trend Ellis noted between 1950 and 1960 has continued over the next decade, an analysis of typical 1970 fare would have spelled out the obscenities in the paragraph above. Ellis's 1950 and 1960 content analysis provides a basis for such a comparison of cultural attitudes. To delineate the changes more precisely, Ellis also made a tabulation of sexual attitudes. He then analyzed the greater acceptance of sex in the mass media in 1960 compared to the restrictions of 1950. The results, shown in Table 4-4, could be statistically treated in the manner of Figure 4-2 to help determine how significantly the attitudes changed in the ten-year period. In the original source, Ellis specified what he operationally defined for each category. This table illustrates how the technique of content analysis in the collection of data can be summarized. This technique is particularly useful in evaluating popular beliefs on a variety of subjects. As such it is an objective check on subjective values which influence behavior in the society.

TABULATION TECHNIQUES Content analysis uses a variety of procedures for deriving data from mass communications. One is *symbol counts*, which Ellis used in tabulating the negative and positive sexual references in his study. Although one might

Table 4-4 An Example of Content Analysis Tabulation — Number and Kinds of Sex Attitudes Expressed in American Mass Media, Classified According to Type of Sex Activity

Type of sex activity	Number of liberal attitudes	Number of conservative attitudes
Extramarital coitus		
1950	182 (49%)	187 (51%)
1960	266 (62%)	163 (38%)
Non-coital sex relations		
1950	125 (81%)	30 (19%)
1960	65 (86%)	11 (14%)
Sex relations leading to pregnancy		
1950	8 (19%)	34 (81%)
1960	75 (72%)	33 (28%)
Sex organs, desires, and expressions		
1950	138 (67%)	68 (33%)
1960	740 (93%)	60 (7%)
Sex perversions and crimes		
1950	5 (20%)	20 (80%)
1960	79 (54%)	68 (46%)
Sex control, censorship		
1950	51 (29%)	136 (71%)
1960	116 (70%)	51 (30%)
Totals		
1950	509 (51%)	475 (49%)
1960	1341 (78%)	386 (22%)

SOURCE: Albert Ellis, *The Folklore of Sex* (New York: Grove Press, 1961), p. 236.

merely count the symbols, it is more accurate to assign positive and negative values to contexts in which the symbols appear. This procedure is called *one-dimensional classification of symbols.*

There is also *item analysis,* classifying the significance or insignificance of sections or passages of material; or material might be classified by themes, explicit and implicit, found in the material. There are other types of analysis as well, but these will serve to give a general view of content analysis procedure (see also Merton, 1959: 515–516).

All these techniques produce tabulations. As Ellis put it, "Modern science apparently cannot escape statistics" (p. 235). Even subjective values expressed in mass communications are tabulated and treated quantitatively.

A FINAL NOTE ON TOOLS OF THE TRADE Given the tendency to quantify information and to look for central tendencies, it is not surprising that sociologists use statistical tables in research reporting. Tables are neat and efficient ways of summarizing information. Hence, most sociological research articles and textbooks, including this one, contain many tables. This checklist will be helpful in making tables useful and easy to read. Several of these points are outlined by Allen Wallis and Harry Roberts (1956: 270–274):

1. Read the title carefully; Table 4-4's title tells that it is an example of content analysis tabulations.

2. Read the headnote or other explanation if any; in Table 4-4, the particular basis of the tabulations is explained.

3. Check the source for reliability; the United States Census is generally reliable.

4. Read footnotes to see how they may affect the data; a text note to Table 4-4 explains that the detailed operational definitions for each category can be found in the original source, which is also footnoted.

5. Check the units used; it makes quite a difference whether birth rates are per 1000, per 100, or per 10.

6. Look at the over-all average to find general trends; the totals in Table 4-4 indicate a general liberalization in acceptance of literary sexual referents.

7. Check the variability in different categories; note in Table 4-4 the generally greater acceptance of various referent categories compared to other categories.

8. When there is more than one variable such as age, color, sex, or social class, see how the averages compare between variables; for example note in Tables 6-3, 6-4, and the selection Work and Sexual Inequality that the sons of skilled and unskilled laborers are more likely to remain in the same occupation than are the sons of professional or managerial fathers.

The data presented in tables and in similar forms, and all the techniques used to gather objective information, are designed to help test the accuracy of our ideas about human behavior.

SUMMARY

Sociology and all other scientific disciplines employ methods of research that provide objective, *empirical** information. Goals in society are value-oriented, but effective implementation of goals depends on reliable social information. A prerequisite to providing such information is the ability to distinguish fact from opinion.

Most sociological knowledge is derived from systematic research. An initial step is the development of *statements* that can be verified. Such statements often result in the collection of data that can be treated on *nominal**, *ordinal**, or *interval* scales*. The accumulation of accurate social information in a given area of sociological interest is generally accomplished by *descriptive research** using the *scientific method** (Appendix B) which also employs *experimental** techniques and the use of *hypotheses**. These are statements about the presumed relationship between two or more social phenomena. Hypotheses are often part of *analytic research**, which attempts to determine how any given variable influences the behavior of another particular variable.

Five of the most widely employed research techniques or tools of the trade are *observations**, *interviews**, *sampling**, *use of available data*, and *content analysis**. Observations include *unstructured** and *structured** methods. *Participant observation** is an anthropological variant used by some sociologists to gain insight into the daily life pattern of some groups in the society. Interviews use both *interview schedules** and self-administered *questionnaires**. Sampling techniques are applied to large populations, as in the *decennial census*, and to *random samples**, in which a representative number of a larger population is analyzed. Since random sampling always involves the risk of error in generalizing to a larger population, statistical measures are used such as the *standard deviation** in a *normal curve** distribution in order to reduce the risk of error. Sampling and statistical control measurements have become so efficient and accurate that the United States Census now employs samples to secure some of its population information. Many universities have established *survey research centers* to sample local and national populations regularly on a variety of questions. The use of available sources of data — data collected and printed by others who may not have had a sociological purpose in its collection — is another common technique for getting information. The richest sources of such data are the Census and other government publications. The mass media are additional sources of material that lends itself in particular to *content analysis** of stories and articles, providing insight into the values and beliefs of the society.

Most *data** collected can be tabulated in some form. Consequently, it is useful to read tables of summarized information carefully. A summary of the Wallis and Roberts checklist for the effective reading of tables is given on page 124.

QUESTIONS FOR DISCUSSION

1. Eyewitness accounts are generally thought to be a particularly accurate kind of evidence. Take an

event at which a number of your friends were present — a classroom discussion, an athletic event, or any other — and a day or so after the event ask each witness to describe independently what happened. Check for consistencies and contradictions in the accounts.

2. Describe some aspect of your community such as local transportation facilities or recreational areas. Differentiate between what you think ought to be and what actually is. How could the collection of additional accurate information help you decide whether the system should be maintained as it is or changed in a particular way? What information should be collected?

3. Objective reporting involves the use of precise language and a minimum of opinion or of descriptive language that stresses a particular point of view. Check a local newspaper and see if you can detect biased reporting. A good place to start is with the sports page, particularly with a story on a game in which a local team took part.

4. How could people with different values and goals use the same scientifically based information to support their differing perspectives?

5. Why is a necessary first step in the scientific method a careful statement of the problem to be investigated?

6. Frame a hypothesis and devise an experimental design to test the hypothesis.

7. Why is it not often possible in sociological research to develop controlled experiments? Cite some practical and some ethical considerations.

8. Why may random samples be better indicators of the total United States population than attempts to count every single individual? Why is it usually considered more desirable to have a probability than a nonprobability sample drawn?

9. How is it possible for participant observation and unstructured observations to provide more accurate data in some social situations than structured interview questions?

10. Review your understanding of the following terms and concepts:

empirical research

nominal scales

ordinal scales

interval scales

descriptive research

Likert scale

Thurstone scale

Guttman scale

validity (of scales)

reliability (of scales)

analytic research

structured observations

interview schedules

decennial census

survey research

mean

median

mode

range

REFERENCES

1971   The American Sociologist: 7:1

Blalock, Jr., Hubert
    1970   An Introduction to Social Research. Englewood Cliffs, N.J.: Prentice-Hall.

Blumer, Herbert
1972 "Presidential address." 43rd Annual Meeting of the Pacific Sociological Association (April 14): Portland, Oregon.

Bright, George W. and Carol-Ann Jones
1973 "Teaching children to think metric." Today's Education (April): 16-17. Washington, D.C.: National Education Association.

1971 1970 Census User's Guide. Washington, D.C.: U.S. Census Bureau.

Chaiklin, Harris and Verl S. Lewis
1964 A Census Tract Analysis of Crime in Baltimore City. Baltimore, Maryland: University of Maryland School of Social Work.

Clemens, Samuel (Mark Twain)
1951 "The evidence in the case." The Wit and Humor of America. Indianapolis: Indianapolis Publishing Company (1907) and W. Leary and J. Smith (eds.), Think Before You Write. New York: Harcourt, Brace.

Durkheim, Emile
1951 Suicide. V. Spaulding and G. Simpson. (trans.) Glencoe, Ill.: The Free Press.

Ellis, Albert
1961 The Folklore of Sex. New York: Grove Press.

Gallin, Bernard
1961 Hsin Hsing: A Taiwanese Agricultural Village. Unpublished Ph.D. dissertation. Cornell University.

Harvey, Patricia
1975 "Job satisfaction: a study of secretarial staff." Unpublished manuscript. Colorado State University.

Johnson, John
1975 Doing Field Research. New York: The Free Press.

Kahn, Robert L. and Charles F. Cannell
1961 The Dynamics of Interviewing. New York: John Wiley & Sons.

Leary, William G. and James Steepe Smith
1951 Think Before You Write. New York: Harcourt, Brace.

Liebow, Elliot
1967 Tally's Corner: A Study of Negro Streetcorner Men. Boston: Little, Brown.

Lenski, Gerhard
1961 The Religious Factor. Garden City, N.Y.: Doubleday.

Loether, Herman and Donald McTavish
1974 Inferential Statistics for Sociologists. Boston: Allyn and Bacon.

Mayer, Milton
1949 "How to read the Chicago Tribune." Harper's (April): 24-35.

Merton, Robert K.
1959 Social Theory and Social Structure. Glencoe, Illinois: The Free Press.

Miel, Alice
1967 The Shortchanged Children of Suburbia. New York: Institute of Human Relations.

Nie, Norman, G. Hadlai Hull, Jean Jenkins, Karen Steinbrenner, Dale Bent
1975 SPSS: Statistical Package for the Social Sciences. New York: McGraw-Hill.

Selltiz, Claire et al.
1962 Research Methods in Social Relations. New York: Holt, Rinehart and Winston.

1973 Some Questions and Answers about the UCLA Survey Research Center. Los Angeles: University of California Press.

1968 Subject Reports: Women by Children Under Five Years Old, Final Report. Washington, D.C.: U.S. Bureau of the Census.

Thomas, W. I.
    1931 "The relation of research to the social process." in Essays on Research in the Social Sciences. Washington, D.C.: The Brookings Institution.

Thomlinson, Ralph
    1965 Sociological Concepts and Research. New York: Random House.

Wallis, W. Allen and Harry Roberts
    1956 Statistics: A New Approach. New York: The Free Press.

Whyte, William Foote
    1955 Streetcorner Society. Chicago: University of Chicago Press.

Wiseman, Jacqueline and Marcia Aron
    1970 Field Projects for Sociology Students. Cambridge, Mass.: Schenkman.

Part 2

ISSUES FACING AMERICAN INDIVIDUALS

What the social scientist ought to do for the individual is to turn personal troubles and concerns into social issues and problems open to reason — [the] aim is to help the individual become self-educating.

C. Wright Mills

Chapter 5

ADOLESCENCE AND THE LIFE CYCLE

Some day a Dr. Salk will probably come along with a vaccine for adolescence. If so, the only question will be which Nobel Prize he should get — the one for medicine or the one for peace.

Richard Armour

ADOLESCENTS AND SOCIETY

You will recall from our discussion in Chapter 3 that one traditional function of the family is to socialize children into the culture. As America has become a mass urban society with greater and earlier socializing influences by educational, economic, and government institutions, the contemporary family faces complex challenges in serving the purpose with which it is still charged by our culture. Therefore, a consideration of the problems of adolescents will tell us something about the challenges of social life that face all age groups in modern society. So great have been the changes that have come about with our atomic, industrial urban age, that this generation of teenagers has arrived in what amounts to a new country. A young person who asks his or her parents whether the world around them has changed much since they were teenagers can pull up a chair for a long discussion.

All age groups in a society must make social adjustments to changing times, but there are additional burdens of inexperience, limited power, and uncertain status among adolescents. This generally challenging situation constitutes what we call adolescent problems.

Our young people have more educational training, more material resources, more leisure, and more exposure to community and world events than any previous generation. A thirteen-year-old girl spots an error of scientific reasoning on *Star*

Trek reruns and writes to the network; another girl of the same age is charged with possession of LSD. She wears a tee shirt that says Fly Me. Our youth have seen much, but what they are to do with all the stimuli to which they are exposed is a problem not only for others but for themselves as well.

This chapter will take up three main points. First, there is a consideration of adolescence as a distinct stage in the general, and particulary in the family, *life cycle**. Second, there is a consideration of adolescence as an imperfect (not fully developed) *subculture** (see the selection entitled Subculture). During the adolescent stage of life when the rudiments of a subculture exist, a variety of *developmental tasks** must be accomplished; *discrimination** toward adolescents as a class must be dealt with. And third, we will look at the relationships that adolescents have with the larger society, including signs among adults of flexibility toward meeting the needs of adolescents.

THE PLACE OF ADOLESCENCE IN THE LIFE CYCLE

Until adolescence, the major socializing influence on individuals is the family. The institutions of education, religion, government, and the economy are secondary. Thus, adolescence has a particular place in the *family life cycle** as well as in the life cycle of the individual. The concept of the life cycle is a useful one by which sociologists and members of the society at large identify certain events in the course of a person's life as particularly important (van Gennep, 1960; Hill, 1964). Many events such as birth, marriage, and death occur within the family life cycle, which in America can be divided into the eight stages indicated in Figure 5-1. These stages can be summarized in the following manner:

I. Beginning families (married couple without children)

II. Childbearing families (oldest child birth to two-and-one-half years)

III. Families with preschool children (oldest child two-and-one-half to six years)

IV. Families with school children (oldest child six to thirteen years)

V. Families with teenagers (oldest child thirteen to nineteen years)

VI. Families as launching centers (first child gone to last child leaving home)

VII. Families in the middle years (empty nest to retirement)

VIII. Aging families (retirement to death of both spouses)

As the title to Figure 5-1 denotes, these are general stages. As such they are statistical averages. Single adults do not experience these stages. The normative range for length of time in each stage varies considerably depending upon such factors as number of children in a given family or such events as divorce or death. For example, in families with three or more children, Stage V, in which there is at least one teenager in the family, would take longer than seven years. As the number of children per family in American society tends to decline and as life spans increase, the average length of time in each stage will show changes in future census years just as this figure is different from those of earlier censuses. Such considerations provide insights not only into the changing American family structure but into changes in the general society as well.

CHARACTERISTICS OF THE FAMILY LIFE CYCLE The family life cycle has one property of special interest: some of its features are inevitable. First, there will always be fixed age differentials among family members; as one family member grows older, so do the others. Second, only at certain maturation levels can some achievements occur, for example, learning to walk or developing secondary sex characteristics. How family members adjust to these inevitable situations is influenced by *norms** and *values**. There are laws about when children must start school and when they may leave it, although public pressure may cause changes in the law. Right now there are proposals for lowering the age for legally leaving school, while most young people are actually extending their schooling. The time at which a parent worries that the child, no longer a child, may become pregnant or cause someone to become pregnant is not culturally negotiable. That potential pregnancy is viewed as worrisome is, however, based on cultural values.

We develop viewpoints about what situations are likely to occur during the family cycle based on these inevitable and negotiable factors. We further specify these conditions by cultural decisions about how long children should be considered children and how long they should remain under their families' care. Adolescence in our society is in fact culturally developed as a period of prolonged transition from childhood to adulthood. In other societies, a single ceremony, typically after puberty, signifies the passage from child to adult. Adolescence serves no useful function for such societies. In our own, it regulates transition into an adult world of work and status attainment. Gradual movement toward adult responsibilities is supposed to reduce strain for young people and their elders, but it isn't always so. The events that characterize any given stage of the family life cycle are of course quite personal to the individuals involved in them, but most such events are common to so many families that they are also social in nature and may be viewed sociologically.

ADOLESCENCE AS A PROBLEM PERIOD The concept of adolescent problems (Stage 5 in Figure 5-1) illustrates the social character — or more accurately, the current stereotype of it — for the teenage

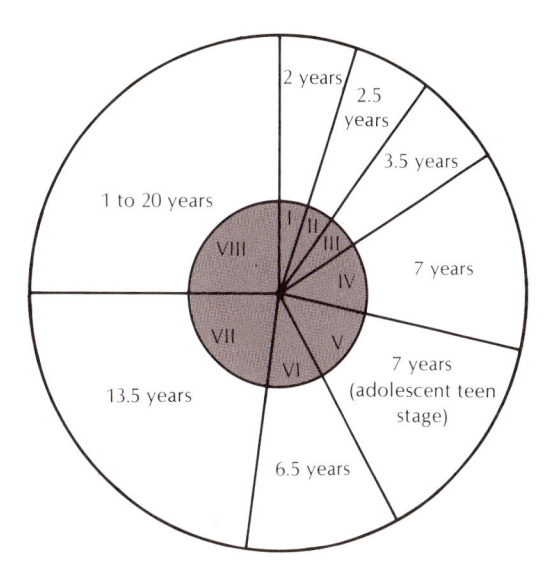

Figure 5-1 Average length of time in each of eight stages in the family life cycle. SOURCE: U.S. Census.

years. It is of course far from true that the adolescent years are always marred by parent–youth conflict, maladjustment to school, unsureness about occupation and the future, or delinquency. But it is true that these and related problems are more common today than they used to be in this country. In America's first century as a nation, the transition from childhood to adulthood was generally smooth. In rural society, parents and youth usually lived pretty much alike (Ramsey, 1967: 18–20).

In modern American society, a paradox occurs. On the one hand, people in their teens are healthier and more aware of the social world around them than was true of past generations. Yet, the changing occupational structure prolongs economic dependency on parents as young people generally go to school longer and take longer to prepare for independent adult status. Just how rapidly social change is occurring is illustrated in the lack of continuity between the occupational status of parents and teenage children. Given the parents' role as socializing agents for their youngsters, the attempt to apply the old patterns to the new cultural content is one of the basic factors in parent–teenager conflict. In light of the rapid changes in the society, this is a conflict inherent in the *birth cycle interval,* the length of time between the birth of one person and his or her procreation of another. Kingsley Davis graphically presents the old and new generational cultural content differences between parents and children in the manner shown in Figure 5-2.

PAST PARENTAL EXPERIENCES AND CURRENT ADOLESCENT REALITIES Both parents and teenagers face the developmental problems of modern society. In socializing their children into society, parents tend to apply past experiences in a context where the schooling, dating patterns, and much else is different for their adolescent children than it was for them. The teenagers enter this period knowing that some of their parents' experiences, including fundamental preparation for a job, will have to be different for them. Employers' needs and expectations may have changed since the parents last applied for a job. The parent often cannot help when the need is there. On the other hand, the parent may feel a responsibility to teach some sexual facts of life, but the teenager's own knowledge of sexuality and birth control may exceed the parents'. The advice is often not wanted: family relationships may become tense.

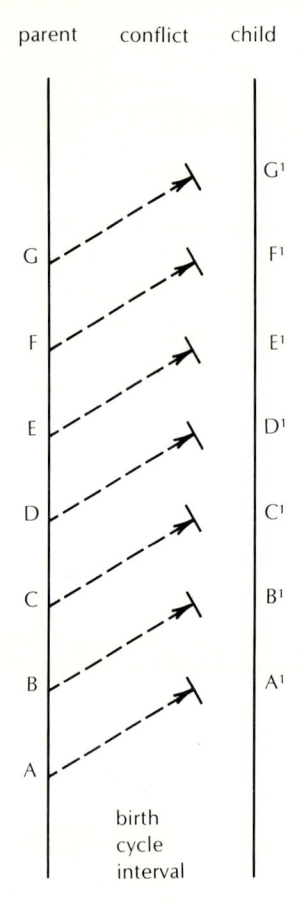

Figure 5-2 Old cultural content acquired at each stage of life.

their children. Today, for the first time, most young people now enter different occupations from those of their parents. This is generally true of urban industrialized societies.

This rapid change in the urban occupational structure is mirrored in other aspects of life; for example, urban families have fewer children than rural families, and they have more leisure time. A consequence for the family is that the values and life pattern acquired by parents when they were adolescents were very different from those of their

DEVELOPMENTAL TASKS OF THE ADOLESCENT YEARS

The role strains facing the current generation of adolescents are not entirely new. They have been growing at an accelerating pace since the nineteenth century, when the Industrial Revolution began to change fundamentally the everyday life styles of most Americans. What this did for adolescents was to shift them, as one author sees it, from an era of apprenticeship to one of rebellion (Ramsey, 1967: 18–28). In the era of apprenticeship, teenagers were socialized directly by their mothers and fathers and by members of their extended families into fairly clear-cut roles and life patterns. In the twentieth century's era of rebelliousness, teenagers have increasingly been influenced by socializing forces outside the family, such as peers, schools, and by their perceptions of the occupational choices before them.

LACK OF CLEAR RITES OF PASSAGE Certainly not all adolescent behavior must be considered extreme enough to be called rebellion. A teenager may be balky or resistant on one issue while generally cooperative. Where resistance becomes common and accommodation is abandoned, rebellion is more likely to occur. When social change happened at a slower pace, and the family, educational, and occupational life of one generation was similar to that of the one before, various *rites of passage* and ceremonies of initiation provided clear guidelines on proceeding from childhood to adult status. Often religious ceremonies, such as confirmations and bar mitzvahs, or educational ceremonies, such as graduations, marked the age at which an individual in her or his teens became an adult, able to establish a separate nuclear family and take on an occupation. The ceremonies served these functions (Eisenstadt, 1972: 18):

The transmission of the cultural lore with its instructions about proper behavior, both through formalized teaching and through various ritual activities; . . . is

The traditional Jewish bar mitzvah ceremony is a rite of passage that once marked the transition from childhood to adulthood but today marks the transition from childhood to adolescence. SOURCE: Grette Manheim/DPI.

combined with: A relaxation of the concrete control of the adults over the erstwhile adolescents and its substitution by self-control and adult responsibilities.

While many in the culture continue to observe the forms of various *rites of passage*, in substance there is no longer a clear passage for adolescents out of that status in family, church, or school into independent adult status. There are symbolic changes, of course, such as acquiring a driver's license, leaving home to attend college, or taking one's first apartment, but these events do not have the formal cultural recognition as symbols given to *rites of passage*.

Jesse Bernard refers to turning points in adolescent development which are tied not to an orderly sequence of changes but to some critical event so that, "a new definition of reality creates a new reality.... [T]he world 'tilts' in a new direction" (Bernard in Dragastin and Elder, 1975: 243). Sexual initiation may be such a turning point. For some, the very absence of such turning point events may have profound effects. The first date may mean as much as the absence of that experience.

The concept of *developmental tasks** is useful in considering the multiple problems of adolescents adjusting to the contemporary social system. From childhood to old age, individuals have developmental tasks which Robert Havighurst defines as (1953:2)

tasks which arise at or about a certain period in the life of an individual, successful achievement of which leads to his (or her) happiness and to success with later tasks, while failure leads to unhappiness in the individual, disapproval by the society, and difficulty with later tasks.

Havighurst delineates eight such developmental tasks in adolescence:

1. acceptance of one's physical characteristics

2. development of appropriate relations with age-sex mates

3. development of appropriate relations with members of the opposite sex

4. development of emotional independence from adults

5. development of a personal set of values

6. development of civic competence

7. preparation for marriage and family life

8. preparation for economic independence

There are so many interrelationships among the developmental tasks that it may be hard to achieve any one of them without mastery of some others. Learning to date requires that an adolescent accept his or her physical characteristics and develop relationships with peers of the same sex who can serve as role models. Where dating leads to marriage, emotional independence from parents is important (lest the bride or groom go home to mother), and in our society, economic independence is considered desirable. Yet it now takes longer to train successfully for economic independence, thereby prolonging dependence upon adults (usually parents), and extending nonadult status.

ACHIEVING A SENSE OF SELF-IDENTITY In the course of finding our way through the labyrinth of developmental tasks, we make and remake our sense of identity. In fact, the achievement of developmental tasks gives us most of our answers to the classic question, Who am I? as the following quotation discusses.[1]

---

[1] "Emergence of Identity," from *Report to the President: White House Conference on Children* (Washington, D.C., U.S. Government Printing Office, 1970) as reported in David Gottlieb, *Children's Liberation,* © 1973. Adapted by permission of Prentice-Hall, Inc., Englewood Cliffs, New Jersey.

ADOLESCENCE AND THE LIFE CYCLE 137

Pushing the "right" image. SOURCE: Reprinted by permission of Dana Perfumes Corporation.

To discuss the problems of emergence of identity, some common understandings about the meaning of "identity" are important. In the behavioral science literature, having a sense of identity has come to mean being able to answer satisfactorily the questions, "Who am I?" and "Where am I going?" Some would add, "Where did I come from?" The "Who am I?" includes knowing what I can do, what I am unable to do, what kind of person I am, and what is my best way of doing things. The "Where am I going?" includes an understanding of such things as what I can become, what I can learn to do, what I cannot learn to do, and what I want to become.

A strong sense of identity, however, is not enough. What is needed is a healthy sense of identity — one both favorable and realistic. The following characteristics have been attributed to the person with a healthy sense of identity:

A feeling of being in one piece, with an integrated rather than confused or diffused self-concept

Certainty about one's place in the world and how to behave

Autonomy as a person and confidence in self, ability to establish and maintain independent judgments without reference to external sources

Insistence upon being oneself rather than playing at being oneself

High capacity for empathy and for respecting the identity of others.

There are many types of identity — family, ethnic and cultural, religious, political, economic, physical, sexual, and intellectual. Identity involves all aspects of a person's being. . . .

A presidential task force charged with reporting findings to the White House Conference on Children identified the following major obstacles to the emergence of strong healthy identities ("Emergence of Identity," 1970):

deprivation (economic, psychological, social, cultural)

sex discrimination and overemphasis on socially determined sex differences unrelated to sexuality

ethnic, racial, and religious prejudice and discrimination

taboos against acceptance of biological identity

taboos against acceptance and expression of affection

failure to learn skills of mastery and competence

overemphasis on conformity and uniformity with a resultant discrepancy between a healthy identity and a functional identity.

Adult responsibilities sometimes come in a particularly stressful way. Some teenagers become parents when they are scarcely out of the nest themselves. Through the loss of a parent, another may be thrust early into the breadwinner role. For others, the pain may come from developing independent points of view that force confrontations with those whom they have loved and respected.

The Bill Mauldin cartoon illustrates the generational dilemma. The cartoon could refer to many issues, for example, a typical adult's admiration for the industrial growth and expansion of the nation's economy, which has provided considerable economic security for most. Viewing the same economic structure, many young people have noted that uncontrolled industrial growth is creating destructive air and water pollution. Taking one side or the other on such a question (even though there are not necessarily opposite views on all questions), may result in disapproval by society, or more precisely by particular segments of society. An adolescent may then find that he or she will have to face disapproval either by parents or by peers. Role strain may result (see Chapter 2).

The rapid changes in social life which have been taking place during the birth cycle interval in our time make for many value conflicts. Whether an adolescent decides to live with a member of the opposite sex while in college, as one-fifth to one-third now do (Hudson and Henze, 1973), whether he or she attempts to modify the profit emphasis of the American work ethic toward a social ethic, which emphasizes the rights of minorities and restricts industrial damage to the environment (Flacks, 1971), or takes a stand on any other contemporary issue, it is inevitable that adolescents will face disapproval by some of their elders and some of their peers. As a culture, American society is long past the era of apprenticeship through family socialization.

ADOLESCENT REBELLIOUSNESS Resistance has taken many forms, including major movements challenging the status quo on civil rights, war, and ecological issues. One tangible result of pressures by youth was the passage of the constitutional amendment lowering the voting age from twenty-one to eighteen years — and implicitly speeding adult status. The experienced cultural anthropologist Margaret Mead questions the popular view that the widespread youth–adult conflict is caused by such alleged factors as the collapse of the family, the triumph of soulless technology, or a final breakdown of the establishment. Rather, Mead notes that (1970b: 23)

behind these attributions there is a more basic conflict between those for whom the present represents no more than an intensification of our existing . . . culture, in which peers are more than ever replacing parents as the significant models of behavior, and those who contend that we are in fact entering a totally new phase of cultural evolution.

SOURCE: Copyright © 1970 Courtesy of Wil-Jo Associates, Inc. and Bill Mauldin.

To a considerable extent, adolescent rebellion is a widespread attempt by young people to adjust to a social world that includes many new elements. Mass communication and rapid land, sea, and air transportation have put an end to cultural isolation. No national, racial, or religious group can remain an isolated social island. The urbanization that brings into close proximity people of different social classes and outlooks is worldwide. If a world community has not yet emerged, world communication has. The future may even bring the global village based on mass communication described by McLuhan and Fiore (1970).

Thus, it is not surprising that the challenge to the status quo in American society — whether on a large social issue such as racial equality or on a mass individual one such as intimate male-female living patterns — has been initiated and practiced by the young (Flacks, 1971). Furthermore, such challenges to the status quo have been worldwide, in urban societies as diverse as Czechoslovakia, Great Britain, Japan, and the Soviet Union (Mead, 1970a).

The general adult response to adolescent challenges has been one of accommodation. Most families continue to stay together; over half of state budgets are allotted to public education. Yet, there is substantial evidence of adult resistance and measurable hostility toward adolescents. Young people are often unsettling to older adults who also grew up in a rapidly changing, though a very different, cultural era. Hostility from adults also arises from our cultural support for youth and beauty, which causes anxiety among those growing older.

ADOLESCENCE AS A TRANSITIONAL STAGE AND AS A SUBCULTURE Adolescence can be considered a transitional stage from childhood to adulthood or a subculture different from the rest of the culture (Berger, 1963; Gazell and Gitchoff, 1973). Until recent years, the standard approach was that the teenage years are basically a stage to go through and grow out of in the process of socialization from childhood to adulthood. The subculture approach holds that teenagers exhibit all the characteristics of a separate cultural group, including association with age-mates, special tastes in music and fashions, a critical view of the status quo, and differential treatment by society in general.

The concept of an adolescent subculture gained popularity with James S. Coleman's *The Adolescent Society* (1961). In more recent literature, however, numerous authors have attacked the concept of stormy and rebellious adolescents in their own small society as inaccurate, stressing evidence of many sources of agreement between adolescents and their parents (Matteson, 1975: 92–95).

SUBCULTURE

From: J. Milton Yinger, "Contraculture and Subculture," *American Sociological Review* 25 (1960), pp. 627–628.

The variety of referents for the term subculture is very wide because the normative systems of sub-societies can be differentiated on many grounds. The groups involved may range from a large regional subdivision to a religious sect with only one small congregation. The distinctive norms may involve many aspects of life — religion, language, diet, moral values — or, for example, only a few separate practices among the members of an occupational group. Further distinctions among subcultures might be made on the basis of time (has the subculture persisted through a number of generations?), origin (by migration, absorption by a dominant society, social or physical segregation, and other sources), and *by the mode of relationship** to the surrounding culture (from indifference to conflict). Such wide variation in the phenomena covered by a term can be handled by careful specification of the several grounds for subclassification... All societies have differentiating roles, but only heterogeneous societies have subcultures... subculture... refers to norms that set a group apart from, not those that integrate a group with, the total society. Subcultural norms... are unknown to, looked down upon, or thought of as separating forces by the other members of a society.

* Emphasis added, as it is the mode of relationship that distinguishes adolescence as a subcultural group.

The transitional view has much to support it. Most adolescents do not exhibit serious delinquent behavior or life styles which totally breach relations with parents or adults generally. Furthermore, teenagers lack the intergenerational continuity and resources of other cultural groups. Given the brevity of adolescence and domination by the adult world, some authors see adolescent culture as a myth (Elkin and Westley, 1955, Bealer, et al., 1965, Matteson, 1975).

Yet clear social forces are at work both within the peer group and from adult sources that have resulted in aspects, if not full development, of an adolescent subculture. Let's look at peer relationships. The adolescent stage in the family life cycle is a time when the generation gap is keenly felt. Thomas Cottle goes so far as to say, "There is no even exchange between generations, nor is there ever a possibility for it. Parents are by definition not peers, and their concern does not imply that they become colleagues" (Cottle, 1971, cited in Gottlieb, 1973: 87-88).

Teenagers share such developmental tasks as a need to achieve emotional independence from parents, deciding on choices about careers, and establishing identities as members of their own generation (see Havighurst, 1953: 11-119, Elder in Dragaston and Elder: 1975: 10). Eisenstadt draws these factors together and argues that there *is* a youth culture that attempts to accommodate to the stresses caused by discontinuity between childhood learning and expectations and later experience.

CONTRACULTURE AND THE HIPPIE MOVEMENT The alternative-life-style movement of the hippies in the period roughly 1967-1970 was an element of adolescent subculture. It is described by John Robert Howard's article "The Hippie Community: Deviant Togetherness."[2]

Howard observed that the hippie movement, which appears to have begun to develop some integrative capabilities in late 1966, had managed by the summer of 1967 to achieve not only some specific objectives among its members but to make itself visible to the nation. Although its major centers were the Greenwich Village area of New York and the Haight-Ashbury (called Hashbury) area of San Francisco, other major communities developed rapidly. Unlike the Beatniks of the late 1950s, whose mode of dress often included black clothing, and whose tendency was to cluster together away from the eyes of non-Beats, the hippies made known their presence by costume and cosmetics (including, for some, body paint). Their defiance of conventional norms shocked some, amused others. While it is not possible to describe an accurate profile for all hippies, because different hippie communities developed individual alternative values and norms, some generalizations regarding beliefs and practices can be made.

The hippies were young. A famous slogan developed by radical media figure Abbie Hoffman, "Don't Trust Anyone over Thirty," caught the essence of a movement of young people, many of them runaways, who had become disenchanted with what they saw as adult hypocrisies and mismanagement, abuses of power, violations of basic human rights, and general tediousness.

The hippies were against the obsession with acquiring wealth and personal property, repressive schooling, the regimentation of work (nine-to-five jobs) in our society, sexual repression, and war.

They were for enhancing creative powers and insight (to which end many used consciousness-expanding drugs, usually illegal), flower power (learning to spread the power of love to right evil), doing one's own thing (as long as it doesn't hurt someone else), and sharing (financially, sexually, intellectually).

As the havens for cultural dropouts became known, large numbers crowded into the urban centers, straining not only the forces of the law but also the resources of those already there. In San Francisco, a group called the Diggers took responsibility for getting food (sometimes restaurant dis-

---

[2] Adapted from "The Flowering of the Hippie Movement" by John Robert Howard in volume no. 382 of *The Annals* of the American Academy of Political and Social Science. Copyright 1969 by The American Academy of Political and Social Science. All rights reserved.

142 ISSUES FACING AMERICAN INDIVIDUALS

Different forms of expression. SOURCE: (a) Jeff Albertson/Stock Boston; (b) Sepp Seitz/Magnum.

cards) for the Hashbury people, a task which rapidly became monumental. Other hippies spread across the land developing communes, or total-living communities, on religious, sexual, or economic bases. This withdrawal from the larger society combined with cohesion around commonly held values and norms is subcultural in nature. Where it actively opposed dominant cultural values and norms, it was named the counter-culture.

The cohesion around basic principles was occasionally demonstrated to the dismay of police, politicians, and conservative Americans in mass demonstrations focused on specific issues, such as protesting the American involvement in Vietnam.

Even the music of the time was influenced by the hippie urge to transcend conventions. The Doors and Jim Morrison urged people to get high ("Light My Fire," "Break on Through"); Jefferson Airplane (now Starship) adapted Alice in Wonderland to contemporary America ("White Rabbit"), Strawberry Alarm Clock encouraged us to dabble in incense and peppermints in the song of that name. Acid rock, raga rock, heavy-metal rock moved forward to enliven the music scene. And rock festivals brought the like-minded in droves. The concept of fellowship and cooperation expressed at Woodstock, even though it was later marred by violent concerts such as Altamont, still lives in the memories of some as the best and most beautiful merging of music and philosophy of hippiedom.

To the non-hippie, the rejection of the work ethic, the renunciation of fashion from Nieman-Marcus for fashion from Goodwill, the apparent unashamed enjoyment of their minds and bodies was enough to stir the deepest passion for violence. So it is not surprising that heads got cracked, noticeably at the 1968 Democratic National Convention.

Not every hippie was together with every other hippie, any more than all other Americans agreed on everything. But the adherence to general philosophical positions, the total living experience in which hippies looked to each other rather than to straight society for religion, financial help, camaraderie, and knowledge represented an attempt to develop functional alternatives for meeting their needs through replacement of existing institutions with varieties more workable for them.

The hippies held together for a time, then as personal experiences and changes in culture and the winding down of the war caused the alternative lifestyle to work less well for individuals, people began to drift away. The deviant threat to the society dissipated, leaving behind the truly criminal who had gravitated to the edges of the movement, the disoriented, the ill, and a few other lost souls. What was their legacy? John Robert Howard answers (1969:55):

In summary, the hippies have commented powerfully on some of the absurdities and irrationalities of the society. It is unlikely that the straight will throw away his credit cards and move to a rural commune, but it is equally unlikely that he will very soon again wear the emblems of his straightness with quite so much self-satisfaction.

ADOLESCENT-ADULT ATTITUDE DIFFERENCES

There are other less dramatic indicators of increasing adolescent independence, in attitudes at least, from the culture of their elders. One such indicator is a change in religious attitudes through the years. One study, the findings of which parallel other research, compared religious attitudes among college students in 1967 with those held in 1948. Since almost half of all adolescents now go to college (*Current Population Reports,* 1971), and since college-trained people fill most influential economic, social, and government positions, such a sample is of particular interest for trend analysis. In both years, the reported early influence of religion on student respondents was much the same: about two-thirds of both groups reported very marked or moderate influence (Hastings and Hoge, 1970). But in 1967, most students indicated a general decline in traditional religious influence among Roman Catholics, Protestants, and to a lesser extent Jews. As the researchers concluded (Hastings and Hoge, 1970: 28):

For both liberal and conservative [religious] groups the picture is one of considerable disaffection, with large numbers of students departing entirely from any traditional religious identification at all.

The study also provides evidence that students question the need for religion; some of them suggested that a new type of religion is needed (Hastings and Hoge, 1970: 18). There is a continuing concern with ethical and moral questions. In more recent data, Daniel Yankelovich found in a sample of college and noncollege youth in 1973 that religion was regarded as a very important personal value by only 42 percent of the noncollege youth interviewed, and 28 percent of college youth (Yankelovich, 1974: 93). The ranking of religion among other important values is found in Table 5-1. For both groups the percentages are far below those reported in 1969.

The decline in interest may be a source of tension with older Americans who are more supportive of traditional religion, and who may be made anxious by this lack of support their beliefs among the newer generation (recall here the discussion on the institution of religion in society).

Adolescent strivings for independence in a changing society pose dilemmas for many parents and other adults. On the one hand, adolescent life patterns are often quite different on such basic issues as occupational choice, marital status, and the desire to have children. Jobs are generally more complex, taking more extended training. Women are more often career oriented, and generally have less desire to have large families (Miles, 1971). The result is the emergence of a large group of young people striving for and exhibiting much independence from adults while still being economically dependent upon them.

Table 5-1 Personal and Social Values: Trend Data by Total Noncollege Youth Versus Total College Youth

	Noncollege % 1973	Noncollege % 1969	College % 1973	College % 1969
Welcome social changes				
More emphasis on self-expression	76	70	83	84
Less emphasis on money	74	54	80	72
More emphasis on law and order	68	81	51	58
More respect for authority	66	86	48	59
More emphasis on technological improvements	61	64	55	56
More acceptance of sexual freedom	47	22	61	43
Less emphasis on working hard	35	32	31	24
Very important personal values				
Love	88	90	87	85
Friendship	87	90	86	84
Privacy	78	74	71	62
Education	75	81	76	80

Table 5-1 Personal and Social Values: Trend Data by Total Noncollege Youth Versus Total College Youth (continued)

	Noncollege % 1973	Noncollege % 1969	College % 1973	College % 1969
Very important personal values (cont.)				
Doing things for others	64	55	56	51
Living a clean, moral life	57	78	34	46
Religion	42	65	28	39
Patriotism	40	61	19	35
Money	34	40	20	18
Changing society	27	29	24	33
Belief in traditional American values				
People should save money regularly	80	89	71	76
Private property is sacred	74	88	67	76
A "strong" person can control own life	70	77	65	62
Competition encourages excellence	66	81	62	72
Hard work will always pay off	56	79	44	57
Activities thought to be morally wrong				
Extramarital sexual relations	65	78	60	77
Having an abortion	48	63	32	36
Relations between consenting homosexuals	47	72	25	42
Casual premarital sexual relations	34	58	22	34
Reasons worth fighting a war for				
Counteracting aggression	53	67	50	57
Containing communism	50	69	30	43
Protecting own national interest	49	66	34	38
Protecting our allies	46	50	34	38
Fighting for our honor	43	59	19	25
Maintaining our position of power in world	40	51	23	25
Keeping a commitment	23	28	11	14
Restraints willingly and easily accepted				
Prohibition against mind-expanding drugs*	71	79	73	73
Power and authority of the police	60	79	48	48
Power and authority of the "boss" in a work situation	57	71	44	49
Prohibition against marijuana	49	71	38	49
Conformity in matters of dress and personal grooming	42	54	33	33
Outward conformity for the sake of career or job advancement	37	35	20	14
Abiding by laws you do not agree with	24	34	12	15

* Asked about "LSD" in 1960. Asked about "mind-expanding drugs" in 1973.

SOURCE: *The New Morality: A Profile of American Youth in the Seventies* by Daniel Yankelovich. Copyright 1974 by McGraw-Hill Book Company. Used with permission of McGraw-Hill Book Company.

SOURCE: Reprinted by permission of Jules Feiffer.

DEPENDENCE VS. INDEPENDENCE This pattern of dependence in need, independence in behavior generates tensions between adults and adolescents. There are fewer tasks for teenagers to perform at home than there were in farm families. Even farms today have automated many tasks, such as the feeding of animals and the milking of cows, just as many urban tasks, such as delivering groceries and running elevators, have been eliminated by automation. Now teenagers must compete with adults for unskilled and semiskilled jobs in a declining market. Adolescents have the highest unemployment rate of any age category (18.4 percent in June, 1976, according to the Labor Department) and are less successful than adults in getting jobs.

There is an analogy between adolescents and newly arrived ethnic minority groups. Both adolescents and immigrants are faced with the developmental task of achieving economic security while they are under pressure to change the life style they adhere to and become socialized into the dominant culture. The general cultural imagery of the two groups shows some similarities. As Edgar Friedenberg notes, both adolescents and minority groups tend to enter the society in a low socioeconomic status, and both are depicted (1967: 50–51)

as childish and irresponsible, warmhearted and lovable, but uncontrolled and unstable — their broad jollity shifts easily to whimsical and destructive brutality. They excel in crude expression, in dancing and jazz and sports; the spirit of Dionysius is barely contained in the body of Apollo.

Faced with changing circumstances, adolescents do not strongly identify with localized institutional structures such as neighborhood or religion. One analyst describes this as a *ghetto situation,* typified by "high exposure to one's own kind, low income, and uncertainty of residential and general future" (Lofland, 1968: 238). Out of these circumstances comes behavior that is often viewed by much of the adult world as deviant and troublesome. This aspect of adolescent behavior calls for attention and we turn to it in the next section.

ADOLESCENTS' RESPONSES TO THEIR POSITION IN SOCIETY

Adolescents' responses to their unclear status in society take many forms. Many seek early adult status. While few marry early, about 90 percent of high schools in the United States report at least one student marriage every year (Ramsey, 1967: 41). About one-third of all students leave high school before graduating, primarily to seek employment (Elliott, 1966: 307).

RULE-BREAKING Given the changing values and practices in sexual conduct, reaction to prolonged schooling, and adaptation to a changing occupational structure, many adolescents respond to social life in a way that is viewed by adults as deviant. *Deviance** means rule-breaking; *deviants* are rule-breakers (Manning and Truzzi, 1972: 176). Not all adolescent rule-breaking takes the form of illegal behavior. Remember that norms are rules, but not all norms are supported by law. Violations of formerly cherished values, such as premarital virginity and obedience to parental authority, may be forms of rule-breaking. Furthermore, it is useful to distinguish between deviant behavior which is not designed to change the society and that which aims to create new acceptable forms of behavior. Examples of the former are deciding to marry at a younger age than is normative or to enter an unpopular occupation or getting involved in delinquent or criminal activity. Some examples of behavior designed to change society are supporting the ecology movement[3] or participating in the civil rights movement for racial and sexual equality. There is frequently considerable overlap between behavior that is not oriented toward change and behavior that is oriented toward change.

Deviant adolescent behavior is so widespread that much research is focused on it (Sebald, 1977; Gazell and Gitchoff, 1973). It is useful to note here that the dominant adult society influences the way allegedly deviant adolescent behavior is viewed by some researchers. As Howard Becker observes about much of this research (1967: 3–4):

What laymen want to know about deviants is: Why do they do it? . . . What is there about them that leads them to do forbidden things? Scientific research has tried to find answers to these questions. In doing so it has accepted the common-sense assumption that there is something inherently deviant (qualitatively distinct) about acts that break (or seem to break) social rules. It has also accepted the common sense assumption that the deviant act occurs because some characteristic of the person who commits it makes it necessary or inevitable that he should. Scientists do not ordinarily question the label "deviant" when it is applied to particular acts or people but rather take it as a given. In so doing, they accept the values of the group making the judgment.

Becker implies that to accept automatically the values of the dominant adult society and to identify certain adolescent behavior as deviant is as dangerous to objective analysis as to reject adult values automatically. After all, there are variations among adults too, and all adolescents become adults. Without implicitly accepting or rejecting any set of values, we shall distinguish between individual and collective forms of adolescent deviancy.

---

[3] Keep in mind that mass behavior not oriented toward change may result in social change, while change-oriented behavior may not. For example, some major goals of the civil rights movement of the 1960s, in which a disproportionately large number of the participants were in their teens, have not yet fully been accomplished. Yet other kinds of mass phenomena of the 1960s (extramarital cohabitation on the part of millions of young people, for example) have been widely and quietly accepted in the 1970s.

INDIVIDUAL DEVIANCE The form of adolescent deviance that causes most adult concern is delinquency.[4] The Presidential Commission on Crime in a Free Society noted that the two main categories of criminal behavior are crimes against persons and crimes against property (*The Challenge of Crime in a Free Society*, 1967). As the commission reported (55–90), crime rates tend to be higher for middle and late adolescents than for any other age category. At least until the student protest movements of the 1960s, injury to persons and loss of property caused by illegal deviant acts was considered to be the major social problem related to adolescence.

We shall not use tables to indicate the extent of juvenile delinquency because they are as imprecise as are crime statistics generally (see Wolfgang, in Gazell and Gitchoff, 1973: 48–51). A reasonable estimate based upon a combination of studies is that somewhere between 2.5 and 5 percent of the teenage population commit acts that clearly violate the law (Ramsey, 1967: 97). Given an adolescent population in the United States of over 12 million (*Statistical Abstract of the United States,* 1971), the lower of these figures would still mean that several hundred thousand young persons each year engage in deviant acts that cause serious personal injury or property loss.

There is wide public agreement that juvenile law-breakers need to be brought under closer control. There is less consensus over illegal acts in which there is no victim. Legal prohibitions against cigarette smoking (not addictive drugs), voluntary sexual relations (not related to rape or venereal disease), and the like, are based more on notions of morality than on measurable damage to persons involved or to others in the community. Such prohibitions involve *labeling** the conduct immoral, and applying legal sanctions against it (Schur, 1965).

Such labeling of certain victimless acts as illegal has resulted in conflict between young people and adults for two main reasons. One is the double standard. Adults generally engage in or accept as lawful such behavior as smoking and drinking, but this behavior is generally prohibited to adolescents even when addictive drugs or drunkenness are not involved. Second, most adolescents do in fact do things unacceptable to general adult values; for example, by the late teens, most have engaged in sexual relations (Hunt, 1960a).

While most illegal juvenile acts do not add up to a social movement to change the society, they sometimes have latent change-inducing consequences. This is true of illegal activities with victims and without victims. Most deviant acts involving victims, such as willful injury or destruction of life or property, are committed not just by adolescents but by poor adolescents living in the central areas of major cities (Morris, 1962). There is a great deal of middle-class delinquency, but it is studied less (Shanley, 1967: 185). Gangs in the inner city have historically been common among adolescents whether among the national minorities of a half century ago (Thrasher, 1936) or the racial minorities of more recent years (Cohen, 1955). Opportunities also exist in inner cities for agents of organized crime to recruit adolescents (Cressey, 1970: 132–135).

The existence of gangs appears to be related to what some theorists call *differential association**; gang members engage in illegal activities because they are part of a peer group that does so (Sutherland and Cressey, 1955: 74–81). Additionally, what appears to cause much of this behavior is a sense of anomic detachment from the general society based on values that hold that the goals of economic security and social status (good jobs and respected roles) are desirable but the institutional means

---

[4] Delinquency is a nontechnical term which refers to a whole range of legal offenses. "Pure types do not exist, and there are many variants along the norm-violating continuum" (Kvaraceus, 1969: 464).

(good schools and jobs for adolescents) to those goals are not available to many poor adolescents (Cohen, 1955).

The *theory of deviant means* (Merton, 1938) helps explain some of the underlying causes of damaging juvenile behavior. Gang behavior takes on some characteristics of a social movement to change established social institutions when it enables a group to achieve generally desired goals. The illegal and damaging means to this end make adolescents reject the normative adult values and place them in sharp conflict with the adult world.

A clearer effort at social change is reflected in many of the protest movements of recent decades. Examples include the Berkeley Free Speech Movement in 1964, the antiwar protest at Kent State in 1970, and the 1975 student strike at Brown University against the alleged discriminatory act of raising tuition that would prevent the enrollment of many minority and low-income students.

DEVIANT ACTS AS COLLECTIVE BEHAVIOR[5]

While illegal deviant behavior helps to produce social change, it is not generally organized for that purpose. Adolescent behavior manifestly aimed at changing the values and behavior patterns in the society is more often associated with technically legal acts of social protest that are widely disapproved.

Reform movements are not new in American history, but the extent of adolescent involvement in them is. The abolitionist movement of the 1850s, and the labor movement of the 1930s were centered around concerns of the general adult population. But in the reform movements of the 1960s — mainly civil rights, antiwar, and ecology — active, organized youth was central (see: Bell, 1968/Braungart, 1972/Flacks, 1971/Lipset, 1971).

Why do analysts of adolescent behavior often combine the separate concepts of *deviance** and *collective behavior**? Peter Manning and Marcello Truzzi provide the answer.[6]

Deviance involves rule-breaking and rule-breakers; collective behavior involves the emergence of new forms of social relationships. In the extreme, the two categories are clearly distinguished: criminals and most deviants do not seek to change the social order or to innovate social arrangements; people involved in most social movements, cults, sects, and crowds do not engage in criminal activities. However, because change-oriented activities generate resistance, legal or informal, which leads to legal charges and enforcement against innovators, and because criminal activity is also used to create sociopolitical change (for example, bombings and terrorism), the line between deviance and collective behavior is rather blurred.

Violating some standard of behavior in a complex society is almost inevitable. The normative standards are vague; the expected degree of response, if specified at all, is uncertain; and response is based on the situation in which the violation occurs. We may, in fact, agree . . . that to deviate is natural. The implication of the above is that an act or behavior itself may be less important than people's response to it. For example, a suit was brought during the fall of 1970 to halt the Michigan–Michigan State football game. A large rock festival had been held in central Michigan in the late summer, and the usual huge crowd of musicians, drug freaks (both buyers and sellers), teeny-boppers, and travelers scandalized the local citizenry. A second hard-rock festival was planned for September 6, but it was cancelled when the county prosecutor obtained a restraining order against it. The suit against the football game was brought by a janitor at the University of

---

[5] *Collective behavior** is a sociological concept taken up at different points in the text, as noted in the subject index. Collective protest and social movements, discussed in this section, are given further attention in Chapter 8 on conflict and intergroup relations.

[6] Peter Manning and Marcello Truzzi, *Youth and Sociology*, © 1972, pp. 176–177. Reprinted by permission of Prentice-Hall, Inc., Englewood Cliffs, New Jersey 97632.

Michigan, formerly a student there and an ex-sports editor for the student paper. He stated, "I've decided to file this suit because Governor Milliken and other so-called law and order political figures in this state have selectively applied the law to repress one form of mass culture while allowing another to exist".... After the August rock festival, the governor of the state had said that if drugs and rock festivals were to be synonymous, there would be no more rock festivals in Michigan. Many localities passed ordinances strictly controlling gatherings of 5,000 or more people.

The suit filer charged that college football games were also synonymous with illegal possession of drugs (for example, alcohol).... The point of the challenge to the legal system is clear: the behavior of the spectators included many illegal acts at both "festivals." However, one was associated with hippie culture, youth, and immorality, while the other event was characterized as mature, adult, clean fun. A hearing dismissed the suit on the afternoon before the game.

Since the First Amendment to the Constitution guarantees the right to petition and assemble for redress of grievances, there is still a question of how youthful participation in lawful protest movements can be considered delinquent or deviant behavior. Edgar Friedenberg succinctly gives the reason (1967: 38):

It is difficult to keep discussion of *any* [emphasis added] topic related to adolescence from turning into a discussion of juvenile delinquency; I have even had participants, referring to a book I had written called *The Vanishing Adolescent,* identify it as *The Vanishing Delinquent,* without apparently noticing [the difference]. ...

SOCIAL MOVEMENTS TO CHALLENGE THE STATUS QUO The relatively high unemployment rates among both college and noncollege adolescents may be an underlying factor in *social movements** to challenge the status quo. It has been the case since the Depression years of the 1930s, that job-seekers in their teens and early twenties have consistently had an unemployment rate of two or more times that of older adults (*Social Indicators,* 1973: 116). While recent youth protesters have been mostly college students or young people working in jobs not requiring college training, this high unemployment factor is a constant worrisome reality.

The strike of young blue-collar workers in the General Motors plant in Lordstown, Ohio, in 1972, and the Free Speech Movement on the University of California, Berkeley, campus in 1964, were dramatic signs of discontent with the status quo among both noncollege and college youth (Levinson, 1973). Both groups are large and significant in potential impact.

Signs of alienation and resistance among young people no longer in school appear mainly among blue-collar workers in factories. Here are many who dropped out of high school or who entered the work force after graduating. Most of them do not like their work. In random sampling conducted by the University of Michigan Survey Research Center, fewer than one-quarter — 23 percent — indicated that they liked their jobs and would try to get into a similar type of work if they could start over again (Wilensky, 1967: 134).

With the significant exception of blacks and other racial minorities, the main concerns of noncollege young people are with their own conditions of life. Where larger social issues come into play, as in questions of civil rights, they often do so in connection with work, as when in 1972 young members of the United Auto Workers union elected blacks to replace older white union leaders in several northern locals (Levinson, 1973: 34). These acts were in the tradition of labor reforms for better working conditions, but instead of the usual demands for more pay, the major demand — supported mostly by young workers — was for less boredom on the assembly lines, and for the right *not* to work overtime, whatever the extra pay involved. (See the selection entitled Assembly Line in Chapter 3.) As reported in the *Wall Street Journal* (O'Donnell, 1973: 1):

The current negotiations between the United Auto Workers union and the nation's giant automobile companies are more than ever focusing on "the system" — the quality of life on the assembly line.

Protest among noncollege youth has received little attention in research and in the mass media, but it has been consequential. While declining in proportion, noncollege youth still represents over half the youthful population, and about one-third of union workers (Levinson, 1973: 34). Yet protest of more consequence emanates from late adolescent college youth, whose numbers are growing, and who already possess potential political power. In addition, they compose that sector of the population out of which emerge the most influential people in the society. Consequently, student protest is of particular interest as a challenge to the social system.

The student activists of the 1960s, and the population base they represented, posed strong challenges to the status quo. The activists tended to be found in the better institutions and were among the brightest students (Lipset, 1972: 123). About one-fifth of all students participated in protest demonstrations on such issues as civil rights or the Vietnam War. At such prestigious institutions as Berkeley, Harvard, and the University of Michigan, nearly half of all students participated (Kahn and Bowers, 1970). Many of them are still active, though in less dramatic ways.[7] Former activists are heavily concentrated in academic and human service work, while former student government members and those not politically involved work in the private sector of the economy (Fendrich, cited in Feldman and Thielbar, 1975: 357). As Fendrich observes: (p. 368)

In sum, the activists have not been co-opted during the ten years since they became involved in civil rights protests. They have resisted the moderating influences of getting married and having children. Nor have they allowed themselves to drift into a retreatist life-style. Instead they have combined ideological commitments with their occupational and political orientations.

Indeed the student movement was not restricted to a mere fringe of radicals in Students for a Democratic Society or the Student Non-Violent Coordinating Committee. This was made clear in a sampling of one hundred colleges and universities in 1966 (see Tables 5-2 and 5-3). These tables provide findings that demonstrate the wide involvement of many college students in the protests of the 1960s and the particularly high rate of involvement

Table 5-2 Percent of Students Active in Protest Movements by School Quality

	Top-ranking	Highly selective	Moderately selective	Not very selective
Percent involved	41	18	13	16
Number involved	110	228	305	214

SOURCE: Roger Kahn and William Bowers, "The Social Context of the Rank-and-File Student Activist: A Test of Four Hypotheses," *Sociology of Education* (Winter, 1970), Tables 5 and 7.

---

[7] Of course some activists remained visible well beyond the activist sixties. Sam Brown, a leader of a major antiwar rally in Washington, D.C., was elected treasurer of Colorado in 1974. Tom Hayden made a strong but unsuccessful bid to replace John Tunney as the Democratic senatorial candidate in California in 1976. Jerry Rubin and Abbie Hoffman are writers of books and screenplays.

Table 5-3 Percent of Students Active in Protest Movements by Indicators of Academic Achievement and School Quality

	Top-ranking	Highly selective	Moderately selective	Not very selective
B and above	47% (N=17)	32% (N=37)	14% (N=49)	11% (N=37)
B to C	47% (N=60)	16% (N=136)	11% (N=153)	16% (N=122)
C or below	27% (N=26)	13% (N=40)	13% (N=70)	16% (N=39)

SOURCE: Roger Kahn and William Bowers, "The Social Context of the Rank-and-File Student Activist: A Test of Four Hypotheses," *Sociology of Education* (Winter, 1970), Tables 5 and 7.

of students at the top-ranking colleges. It is interesting to note that as open protest appeared to subside in the early 1970s, increasing numbers of young women maintained an activist student role through the women's liberation movement. As with earlier protests, the greatest activity occurred at such prestigious institutions as Wesleyan and Dartmouth (Howe, 1973).

To maintain a fair perspective on youthful protest, it should be noted that most youth, whether college students or young union workers (who often have voted conservatively) did not take part in protests. Most seem to accept the system (Lipset, 1971). Although there are clear trends toward challenging the status quo on religious, sexual, and social attitudes and behavior, a high proportion of young people continue to accept the attitudes of the prevailing adult social world.

Taylor reports a Yankelovich poll on political orientations of the young and concludes from the data that even radicals seem to be middle-of-the-road on traditional values regarding patriotism, sex, and religion; many of them (55 percent) are from working class families or nonwhite groups (26 percent) who hold conventional standards of personal morality (Taylor, in Howe and Harrington, 1972: 182-183). Deviant political views may be more specialized than generalized.

LEGITIMACY OF LEGAL PROTESTS By common definitions of deviance, it is not easy to consider the participation of young people in legal protests as deviant behavior. A social phenomenon that is identified as a social problem involves *subjective* recognition that some condition in the society is a problem, an *objective* basis for the alleged problem, and *alleviation,* that is measures to correct the condition (Fuller and Myers, 1941). The first criterion is clearly met in the general adult opposition to the protesters' views. In one, perhaps extreme, case, the mother of a Kent State University student remarked, following the fatal shooting of four students by National Guardsmen, that had her son been a protester, he too would have deserved to die.

It is less easy to meet the second and third criteria, objective recognition and alleviation. Youth's involvement in protest is often viewed as problematically deviant behavior. Yet after reviewing the findings on student protests nationally on such issues as civil rights, war, and ecology, the Cox Commission reported that (1968: 4):

Today's students take seriously the ideals taught in schools and churches, and often at home, and then they see a system that denies its ideals in its actual life. Racial injustice and the war in Vietnam stand out as prime illustrations of our society's deviation from its professed ideals and of the slowness with which the system reforms itself.

The report, set up to analyze deviant behavior in young people, noted that the system — which is dominated by adults — has itself deviated from its own professed ideals. Furthermore, some issues that had been unpopular with the general public, including many provisions of the Civil Rights Act of 1964, have become more generally accepted.

ADOLESCENCE AND THE LIFE CYCLE 153

Young people have been involved in a wide variety of protest movements. SOURCE: (a) Copyright Tarentum, Pa. *Valley News Dispatch*; (b) Wide World Photos; (c) Bruce Davidson/Magnum; (d) Roger Malloch/Magnum.

Young protesters have become a more normative group, owing to changes in subjective social boundaries. This shift suggests some accommodation in society toward previously disapproved individual and collective adolescent behavior.

SOCIETAL ACCOMMODATION TO ADOLESCENT PROBLEMS

Given the considerable gap between adolescent and adult attitudes in general and behavior on a variety of social issues, what are the prospects for accommodation? With the notable exception of slavery and later racial friction, Americans have shown throughout their cultural history a good deal of flexibility and adaptation in the face of intergroup problems.

HISTORICAL ACCEPTANCE OF DISSENTING VIEWS Since the founding of the nation, there has been a continuous stream of challenges to the status quo. The past century and a half has seen people who own no property attain political rights, has seen slavery abolished, women's suffrage achieved, the labor movement begun, affirmative action programs developed, and so on. Over time, the perspectives and demands of the dissenters have often become part of the normative structure.

One reason for the success of such groups is that they were too large for others to ignore without losing social stability. Adolescents are now a large age group in the United States — over 12 million in a population of 210 million (*Statistical Abstract of the United States,* 1971). Given the age distribution at present, they will remain a sizable group until at least the 1990s. The large population of adolescents gives added meaning to the widespread deviant behavior discussed earlier. In the areas of victimless rule-breaking, past cultural experience suggests that there will be accommodation, and there is evidence that this is now occurring.

The Prohibition era of the 1920s may be instructive. At that time the Eighteenth Amendment to the Constitution, prohibiting the use of alcohol, was in effect. But so many people sold, bought, and drank liquor that the law could not be enforced; it was repealed by the Twenty-first Amendment in the early 1930s. Enforceable laws were passed to curb objectively damaging behavior, such as driving when drunk, which remains illegal, though the drinking of alcohol as such does not.

It was not true in the 1920s that everybody wanted to drink or even to allow others to do so. Nor is it true now that all adolescents are challenging prevailing values. For all their disaffection from adult values and behavior, most adolescents accept much of the system as it is. The adult world itself is divided in American society. There have always been political and social conservatives and liberals. Research shows that young people do not break totally from parental values but rather act out those values as their elders often do not (Braungart, 1972). While this does not alter the fact that differences exist between adolescent and adult life styles and responses to new occupational and social conditions, it argues against the probability of a total breach between the generations.

RESISTANCE VS. ACCEPTANCE One adult response to dissident adolescent behavior is the violent backlash, as after the 1968 Democratic national convention (Walker, 1968) and the shootings of students at Kent State and Jackson State Universities in 1970 (Scranton, 1970). The chief adult response, however, seems to be accommodation, much like that in the Prohibition era. This accommodation underlies the action of two-thirds of the states in dropping the voting age from twenty-one to eighteen in federal elections in 1972, and passage of a constitutional amendment for all states, although it is noteworthy that most young people eligible to vote have not done so. This national move to extend adult political rights to adolescents has been accompanied by other signs of accommodation. Until the 1960s, every state had laws against extramarital sexual relations. Given the realities of youthful activity, it was a clear act of accommodation when, in the early 1970s, nine states[8] eliminated laws restricting private sexual conduct between consenting adults, an age category that now includes at least those in the late adolescent years.

Perhaps more fundamental than this broadening of personal civil liberties are the more basic effects of extending the right to marry without parental consent and to assert political power through the vote. There are more and more young people on representative committees and boards in schools, and on policymaking bodies such as the various platform subcommittees of the Democratic and Republican parties. As with the end of Prohibition, these accommodations have decriminalized a good deal of previously forbidden but widely practiced adolescent behavior. Many activities which had been labeled deviant and illegal are now, if still sometimes deviant, no longer illegal or so widely viewed as delinquent. Quite aside from the issue of deviancy, such accommodations increasingly let adolescents take part in the society in a way that meets more of their individual and group needs. Yet, there still remain formidable subjective labeling and objective adjustment problems that confront adolescents in the society.

---

[8] Colorado, Connecticut, Delaware, Hawaii, Illinois, North Dakota, Ohio, Oregon, and Pennsylvania.

SUMMARY

The adolescent years are a period in which age-related problems become evident. As a stage in the general and family *life cycle**, adolescence is the time when the gulf between generations is wider than at any other stage. The *developmental tasks** adolescents face in moving from childhood to adulthood have become more complex in rapidly changing modern society. In the first century of our national existence, there was greater continuity of roles between the adolescent and parental generations. This has been called the *apprenticeship era*, in which transitional *rites of passage* from childhood to adulthood were made clear. New educational, occupational, and sex roles have brought new patterns of social life in the *birth cycle interval* between the adolescent and adult generations. The intergenerational conflicts that have emerged have given rise to what Ramsey has called "the era of adolescent rebellion."

One consequence is that contemporary adolescents have increasingly been characterized as an imperfect (not fully developed) *subculture** with minority status in the society. Until recently, hippies constituted a more developed subculture. As a subculture, adolescents have developed values and life styles that differ from the general adult forms. Responses of adolescents to their new position in society show a variety of both individual and collective behavior often viewed by adults as deviant. Individual behavior includes symptoms of seeking early adulthood status by marrying or dropping out of school to seek employment. Moreover, a higher proportion of adolescents than of any other age group engage in various forms of delinquency. Such behavior has led to research-based explanations including *labeling theory* and the *theory of deviant means*. Another response is collective protest designed to change the status and roles of adolescents and to alter other aspects of the social system. A relatively high proportion of adolescents engage in civil rights, ecological, and other social movements.

There are signs that adults are accommodating to the problems of adolescents. This reflects the American cultural tradition of flexible adaptation to challenges in the normative scheme of things. The lowering of the voting age to eighteen by constitutional amendment, and the increasing numbers of adolescents on policymaking bodies, are signs of societal accommodation, a process that results in policies which meet the individual and group needs of adolescents.

QUESTIONS FOR DISCUSSION

1. What makes the adolescent years particularly difficult in the United States? Is adolescence dysfunctional for our society? Does it have functional attributes?

2. Adolescents are being socialized into the larger society by a variety of social groupings. What complementary or conflicting socialization is likely to come from parents, teachers, and peers?

3. Robert Havighurst lists eight developmental tasks of the adolescent period. How are the tasks interrelated? Does the interrelationship affect the likelihood of accomplishing the tasks? How so?

4. Define the term *subculture*. To what extent do you believe adolescents do or do not constitute a subculture?

5. To what extent would you agree with Edgar Friedenberg's comparison of minorities with adolescents?

6. Merton's theory of deviant means and Becker's labeling theory have been used to explain various forms of individual deviant adolescent behavior. What are some examples of adolescent behavior that could be explained by one or the other of these perspectives?

7. Even legal activities of adolescents, such as engaging in unpopular social movements, may be viewed as deviant. What are some social costs of engaging in such forms of collective deviancy?

8. Why do some analysts refer to the adolescent subculture as *imperfect*? What would be a *perfect* subculture in Yinger's terms?

9. What has happened to the activist student leaders of the 1960s? Do you believe that they have been co-opted into the system, or has the system changed to accommodate the changes they advocated? Explain.

10. Review your understanding of the following terms and concepts:

family life cycle

birth cycle interval

deviance

subculture

developmental tasks

apprenticeship era

era of rebellion

labeling

differential association

theory of deviant means

REFERENCES

Bealer, Robert, Fern B. Willits and Peter Maida
   1965   Rural Youth in Crisis: Facts, Myths and Social Change. Washington, D.C.: United States Department of Health, Education and Welfare.

Becker, Howard
   1963   The Outsiders. Glencoe, Ill.: The Free Press.
   1967   Social Problems. New York: John Wiley & Sons.

Bell, Inge Powell
  1968 CORE and the Strategy of Non-Violence. New York: Random House.

Berger, Bennett
  1963 "On the youthfulness of youth cultures." Social Research 30: 319–342.

Bernard, Jesse
  1975 "Adolescence and socialization for motherhood." Sigmund E. Dragastin and Glen H. Elder, Jr. (eds.), Adolescence in the Life Cycle: Psychological Change and Social Context. Washington, D.C.: Hemisphere Publishing Corporation: 227–252.

Braungart, Richard
  1972 "Parental identification and student politics: an empirical reappraisal." P. Manning and M. Truzzi (eds.), Youth and Sociology. Englewood Cliffs, N.J.: Prentice-Hall: 357–366.

  1967 The Challenge of Crime in a Free Society: A Report by the President's Commission on Law Enforcement and the Administration of Justice. Washington, D.C.: Government Printing Office.

Cohen, Albert
  1955 Delinquent Boys: The Culture of the Gang. Glencoe, Ill.: The Free Press.

Coleman, James
  1961 Adolescent Society. Glencoe, Ill.: The Free Press.

  1971 Current Population Reports. Series P-20, Number 215 (March 5). Washington, D.C.: Government Printing Office.

Cottle, Thomas
  1971 Parent and Child — The Hazards of Equality from Time's Children: Impressions of Youth. Boston: Little, Brown. 1969. Cited in David Gottlieb (ed.), Children's Liberation. Englewood Cliffs, New Jersey: Prentice-Hall 1973: 87–101.

Cox Commission
  1968 Report of the Fact-Finding Commission Appointed to Investigate the Disturbances at Columbia University. New York: Vintage Books.

Cressey, Donald
  1970 "Organized crime and inner-city youth." Crime and Delinquency 16 (April, 1970): 132–135.

Davis, Kingsley
  1940 "The sociology of parent-youth conflict." American Sociological Review 5: 523–535.

Eisenstadt, S. N.
  1956 From Generation to Generation. Glencoe, Ill.: The Free Press.
  1972 "Archetypal patterns of youth." P. Manning and M. Truzzi (eds.), Youth and Sociology. Englewood Cliffs, N.J.: Prentice-Hall: 15–19.

Elder, Jr., Glen
  1975 Adolescence in the Life Cycle: An Introduction. Sigmund E. Dragastin and Glen H. Elder, Jr. (eds.), Adolescence in the Life Cycle: Psychological Change and Social Context. Washington, D.C.: Hemisphere Publishing Corporation.

Elkin, Frederick and William Westley
  1955 "The myth of adolescent culture." American Sociological Review 20: 680–684.

Elliott, Delbert
  1966 Delinquency, School Attendance and Dropout. Social Problems 13: 307–314.

Fenrich, James
1975 "Radicals revisited: long range effects of student protest." Originally in Journal of Voluntary Action Research, Association of Voluntary Action Scholars, Boston College, Chestnut Hill, Mass. Reprinted in Saul D. Feldman, and Gerald W. Thielbar (eds.), Life Styles: Diversity in American Society. Boston: Little, Brown: 349–359.

Flacks, Richard
1971 Youth and Social Change. Chicago: Markham Publishing Company.

Friedenberg, Edgar
1967 "Adolescence as a social problem." H. Becker (ed.), Social Problems. New York: John Wiley and Sons: 35–75.

Fuller, Richard and Richard Myers
1941 "The natural history of a social problem." American Sociological Review 6: 320–328.

Gazell, James and G. Thomas Gitchoff (eds.)
1973 Youth, Crime, and Society. Boston: Holbrook Press.

Gibbons, Don
1976 Delinquent Behavior. Engelwood Cliffs, New Jersey: Prentice-Hall.

Gottlieb, David (ed.)
1973 Children's Liberation. Englewood Cliffs, New Jersey: Prentice-Hall.

Hastings, Philip and Dean Hage
1970 "Religious change among college students over two decades." Social Forces 49: 16–28.

Havighurst, Robert
1953 Human Development and Education. New York: Longman, Green.

Hill, Richard
1964 "Methodological issues in family development research." Family Process, March, 1964, 3: 186–206.

Howard, John Robert
1969 "The flowering of the hippie movement." The Annals of the Academy of Political and Social Science 382: 43–55.

Howe, Florence
1973 "Women in higher education: no ivory towers." Ms. Magazine (September): 46–47; 78–80.

Howe, Irving and Michael Harrington (eds.)
1972 The Seventies: Problems and Proposals. New York: Harper and Row.

Hudson, John and Lura Henze
1974 "Personal and family characteristics of cohabitating college students." Journal of Marriage and the Family 36: 722–727.

Hunt, Morton
1973a Sexual Behavior in the 1970's. Chicago: Playboy Press.
1973b Sexual behavior in the 1970's. Playboy (October): 84–88; 194–207.

Kahn, Roger and William Bowers
1970 "The social context of the rank-and-file student activist: a test of four hypotheses." Sociology of Education 43: 38–55.

Kvaraceus, William
1969 "Delinquency prevention." Crime and Delinquency 15 (October): 463–470.

Levison, Andrew
1973 "The rebellion of blue collar youth." Annual Editions: Readings in Social Problems '73/'74. Guilford, Conn.: Dushkin Publishing Group: 31–35.

Lipset, Seymour
1971 "Youth and politics." R. Merton and R. Nisbet (eds.), Contemporary Social Problems, 3rd Edition. New York: Harcourt Brace Jovanovich: 743–791.
1972 Rebellion in the University. Boston: Little, Brown.

Lofland, John
   1968   "The youth ghetto." Journal of Higher Education 39: 121-143.

Manning, Peter and Marcello Truzzi
   1972   Youth and Sociology. Englewood Cliffs, N.J.: Prentice-Hall.

Matteson, David
   1975   Adolescence Today: Sex Roles and the Search for Identity. Homewood, Illinois: Dorsey.

McLuhan, Marshall and Quentin Fiore
   1970   The Medium is the Massage. New York: Random House.

Mead, Margaret
   1970a   Culture and Commitment. New York: Doubleday.
   1970b   "Youth revolt: the future is now." Saturday Review (January 10): 23-25; 113.

Merton, Robert
   1938   "Social structure and anomie." American Sociological Review 3: 677-682.

Michener, James
   1971   Kent State: What Happened and Why. New York: Random House.

Miles, Rufus
   1971   "The future population of the United States." Population Bulletin 27: 5-31.

   1970   "Monthly vital statistics report." Annual Summary for the United States (October 21). Washington, D.C.: Government Printing Office.

Morris, Terrance
   1962   "A critique of area studies." M. Wolfgang, L. Savits and N. Johnstone (eds.), The Sociology of Crime and Delinquency. New York: John Wiley and Sons: 191-198.

Neugarten, Bernice
   1967   "The aged in American society." H. Becker (ed.), Social Problems. New York: John Wiley and Sons. 167-196.

O'Donnell, James
   1973   "On the line." The Wall Street Journal (July 25): 1 and 21.

Ramsey, Charles
   1967   Problems of Youth. Belmont, Cal.: Dickenson.

Schur, Edwin
   1965   Crimes Without Victims. Englewood Cliffs, N.J.: Prentice-Hall.

Scranton Report
   1970   Presidential Commission on Campus Unrest. Washington, D.C.: Government Printing Office.

Sebald, Hans
   1977   Adolescence: A Sociological Analysis. Englewood Cliffs, N.J.: Prentice-Hall.

Shanley, Fred
   1967   "Middle-class delinquency as a social problem." Sociology and Social Research 51: 185-198. Reprinted in James A. Gazell and G. Thomas Gitchoff (eds.), Youth, Crime, and Society. Boston: Holbrook Press: 298-313.

   1973   Social Indicators. U.S. Bureau of the Census, Washington, D.C.: Government Printing Office.

   1971   Statistical Abstract of the United States. Washington, D.C.: Government Printing Office.

Sutherland, Edwin and Donald Cressey
   1955   Principles of Criminology. Philadelphia: Lippincott.

Taylor, Gus
   1972   "Generation gap or gap within a generation?" Irving Howe and Michael Harrington (eds.), The Seventies: Problems and Proposals. New York: Harper and Row.

Thrasher, Edwin
   1936   The Gang. Chicago: University of Chicago Press.

Van Gennep, Arnold
   1960   The Rights of Passage. Chicago: University of Chicago Press.

Walker, Daniel
   1968   Rights in Conflict. New York: New American Library.

Wilensky, Harold
   1967   "Work as a social problem." H. Becker (ed.), Social Problems. New York: John Wiley and Sons: 117–166.

Wolfgang, Marvin
   1967   "The culture of youth." Ronald Steel (ed.), New Light on Juvenile Delinquency. New York: The H. W. Wilson Company: 101–107. Reprinted in James A. Gazell and G. Thomas Gitchoff (eds.), Youth, Crime, and Society. Boston: Holbrook Press: 43–51.

Yankelovich, Daniel
   1974   The New Morality: A Profile of American Youth in the 70's. New York: McGraw-Hill.

Yinger, Milton
   1960   "Contraculture and subculture." American Sociological Review 25: 625–635.

Chapter 6

SOCIAL CLASS AND POVERTY

All animals are equal, but some are more equal than others.

George Orwell

SOCIAL CLASS AND SOCIAL OPPORTUNITY

How is it that one individual attends a costly private college, another a state university, a third a junior college, and a fourth drops out of high school? Why does one individual earn twice the average national income while another earns half as much and has trouble maintaining a home and family? Is it entirely a matter of individual talent and motivation, or do social factors influence the way in which personal qualities are developed?

One way of gaining insight into these questions is to look at *social classes**, or groupings of people with common social and economic — socioeconomic — positions in society. The social class a person is born into influences specific roles and tasks throughout the life cycle. Affected are the kind of neighborhood one grows up in, the dating pattern pursued, educational aspirations, occupational goals, and every other aspect of one's life style. This is not only a matter of personal taste and talent. It is unlikely that even a Michelangelo, born of poor parents, could have exhibited his special artistic talents if he had not been supported by members of a more secure social class in Italian society who recognized and encouraged the development of his talent. What was true for Michelangelo is true for most of us, whatever our talents and interests.

SOCIAL CLASS AS A BASIS FOR ANALYZING SOCIETY Social class is a popular concept, but only part of its more general meaning is widely understood. When someone is said to have *class*, the intent may be similar to calling a person cultured. *Class* is also used to refer to a person who performs a role particularly well. Such popular conceptions call attention to major differences in the everyday life styles of different social classes. Yet these differences in life style are symptomatic of the profound meaning which social-class status has for individuals and the whole society.

One of the earliest social scientific analyses of social class was made by Karl Marx in the nineteenth century. Marx defined social classes entirely in economic terms, as economic interest groups. In modern industrial society, he said, the two major classes are the working proletarian class and the managerial bourgeois class (Marx, 1956 trans.).

Marx, who with his associate Friedrich Engels wrote *The Communist Manifesto*, believed that history bore out a pattern of exploitation of the lower class (proletarians) by the owners of the instruments of production (the controllers of the economy or bourgeoisie). He believed that only through revolution based on development of class consciousness (awareness of common problems) could the *have nots* gain society's rewards. Such consciousness, he said, is blocked by the *haves'* manipulations of the major social institutions.

Marx's view, which puts the economic order at the basis of society's workings, is called *economic determinism*; it is based on the *cash nexus*, or hub, around which the spokes of society's wheel are mounted. Whoever controls the economy exploits those who lack control. In an industrial society, the owners of the instruments of production (the factories, the tools, and the capital) control the workers. This raw economic control is masked by manipulation of the major institutions, or superstructure, which rest on this economic base. The idea is shown diagrammatically in Figure 6-1.

BROADENING THE MEANING OF CLASS Early in the twentieth century, Max Weber, another German analyst, broadened the definition of class by adding to Marx's *economic order* the *social order*, based on the distribution of social honor or prestige, and the *political order*, based on the distribution of political power (Weber, 1946 trans., 180–184). More recent social class theorists have added other criteria for measuring social class position. Gerhard Lenski (1966) observes that modern society stresses credentials such as academic degrees and considers educational achievement a major class factor.

Figure 6-1 Marx's superstructure.

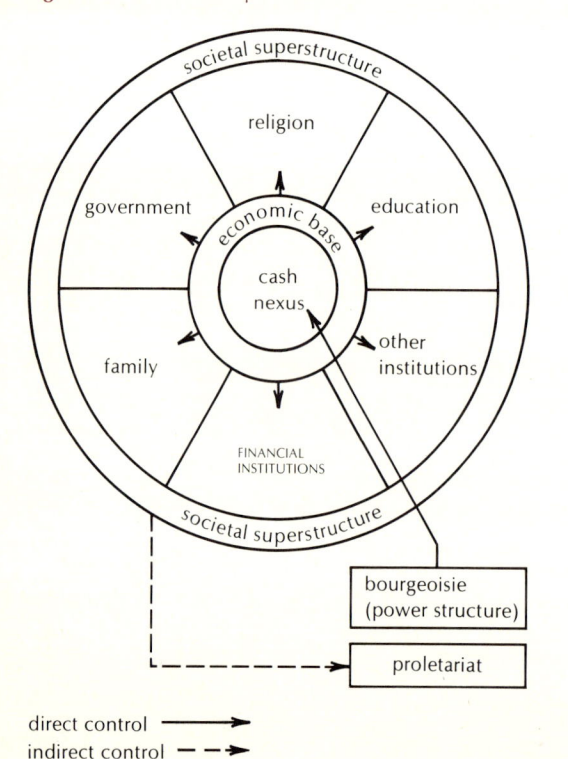

Other theorists note the need to consider the consequences of subjective class factors. For example, people's perception of their class status may differ from their objective position based on such criteria as occupation and education (Centers, 1949; Hodge and Trieman, 1968). Such self-perceptions have a real effect on individual values and life styles. Another mode of subjective criteria used in evaluating social class is the rating of others through the *reputational approach,* by which people in a community identify and rate others as having much or little prestige in a community. Informal rating processes are happening in every community and greatly influence who has power and what kind — political, economic, or other (Kornhauser, 1966). While a society may develop consistent indicators of social class, additional stratification systems based on other criteria may emerge within the larger framework. (See the selection entitled "Stratification Among Autocrossers.")

STRATIFICATION AMONG AUTOCROSSERS: ALTERNATIVE CRITERIA FOR STRATIFICATION

From: Adrian F. Aveni, "Alternative Stratification Systems: the Case of Interpersonal Respect Among Leisure Participants," *The Sociological Quarterly* 17 (Winter, 1976): 53–64.

Contemporary theory and research on stratification tend to be conducted as if a single stratification system existed throughout society. The present study suggests that multiple stratification systems exist and provides an empirical analysis of one such system. . . .

The present research examines stratification among participants in a leisure activity known as "autocrossing." In particular, the hierarchy of interpersonal respect among the autocross participants is examined. Various sets of criteria are then introduced and their relationship with the respect hierarchy is analyzed in order to determine how well they can "account" for the hierarchy. The first set of criteria that is examined consists of occupational, financial, and educational attainment. These are all commonly employed criteria of stratification which are typically assumed to operate throughout the entire society. . . . If occupation, income, and education are related to the respect that leisure participants feel toward one another, then there is evidence that a single stratification system is operating. On the other hand, it is possible that other criteria may be related to the interpersonal respect among the leisure participants. . . .

Autocrossing is an increasingly popular form of auto racing. Typically the events are conducted in empty parking lots although occasionally air strips and sections of race tracks are used. The objective of autocrossing is to drive through a predetermined course, marked by rubber cones or pylons, in the fastest possible time. The courses consist of many slaloms and sharp curves so that drivers are continually forced to maneuver their cars as well as to brake and accelerate. The nature of the sport, therefore, tests the maneuverability and dexterity of both driver and machine. Most clubs place cars in one of about 12 classes, based upon the make and model of the car and the nature of any modifications that have been made to it. Only the drivers of those cars in the same class compete against one another. Usually each participant is given three timed "runs" through the course. The best of the driver's three times determines the finishing position of the driver. Since the actual length of time that autocross participants are "racing" is quite short, perhaps one minute per run, the vast majority of any day at an autocross event is spent waiting. This is significant because it means that the participants have the opportunity to get to know one another.

Two of the characteristics of autocrossing make it well-suited for an examination of the problem. . . . One is that the nature of autocrossing activities fosters the establishment of a community of autocross participants. These individuals meet regularly for long periods of time at autocross events. This provides a substantial basis for the establishment of a stable set of expectations regarding respect among the participants. The second characteristic of importance is that autocrossing can potentially be an expensive leisure pursuit, due to the associated costs of automobiles. This means that persons with large incomes have some advantages over others. This, in turn, could have an indirect effect upon the amount of respect they receive. Compared to most other leisure pursuits, autocrossing may thus tend to emphasize the importance of money. If leisure participants use occupation and income as factors in determining the respect they show toward one another, it might be expected to be especially visible among the autocross participants.

Here the author gives a detailed statement of method used in collecting information. Briefly, three autocrossing clubs in Columbus, Ohio, were studied, using two questionnaires identical in content except for five items. On one form, respondents were asked to nominate three other autocross drivers who they felt were the best drivers and also to nominate three persons having the greatest mechanical knowledge and three persons whom they most respected.

On the second form, participants were asked to rank in order of importance five qualities which might affect the amount of respect they felt toward other autocross participants. They were also asked to rate twenty different autos on their performance in autocross events. Prestige scores could then be assigned to autos. Most respondents were male, in the age range of twenty to twenty-nine with at least a high school education. Some were college students. Only 18 percent earned $15,000 or more per year.

Taken together, the findings . . . indicate that the commonly used, societal-level criteria of stratification are of little importance in determining the amount of respect which individuals receive. This being the case, it is worthwhile to determine what kinds of factors are being related to respect.

One potential source of respect among autocross participants is the automobile. . . . [But] the findings regarding the relation between each of the four measures of auto quality [condition, modifications, performance rating, classification] and the number of respect nominations suggest that the autos themselves were not of great importance in determining the amount of respect received by the participants. . . . One conclusion from these findings is that respect generally cannot be "bought" through the purchase of an expensive, sophisticated car. This is consistent with the previous findings regarding the relation between income level and respect. The data suggest that respect is achieved in other ways. . . .

The findings . . . indicate a moderate to strong association between respect nominations and all three measures of ability [driving and mechanical abilities, finishing position]. . . .

Average Rank, Percent Indicating Most Important and Least Important, for Five Factors Affecting the Amount of Respect Felt Toward Other Participants

FACTOR	Average rank	% Indicating most important	% Indicating least important
Driving ability	4.4	55.7	1.7
Personality factors	3.4	34.5	16.4
Finishing position	2.6	5.2	23.5
Mechanical ability	2.5	0.8	24.1
Type of car driven	2.1	3.5	35.4

[The author also reported moderate association between several measures of commitment and number of respect nominations. These measures were number of local autocross events in which each individual had participated, number of years of participation, number of autocross clubs in which the individual has membership, and three measures of the individual's providing assistance at autocross events during the year.]

(a) Karl Marx (1818–1883) advanced a general theory of society that has been a continuing influence on those who accept, modify, or reject his economic class-conflict thesis. (b) Max Weber (1864–1920) provided some of the most influential analyses of the distinctive aspects of the capitalist social and economic order. SOURCE: (a) The Bettmann Archive; (b) Brown Brothers.

Data from this study of autocross participants have indicated that such conventional indices of stratification as occupation, education, and income levels have little or no effect upon the amount of respect that participants have for one another. In contrast, respect was found to be highly related to the possession of those abilities specifically emphasized in the leisure pursuit: driving and mechanical abilities, and finishing position. Additional findings have shown that several indicators of commitment to the leisure pursuit are moderately related to respect, and that the participants themselves rank personality factors quite high in importance. The overall context of the findings therefore indicates that a system of stratification exists among the leisure participants which is considerably different from that commonly assumed to operate throughout the society. The system may be considered as evidence of one of the alternative stratification systems in operation among various groups throughout the society.

Much of the literature on social class conveys the impression that by virtue of their class position working class and lower-middle class persons lead lives that are relatively bleak. Their occupations have low prestige and often involve meaningless work. Incomes are relatively low. Assuming such persons reacted to their low positions in society as they have been portrayed, one might wonder how they maintain any self-respect. It might be argued that other concerns, such as family and kin, take on increased meaning to working and lower-middle class persons. However, part of the answer may lie in the recognition that individuals are members of several stratification systems. One such system, that was found among leisure participants, may provide an avenue for the emergence and sustenance of self-respect. The findings of this study are consistent with this interpretation.

The central concept of this chapter, social class stratification, is considered in the light of the nature of social class, the major consequences of social class status, the degree of *social mobility** or shift from one social position to another (Matras, 1975: 12) that exists in American society, and the lack of upward mobility found in the lower strata in what some analysts now call the *culture of poverty*.

THE CHANGING STRUCTURE OF SOCIAL CLASS

In America, social class analysis was stimulated by the work of W. Lloyd Warner who, with his associates at Yale University in the 1930s, made his now classic *Yankee City* study (Warner and Lunt, 1941). Warner, who was trained as a cultural anthropologist, selected for research Newburyport, Massachusetts, a town of about 17,000 residents, within a day's drive of the metropolitan areas of Boston and New York. He developed an Index of Status Characteristics (ISC) using the demographic or population characteristics of occupation, source of income, house type, and dwelling area (1941: 39–43). He relied greatly on the occupational index in determining social class position; using the following categories: unskilled labor, skilled factory, skilled craft, management-aid, management, and professional.

CRITERIA FOR SOCIAL CLASS STATUS Warner's measurements of social class have been modified extensively since the 1930s, but his occupational criteria are still an excellent way of evaluating social class. Using the occupational index, Warner placed people in five major class strata: *lower-lower* class (viewed by the larger community as not respectable, lazy, dependent, and lacking good middle-class virtues); *upper-lower* class (perform a decreasing number of needed tasks and are viewed as poor but honest workers — the semiskilled workers in factories, service workers, and small tradesmen); the *lower-middle* class (some skilled workers, small businessmen, clerical workers, and lower level white-collar workers); *upper-middle* class (solid, highly respectable people but not society — substantial business and professional men and women who aspire to be upper class and who participate in community and civic activities); and the *upper* class — wealthy people (*upper-upper* class if the wealth is inherited, influential merchants, financiers, or people in the higher ranks of their professions, such as surgeons and judges).

Warner diagramed his findings in what has become a famous sociological triangle (Figure 6-2). This summary of social class stratification is useful in understanding studies of a generation ago and provides a basis for evaluating the continuities and changes in the American stratification pattern. The social class categories in Yankee City were based largely upon the occupational ranking noted to the left of the diagram. There are many uses for Warner's social class categories, even with the modifications noted in this chapter. It is possible to measure the proportion of Americans in each category according to occupational and other life style activities. It is also possible to measure trends in the generally upward social class movement in American society between the end of the Great Depression in 1940 and in more recent years.

```
occupational                    class                    1940 Yankee
status                          structure                City proportions

                                   U        upper              3
managerial
and
professional                     UM        upper              10
                                           middle
skilled craft
----------------
management-aid                   LM        lower              28
                                           middle

skilled factory                  UL        upper              33
semi-skilled                               lower
----------------
                                 LL        lower              25
unskilled                                  lower
                                                             ____
                                                             99%
```

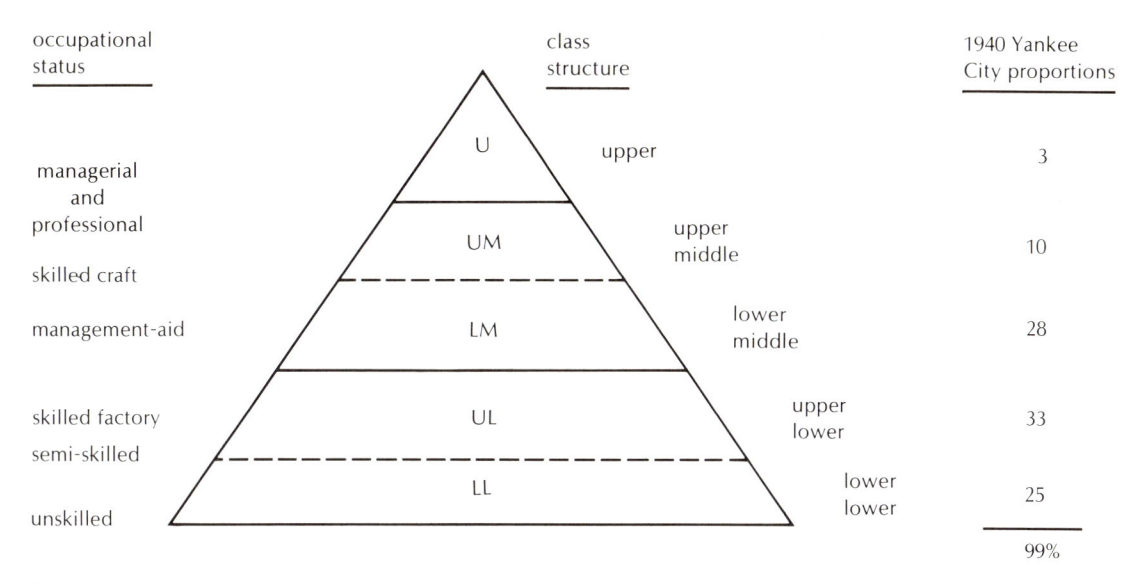

Figure 6-2 The social class structure of Yankee City in 1940. SOURCE: Copyright © 1941 by Yale University Press.

Note that, in Table 6-1, the numbers increase toward the bottom of the scale. When Warner first constructed his pyramid in the late 1930s, it generally reflected social reality. There were more people in the lower classes (upper-lower and lower-lower totaled well over half) than in the middle and upper classes (less than 41 percent of the total). The table also indicates the changes in the American social class pattern. Next to Warner's 1940 proportions for each class level are the approximate proportions of these classes based on 1970 census data. No longer do the proportions get larger as you go down the scale; the largest group of people is now the middle class.

DEGREES OF SOCIAL ACCLAIM AND PRESTIGE

Those in the upper and many in the middle class have occupations to which the American work ethic grants a high degree of social status. As we discussed earlier, status involves the degree of social

Table 6-1 The Changing American Social Class Structure

Occupational status	1940[a] — Yankee City class proportions	1970[b] — United States class proportions
Managerial & professional	3	15
Skilled craft	10	25
Management-aid	28	25
Skilled factory	33	15
Unskilled	25	20
	99%*	100%

* The total percentage came to less than 100% because numbers were rounded off.

[a] SOURCE: Based on Table 7 data in Lloyd Warner and Paul Lunt, *The Social Life of a Modern Community* (New Haven: Yale University Press, 1941), p. 225. Copyright © 1941 by Yale University Press.

[b] SOURCE: Based on percentages from Table 9 in *Current Population Reports,* Series P-60, No. 80, October 4, 1971 (Washington, D.C.: Government Printing Office).

acclaim and prestige a given social role receives. High status brings admiration and respect. Conversely, low status results in lack of admiration, social rejection, and avoidance. Even for low status individuals who move up, this low esteem has some continuing effects. A study at Stanford University indicated that among freshmen, 32 percent of lower-class youth were socially withdrawn and isolated compared to 11 percent from other classes (Ellis, Lane and Olesen, 1963).

The status differentials by occupational position can be seen in Table 6-2. In this table, the general categories noted by Warner can be evaluated in more detail. Such managerial and professional occupations as building contractor and lawyer rank near the top. The less skilled occupations such as garbage collector and janitor rank near the bottom, in status if not necessarily in functional usefulness and sometimes in payment for services rendered, as the highly paid trolley drivers (or streetcar motormen) of San Francisco can attest. Still, the people in the low-prestige occupations are so often among those whose earnings are low and who are often underemployed, that they compose the highest proportion of those in the poverty class.

The fact that the lower class categories are a declining proportion of the total population (see Table 6-1) has weakened the position of those left at the bottom. The lower-lower and upper-lower classes no longer have the social and political influence they had in the 1930s when Warner first analyzed American social classes.

DETERMINING SOCIAL CLASS RANKINGS

What are the social class ratings based upon? Two sets of criteria are used. There are *objective* criteria, such as income and level of education, and there are *subjective* criteria, such as the high prestige accorded certain occupations regardless of income and level of education. For example, note in Table 6-2 that ministers and priests rank higher in prestige than do bankers or economists, who generally earn more.

Such occupational categories as professional, managerial, skilled, unskilled are objective descriptions of occupational differences. The average income from each category can be precisely measured by census and other data. Thus we know that professionals average over $15,000 a year and generally have college training, while unskilled workers average less than $10,000 a year and generally have not had more than an elementary or

A lifestyle that can only be experienced at the top of the social class structure. SOURCE: Rudolph Edward Leppert, Jr./Globe Photos.

Table 6-2   Prestige Ratings of Occupations

Occupation	Score	Occupation	Score
U.S. Supreme Court justice	94	Railroad engineer	76
Physician	93	Owner-operator of a printing shop	75
Nuclear physicist	92	Trained machinist	75
Scientist	92	Farm owner and operator	74
Government scientist	91	Undertaker	74
State governor	91	Welfare worker for a city government	74
Cabinet member in the federal government	90	Newspaper columnist	73
College professor	90	Policeman	72
U.S. Representative in Congress	90	Average	71
Chemist	89	Reporter on a daily newspaper	71
Diplomat in the U.S. Foreign Service	89	Bookkeeper	70
Lawyer	89	Radio announcer	70
Architect	88	Insurance agent	69
County judge	88	Tenant farmer — one who owns livestock and machinery and manages the farm	69
Dentist	88	Local official of a labor union	67
Mayor of a large city	87	Manager of a small store in a city	67
Member of the board of directors of a large corporation	87	Mail carrier	66
Minister	87	Railroad conductor	66
Psychologist	87	Traveling salesman for a wholesale concern	66
Airline pilot	86	Plumber	65
Civil engineer	86	Barber	63
Head of a department in a state government	86	Machine operator in a factory	63
Priest	85	Owner-operator of a lunch stand	63
Banker	85	Playground director	63
Biologist	85	Corporal in the regular army	62
Sociologist	83	Garage mechanic	62
Captain in the regular army	82	Truck driver	59
Accountant for a large business	81	Fisherman who owns his own boat	58
Public school teacher	81	Clerk in a store	56
Building contractor	80	Milk route man	56
Owner of a factory that employs about 100 people	80	Streetcar motorman	56
Artist who paints pictures exhibited in galleries	78	Lumberjack	55
Author of novels	78	Restaurant cook	55
Economist	78	Singer in a nightclub	54
Musician in a symphony orchestra	78	Filling station attendant	51
Official of an international labor union	77	Coal miner	50
County agricultural agent	76	Dock worker	50
Electrician	76	Night watchman	50
		Railroad section hand	50

Table 6-2   Prestige Ratings of Occupations (continued)

Occupation	Score	Occupation	Score
Restaurant waiter	49	Soda fountain clerk	44
Taxi driver	49	Sharecropper — one who owns no livestock or equipment and does not manage farm	42
Bartender	48	Garbage collector	39
Farmhand	48	Street sweeper	36
Janitor	48	Shoe shiner	34
Clothes presser in a laundry	45		

SOURCE: Hodge, Robert W., Paul M. Siegel, and Peter A. Rossi, "Occupational Prestige in the United States, 1925–1963," *American Journal of Sociology* 70 (1964), pp. 286–302. © 1964 by The University of Chicago. All rights reserved.

partial secondary school education. On the other hand, prestige ratings of occupations are based in part on the subjective feelings and values people have about various occupations. Income alone is not enough to explain high or low status. After all, truck drivers may earn considerably more than schoolteachers, yet the latter have a higher prestige rating, which points to the need to consider many factors — education, reputation, power or influence, and organization memberships — before an accurate assessment of anyone's social class status can be determined. Social class is a sociopsychological phenomenon (Page, 1961: 48). The selection by Sorokin denotes some of the complexities and consequences to the society of the social class structure.

SOCIAL CLASS

From: Pitirim Sorokin, "What Is A Social Class?" *Journal of Legal and Political Sociology* (1947), pp. 21–22 and 27–28.

Sorokin, a grand theorist (one who develops a comprehensive theory to account for societal stability and change) introduces the idea of mobility directions — vertical mobility up or down the stratification ladder, and, by inference, horizontal mobility, or movement from place to place at about the same level in the hierarchy. (See also the section on Social Mobility.)

Our task consists in determining whether there is a specific multibonded group, different from the family, tribe, caste, order, or nation, that in modern times has exerted a powerful influence. We are not seeking for any of the enumerated powerful multibonded groups, which have already been analyzed. Whether we designate the group in question as a social class or by some other term is unimportant. We may call it X, if we prefer.

SOURCE: Reprinted by permission of Robert Censoni.

"We both get a tour of Japan—you get a tour of the polluted waters; I see Expo and go to the baths."

The answer to the question is in the affirmative. There has been and is such a group. Its formula is as follows: It is (1) legally open, but actually semiclosed; (2) "normal"; (3) solidarity; (4) antagonistic to certain other groups (social classes) of the same general nature, X; (5) partly organized but mainly quasi-organized; (6) partly aware of its own unity and existence and partly not; (7) characteristic of the Western society of the eighteenth, nineteenth, and twentieth centuries; (8) a multibonded group bound together by two unibonded ties — occupational and economic (both taken in their broad sense) and by one bond of social stratification in the sense of the totality of its essential rights and duties as contrasted with the essentially different rights and duties of other groups (social classes) of the general nature, X....

It is to be observed... that the sharpness of the class division in a population and the conspicuousness of the class traits in each member depend largely upon the length of time during which the members remain in their class and its unibonded groups. As a rule, other conditions being equal, the longer the period of membership the more class-minded they become. For the same reason, in societies like that of the United States (especially in the past), in which vertical social mobility is strongly developed, the class differentiation is bound to be less clear and effective than in populations with weak vertical mobility. This explains why the proletariat in America has been less clear-cut than in many European countries, and why the social class has played a less conspicuous role in the United States than in Europe.

CHANGING CLASS STATUS Over time, the objective awards and subjective evaluations of occupational positions change with changing conditions. Thus, in recent history, there have been a number of changes in middle- and high-status occupations. A comparison of the data collected in 1963 (see Table 6-2) with data collected in 1947 shows that striking changes can occur in little more than fifteen years. *Nuclear physicist* moved up from a rank of 18 to a rank of 3 (probably reflecting the development of nuclear energy for peacetime and military purposes); *public schoolteacher* moved up from rank 36 to rank 29 (probably reflecting the increased emphasis on education as a route to upward mobility and higher status); and *minister* moved down from rank 13 to rank 17 (probably reflecting the declining influence of formal religious institutions, as discussed in Chapter 3).

As one moves down the social ladder, there is increasing objective and subjective agreement. For example, in both the 1947 and 1963 samples, such low-paid occupations as shoe shiner, street sweeper, and janitor remained at the bottom (Hodge, Siegel and Rossi, 1964: 290–293). The people in the lowest category earn the least, with negative consequences to their health, quality of life, and longevity (see Matras, 1973).

As has become evident over the past few decades, in protest movements by minorities and poor people generally, those at the bottom feel unhappy about their low status. Not only is everybody else objectively better off but there is a tendency for those of higher status to label those in the lower strata no account and shiftless (Warner, 1960: 19).

Since Warner's *Yankee City* and other class studies in the 1930s and 1940s, there has been considerable movement within the American social class hierarchy. Most of this movement has been upward and has occurred within the upper-middle and upper classes. As we shall see, this movement appears to reflect the nature of opportunity in the emerging American social class structure more than it does the nature of the people at the bottom.

UPWARD AND DOWNWARD MOBILITY

John Kenneth Galbraith's *The Affluent Society* (1958) is a widely read economic analysis of American society. The book shows that most Americans, more than any other mass of society, enjoy a high standard of living. Yet for several million Americans, the old Soviet peasant query is appropriate: "If everything is so good then why is everything so bad?" The fact is that American affluence is still so unevenly distributed that, while most Americans judge themselves to be middle class, there are other class dimensions, including a wealthy upper class and an impoverished lower class.

OPEN AND CLOSED SYSTEMS A central question about American social classes is not so much whether widely different classes exist but whether the system is open or closed. Are people born into a *closed class* category that determines their social and occupational roles for life (as in the traditional caste system of India, based on inheritance)? Or do people have the opportunity to move in an *open class* system that holds all persons to be created equal?

To some extent, the answers to these questions may be affected by whether one is black or white, male or female, and by other social characteristics.

American society, like other modern technological societies, has a somewhat open class structure based on one's ability to perform in various occupational and other positions. This does not mean that the class one is born into (remember the placing function of families) is not a major influence on one's life pattern. Indeed, there are major class influences on the amount of social mobility of both individuals and groups. Yet, as Tables 6-3 and 6-4 suggest, most Americans, as well as most Britons and Danes, who also live in modern urban societies, do in fact have a different occupational status from that of their parents. They may not change in Horatio Alger rags-to-riches style, but as Otis Dudley Duncan concluded in analyzing data for the 1920 to 1965 period, intergenerational social mobility appears to have increased moderately in the most recent decades (1965: 491).

Matras identifies a number of factors (some achieved, some ascribed) that affect the move to higher occupational socioeconomic status. These are (Matras, 1975: 273):

Table 6-3 British and Danish Occupational Status – Father and Son Comparisons by Percentages

			British son's status*								Danish son's status*				
			1	2	3	4	5				1	2	3	4	5
			(Number)								(Number)				
	1	(129)	39	36	5	14	5		1	(57)	32	17	30	5	2
	2	(495)	6	35	17	31	11		2	(318)	8	33	34	18	7
Father's status*	3	(521)	4	13	22	43	18	Father's status*	3	(672)	3	13	43	32	9
	4	(1514)	2	10	13	46	29		4	(778)	1	6	22	45	26
	5	(845)	0	2	9	40	49		5	(530)	1	2	13	37	47

* Italics added where fathers' and sons' occupational status were the same. The status categories would be equivalent to Warner's classification system, in which 1=upper, 2=upper-middle, 3=lower-middle, 4=upper-lower and 5=lower-lower.

SOURCE: Adapted from Leon A. Goodman, "How to Ransack Social Mobility and Other Kinds of Cross-Classification Tables," *American Journal of Sociology* vol. 75, no. 1 (July 1969), p. 35. © 1969 by The University of Chicago. All rights reserved.

Table 6-4 American Occupational Status — Father and Son Comparisons by Percentages

			Son's status*				
			Professional	Managerial	Clerical	Skilled	Unskilled
		(Number)					
	Professional	(28)	25	18	21	32	4
	Managerial	(95)	19	27	17	25	12
Father's status*	Clerical	(36)	28	14	19	22	17
	Skilled	(209)	9	15	10	54	12
	Unskilled	(69)	3	11	13	38	35

* Italics added where fathers' and sons' occupational status were the same. Note that the farm owner category, which appeared in the original table, has been combined with the managerial category because of the small proportion of cases and overlapping occupational functions.

SOURCE: Adapted from Seymour Martin Lipset and Reinhard Bendix, *Social Mobility in Industrial Society* (Berkeley: University of California Press, 1959), p.89. Copyright © 1959 by Regents of the University of California; reprinted by permission of the University of California Press.

1. the individual's initial occupational status or the occupational status of his parents

2. his own education

3. his residential history (farm origin or not, migrant or not)

4. the size of his family, his position among siblings

5. his race, ethnicity, national origin, region, and community size or type

6. his marital status, the number of his children

7. his intelligence

8. his motivation or aspirations

9. his age, year of birth, and year of entrance into the working force

The stratification structure does yield to the efforts of individuals and groups. An underlying reason for flexibility in the social class structure is that, in our technological society, rapid changes occur in the demand for skills. As no upper-class elite has a monopoly on ambition and talent, there are constant pressures from below. There are demands for competent performance in new and expanding jobs, while there are people at every social level eager to move up in the opportunity structure. The consequence of the upward push and the loss of status of some in the higher ranks creates a variety of tensions and conflicts of interest. For example, early in the century, while such auto manufacturers as Henry Ford were moving up, the manufacturers of horse-drawn carriages were often moving down. This upward-and-downward (vertical) mobility reflects the changing economic and social structure in modern society.

THE NATURE OF CLASS BOUNDARIES After Warner and his associates laid the groundwork, sociologists began to debate the nature of class boundaries in American society: Is it characterized by a *hierarchical class structure* or by an overlapping *status continuum*?

Those favoring hierarchical class argue that American society is composed of distinct structural units, described in terms of a limited number of classes (Landecker, 1960: 868). Advocates of the continuum hold that status differences in American society are thought to be of a gradual character and to lack natural breaks (Landecker, 1960: 868). In contrast to the structural argument, this thesis holds that status differences are continuous and overlapping, not clear cut and separate.

VERTICAL MOBILITY Vertical mobility from one social stratum to another is much affected by the social organization of a given society, in that societies are based primarily on either status by *ascription* (attributes with which one is born) or status by *achievement* (ability to alter attributes by one's own actions). Matras observes that (1975: 256–257):

[S]ometimes persons are born, not with position-determining attributes themselves, but into families or groups in which membership promises favorable *access* to certain attributes. Thus, belonging to a certain family, or living in a certain town, suburb, or neighborhood, or belonging to a given church, ethnic association, or club may give a person special opportunities for earning money, for getting an education, or for attaining influence or power.... [I]ndividuals may obtain such attributes by their own actions or efforts: by saving money or buying property, by obtaining a high-paying job, by being elected to office or engaging in some other political activity, or perhaps by demonstrating personal heroism, or piety, or cultural or literary achievements. Such attributes constitute *achieved* bases of position and status attainment....

The individual learns quite young to accept the idea that persons are placed in an arrangement vis-à-vis each other, and that there are limits placed by the society on his or her ability to move from one place to another. Particularly in achievement-oriented societies, which often employ a competitive stimulus, the individual is encouraged to move up the social ladder. Furthermore, downward movement is a subject of scorn. Thus, a manual laborer hopes to move to a white-collar occupation, but it is rare that a white-collar jobholder seeks a manual occupation. This *upward vertical mobility* is valued in the United States. To engage in *horizontal mobility*, or the exchange of occupations at about the same level, say from bus driver to taxi driver, is not regarded as fulfilling the American value of bettering oneself.

In the United States, both ascribed roles and achieved roles account for mobility. There are fewer female than male executives because women have historically held an inferior ascribed status, as have members of other minority groups. There are no women Catholic priests because ascription excludes women from that role. There are women executives, though few in number compared to men, because the executive role is not completely dictated by ascribed characteristics. Even though discrimination against those with certain ascribed characteristics may make the achievement more difficult, a woman can become an executive if she fulfills other criteria, say decision-making ability.

Mobility may also be *individual* or *group* in nature. *Individual mobility* refers to an individual's making a new place for him- or herself, perhaps through hard work, saving, and investment, or perhaps by charisma. The four Beatles, for example, came from the lower-class industrial city of Liverpool. Each used his talent to achieve stardom. Although the four performed as a group, the individual capabilities of each made the occupational opportunity possible. The Beatles didn't become famous entertainers in order to provide jobs for the working class of Liverpool.

Group mobility refers to the ability of people to move collectively in large numbers because of structural changes in society which affect those with common attributes. For example, as a result of civil rights activity and the installation of affirmative action programs, minorities now find themselves at the head of the line for certain occupations because, in addition to whatever job qualifications a minority member may have, there is now a structural stimulus to fill the occupational slot with a black, a woman, or a Chicano. Blacks as a group, or women as a group, are automatic beneficiaries, at least on paper, of a single legislative act designed to alter the opportunity structure. Formerly privileged groups may face *downward mobility* as a result of these same changes. White male college graduates have recently charged reverse discrimination in that they experience difficulties in moving into occupations formerly available first to them, then to others.

In *closed societies,* little vertical mobility occurs. In *open societies,* where achieved attributes are more valued, mobility is higher. These are ideal types; few societies are based fully on ascribed characteristics, none on purely achieved ones. While there is much disagreement on whether or not the United States allows a great deal of social mobility, it is certainly true that the socialization process begins early to prepare us to try.

The question of where class boundaries lie makes it more difficult to answer an important question — is vertical mobility increasing or decreasing in the United States? Some of the class factors to consider in making an assessment are denoted in the Matras excerpt on social mobility. The complex issue of increasing versus decreasing mobility in America is so related to the economic system, that some main historical currents need to be considered in order to understand what is happening. In particular, advances in technology since 1900 affect the contemporary system from top to bottom.

AUTOMATION AND CYBERNATION

From the mid-nineteenth until the mid-twentieth century, the stratification system was basically a continuum at all social class levels. The last quarter century has produced upward mobility for most but static or downward mobility for many in the lower strata. Both movements are effects of *automation* and *cybernation.*

MASS PRODUCTION AND A MASS WORK FORCE Early industrialization brought increasing automation, in which Henry Ford's mass production line became a dominant form. *Automation* means that products are manufactured by machines rather than by human handcraft. In the early days of mass production, the products still needed to be assembled by human hands. Large numbers of factory workers performed simple, unskilled but essential functions on the line. The machine-tender was a necessary part of the production process. Immigrants in the late nineteenth and early twentieth centuries came to this country seeking not only political freedom but jobs as well. Business leaders also encouraged internal migration from farms to cities.

Efficient automative processes brought a decline in the need for unskilled machine-tenders. Restrictive immigration acts beginning in 1921 reflected the changes in the labor requirements of manufacturers. Even during the period of greatest need for unskilled factory labor, the average pay was near the poverty level. In 1904, the average annual wage of a full-time factory worker was $566 (Hourwich, 1912: 258). This represented a very low standard of living. But there were factors operating that made even the lower strata of society part of a fluid class system.

THE FRONTIER AND THE OPEN CLASS SYSTEM One major influence in maintaining an open class system throughout the nineteenth century was the expanding western frontier. The availability of vast lands west of the Mississippi acted as a safety valve. That is, no matter how difficult life became for those in the lower strata of the society, there were always new opportunities in the relatively unsettled and undeveloped West. The moving frontier helped stabilize and maintain opportunity, a belief epitomized in Horace Greeley's famous advice, "Go west, young man, go west." Particularly in the nineteenth century, the existence of the frontier helped prevent a stagnant situation in the increasingly industrialized Northeast and Midwest. As the historian Frederick Jackson Turner put it (Wish, 1960: 190):

The existence of an area of free land, its continuous recession, and the advance of American settlement westward, explain American development.... This perennial rebirth, this fluidity of American life, this expansion westward with its new opportunities ... furnish the forces dominating American character.

Turner probably exaggerated the effects of the expanding frontier, and he neglected its disruptive impact on the Indians. Yet there is much in what he said. The presence and availability of a vast, sparsely developed frontier was a major force in American history.

At the same time, the development of automated manufacturing ensured a place in the economy for the masses of unskilled workers. Accordingly, these people were able to exercise effective political leverage, bringing about, by the 1930s (Warner and Lunt, 1941) adoption of such measures as minimum wage laws, work safety standards, social security, and the right for labor union representatives to bargain with corporate owners on wages and work conditions (Schlesinger, 1962).

CLASS EFFECTS OF THE CYBERNETIC REVOLUTION The forward thrust of the lower classes was accelerated in the case of union members. However, for many young workers with few skills, upward mobility was stopped by a new development in technology, the *cybernetic revolution**. Beginning in the 1940s, cybernetics — that is, automation coupled with computer control and analysis — rapidly increased productivity and at the same time reduced the need for unskilled and semi-skilled machine-tenders (Michael, 1962). Cybernetics is thus a kind of automation, but it is so advanced technologically that it has changed the occupational status of millions in most major industries; a minority of workers are now in unskilled positions (see the table in the selection on work and sexual inequality).

Table 6-5 shows the percentage of workers engaged in production and as laborers in comparison with the percentage of workers in other occupations. Paul Samuelson illustrates the relationship of automation and employment in a model which shows that effects of automation on unemployment and the economy in general are influenced by the ability of the economy to increase consumption, investment, and government spending (Samuelson, 1973: 340–344). These alterations, however, are controlled not by the worker but by forces largely outside the worker's influence.

Computerized technology is now able to detect and correct breakdowns in equipment and to perform other processes with a minimum of human maintenance. What Donald Michael calls the silent conquest of cybernation is resulting in a shift at the bottom of the stratification system from a continuum of overlapping classes to a structure with increasing rigidity. Even the great industrial unions in the American Federation of Labor, which has over 15 million members, no longer afford the protections and provide as much upward mobility for as many as they did during the period of automation. By the mid-1970s, the industrial unions were no longer growing as rapidly as they had between the mid-1930s and mid-1950s; the unions have slowed in gaining members in relation to the growth of the total labor force (Samuelson, 1973: 132).

Table 6-5 United States: Structure of the Economically Active Population, 1974

	Occupational group	Employers, workers on own account	Salaried employees and wage earners	Family workers	Others and status unknown	Total and percent
0-1	Professional, technical and related workers	1,001,000	11,325,000	12,000	285,000	12,623,000 (13.5)
2	Administrative and managerial workers	1,784,000	7,132,000	26,000	168,000	9,109,000 (9.8)
3	Clerical and related workers	119,000	14,682,000	242,000	725,000	15,767,000 (16.9)
4	Sales workers	561,000	4,777,000	79,000	240,000	5,657,000 (66.1)
5	Service workers	689,000	10,614,000	70,000	764,000	12,137,000 (13.0)
6	Agricultural, animal husbandry, and forest workers, fishermen and hunters	1,622,000	1,050,000	376,000	79,000	3,127,000 (3.4)
7-9	Production and related workers, transport equipment operators, and laborers	1,611,000	28,094,000	71,000	2,138,000	31,914,000 (34.2)
	Members of armed forces		2,229,000			2,229,000 (2.4)
	Persons seeking work for the first time				670,000	670,000 (.7)
	Total (percent)	5,911,204	72,235,920	404,210	3,497,447	93,240,000 (100.0)

SOURCE: Adapted from *Yearbook of Labour Statistics.* (Geneva: International Labour Office, 1975), pp. 202-203.

CLASS STATUS REWARDS AND PENALTIES The general upward shift in class status evident in Table 6-1 shows that an expanding economy benefits those who fill its functional needs. Also, the less needed industrial workers are protected by unions. For those workers (particularly the young and, until recently, unskilled) who are not in the new work force of skilled technicians, professionals, and management, unemployment and underemployment remain far above the national average. Women, white-collar workers, and southern workers continue to be slow to join unions. Note in Figure 6-3 that there were fluctuations in union membership in the 1950s and 1960s when automation was occurring rapidly. With the decline of blue-collar unions — reflecting the effects of cybernation — the unemployment rates of the unskilled range from 10 percent to 30 percent, compared to a general unemployment rate of under 7.5 percent (Bureau of Labor Statistics, June 1976).

While there may be proportionately fewer at the bottom of the scale now than in the past, their relative condition appears to be deteriorating — in social distance from other classes, in quality of education, in housing, and in other ways.

An interpretive note is called for here. The assumption of a decline in the number and proportion of people in a state of poverty is based on official government figures. According to a 1969 report of the Bureau of the Census, "Poverty in the United States, 1959 to 1968," the number of people living in absolute poverty dropped from near 40 million, or 22.4 percent of the population in 1959, to somewhat more than 25 million, or 12.8 percent of the 1968 population. These figures are based mainly on the effects of the rising price of food matched by income in constant dollars (what dollars would buy in 1959). The rise of 16.7 percent in the Consumer Price Index for food between 1959 and 1968 was taken into account when computing the apparent decline in the number and proportion of those in a state of absolute poverty; but this singular price index provides only a partial measure of the cost of living for the poor.

David Gordon came up with significantly different results using several other major cost factors. He noted that in 1959–1968, the cost of public transportation rose by 38.5 percent, medical care by 45.1 percent, and general services by 34.9 percent. He then calculated that the number in absolute poverty in 1968 was roughly 50 percent higher than the official estimates, or around 37.5 million persons, close to 20 percent of the population, rather than 25 million persons (Gordon, 1972: 99).

Thus, for the large majority, from the lower-middle to the upper class, general upward mobility continues; but for the minority at the bottom, there is a structure of distinct units increasingly rigid and difficult to move out of. We may indeed have an affluent society, as Galbraith suggests, but it is also one in which there is poverty in affluence (Will and Vatter, 1970).

Figure 6-3 Membership in labor unions. SOURCE: From *Economics* by Paul A. Samuelson. Copyright 1973 McGraw-Hill Book Company. Used with permission of McGraw-Hill Book Company.

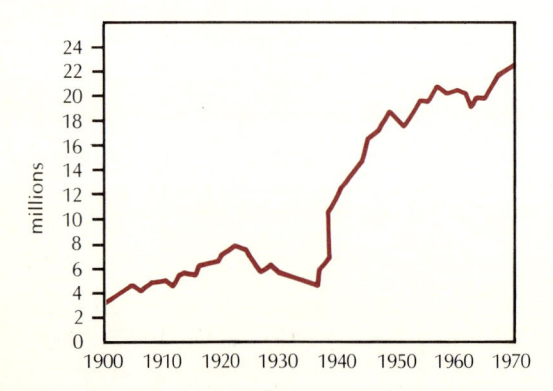

THE RACIAL FACTOR

CURRENT CONSEQUENCES OF A FORMER CASTE SYSTEM As we shall see in the next chapter, any discussion of low income groups must consider minority status. Certainly blacks, who are the largest racial minority, are concentrated in the low income categories. The same could be said for Spanish-Americans, including Chicanos and Puerto Ricans, and American Indians. In addition to other socioeconomic characteristics such as income and education, racial minorities have been treated in a way that has led to and sustained a state of poverty for many.

The similarities and differences between racial minorities and poor whites (*Current Population Reports*, 1971) were discussed in Sidney Willhelm's provocative book *Who Needs the Negro?* (1970), which touched upon two interrelated problems. First, the economic functions that blacks at the bottom of the occupational ladder once fulfilled in cotton fields or early factories no longer exist to any substantial degree. Second, since there are more whites in the population, most of the poor are white; however, a far higher *proportion* of blacks, Spanish-Americans, and Indians live in a state of poverty. The effect of minority status is evident in the census data, which document that while less than one white in ten is at the poverty level, approximately one in three blacks, and one in four Spanish-speaking people is, as are over half of the American Indians (Thurow and Lucas, 1974: 81).

All this did not happen in the last decade or two. Just as by birth people may inherit great fortunes that took generations to build, great poverty is often inherited by people who did little or nothing to create it.

THE LEGACY OF THE OLD RACIAL CASTE SYSTEM   The class position of blacks can usefully be viewed in historical perspective. The end of slavery after the Civil War did not provide blacks with either full social equality or equality of opportunity. Until the mid-twentieth century, most blacks remained in the South, where various forms of racial segregation, such as in schools, existed by law until the landmark 1954 *Brown* school desegregation decision of the Supreme Court. Almost half of the South's approximately 20 million blacks moved to the urban centers of the North, West and, most recently, the South itself (Taeuber, Chiazze, and Haenszel, 1968). They came with the very kind of labor experience that was being eliminated by cybernation (Ferman, 1968).

In effect, blacks and other racial minorities[1] have come out of a class hierarchy that cannot be explained adequately either in terms of continuum or of structure, but rather in terms of caste. A caste system is the most rigid form of stratification. Castes are characterized by *endogamy**, or exclusive in-group association, including marriage, and no vertical movement from one social stratum to another. For almost a century after the Civil War, there was a racial caste system in the Deep South. While there were class differences among blacks, the highest was below anyone in the upper class in the white community, as the diagram in Figure 6-4 indicates. The caste line (AB) means that all blacks, whatever their socioeconomic level, had a class status lower than any whites.

URBAN OPPORTUNITIES   Because young blacks learned that the more desirable jobs were closed to them whatever their abilities and ambitions, many moved to such cities as New York, Philadelphia, Detroit, Chicago, and Los Angeles (Ginsberg, 1960), bringing their long history of forced low caste status with them. So it is no surprise that a breakdown

---

[1] For good analyses of the historical factors that have influenced the class status of Indians and Chicanos (Mexican-Americans were categorized as non-whites in the 1940 U.S. Census) see: Beatrice Medicine, "The Native American," in D. Spiegel and P. Keith-Spiegel (eds.), *Outsiders, U.S.A.* (San Francisco: Rinehart Press, 1973), pp. 391–407 and Rudolfo Alvarez, "The Unique Psycho-Historical Experience of the Mexican American People," *Social Forces* vol. 52 (June 1971), pp. 15–29.

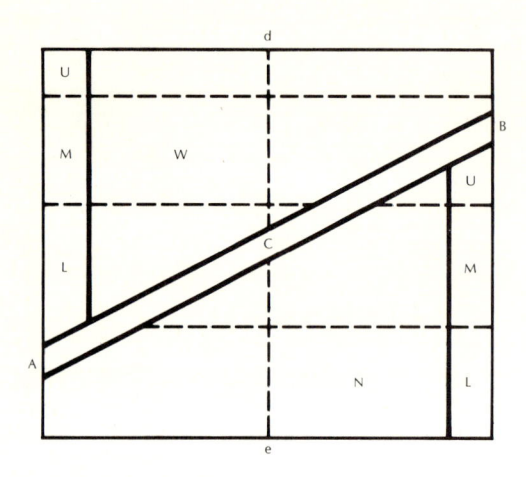

W — white social class structure
N — black social class structure
U — upper class   AB — caste line
M — middle class   de — ultimate position of caste line
L — lower class   C — axis of caste line

Figure 6-4 The social caste system in the Deep South sixty-five years after the Civil War. SOURCE: From *Deep South* by Allison Davies (University of Chicago Press, 1941).

of occupational categories by ethnic groups shows about two-thirds of all blacks in the un- or semi-skilled occupational categories of operatives, service workers, and laborers. For similar historical reasons, American Indians and Chicanos are also concentrated in these increasingly obsolete positions (see Table 6-6).

About one-third of all blacks have made substantial progress upward (Thurow and Lucas, 1974). For these people, there still remains a problem of discrimination. As S. M. Miller and Martin Rein report of a study performed at the University of Michigan (1967: 455):

...a multivariate analysis of salary differentials between whites and nonwhites [was made], taking into account education, rural background, and skills. This analysis made possible a close assessment of the impact of discriminatory practices on nonwhites. When all these factors were considered, the nonwhites earned almost $900 less than whites. Thus pure discriminatory factors rather than skills and the like operate to reduce Negro income.

Most blacks as well as Spanish–Americans and Native Americans have come into an urban industrial setting that structurally excludes them from upwardly mobile occupations, even when prejudice and discrimination may no longer be the prime factor working against them. This situation is a major source of interracial conflict, a topic considered in Chapter 8.

THE NEGLECTED ETHNICS So far, the ethnic groups we have considered represent the poor; but the not-so-poor also have severe class problems. These are people of the lower-middle class and the upper-lower class, out of the poverty range. Their life circumstances and attitudes about poverty and the poor are crucial to our understanding of what is happening to those at the bottom.

THE ALMOST POOR Unlike persons of managerial and professional status, those in the lower-middle and upper-lower classes are close to the poor both socially, in class, and physically, in residential living patterns within cities. Indeed, this very closeness, coupled with difficult living circumstances, may arouse a sense of group consciousness (often class-related) to differentiate each from the other. It has become increasingly clear in the 1960s and 1970s that programs to assist those in poverty — known popularly in their early days as the war on poverty — may be viewed as a threat to the precarious position of many in the upper-lower and lower-middle classes in a society whose need for their services is also declining.

Who are these not-so-poor? While many are white Protestants and others are from racial minorities, most are white ethnics (Inglehart and Mangline, 1974: 2) — children and grandchildren of

Table 6-6 Employment of Minority Groups and Anglos[a], 1966 (Numbers in Thousands; Percent Distribution)

	Men[b]				Women[b]			
Occupation[c]	Black	American Indian[d]	Chicano[e] (Spanish American)	Anglo	Black	American Indian	Chicano (Spanish American)	Anglo
Professional and technical workers	2.0	6.6	4.7	13.9	6.1	5.6	3.6	7.4
Managers, officials and proprietors	1.0	6.5	2.5	12.0	.7	2.2	.8	2.6
Clerical workers	2.7	3.9	5.1	7.1	17.5	21.7	24.1	40.8
Sales workers	1.3	4.7	3.0	7.4	4.0	12.5	6.9	9.3
Craftsmen	7.9	19.3	13.9	20.4	2.4	5.1	4.8	2.8
Operatives	37.2	29.9	32.1	25.5	24.9	24.2	29.8	21.7
Service workers	18.1	6.7	12.2	5.4	30.3	16.9	12.4	9.1
Laborers	29.8	22.3	26.4	8.4	14.1	11.8	17.6	6.4
Percent of total population	8.2	.2	2.5	88.6	7.9	.2	2.5	88.9
Total: Percent	100	100	100	100	100	100	100	100
Number	1,472	39	453	15,962	648	17	202	7,228

[a] "Anglos" compose over 85 percent of the whites in the U.S. Census.
[b] Orientals, primarily Chinese and Japanese, who compose less than one half of one percent of the population and who are concentrated in skilled and professional occupational statuses are not included.
[c] The data was collected from employers with 100 or more workers.
[d] Nonreservation Indians
[e] Includes Mexican-Americans and Puerto Ricans

SOURCE: *Manpower Report of the President,* U.S. Department of Labor (Washington, D.C.: Government Printing Office, 1968), p. 64.

States in the early industrialization period of the late nineteenth and early twentieth centuries. By the 1930s, still on the eve of the cybernetic revolution, there were more of these white ethnics in the upper-lower class than either native white Protestants or blacks.

STRAIN IN THE UPWARD MOBILITY AMONG WHITES Much of the upward mobility between 1940 and 1970 (see Table 6-1) was by white ethnics. More are now in the lower-middle than in the upper-lower class, and fewer than 10 percent are in the lower-lower (poverty) class, compared to over 30 percent in the 1930s. What does this mean in terms of practical living? It means that about a third of the blue-collar working-class of white ethnic background have an average family income of $5,000 to $10,000 at a time when most American families average over $10,000 a year (Moyers, 1969: 2). The strain of *making it* becomes clear when we look closer at a specific example. An Italian family of four on Long Island, the Cappellis (husband a hospital attendant and wife a part-time secretary), budgeted their yearly income on a monthly basis (see Table 6-7). Higher average wages in the 1970s were matched by higher costs, so that the strained circumstances of this working-class family continue.

Table 6-7 Monthly Expenses of a Working-Class Family

Husband's monthly income	$403.50
Wife's monthly income	56.00
Total yearly income	$5,409.50
Monthly expenditures	
State health insurance	$ 7.26
Social security	19.36
State income tax	2.06
Federal income tax	25.08
Mortgage principal	16.95
Mortgage interest	62.20
Property taxes, insurance	71.85
Life insurance	26.00
Oil	24.00
Electricity	9.00
Phone	6.00
Car maintenance	40.00
Entertainment	4.00
Cigarettes	15.00
Newspapers	1.20
Clothing	10.00
Credit charge	15.00
Food	80.00
Garbage collection	3.75
Medical expenses, drugs	12.00
Haircuts	4.00
Miscellaneous	4.25
Total expenses	$ 459.50

SOURCE: Aronson, Harvey, "Life with Cappelli on $101 a Week," *Newsday Report* (New York: Institute of Human Relations, 1969), p. 9. Copyright 1969, Newsday, Inc. Reprinted by permission.

Millions of others have problems similar to the Cappellis'. Their monthly budget has little give to it. Cutting back on entertainment and cigarettes would provide little more for basic necessities, even on the dubious assumption that no diversion from work and mere survival is necessary. Unusual expenses because of an accident, an illness, a trip to visit a distant relative, or the like, would put tremendous strain on the precarious family budget. Most people like the Cappellis live in old residential sections close to the poorest areas of a city. Urban renewal and the leveling of slum dwellings often increases the pressure on their neighborhoods, as the displaced poor seek new places for themselves. Irving Levine and Judy Herman observe that basic issues for these people are fear of urban renewal and the need for more police protection and more low-income housing (1972). They further note that these are the same underlying issues facing poor blacks and others generally of lower-class status. If we add the needs for quality education and secure employment, we have the major issues for both the poor and the not-so-poor. These common needs provide the basis of interaction between these strata in the society.

The result is a permanent condition of strain. Pressures for change, which are considerable, can lead to a coalition to accomplish common goals, or they can lead to greater competition for scarce supplies. The roles of the upper-middle and upper classes have not been explored here. Nor has the relationship between sex and earning capabilities based on available occupations (see Table 6-8). However, it is worth noting that the success, attitudes, and behavior of the more influential groups affect what the lower classes will do in response to their own felt needs.

Table 6-8   Work and Sexual Inequality

Occupation Group	Distribution (%) Males	Females
Total employed	100.0	100.0
White-collar workers	40.9	60.6
Professional and technical	13.7	14.5
Managers, officials and proprietors	14.6	5.0
Clerical workers	6.7	33.9
Sales workers	5.9	7.2
Blue-collar workers	45.9	15.4
Craftsmen and foremen	19.9	1.3
Operatives	18.3	13.3
Nonfarm laborers	7.7	0.8
Service workers	8.2	22.3
Private household workers	0.1	4.9
Other service workers	8.1	17.4
Farmworkers	5.1	1.7
Farmers and farm managers	3.2	0.3
Farm laborers and foremen	1.9	1.4

SOURCE: *Manpower Report of the President* (Washington, D.C.: U.S. Department of Labor. March, 1972), p. 173.

THE QUALITY AND INEQUALITY OF LIFE

Money may not be everything, but when there isn't enough of it life can be hard. Money is so basic to social class that all four dimensions of Lloyd Warner's Index of Status Characteristics (ISC) — occupation, source of income, house type, and dwelling area (Warner and Lunt, 1941: 41) — depend upon it. Other basic factors in class status, such as the achieved characteristic of educational level and the ascribed characteristic of race, are often related to economic ability. Children of people whose occupational status is low and who live in poor areas are less likely than others to go to good schools. Since racial minorities are likely to live in such conditions, many of them develop a poverty syndrome from which it is difficult to escape. This is what Eugene O'Neill was talking about when he said, "The child was diseased at birth, stricken with a hereditary ill that only the most vital men are able to shake off. I mean poverty — the most deadly and prevalent of all diseases."

CRITERIA USED TO MEASURE POVERTY The federal government bases much of its definition of poverty on income levels, which vary from year to year and area to area depending on the cost of living. At any given time, the figure established to determine who qualifies for federal welfare assistance is an arbitrary one. In 1970, the poverty threshold was $3,680 for an urban family of four; average family income was over $10,000 a year (*Characteristics of Low Income Population,* 1970). By 1976, the poverty line had become $5,500 per year, but the income of the poor had not kept pace.

In reality, circumstances such as having to travel long distances to and from a job may make it difficult for a worker and his family to live on $6,000, even though they are not officially in a state of poverty. Whatever the exact figure, low income is associated with certain pathological conditions of life. Consider these:

Even with a relatively high unemployment rate, most of the poor work full time at unskilled jobs that bring in earnings near or below the poverty line (*Manpower Report of the President,* 1970).

Between 30 to 70 percent of children from poverty backgrounds are found to have nutritional anemia, a form of slow starvation (*Citizen's Board of Inquiry,* 1968: 8).

Poor children in the South receive only 50 percent of the calories they need, and worms reduce nutrition further. The premature birth rate of the poor is three times that of the affluent. Half the premature children mature with inadequate mental development; children of the poor show impaired learning ability up to five times as often as other children (Parker, 1972: 11).

Nearly one out of every three persons living in poverty suffers from a chronic condition that limits the person's activities; for middle-class families the figure is one in thirteen (Humphrey, 1968: 2).

Low income persons do not usually have access to legal assistance, nor do they usually receive the same equitable treatment when their cases are presented in court as do middle- and particularly upper-class persons (Handler, 1971: xiii–xix).

SOCIAL RECOGNITION OF POVERTY The disadvantages of poverty apply to all. "The poor shall always be with you," says the New Testament. Yet the recognition of poverty as a social problem is recent. Until the 1930s, the poor were held to be paupers or bums, generally ignored and viewed, much like Alfred P. Doolittle in Shaw's *Pygmalion,* as the undeserving poor (Gladwin, 1967: 12). In the 1930s, President Roosevelt observed that he saw "one-third of a nation ill-housed, ill-clad, ill-nourished"; he dedicated much of his domestic program to reducing this high level of poverty.

Since the 1930s was the time of the Great Depression, it might be surmised that the recognition of poverty as a social problem grew out of that experience. Yet the concept and programing of the War on Poverty occurred in the midst of prosperity in the 1960s. Some insight can be gained into this phenomenon if we think of poverty as either rural or urban, and keep in mind that, since the census year of 1920, more and more Americans have lived in urban areas. There are sharp differences between average income levels for rural states and states where most of the populace live in large metropolitan areas. The average income on the eve of the cybernetic revolution was near the poverty level in such states as Alabama and Mississippi and was less than half the average income of such urban states as California and Michigan.

Since poverty is more severe in rural than in urban communities, it could reasonably be expected that pressures from the poor come from rural areas. In this case, common sense leads us astray. The record is clear that both in terms of organized social action by poor people and civil disorder among the poor, particularly the minority poor, the pressures have come primarily from the cities, not the small towns and rural communities. The 1968 poor people's march on Washington led by Martin Luther King included blacks, Chicanos, Indians, and poor whites, mainly from the slum areas of what they hoped would become model cities (Will and Vatter, 1970: 209–210). Major civil disorders in which poverty was a factor (*Report of the National Advisory Commission,* 1968) occurred in Los Angeles (1965), Cleveland (1966), Detroit (1967), and Newark (1967).

THE URBAN SETTING AND RELATIVE DEPRIVATION Why is poverty more keenly felt in urban than in rural areas, and why is urban protest more

SOCIAL CLASS AND POVERTY 185

evident? It may simply be that the urban poor have a greater opportunity to protest. The poverty of both black and white rural poor has long been widespread. In 1973, 10 million rural poor fell below the poverty line (Samuelson, 1973: 417), but the nature of small farming is to be independent and to live far from one's neighbor. In this century, most rural poor simply left the farms and came to the cities. Once in the cities, the poor live closer to each other, can organize more effectively, and support each other's feelings and actions. These observations are supported by the research-based concept of *relative deprivation** (see the selection that discusses this concept), one group recognizing more sharply its own deprivation through close interaction with others who are better off (Stouffer, 1949: 125; Merton, 1957: 227–234).

RELATIVE DEPRIVATION

From: Nona Glazer and Carol Creedon, *Children and Poverty: Some Sociological and Psychological Perspectives* (Chicago: Rand McNally, 1968), pp. 3–4.

The concept of relative deprivation . . . is useful in understanding the relationship of the civil rights movement and an economy of relative abundance to a growing concern with eliminating poverty. Why did blacks — and now, the other poor — wait until there was a rise in their own standard of living to demand a greater share of social and economic rewards? The factors which led to the burgeoning of the civil rights movement, especially in the early 1960s, are complex; some insight into the acceleration of the movement can be gained by contrasting the experience of deprivation in the context of mass affluence.

Relative deprivation was developed by the authors of *The American Soldier*[1] to explain certain apparently incongruous attitudes of soldiers toward their army experiences. The incongruity was that the absolute level of reward (e.g., rate of promotion in a given military unit or place of duty) was not directly related to the degree of satisfaction which the men expressed. For example, men with college educations were more dissatisfied with the rates of promotion than men with grade school educations, even though college men experienced a more rapid rate of promotion; [black] soldiers stationed in the South were no less satisfied than [black] soldiers stationed in the North; high-ranking officers were not necessarily more satisfied with their rank than were low-ranking officers. Clearly, the magnitude of reward or deprivation is not the crucial element in determining satisfaction and dissatisfaction. The concept of relative deprivation suggests that it is the comparison which an individual makes between his own situation and the situation of others which is critical in determining satisfaction, rather than the objective situation in which he finds himself. The "others" with whom [one] compares [one]self are "reference groups" (with whom the self may or may not interact, and with whom the self may or may not be similar in social status or social category). Satisfaction is a function, then, of relative deprivation and relative reward rather than of an absolute level.

[1] Samuel F. Stouffer et al., *The American Soldier*, vol. I (Princeton, N.J.: Princeton University Press, 1949), p. 250.

A CASE OF NONMATERIAL RELATIVE DEPRIVATION   In this poem by Edwin Arlington Robinson, we learn that even the wealthy may experience relative deprivation of a nonmaterial nature. What did Richard Cory lack? Friends? Ability to come to grips with personal tragedy? We don't know. But we know material wealth was not enough (Robinson, 1934):

RICHARD CORY[2]
Edwin Arlington Robinson

Whenever Richard Cory went down town,
   We people on the pavement looked at him;
He was a gentleman from sole to crown,
   Clean favored, and imperially slim.

And he was always quietly arrayed,
   And he was always human when he talked;
But still he fluttered pulses when he said,
   "Good-morning," and he glittered when he walked.

And he was rich — yes, richer than a king,
   And admirably schooled in every grace:
In fine, we thought that he was everything
   To make us wish that we were in his place.

So on we worked, and waited for the light,
   And went without the meat, and cursed the bread;
And Richard Cory, one calm summer night,
   Went home and put a bullet through his head.

THE SOCIAL CONSEQUENCES OF MATERIAL RELATIVE DEPRIVATION Giving credence to the relative deprivation thesis is the fact that as poor people have moved into the cities, this syndrome has occurred: while they are generally better off than their poor rural kin, they remain poor; and they have been involved in far more extensive protest efforts against their condition than have the rural poor.

The fact that the stronger protest against poverty occurs where there is relatively less deprivation does not obscure the reality of actual deprivation for the urban poor. The bases for their protests are to be found not only in per capita income, poor education, and higher incidence of disease and death. The conditions of life for the poor are such that Michael Harrington's popular and influential *The Other America* (1963) is an apt and descriptive title. These excerpts from testimony before the United States Commission on Civil Rights show the sense of hopelessness and powerlessness that colors the lives of the urban poor in their locked-in condition in this cybernetic age ("Testimony," 1968: 14–15):

Mrs. Charlie Jones of Gary: Well, where I live this is really a slum neighborhood is what you would call it. And, well, you know, a lot of people that doesn't live there. It's whiskey stores there. They will come and they will buy the whiskey and they sit in the car and drink it in this neighborhood because this is just a slum and who cares. And all this, your children see this. They have to grow up right with all this.

Robert Jacobs of Potrero Hill, San Francisco: On certain occasions I have waited for something like four or five hours just to get a taxi to come four or five blocks with groceries for my family. You cannot get a taxi at night. At one time I had sickness in my family and I tried to get a taxi. I had to pay an additional $35 just to get my child to the hospital, because the taxi said they couldn't find it and they didn't want to come out here.

Rev. Virgil Wood of Roxbury, Boston: One family had called the police because of an incident in the area. They waited 10 minutes, 15 minutes, 20 minutes and there was no response. Then someone was smart enough to think of calling the police, saying, "Get out here quickly, there is a Negro beating up a white man." The police were there in two minutes.

What the young and everyone else can see on a crowded inner-city slum street is open sporadic violence in a hostile environment. The impact on the socialization of young people was indicated by Claude Brown's description of his childhood experiences in the streets of Harlem (1966: 429):

[2] Source: "Richard Cory" is reprinted by permission of Charles Scribner's Sons from *The Children of the Night* by Edwin Arlington Robinson.

SOCIAL CLASS AND POVERTY 187

Unemployment lines in the thirties and in the sixties. Today many of the unemployed are victims of our cybernetic economy. SOURCE: (a) Leonard Freed/Magnum; (b) Library of Congress.

You might see somebody get cut or killed. I could go out in the street for an afternoon, and I would see so much that, when I came in the house, I'd be talking and talking for what seemed like hours. Dad would say, "Boy, why don't you stop that lyin'? You know you didn't see all that. You know you didn't see nobody do that." But I knew I had.

PROPOSALS TO END POVERTY

According to *The Report of the National Advisory Commission on Civil Disorders*, "What the American economy of the late nineteenth and early twentieth century was able to do to help the European immigrants escape from poverty is now largely impossible. New methods of escape must be found for the majority of today's poor." Effective efforts to

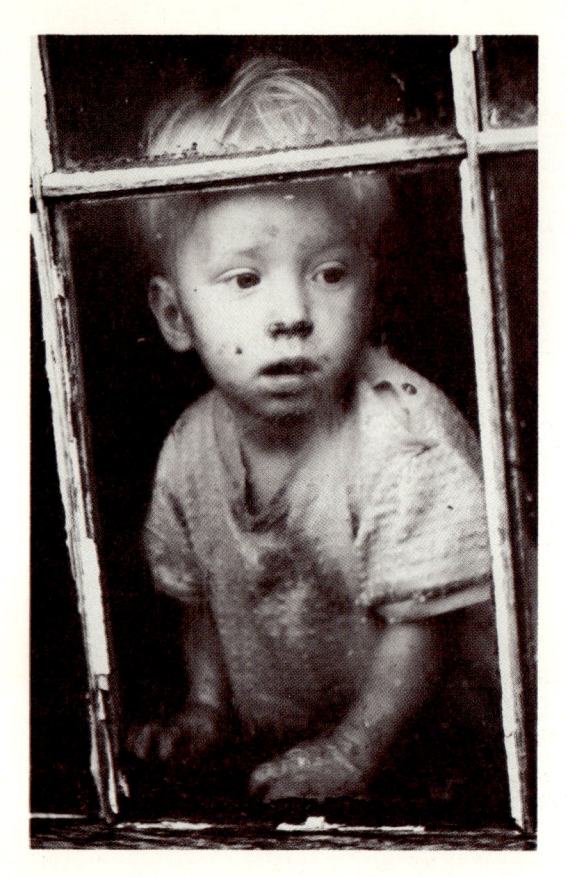

"Relative deprivation." SOURCE: Arthur Tress/Photo Researchers.

reduce and ultimately end poverty depend on an accurate assessment of why poverty persists. For those at the bottom of the scale, the commission supports the "class structure" as opposed to the "class continuum" idea discussed earlier. The evidence cited in this chapter, including the effects of the cybernetic revolution, gives substantial support to the view that the poor of today cannot generally use unskilled occupational roles for upward mobility as did the poor of earlier generations.

SELF-HELP DOCTRINES It is increasingly recognized by analysts that proposals which actually lessen poverty are based on an understanding of the facts of contemporary social life for the poor. The traditional American doctrines of self-help, rugged individualism, and voluntary assistance to people in difficulty have worked well for many, and when opportunity exists can probably continue to do so. The qualifying phrase here is *when opportunity exists*. What became evident to most Americans during the Hey-buddy-have-you-got-a-nickel-for-a-cup-of-coffee Depression days of the 1930s was that there were times when hardworking men and women could not escape poverty without broad government and private help. What is no longer so evident to most Americans who have been removed from poverty since the 1940s is that those at the bottom of the social hierarchy are still in an economic depression.

It is possible to pick yourself up by your bootstraps if you have the bootstraps. But some of the bootstrap measures of the 1930s do not apply to the poor of today. For instance, social security provides income benefits at retirement, but only to those employed in jobs where social security payments have been made — which does not include the unskilled, nonunion jobs of most poor. Also, the benefits derived from industrial union contracts since the 1935 National Labor Relations Act come only to union members (who have been declining as a proportion of the total work force since the mid-1950s). What now appears to have emerged among those poor who can't get out of it is a *culture of poverty*, which operates for survival. According to Oscar Lewis (1966: 19):

[The culture of poverty is] a subculture of Western society with its own structure and rationale, a way of life handed down from generation to generation along family lines . . . a culture in the traditional anthropological sense that it provides human beings with a design for living, with a ready-made set of solutions for human problems.

SOCIAL CLASS AND POVERTY 189

The common language of poverty. SOURCE: (a) Martin J. Dain/Magnum; (b) Burk Uzzle/Magnum; (c) Paul Fusco/Magnum; (d) Burk Uzzle/Magnum.

THE POVERTY SYNDROME   While Lewis' culture of poverty gives us some sense of a whole picture of poverty, it should be noted that not all social scientists are willing to see those in poverty as having such a fully developed, purposive design for living as Lewis suggests (see Eames and Goode, 1973: 7–9). An alternative view to the culture of poverty is the idea of a *cycle of poverty,* which predestines certain people to a life of poverty based on color, economic status, or other characteristic. You might say that one inherits poverty (Wilber, 1975: 8–9).

Here, then, is a situation in which a modern technological economy structurally excludes those in the lower class, and traditional measures to assist those at the bottom do not help them. As noted earlier in the testimony of one urban slum dweller: "Just like you step into something, you just sink and you can't get out of it." In fact, most cannot get out of it without major changes in the opportunity structure of the society.

What is being done? What can be done? A useful framework is needed for considering specific steps that have been and are being taken to consider the major disabilities created by poverty. In *Poverty, U.S.A.* (1967), Thomas Gladwin provides just such a useful framework. Gladwin notes that: poverty is being poor, poverty is being despised, poverty is being incompetent, and poverty is being powerless. Let's consider the policy and program implications of these four points.

POVERTY IS BEING POOR   It is self-evident that poverty is being poor. What is not self-evident is *why* the poor stay poor. Before the Great Depression, the focus was traditionally on the poor themselves. Some influential recent efforts to minimize poverty have drawn on this tradition. Examples of this are particularly evident in efforts aimed at the poor members of minority groups. The racial integration movement from the mid-1950s to the mid-1960s was founded on the assumption that breaking down discriminatory barriers would be enough to ensure upward social mobility for blacks as for other poor people (Makielsky, 1973: 170–172).

THE MOYNIHAN REPORT   An influential analysis of the failure of upward mobility was the Moynihan Report (1965). In this policy-oriented analysis, Daniel P. Moynihan, who worked in the Kennedy, Johnson, Nixon, and Ford administrations, presented the idea that the lack of family cohesion among poor black families was the major factor inhibiting upward mobility. (This point of view was not well-received by blacks and by some scholars.) Moynihan attributed the breakdown of many black families to the aftermath of slavery and segregation perpetuated by a welfare system that offers aid to families *without* fathers. This welfare system was first developed in the Depression and was designed to aid the most needy. The more recent effect was to encourage men earning a low income to leave their families so that their wives and children could qualify for public assistance. Some effort has been made to rid welfare programs of this dysfunction. Moynihan saw larger social factors in the poverty syndrome but focused on the poor individual in the context of his family, using a culture of poverty analysis (see Table 6-9).

With all its insights, there are difficulties with the Moynihan thesis. The research of Hyman Rodman and others shows that the apparently disorganized form of much poor black family behavior — which is generally found in the lowest class levels of other groups as well — may represent the most effective solution to their problems of social and economic deprivation (Rodman, 1959). While poverty does often appear in the same families from one generation to another, the subculture of poverty (if it can be so identified) does not appear to be independent of the values and goals of

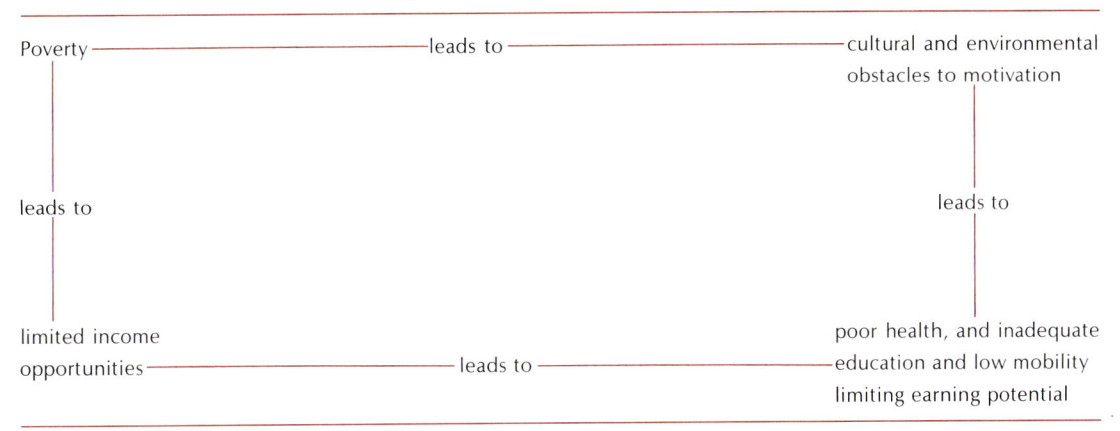

Table 6-9   The Cyclical Nature of Intergenerational Poverty

Poverty ——————————— leads to ——————————— cultural and environmental obstacles to motivation

| leads to | leads to |

limited income opportunities ——————————— leads to ——————————— poor health, and inadequate education and low mobility limiting earning potential

SOURCE: Prepared by Daniel P. Moynihan for the Council of Economic Advisers to President Kennedy, 1963.

the larger society. In his analysis of young poor urban black males who live much of their lives un- or underemployed on street corners, Liebow observed that (1967: 222):

> ... the street corner man does not appear as a carrier of an independent cultural tradition. His behavior appears not so much as a way of realizing the distinctive goals and values of his own subculture, or of conforming to its models, but rather as his way of trying to achieve many of the goals and values of the larger society, of failing to do this, and of concealing his failure from others and himself as best he can.

DISRUPTING EFFECTS OF LARGE SOCIAL FORCES (Note that Liebow's "subculture" is based on minority status as well as poverty.)

The failure of poorly educated and unskilled individuals to succeed in the cybernetic age appears to be related as much to social forces in the larger society as to difficulties in the family structure of the poor. There is some confusion between *demographic characteristics*, such as number of households without fathers, and *social structure*, which may appear quite different from the middle-class norm as people try to maximize adjustment to surrounding conditions. It is in this sense that people develop a culture of poverty. It has functional value for the purpose of survival even as people seek to improve their circumstances. Thus, the intergenerational poverty syndrome appears to be more related to the larger economic, educational, and social conditions of the poor than to inherent characteristics of their family structures. Policies which fail to recognize these relationships have little chance of success.

INCOME MAINTENANCE PROPOSALS Perhaps the major poverty policy today favors some form of *income maintenance* program. Such proposals now appear to cut across the conservative–liberal political spectrum and to extend beyond the limited resources of the local communities where the poor are concentrated. While the war on poverty is associated with the liberal domestic policies of John Kennedy's and Lyndon Johnson's administrations, Richard Nixon in the first year of his conservative administration, made the following proposal in regard to welfare reform (1970: 204):

I propose that the federal government build a foundation under the income of every American family with dependent children that cannot care for itself — wherever in America that family may live.

Mr. Nixon's proposal, in some respects reminiscent of Moynihan's focus on families rather than individuals, no longer assumed that the normal opportunity structure in the society would enable all poor people to work themselves out of poverty without substantial assistance.

In recent years, another technique advocated to create a guaranteed income above the poverty line is the *negative income tax* (Green, 1968). Under the current system, people pay federal income taxes on earnings over a certain amount, including $750 per dependent or certain business and professional expenses. Income above these exemptions is taxed on a sliding scale. A negative income tax would provide an individual or family below the taxable level enough additional income to exceed the poverty line, also according to a sliding scale. The scheme is thus intended not only to supplement all inadequate incomes up to a certain level but also to preserve the American work ethic — though it might make some people work less, not more.

The fact that both conservative and liberal administrations have advocated minimum income proposals suggests, on the one hand, that there has been widespread recognition of the locked-in condition of the poor and on the other, that there may be emerging a consensus in the society to establish and maintain an income level above poverty for all. The poor themselves are becoming increasingly active in support of such plans (Blanchard, 1972).

POVERTY IS BEING DESPISED Poverty is not likely to be ended by a minimum income alone. In the tradition of the American work ethic, even those now on welfare — most of whom are aged, ill, or dependent children — are often branded as undeserving. As David Matza observes (1966: 312):

The disreputable poor are the people who remain unemployed, or casually or irregularly employed, even during periods approaching full employment and prosperity; for that reason . . . they live in disrepute.

POLICY EFFECTS OF BEING AN OUT-GROUP This attitude strongly inhibits any such help to the poor as a guaranteed minimum income and works against other approaches. Poor people are an *out-group**, whereas those higher in social status tend to be *in-groups**; thus, a double standard is created (Merton, 1957: 428–429). Leaders of large bankrupt corporations like the Penn Central Railroad or the Lockheed Corporation are not considered disreputable. They receive billions of dollars in public underwriting of their losses. In contrast, the disreputable poor out-group are often granted assistance grudgingly. The government "utiliz[es] a 'means test' and demand[s] behavior which evidences a 'deserving poor'" (Miller and Rein, 1967: 513).

This approach to poverty programming[3] is evident in both Democratic President Lyndon Johnson's and Republican President Richard Nixon's policy statements. As President Johnson stated in his Message on Poverty in 1964 (10):

[A poor person] does not have the skills demanded by a complex society. He does not know how to acquire those skills. He faces a mounting sense of despair which drains initiative and ambition and energy.

---

[3] An excellent treatment of the relationship of the "work ethic" to problems of the poor in crosscultural perspective is found in Edwin Eames and Judith Granich Goode, *Urban Poverty in a Cross-Cultural Context,* The Free Press, 1973: 258–262.

And as President Nixon stated in his address to the nation on welfare reform in 1969 (205):

Under this [minimum income] proposal, everyone who accepts benefits must also accept work or training provided suitable jobs are available....

President Ford, in his 1976 budget address, suggested limiting food stamps to those at or below the poverty line, and setting a limited standard deduction for all, except the elderly, at $100 per month. Elderly persons were to receive a deduction of $125 per month. He also advocated allowing two unemployment compensation programs to expire in 1977 (see the New York *Times,* January 22, 1976).

These attitudes weaken poverty programs in both subjective and objective ways. On the subjective level, poor people tend to develop a negative view of themselves that sharply limits their response to assistance programs, leading others to hold them in low esteem (Deutsch, 1960). On the objective level, proposals to maintain income do not consider all persons in a state of poverty. Figure 6-5 indicates who the beneficiaries of public assistance are. HEW estimated that fewer than one percent are able-bodied adult males. It is questionable whether the others could work more than they have been doing. See Table 6-10 also.

PROBLEMS WITH THE WORK–MEANS TEST FOR THE UNSKILLED Another objective problem with the work–means test approach is that the structure of employment in the American cybernetic economy is such that even if all the able-bodied adults were trained effectively, there would still not be sufficient employment for the poor. To see why, let us consider some observations Nelson Rockefeller made while he was governor of the urbanized state of New York. Governor Rockefeller noted the need for advanced educational training for most people, including most of the poor, in order to be economically successful. He observed that his grandfather,

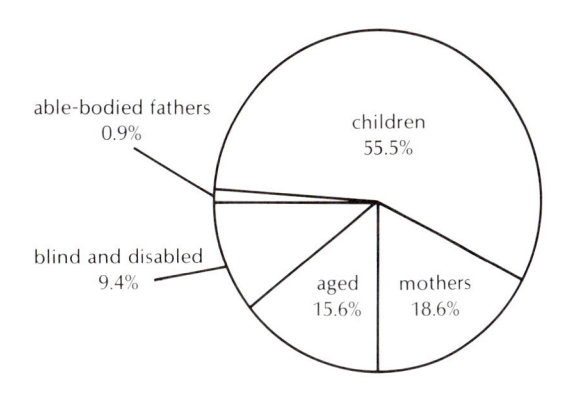

Figure 6-5 Characteristics of social welfare assistance recipients.

- able-bodied fathers 0.9%
- children 55.5%
- blind and disabled 9.4%
- aged 15.6%
- mothers 18.6%

oil tycoon John D. Rockefeller, was a school dropout at age fourteen, which would have precluded economic success today. The governor reported that (1966: 2):

There were scads of unskilled jobs around in my grandfather's day. Now these kinds of jobs have gone the way of the buffalo.... Young people today need all the education, training and guidance they can get. There are more opportunities than ever, thanks to our boom-

Table 6-10 Number of Recipients of Public Assistance (1972)

Program	Number of recipients in millions
Old Age Assistance (OAA)	1.9
Aid to Blind (AB)	0.1
Aid to Permanently and Totally Disabled (APTD)	1.2
Aid to Families with Dependent Children (includes unemployed father provision, AFDC-UF)	11.2
Total	14.3

SOURCE: U.S. Bureau of the Census, *Statistical Abstract of the United States,* 1973, Table 500.

ing American economy, but not for those people without skills.

UNEMPLOYMENT ON THE CLASS SCALE While the unskilled are particularly vulnerable to joblessness, it would be unfair to omit mentioning that unemployment has become a national problem, affecting higher as well as lower classes. In 1975, unemployment rose to nearly 9 percent. By June 1976, it had dropped to 7.5 percent, but that is still a high percentage and does not include those who have become so depressed in their quest for work that they no longer declare themselves to be actively looking. In 1975, *Time* magazine gave a general breakdown of the unemployed (*Time*, March 17, 1975: 20):

1 out of 16 adult men
1 out of 12 adult women
1 out of 5 teen-agers
1 out of 6 young Viet Nam veterans
1 out of 14 whites
1 out of 7 non-whites
1 out of 9 blue-collar workers
1 out of 19 heads of households.

A year later the same magazine ran a story on employment, "Slim Pickings for the Class of '76." Numerous stories were told of underemployed persons, an office messenger with a Ph.D. in medieval history for one. The article discusses by implication a problem called *status inconsistency*, in which the individual does not line up appropriately on all dimensions of status and receive rewards compatible with some aspects of status; a highly educated person, for example, expects high status, a successful career, and a high salary.

The *Time* article shows that status inconsistency for upper-level groups is considered dysfunctional for the society (*Time*, March 29, 1976: 48):

What is bad, however, is to have a college graduate stuck in a lower-level job too long. Society is ill served by the dissatisfaction he feels as the job that once seemed a temporary expedient begins to look like a career. And there is an insidious ripple effect to the under-employment of the well-educated. When Ph.D.s take jobs away from the B.A.s, the B.A.s find positions — in retail sales for example — that used to go to high school graduates. . . .

Sooner or later, the best-educated young Americans find jobs, if only ones for which they are overqualified, and during a lifetime they will still make much more money than youths with less education. In the process, however, the college-educated under-employed aggravate a social problem even more disruptive than their own: the travail of the non-college youths for whom there are no jobs at all.

Programs for the poor are typically tied to notions regarding the willingness of the poor to work. But what if there is no work? The development of effective programs to end poverty is related to the attitudes and values of those in a position to support the programs. Reformers argue for more recognition of the fact that most poor are excluded from opportunity and a revision of attitudes concerning the poor. Philip Wogaman, professor of Christian social ethics at the Wesley Theological Seminary, argues strongly for more objectivity in the handling of poverty programs (1968: 76–77):

One of the striking aspects of most welfare programs . . . is the expectation that the recipient will humbly acknowledge his indebtedness and properly express his gratitude to the giver. The outraged public response to the Welfare Rights Movement was revealing. More than anything else, the members of this movement [of poor people] sought to have their aid payments considered as a basic right, not as a gift, and it is believed that the recipients should be grateful to the givers . . . but [giving in such a manner] . . . leaves the humiliated poor in a scarcely improved condition. There is much to be said for an objective handling of the basic conditions of life, treating them rather as a basic human right. . . .

The minimum income proposal is not likely to get far as long as any gain made by the poor stigmatizes their improved status. Indeed, such blame is one reason why the poor are excluded from the opportunity structure beyond the minimum level (Miller, 1967). Yet there are practical as well as idealistic reasons for improving the conditions of the poor. The American secular democratic and the Judaeo–Christian religious traditions hold to the dignity of every individual whatever his or her circumstances. This fact aside, the poor, who are increasingly squeezed into deteriorating urban industrial centers, no longer suffer in silence. As Henry Ford II noted after the Detroit riots of 1967: "It is difficult building automobiles in burned down factories." And as Paul Samuelson, the economist, remarks (Samuelson: 1973: 765):

For conscience's sake, we are impelled to help. Besides, history teaches us that men do not always starve quietly.

POVERTY IS BEING INCOMPETENT One theme in this view of poverty is the lack of desirable skills for employment among those at the bottom of the ladder. As noted in the preceding section, such competence does not guarantee upward mobility, but it is a prerequisite and greatly increases the chances of mobility. Competence would lessen the rigidity of an increasingly closed system by providing the lower classes more of the opportunities that are available to others in an open system.

EDUCATION AND TRAINING NEEDS There are two routes to occupational competence on the part of the poor: education for children and training or retraining for adults. Since the future is with the young, let us consider education first. In American society, the belief has long been held that widespread opportunity for schooling is the best way to avoid a hardened class structure (Brookover and Gottlieb, 1964: 177). This old ideal has become widespread as we have moved from a *Gemeinschaft* (small town) society with continuity of occupations and life styles from one generation to the next to a *Gesellschaft* (metropolitan) society with intergenerational discontinuity of occupations, particularly in the lower classes. As the society becomes increasingly based on secondary rather than primary ties, and as it becomes credentials-oriented, education becomes more than ever the road to betterment.

POOR SCHOOLS FOR POOR CHILDREN Unfortunately, the quality of the schools available to poor children has been static or deteriorating just when the need for quality has grown (Bommarito and Kerber, 1965). Census data show that most middle-class people have moved out of the central cities, which have the heaviest concentration of the poor. Since about half the school tax support is from local sources, city schools now get less tax money than before and have less to offer poor children. The limited resources of rural school districts mean that the rural poor are no better off. The national study on equal educational opportunity conducted by James Coleman (1966) identified the social class status of families and the larger community setting as the two most influential factors in academic and later occupational success — one reason for the controversial court-ordered busing of children from poor to better quality schools (see Makielski, 1973).

THE ELEMENTARY AND SECONDARY EDUCATION ACT The Elementary and Secondary Education Act (ESEA) of 1965 was the first major federal funding bill for schools below the college level. The act is designed to meet some of the problems and to stimulate communities and states to increase their support for schools in poor areas. The major provisions of the act would improve education as a source of opportunity for the young poor. These provisions include (*Federal Role in Education*, 1966: 46–49):

1. federal aid for school operation and maintenance in districts where there are families with incomes under $2000 (later increased)

2. authorization of grants for the acquisition of school library resources, textbooks, and other printed instructional materials for the use of children and teachers

3. authorization of grants to the states for supplementary educational centers and services to provide vitally needed educational services and to establish model school programs.

In many ways, the ESEA turned out to be more a statement of aims than an actual benefit. As Detroit's superintendent of schools Norman Drachler noted in an interview in 1971, federal funding has not offset the sharp decline in local tax support. In consequence, federal aid has slowed the deterioration without significantly advancing educational quality for the poor. Nevertheless, the basic concept of offering more resources to schools in disadvantaged areas is now law and is widely recognized.

THE ECONOMIC OPPORTUNITY ACT To help meet the needs of the adult poor, Congress passed the Economic Opportunity Act (EOA) in 1965, which calls for the use of public schools and private businesses to rehabilitate and train unskilled adults. Even this approach offers only a partial solution to the problem of poverty. The economic effectiveness of retraining for adults and education for the young depends on the availability of jobs at the end of the process.

Perhaps the best approach to cracking the occupational exclusion of the poor is quite recent. Major new programs were advanced to assist the third of the nation living in poverty during the Great Depression of the 1930s. Beginning in the Hoover administration in 1932, the Reconstruction Finance Corporation was chartered and authorized millions of dollars in loans to save banks, railroads, building and loan associations, and other financial institutions (Schlesinger, 1960: 225–226). By the end of the 1930s, there was an alphabet soup of new government agencies to help the poor, including the AAA (Agricultural Adjustment Administration) to stabilize farm prices, the FHA (Federal Housing Administration) to offer low-interest loans to people endangered by foreclosure of mortgages on their homes, the CCC (Civilian Conservation Corps) to employ young people and aid in the preservation of natural resources, the NLRB (National Labor Relations Board) to assist in collective bargaining between unions and employers — and many others.

ECONOMIC EXPANSION AND SOCIAL PROGRAMING Since the 1930s, the American economy, based on government controls and free enterprise, has expanded far beyond that of any other nation. Hence, it would be hard to argue that the changes in the social system in the 1930s undermined the growth and potential of the society. The very opposite is true. The poor had become a small proportion of the population by the early 1970s. The problems now facing Americans are largely a consequence of enormous economic expansion, which has meant greater dependence on foreign sources of raw materials and foreign markets for our products. This system of global interdependence has great potential benefits. However, it can reduce stability unless we use the skills of Americans in the lower strata to increase our competitiveness in the world economy.

POVERTY IS BEING POWERLESS The problem of starting new programs and expanding old ones may be difficult because of the relatively small poor population in American society today. Yet most poor people, individually and as a group, have been relatively powerless to change their circumstances. As Gunnar Myrdal observed, "No privileged class in history has ever climbed down from its privileges and opened its monopolies just out of goodwill. . . . idealism plays its role only when there is pressure from below" (1970: 209).

ACQUIRING POLITICAL POWER Lacking economic and political power, how can the poor influence society to press for the elimination of poverty? Increasingly, policy-oriented theorists have advocated a coalition of the various poverty groupings in the society — rural and urban, black and white, and so on. This was the thrust of Bayard Rustin's article "From Protest to Politics" (1965). It was the concept behind Martin Luther King, Jr.'s, poor people's march on Washington in 1968, and of Gunnar Myrdal's analysis of that march (1970: 209):

If you attack poverty, you must do it on a broad scale. Martin Luther King knew this. What I have is the fear that the poor people of a different ethnic character will fight each other as they have always done; what I also have is the hope that they will stand together and ask for their rights.

Political action for the poor requires effort at various levels of society. The poor people's march was aimed at creating national pressure to expand such programs as those under the Elementary and Secondary Education and Economic Opportunity Acts passed in the mid 1960s, as well as to press for new programs like income maintenance. Such action often requires effort at the grass-roots level. Rent strikes in Chicago led by the late Saul Alinsky, and in New York by Jesse Gray, are examples. Organizing to elect sympathetic local leaders are others.

BREAKING THE POVERTY SYNDROME In practical social and political terms, what are the chances that a coalition of the poor will succeed? Any major moves to increase opportunities for the poor to achieve upward mobility may meet with a backlash from others as they have in the past. At the same time, there are recent signs that coalition can bring the poor some ability to break out of the poverty syndrome. As Charles Valentine observes (1970: 170–171):

Urgent public issues sometimes require and bring to reality what had seemed to be visionary theoretical solutions. The precedents of recent national legislation in civil rights and related fields show that there is potential for seemingly improbable political responses to massive and urgent public pressure. . . . The result may be that very great previously wasted or destructive human energies would be liberated in a regenerative movement of potentially transcendent importance for the whole society. To compare this potentiality with what has actually been taking place in our cities . . . brings home the need for a bold new approach.

SUMMARY

We have discussed the nature of social classes and of social mobility in American society. The problem of continuing poverty is of particular concern to our discussion. Some major points are:

*Social classes** characterize all modern societies, though some societies have more upward and downward *social mobility** than others. The measurement of social class position and life style involves a variety of factors, including occupational status, educational attainment, political influence, social prestige, and related characteristics.

With the *cybernetic* (computer) *revolution** and a generally expanding economic base, most Americans have moved upward. For them, the social class system has been a fluid *social continuum.* But the unskilled have remained static or moved downward. In consequence, using standard occupational and related class measurements, about one-fifth of the population is near or below the poverty line. While this is a smaller proportion than a generation ago, poverty is still a major social problem.

Because of discrimination, including a former racial *caste** system in the Deep South, a high proportion of racial minorities still occupy the lowest stratum. To them, as to others with poor educational and occupational training, modern technological society has not given the opportunity for upward mobility. Within such groups, functional patterns emerge for living in poverty. Some consider these patterns sufficiently developed to be called a *culture of poverty.*

Concentration in cities has made the poor more visible. Concentration also intensifies feelings of *relative deprivation**, leading to organized protest.

Poverty means being poor, despised, incompetent, and powerless.

Largely in response to organized protest, an increasing number of private and public programs have been proposed to reduce or end poverty in American society. Prominent proposals are income maintenance plans, negative income tax, better quality schools, and job retraining.

Changing the view of the poor as disreputable violators of the work ethic would make it easier to put into effect these and related proposals. The goal is to end widespread impoverishment, once believed inevitable but no longer thought to be so.

QUESTIONS FOR DISCUSSION

1. In what social class would you place yourself? Take into account the occupational status of your family and your own educational and occupational goals. What other criteria might you use?

2. In modern technological society, there is both upward and downward social mobility. Give an example of each. Horizontal mobility also occurs. Give an example.

3. Max Weber and others note that power is a major factor in social class stratification. Why is it said (see Gladwin) that being poor is being powerless?

4. To what extent do you think social class affects the personality and behavior of people? How might it affect how you treat someone else?

5. Do you believe that there is still a racial caste system in the United States like the one described by Davis and the Gardners in *Deep South*?

6. In what ways does the traditional status of racial minorities and of women improve the opportunity for others not in these groups in the society?

7. How can the concepts of *relative deprivation* and *class conflict* be related to each other?

8. Invent and discuss a stratification system based on characteristics other than wealth, power, and prestige, for example athletic ability, IQ, or physical attractiveness.

9. Based on your understanding of how well antipoverty programs have worked, do you believe that class consciousness (awareness of common situation and problems) is growing or declining in American society?

10. Review your understanding of the following terms and concepts:

social class

Index of Status Characteristics (ISC)

social mobility

class structure thesis

status continuum thesis

white ethnics

racial caste system

cybernetic revolution

relative deprivation

culture of poverty

income maintenance plan

work ethic

REFERENCES

Alvarez, Rudolfo
- 1971 "The unique psycho-historical experience of the Mexican-American people." Social Science Quarterly 52: 15–29.

- 1975 America's New Joblessness: The Frustration of Idleness. *Time* (March 17): 19–26.

Aveni, Adrian
- 1976 "Alternative stratification systems: the case of interpersonal respect among leisure participants." The Sociological Quarterly 17: 53–64.

Blanchard, Eric
- 1972 "The poor people and the 'white press.'" R. Turner and L. Killian (eds.), Collective Behavior. Englewood Cliffs, N.J.: Prentice-Hall: 217–221.

Bommarito, Barbara and August Kerber
- 1965 The Schools and the Urban Crisis. New York: Holt, Rinehart and Winston.

Brookover, Wilbur and David Gottlieb
- 1964 A Sociology of Education. New York: American Book Company.

Brown, Claude
- 1966 Manchild in the Promised Land. New York: The New American Library.

Carman, Harry and Harold Syrett
- 1955 A History of the American People, II. New York: Knopf.

- 1970 Characteristics of the Low-Income Population. U.S. Census Bureau. Report P-60, No. 81. Washington, D.C.: Government Printing Office.

Centers, Richard
- 1949 The Psychology of Social Classes. Princeton, N.J.: Princeton University Press.

- 1968 "Citizens' board of inquiry into hunger and malnutrition in the United States." Hunger, U.S.A. Washington, D.C.: New Community Press.

Coleman, James
- 1966 Equal Educational Opportunity. Washington, D.C.: Government Printing Office.

- 1971 Current Population Reports. Series P-60, No. 77. Washington, D.C.: Government Printing Office.

Davis, Allison, Burleigh Gardner, and Mary Gardner
- 1941 Deep South. Chicago: University of Chicago Press.

Deutsch, Martin
- 1960 "Minority group and class states as related to social and personality factors in scholastic achievement." The Society for Applied Anthropology, Monograph #2. Ithaca, New York.

Duncan, Otis Dudley
- 1965 "The trend of occupational mobility in the United States." American Sociological Review 30: 491–498.

Eames, Edwin and Judith Granich Goode
　1973　Urban Poverty in a Cross-Cultural Context. New York: Free Press.

Ellis, Robert, W. Clayton Lane and Virginia Olesen
　1963　"The index of class position: an improved intercommunity measure of stratification." American Sociological Review 28: 271–277.

　1966　Federal Role in Education. Washington, D.C.: Congressional Quarterly Service.

Ferman, Louis
　1968　The Negro and Equal Employment Opportunities. New York: Praeger.

Ford, Gerald
　1976　Budget Message to the Congress of the United States. Reported in New York Times (January 22).

Ginsberg, Eli
　1960　"Segregation and manpower waste." Phylon 21: 311–316.

Gladwin, Thomas
　1967　Poverty U.S.A. Boston: Little, Brown.

Glazer, Nona and Carol Creedon
　1968　Children and Poverty: Some Sociological and Psychological Perspectives. Chicago: Rand McNally.

Glenn, Norval
　1963　"Some changes in the relative status of American nonwhites." Phylon 24: 109–122.

Goodman, Leon
　1969　"How to ransack social mobility and other kinds of cross classification tables." American Journal of Sociology 75: 1–40.

Gordon, David
　1972　Theories of Poverty and the Underemployed. Lexington, Mass.: D.C. Heath.

Green, Christopher
　1968　Improving Income Maintenance Through Negative Taxation. Federal Programs for the Development of Human Resources. Washington, D.C.: Joint Economic Committee, Subcommittee on Economic Progress.

Handler, Joel
　1971　Family Law and the Poor. Westport, Conn.: Essays by Jacobus Tenbroek.

Harrington, Michael
　1963　The Other America. Baltimore: Penguin.

Hodge, Robert, Paul Siegel, and Peter Rossi
　1964　"Occupational prestige in the United States, 1925–1963." American Journal of Sociology 70: 286–302.

Hodge, Robert W. and D. J. Trieman
　1968　"Class identification in the United States." American Journal of Sociology 73: 535–542.

Hourwich, Isaac
　1912　Immigration and Labor: The Economic Aspects of European Immigration to the United States. New York: G. P. Putnam's Sons.

Humphrey, Hubert
　1968　"The future of health services for the poor." Public Health Reports. Washington, D.C.: U.S. Department of Health, Education and Welfare: 1–5.

Inglehart, Babette and Anthony Mangione
　1974　The Image of Pluralism in American Literature: An Annotated Bibliography. New York: Institute of Human Relations.

Johnson, Lyndon
   1970   "The great unfinished work of our society" (from President Johnson's Message on Poverty, March 16, 1964). R. Will and H. Vatter (eds.), Poverty in Affluence. New York: Harcourt, Brace and World: 9–11.

Kirchner, Walter
   1955   History of Russia. New York: Barnes & Noble.

Kornhauser, William
   1966   "'Power elite' or 'veto groups'?" R. Bendix and S. Lipset (eds.), Class, Status, and Power. New York: The Free Press: 210–218.

Landecker, Werner
   1960   "Class boundaries." American Sociological Review 25: 868–877.

Lenski, Gerhard
   1966   Power and Privilege. A Theory of Social Stratification. New York: McGraw-Hill.

Levine, Irving and Judy Herman
   1972   "The life of white ethnics." Dissent (Winter): 1–8.

Lewis, Oscar
   1966   "The culture of poverty." Scientific American 4: 19–25.

Liebow, Elliot
   1967   Tally's Corner: A Study of Negro Streetcorner Men. Boston: Little, Brown.

Lipset, Seymour and Reinhard Bendix
   1959   Social Mobility in Industrial Society. Berkeley, Cal.: University of California Press.

Makielski, S. J.
   1973   Beleaguered Minorities. San Francisco: W. H. Freeman.

   1976   Manpower Information Service Bulletin. Bureau of National Affairs, Inc., vol. 7, nos. 16 and 18.

   1970   Manpower Report of the President. U.S. Department of Labor. Washington, D.C.: Government Printing Office.

Marx, Karl
   1956   Karl Marx: Selected Writings in Sociology and Social Philosophy. T. Bottomore and M. Rubel (eds.), New York: McGraw-Hill.

Matras, Judah
   1973   Population and Societies. Englewood Cliffs, New Jersey: Prentice-Hall.

   1975   Social Inequality, Stratification, and Mobility. Englewood Cliffs, New Jersey: Prentice-Hall.

Matza, David
   1966   "The disreputable poor." N. Smelser and S. Lipset (eds.), Social Structure and Social Mobility in Economic Development. Chicago: The Aldine Press: 311–339.

Medicine, Beatrice
   1973   "The native American." D. Spiegel and P. Keith-Spiegel (eds.), Outsiders, U.S.A. San Francisco: Rinehart: 391–407.

Merton, Robert
   1957   Social Theory and Social Structure. New York: The Free Press.

Michael, Donald
   1962   Cybernation: The Silent Conquest. Santa Barbara, Cal.: Center for the Study of Democratic Institutions.

Miller, S. M. with M. Rein, P. Roby, and B. Gross
   1967   "Poverty, inequality, and conflict." The Annals of the Academy of Political and Social Science (September): 18–25.

Miller, S. M. and Martin Rein
1967 "Poverty, inequality, and policy." H. Becker (ed.), Social Problems. New York: John Wiley & Sons: 426–516.

Moyers, William
1969 Group Life Report. New York: Institute of Human Relations.

Morgan, James et al.
1962 Income and Welfare in the United States. New York: McGraw-Hill.

Moynihan, Daniel
1965 The Negro Family: The Case for National Action. Washington, D.C.: U.S. Department of Labor.

Myrdal, Gunnar
1970 "Backlash, privilege, and pressure." R. Will and H. Vatter (eds.), Poverty in Affluence. New York: Harcourt, Brace & World: 210.

Nixon, Richard
1970 "Welfare alternatives" (from President Nixon's Address to the Nation on Welfare Reform, August 8, 1969). R. Will and H. Vatter (eds.), Poverty in Affluence. New York: Harcourt, Brace & World: 203–208.

Page, Charles
1961 "Social class and American sociology." R. Bendix and S. Lipset (eds.), Class, Status and Power. New York: The Free Press: 45–48.

Parker, Richard
1972 The Myth of the Middle Class. New York: Liveright.

Passow, A. Harry
1963 Education in Depressed Areas. New York: Teachers College Bureau of Publications.

1968 Report of the National Advisory Commission on Civil Disorders. Washington, D.C.: Government Printing Office.

Rist, Ray
1972 The Quest for Autonomy: A Socio-Historical Study of Black Revolt in Detroit. Los Angeles: UCLA Center for Afro-American Studies.

Rockefeller, Nelson
1966 "Dropouts — one man's answer." *This Week* (January 23): 2.

Robinson, Edwin Arlington
1934 Collected Poems. New York: Macmillan.

Rodman, Hyman
1959 "On understanding lower-class behavior." Social and Economic Studies 8: 441–449.

Rustin, Bayard
1965 "From protest to politics: the future of the civil rights movement." A Commentary Reprint (February). New York: Institute of Human Relations.

Samuelson, Paul
1973 Economics. New York: McGraw-Hill.

Schlesinger, Arthur
1960 The Politics of Upheaval. Boston: Houghton Mifflin.

1976 "Slim pickings for the class of '76." *Time* (March 29): 45–49.

Sorokin, Pitirim
1947 "What is a social class?" Journal of Legal and Political Sociology: 21–28.

Spiegel, David and P. Keith-Spiegel
1973 Outsiders, U.S.A. San Francisco: Rinehart.

Stouffer, Samuel
1949 The American Soldier, I. Princeton, N.J.: Princeton University Press.

Taeuber, Karl, Leonard Chiazze, and William Haenszel
   1968   Migration in the United States: An Analysis of Residence Historics. Washington, D.C.: Government Printing Office.

   1968   Testimony (to the U.S. Commission on Civil Rights). The City (January): 14–15.

Thurow, Lester and Robert Lucas
   1974   "The American distribution of income: a structural problem." L. Rainwater (ed.), Social Problems and Public Policy. Chicago: Aldine: 75–88.

Valentine, Charles
   1970   Culture and Poverty. Chicago: University of Chicago Press.

Warner, Lloyd
   1960   Social Class in America. New York: Harper Torchbooks.

Warner, Lloyd and Paul Lunt
   1941   The Social Life of a Modern Community. New Haven, Conn.: Yale University Press.

Wattenberg, Ben
   1976   The Real America. New York: Capricorn Books.

Weber, Max
   1946   From Max Weber: Essays in Sociology. H. Gerth and C. Wright Mills (trans.). New York: Oxford University Press.

Wilber, George
   1975   "Determinants of poverty." George L. Wilber (ed.), Poverty: A New Perspective. Lexington, Kentucky: University of Kentucky Press.

Willhelm, Sidney
   1970   Who Needs the Negro? Cambridge, Mass.: Schenkman.

Will, Robert and Harold Vatter
   1970   Poverty in Affluence. New York: Harcourt, Brace and World.

Wish, Harvey
   1960   "Turner and the moving of the frontier." The American Historian. New York: Oxford University Press: 181–208.

Wogaman, Philip
   1968   Guaranteed Annual Income: The Moral Issue. Nashville: Abington Press.

   1974   Yearbook of Labour Statistics. Geneva, Switzerland: International Labour Office.

   1975   Yearbook of Labor Statistics. Washington, D.C.: Government Printing Office.

Chapter 7

ANOMIE AND THE ELDERLY

Of old when folk lay sick and sorely tried,
The doctors gave them physic and they died:
But here's a happier age, for now we know
Both how to make men sick and keep them so!

Hilaire Belloc

THE ELDERLY AND SOCIETY

The elderly are creating a new social problem in American society. Only recently has there been a large enough number of elderly citizens in the population to create a problem. Our rising standard of living, combined with medical advances, has enabled people to live longer. Just how rapidly the elderly have become a significant segment of society is clear if we compare the picture today with that at the turn of the century. In 1900, one in twenty-five Americans was over age sixty-five. By 1970, one in ten was over sixty-five. In 1900, life expectancy was forty-seven years; in 1970, it was nearly seventy years *(Population and the American Future,* 1972: 11). In the mid-nineteenth century, there were only ten persons over sixty for every hundred under fifteen. By the mid-twentieth century, there were forty-five persons over sixty for every hundred under fifteen (Sheldon, 1960: 28). In 1900, there were slightly more than 3 million older persons in the United States. In 1970, there were over 20 million — a sixfold increase, and double the increase for the general population (Atchley, 1972: 9).

SOCIAL GERONTOLOGY What are some social consequences of this shift toward greater age? How does the presence of the old affect other age groups? How do the elderly get along in a rapidly changing society? These and related questions are asked increasingly often by social scientists and by

Americans in general. In a variation on Horace Greeley's "Go west, young man, go west," a bright young sociologist could well be advised, "Go to the old, young colleague, go to the old." The field of *social gerontology**, which specializes in the societal aspects of aging, is of recent origin. The term itself was not introduced until the mid 1950s. By then, the average life span of Americans had so increased that a new population group had appeared (Tibbitts, 1960). The long-term trend of a growing population of the elderly can be seen in Figure 7-1.

MAJOR PROBLEMS CONFRONTING THE ELDERLY
There are two kinds of problems confronting the elderly. First is the general problem of adjusting to roles that are satisfying to them and to others. This problem exists in the context of rapid social change in a youth-oriented society. Second, a high proportion of the elderly suffer from poverty, illness, and social isolation. Easing these problems involves personal and family adjustments and broad questions of social policy.

Emile Durkheim, the great French sociologist, presented at the turn of the century a classic statement on the meaning of *anomie** in his analysis of the specific problem of suicide (1954, viz. 1897). He cited a lack of rules and normlessness as a cause not only of anomie but of a general social rootlessness, alienation, of certain individuals and groups in modern society, a problem increasingly affecting the elderly, who experience relatively high rates of emotional disorders.

Discussion of the problems of the old lends itself to understanding Durkheim's concept of anomie, particularly as that term relates to social isolation (see the selection on anomie). Another concept stressed in this chapter is that of stereotyping, here referring to negative overgeneralizations about groups of people.

ANOMIE

From: Emile Durkheim, *Suicide*, John Spaulding and George Simpson, trans. (Glencoe, Ill.: The Free Press, 1951), p. 246. Copyright 1951 by The Free Press, a corporation. Permission to quote also granted by Routledge and Kegan Paul, Ltd., London.

This is an excerpt from Durkheim's *Suicide* on the concept of anomie that illustrates its general applicability. Note that Durkheim's use of the term *regulation* refers to the informal norms of society rather than legislative rules.

It is not true ... that human activity can be released from all restraint. Nothing in the world can enjoy such a privilege. All existence being part of the universe is related to the remainder; its nature and method of manifestation accordingly depend not only on itself but on other beings, who consequently restrain and regulate it. Here there are only differences of degree and form between the mineral realm and the thinking person. Man's characteristic privilege is that the bond he accepts is not physical but moral; that is, social. He is governed not by a material environment brutally imposed on him, but by ... society.

But when society is disturbed by some painful crisis or by beneficient but abrupt transitions, it is momentarily incapable of exercising this influence.... If the disturbance is profound, it affects even the principle controlling the distribution of men.... Since the relations between various parts of the society are necessarily modified, the ideas expressing these relations must change.... The state of deregulation or anomie is thus further heightened.

Anomie ... is a regular and specific factor in suicide in our modern societies: one of the springs from which the annual contingent feeds. So we have here a new type to distinguish from the others. It differs from them in its dependence, not on the way in which individuals are attached to society, but on how it regulates them ... one basis for suicides ... results from man's activity's lacking regulation and his consequent sufferings.

FROM SOCIAL RESPECT TO SOCIAL ISOLATION An irony of American cultural history is that, until early in the twentieth century, when there was a small proportion of elderly people in the population, old people tended to have clear and respected roles. Then, as our society matured (see Figure 7-1), the much greater numbers of the elderly found their roles becoming unclear and ignored. This process now affects many of the over 20 million elderly in the United States.

In summarizing a collection of essays on aging in crosscultural perspective, Cowgill and Holmes find that modernization plays a strong part in establishing the place of the old. The concept of old age itself is altered in modern societies, for people in nonliterate societies age earlier. The measure of age in modern societies is chronological age rather than a person's capabilities (Cowgill and Holmes, 1972: 308). The collection shows strong support for the proposition that the status of the elderly is high in nonliterate societies and lower and more ambiguous in modern societies (p. 310).

INDUSTRIALIZATION AND THE INDEX OF AGING Researchers occasionally use the *index of aging* as a measure. This index is based on the ratio of the number of persons sixty years old and over to the number of children under fifteen. One of the consequences of industrialization and rising standards of living is a marked extension of life spans. For example, Great Britain and Sweden both began industrializing earlier than did the United States and also showed an increase in the proportion of old people earlier. From the mid-nineteenth to the mid-twentieth century, the younger American society had more than quadrupled its index, compared to a tripling in Great Britain and Sweden, though America continued to have a lower index of aging than the two European countries (Sheldon, Chapter 2 in Tibbitts, 1960: 28).

Figure 7-1 illustrates the underlying basis for the emergence in mid-century of the field of social gerontology, which specializes in the study of the social and psychological aspects of the human

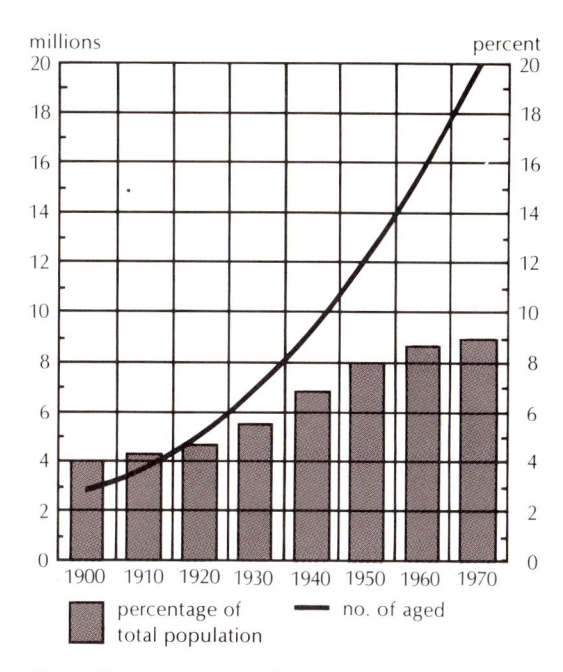

Figure 7-1 Aged population of the United States, number and percentage of total population, 1900–1970. SOURCE: U.S. Census.

aging process. Between 1900 and 1950, the total proportion of the population sixty-five years old or older doubled from 4 to 8 percent. The long-range continuation of this trend was evident in the 1950s when this chart was developed and has been confirmed by the 1970 census and other recent population reports.

As with adolescents, a useful perspective in evaluating the contemporary status of many of the elderly is the family life cycle (see Figure 5-1). Of the eight stages in the normal cycle, Stage V, in which there are adolescents, and Stage VII, which encompasses the old age of the parents, are most problematic in role strain and conflict. Both age groups generally have few clear functional roles within the family and are marginally related to the larger occupational and social structure. This was not always true in American society. Neither adolescents nor the elderly were always distinguished

208 ISSUES FACING AMERICAN INDIVIDUALS

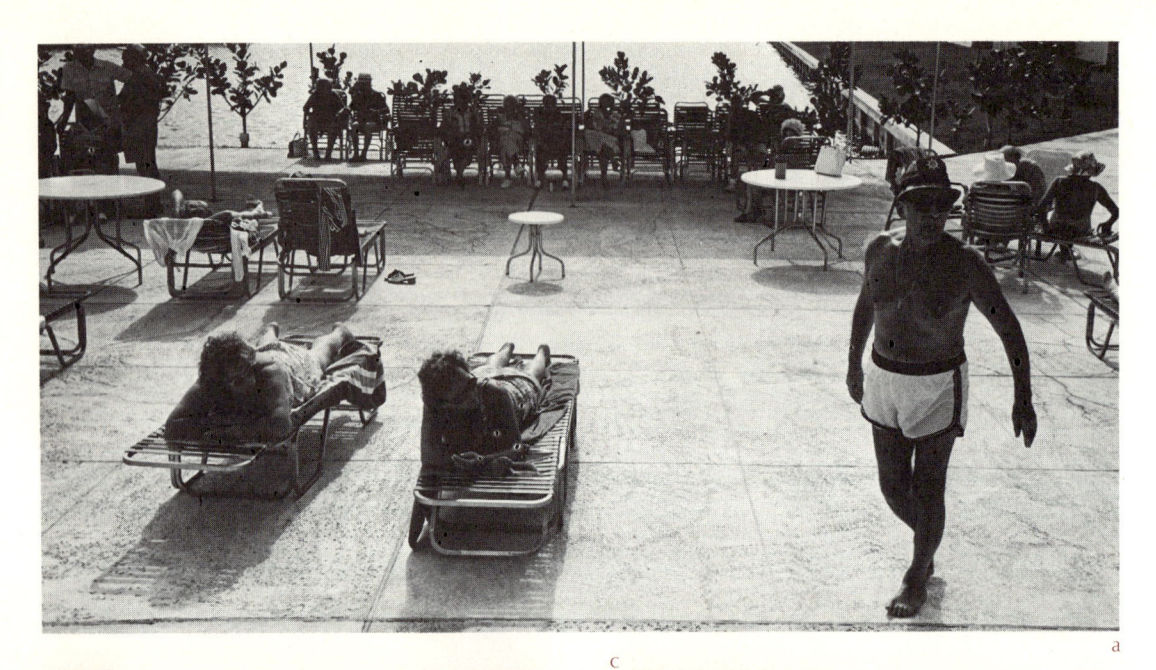

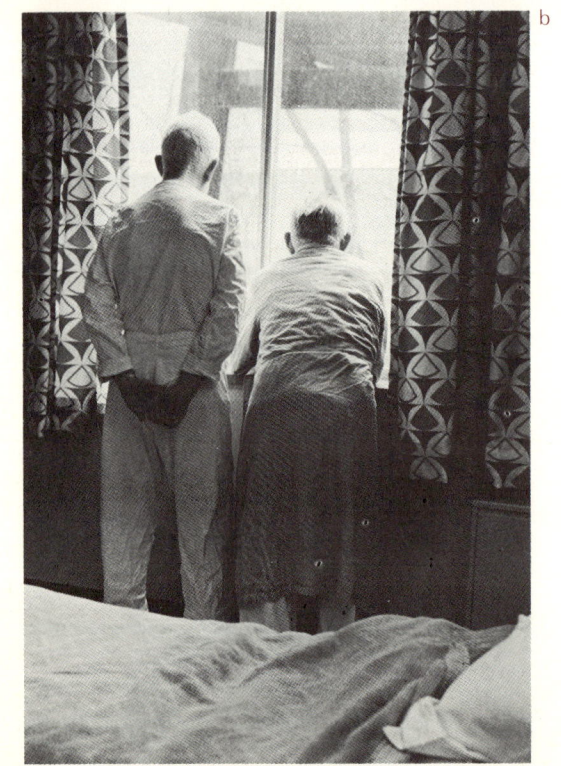

Three different lifestyles among the elderly. SOURCE: (a) Alex Webb/Magnum; (b) Sepp Seitz/Magnum; (c) Suzanne Opton.

as social groups with a wide range of social problems. Throughout the colonial period, and at least through the nineteenth century, when the society was predominantly agrarian, there persisted what Bernard Farber refers to as the *natural-family* system of continuity (1973: 115–142). Until the twentieth century, there was generally a great deal of stability among generations. As we discussed in Chapter 3, Americans tended to live in the same small communities from one generation to another, have large families and extended kin, perform manual work and activities at home, and have a life pattern similar to that of earlier generations. In this situation, the elderly played a highly functional role in socializing younger members of the family.

Family and community customs and mores were so long established that they seemed to be a natural way of life. Modern urban society has demonstrated that while the natural-family model once worked well for every age group, including the old, it no longer does. The elderly are no longer in a position to help socialize young people. Many of them began life in small communities or in cities which have changed radically over the years. Young families tend to be much smaller and more mobile than in the past, leaving behind a large proportion of the elderly, who increasingly find themselves without traditional family, occupational, and community roles.

THE FUTURE OF THE ELDERLY In the future, older Americans will have certain common experiences that the elderly of the present do not. In the future, a higher proportion of the aged will be native born, will have been born and socialized in urban areas, will have a higher average formal education, and will be the recipients of social security and health plans that have been evolving since mid-century. In contrast, many of today's elderly are either foreign-born or raised in rural areas, have experienced such traumatic events as the Great Depression of the 1930s, and have faced the problems of rising health costs and low income (social security, pensions, and health programs have been limited in scope until quite recently).

The pace, way of life, and many of the values of the elderly are drawn from a different set of social experiences and are often at variance with those of younger members of society with whom they coexist. The elderly experienced different kinds of, and attitudes toward, general education, religious practices, sexual mores, occupations, and general lifestyle.

VALUES AND LIFESTYLES Of course, some older Americans find the life styles of the young both acceptable and functional for themselves. Increasingly more old people are living together without getting married, both for companionship and as a means of easing financial pressures. Old people who marry risk losing some or all of their social security benefits. For this reason and others, elderly people are more socially isolated and alienated than in the past. This isolation produces a state of anomie.

The elderly do not constitute a cohesive group. Though they share a variety of problems, they differ from each other in social class and ethnic, racial, religious, and occupational background. Thus, the elderly have not been able to agree upon goals or means to achieve them as have other, more cohesive groups, such as members of labor unions or civil rights organizations.

THE PHYSIOLOGICAL FACTOR IN AGING

Social and psychological factors are the primary causes of the difficulties most elderly people face in modern society. Before we consider the aspects of modern society that isolate the elderly, we must consider aging as a biological process. Some of the limits imposed by aging are self-evident. People in all walks of life tend to slow down as they advance in years. Just how extensive this slowing-down process is can be seen in Table 7-1.

Theories of aging are concerned with physiological changes over time. While medical science has modified the process, human cells nevertheless undergo such increasingly delimiting processes as the accumulation of metabolic waste products and the wearing out of protoplasm (Chown, 1972: 9). While different kinds of human cells vary in expected length of life, and some, like long-lasting nerve cells, have no powers of replacement, there does appear to be a general constant loss of neurons and other cells.

Table 7-1 Percent of Population Limited in Activity and Mobility by Chronic Health Conditions; by Age

	All ages	Age sixty-five and over
Total population	100.0	100.0
Persons with no chronic conditions	58.1	21.3
Persons with one or more chronic condition(s)	41.9	78.7
Persons whose condition limits activity	10.9	45.1
Hindered in going to school, working, or keeping house	5.8	22.8
Prevented from going to school, working, or keeping house	2.3	15.5
Persons whose condition limits mobility	2.7	17.8
Trouble in getting around alone	1.6	9.9
Unable to get around alone	0.6	4.1
Confined to house	0.5	3.8

SOURCE: Adapted from "Health, Education and Welfare Indicators" (Washington, D.C.: Government Printing Office, October, 1962), p. xxi.

CROSS-CULTURAL EFFECTS OF AGING One interesting attempt to evaluate the physiological effects of aging was a cross-cultural study made by David Gutmann of the University of Michigan–Wayne State University Institute of Gerontology. He analyzed data collected in 1969 on elderly persons in four different cultures: residents of Kansas City, Missouri; Druze tribesmen in the Middle East; lowland and highland Mayas in Latin America; and American Navajo Indians. For all the wide cultural differences between these groups, there were common aspects of the behavior of the elderly that appeared to be related to the intrinsic nature of the aging process. One such common denominator was the awareness of the imminence of death. As Gutmann puts it, "The common reality that unites older men is the universal recognition of death" (1969: 36). Gutmann cited this common recognition to explain certain psychological changes. Whether in nonliterate Indian cultures or in urban America, older men changed from being active and assertive to being passive; they dwelt on the past rather than the future. As Gutmann put it, "It appears that aged men across cultures have their own 'country of old men' — a dominion that they do not share even with their own sons in their own societies" (1969: 35).

Table 7-1 demonstrates some physiological effects of age. The National Health Survey definition of chronic health conditions includes diagnosed diseases as well as complaints such as stiffness in the joints and susceptibility to chilling, conditions that restrict individuals' participation in social activities beyond any culturally induced limitations. Additional physiological signs of aging are that the heart rate slows down (Frolkis, 1966), vision tends to decline (Sheldon, 1948), kidney function is reduced (Atchley, 1972), sensory–motor activities become more difficult (Welford, 1962), and general energy level is lower (Sheldon, 1948).

WOMEN AND AGING Physiological problems may nevertheless be less inherently limiting than many studies suggest. For example, in Gutmann's cross-cultural analysis, the focus was entirely on old men. When women are included, a different picture emerges. Most elderly women who are still homemakers feel less of a break in their life pattern than do men, who are usually retired. There is evidence that retirement causes men to withdraw psychologically from social interaction more than do women affected by a parallel change (Cumming et al. 1960: 27). Sex is not the determining factor, for men who continue to work, particularly at well-paying jobs (Blau, 1956; Blau, 1973), also continue in an active social role. Furthermore, there is growing evidence that older people are capable of considerable psychological and social adaptability (Burgess, 1960: 20; Neugarten, 1971).

RISING LIFE EXPECTANCY An irony is that the biological limitations that accompany the aging process are in large measure a latent consequence of our success in extending life expectancy. At the turn of the century, Americans could expect to live less than fifty years; most Americans can now look forward to an extra quarter of a century (*Population and the American Future*, 1972: 11). Furthermore, by the end of this century, doctors will probably be able to double the thirty or forty years of healthy adult life that we enjoy at present (Strehler, 1973). Even today, in some societies, people well over one hundred are very active.

THE ELDERLY AS A MINORITY GROUP

According to this definition from Hoult's *Dictionary of Modern Sociology*, the elderly qualify as a minority group (1969: 205):

Minority group. In any society, a group that because it is made up of persons having particular biological or social characteristics, is an object of prejudice and/or is subjected to negative discriminatory treatment....

As noted earlier, the elderly possess particular biological characteristics. Increasingly isolated in the retirement years from younger members of the society, they tend also to possess particular social characteristics. And as we shall now see, the aged are subject to widespread *prejudice** and *discrimination**.

THE ROLELESS IMAGE OF THE ELDERLY The elderly, according to Ernest Burgess:[1]

first ... lost their economic independence. They were demoted from the status of employer to that of employee. Their place of work was no longer the factory or office but the home. Second, in increasing numbers they had to give up rural residence for urban living. Third, they were now forced to retire from work by the decision of the employer rather than of their own free will as in the past. Fourth, they lost their former favored position in the extended family. No longer were the grandfather and the grandmother the center of the absorbing social life of their descendants but often became unwanted hangers-on, taking part by sufferance in the activities of their children and grandchildren. Fifth, deprived of the society of their family and having lost associates on the job and other friends by death or departure to other communities, they found themselves cursed instead of blessed by leisure time in abundance and little or nothing to do with it.

In sum, retired older men and women are, in Burgess' words, "imprisoned in a roleless role."

This roleless image in itself constitutes a problem for the old. As they interact with their significant others, such as younger kin, former co-workers, and neighbors, they see themselves as

---

[1] © 1961 by the University of Chicago. All rights reserved.

socially irrelevant. The younger generation's perceptions of the old inevitably shapes their self-image. They withdraw, living out a self-fulfilling prophecy (Vander Zanden, 1975: 111–115).

AGEISM The minority status of the elderly is so prevalent that *Newsweek* characterized the phenomenon as *ageism* (1974: 80), much as prejudice and discrimination toward blacks is called racism. The *Newsweek* report cites some examples of ageism. A thirty-eight-year-old Chicago man cannot become a trainee fireman because he is too old; in Scottsbluff, Nebraska, a newspaper advertisement for a sports editor requires the applicant to be "youthful"; in Phoenix, Greyhound refuses to hire drivers over thirty-five.[2] While these cases may not be typical of the experiences of most older people, an individual has little choice when placed in a category regardless of his or her individual merits.

For people in their sixties and beyond, exclusion based on age is significantly more intense and arbitrary. Whether in private business or in government, the elderly are usually faced with compulsory retirement. In addition, they find themselves no longer actively involved in raising families. As a result, they experience what Zena Blau calls *role exit* (1973: 14). Many of the elderly may well want to retire from work and family responsibilities, but unlike younger adults, they often have no choice.

STEREOTYPES *Role exit* is a useful means of describing the social isolation of many old people. How this process relates to minority group status is made clear by the emergence of *negative stereotypes* toward the elderly. Stereotypes are so much a part of everyday life that it is necessary to distinguish arbitrary and hostile stereotyping toward any group, including the old, from other kinds. As Bogardus points out, "It's almost impossible for most people in a busy world of activities to weigh every reaction of every person, minute-by-minute, in terms of individual meanings and merits.... Thus persons and also groups are typed in snap-judgment style" (1950: 286). Stereotypes become dangerous when we refuse to alter judgments even when objective evidence demonstrates the stereotype to be wrong, when we refuse to judge individuals on their own merits. One group active in combating discrimination and stereotyping is the Gray Panthers who have about 7,000 members ("How to Fight Age Bias," 1975: 91). The willingness of the Gray Panthers to pattern its activities after radical youth and racial minority groups shows the capability of older Americans for flexibility and the acceptance of unconventional lifestyles.

STEREOTYPES

From: Walter Lippmann, *Public Opinion* (New York: Macmillan, 1922), pp. 73–74. Copyright 1922 by the Macmillan Company.

[The] hallmark [of the stereotype] is that it precedes the use of reason; is a form of perception, imposes a certain character on the data of our senses before the data reach the intelligence. The stereotype is like the lavender windowpanes on Beacon Street, like the doorkeeper at a costume ball who judges whether the guest has an appropriate masquerade. There is nothing so obdurate to education or to criticism as the stereotype. It stamps itself upon the evidence in the very act of securing the evidence. That is why the accounts of returning travellers are often an interesting tale of what the traveller carried abroad with him on his trip.

---

[2] The law now protects older workers. It is illegal to discriminate in hiring on the basis of age as well as race, ethnic origin, or sex. Much *de facto* discrimination still exists, of course.

If he carried chiefly his appetite, a zeal for tiled bathrooms, a conviction that the Pullman car is the acme of human comfort, and a belief that it is proper to tip waiters, taxicab drivers, and barbers, but under no circumstances station agents and ushers, then his Odyssey will be replete with good meals and bad meals, bathing adventures, compartment-train escapades, and voracious demands for money. Or if he is a more serious soul he may while on tour have found himself at celebrated spots. Having touched base, and cast one furtive glance at the monument, he buried his head in Baedecker, read every word through, and moved on to the next celebrated spot; and thus returned with a compact and orderly impression of Europe, rated one star, or two.

In some measure, stimuli from the outside, especially when they are printed or spoken words, evoke some part of a system of stereotypes, so that the actual sensation and the preconception occupy consciousness at the same time. The two are blended, much as if we looked at red through blue glasses and saw green. If what we are looking at corresponds successfully with what we anticipated, the stereotype is reinforced for the future, as it is in a man who knows in advance that the Japanese are cunning and has the bad luck to run across two dishonest Japanese.

If the experience contradicts the stereotype ... if the man is no longer plastic, or if some powerful interest makes it highly inconvenient to rearrange his stereotypes, he pooh-poohs the contradiction as an exception that proves the rule, discredits the witness, finds a flaw somewhere, and manages to forget it.

The perceptions, or stereotypes, we hold about the elderly are at odds with the positive stereotypes Americans tend to hold of themselves. The findings in Table 7-2 closely match others gathered over the years (see Katz and Braly, 1933; Gilbert, 1951; Karlins et al., 1969). The table illustrates that stereotypes may be positive. The category, American, is an *in-group*, to which the traits ascribed are positive ones in the society's system of values. If a

Table 7-2 Stereotypes Considered Most Typical of Americans

Stereotype trait	Percent	Rank
Ambitious	67	1
Industrious	62	2
Materialistic	56	3
Efficient	49	4
Practical	48	5

SOURCE: Adapted from Gerhart Saenger and Samuel Flowerman, "Stereotypes and Prejudicial Attitudes," *Human Relations* 7 (1954), p. 220. Originally published by Plenum Publishing Corporation. Based on a sample of 229 college students.

group is an *out-group*, such as the Germans were during World Wars I and II, they may remain socially isolated even though they are viewed as having these traits. In the case of the elderly, their social isolation is intensified over a long period of time because they are not thought to possess these admirable traits.

The picture of Americans as assertive and independent contrasts sharply with stereotypes about the elderly. Ernest Burgess summarizes these negative stereotypes (1960: 20):

1. *Passive behavior* is the expected pattern for the older person in retirement. He should take it easy, loaf, and fish. He has worked so hard all his life that now he wants only to rest.

2. *Dependence* on others for advice and assistance is the natural and inevitable consequence of advancing years. Ethel Shanas, in an unpublished paper, has analyzed this as a reversion in second childhood to the baby role.

3. *Custodial care* in institutions is the answer to the chronic illnesses and mental disturbances that increase with old age. Accordingly, the proportion

of older persons with physical and mental illnesses occupying hospital beds has increased faster than their percentage of the population.

4. *Withdrawal from social participation* tends to accompany departure from employment. Often the older person feels elbowed out of groups by subtle pressures.

5. *No preparation* for retirement is required or expected. Older persons, it is asserted, need only to relax, read, and listen to radio and television.

6. *Circulation of myths* which have no basis in fact is prejudicial to older persons. Typical of these are that older workers are unable to learn new skills and have more accidents, more absences, and less productivity than younger workers.

SEX AND THE ELDERLY All this constitutes an image of human beings who no longer have human feelings, interests, or activities. One consequence is the general assumption that the elderly do not engage in sexual activity. We know as a matter of fact that sexual interest and activity continue, though at a slower pace, for healthy people into their eighties and beyond (Hunt, 1974). One analyst became aware of the general attitude toward sex among the elderly when she could not find the subject even mentioned in research material on problems and life styles of the elderly (Cabot, 1961: 69). The impact of the stereotype is evident in the anxiety old people feel about their continued interest in sex (see Masters and Johnson, 1966). Moreover, among the unmarried, widowed, and divorced, sexual activity may be cut off for want of a suitable mate. For women, who bear the burden of our society's belief that attractiveness is tied to youth, sexual partners become more difficult to find as one ages (Sontag, 1972).

The lack of clear-cut and active roles for the elderly further exaggerates the image of old age. As Birren and Gibbon observe (1973: 76–77), doctors tend to see only sick old people and so feel that all old people are sick; social workers see only the indigent and so assume that all old people are poor; ministers see those with religious concerns and so feel that all old people are concerned with the hereafter; and the public sees the visible few elderly who sit on benches in the park day after day and so assume that all old people are inactive and have no interests to keep them involved with society.

Negative stereotyping of the old is probably more the result of their minority group status than a cause of it, although certainly there is an interdependent relationship. Even when some older people are perceived as having admirable, assertive, and independent traits, they tend to be viewed as out-group members. The combination of minority status and a stereotyped image of dependency leaves the old with more economic and related problems than any other adult age group.

The differential and relatively low income of the aged is general throughout American society. A group with minority status based on one characteristic, that of age, may find its economic base lowered further when that same group has other minority group characteristics, such as being black and/or female.

The income of the elderly is comparable more to that of other minorities than to the general income level (see Figure 7-2). The picture is the same for the income of black and white females. Moreover, the elderly often have a fixed income, so that inflation causes them additional hardship. Over half the income of the elderly is derived from three sources (Birren and Gibbon, 1973: 78–79): 32 percent from earnings in low-paying occupations or jobs that pay small amounts to those over retirement age; 15 percent from dividends and rents; and 3 percent from private pensions. Social security benefits (30 percent) constitute one hedge against rising costs, but historically have trailed inflation.

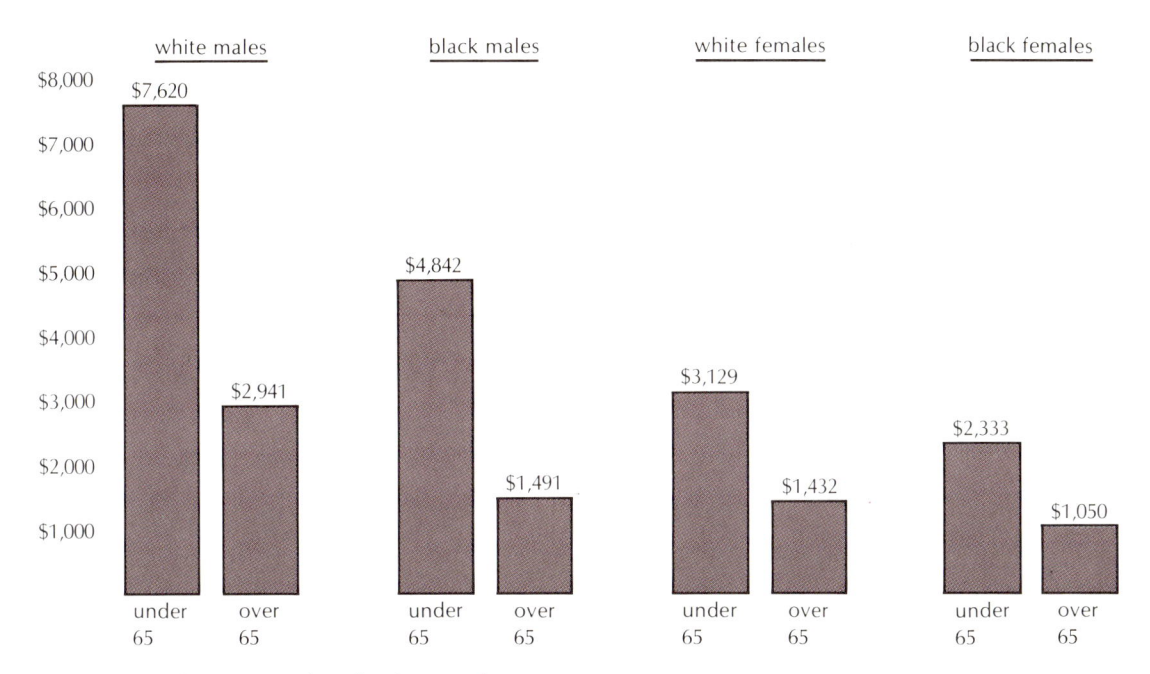

Figure 7-2 Comparison of median incomes, by age, race, and sex, 1969. SOURCE: U.S. Census.

The combination of declining roles, negative stereotyping, and marginal income has left a large proportion of the old in a state of poverty. According to the 1970 Census, people sixty-five and over make up 20 percent of the poor but are only 10 percent of the total population (*Facts and Figures on Older Americans*, 1971: 1). One elderly person in four lives in a state of poverty. In short, low income and a prevailing image of dependency have created a new set of conditions for the old in America; as a result, life is not easy for them.

DISENGAGEMENT AND THE AGING PROCESS

There is a growing consensus in the research literature that the elderly become *disengaged* from others in the society (Cumming and Henry, 1961; Lowenthal and Boler, 1965; Blau, 1973). There is less agreement as to whether this disengagement is a harmful or a helpful response to aging in modern society. Let us explore this *theory of disengagement*. Does the general removal of the old from active social involvement represent unwanted social discrimination (a dysfunction) or does such withdrawal represent the desire of old people themselves to reduce their involvement (a functional device)?

Table 7-3 presents findings showing that people tend to withdraw from many social roles as they go beyond age sixty-five. Elaine Cumming and her associates drew a sample of over 200 persons in Kansas City, Missouri (1960: 23–35). Evaluating such common social roles as parent, spouse, worker, community volunteer, and others, they found that after sixty-five, a substantial majority found themselves with fewer than six active social

Table 7-3   Small Number of Roles, by Age

Total	Percentage with fewer than six roles*
Age 50–54	39%
55–59	38
60–64	41
65–69	60
70–74	78
75 and over	92

* The roles in which the respondents act are typical in the course of life, such as spouse, parent, and worker.

SOURCE: Elaine Cumming, Lois Dean, David Newell, and Isabel McCaffrey, "Disengagement: A Tentative Theory of Aging," *Sociometry* 23 (1960), p. 27.

roles for the first time in their adult lives. These findings confirm what we have called the process of *role exit* (Blau, 1973: 14–20).

Until the 1960s, most social gerontologists assumed that this disengagement process was inherently a problem for the old. They developed an *activity theory* (Cavan, Burgess, Havighurst and Goldhamer, 1949; Havighurst and Albrecht, 1953), holding that if the elderly are to remain healthy and happy, the disengaging process must be halted and reversed, and elderly persons must continue to be active, socially and otherwise.

CHALLENGES TO THE ASSUMPTIONS OF CONTRASTING THEORIES In 1961, Cumming and Henry challenged the assumptions of both the activity theory and the disengagement theory. They held that the health and welfare of the old was not inherently a matter of continued social activity. They advanced the proposition that the mutual withdrawal of the elderly from society and of the rest of society from the elderly was often related to *successful* aging, finding a living pattern that is satisfying to many of the elderly. They thus redefined disengagement as "an inevitable process in which many of the relationships between a person and other members of society are severed, and those remaining are altered in quality" (1961: 25). This interpretation stimulated new formulations that have revealed some of the complexities of a socially satisfying aging process. The result is a perspective that embraces aspects of both the activity and the disengagement theories.

The crucial issue for the old is whether social withdrawal or continued activity is voluntary or involuntary (Lowenthal and Boler, 1965). The elderly often find themselves pigeonholed into roles that they may not want to fulfill. Ernest Burgess notes that most younger adults tend to approve of the following activities for the aged (1960: 343):

goes out and visits with other people the same age a great deal

keeps up by mail and telephone or by personal visits with a large number of friends

spends more time than formerly in visiting friends and writing to them

visits friends and receives visits in his (her) own home

spends several hours a day at club or lodge rooms with old friends

As Burgess further notes, younger adults tend to disapprove of the following activities on the part of the elderly:

visits relatives or friends for long periods of time

no longer entertains groups of friends at home

has lost touch with former friends

very seldom visits with friends although has friends and is able to do so lives a quiet life with no social contacts other than husband or wife

Many elderly people may agree with this general *public opinion**, which approves activity only with age mates. Those who do not are often in no position to act on their preferences.

OBJECTIVE AND SUBJECTIVE FORMS OF DEPRIVATION For the old who are also poor, the lack of an independent role in modern society is an objective deprivation. Yet, full participation in the larger society is often denied even those who can afford a middle- or upper-class life style. Middle-class neighborhoods tend to cater to people in middle age, particularly families with young children. The growing separation from family and general community life has spawned a number of retirement communities for people in the middle class and above (Cowgill, 1972: 249). These communities are often far removed from the original homes of the elderly and are often restricted to people fifty and older. The result may be a more subjective form of deprivation. As Friedenberg observes of such middle-class "paradise towns" (1967: 36):

... Our lives run downhill and waste away into the sands often enough to suggest that growing up in America is not a process of maturation so much as of surrender; of atrophy and renunciation of the human qualities for spontaneous feeling, action, and commitment that, under more favorable social circumstances, would be the expected outcome of normal growth. The Senior Citizens of Paradise Town, pretending to themselves as long as they can that strangers, if friendly, are as good as friends and that heart attacks can be fun, are not, in their present form, a part of God's creation. They become what they are, as we all are doing, through such growth as is possible to them under the conditions of their life.

For the elderly of all social classes, there is often a consequent feeling of *relative deprivation** that goes beyond immediate economic and general social circumstances. The elderly tend to compare their condition not only with that of other age groups but also to their status earlier in their adult lives. By their mid-sixties, most people quite suddenly find themselves less independent than they were and less able to choose their own roles. This is so for those who want to enter a state of social disengagement and also for those who would prefer to remain active. It is particularly difficult to find oneself in a position of low status when one is accustomed to higher status. In this sense, a good deal of the alienation, mental distress, and general anomie afflicting the old can be understood as aspects of relative deprivation.

The concept of relative deprivation also helps to explain the particular difficulties faced in old age by males. Females live longer than males in American society — seventy-four years for women, sixty-seven for men (*Information Please Almanac*, 1970: 852), though older women show consistently higher rates of illness than do older men (Atchley, 1972: 130).

PROBLEMS FACING ELDERLY MEN AND WOMEN While the roles of females in American society may now be undergoing radical educational, familial, and career changes, this is less true for elderly women, who generally were housewives throughout their adult lives. Table 7-4 shows that

Table 7-4   **Perceived Constricted Life Space, by Age and Sex**

	Males (N=107)	Females (N=104)
Age 50–54	37%	42%
55–59	44	69
60–64	42	53
65–69	82	63
70–74	89	80
75 and over	100	92

SOURCE: Adapted from Elaine Cumming, Lois Dean, David Newell, and Isabel McCaffrey, "Disengagement: A Tentative Theory of Aging," *Sociometry* 23 (1960), p. 27.

most women in their late fifties and early sixties view their life space as *constricted*. They meet fewer people, play fewer roles, visit fewer places. One's social world shrinks. A minority of men feel constricted during these years, but such feelings almost double at the retirement age of sixty-five. Indeed, after sixty-five, a higher proportion of males than females report that their life space is constricted. The Protestant work ethic into which they were socialized weighs heavily on males. As Blau reported in an urban study, among men over sixty-five, one in three among the retired felt old while among those still working, only one in five felt old (1956: 198–203). As one man put it (200):

When did I start to feel old? Why when I stopped working. I was always real proud that I'd come to Chicago and got a job and supported myself. Then when I couldn't work anymore, why I wasn't good for anything.

The traditional male role of independence and status through occupation is apparently dysfunctional

A symbolic depiction of the constricted life space so many of the elderly feel. SOURCE: Drawing by Charles Addams; © 1974 The New Yorker Magazine, Inc.

for elderly men when they compare their present roles to their former roles and also to the approved roles of young men.

While alienation after retirement appears to be the dominant pattern, it is worth noting that, among a minority — high income professionals, corporate executives, skilled technicians — men enjoy retirement as much as they enjoyed working (Shanas, 1968: 330–340). Since they have more money, they are more able to enjoy their new leisure. This emerging pattern among the affluent elderly appears to be gaining social approval among both retired people and the general public (Atchley, 1974).

Since most men do not live as long as women, women are often left in a vulnerable and anomic position (see Lopata, 1973). Over 80 percent of elderly women (*Health, Education and Welfare*, 1972) are widows or were always single; of nearly a million elderly in nursing homes, about three-quarters are women. The social isolation of millions of old women can be seen in many ways. While three-quarters of elderly men are licensed drivers, only one-fifth of elderly women are (Carp, 1971). Thus old women often experience social disengagement even though their life style creates less of a break from earlier life patterns than is true for men.

DISENGAGEMENT AND INDIVIDUAL DIFFERENCES For both men and women, there is conflicting evidence with regard to the traditional view that disengagement is inherently pathological and social activity inherently healthy. This conflict may be due to broad individual and group differences. Elderly people come from every conceivable social, racial, religious, and ethnic background. The larger social question is: What social conditions will enable the elderly to enjoy a satisfying life, whatever their backgrounds?

SOCIETAL ACCOMMODATIONS TO THE PROBLEMS OF THE ELDERLY

A concept useful in discussing the problems of old age is *accommodation**, defined by Ogburn and Nimkoff as a two-way process in which there is a "working together of individuals and groups in spite of differences or latent hostility" (1964: 148). There are signs that younger and older people are beginning to cooperate on new policies to assist the elderly. Yet the limited extent to which this has occurred, under increasing pressure from the growing numbers of the elderly, suggests continuing difficulties.

The elderly themselves have taken the lead in pressing for reforms. A substantial majority of old people take part in the political process almost as much as those in their forties and fifties, and more than those still younger (Lipset, 1963: 189, 221; Schmidhauser, 1970: 70–82). With the weakening of the extended kinship system, which provided informal family care, government programs have paid increasing attention to the elderly, beginning with the Townsend Plan of the 1930s.

Rallying behind the leadership of Francis E. Townsend, a country physician, hundreds of thousands of elderly people across the nation organized to support the idea of a guaranteed minimum income of $200 a month for everyone over sixty. In 1935, the influential Senator William E. Borah of Idaho called the Townsend movement "the most extraordinary social and political movement in recent years and perhaps in our entire history" (Schlesinger, 1960: 40). The program was, at that time, too radical for most Americans to accept.

While the Townsend movement did not achieve its goal, it helped bring about the passage of the Social Security Act of 1935, which guaranteed some government income for most elderly retired workers. The movement marked the emergence of the elderly as a political force on issues directly affecting their interests.

The record of federal legislation since the Townsend movement reflects this growing influence. As part of the social security legislation of 1935, there was passed the Old Age, Survivors, and Disabilities Act, which provided limited but direct welfare grants to the elderly poor. Beginning in the 1940s, a series of amendments to the Social Security Act has extended coverage to more retired workers and has increased benefits. The Housing Act of 1956 contained a specific provision authorizing the Federal Housing Administration to provide low-interest mortgages, especially for the elderly. Then, as part of the civil rights movement, legislation was developed in the 1960s to end age discrimination in employment under provisions of the Manpower Development and Training Act of 1962, the Age and Discrimination Act of 1967, and the Middle-Aged and Older Workers Full Employment Act of 1968.

LIMITATIONS OF REFORM LEGISLATION Perhaps most symbolic of the growing influence of and concern for the old were the 1961 and 1971 White House conferences on aging. Out of the 1961 conference came the most far-reaching of all Congressional measures respecting the elderly, the Older Americans Act of 1965. An Administration on Aging was developed within the Department of Health, Education and Welfare, with the objectives of developing programs with and for the elderly that were designed to provide:

1. an adequate basic income

2. the best possible physical and mental health

3. suitable housing

4. full restorative and rehabilitative services

5. opportunity for employment without age discrimination

6. retirement in health, honor, and dignity

Maggie Kuhn, leader of the Gray Panthers, an activist group that fights for the rights of the elderly. SOURCE: Courtesy of the Gray Panthers.

These were statements of national aims. While the act itself did not provide any specific programs, it stimulated them. The development and expansion of Medicare in the late 1960s and early 1970s is a prime example. Given the high cost of medical care and the increasing medical needs of people as they enter old age, the provision of health care is crucially related to the economic stability of most elderly.

With all these developments since the 1930s, one might wonder if a problem still exists. The answer is yes. While the elderly constitute the kind of political force that can *secure* legislation, they do not have the force to *implement* it. Their average income is about half that of younger people (Farley and Hermalin, 1972: Tables 4 and 6). They are a minority of all voters (about one in six). The social isolation that accompanies their low status has halted momentum on programs for the elderly. In effect, they are outside the power structure and are unable to insist that programs bearing directly on their own lives be implemented. Hence, efforts to ease the plight of many elderly have not kept pace with their objective needs. Increases in social security benefits have consistently fallen behind inflationary rises in cost of living, just as Medicare coverage fails to keep up with the geometrically rising cost of medical care (Gordon, 1972: 99).

Many old people retain close and warm relationships with their children and grandchildren, who are themselves adjusting to a changing society and are often not able to help them materially. Hence, many of the elderly live in nursing homes — almost one million of the over 20 million in the United States. David Pryor (1970: 15–17) found that, while over $2 billion a year of tax funds now go to such homes, the lack of care is evident:

The scarcity of medical care for the nursing home patient constitutes a national scandal.

One-seventh of drug prescriptions to nursing home patients are administered wrongly, and drugs are commonly used to make patients easier to handle.

Nursing homes that spend an average food-cost per patient of less than $1 a day still qualify for continuing government grants.

A Senate committee investigation in 1975 also documented the low quality of nursing-home care. It found that, while the government supplies most of the funds that make nursing homes profitable, there is little overseeing of how the money is used. The result is often a series of major abuses of patients' rights and public trust. One investigation of fifty-five nursing homes operated by one man estimated his unreported earnings to be as high as $24 million (*The Nursing-Home Scandal*, 1975: 23):

Care in nursing homes is often minimal or worse, with helpless patients left untended for hours; at last week's hearing [a] city physician ... testified that nursing-home residents are often admitted to city hospitals feverish, dehydrated, and ridden with bedsores. "Some of these patients are so dry they no longer salivate ... or form tears." But despite complaint and documented charges of abuse, Federal officials are reluctant to close nursing homes, arguing that the patients have nowhere else to go.

Moreover, life in many nursing homes is bureaucratized, routinized, and isolated. Daily contacts are limited to other inmates and members of the staff. Status in such an institution often carries over to other settings, so that informal gatherings with family and friends outside increasingly come to resemble those within (Hochschild, 1973: 140). Routine takes over even at the time of death. As Jaber Gubrium observed, reactions to death are determined by the social practices in the home; nurses and other staff tend to be impersonal and businesslike, and fellow patients may show a limited amount of sympathy (Gubrium, 1975: 197–216).

FIGHTING HUMAN OBSOLESCENCE IN AND OUT OF INSTITUTIONS Jules Henry, an American anthropologist, investigated three nursing homes — two private, one public — and reported his findings in his famous work *Culture Against Man*. Henry chides us for our indifference to the *low-visibility* inmates of institutions who have been discarded as obsolete when their working years are past. As he observes in his perceptive article on human obsolescence (1963: 392–393):

Public institutions for sick "social security paupers" — those who have no income but their social security checks — are ruled by the social conscience; that is to say, obvious things that readily excite conventional feelings of right and wrong are taken account of within the limits of miserly budgets, but everything else is slighted. For example, an institution may have plenty of medicine and an abundance of sterile gauze, but the medicine is often administered by ignorant persons and the gauze contaminated by ill-trained aides. Bedding, even when sufficient, may be dingy grey because of penny-pinching on soap and bleach. Food may be adequate but distributed in assembly-line fashion and eaten within obligatory time limits. Every bed may have a thin blanket sufficient for the regulated temperature of the institution, but if the heating breaks down or the staff decides to open the windows when the outside temperature is freezing, the patients are unprotected. Thus, were the social conscience to inquire whether the inmates had enough of what they need, the answer would be "yes," and the social conscience, easily lulled by appearances and small expenditures, would sleep on.

Always interested more in outward seeming than inner reality, always eager not to be stirred or get involved too much, always afraid of "pampering" its public charges and more given to the expression of drives than of values, the social conscience cannot be stirred to a concern with "psychology" unless some terrible evil, like juvenile delinquency, rages across the land. Hence, the spiritual degradation and hopelessness of its obsolete charges seem none of its affair. The social conscience is affected by things having "high visibility," like clean floors, freshly painted walls, and plenty of medical supplies, rather than by those having "low visibility," like personal involvement. A nurse in a mental hospital once put it to me this way: "When you go off duty they can tell if you've got a clean dressing room, but they can't tell if you've talked to a patient." In an institution for obsolete social security paupers the supervisor can tell whether or not a patient has been bathed but not whether the aide who did it spent a little extra time bathing the patient as if he was a human being rather than something inanimate. Since too many minutes devoted to being human will make an aide late in getting her quota of patients "done," they are washed like a row of sinks, and their privacy is violated because there is no time to move screens around or to manipulate the bedclothes in a way that preserves the patient's sense of modesty.

In many primitive societies the soul is imagined to leave the body at death or just prior to it; here, on the other hand, society drives out the remnants of the soul of the institutionalized old person while it struggles to keep his body alive. Routinization, inattention, carelessness, and the deprivation of communication — the chance to talk, to respond, to read, to see pictures on the wall, to be called by one's name rather than "you" or no name at all — are ways in which millions of once useful but now obsolete human beings are detached from their selves long before they are lowered into the grave.

Adjusting to old age, and often to retirement, is a complex task at best. What goes on in many nursing homes magnifies the problem. Elderly people have to adapt to new physical and social challenges. Being economically dependent and socially isolated makes aging happily difficult. The problems of the elderly are likely to grow along with the proportion of old people in the population — likely to exceed 15 percent by the year 2000 (*Population and the American Future*, 1972: 98). Medical technology and rising standards of living will probably continue to expand life span. What does one do from age sixty-five to eighty-five? ninety? one hundred? What happens to the pension funds and social security benefits designed for a life pattern of twenty years spent growing up, forty years working, and ten years in retirement? We must find ways to extend good health into old age and provide the elderly with a genuine choice between withdrawal and activity.

SUMMARY

The elderly constitute a significant social group. From less than 5 percent of the population at the turn of the century, they have grown to over 10 percent now, and their problems of social adjustment have also increased. These developments have stimulated the growth of *social gerontology*, the study of the societal aspects of aging.

The growth of the elderly population has occurred simultaneously with the growth of American industrial urban society. The shift from rural agrarian to modern society has left old people with fewer clear and respected roles. A major consequence is widespread *anomie** among the elderly, who tend to be socially isolated and alienated from younger groups.

While most restrictions on the activities of the elderly can be attributed to social factors, others have physiological causes. The body slows down so that certain activities can no longer be performed efficiently. Aging may also affect mental processes, although there is increasing evidence that social isolation may have the greater effect, particularly as medical technology extends the present thirty or forty years of vigorous middle life. The difference between the problems of retired males and women sixty-five to seventy argues that the social environment is the chief cause.

The elderly have been subject to job, income, and other forms of discrimination, and so can be considered a *minority* group*. Like other minority groups they are often the target of negative *stereotyping** which stresses their passive and dependent social role.

The old tend to become disengaged from many earlier social activities. The *theory of disengagement* developed in an attempt to understand why. The *activity theory* held that disengagement was an inherent problem of the old. The view now is that the basic problem facing the elderly is not their level of social disengagement or social activity but their general lack of resources and the anomie that often precludes their choice of a satisfying life style.

The elderly often view themselves in relation to their former roles in society and relative to other adults. In doing so, they develop a sense of *relative deprivation.*

Since the Townsend movement of the 1930s, the elderly have constituted a political force on issues that directly affect their lives. As a consequence, they have influenced the passage of a series of congressional acts from the social security legislation of the 1930s to the equal opportunity and Medicare acts of the 1960s and 1970s.

Old people are still victimized by corruption in the nursing-home industry and by low income that has not kept pace with rising cost of medical care. These conditions may change as the elderly show an increased desire to play a part in society.

QUESTIONS FOR DISCUSSION

1. What are some immediate consequences for the society of having a population of old people representing 10 percent of the total?

2. Is it necessarily true that the elderly of the future will be a conservative group?

3. How can stereotyping the elderly become a self-fulfilling prophecy?

4. How much of the *successful disengagement* of the elderly could be due to resignation to one's fate rather than healthy adjustment?

5. Because of the earlier average death rate of men, what kinds of status problems are often faced by women?

6. What are some examples of differences between younger and older Americans on basic values? What are their consequences?

7. What are some ways in which old people exhibit the characteristics and responses of a minority group in American society?

8. Are the disengagement and activity theories of successful aging necessarily in conflict?

9. What are the social policy implications for the elderly of the cultural value of guaranteeing life, liberty, and the pursuit of happiness?

10. Review your understanding of the following terms and concepts:

social gerontology

anomie

stereotyping

ageism

index of aging

human obsolescence

chronic health conditions

constricted life space

disengagement theory

activity theory

Older Americans Act

REFERENCES

Atchley, Robert
    1972   The Social Forces in Later Life. Belmont, Cal.: Wadsworth.

Birren, James and Kathy Gibbon
    1973   "The elderly." D. Spiegel and P. Keith-

Spiegel (eds.), Outsiders: USA. San Francisco: Rinehart: 75–95.

Blau, Zena
- 1956 "Changes in the status and age identification." American Sociological Review 21: 198–203.
- 1973 Old Age in a Changing Society. New York: Franklin Watts.

Bogardus, Emory
- 1950 "Stereotypes versus sociotypes." Sociology and Social Research 34: 286–291.

Burgess, Ernest
- 1961 Aging in Western Societies. Chicago: University of Chicago Press.

Cabot, Natalie
- 1961 You Can't Count on Dying. Cambridge, Mass.: Riverside.

Carp, Frances
- 1971 "On becoming an ex-driver." Gerontologist 11: 101–103.

Cavan, Ruth, E.W. Burgess, R.J. Havighurst, and H. Goldhamer
- 1949 Personal Adjustment in Old Age. Chicago: Science Research Associates.

Chown, Sheila
- 1972 Human Aging. New York: Baltimore: Penguin.

Cooley, Charles
- 1922 Human Nature and the Social Order. New York: Scribners.

Cowgill, Donald
- 1972 "Aging in American society." Donald O. Cowgill and Lowell D. Holmes (eds.), Aging and Modernization. New York: Meredith Corporation.

Cowgill, Donald and Lowell Holmes
- 1972 "Summary and conclusions: the theory in review." Donald O. Cowgill and Lowell D. Holmes (eds.), Aging and Modernization. New York: Meredith Corporation.

Cumming, Elaine, Lois Dean, David Newell, and Isabel McCaffrey
- 1960 "Disengagement: a tentative theory of aging." Sociometry 23: 23–35.

Cumming, Elaine and William E. Henry
- 1961 Growing Old. New York: Basic Books.

Durkheim, Emile
- 1951 Suicide. (First published 1897.) J. Spaulding and G. Simpson (eds.) Glencoe, Ill.: The Free Press.

- 1971 Facts and Figures on Older Americans. Washington, D.C.: United States Administration on Aging.

Farber, Bernard
- 1973 Family and Kinship in Modern Society. Glenview, Ill.: Scott-Foresman.

Farley, Reynolds and Albert Hermalin
- 1972 "The 1960's: decade of progress for blacks?" Demography 9: 353–367.

Friedenberg, Edgar
- 1967 "Adolescence as a social problem." H. Becker (ed.), Social Problems. New York: John Wiley & Sons: 35–75.

Frolkis, V.V.
- 1966 "Neuro-humoral regulation in the aging organism." Journal of Gerontology 21: 161–167.

Gilbert, George
- 1951 "Stereotype persistence and change among college students." Journal of Abnormal and Social Psychology 46: 245–254.

Gordon, David
- 1972 Theories of Poverty and Underemployment. London: D.C. Heath.

Gubrium, Jaber
- 1975 Living and Dying at Murray Manor. New York: St. Martin's Press.

Gutmann, David
    1969   The Country of Old Men: Cultural Studies in the Psychology of Later Life. Ann Arbor, Mich.: University of Michigan–Wayne State University Institute of Gerontology.

Havighurst, Robert and R. Albrecht
    1953   Older People. New York: Longmans, Green.

    1972   Health, Education and Welfare Indicators. Washington, D.C.: Government Printing Office.

Henry, Jules
    1963   Culture Against Man. New York: Random House.

Hochschild, Arlee
    1973   The Unexpected Community. Englewood Cliffs, N.J.: Prentice-Hall.

Hoult, Thomas Ford
    1969   Dictionary of Modern Sociology. Totawa, N.J.: Littlefield, Adams.

    1975   "How to fight age bias." Ms. Magazine 3 (12): 91.

Hunt, Morton
    1974   Sexual Behavior in the 1970's. Chicago: Playboy Press.

    1970   Information Please Almanac. New York: Atlas and Yearbook.

Karlins, Marvin, Thomas Coffman and Gary Walters
    1969   "On the fading of social stereotypes: studies in three generations of college students." Journal of Personality and Social Psychology 13: 1–16.

Katz, David and K.W. Braly
    1933   "Racial stereotypes of 100 college students." Journal of Abnormal and Social Psychology 28: 280–290.

Lippmann, Walter
    1946   Public Opinion (First published 1922). New York: Penguin.

Lipset, Seymour
    1963   Political Man: The Social Bases of Politics. New York: Anchor.

Lopata, Helena
    1973   Widowhood in an American City. Cambridge, Mass.: Schenkman.

Lowenthal, Marjorie and Deetje Boler
    1965   "Voluntary vs. involuntary social withdrawal." Journal of Gerontology 20: 363–371.

Masters, William and Virginia Johnson
    1966   Human Sexual Response. New York: Little, Brown.

Mead, George Herbert
    1934   Mind, Self and Society. Chicago: University of Chicago Press.

    1976   "The Medicaid scandal." Time Magazine. February 26: 37.

Mendelson, Mary Adelaide
    1974   "Tender Loving Greed." New York: Knopf.

Morgan, James
    1962   Income and Welfare in the United States. New York: McGraw-Hill.

Neugarten, Bernice
    1971   "Grow old along with me! the best is yet to be." Psychology Today 5 (December): 45–48, 79, 81.

    1975   "The nursing-home scandal." Newsweek (February 3): 23–24.

Ogburn, William and Meyer Nimkoff
    1964   Sociology. Boston: Houghton Mifflin.

1972 Population and the American Future. The Report of the Commission on Population Growth and the American Future. New York: New American Library.

Pryor, David
1970 "Where we put the aged." The New Republic (April 25): 15–17.

Saenger, Gerhart and Samuel Flowerman
1954 "Stereotypes and prejudicial attitudes." Human Relations 7: 217–238.

Schlesinger, Arthur
1960 The Politics of Upheaval. Boston: Houghton Mifflin.

Schmidhauser, J. R.
1970 "The elderly and politics." A. Hoffman (ed.), The Daily Needs and Interests of Older People. Springfield, Ill.: Charles C. Thomas: 70–82.

Shanas, Ethel et al.
1968 Older People in Three Industrial Societies. New York: Atherton.

Sheldon, Henry
1960 "The changing demographic profile." C. Tibbitts (ed.), Handbook of Social Gerontology. Chicago: University of Chicago Press.

Sheldon. J. H.
1948 The Social Medicine of Old Age. London: Oxford University Press.

Sontag, Susan
1972 "The double standard of aging." Saturday Review 55: 29–38.

Strehler, Bernard
1973 "A new age for aging." Natural History (February).

1974 "Thinking young." Newsweek (April 29): 80.

Tibbitts, Clark
1960 Handbook of Social Gerontology. Chicago: University of Chicago Press.

Vander Zanden, James
1972 American Minority Relations. New York: Ronald Press.

Welford, A.T.
1962 On changes of performance with age. Lancet 17: 335–3.

Part 3

ISSUES FACING AMERICAN GROUPS

Groups vary in size, duration, stability, mode of contact, objectives, manner of admission, sanctions, formality, role prescriptions, degree of acquaintance among members, and in many other ways.

George Lundberg

Chapter 8

COLLECTIVE CONFLICT AND INTERGROUP RELATIONS

Everywhere they say 'Go to California!' California's the great pot o' gold at the end of the rainbow. Well, now we're here in California, and there ain't no place else to go, and the only pot I seen's the kind they peddle at Sixtieth and Avalon.

A black Watts rioter, Los Angeles, 1965

MINORITY GROUPS IN SOCIETY

Certain historical moments so dramatize a problem that they spark widespread concern. Perhaps the most powerful such event was the dropping of the atomic bomb on Hiroshima at the end of World War II. Americans immediately became aware of the importance of international stability; the alternative was another global war, this time one in which American society could be severely damaged.

Of similar significance to our society was the series of urban racial disorders in the 1960s that grew out of the black civil rights movement. After hundreds of civil rights marches in the early 1960s, and over two dozen major riots in the mid and late 1960s *(Report of the National Advisory Commission on Civil Disorders,* 1968: 583–631), the degree of interracial conflict in the United States became widely evident to black and white alike.

HISTORY OF MINORITY PROBLEMS The intensity of our interracial problems is not new. The issue has been developing for generations, as has the interest of sociologists in it. American society is so diverse racially, ethnically and religiously, that intergroup relations became a focus for early research. Much of the history of intergroup relations has been a series of problems, from the days of slavery and exclusion of Native Americans from their traditional lands, to the restrictive immigration acts of this century aimed at Orientals and at southern and eastern Europeans.

In America, certain groups have been more equal than others — particularly white male Protestants, who have been the most influential group in the society. Controversy and conflict have resulted, since no group is willing to accept second-class citizenship. In recent years, strong feelings have arisen among blacks, Spanish-Americans, native Americans (Indians), women, and other groups about this unequal treatment and unequal opportunity. Though this chapter makes some reference to each of these groups, the main emphasis is on black-white relations, for blacks in American society have long been excluded systematically from opportunities available to others.

ANALYZING INTERGROUP RELATIONS A number of specialized terms and concepts are used in discussing intergroup relations. Generally hostile attitudes often result in *discrimination** against *minorities**; this behavior may in turn become a source of prejudice. *Segregation**, forced separation based on racial or other group characteristics, is often a result. Two more general concepts useful in discussing the status of minorities are *race relations* and *intergroup relations*.

The concept of *conflict** is central to understanding tense social interaction between individuals or groups.[1] Another important concept is *social movement**, which is a form of *collective behavior**, or relatively spontaneous crowd action.[2] In this chapter, we shall discuss collective behavior in *social movements*, which are generally group efforts to change the status quo. Social movements tend to be accompanied by *social conflict**, because those with a stake in maintaining things as they are may oppose change.

THE MEANING OF MINORITY STATUS

Since the position of minority groups in society involves the status of people in racial, religious, and other groupings, let us recall our definition of *status:*

Status involves the degree of social acclaim and prestige a role receives. High status brings admiration and respect, and is a source of positive attraction. Conversely, low status results in lack of admiration, social rejection, and avoidance.

In American society, certain ascribed group characteristics including race, national origin, religion, and sex, have been considered to have either high or low status, independent of such achieved status factors as income and education. A number of low-status groups have not been afforded the opportunities that go with high status. Whites still tend to be of higher status than blacks, northern Europeans of higher status than southern Europeans, males of higher status than females.

---

[1] *Conflict** is, of course, not the only possible relationship. For example, groups may develop *accommodations** to each other to minimize tensions. (Accommodation is discussed later in the chapter.) Or a group may *assimilate** so completely that it blends into the dominant population, and hence no longer has a minority identification. Collective conflict, emphasized here, occurs when the social forces that seek to maintain stability are brought dramatically into play against divisive forces, producing a great potential for social change.

[2] It is useful to note here the two basic forms of collective behavior treated in other chapters. They are short-lived, spontaneous *crowds** (see pages 278–279 for a discussion of crowd convergence in disaster situations) and *publics** and *public opinion** (see pages 472–473 for a discussion on political parties and pages 453–455 for a discussion of *groupthink*). A good basic source on collective behavior is Ralph Turner's and James Killian's *collective behavior* (1972).

MINORITY GROUP CHARACTERISTICS People are members of a minority when their low status is based on the ethnic background, race, religion, sex, or life style of their group. Wagley and Harris suggest that minorities share five characteristics (1958: 10): (1) they are subordinate groups in complex societies; (2) they have special physical and/or cultural traits that are held in low esteem by the more dominant members of the society; (3) they are self-conscious units bound together by the special disabilities that their disvalued traits bring; (4) membership is transmitted by a rule of descent, which results in group identification by succeeding generations even in the absence of readily apparent cultural or physical traits; and (5) by choice or necessity, they tend to marry within the group.

MINORITIES

From: Louis Wirth, "The Problem of Minority Groups," in R. Linton (ed.), *The Science of Man In The World Crisis* (New York: Columbia University Press, 1945), pp. 347-348.

To understand the nature and significance of minorities it is necessary to take account of their objective as well as their subjective position. A minority must be distinguishable from the dominant group by physical or cultural marks. In the absence of such identifying characteristics it blends into the rest of the population in the course of time. Minorities objectively occupy a disadvantageous position in society. As contrasted with the dominant group they are debarred from certain opportunities — economic, social and political. These deprivations circumscribe the individual's freedom of choice and self-development. The members of minority groups are held in lower esteem and may even be objects of contempt, hatred, ridicule, and violence....

Aside from these objective characteristics by which they are distinguished from the dominant group and in large measure as a result of them, minorities tend to develop a set of attitudes, forms of behavior, and other subjective characteristics which tend further to set them apart. One cannot long discriminate against people without generating in them a sense of isolation and of persecution and without giving them a conception of themselves as more different from others than in fact they are. Whether, as a result of this differential treatment, the minority comes to suffer from a sense of its own inferiority or develops a feeling that it is unjustly treated — which may lead to a rebellious attitude — depends in part upon the total social setting in which the differential treatment operates. Where a caste system has existed over many generations and is sanctioned by religious and other sentiments, the attitude of resignation is likely to be dominant over the spirit of rebellion. But in a secular society where class rather than caste pervades the stratification of people, and where the tradition of minority status is of recent origin, minorities, driven by a sense of frustration and unjustified subordination, are likely to refuse to accept their status and their deprivation without some effort to improve their lot.

Not all minorities have all the characteristics listed by Wagley and Harris, particularly the last two. Jews, who are of virtually every racial and ethnic background, may not display apparent cultural or physical traits (Froman, 1972: 79-81). And, while women in most respects constitute a minority group, they do not intramarry.

This last fact points up another, often misunderstood, characteristic of minorities. They need not be a *numerical* minority within a society. It is only necessary that they be of low status and be discriminated against by more dominant members of

Table 8-1 General Characteristics of Persons of Selected Ethnic and Racial Groups: United States, 1970

Ethnic group	Numbers in millions	Percentage
Total population	203.2	100.0
Female	103.9	51.1
Male	99.3	48.9
Native [born] of native parentage	169.6	83.5
White	146.2	71.9
Persons of foreign stock:		
Second generation in U.S.	24.0	11.8
First generation in U.S.	9.7	4.7
Second generation from:		
United Kingdom	1.8	.9
Canada	2.2	1.1
Ireland	1.2	.6
Germany	2.8	1.4
U.S.S.R	1.5	.7
Poland	1.8	.9
Italy	3.2	1.6
Mexico	1.6	.8
First generation from:		
United Kingdom	.7	.3
Canada	.8	.4
Ireland	.3	.1
Germany	.8	.4
U.S.S.R.	.5	.2
Poland	.5	.2
Italy	1.0	.5
Mexico	.8	.4
Persons of Spanish origin:		
Mexico	9.1	4.5
Puerto Rico	4.5	2.2
Cuba	.5	.2
Racial groups:		
White	177.7	87.5
Black	22.6	11.1
American Indians	.8	.4
Asian:		
Japanese	.6	.3
Chinese	.4	.2

SOURCE: *Population of the United States: Current Population Reports, 1974.* Washington, D.C.: U.S. Department of Commerce. Series P-23, p. 93.

the society. Women in American society in fact constitute a slight majority in numbers, though they have minority status. (See, for example, the section Work and Sexual Inequality in Chapter 6.) A more dramatic disparity between the status and size of a minority exists in South Africa, where blacks, who represent nearly 80 percent of the population, are subjugated by the official segregationist policy of *apartheid*, enforced by the white *numerical* minority, which is in fact a *power* majority.

MINORITY ACCEPTANCE OF EGALITARIAN IDEOLOGY Unlike South Africa, the United States has an ideology and legal structure that call for equality. Minorities seek practical support of these values from others. Minorities, by definition, are of lower status than dominant groups. Vander Zanden notes that minorities' responses to their status form a continuum between the poles of *acceptance* and *aggression* (1972: 306).

As Louis Wirth observed [see the selection on minorities], in a secular and urban society such as the United States, "minorities ... are likely to refuse to accept their status or their deprivation without some effort to improve their lot." Aggressive minority challenges to the dominant majority were established practices long before the forces of urbanism and secularism became dominant.

HISTORICAL INTERGROUP CONFLICT

Social conflict is a process of interaction involving two or more parties opposing one another on issues such as equality of treatment and economic security. The parties may be individuals or groups. Intergroup conflict is an important characteristic of contemporary American society. Ever since colonial times, there have been efforts by a great variety of groups to exchange their minority status for co-equal status and *accommodation**, in which groups aim to reduce conflict and live cooperatively together (Gordon, 1964). The earliest such efforts were made by religious minorities. Those that followed were made primarily by ethnic nationality groups, and most recently by racial minority groups. In this process, general patterns emerge: movement from interreligious conflict to accommodation (seventeenth and eighteenth centuries); movement from interethnic conflict to accommodation (nineteenth and early twentieth centuries); and movement from interracial conflict to continuing attempts at accommodation (twentieth century).

CONFLICT

Source: Lewis Coser, "Conflict: Social Aspects," *International Encyclopedia of the Social Sciences*, vol. 3 (New York: Macmillan, 1968), pp. 232–234. Copyright © 1968 by Crowell-Collier and Macmillan, Inc.

Social conflict may be defined as a struggle over values or claims to status, power, and scarce resources, in which the aims of the conflicting parties are not only to gain the desired values but also to neutralize, injure, or eliminate their rivals. Such conflicts may take place between individuals, between collectivities, or between individuals and collectivities. Intergroup as well as intragroup conflicts are perennial features of social life.

Conflict is an important element of social interaction. Far from being always a "negative" factor that "tears apart" social conflict may contribute in many ways to the maintenance of groups and collectivities as well as to the cementing of interpersonal relations. . . .

The impact of conflict on social structures varies according to the type of such structures. In loosely structured groups and in open, pluralistic societies, conflict that aims at a resolution of tension between antagonists is likely to have stabilizing functions. If the direct expression of rival claims is permitted, such conflicts may serve to eliminate the causes for dissociation and to re-establish unity. In such flexible structures, multiple affiliations of individuals make them participate in a variety of group conflicts so that those who are antagonists in one conflict are allies in another. Thus, multiple conflicts, although varying in intensity, are likely to crisscross one another and thereby prevent cleavages along one axis. The pluralism of associations in such types of societies leads to a plurality of fronts of conflict, and the intensity of any one of these conflicts is likely to be relatively low. Segmental participation in a multiplicity of conflicts constitutes a balancing mechanism within the structure. In this way, conflicts may be said to sew pluralistic societies together.

In rigid social structures and in closed groups, on the other hand, the impact of conflict is likely to be quite different. The closer the group, the more intense are conflicts likely to be, that is, the more highly involved the parties. Such groups tend to inhibit the open acting out of hostility since they fear its disruptive effect. Closed groups tend to absorb the total personality of their members; they are jealous of members' affiliation with other groups and desire to monopolize their loyalty. The resultant deep involvement of the members and the intimate association among them is likely to lead to a great deal of hostility and ambivalence, a hostility, however, to which the group denies legitimate outlets. Hence, if conflicts break out in groups that have tried to prevent them, they are likely to be peculiarly intense. This is so because, first, the personality absorption in such groups tends to favor the mobilization of all psychic energies in the conduct of the struggle, and, second, because these conflicts now are not likely to remain limited to the issues at hand but to revive all those grievances that were denied expression previously. All the previously latent causes for conflict are now superimposed upon one another.

Like all ideal types (see Chapter 2), these general patterns of change call for qualification. Not all interreligious conflict was resolved in American society in the colonial period, nor were ethnic or national group conflicts ended early in this century, nor has there yet been full interracial accommodation. These characterizations merely denote the periods of most intense conflict. The nature of these interactions and their resolution provides a necessary background for understanding current intergroup relations in American society. Let us consider developments in each of the three periods mentioned.

FROM INTERRELIGIOUS CONFLICT TO ACCOMMODATION In 1773, Reverend Jonathan Mayhew of Boston remarked:

> ... When we consider what our forefathers suffered ... for nonconformity to a non-instituted mode of worship.... When we consider the narrow, censorious and bitter spirit that prevails in too many of the Episcopalians among us ... we cannot well think of that church's gaining ground here to any great degree.... Will they never let us rest in peace, except where all the weary are at rest? Is it not enough that they persecuted us out of the old world? Will they pursue us into the new and convert us here?

This statement, published on the eve of the American Revolution, marks the first major overt intergroup conflict in American society. A Protestant minister expressed the strong American opposition to the Anglican, or Episcopalian, Church's establishing on American shores the formal religious controls operating in England.

RELIGIOUS LIBERTY AND THE AMERICAN REVOLUTION The impact of the religious issue on the development of American society is evident in the analysis by two prominent historians of the factors that led the colonists to revolt against Great Britain.

Leopold and Link note five such factors (1952: 45–54): (1) the economic factor (No taxation without representation); (2) the political factor — the growth of more democratic and independent political institutions than those then existing in England; (3) the religious factor — the resistance of many non-Anglican Protestants and other religious minorities to any attempt to establish an official church (Episcopalian or any other); (4) the social factor — the mixture of many non-English immigrants from France, Germany, and other nations with little prior loyalty to England; and (5) the psychological factor — the growth of national self-consciousness. Thus one of the five major causes of the American Revolution — religion — is defined as an intergroup conflict.

EARLY SIGNS OF FUTURE CONFLICTS Many minority group conflicts that were to flare up later did not appear during the colonial period. Black slavery was legal throughout the colonies, although most slaves were concentrated on the plantations of the South. In 1760, on the eve of the American Revolution, there were on the small farms of the North, where slaves were generally not economical, only 87,000 blacks; in the South there were 299,000 (Channing, 1908: 491–492).

The status of slaves was not entirely a matter of economics. As Froman points out, whites, because of their tradition of liberty, found it necessary to use the excuse of alleged black inferiority to justify their enslavement. In addition, blacks, unlike Indians, found escape difficult because of their lack of knowledge of the land. Finally, slavery provided those whites with low self-esteem a philosophy that gave them a sense of racial superiority (Froman, 1972: 42–45). Certainly not all whites accepted these rationales; blacks obviously could see their

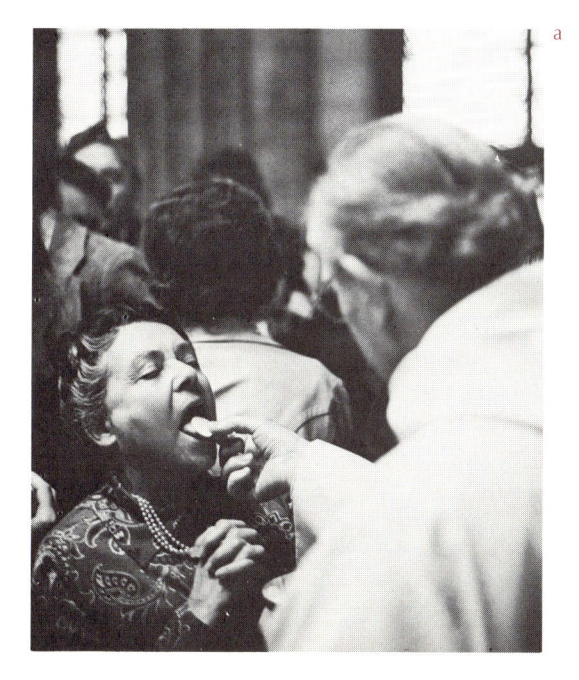

COLLECTIVE CONFLICT AND INTERGROUP RELATIONS 235

Early conflict between religious groups in American society has largely given way to religious pluralism. SOURCE: (a) Erich Hartman/Magnum; (b) Louis Goldman/Photo Researchers.

disadvantaged place in society, and many whites, among them the abolitionists, could not shut their eyes to inequality.

Other important minority groups, unlike the blacks, for various reasons did not engage in major organized efforts to change their status. Indians are members of separate tribal nations, and the intense conflicts among them were comparable to international conflicts. Ethnic minorities, such as the Irish and Italians, did not enter the society until well along in the nineteenth century. Women did not begin to organize for their rights until the development of mass public education in the last century. They generally accepted a socialization process which denied them rights.

MINORITY RELIGIOUS CHALLENGES IN THE COLONIAL PERIOD   Thus the only minorities that could effectively challenge their minority status in the colonial period were religious groups. The seeds of discontent were sown in the very reasons why the early colonists came to the New World. The Puritans had been driven out of England by the Anglican Episcopalians. Resistance came naturally to them. As early as 1635, dissidents led by Roger Williams challenged the Puritans. The establishment of independent colonies in Rhode Island and Connecticut set the stage for the kind of protest noted in Reverend Mayhew's statement.

By the mid-eighteenth century, religious pluralism in America was evident in the proliferation of Protestant groups and in the settlements of Catholics in Maryland, Quakers in Pennsylvania, and Jews in New York. The importance of religious pluralism in the colonies is seen in the Bill of Rights and in the language of the First Amendment: "Congress shall make no law respecting an establishment of religion, or prohibiting the free exercise thereof...." As Vander Zanden has observed, by the mid-eighteenth century "the great multiplicity of faiths made [religious] intolerance impractical and disruptive of the social fabric" (1972: 412). Yet past restrictive values and practices had continuing effects. The Mormons, with their unorthodox Christian theology, often faced violent opposition. Even in Utah, where they were dominant, the Mormons had to forsake their religiously sanctioned practice of polygamy before the state was allowed to enter the Union (Kephart, 1972: 162).

FROM INTERETHNIC CONFLICT TO ACCOMMODATION   From the establishment of the Republic until the restrictive immigration acts of the 1920s, over 30 million immigrants became American citizens (*Statistical Abstract,* 1966: Tables 123 and 125). Sowell reports that, prior to the development of steamships, which made voyages shorter, more dependable, and more economical, immigration was biased toward departure from those European ports engaged in large-scale commercial trade with the United States. Those living closest to these ports could best afford to emigrate (Sowell, 1975: 64–65).

MINORITY GROUPS AND IMMIGRANTS   Many of the immigrants were motivated primarily by persecution. This was true of European Jews throughout most of the nineteenth and early twentieth centuries. In other cases, minority status was coupled with additional problems. For example, in the 1840s economic depression and a potato famine in Ireland and the crushing of dissident political beliefs in Germany stimulated millions to emigrate to America. In the 1870s and 1880s, severe economic problems in China encouraged hundreds of thousands to seek work as railroad laborers in the American West; and from late in the nineteenth century until the 1920s, the growing American industries employed masses of unskilled laborers, who came largely from Italy, Poland, and Russia. In these cases, minority members chose to emigrate rather than adjust to minority status in their own society.

CONFLICTS WITH THE NATIVE-BORN Even with a rapidly growing industrial economy and an expanding western frontier, the native-born began to view the entry of millions of immigrants with increasing concern. Such derogatory group terms as mick ditchdiggers for the Irish, kikes for the Jews, wops for the Italians, and chinks for the Chinese became commonplace. By the turn of the century, the United States was becoming increasingly urbanized, and in American industry, the demand for immigrant labor declined. The cities developed ethnic enclaves (pockets) — Little Italys, Little Polands, and Chinatowns.

World War I crystallized sentiment of the American-born against foreigners. The first discriminatory legislation had been the Chinese Exclusion Act of 1882. Now, in the wake of isolationist sentiment, antagonism was widely directed at European aliens, many of whom were considered anarchists, radicals, and "Reds." Prominent academicians of the day lent their analytical support to the rising tide of hostility toward southern and eastern European immigrants. Robert DeWard, a Harvard professor of geology, argued for the need to restrict the immigration of southern and eastern Europeans on the grounds that (1919: 516)

> ... to grant free admission to all who want to come may give us, for the moment, a comfortable feeling that we are providing a "refuge for the oppressed," but it is in the highest degree "ungenerous" in us, the custodians of the future heritage of our race, to permit to land on our shores mental, physical and moral defectives, who themselves and through their descendants, will not only lower the standards of our own people, but will tremendously increase all future problems of public and private philanthropy. It is in the highest degree "un-American" for us to permit any such influx of alien immigrants as will make the process of Americanization any more difficult than it already is.

This was the period of the second rise of the Ku Klux Klan. The Klan turned from terrorizing blacks to persecuting the foreign-born.

THE FIRST RESTRICTIVE IMMIGRATION ACTS In 1921, the first restrictive immigration act was passed. As we discussed in Chapter 2, its purpose was to limit total immigration sharply and to favor immigrants from Great Britain and western and northern Europe. Ethnic minorities reacted to these hostile developments in a variety of ways. Delinquency rates rose among adolescents in urban ethnic enclaves. Concerted efforts were made by various ethnic groups to take over city hall as a means of increasing their political influence and stabilizing their lives. Recall also the discussion of the functions of the political machine (Chapter 1) for meeting needs of the otherwise powerless.

The rise of John F. Kennedy to the presidency can be traced to the Irish domination of Boston politics, including the election of Kennedy's grandfather as mayor of Boston, which provided him with the political base from which to move into national politics. Irish, Italian, Polish, Russian, and other ethnic minorities also began to assert influence in the trade union movement. Most of the workers who joined the American Federation of Labor at the turn of the century and later the Congress of Industrial Organizations (now merged into the AFL-CIO) were of ethnic minority stock (Warner and Low, 1941).

SYMBOLS OF ETHNIC ACCEPTANCE Two developments symbolized the successful efforts of ethnic minorities to become an accepted, indigenous part of American society. The first of these was the passage of the National Labor Relations Act (NLRA) of 1935. Second was the enactment of the nondiscriminatory Immigration Act of 1965. The NLRA, a major development in the economic stabilization of ethnic minorities, gave labor unions the right to enter into collective bargaining agreements with corporations. Violence gave way to negotiations and sanctioned strike activity. As a result, such ethnic groups as the Irish, Italians, and Poles are now generally members of the middle class (Blauner, 1969).

Evidence of the growing economic and political influence of ethnic minorities is seen in the 1965 immigration legislation. An Irish Catholic senator from Michigan, Patrick McNamara, introduced a bill, which passed both houses of the Congress, abolishing the national origins quota system of earlier acts. By the provisions of the new act, since June 30, 1968, the annual ceiling on immigration has been set at 179,000, compared to an annual total of close to a million at the turn of the century (Bernard, 1950: 24).

Official immigration (excluding an unknown number of illegal immigrants mostly from Mexico) has slowed to a trickle from a rate of 5.89 per 1,000 population in 1900 to 1.84 per 1,000 in 1972 (Office of Management and Budget, *Social Indicators*, 1973: 257). The new quota applies equally to all nations outside the western hemisphere; there is no country-by-country quota. This act was a fundamental reversal of the former discriminatory policy, but not a total one. The act also specified that preference would be given to applicants on the basis of family ties to Americans and occupational skills in short supply in the nation. Given the large existing population base of people whose national origins were in Great Britain or western or northern Europe — as well as the industrialized nature of those countries — the new provisions continue to favor the earlier favored nations.

FROM INTERRACIAL CONFLICT TO CONTINUING ATTEMPTS AT ACCOMMODATION To understand twentieth-century racial conflicts, it is necessary to know the background from which current pressures have emerged. The language of the United States Constitution is instructive in respect to the state of race relations at the time of the founding of the republic. Recall this discussion in Chapter 2 of Article 1, Section 2 of the Constitution, dealing with the basis of representation from each state in the House of Representatives. The "free persons" referred to included indentured servants, who were generally white immigrants from Great Britain bound to work for someone for up to ten years. Excluded as free persons were "Indians not taxed," which included most, since they were viewed as citizens of separate tribal nations. By the terms of the "three fifths of all other persons" provision, each Negro slave was to be counted as three-fifths of a person in determining how many representatives a state was entitled to have.

LEGAL EMANCIPATION AND PRACTICAL SUBJUGATION Even when this provision was eliminated by the Fourteenth Amendment, passed after the Civil War, its symbolic meaning has continued into the present. For most blacks, emancipation has

Symbols of social status. SOURCE: George Gardner.

A scene from "Roots" and part of the record-breaking television audience that watched the show. SOURCE: (a) John Soto/New York Times Pictures; (b) Ben Tucker-Savannah.

not been a reality. The movement toward equal status in the decade following the Civil War was stopped primarily because of the political compromise of 1877, in which Rutherford B. Hayes won the election in the electoral college thanks to bargained-for southern votes. Hayes had lost the popular election to Samuel J. Tilden. The compromise consisted of Hayes's prior agreement to abolish the Freedman's Bureau in the former confederate states, thereby ending the national effort to assist the newly freed black citizens participate fully in the social, economic, and political life of the society (Carman and Syrett, 1955: 39–45).

The result was a systematic elimination of any rights blacks had recently secured. Numerous laws were passed in southern states to keep blacks from voting, in violation of the Fifteenth Amendment (granting citizens the right to vote despite "race, color, or previous condition of servitude"). The most common laws required literacy and other tests, poll taxes, and property qualifications before a person could vote. To ensure that these laws affected only black citizens, *grandfather clauses* were generally included, by which any man who could not meet the educational or property qualifications could still vote so long as he was the son or grandson of a person who had voted. Slaves, of course, had not voted.

BLACK MIGRATION TO THE CITIES Such measures stimulated millions of blacks to migrate to the expanding industrial cities of the North. The extent of this movement is indicated by the changing proportion of blacks to whites in the South and in the North. At the end of the Civil War, nearly half the total southern population was black, compared to less than one percent of the northern population. In 1970, 52 percent of the blacks lived in the North and West (Fellows, 1972: 24).

BARRIERS IN THE NORTH Overt barriers to equal treatment also existed in the North. The labor unions, instrumental in helping ethnic minorities achieve equal status, were generally closed to blacks. The large and powerful American Federation of Labor (AFL), had grown in the quarter of a century between 1890 and 1914 from 550,000 members to over 2 million. Yet, the policy of the AFL specifically excluded both Negroes and women. It had forgotten its own immigrant heritage in its restrictionist policy (Higham, 1975: 49). By mid century, blacks, now heavily concentrated in cities in the North and increasingly in cities of the South, became assertive in a variety of ways. Like early religious and ethnic minorities, blacks expressed their demands for equality of treatment and opportunity. Recent efforts of blacks have stimulated major intergroup tensions in America.

THE AMERICAN RACIAL DILEMMA

In the late 1930s and early 1940s, the Carnegie Foundation sponsored the first society-wide in-depth analysis of race relations in American society. The investigation was headed by the Swedish socioeconomist Gunnar Myrdal, who worked with a team of American sociologists. The result was the publication of the monumental *An American Dilemma*. Myrdal developed the thesis that the major conflict in American race relations is moral, in that the egalitarian values of the culture are at odds with the unequal treatment afforded black people (1944: XLVII):

Though our study includes economic, social, and political race relations, at the bottom our problem is the moral dilemma of the American — the conflict between his moral valuations on various levels of consciousness and generality. The "American Dilemma," referred to in the title of this book, is the ever-raging conflict between, on the one hand, the valuations preserved on the general plane which we shall call the "American Creed," where the American thinks, talks, and acts under the influence of high national and Christian precepts, and, on the other hand, the valuations on specific planes of individual and group living, where personal and local interest; economic, social, and sexual jealousies; considerations of community prestige and conformity; group prejudice against particular persons or types of people; and all sorts of miscellaneous wants, impulses, and habits dominate his outlook.

PREJUDICE AND DISCRIMINATION Myrdal was pointing to the society-wide racial discrimination in the nation, which contradicted the American creed of equality. The far-ranging analysis presented evidence of prejudice — hostile prejudgments and attitudes toward blacks and other groups, whatever their personal qualities or social position. However, the central focus of analysis was discrimination — overt action in which minorities are subject to unfavorable treatment on the basis of race or some other characteristic such as age, nationality, religion, or sex (see the selection on prejudice and discrimination). In all areas of American social life — close interpersonal relations, schooling, job opportunities, availability of housing, or other normal activities — blacks were viewed and treated as inherently inferior to others.

PREJUDICE

From: Gordon Allport, *The Nature of Prejudice* (Reading, Mass.: Addison-Wesley, 1954), pp. 6–10.

The word *prejudice*, derived from the Latin noun *praejudicium*, has, like most words, undergone a change of meaning since classical times. There are three stages in the transformation.

1. To the ancients, praejudicium meant a precedent — a judgment based on previous decisions and experiences.

2. Later, the term, in English, acquired the meaning of a judgment formed before due examination and consideration of the facts — a premature or hasty judgment.

3. Finally the term acquired also its present emotional flavor of favorableness or unfavorableness that accompanies such a prior and unsupported judgment.

Perhaps the briefest of all definitions of prejudice is: *thinking ill of others without sufficient warrant.* This crisp phrasing contains the two essential ingredients of all definitions — reference to unfounded judgment and to a feeling-tone. It is, however, too brief for complete clarity.

In the first place, it refers only to *negative* prejudice. People may be prejudiced in favor of others; they may think *well* of them without sufficient warrant . . . while it is important to bear in mind that biases may be *pro* as well as *con*, it is none the less true that *ethnic* prejudice is mostly negative. A group of students was asked to describe their attitudes toward ethnic groups. No suggestion was made that might lead them toward negative reports. Even so, they reported eight times as many antagonistic attitudes as favorable attitudes. . . .

It is not easy to say how much fact is required in order to justify a judgment. A prejudiced person will almost certainly claim that he has sufficient warrant for his views. He will tell of bitter experiences he has had with refugees, Catholics, or Orientals. But, in most cases, it is evident that his facts are scanty and strained. He resorts to a selective sorting of his own few memories, mixes them up with hearsay, and overgeneralizes. No one can possibly know *all* refugees, Catholics, or Orientals. Hence any negative judgment of these groups *as a whole* is, strictly speaking, an instance of thinking ill without sufficient warrant. . . .

Overcategorization is perhaps the commonest trick of the mind. Given a thimbleful of facts we rush to make generalizations as large as a tub. One young boy developed the idea that all Norwegians were giants because he was impressed by the gigantic stature of Ymir in the saga, and for years was fearful lest he meet a living Norwegian. A certain man happened to know three Englishmen personally and proceeded to declare that the whole English race had the common attributes that he observed in these three.

There is a natural basis for this tendency. Life is so short, and the demands upon us for practical adjustments so great, that we cannot let our ignorance detain us in our daily transactions. We have to decide whether objects are good or bad by classes. We cannot weigh each object in the world by itself. Rough and ready rubrics, however coarse and broad, have to suffice.

Not every overblown generalization is a prejudice. Some are simply *misconceptions*, wherein we organize wrong information. One child had the idea that all people living in Minneapolis were "monopolists." And from his father he had learned that monopolists were evil folk. When in later years he discovered the confusion, his dislike of dwellers in Minneapolis vanished.

Here we have the test to help us distinguish between ordinary errors of prejudgment and prejudice.

If a person is capable of rectifying his erroneous judgments in the light of new evidence he is not prejudiced. *Prejudgments become prejudices only if they are not reversible when exposed to new knowledge.* A prejudice, unlike a simple misconception, is actively resistant to all evidence that would unseat it. We tend to grow emotional when a prejudice is threatened with contradiction. Thus the difference between ordinary prejudgments and prejudice is that one can discuss and rectify a prejudgment without emotional resistance.

Taking these various considerations into account, we may now attempt a final definition of negative ethnic prejudice.... Each phrase in the definition represents a considerable condensation of the points we have been discussing:

Ethnic prejudice is an antipathy based upon a faulty and inflexible generalization. It may be felt or expressed. It may be directed toward a group as a whole, or toward an individual because he is a member of that group.

The net effect of prejudice, thus defined, is to place the object of prejudice at some disadvantage not merited by his own misconduct.

DISCRIMINATION

From: Brewton Berry, *Race and Ethnic Relations* (Boston: Houghton Mifflin, 1965), p. 341. Permission to quote also granted by Routledge & Kegan Paul, Ltd., London.

Dominant peoples everywhere have resorted to various devices for restricting economically, politically, and socially the racial and ethnic groups over whom they have set themselves. The term commonly applied to such practices is *discrimination,* which F. H. Hankins has defined as the "unequal treatment of equals, either by the bestowal of favors or the imposition of burdens." Discrimination touches upon every phase of life. Subordinate groups are often restricted in their use of hotels, restaurants, transportation, and such public facilities as parks, playgrounds, swimming pools, and libraries. Churches and hospitals are often closed to them; intermarriage is opposed; and social contacts between master and servant are hedged about with an elaborate system of etiquette. In the economic realm members of minority groups are barred from trade unions and professional associations, they are effectively excluded from many occupations, they are the "last to be hired, and the first to be fired," and, where they are permitted to work, they are kept down by the imposition of a "job ceiling." One function of these discriminations is to isolate the dominant and subordinate groups and to limit contact and communication between them.

THE MORAL DILEMMA Myrdal's identification of a moral dilemma felt by whites makes an assumption that has lately been criticized empirically. The assumption is that white Americans apply the American creed of equality to all members of the society. While recent analyses of social distance (see Bogardus, 1968) and stereotyping (see Gordon, 1973) suggest that there has been a lessening of hostility toward blacks, there is considerable evidence to suggest that, for many white Americans, continuing prejudice toward blacks constitutes no moral dilemma.

In the early 1960s, a sample was taken of households in Indianapolis (Westie, 1965). People were asked to agree or disagree with such statements as: "Everyone in America should have equal opportunity to get ahead" (a general value) and, "I would be willing to have a Negro as my supervisor in my place of work" (a specific application of the value). While 81 percent of the general statements were accepted, only 56 percent of the specific ones were.

The fact that many whites could agree in general with the egalitarian American creed while refusing to apply it to blacks creates a profound dilemma for blacks, if not for whites, and is a major factor in racial tension.

Prejudice and discrimination do not always go hand in hand. A way to understand and interpret people's attitudes is demonstrated by this prejudicial attitude–discriminatory behavior typology developed by Robert Merton (Robert Merton, "Discrimination and the American Creed," in R. MacIver (ed.), *Discrimination and the National Welfare*, New York: Harper & Row, 1949, p. 103):

	Attitude Dimension: Prejudiced (−)* and Un-Prejudiced (+)*	Behavior Dimension: Discriminator (−)* and Non-Discriminator (+)*
I. Unprejudiced non-discriminator[1]	+	+
II. Unprejudiced discriminator	+	−
III. Prejudiced non-discriminator	−	+
IV. Prejudiced discriminator	−	−

[1] The value of being unprejudiced and the behavior of being nondiscriminatory constitute the American creed.
* Where (+) = conformity to the creed, and (−) = deviation from the creed.

These are not merely prototypes. Each type exists extensively in American society. This typology points out clearly that attitudes (prejudice) and behavior (discrimination) do not always go together. As Albrecht, DeFleur, and Warner note (1972), it is necessary to evaluate the *contingency conditions,* or the pressures, operating on people in different social situations that affect whether or not people will act on their beliefs. An examination of each of thee types illustrates common consistent and inconsistent reactions (Merton, 1949: 103–110).

UNPREJUDICED NONDISCRIMINATORS These individuals believe in the American creed and act upon their beliefs. They can often be found as leaders or general members of organizations devoted to equal treatment of all American citizens, such as the American Civil Liberties Union (ACLU) or the National Association for the Advancement of Colored People (NAACP). Merton notes that these individuals occupy a strategic position in society in the campaign against prejudice and discrimination.

UNPREJUDICED DISCRIMINATORS These people deny that they are prejudiced, yet they support discriminatory practices that appear to be to their immediate advantage. (See Westie's sample, in which some who professed agreement with the American creed did not want a black person as a supervisor.) Robert Kahn's *Discrimination Without Prejudice* (1968) presents a prototype of this pattern. Kahn and his associates documented the manner in which middle-level executives express nonprejudicial attitudes but avoid hiring or promoting minority persons because they fear negative reactions from their corporate superiors.

PREJUDICED NONDISCRIMINATORS These individuals reluctantly follow the creed. They do not believe in it and are openly prejudiced. Yet they tend to conform in treating minority members equitably for fear of being penalized. Others of this type are people in business who have minority customers, politicians who have a number of minority constituents, and trade-union leaders who may be personally opposed to allowing blacks or other minorities in their unions but who bow to pressure from union members. These people are particularly affected by strong legal measures to ensure equality of treatment.

PREJUDICED DISCRIMINATORS These individuals are consistent in their attitudes and behavior; they are unabashed bigots. They can be found in racist organizations such as the Ku Klux Klan. In some areas, such as places in the rural South where racial prejudice and discrimination is an accepted way of life, they are social conformists. However, in most parts of the nation, including the urban parts of the South, such people are considered deviant. They may provoke incidents of violence when community tensions run high, for example, during efforts to desegregate schools or neighborhoods.

THE THOMAS THEOREM EFFECT   As W. I. Thomas observed, whatever beliefs people hold, they are real in their consequences (1931: 139). (Recall the discussion of the Thomas theorem in Chapter 2). In race relations, the disparity between the egalitarian American Creed and actual practice has led to real tensions and conflict.

THE CONTINUING DILEMMA   Widespread racial discrimination was legally sanctioned in the United States until quite recently. While such discrimination was most widespread in the South, it existed in every region of the nation and in virtually every social setting. The consequence has been the structural exclusion of many blacks in the society from most of our affluent suburbs and from the best schools and jobs.

THE SEGREGATION ISSUE   The effects of discriminatory practices can be seen in the degree of racial *segregation* (separating people on the basis of group characteristics), a continuing practice in American institutions. After the Compromise of 1877, white southern politicians developed a campaign to dehumanize Negroes along the lines of their former slave image (Friedman, 1970). Most blacks lived in the South then, and northern politicians increasingly acquiesced to southern proposals. The result was a wide assault on individual blacks and black communities. In the 1890s, an average of two to three blacks were lynched each week (Berry, 1965: 108), and white riots in black communities resulted in loss of life and property (Logan, 1925). In this context, the meaning of the Fourteenth Amendment's provision for equal protection under the law began to be reinterpreted by the federal courts.

A key decision of the Supreme Court was the 1896 *Plessy* decision. Like all Supreme Court cases, this one concerned a specific case but had broad implications. The Court ruled that blacks and whites could be seated separately in railroad cars. The Court advanced the doctrine that *separate but equal* treatment of the races was constitutional, and thus sanctioned the principle of racial segregation in other areas of social life, leading to treatment that was separate but not, in fact, equal. The races were separated in schools, in employment, in housing, in interpersonal relations, as well as in the initial focus of the Court's concern, mass transportation.

Encouraged by this judicial doctrine, southern states moved to separate the races de jure (by law). Such legally based segregation was less extensively practiced in the North and the West, but it was common even there to find *restrictive covenant* clauses in the deeds of private houses that restricted their sale to whites only. (In 1948, the Supreme Court ruled that such practices were unconstitutional.) Furthermore, housing developments in which Federal Housing Administration (FHA) mortgage money was involved were racially segregated on the fallacious grounds that racial homogeneity was essential to a neighborhood's financial stability[3] (Abrams, 1966: 690).

---

[3] Concerning the popular view that property values decline in racially changing neighborhoods: by gathering extensive data over a twelve-year period for San Francisco, Oakland, and Philadelphia, Luigi Laurenti and his research associates at the University of California at Berkeley discovered that, except for brief panic-selling periods of a few weeks or months, the evidence overwhelmingly showed that values either remained the same or increased. See: Luigi Laurenti, *Property Values and Race* (Berkeley: University of California Press, 1960).

DE JURE AND DE FACTO SEGREGATION   All such legally sanctioned segregation has ended. Beginning in the 1920s, the NAACP initiated over a dozen judicial challenges to segregation (Ivy, 1964: 285-289). The key decision was the *Brown* case of 1954. Like *Plessy*, it has both a narrow and a broad meaning. Citing social scientific evidence gathered since the *Plessy* decision, the Court held unanimously that schools racially segregated by law were inherently unequal, thereby reversing the *Plessy* decision. Thus, the Court ended any sanctioning of the de jure segregation of public schools. By implication, this new position ended segregation on all levels of interaction, as was indicated by the Court's response to a case challenging Virginia's antimiscegenation law (Graham, 1966: 12E). In 1967, the Supreme Court held that Virginia's law banning interracial marriage was unconstitutional. This decision had the effect of nullifying similar laws in twenty other states.

Most of these decisions were aimed at the South, where there was a body of law supporting segregation. In the North and the rest of the nation, there did not exist as much de jure racial segregation. Yet the degree of de facto segregation (supported by practice rather than by law) was as extensive as in the rural South (Taeuber, 1964: 48).

In effect, blacks have faced continuing *institutional racism*. They experience the dual frustration of being blocked from jobs on the grounds that they are unqualified and of being discouraged and intimidated in efforts to find housing. In being prevented from finding suburban housing, blacks are also kept away from new jobs in suburban areas. Not informed about such jobs, and lacking transportation to them, they are thus confined to the city with its inferior schools, inferior housing, and other ills (Froman, 1972: 108-109).

The consequences of continuing segregation, and of the minority status of racial and other groups, are quite different in urban than in rural agrarian areas. People live closer together in cities. They are able to communicate their discontents more regularly and more extensively. These discontents become expressed in a variety of organized and disorganized ways, but always as a challenge to dominant society.

BLACK-LED CHALLENGES TO THE STATUS QUO

THE LATE FIFTIES AND EARLY SIXTIES: HOPE FOR CHANGE   Long before the *Brown* decision, it was evident that blacks were discontented with their status. There had been black revolts since pre-Civil War days in the South. The insurrections of Denmark Vesey in South Carolina in 1822 and of Nat Turner in Virginia in 1832 were two of the early demonstrations against minority status (Berry, 1971: 24-27). After the Civil War, articulate black leaders such as Frederick Douglass and W.E.B. DuBois rose to prominence, but it was not until the *Brown* decision that mass protest emerged. Urban crowding, unemployment, and other problems provoked blacks to be receptive to arguments in favor of organized action.

The conditions were right for such protests; the spark came a year after *Brown*, in 1955. In Montgomery, Alabama, a black woman, Rosa Parks, refused to move to the back of a bus to give a white woman her seat. The bus driver had Mrs. Parks arrested. Led by the Reverend Dr. Martin Luther King, Jr., the black community of Montgomery responded by organizing a successful boycott of the city's buses. Within a year, the buses of Montgomery were integrated. This event launched Dr. King and his organization, the Southern Christian Leadership Conference (SCLC), into national prominence.

By the late 1950s and early 1960s, such older black organizations as the NAACP and the Urban League began to support the more aggressive efforts of the SCLC. Other black-led organizations began to emerge, of which the Student Non-Violent Coordinating Committee (SNCC) and Congress of Racial Equality (CORE) were particularly active. Thus, a major *social movement** was launched, involving collective action to achieve equal status for black Americans. The guiding principle of the early civil rights movement was *nonviolence,* articulated by Dr. King, who had been deeply influenced by the philosophy of Gandhi; Gandhi's mass nonviolent demonstrations, also including hunger strikes, had succeeded against British colonial rule in India (King, Jr., 1968: 99).

A NOTE ON THE GENERAL MEANING OF SOCIAL MOVEMENTS In Herbert Blumer's now classic definition of social movements he identifies a dimension of *collective behavior* besides *crowds** and *publics**. While this definition serves to highlight minority social movements, it is useful to keep in mind the broader implications of social movements, which can also be led by dominant groups in the society (1951: 168-169):

Social movements can be viewed as collective enterprises seeking to establish a new order of life. They have their inception in a condition of unrest and derive their motive power on the one hand from dissatisfaction with the current form of life and, on the other hand, from wishes and hopes for a new scheme or system of living. The career of a social movement depicts the emergence of a new order of life. In its beginning, a social movement is amorphous, poorly organized, and without form; the collective behavior is on the primitive level ... and the mechanisms of interaction are elementary, spontaneous mechanisms. ... As a social movement develops, it takes on the character of a society. It acquires organization and form, a body of customs and traditions, established leadership, an enduring division of labor, social rules and social values — in short, a culture, a social organization, and a new scheme of life.

AN AGGRESSIVE NONVIOLENT STRATEGY Nonviolence is not a quiet strategy. It makes use of a variety of aggressive techniques — sit-ins in segregated restaurants, marches in segregated neighborhoods, voter registration drives in predominantly black precincts, the active search for white allies, boycotts, and a variety of other tactics (Bell, 1968: 29-45).

The nonviolent civil rights movement culminated in the 1963 march on Washington, which drew over 200,000 participants (Waskow, 1967: 236). Organizational representatives of all the major black civil rights organizations were joined by white spokesmen for the Protestant National Council of Churches, the American Jewish Committee, the Anti-Defamation League, and various Catholic archdiocesan committees. Labor leaders were there from the American Federation of Labor and the United Auto Workers. It was a time for both anger and hope, sentiments that Dr. King expressed in his famous "I have a dream" speech, delivered at the march (1971: 347-349):

... In a sense we have come to our nation's capitol to cash a check. When the architects of our republic wrote the magnificent words of the Constitution and the Declaration of Independence, they were signing a promissory note to which every American was to fall heir. This note was a promise that all men would be guaranteed the inalienable rights of life, liberty, and the pursuit of happiness.

It is obvious today that America has defaulted on this promissory note insofar as her citizens of color are concerned. Instead of honoring this sacred obligation, America has given the Negro people a bad check; a check which has come back marked "insufficient funds". ...

I say to you today, my friends, that in spite of the difficulties, and frustrations of the moment I still have a dream deeply rooted in the American Dream.

I have a dream that one day this nation will rise up and live out the true meaning of its creed, "We hold these truths to be self-evident; that all men are created equal."

The hopes expressed at the march were soon disappointed. Two weeks later, a bomb was set off at an all-black church in Birmingham, Alabama, killing four children attending Sunday school (Waskow, 1967: 238). Two months later, President John Kennedy was assassinated, thereby removing a national leader who had expressed public support for the march and for the civil rights movement (Schlesinger, 1967: 886–888).

MAJOR CIVIL RIGHTS LEGISLATION These dramatic developments, coupled with strong presidential leadership by Lyndon Johnson, led to public support for civil rights legislation. Acts were passed in 1964 and 1965 that provided the legal basis for achieving the widespread aims of the civil rights movement, including specific programs to achieve equality of opportunity in jobs and education, and other basic issues.

The Civil Rights Act of 1964, the most comprehensive civil rights legislation since the end of the Civil War, guaranteed that the same standards for voter registration be applied to all citizens in federal elections, prohibited discrimination on account of race in businesses serving the public, and established a provision ensuring fair employment practices by employers or unions with twenty-five or more employees or members. Other civil rights acts followed, in 1965 extending voting rights protection to state and local elections, and in 1968 barring discrimination in the sale or rental of houses paid for by Federal Housing Administration or other federal funds.

In addition to this legislation, other acts passed in 1965 were addressed to the programmatic goals of the civil rights movement. The Economic Opportunity Act funded the training of unskilled blacks and others in order to secure good jobs in a rapidly changing economy. (That economic opportunity has not yet been fully equalized can be seen in Table 8-2.) The Elementary and Secondary Education Act was designed to stimulate more funding for quality education for poor young blacks and others.

Table 8-2 Persons Below the Low-Income Level[a] in 1970, by Ethnic Origin of Head, for the United States (Numbers in Thousands)

Ethnic origin	Number below low-income level	Percent below low-income level
All persons	25,522	12.6
White	17,480	9.9
Black	7,650	33.6
Spanish origin	2,177	24.3
Mexican	1,407	28.0
Puerto Rican	424	29.2
Cuban	86	13.7
Other	260	14.0

[a] The low-income thresholds ranged from $1,950 for an unrelated adult individual to $6,470 for a family of seven or more persons. The threshold for a nonfarm family of four was $3,968.

SOURCE: Adapted from *Current Population Reports*, Series P-20, no. 224, 1971, p. 8.

SOURCE: Reprinted by permission of the *Plain Dealer*.

'Guess what? I learned what de jure and de facto mean'

SOURCE: (a) Alon Reinnger/DPI; (b) Wide World Photos.

RESISTANCE TO DESEGREGATION EFFORTS The Coleman Report (1966) recommended that poor, low-achieving blacks and whites, interact with high-achieving students in order to provide equality of educational opportunity. The NAACP led efforts to enforce these acts by means of court-ordered busing in order to achieve integrated schooling.[4] Court orders to bus children met vio-

---

[4] In 1976, James Coleman testified in a Senate committee session that he felt that the Court's position in support of busing had not produced beneficial results. In response, Reynolds Farley and other demographers noted that busing had not encouraged whites to move to the suburbs at an accelerated rate (1975: 1).

lent white opposition in Detroit, Boston, and other cities. President Richard Nixon declared his opposition to the busing of pupils to achieve racial integration and urged steps to offset court decisions requiring such busing (Pinckney, 1973: 352). In 1976, President Gerald Ford advised his attorney general to place a test case on busing before the Supreme Court. Although the plan was dropped, the President's opposition to busing was on the record.

Resistance took a variety of forms, reminiscent to many blacks of the period after the Compromise of 1877. Even as the acts of the mid-1960s were being passed, the actual living conditions of masses of poor blacks concentrated in the cities was deteriorating, and racial segregation was increasing (Abrams, 1965). Most upper-middle-class whites were moving into the suburbs (as we shall see in Chapter 10). Less tax money was available to meet the needs of the urban population, increasingly black, lower-middle class, and elderly. Urban renewal projects demolished substandard low-cost housing but did not replace it, leaving blacks in more strained circumstances than before (Abrams, 1965).

Sowell reports that urban renewal subsidies go mainly to businesses and to middle- and upper-income families who relocate. In the first ten years, more than two-thirds of the people displaced by urban renewal programs were black or Puerto Rican, although low-income Italian, Irish, and Mexican–Americans were affected too (Sowell, 1975: 197). He goes on to cite other factors in problems of urban renewal: special interest groups influence government officials; program administrators are defensive about criticism; social reformers and the affected ethnic and racial groups lack common goals; and experts are often uninformed about the real problems of disadvantaged minorities (Sowell, 1975: 198–204).

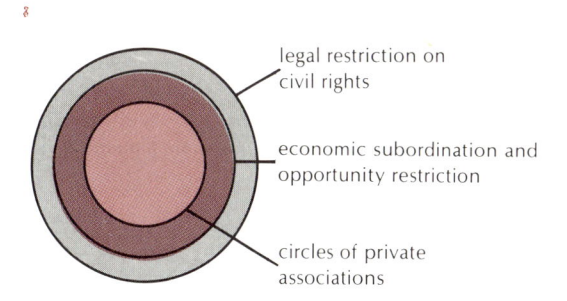

Figure 8-1 Bands of barriers to the achievement by minorities of co-equal status and opportunity. SOURCE: Adapted from the narrative of Herbert Blumer, "The Future of the Color Line" in J. McKinney and C. Thompson (eds.), *The South in Continuity and Change* (Durham, N.C.: Duke University Press, 1967), pages 329–330. Copyright 1965 by Duke University Press.

MULTIPLE BARRIERS TO EQUAL OPPORTUNITY Even if all the aims of the civil rights movement had been attained, other barriers to racial equality would remain. Herbert Blumer discusses some of them (1967: 329–330):

It is a serious mistake . . . to regard the achievement by Negroes of civil rights, as at present defined, as equivalent to removing the color line. . . . The tested area of civil rights is . . . but the outer band of the color line. Inside it lies the crucial area of economic subordination and opportunity restriction — an area of debarment of Negroes, which is exceedingly tough because it is highly complicated by private and quasi-private property rights, managerial rights, and organizational rights. Still further inside of the color line are the varied circles of private association from which the Negro is grossly excluded. Thus the successful achievement of civil rights merely peels off, so to speak, the outer layer of the color line. By itself, it does not significantly alter the social positions of the two racial groups.

THE MIDDLE AND LATE 1960s: DESPAIR AND CHALLENGE In the late 1960s, a combination of social forces produced mass despair among blacks. Rising white resistance was increasingly evident, while the civil rights movement continued to encourage rising aspirations among blacks. As blacks saw and wanted more of the good life enjoyed by most whites, such new black leaders as the writers Malcolm X *(Malcolm Speaks)*, Eldridge Cleaver *(Soul on Ice)*, and Stokely Carmichael *(Black Power)* began to give expression to their discontent. Malcolm X testified to and articulated this growing black discontent with establishment leadership in both the black and white communities in a speech in Detroit shortly after the march on Washington. He took aim at the Council for United Civil Rights Leadership that had planned the march, charging that (1971: 42–43)

once they formed it, with the white man over it, he promised them and gave them $800,000 to split up among the Big Six; and told them that after the march was over they'd give them $799,000 more. A million and a half dollars — split up between leaders that you have been following, going to jail for, crying crocodile tears for. And they're nothing but Frank and Jesse James. . . . It was a sellout.[5]

CIVIL DISORDERS The discontentment of the blacks in the urban ghettos of America soon became evident. In 1964, civil disorders broke out in Jacksonville, Florida, Jersey City, and New York City. Then in August 1965, in the Watts section of Los Angeles, a riot resulted in thirty-four deaths, hundreds of injuries, and $35 million in damage. Over the next two years, a number of cities in all sections of the nation experienced similar racial disorders. Tampa, Cincinnati, Atlanta, and Newark were among the hardest hit. In July 1967, Detroit experienced the worst racial riots in the history of the nation, and the worst rioting any city had seen since the Irish draft riots in New York during the Civil War. The Detroit riots left forty-three dead, over a thousand injured, over seven thousand arrested, and at least $50 million in property

Martin Luther King (1929–1968) had charismatic qualities that continued to influence the civil rights movement even after his assassination. SOURCE: Brown Brothers.

---

[5] The "Big Six" referred to by Malcolm X were the black leaders Martin Luther King, Jr., of SCLC, Roy Wilkins of the NAACP, Whitney Young of the Urban League, James Farmer of CORE, John Lewis of SNCC, and the march's coordinator Bayard Rustin of Freedom House.

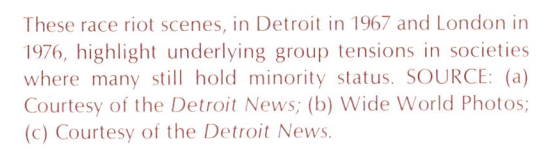

These race riot scenes, in Detroit in 1967 and London in 1976, highlight underlying group tensions in societies where many still hold minority status. SOURCE: (a) Courtesy of the *Detroit News*; (b) Wide World Photos; (c) Courtesy of the *Detroit News*.

destroyed (*Report of the National Advisory Commission*, 1968: 35–108).

Though unplanned and spontaneous, the civil disorders became so extensive that researchers increasingly began to identify them in terms of *violence as protest* (Fogelson, 1971). Black leaders expressed the need to establish *black power* to secure their rights and the programs that would offer them real opportunities to exercise those rights (Carmichael and Hamilton, 1967).[6] While moderate black leaders, including those who had organized the

---

[6] Stokely Carmichael of the Student Nonviolent Coordinating Committee used the term *black power* extensively. His fiery rhetoric and urging of militant actions (no more nonviolence) did much to move SNCC in a new direction.

march on Washington, continued to urge nonviolent means to secure their rights, more militant leaders such as Eldridge Cleaver and Huey Newton of the Black Panther party urged people to use any effective means. Moderate or militant, black leaders were united on one issue: they wanted a major improvement in the status of blacks in American society.

Eventually, Cleaver fled the country, and found in exile that other countries may offer fewer opportunities than the United States. He came home to face legal action. Malcolm X and Martin Luther King, Jr., were assassinated. The costs of speaking out were high.

THE WOMEN'S MOVEMENT AND OTHER ORGANIZING MINORITIES The civil rights movement brought increasing self-awareness and organized efforts to other minority groups. It has long been recognized that minority status is associated with race, religion, and nationality. It is now widely recognized that minority status is also associated with such additional group characteristics as age, sex, physical condition, and life style. Adolescents, the elderly, women, the disabled, and those who adhere to deviant life styles such as homosexuality are all subject to prejudice and discrimination.

RECOGNITION THROUGH SOCIAL MOVEMENTS The wide recognition of any given minority group's status is generally a consequence of social action initiated by members of the group. An example is the contemporary reemergence of the feminist movement. The suffragettes of the nineteenth and early twentieth centuries had their greatest success when a constitutional amendment was passed in 1920 enabling women to vote in national elections. That early feminist movement was also sparked by the civil rights issues surrounding blacks in the form of the abolitionist movement. Many women who were active in the abolitionist movement saw a clear analogy between the position of women in society and that of black slaves. Gunnar Myrdal, in *An American Dilemma*, notes this parallel low status (1944: 1073):

... [the] present status, as well as [women's] history and problems in society, reveal striking similarities to those of Negroes.

In the historical development of these problem groups in America there have been much closer relations than is now ordinarily recorded. In the earlier common law, women ... were placed under the jurisdiction of the paternal power. When a legal status had to be found for the imported Negro servants in the seventeenth century, the nearest and most natural analogy was the status of women.... The ninth commandment — linking together women, servants, mules, and other property — could be evoked, as well as a great number of other passages of Holy Scripture ... the paternalistic idea ... held the slave to be a sort of family member and in some way — in spite of all differences — placed him beside women ... under the power of the *paterfamilias* [male head of the family].

Feminists called the Seneca Falls Women's Rights Convention of 1848, led by such leaders as Elizabeth Cady Stanton and Lucretia Mott (Fidell and Keith-Spiegel, 1973: 452). Years of organizing efforts, including picketing, marches and lawsuits as well as the involvement of women in industry during World War I culminated in the successful drive for voting rights. Yet, when the Third National Conference of Commissions on the Status of Women was convened under the leadership of Eleanor Roosevelt in the early 1960s, the low status of women in society had not changed in a number of respects. The commission reported that, despite having won the right to vote, women were discriminated against in virtually every aspect of life (Stanton, 1975: 22). (See also in Chapter 6 the selection on Work and Sexual Inequality.)

EVALUATING STATUS BY POSITIONS OF INFLUENCE One ironic sign of the unequal status of women in American society is the fractional involvement of women in positions of political influence. A half century after gaining the vote, women held fewer than 10 percent of the key elected and appointed positions in government even though they composed 51 percent of the total population (see Table 8-3 summarizing female representation in a variety of government positions as of 1975).

In this context, the National Organization of Women (NOW) was formed in 1966 and soon became widely known in its fight for the Equal Rights Amendment (ERA), designed to protect the rights of women. Feminist leaders such as Betty Friedan, Gloria Steinem, and Shirley Chisholm became as well known nationally as had been Martin Luther King, Jr., Malcolm X, and Roy Wilkins. Like the black movement, the feminist movement affected virtually every area of American life. Figure 8-2, depicting a large number of women's magazine endorsements of the ERA, demonstrates the cross-section of American women who seek equality of treatment and opportunity.

SIGNS OF GENERAL CHANGE WITHIN THE DISCIPLINE Signs of minority *social movements* appeared within sociology itself, which has seen since the late 1960s the rise and institutionalization of black, feminist, and gay caucuses at the annual conventions of the American Sociological Association (ASA) and regional associations. The ASA sponsored a report, *The Status of Women in Sociology:*

Table 8-3   Where Women Stand — 1975

Cabinet, Supreme Court, judiciary
There is only one woman in the Cabinet. No women have ever been appointed to the U.S. Supreme Court; of 675 federal judgeships, only eight are filled by women.

Women in Congress
In the 1974–1976 Congress, there were nineteen women representatives, and there are no women in the Senate. The peak year was 1962, when a total of twenty women served, constituting 5 percent of the membership:

California	Yvonne Brathwaite Burke	Massachusetts	Margaret Heckler
	Shirley Pettis	Missouri	Leonore Sullivan
Colorado	Patricia Schroeder	Nebraska	Virginia Smith
Hawaii	Patsy Mink	New Jersey	Millicent Fenwick
Illinois	Cordiss Collins		Helen Meyner
Kansas	Martha Keys	New York	Shirley Chisholm
Louisiana	Lindy Boggs		Elizabeth Holtzman
			Bella Abzug
Maryland	Marjorie Holt	Tennessee	Marilyn Lloyd
	Gladys Noon Spellman	Texas	Barbara Jordan

Table 8-3 Where Women Stand — 1975 (cont.)

Government policy-making positions
4.5 percent of the approximately 100,000 government jobs paying $20,000 and higher are filled by women. In 1968, women held 3.7 percent of those positions.

State leaders
Only one woman, Ella Grasso of Connecticut, is governor of a state — the first woman to win this post without riding on her husband's coattails.

In state legislatures

Total # legislators	7561
Total # women legislators	604
Percent of women in legislatures	8.06%

Top five legislatures by percent of women:		Bottom five legislatures by percent of women:	
New Hampshire	24.5	Alabama	.7
Arizona	20.0	Louisiana	1.4
Delaware	16.1	California	1.7
Colorado	16.0	Arkansas	2.2
Alaska	15.0	Nebraska	2.0

Eight states have no women in the state senate.

Mayors
According to the National League of Cities, in 1972, 4.2 percent of the mayors of the 100 largest cities were women.

School board members
12 percent of school board members in 1972 were women.

SOURCE: *AAUW Journal*, Volume 69, Number 3 (November 1975), p. 10.

1968-1972, edited by Helen MacGill Hughes (1973), which presented detailed documentation on the lack of equal treatment for equal performance.

The report also made a more general observation that extends beyond the male resistance to the equality of women in sociology (Hughes, 1973: 2-3):

As Virginia Woolf observed, the history of men's opposition to the emancipation of women is perhaps more interesting than the story of the emancipation itself. It is a history that keeps repeating itself, in which prejudice is given expression in many guises. Thus course material is sometimes, no doubt quite unconsciously, chosen exclusively from the male perspective: the data presented in class concern, for example, male delinquency, male adolescence, male mobility, and so on, as though the behavior and vicissitudes of the other half of the human race did not count. And if the women students object, their comments are sometimes disparaged, or ridiculed, or perhaps, with devastating consistency, ignored.

Figure 8-2 SOURCE: Courtesy of American Association of University Women.

GLAMOUR
Can you support the **ERA** and still
- scrub your floors until they gleam? ☐ Yes ☐ No
- keep the American family whole? ☐ ☐
- let your husband call you baby? ☐ ☐

Good Housekeeping
Thus far, the Equal Rights Amendment has been ratified by the following 34 states: Alaska, California, Colorado, Connecticut, Delaware, Hawaii, Idaho, Iowa, Kansas, Kentucky, Maine, Maryland, Massachusetts, Michigan, Minnesota, Montana, Nebraska, New Hampshire, New Jersey, New Mexico, New York, North Dakota, Ohio, Oregon, Pennsylvania, Rhode Island, South Dakota, Tennessee, Texas, Vermont, Washington, West Virginia, Wisconsin and Wyoming.

McCall's
The wife who is eligible for child support now would also be eligible under ERA. The welfare of the child would be the determining factor in custody cases, as it already is in most states.

REDBOOK
My daughter Susan and American women of all ages would benefit from the improvements the Equal Rights Amendment would promote in our society. ERA will open up options for women and it will mean more choices for women and greater respect for the decisions they make in the home or in the market place.

BETTY FORD
THE WHITE HOUSE

True Romance
What that means is that, under the Equal Rights Amendment, your little girls will grow up entitled to the same educational and job opportunities that are now open to men and boys.

COSMOPOLITAN
We are, in voting yes to ERA, giving them a principle and asking them to make it work by respecting the spirit of the amendment. And that spirit is one of expanding—not shrinking—human rights. The specifics of the laws our lawmakers write will change and change again to suit the needs of the times, but the principle will have been established: Men and women will have equal rights or they will have unequal ones, as they have today.   Linda Wolfe

"It seems incredible to me that, 200 years after the founding of our country, we are still trying to establish equal rights for all citizens. It's not a question of women against men, but a question of realizing and compensating equally for the full potential of all people.

"Yes, I support the Equal Rights Amendment. It's time we started thinking of ourselves as full human beings."

Ms.
Joan Bennett Kennedy

womenSports
Personally, I wish we would have called the Equal Rights Amendment the Equal *Opportunity* Amendment from the beginning, because people get upset and confused about the word *rights*, and a negative feeling swells up. People are not going to think positively about something that makes them feel negative on a gut level. I looked up the word *equal* when I started thinking about this, and Webster defines it as "regarding or affecting all objects in the same way, impartial."

Billie Jean King

VOGUE
For behind the slogan of "equality" lies the specter—half-tempting, always frightening—of independence. Women are trained not to perceive themselves as autonomous and capable of enterprising acts, not in the way men are. And behind independence lies the greater specter—more tempting, more threatening—of power. Women are afraid of competing for power, and not just because they are used to their servile status. They are afraid, with good reason, of the retaliation of men. No women could have read the immortal comment of that soldier, statesman, and cultural revolutionary, Colonel Qaddafi of Libya—"I'll agree that women are the equals of men when I see pregnant women in the paratroop corps"—without feeling a visceral shudder. When power is at stake, men will not always be kind.   Susan Sontag

LADIES' HOME Journal
JULY '76
I am an optimist about both women and men ... about women's aptitude to grow and live multi-personal, achieving lives and about men's ultimate abilities to live with women who aren't necessarily slaves.

ESSENCE
The Equal Rights Amendment
1. Equality of rights under law shall not be denied or abridged by the United States or by any state on account of sex
2. The Congress shall have the power to enforce, by appropriate legislation, the provisions of this article
3. This amendment shall take effect two years after the date of ratification

BRIDE'S
● By the time you celebrate your silver or golden anniversary, the ERA could mean more. At present, a wife who has worked long enough to earn social security retirement benefits (ten years if born before 1930) has her choice. She can take one-half the amount her husband gets, the way a non-working wife can. Or she can receive what she's entitled to on her own—whichever is more. Say you'd been a part-time piano teacher, and he'd been an accountant. Your benefits would probably be less than half of his, so you'd take the half (just as if you hadn't worked). A husband rarely has this option. If he'd been the piano teacher, and you the accountant, he probably couldn't take that bigger half, and you wouldn't have as much to live on as a couple. The ERA would give husbands all the social security benefits wives now enjoy.

Playgirl
Thus, the struggle over ERA has begun ERA's work before the amendment is actually ratified. Women on both sides have gained a sense of womanpower by dealing with a woman's issue.

For other women, the struggle has been an enjoyable maiden voyage into a larger world, and they will continue to travel. ERA, if it passes, is their passport to independence. ■

New Woman
"The idea of erasing protective labor laws for women, for which many had fought hard, bothers me. Changes in domestic relations laws worry me too. But it's important to both women and men that women be regarded as *human* individuals entitled to equal protection and equal responsibility under the law."

MADEMOISELLE
Will the ERA legalize homosexual marriages?
Ross: Of course not. There's been a case on that issue already under a state ERA, not under the federal ERA, in the state of Washington, and the court found that all the ERA means is that if you are going to prohibit homosexual marriage between men, you have to prohibit it between women.

VIVA
I've seen those women's libbers who push the ERA. Why should I go along with that bunch?

There are many individuals and organizations supporting the ERA that do not fall into the category of "women's libbers." These include Gerald and Betty Ford, Alan Alda, Howard Cosell, Mary Tyler Moore, Jean Stapleton; and the National Council of Churches, the AFL-CIO, the United Auto Workers, the League of Women Voters, and, according to the 1975 end-of-the-year poll taken by NBC, 58 percent of all men.

Family Circle
● *Myth*: ERA will invalidate all state laws which require a husband to support a wife.
● *Fact*: Who says husbands are legally required to support their wives, even now? Although some state laws require this, they are rarely enforced.

Woman's Day
One woman says quietly to a friend, "I don't see why we even have to *argue* about ERA here in Illinois, the land of Lincoln. This amendment ought to be about as controversial as Girl Scout cookies."

ERA! ERA! ERA! ER

All material copyrighted by the publication in which it appeared in July, '76.
©Copyright 1976 American Association of University Women

Reprinted from August '76 AAUW Journal
American Association of University Women
2401 Virginia Avenue, N.W.
Washington, D.C. 20037

As in the case of the black movement, legal successes for women have been substantial, though the economic and private barriers Blumer noted (see Figure 8-1) are giving way less readily. Out of the women's movement have come laws on sex discrimination in education, inheritance taxes, rape, housing, and credit (Safilios-Rothschild, 1974; McKee, 1975).

INCREASING VISIBILITY OF OTHER MINORITIES Other minorities have also begun to be visible. Don Spiegel and Patricia Keith-Spiegel (1973) in their survey, "Outsiders: U.S.A.," note the emergence of such age-related minority groups as adolescents and the elderly, such health-related minority groups as the physically disabled, such economic minority groups as the intergenerational poor and school dropouts, such deviant-behavior minority groups as homosexuals and exprisoners, and such ethnic-heritage minority groups as Asians, Spanish-Americans, and Native Americans.

Altogether, the minority groups in American society compose a substantial majority of the population. Given the rising consciousness of minorities in the United States, it is likely that minority social movements will have a profound impact, ultimately going beyond civil rights legislation toward genuinely equal treatment and opportunity for all.

Congresswoman Shirley Chisholm's book *Unbought and Unbossed* is an articulate statement of new black political leadership. SOURCE: Charles Gatewood.

COLLECTIVE CONFLICT AND INTERGROUP RELATIONS 257

SOURCE: © 1973 United Feature Syndicate, Inc.

SIGNS OF INTERGROUP ACCOMMODATION

*Accommodation** is a process by which conflict between competing groups is reduced. It is hard to say whether American society is moving toward increasing interracial accommodation or more conflict. The conditions of most blacks continue to create interracial tension. The same can be said for other minorities, such as Chicanos, Puerto Ricans, and, increasingly, Native Americans (Howard, 1972). Yet there are objective and subjective indicators that some accommodation is occurring:

Objective Indicators
1. limited signs of upward socioeconomic mobility

2. increasing political influence

Subjective Indicators
1. the revolution in minority self-image and self-expression

2. signs of more accepting general attitudes toward minorities

Let's consider each of these indicators.

OBJECTIVE INDICATORS OF ACCOMMODATION *Limited signs of upward socioeconomic mobility of minorities.* The narrowing gap in real income and occupational status between black and white males from 1959 to 1969 (Table 8-4) is a trend reflective of other minority–dominant group trends, with some exceptions, notably the male–female gap.

The data in Table 8-4 call for careful analysis. For example, in reviewing this and related census data, Wattenberg and Scammon hold that, when one controls for age (when the gap is narrower at the younger age groupings), it can be reasonably argued that, in this generation, blacks have made the breakthrough to coequal status (1973: 34–44). Caution is called for in evaluating the pace of minority groups' upward mobility. As Tautfest observes of the same data, it is necessary to consider specific aspects of the circumstances of blacks and others living in the cities in which the data are collected (1974: 2–3). Blacks, including the younger age groups who are closing the income gap, tend to be concentrated not only in cities but in or near the ghettos where housing is crowded and living expenses high. Given these qualifications, there has been some progress of blacks and other minorities, which was a major aim of the civil rights movement of the 1950s and 1960s. If white middle-class males accept this trend and let it continue, then the trend will provide some resolution and accommodation of intergroup conflict. Such trends slow down somewhat in periods of economic recession, such

Table 8-4   Income of Black and White Males, in 1969 Dollars, by Age and Occupation, 1959 and 1969

Characteristics	Median income in 1959 White men	Black men	Ratio of black to white*	Median income in 1969 White men	Black men	Ratio of black to white[a]
Age						
20–24	$3408	$2183	64	$3822	$3466	91
25–34	6349	3667	58	8311	5558	67
35–44	7156	4050	57	9399	5810	62
45–54	6708	3543	53	9001	5117	57
55–64	5797	2833	49	7576	4263	56
65 and over	2307	1213	53	2941	1491	51
Total[b]	5464	2919	53	6765	3935	58
Occupation						
Professionals	8952	5254	59	11860	8606	73
Managers	8842	4725	53	11157	6598	59
Clerical	5602	5380	96	8032	7263	90
Craftsmen	6660	4498	68	8905	6488	73
Operatives	6262	4485	72	7525	5824	77
Service	5401	3515	65	6671	4865	73
Laborers	5448	3893	71	6278	5328	85

[a] The ratio can be interpreted as meaning that, on the average, for every $100 earned by whites, blacks earned the lesser amount noted.

[b] Includes some men under 20 who report income.

SOURCE: *Current Population Reports*, U. S. Department of Commerce, Bureau of the Census, 1960. Series PC (1) –ID, Table 219; PC (2) –5B, Table 7; and *Current Population Reports*, U.S. Department of Commerce, Bureau of the Census, 1970. Series P-60, No. 75, Table 45.

as the one the country experienced through most of the 1970s. In this context, unemployment rates are high, ranging up to 10 percent generally, but are intensely higher — over 20 percent — for city-dwelling young blacks. Such experiences intensify a sense of hopelessness and increase crime rates and violent protest orientations.

Increasing political influence. Though the migration of middle-class whites to the suburbs has generally had bad effects on blacks, it has had at least one major benefit. It has enabled blacks to exercise political power in a way reminiscent of the ethnic power blocs of a half century ago (see Table 8-5).

In the 1970s, Cleveland, Detroit, and Los Angeles elected black mayors for the first time in history. Furthermore, the election of Mayor Thomas Bradley in Los Angeles, where voting-age blacks constituted less than 20 percent of the population, demonstrated that significant numbers of whites were willing to accept blacks in a position of status and influence. More generally, urban blacks, by exercising power, can pressure suburbanites on certain issues. Suburban communities are linked to central cities in a variety of ways, including water and transportation systems, and in a variety of business enterprises. Political bargaining between blacks and whites resembles the bargaining that once took place between immigrants and the dominant group. Chicanos hold the same position in Phoenix, Los Angeles, and other southwestern cities that Puerto Ricans have in New York. The weakness in this picture is that in earlier times, all bargaining parties lived within the city. Thus, minorities of the day were more effective than current minorities can be in applying political pressure.

It is also worth noting that minorities other than urban blacks and Hispanics are organizing effectively. Moreover, on issues that affect the interests of their group, there is also growing political activity among women, the elderly, and adolescents.

SUBJECTIVE INDICATORS OF ACCOMMODATION *The revolution in minority self-image and self-expression.* Kurt Lewin, the social psychologist, documented that minority members often accept the negative definition of themselves that has been developed by dominant groups (1948). Blacks and other minorities no longer tend to accept such definitions. To blacks, "black is beautiful" is more than a slogan.

The consequences of this self-assertion is visible in the attempt to secure equal status and power. As we have noted, the black power movement is finding practical expression in big city politics. Other similar consequences are the fight for the passage of the Equal Rights Amendment, led by women, Mexican-Americans' *la raza* efforts to organize migrant laborers into effective unions, the American Indian Movement's (AIM) efforts to pressure the federal government to enable Native Americans to run their own affairs on their reservations, and the Puerto Rican Independence Movement, aimed at gaining independence or statehood for that American protectorate.

These developments have been accompanied by what Robert Perrucci and Marc Pilisuk call "the revolution in expression" (1971: 561), which extends from moderate to radical groups. An example is clear from the words of Eldridge Cleaver who, as a Black Panther party advocate, stated (1968: 137):

Table 8-5 Percent of Black Population in the Ten Largest Cities, 1970

	Percent of total population	Blacks as a percent of total voting-age population[a]
New York	21	18
Chicago	33	28
Los Angeles	18	16
Philadelphia	34	30
Detroit	44	39
Baltimore	46	41
Houston	26	23
Cleveland	38	35
Washington, D.C.	71	64
St. Louis	41	35

[a] Voting-age population refers to persons eighteen years old and over.

SOURCE: "The Social and Economic Status of the Black Population in the United States," *Current Population Reports*, U.S. Department of Commerce Publication, 1970. Tables 98 and 105.

... blacks are looking on and asking tactical questions. They are asked to die for the System in Vietnam. In Watts they are killed by it. Now — Now! — they are asking each other, in dead earnest: Why not die right here in Babylon, fighting for a better life like the Viet Cong? If these little cats can do it, what is wrong with big studs like us?

Malcolm X, who broke from the Black Muslims, and Stokely Carmichael and Rap Brown of SNCC, among other radical leaders, used similarly violent language. One of the effects of such aggressive expression, coupled with mass expressions of black discontent, was to move nonviolent black leaders to confront whites with the need to accept change. As Roy Wilkins, a spokesman of the NAACP, which has the largest black membership of any civil rights organization, put it (1963: 44):

Stokely Carmichael, an advocate of aggressive rhetoric in the pursuit of equal rights and equal treatment for blacks. SOURCE: United Press International.

In his drive, the Negro citizen will use every available weapon short of violence. No sector of race relations, North or South, will escape the pressures. As with any other population of its size there will be differences on methods, on priorities, and on the degree of concentration. There will be no differences on objectives, except for that minute minority which rejects integration into American life.

Since Mr. Wilkins made this statement in the early 1960s, one of the continuing signs of changing self-expression is the insistence of minorities on creating their own name designations. The United States Census now includes the designation *black* as well as *Negro*. A corollary of this development is the increasing use of the term *Chicano* for Mexican-Americans, and *Ms.* instead of *Miss* or *Mrs.* in addressing women. What it all appears to represent is a step toward individual and group self-determination.

Signs of generally more accepting attitudes toward minority groups. What about the subjective indicators among the more dominant members of the society? While there has been *white backlash* and violent efforts to prevent integration of schools and housing, there also are clear signs that people are accepting minority group members more than in the past. Recall the results reported in Chapter 2 (Table 2-1) on the Bogardus Social Distance scale. All minorities have advanced significantly toward equal acceptance since the 1920s. In 1926, Americans surveyed listed five groups, including blacks, whom they would not welcome as neighbors. By 1966, most people no longer expressed such a feeling about any group.

Young college graduates, who will occupy influential economic and social positions, have expressed similar feelings. Samples taken among college students in 1933, 1951, and 1967 showed a sharp drop in negative and hostile perceptions of minorities (Karlins, Coffman and Walters, 1969: 4-5). Negative traits associated with Negroes — superstitious (1933: 84 percent, 1951: 41 percent, and 1967: 13 percent), lazy (1933: 75 percent, 1951: 31 percent, and 1967: 26 percent) and stupid (1933: 22 percent, 1951: 10 percent, and 1967: 4 percent) — all declined sharply. The same trend was evident in the opinions about ethnic and religious minorities. Italians were viewed as revengeful by 17 percent in 1933 but by less than one percent in 1966; and Jews were viewed as being sly by 20 percent in 1933 but only 7 percent in 1967.

Affirmative action programs are designed to admit minority group members to good schools and good jobs. Consequently, some white males charge that the practice amounts to reverse discrimination. In the *De Funis* case of 1975, the Supreme Court left unresolved the issue of the constitutionality of admitting to law school minority group members whose entrance examination scores were lower than those of some white males who were not accepted. (See also the *Bakke* case of 1978.) Some analysts argue that affirmative action means affirmative discrimination (see Glazer, 1975). If people continue to abandon their prejudices, they ought to be able to settle such conflicts in an orderly fashion.

The general shift toward the acceptance of minority groups may be a major accommodating factor in ensuring equality of opportunity in our society. It is no longer acceptable to express racist attitudes. People who do hold prejudices are becoming less willing to expose them by overt rejection of minorities. As a result, intergroup communication is increasing, moving us, if haltingly, toward a future of true equality.

SUMMARY

In American society, the concept of *conflict**, including the resolution of conflict, helps us interpret the relations between minority and dominant groups. A number of other sociological concepts also shed light on minority group relations.

The civil rights movement from the mid-1950s to the mid-1960s and the civil disorders in the mid-1960s and early 1970s changed intergroup ethnic relations in the society.

*Minority** group status is conferred by dominant groups to minimize social participation by disadvantaged groups. We focused primarily on urban black–white relations. The *Report of the National Advisory Commission on Civil Disorders* and critiques of the report are useful in understanding the extent of the racial crisis in American society.

Minorities in the egalitarian American value structure have challenged the status quo in order to achieve equality of treatment. In the colonial period, such challenges emanated mostly from religious minorities, in the nineteenth century from national minorities, and in the twentieth century from racial minorities and women.

Gunnar Myrdal's classic thesis concerning the *American dilemma* states that there is a conflict between the American ideal of equality and the practice of inequality. Robert Merton's *prejudice**/*discrimination** paradigm illustrates the difference between these two interrelated concepts (attitudes on the one hand, behavior on the other) and provides an analytical vehicle for understanding why there is a dilemma for some Americans and not for others.

The Supreme Court's 1954 *Brown* decision challenged legal, or *de jure,* racial *segregation** in public schools and in other areas of social life. We outlined various dimensions of informal, or *de facto,* segregation and a number of consequences that flow from segregation, particularly segregation by community.

The civil rights movement, extending from the *Brown* decision to the march on Washington in 1963, led to the emergence of black activist organizations such as SCLC, SNCC, and CORE. Black *social movements** inspired social action among other minorities, including Spanish–Americans, Native Americans, and women.

There are four general indicators of intergroup *accommodation**. Two are objective: the limited signs of upward socioeconomic mobility of minorities and the increasing political influence of minorities in national political life (for example, the civil rights legislation of the 1960's). Two are subjective: the revolution in minority self-images and self-expressions and the reduction in social distance indices and other signs that dominant groups are adopting more accepting attitudes toward minorities, a trend which could ultimately reduce or end minority status.

QUESTIONS FOR DISCUSSION

1. Discuss the idea that there would be no minority problem in America today if everyone were prejudiced but no one discriminated.

2. According to some black social psychologists, there exists a campaign to make black males seem to be less than men, especially through television. Discuss this idea in relation to characterizations of black males on television shows. Along similar lines, how are Hispanics and Native Americans portrayed?

3. English is full of black/white imagery and of generic uses of *he* rather than *she*. What effects do you think these usages have had on black, female, and white male self-images?

4. Explain some of the ways in which a person may develop a prejudice. In what forms may prejudice be manifested?

5. According to Lewis Coser, when a group is long denied legitimate outlets for expressing dissent, subsequent intergroup conflict tends to be more intense and dysfunctional than it might originally have been. Discuss the implications of this point with respect to current minority relations.

6. Are there minority social movements going on today? If so, who are the leaders and toward what goals are they striving?

7. Discuss the idea that prejudicial attitudes and discriminatory actions depend on the attitudes and actions of the groups of which one is a member.

8. Support or dispute the point that American society has been a melting pot for various ethnic groups.

9. Review your understanding of the following terms and concepts:

minority groups

ethnic groups

prejudice

discrimination

conflict

the American dilemma

de jure and de facto segregation

social movements

accommodation

REFERENCES

Abrams, Charles
1965   "The housing problem and the Negro." Daedalus (Winter): 64–76.

Albrecht, Stan with Melvin DeFleur and Lyle Warner
1972   "Attitude–behavior relationships: a reexamination of the postulate of contingent consistency." Pacific Sociological Review 15: 149–168.

Allport, Gordon
1958   The Nature of Prejudice. New York: Anchor.

1963   Articles on the march on Washington. The New York Times (August 27, 28, and 29).

Bell, Inge Powell
1968   CORE and the Strategy of Non-Violence. New York: Random House.

Bernard, William
1950   American Immigration Policy: A Reappraisal. New York: Harper & Brothers.

Berry, Brewton
1965   Race and Ethnic Relations. Boston: Houghton Mifflin.

Berry, Mary
    1971   Black Resistance/White Law. New York: Appleton-Century-Crofts.

Blauner, Robert
    1969   "Internal colonialism and ghetto revolt." Social Problems (Spring): 393–408.

Blumer, Herbert
    1951   "Social movements." A.M. Lee (ed.), Principles of Sociology. New York: Barnes & Noble: 168–169.
    1967   "The future of the color line." J. McKinney and E. Thompson (eds.), The South in Continuity and Change. Durham, N.C.: Duke University Press: 329–331.

Bogardus, Emory
    1968   "Comparing racial distance in Ethiopia, South Africa, and the United States." Sociology and Social Research 52: 149–156.

Carman, Harry and Harold Syrett
    1954   A History of the American People, vol. I. New York: Knopf.
    1955   A History of the American People, vol. II. New York: Knopf.

Carmichael, Stokely and Charles Hamilton
    1967   Black Power. New York: Random House.

Chaiklin, Harris and Verl Lewis
    1964   A Census Tract Analysis of Crime in Baltimore City. Baltimore: University of Maryland School of Social Work.

Channing, Edward
    1908   History of the United States: A Century of Colonial History, 1660–1760, vol. II. New York: Macmillan.

Cleaver, Eldridge
    1968   Soul on Ice. New York: McGraw-Hill.

Coleman, James et al.
    1966   Equality of Educational Opportunity. Washington, D.C.: Government Printing Office.

Coser, Lewis
    1968   "Conflict: social aspects." International Encyclopedia of the Social Sciences, vol. 3. New York: Macmillan: 232–234.

DeWard, Robert
    1919   "Americanization and immigration." American Review of Reviews LIX: 513–516.

Ellison, Ralph
    1973   "An American dilemma: a review." J. Ladner (ed.), The Death of White Sociology. New York: Vantage Books: 81–95.

Farley, Reynolds
    1975   "White flight to suburbs not caused by busing." Information: Quarterly Journal of the National Institute of Education (Fall): 1.

Fellows, Donald
    1972   A Mosaic of America's Ethnic Minorities. New York: John Wiley and Sons.

Fidell, Linda and Patricia Keith-Spiegel
    1973   "The woman." D. Spiegel and P. Keith-Spiegel (eds.), The Outsiders: U.S.A. San Francisco: Rinehart: 435–469.

Fogelson, Robert
    1971   Violence as Protest: A Study of Riots and Ghettos. New York: Anchor.

Frazier, E. Franklin
    1962   Black Bourgeoisie: The Rise of a New Middle Class in the United States. New York: Collier.

Friedman, Lawrence
    1970   The White Savage: Racial Fantasies in the Post-bellum South. Englewood, N.J.: Prentice-Hall.

Froman, Robert
    1972   Racism. New York: Delacorte.

Glazer, Nathan
    1975   Affirmative Discrimination. Cambridge: Harvard University Press.

Gordon, Leonard
    1973   "The fragmentization of literary stereotypes of Jews and of Negroes among college students." Pacific Sociological Review 16: 411-425.

Gordon, Milton
    1964   Assimilation in American Life. New York: Oxford University Press.

Graham, Fred
    1966   "Miscegenation nears test in high court." The New York Times (March 13): 12E.

Higham, John
    1975   Send These to Me: Jews and Other Immigrants in Urban America. New York: Atheneum.

Howard, John
    1972   Awakening Minorities: American Indians, Mexican Americans, Puerto Ricans. New Brunswick, N.J.: Transaction Books.

Hughes, Helen McGill
    1973   The Status of Women in Sociology: 1968-1972. Washington, D.C.: The American Sociological Association.

Ivy, James
    1964   "Highlights in school desegregation." The Crisis (May). New York: Official Organ of the National Association for the Advancement of Colored People: 285-289.

Kahn, Robert et al.
    1968   Discrimination Without Prejudice. Ann Arbor: University of Michigan Press.

Karlins, Marvin, Thomas Coffman, and Gary Walters
    1969   "On the fading of social stereotypes: three generations of college students." Journal of Personality and Social Psychology 13: 1-6.

Kephart, William
    1972   The Family, Society, and the Individual. Boston: Houghton Mifflin.

King, Jr., Martin Luther
    1968   The Quotations of Martin Luther King, Jr. L. Hoskins (ed.). New York: Grosset & Dunlap.
    1970   "The Montgomery bus boycott." W. Chace and P. Cooier (eds.), Justice Denied. New York: Harcourt, Brace: 319-325.
    1971   "I have a dream." A. Meier, E. Rudwich, and F. Broderick (eds.), Black Protest Thought in the Twentieth Century. New York: Bobbs-Merrill: 346-351.

Laurenti, Luigi
    1960   Property Values and Race. Berkeley, Cal.: University of California Press.

Leopold, Richard and Arthur Link
    1952   Problems in American History. Englewood Cliffs, N.J.: Prentice-Hall.

Lewin, Kurt
    1948   Resolving Social Conflicts. New York: Harper and Brothers.

Link, Arthur
    1955   American Epoch: A History of the United States Since the 1890s. New York: Knopf.

Logan, Rayford
    1925   The Negro in American Life and Thought: The Nadir, 1877-1901. New York: Dial.

Malcolm X
    1971   "Message to the grassroots." L. Gordon (ed.), A City in Racial Crisis. Dubuque: Wm. C. Brown: 33-44.

McKee, Alice
    1975   "Raising the status of women." AAUW Journal, vol. 69, no. 3: 25.

Merton, Robert
    1949   "Discrimination and the American creed." R. MacIver (ed.), Discrimination and National Welfare. New York: Harper & Row: 100–110.

Myrdal, Gunnar
    1944   An American Dilemma: The Negro Problem and Modern Democracy. New York: Harper & Row.

Perrucci, Robert and Marc Pilisuk
    1971   The Triple Revolution. Boston: Little, Brown.

Pinckney, Alphonso
    1973   "The black American." D. Spiegel and P. Keith-Spiegel (eds.), Outsiders, U.S.A. New York: Rinehart: 347–370.

Safilios-Rothschild, Constantina
    1974   Women and Social Policy. Englewood Cliffs, N.J.: Prentice-Hall.

Schlesinger, Jr., Arthur
    1967   A Thousand Days: John F. Kennedy in the White House. New York: Fawcett Crest.

    1969   Social and Economic Status of Negroes in the United States. Washington, D.C.: U.S. Department of Commerce.

Sowell, Thomas
    1975   Race and Economics. New York: David McKay.

Spiegel, Don and Patricia Keith-Spiegel
    1973   Outsiders: U.S.A. San Francisco: Rinehart.

Stanton, Esther
    1975   "Newer voices are being heard." AAUW Journal, vol. 69, no. 3: 22.

Suter, Larry and Herman Miller
    1973   "Income differences between men and career women." American Journal of Sociology 78: 962–974.

Taeuber, Karl
    1964   "Negro residential segregation: trends and measurements." Social Problems 12: 42–51.

Tautfest, Claudia
    1974   Black Economic Progress in America: A Reappraisal. Unpublished M.A. Thesis, Department of Sociology, Arizona State University.

Thomas, William I.
    1931   "The relation of research to the social process." Essays on Research in the Social Sciences. Washington, D.C.: The Brookings Institution.

Thrasher, Frederic
    1927   The Gang. Chicago: University of Chicago Press.

Turner, Ralph and James Killian
    1972   Collective Behavior. Englewood Cliffs, N.J.: Prentice-Hall.

Vander Zanden, James
    1972   American Minority Relations. New York: Ronald Press.

Wagley, Charles and Marvin Harris
    1958   Minorities in the New World. New York: Columbia University Press.

Warner, W. Lloyd and J. O. Low
    1941   The Social System of the Modern Factory. New York: Yale University Press.

Waskow, Arthur
    1967   From Race Riot to Sit-In. New York: Anchor.

Wattenberg, Ben and Richard Scammon
   1973   "Black progress and liberal rhetoric." Commentary 51 (April): 34–44.

Westie, Frank
   1965   "The American dilemma: an empirical test." American Sociological Review 30: 527–538.

Wilkins, Roy
   1963   "Emancipation and militant leadership." R. Goldwin (ed.), 100 Years of Emancipation. Chicago: Rand McNally: 25–46.

Wirth, Louis
   1945   "The problem of minority groups." R. Linton (ed.), The Science of Man in the World Crisis. New York: Columbia University Press: 347–372.

Yetman, Norman and C. Roy Steele
   1975   Majority and Minority. Boston: Allyn and Bacon.

Chapter 9

COMMUNITY ORGANIZATION AND DISASTER

You keep goin' your way, I'll keep goin' my way, River, stay 'way from my door.[1]

---

[1] From: Mort Dixon and Harry Woods, 1929. Copyright © MCMXXXI by Shapiro, Bernstein & Co., Inc. New York. Copyright renewed MCMLVIII and assigned to Shapiro, Bernstein & Co., Inc. New York, New York 10022. All rights reserved. Also copyright © 1929. Reproduced by permission of B. Feldman & Co. Ltd., 138-140 Charing Cross Road, London WC2H OLD. England.

DISASTER AND SOCIETY

These lines from the old song are about the Mississippi River, the "father of waters." With many tributaries, the Missouri, the Ohio, and the Tennessee, the Mississippi reaches into over half of the forty-eight continental states and into parts of Canada. The floods of the Mississippi are a continuing fact of life for many people; the spring floods of 1973 were the most damaging in the recorded history of the United States (Kentfield, 1973: 14).

Floods are only one of many types of disasters that swiftly create emergencies for large numbers of people. Considering the range of natural and man-made disasters, including earthquakes, tornadoes, hurricanes, riots, and explosions, there are few people who never experience, or have close relatives and friends who experience, the damaging effects of a disaster.

Disasters highlight the nature of *community organization** in an initially disruptive and disorganizing context. Communities tend to be surprisingly resilient in times of emergency. *Collective behavior** specialists Ralph Turner and James Killian (1972) have shown that communities respond to disasters with the same solidarity and *division of labor** seen in normative times. By considering disasters, we learn a good deal about the general nature of community organization.

Disasters strike frequently enough to be a popular theme in fiction. One of the most realistic of such books was Morgan Robertson's *Futility,* pub-

"...TALK ABOUT WATER POLLUTION!"

SOURCE: Copyright © 1972 the *Chicago Sun-Times.* Reproduced by courtesy of Wil-Jo Associates, Inc. and Bill Mauldin.

lished in 1898, the tale of a huge and presumably unsinkable luxury liner much like the *Titanic*. In the foreword to his book on the sinking of the *Titanic*, Walter Lord describes the parallels between Robertson's fictional account and the real disaster that occurred in 1912 (Lord, 1955: 9):

In 1898 a struggling author named Morgan Robertson concocted a novel *(Futility)* about a fabulous Atlantic liner, far larger than any that had ever been built. Robertson loaded his ship with rich and complacent people and then wrecked it one cold April night on an iceberg....

Fourteen years later a British shipping company named the White Star built a steamer remarkably like the one in Robertson's novel. The new liner was 66,000 tons displacement; Robertson's was 70,000 tons. The real ship was 882.5 feet long; the fictional one was 800 feet. Both vessels were triple screw and could make 24–25 knots. Both could carry about 3000 people and both had enough lifeboats for only a fraction of this number. But, then, this didn't seem to matter because both were labeled "unsinkable."

On April 10, 1912, the real ship left Southampton on her maiden voyage to New York. Her cargo included a ... list of passengers collectively worth $250 million dollars. On her way over she too struck an iceberg and went down on a cold April night.

Robertson called his ship the *Titan;* the White Star Line called its ship the *Titanic.*

Learning how people respond to disasters tells us a good deal about community processes in times of stress. Though initially disorganizing, disasters do not generally result in *community disorganization**. The prior network of social relationships, including various types of *voluntary associations**, comes into play.

DIMENSIONS OF DISASTER

What constitutes a disaster? To baseball fans, the loss of a World Series can be a disaster. More objectively, many consider the several hundred traffic deaths that occur daily a national disaster. However, neither of these is a *community disaster*, like a flood, an earthquake, or a tornado, that strikes swiftly and in a short time disrupts a community of people or a limited area within a community. Fritz defines a *disaster* as (1961: 655)

... an event, concentrated in time and space, in which a society or a relatively self-sufficient subdivision of a society undergoes severe danger and incurs such losses to its members and physical appurtenances that the social structure is disrupted and the fulfillment of all or some of the essential functions of the society is prevented.

Such disastrous events may affect the lives of hundreds of thousands at a time. For survivors, of course, the loss of homes or places of employment constitutes a disastrous situation no matter how many other people have suffered similar losses.

NATURAL AND MANMADE DISASTERS Data for a number of disasters are presented in Table 9-1. Most resulted from *natural causes* — earthquakes, floods, or tornadoes. Others were *manmade* — explosions and civil disorders. All these events are concentrated in time and space and affect a relatively self-sufficient subdivision of society, a community.

Disasters cause collective stress, since many members of a social system fail to receive expected conditions of life from the system (Barton, 1970: 38). People become aware of the components of a social system and of the importance of orderly social life. As Brown and Goldin have remarked, "Disaster brings to public notice everyday life as a vulnerable condition and as a total social endeavor that must be actively sustained and protected" (1973: 44). Responsibilities are shifted to those able to take on the roles. The physical facilities of institutions may be altered to accommodate needs other than those for which they were intended. The breakdown in normal operations of the *institutions** of a community, from the family to the government, is temporary but severe. Disaster relief efforts are aimed at restoring the system rather than changing it. This summary of damage resulting from five disasters — three from natural causes and two from human causes — makes it clear why disasters are so disruptive:

HIROSHIMA, JAPAN, AUGUST 6, 1945 Toward the end of World War II, a United States Army Air Force B-29 airplane dropped an atomic bomb on the city. Of the population of 250,000, approximately 30 percent, or 75,000 people, died; another 30 percent were seriously injured; and the rest, about 100,000, were uninjured. Property damage ranged into the hundreds of millions of dollars

Table 9-1 A Sampling of Specific Disasters with Fatalities and Approximate General Frequency of Each Type

Type	Date	Location	Deaths	General frequency
Hurricane	September 11, 1961	Louisiana and Texas	40	several annually
Earthquake	March 27, 1964	Alaska	114	irregular intervals
Flood	June 11, 1965	Sanderson, Texas	26	several annually
Explosion	November 24, 1966	Keokuk, Iowa	21	irregular but increasing with modern technology
Tornado	April 21, 1967	Illinois	55	several major ones annually
Civil disorder[a]	July 23-27, 1967	Detroit, Michigan	43	infrequent but clustered when occur

[a] The figures on the July 1967 civil disorders in Detroit are from *Report of the National Advisory Commission on Civil Disorders* (New York: Bantam Books, 1968), p. 358.

SOURCE: Adapted from: Garb, Solomon and Evelyn Eng, *Disaster Handbook* (New York: Springer Publishing Co., 1969), pp. 145, 162-163, 174-175, 195, 207-208.

(Barton, 1970: 21-23; Heer, 1965: 311-312; Hershey, 1959).

WORCESTER, MASSACHUSETTS, JUNE 9, 1953 A tornado struck the northeast residential section of Worcester at 5:08 P.M. By 5:16 P.M., ninety-four persons lay dead and 327 were seriously injured. Physical damage to the area was estimated at $32 million (Dynes, 1970: 1-3).

CAMERON PARISH, LOUISIANA, JUNE 25, 1957 Hurricane Audrey inundated much of Cameron Parish on the gulf coast with powerful wind-driven waves. Over 400 lives were lost, half of the buildings and most community facilities were destroyed (Bates, 1963: 292; CBS News Almanac, 1976: 910).

CRESCENT CITY, CALIFORNIA, MARCH 28, 1964 Following an earthquake in Alaska on the evening of March 27, a *tsunami*[2] struck the community of Crescent City, California, with a population of about 3,000. Eleven persons died, and twenty-nine blocks of coastal buildings were damaged (Anderson, 1969: 96).

DETROIT, MICHIGAN, JULY 23, 1967 Racial rioting broke out in the early morning hours and lasted four days. By the end of the rioting, which extended to the city limits, forty-three persons were dead, several hundred were seriously injured, 7,200 had been arrested, and there had been at least $50 million in property damage (*Report of the National Advisory Commission*, 1968: 107-108).

---

[2] A *tsunami* is a series of traveling ocean waves caused by underwater earthquakes and volcanic eruptions. Island communities like Japan, where the term was coined, and coastal communities like Crescent City, California, are vulnerable to *tsunamis*. For further details see: *Tsunami: The Story of the Seismic Sea Wave Warning System* (Washington, D.C.: U.S. Department of Commerce, 1965).

COMMUNITY RESPONSE These disasters differ quantitatively. At one extreme is Hiroshima, with 75,000 dead. At the other is Crescent City with a loss of eleven lives (although if Crescent City were the same size as Hiroshima, the proportionate loss of life would have been over 900, making that disaster more severe than those in Worcester, Cameron Parish, or Detroit).

The first devastating effects of the nuclear disaster in Hiroshima paralyzed the people and their community. As a physician noted in his diary after the attack (Hachiya, 1955: 54-55):

> ... the entire population had been reduced to a common level of physical and mental weakness. Those who were able walked silently toward the suburbs and the distant hills, their spirits broken, their initiative gone. When asked whence they had come, they pointed to the city and said, "that way"; and when asked where they were going, pointed from the city and said, "this way." They were so confused that they moved and behaved like automatons.

Given the debilitating consequences of the disaster, and the subsequent looting and black marketeering, it is remarkable that, within weeks, hospitals were reequipped and operating, daily papers were being printed, railroad service had resumed, water service was restored, and reconstruction of buildings had begun (Jungk, 1961: 91-94). Within ten years after the attack, not only had Hiroshima been rebuilt but it had grown in population by over 100,000 (Trumbell, 1957: 129).

REORGANIZING IN EXTREME CIRCUMSTANCES The story of Hiroshima is a dramatic illustration of the resilience of people and their ability to reorganize their lives — and in this instance their

COMMUNITY ORGANIZATION AND DISASTER 271

SOURCE: (a) Henri Cartier-Bresson/Magnum; (b) NOAA Photo; (c) Michael Abramson/Black Star.

entire social system — after a disaster. If the attack had been made with a more powerful hydrogen bomb, the effect might have been total annihilation. (We shall discuss this possibility in Chapter 12 on cold and limited hot wars.) As the people of Hiroshima demonstrated, people respond to disaster with redevelopment and reconstruction.

The problems faced by communities in reorganizing after disasters are not new. The destruction wrought by the 1906 San Francisco earthquake, with its great loss of life, injuries, and $.5 billion in property damage (Downey, 1938: 125), has been equaled and even surpassed in a number of communities, including Hannibal, Missouri, and Capsville, Illinois, struck by the spring floods of the Mississippi River in 1973 (Kentfield, 1973: 16–17).

FROM COMMUNITY DISORGANIZATION TO COMMUNITY ORGANIZATION   For a short period following a disaster, there appears to be more community disorganization than community organization. As James Coleman notes, community disorganization comes about in two ways. One is the absence of any collective effort. The second is the existence of conflicting efforts that cancel each other out. As a rule, community organization soon emerges, enabling people to take coordinated community action. As Coleman observes (1971: 659):

Social organization is important for one reason alone: to enable the social unit to take action as a unit. If bridges are to be built, wars won, food grown, criminals caught, then there must be [community] organization. Thus ... community disorganization ... concern[s] the community's inability to *act* as a community. If a community can act collectively toward the problems that face it, then it is well organized. If it cannot, then it is disorganized relative to these problems, though there may be a great amount of apparent organization.

Such inability to act can come about in two ways: through an absence of any collective effort, or through the existence of conflicting collective efforts that cancel each other out. That is, in some systems, there is no collective energy available for unitary action; in others, there is collective energy, but in mutual opposition, thereby setting up tension without action. The first can be likened to the wasting away of tissue in a body, the second to paralysis.

SOME POPULAR MISCONCEPTIONS ABOUT DISASTERS   There are a number of popular misconceptions about how people respond in extreme situations. Television and news photographs usually show people who have performed individual acts of heroism or victims who have experienced personal tragedies and are in shock (Dynes, 1970: 1). The reports are often accompanied by accounts of a breakdown in local authority with such consequent problems as mass panic and random looting and pillaging (Fritz, 1961: 682). Disaster research specialist Enrico Quarantelli lists six popular beliefs (1973: 58–70):

1. The idea that people will panic in the face of a great threat or danger is not borne out in reality. [People have strong tendencies to continue behavior rather than initiating new courses of action.]

2. It is also incorrect to assume that people cannot adequately organize themselves in the face of danger, and take adaptive steps to deal with a threatening situation. [People generally take whatever protective measures seem possible; people who fail to act may be prudently waiting for better information. Official personnel may have extraordinary problems at times of disaster, but they are not the problems of failure to take adjustive measures.]

3. The view that disasters leave victims dazed and disoriented is also incorrect. [Most disaster victims are not immobilized, passive, or dependent. Shock, or *disaster syndrome,* does occur but does not affect great numbers of people, is usually confined to the

most sudden, traumatic kinds of disasters, has been reported only in certain cultural settings, and is of short duration. Most victims are quite active.]

4. The assumption that local organizations are unable to cope with disasters is based both on the notion that these organizations and the communities in which they are located are so overwhelmed by disaster impact that their efficiency is reduced. [Neither idea stands up well under observation. The belief that communities are overwhelmed is usually derived from overestimating the demand on facilities and underestimating the number of resources still available. The need for food or clothing, for example, may be overestimated; available personnel may be underestimated, as people who are not able to go to their regular jobs are free to assist others. The degree to which role conflict hampers the effectiveness of people assisting others during the emergency is overstated. They're not happy about their situation, but they do not desert their work.]

5. The idea that disaster aftermath creates the conditions for the development of anti-social behavior is widespread. In particular, there is the assumption that widespread looting takes place.... In addition to reports about looting, other stories about various forms of exploitative behavior also are likely to be circulated. [While there are many stories of looting,[3] there are few verified cases of it. Isolated cases of exploiting victims, say, selling food at inflated prices, exist, but altruistic behavior is more common. Differences in status, class, age, race, and sex tend to be minimized.]

6. Contrary to the popular image, morale in disaster impacted communities is not low. Partly as a result of an orientation of altruism and the reaffirmation of equality just described, the short term result is an increase in collective morale. [Many are consoled by the thought that things could have been worse for them. Some feel they are participating in a historic event. A sense of in-group versus out-group, including outside help agencies in some cases, develops. It is typical for communities to adopt an optimistic view of their future.]

DISTORTION BY DRAMATIC MEDIA COVERAGE Disasters are highly dramatic. Consider the difference between public response to an automobile accident and to an airplane crash. On any given day, more people are killed in traffic accidents than in an airplane crash with fifty or a hundred victims. Yet, the air crash gains the attention of the masses. As Merton notes (1970: 713): "[It is] the dramatic quality of unitary events that evokes popular interest. The airplane disaster is perceived as a single event." Attention is focused on the recollections of such persons as the flight crew, ground personnel, hospital emergency units, and others whose role it is to minimize the damage caused by the crash.

Given the nature of the experiences involved in a disaster, the interest in the dramatic is understandable. Human interest stories capture the imagination. Consider this account of one of the survivors of the tornado that struck Flint, Michigan, in 1954 (Form and Nosow, 1958: 34):

I ran for the house. As I ran, I saw the tornado pick up a car on Clio Road. As I put my foot on the front door steps, it came down the driveway and took me. It didn't seem to come from the west because it carried me north. It threw me into a tree first, then slid me along the grass ... I was conscious all the time. It threw me against the basement wall of my house on my head. I just laid there, then looked up and saw the house raising on the foundation. I got up on my hands, raising up; the wind grabbed me again and took me up in the air. While I was going up, something swatted me on top of

---

[3] An exception may be in civil disorders where intergroup conflict exists (see Chapter 8)

The Guatemalan earthquake of 1976. SOURCE: (a) United Press International Photo; (b) Newsweek — Fenga and Freyer; (c) Wide World Photos.

my head, and I landed right in my basement (the house was gone by then). Incidentally, while I was laying against the basement wall the porch fell on my leg.

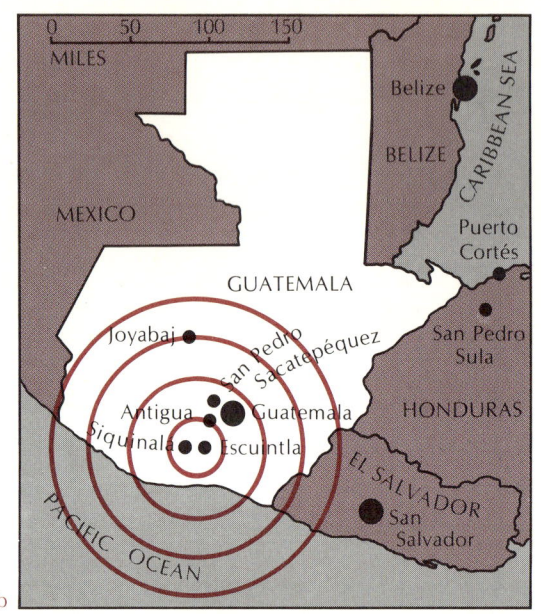

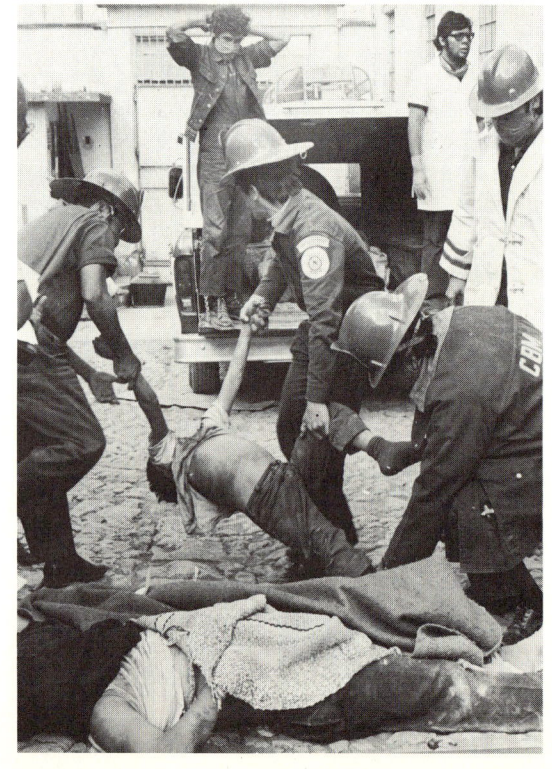

It is understandable that the general image of a disaster is of individual helplessness in the face of little effective community response. Yet in fact, people quickly begin, both individually and in an organized manner, to help those in danger, repair damage, and reconstruct their lives and their community. As this happens, the news value of the event lessens very quickly. Thus, the public impression of disasters is a distortion of what actually occurs overall. Charles Fritz comments (1961: 682):

If people throughout history had engaged exclusively in all the mass panics, stampedes, looting, pillaging, mutual exploitation, and other forms of behavior that are commonly attributed to disaster-struck societies, organized human societies would have long ago ceased to exist.

This is not to imply that a disaster does not cause severe disorientation. However, community disorganization soon gives way to community organization. The actual behavior of most people in disaster-stricken communities recalls the definition of social organization given in Chapter 3: "it is in the operation of social organization by which a society meets the functional prerequisites of providing the necessities of life for physical and social survival."

SHOCK AND RESPONSE

Disasters are so disruptive to a community and its members that the initial impact is one of severe shock. Yet as we have seen, even in the extreme case of the atomic disaster at Hiroshima, within days members of the community were organizing efforts to restabilize their lives and community (Jungk, 1961, 91–94). Such reorganizing efforts are general but do not happen all at once.

STAGES OF RESPONSE Once a disaster has struck, a community tends to go through two general stages within a matter of hours. The initial response is informal, sporadic, individualized. The second response, though not related to formal organized efforts, is more organized than the early response. This organization emerges on the spot and may take shape through the efforts of trained or experienced persons or from organizations such as church groups that develop innovative ways of assisting victims. In what could be considered a third stage, formal government and private relief agency efforts emerge to assist victims and to reestablish essential community functions such as medical care and transportation. We shall consider this third phase in depth later in this chapter.

THE INFORMAL SPORADIC PERIOD Even when a community has effective warning systems, disasters strike giving notice of only hours or even minutes. People are often taken by surprise in the midst of their normal daily activities. Recall the account of the eruption of the volcano Mount Vesuvius in Italy in 79 A.D. The eruption buried the city of Pompeii so rapidly that many Pompeiians were caught and preserved under volcanic ash in their homes, at work, shopping, and in other everyday activities.

The case of Pompeii is particularly dramatic, but it points up the swiftness with which most severe disasters strike. There is little coordinated activity in the first minutes or even hours. In this period of aftershock, no particular response separates uninjured persons trained to combat disaster from those who are untrained and inexperienced (Barton, 1970: 74). If panic and chaos occur, they are most likely to happen in this period (Barton, 1970: 132–138). This is also the stage that attracts the attention of the mass media.

A resident of Minot, North Dakota, reported that the townspeople waiting for the flood crest in April 1976 (the dikes fortunately held), were amused or dismayed by television reports of events that the participants in the flood control effort knew nothing about. This cynical resident suggested that the journalists were manufacturing excitement.

Immediately after disaster strikes, individuals and small groups extricate themselves and others around them from the most severe effects of the damage. Total panic or chaos is extremely rare. Next, most people look after their family and friends before going on to join any formal organization they belong to, such as a government unit or a private business.

ROLE CONFLICTS IN THE EARLY RESPONSE STAGE In this initial stage, people often experience severe *role conflict**. A disaster is so disruptive at impact that one's family, friends, colleagues, and others are all affected simultaneously. People at work become anxious about their families. People at home may also feel the need to assist friends or help out at work. As one patrolman reported (Killian, 1952: 312):

> ... I realized the best thing I could do was to try to make contact with the outside and get help from there.... As I drove out of town people I knew well would call me by name and ask me to help them find their relatives. Driving by and not stopping to help these people who were looking to me as a friend was one of the hardest things I ever had to do.

In this case, the patrolman performed his occupational role from the start and immediately began recruiting and organizing a force of rescue workers from a nearby community. In the immediate wake of disaster, though, even those with such clearly designated roles as police officer may respond in other ways when faced with role conflicts. For example, in the Flint-Beecher, Michigan, tornado of 1954 (Form and Nosow, 1958: 168):

> Only one-quarter of the firemen ... went to the station *before* they did anything in the field. Most of them did something else because they defined [the] disaster as one which they, as firemen, could not deal with in a traditional and expected way ... the firemen were most concerned about getting their friends and neighbors out from under the debris. ...

This type of behavior, whether directed toward one's family, friends, or neighbors, while often eliciting heroic efforts, did not facilitate the functioning of a coordinated and integrated rescue system.

THE EMERGENT ADAPTIVE STAGE It is in this period of shock to a community's normal operations that the next stage of adaptive organized response begins — even before government agencies and other support organizations start to operate.

In most crisis situations, individuals seek to understand and interpret events by turning to friends and acquaintances for reassurance. The role that these previous relationships play should be understood, for these relationships often provide the basis for much of the coordinated response to a crisis (Forrest, 1971: 88).

This general observation, by a staff member of the Ohio State University Disaster Research Center, points out the underlying process of coordinated response to a disaster. As local government assembles its fire, police, and other personnel, relief organizations begin to move into the disaster area, businesses that are able to operate begin to offer services, and other intermediate adaptive efforts spring up.

An example of this adaptive response occurred during the July 23-27, 1967, race riot in Detroit. A *participant observation** field report describes the coordinated efforts made during the crisis (Gordon, 1967: 3-4):

> In ... the first few days of the crisis the government took no steps to provide food, medicine, housing accommodations, and the like for victims of the riot in the ghetto areas ... where whole blocks of businesses

and dozens of residences... were demolished. The organized religious community reacted to this situation quickly. On Monday, July 24, a meeting was set up at a Catholic center in downtown Detroit. About 15 people participated in this meeting.... there were representatives from the Archdiocese, Council of Churches... Jewish Community Council... and the interfaith Ministerial Alliance of [black] Ministers. We met for over two hours and organized the Interfaith Emergency Center. The center was established at the Episcopal Diocese located near Wayne State University, and close to the ghetto areas. For several days it operated on a 24-hour a day basis. This Center was the central organizing structure for the massive effort to coordinate food, medical, and clothing supplies for people burned out in the ghetto areas... a couple of dozen churches in the ghetto including the Episcopal Diocese served literally as refuge stations for a few days and filled in the gap of lack of services until government began to move in this direction toward the end of the week of rioting.

NORMS, GOALS, ROLES AND FACILITIES What happened in Detroit happens in other places: *the creation of norms* in an unusual situation. The emergency center *established goals* (to fill the immediate needs of riot victims), *developed roles* (assigned personnel to an emergency center to coordinate supply and delivery systems), and had the *facilities* from which to operate (churches and synagogues were converted into relief and distribution centers). By the second day of the rioting, a clear organization had emerged. Internal sources of aid were generated until external sources could be activated.

Taylor et al. in a study of the Topeka, Kansas, tornado of June 8, 1966, document the same steps toward recovery in a natural disaster. The authors refer to the development of temporary ("ephemeral") roles, groups, and uses of institutions in new ways. A series of volunteer centers was set up in three churches, bypassing the more formal approaches of traditional relief agencies such as the Red Cross. Specific goals were set: finding victims and beginning to help them; providing a full range of services at each center — legal aid, clothing, food, housing information; and establishing a corps of volunteers to clean up the city (Taylor et al., 1970: 11–116).

Such innovative responses enable people with special skills to apply them until established agencies reassemble themselves. One professional social worker described her experiences as a volunteer in the Interfaith Emergency Center, where she worked until her agency began functioning several days after the disorders (Kalichman, 1968: 1):

Noise, activity and commotion pervaded the [Episcopal] Diocese office adjoining the Cathedral. Beautifully appointed offices had been taken over; the Bishop's office had become the command post. There was a wide variety of people.... Many looked as if they hadn't slept all night and I think this was true. Slowly I began to recognize some faces. There were some workers from Central District Family Service. I saw Len Gordon and he explained roughly what was happening and took me to a meeting of the Interfaith Emergency Council.... The Needs Section was manned by the social workers and handled calls for help. The Center worked on a twenty-four hour basis for several days.

The highly structured, innovative response to the Detroit disaster took place in part because the people knew each other and had worked together before the crisis (Forrest, 1971: 88). In a similar riot in the Watts section of Los Angeles, where there was no such prior activity, no highly structured process emerged (Conot, 1965). In general, though, in all types of disasters, some form of adaptive organized activity emerges and operates until established group structures begin operating effectively (Barton, 1970: 132).

SUPPORTIVE AND NON-SUPPORTIVE COMMUNITY BEHAVIOR This general adaptive behavior still leaves unanswered the question advanced by sociologist Robert Merton: "Why do some situations of large-scale human suffering generate a high rate of supportive behavior toward victims while others do not?" (1970: xxxvi). All social reality involves a number of variables, from the age distribution in the community to the degree of preparedness to the location of the community. Another key factor is the *specificity* or *randomness* of a given disaster. There was more structured activity in Detroit than under similar circumstances in Los Angeles. It is significant that the Los Angeles riot was confined to the Watts section of the city (Conot, 1965), whereas the Detroit disorders ranged over most of the city (Gordon, 1971; *Report of the National Advisory Commission,* 1968).

When disaster strikes a restricted area, people outside the area who are not directly affected continue to operate within the normal behavior patterns of their *reference group*. A disaster confined to a small area may fail to be met with widespread responses because of the similarity of the problem to other isolated types of tragedy that do not trigger mass efforts for relief; and because of the lack of impact on class and other distinctions existing in a community. Limited disasters are usually not frequent enough or widespread enough to threaten the functioning of a community. Narrowly localized disasters can be ignored and normal equilibrium maintained (Fritz, 1961: 658).

The relationship between underlying social class distinctions in a community and concern about disaster was shown in the Rapid City, South Dakota, flood of 1972, in which a great deal of slum housing was swept away. That the destroyed area meant loss of living quarters for some Rapid City residents (many transients) was not a matter of much concern among people of higher status.

DISASTER AND DISCRIMINATION Some years ago Lang and Lang (1964) suggested the concept of dimensions of disaster, which included the idea of distribution of its effect. An *undiscriminating disaster* is one that fits the concept of randomness of impact. A *discriminating disaster* is specific or localized. The discrimination concept may also include social discrimination. Discriminated-against minorities — the black, the poor, and others — are more likely to live in areas of poor quality housing, which is vulnerable to earthquake, flood, fire, or riot damage. (In fact, the slum is more likely to be the location of riot.) The more affluent live in better quality housing, made of brick or stone. In some cases, the location may act as protection; the wealthy can afford homes on higher ground, less vulnerable to flood. Wealthy San Franciscans can afford more architectural features to minimize earthquake damage.

There is evidence that poorer housing once destroyed is less likely to be replaced. The poor frequently have no insurance, no capital for rebuilding, and few skills or incentive for doing their own rebuilding. Promises of assistance are not always made good. The ghetto of Washington, D.C., which suffered damage in the 1967 rioting and burning, still has large areas of damaged structures scheduled for rebuilding.

Even in the short period of adjustment following a disaster, class differences show. As Moore et al. noted, regarding the aftermath of Hurricane Carla, which hit the Gulf Coast area of Texas September 11, 1961 (1963: 124):

The higher the income, the greater the likelihood that the family would remain in the home. This probably is related to possession of sturdier houses by higher income families. The low-income group was more likely to remain in the home community, as was the high-income group, than were the middle-income families. The empirical action is similar between low- and high-income groups; the probable explanations are entirely different. In general, the poor went to public shelters. Middle-income families went to private homes, or motels. The high-income families remained in their own homes, or went to homes of friends or relatives, or to hotels or motels. The rich had access to all types of facilities; the middle- and lower-income families had fewer choices open to them.

REFERENCE GROUP INFLUENCE ON RESPONSES The specific locale of disasters may encourage *particularized reference group behavior.* Consider the reactions of different groups of Americans when disasters strike particular locales overseas. Some American Irish Catholics strongly identify with the Catholic minority in Northern Ireland, just as some American Protestants of English ancestry identify with the Protestant cause there. American Jews rally to the defense of Israeli Jews, and Americans of Arabic background support the Palestinian Arab cause. This reference-group identification was strikingly illustrated during the 1973 West African drought that ravished several black African societies. As the New York *Times* reported, "A number of local black organizations have begun a drive to aid Africans facing starvation in the West African drought" (Johnson, 1973: 20).

Narrow group identification breaks down when a disaster has widespread and random impact. In this case, there is community-wide sympathy and identification with the victims, and an organized response for relief and reconstruction (Barton, 1970: 245). Such disasters as the Flint–Beecher tornado of 1954, the Detroit disorders of 1967, and the Mississippi flooding of 1973, which struck large areas and caused extensive injuries and property damage, unified the community. As Fritz notes about widespread disasters that affect every segment of a community (1961: 685):

Culturally derived discriminations and social distinctions tend to be eliminated because all groups and statuses in the community are indiscriminately affected: danger, loss, and suffering become public rather than private phenomena.

One might expect that the greater damage a disaster causes to persons and property, the greater would be the victims' feelings of deprivation. Actually, the opposite tends to be true. When only a few people are injured and property damage is localized, people in the disaster area feel isolated and have a greater sense of *relative deprivation** (see Chapter 6).

When injuries are widespread and property losses extensive over wide areas, there is often a feeling of sharing and less sense of subjective deprivation. For example, in the Judsonia, Arkansas, tornado of 1952, 65 percent of the residents suffered serious injuries or property loss (Barton, 1970: 252). In the nearby community of Doniphan, 33 percent experienced losses. Yet about half (51 percent) the residents of Judsonia felt less deprived than others. In contrast, only 29 percent of the people of Doniphan felt less deprived than others, even though they actually had suffered less deprivation (Barton, 1970: 252). Such feelings relate to the ability and willingness of people to start helping themselves and others and help to explain why some disasters immediately generate a lot of support for victims while others do not.

SPONTANEOUS DIVISIONS OF LABOR Do disaster victims play roles according to a division of labor by age, sex, or race? A review of the literature on the subject over several decades, compiled by Allen Barton (1970), indicates that children play little part except as victims to be removed to safe quarters. Among adults, the one notable division of labor is that women with children generally concentrate on caring for their family, while men more often work in the general community, although there is considerable overlap in their activities (Barton, "Individual Behavior in the Emergency

Social System" 1970: 62–121). There are nonetheless many women volunteers in aid programs.

Unlike young children, adolescents are often involved in early relief efforts. Unlike adults, they generally do not lead others or act on their own, perhaps because they have not yet acquired clearly defined roles or experience as leaders (see Chapter 5).

During the 1973 Mississippi River flooding, a number of adolescents spontaneously joined adults in sandbagging a medical center in Hardin, Illinois. One sixteen-year-old girl said (Kentfield, 1973: 17):

Actually I'm on a date. That's my boyfriend over there. We're having a ball. I mean, how many times does a guy ask you to a flood?

In the Detroit riot of 1967, several small groups of black teenagers worked with the Interfaith Emergency Center. The Center's executive board leadership asked black teenagers in the hardest-hit rioting areas to communicate with other black adolescents who were rioting. Supplied with walkie-talkies and special armbands, they did play a role in controlling the riot, though they did not initiate the activity, and they operated under the direction of adults.

The general picture of adolescent behavior in a number of case studies is similar to the finding in the Flint–Beecher tornado disaster of 1954, where it was observed (Form and Nosow, 1958: 46):

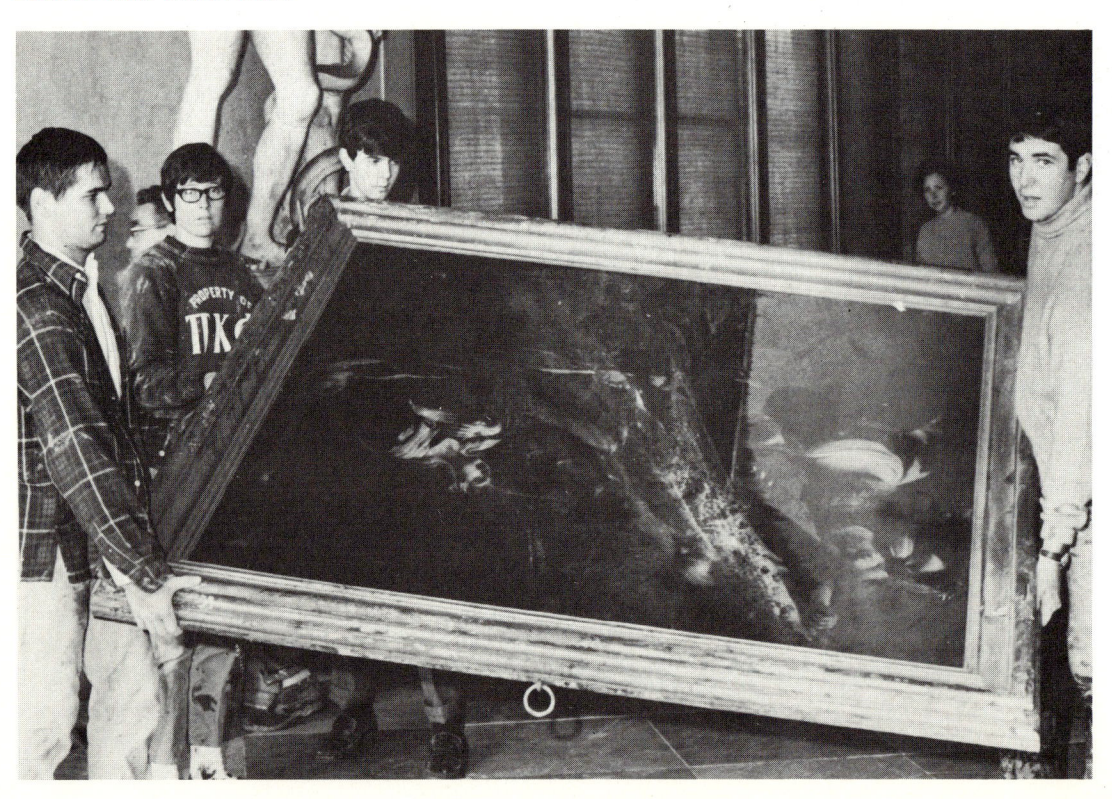

Young people assisting in the salvation of art treasure in the aftermath of the 1967 floods in Florence, Italy. SOURCE: Wide World Photos.

In general, their [adolescent] activity was regulated by others, and they showed only little initiative. At no time did they handle any of the injured, nor did they indicate any desire to do so . . . [they] . . . did not work out a plan for a division of labor. Any opportunity to utilize their skills was largely dissipated because they remained together and did essentially what was a one-person job . . . [suggesting] . . . that they needed one another for moral support.

Once adults have directed them, adolescents render considerable assistance in disaster relief. As an elderly woman caught in the Mississippi River flooding noted, "Never again will I say a word about a long-haired kid. I love every one of them." This elderly woman, watching youth at work, exemplifies a typical role of the aged in disasters: to be treated, if victims, and left to observe rather than to assist. Of course, some elderly persons take an active role.

RECOVERY AND RECONSTRUCTION

Immediately after a disaster, a sense of *community cohesion* emerges. Disasters, whether specific or random, usually result in "the widespread sharing of danger, loss, and deprivation produc[ing] an intimate, primary group solidarity among survivors, which overcomes social isolation and provides a channel for intimate communication and expression" (Fritz, 1961: 689). (See the selection entitled "Disaster Utopia.")

DISASTER UTOPIA

Source: James B. Taylor, Louis A. Zurcher, and William H. Key, *Tornado: A Community Responds to Disaster* (Seattle: University of Washington Press, 1970), pp. 156–162.

We shall look first at the development of the "post-disaster Utopia" as a kind of perspective. We have described how, after disaster, formal rules and regulations were laid aside, the usual distinctions between rich and poor disregarded. For a time there was an almost palpable sense of community cohesion, and many people felt an unselfish concern for the welfare of others. Those who remembered World War II compared this period to the spirit of the London blitz. For a brief time, it seemed as if the golden rule might indeed serve as a guide to action.

Such a utopian mood is common to disasters. . . . It is not, however, unique to them; it has been reported for other times and places as well. Especially is it seen in the early phases of social movements, and among small sectarian associations. [Other examples include the spirit of the French Revolution, Nazi party zealousness in Germany, such sectarian movements as the Diggers or early Quakers, or the mood of the 1969 Woodstock rock festival.] The utopian mood is a concomitant of the kind of communal order which Ferdinand Toennies has described as *gemeinschaft* — a society based on shared sentiments rather than legalistic exchange and rational calculation. It is precisely this kind of communal order which (in less extreme and dramatic form) also seems to underlie much informal organization.

Since the utopian mood has collective consequences, its sources need clarification. What are the conditions which lead to its development? to its decline? What are its limits? And how can it be understood within the general theory of collective behavior? The experience of Topeka may provide a fruitful source of understanding.

. . . Without . . . strong motivation it is doubtful that the usual concerns of role and status could have been held in temporary abeyance. The group task of tornado recovery had high priority, in part because it provided a means of accomplishing pressing individual tasks as well. . . .

The development of group consensus made possible the emergence of new forms of coordinated action and reciprocal expectation, even when individuals acted for themselves and not as members of an organized group. . . . The few cases in which the donor departed from the emergency norms and tried to set limits to his charity (one man tried to donate new suits and asked that they be given only to people who were in the business world) were greeted with annoyance and antagonism. In short, the group norms developed from the collective processes of task definition; they provided cues to individual task-oriented action; and they set limits on acceptable behavior.

In Topeka the utopian mood grew from the perception that common tasks were shared by the entire community. The same dynamics explain other situations in which the utopian mood is found — the early development of nationalistic fervor, commitment to total war, initial stages of revolution, and sectarian social movements. Such situations usually are found at times of intense social stress, of economic insecurity, of physical attack, or precipitous social change, of despair with the present and of status decline. The utopian mood develops if and only if the community or group feels it has "found an answer" to its problems — that is, that it has arrived at a group consensus. . . . This stepwise process may be diagrammed as follows for the general case:

shared common tasks of high priority

+

communication and perception of the shared nature of the task

+

shared agreement on reciprocal individual behavior appropriate to task accomplishment (leads to)

1. A sense of shared closeness with others involved in accomplishing task — i.e. the group or community

2. Enhanced group cohesion, sentiments of warmth and concern

3. Emergence of novel personalistic patterns of interaction with others

4. Relative disregard of status distinctions

5. Relative disregard of status norms governing transactions between groups

equals

THE UTOPIAN MOOD

Utopia and Reality. The utopian mood is transient, and in Topeka its disappearance caused some sense of loss. "The tornado brought out the best in people," we were told; and regrets were voiced that "people couldn't be like that all the time." The foregoing analysis makes clear why the post-disaster Utopia would lead to change in the final outcome. The priority of the shared tasks may lessen; or people may come to perceive that the task is not so shared as they had thought; or disagreement about the kind of individual behavior appropriate may arise. All of these shifts could be observed within a few days after the tornado. The demand for immediate and flexible help was met in the main, and help-giving itself was increasingly routinized and handled by specialists. People no longer had pressing and immediate needs which called for immediate action. The dangerous trees had been cut down; roofs had been patched temporarily with plastic. The long-term tasks of recovery required a specialized bureaucracy with specialized roles and rationalized procedures — insurance adjusters, claim investigators, street crews, and so forth. The decreased priority of the shared collective task signaled the disappearance of the post-disaster Utopia.

A similar process of emergence and decay seems to occur in the early stages of development of many types of collective behavior. If the social stresses have resulted in the shared definition of common and reciprocal tasks, the utopian mood emerges. The mood then promotes a period of enthusiasm and high morale, which inevitably fades as priorities shift, or as different strategies of task accomplishment vie for adherence.

In their review of disaster research, Form and Loomis focus on the persistence of social and cultural systems following disasters. They find a pattern of increasingly effective organization (1956: 181):

Almost immediately after the impact of the destructive agent, a disaster system arises spontaneously to meet the human problems created and to restore a social equilibrium. Far from having a condition of social *anomie** [emphasis added], social systems continue to operate through *all* of the disaster stages, and continuity is found between the old and the emergent systems.

With the possible exception of some civil disorders, disasters generally produce the kind of group identification that speeds the reallocation of human tasks (Dynes, 1970: 209). This involves the immediate adaptation of tasks for personnel or public agencies that have few volunteers, such as fire and police departments. It includes setting up organizations to meet other needs with professional staff augmented by volunteers, such as the Red Cross and social welfare agencies. Other groups rely primarily on volunteers, such as church groups or ham radio operators.

VOLUNTARY ASSOCIATIONS

Source: David Sills, "Voluntary Associations: Sociological Aspects," *International Encyclopedia of the Social Sciences*, vol. 16 (New York: Macmillan and The Free Press, 1968), pp. 362–363. Copyright © 1968 by Crowell-Collier and Macmillan, Inc.

Definitions of the term "voluntary association," as it applies to organizations in modern societies, differ widely, but they generally contain three key elements. A voluntary association is an organized group of persons (1) that is formed in order to further some common interest of its members; (2) in which membership is voluntary in the sense that it is neither mandatory nor acquired through birth; and (3) that exists independently of the state. Even this broad definition admits some exceptions. Membership in such voluntary associations as labor unions or professional societies may be a condition of employment or professional practice, and thus may not be truly voluntary. Membership in a church or in a family society may be "inherited" from one's parents and, in that sense, not voluntary. Many voluntary associations are subject to state control to the extent that they must be registered and agencies of the state often create or sponsor voluntary associations in order to achieve their own ends....

Defined in these broad terms, voluntary associations include all nonstate organizations — churches, business firms, labor unions, foundations, private schools and universities, cooperatives and political parties. In most of the writings on voluntary associations ... a much narrower definition is used. The broad definition is of great interest historically, however, since it is central to the principle of the freedom of association upon which all voluntary associations depend for their existence. It is also relevant to studies of contemporary associations, since it forces the researcher to pay attention to what he is actually studying when he seeks to study the extent of membership in voluntary associations or the functions which voluntary associations serve for their members or for society.

VOLUNTARY ASSOCIATIONS While a variety of *voluntary associations** (see selection) and more formal organizations work to reestablish a community's equilibrium, they are not all rated equally capable by people on the spot. The findings in the Waco and San Angelo, Texas, tornado of 1953 are typical. Note in Table 9-2 that the three highest-ranked relief organizations in Waco were military groups. Among community organizations, churches were rated higher than municipal government (other than city police) or the national Red Cross. The relatively low ratings of the latter two groups is consistent with the findings of other disaster researchers (see Form and Nosow, 1958: 119; Marks and Fritz, 1954: 275; Moore, 1958: 101). Voluntary local associations often fill important community needs in the early stage following disasters.

The disadvantage of formal units such as municipal governments and the Red Cross is that their normal lines of communication are disrupted by disasters (the military, in contrast, comes in from outside the disaster area), and people have high expectations of them. Table 9-2 shows two characteristics of social organization in the aftermath of a disaster: the activation of a broad range of organized efforts to reestablish the equilibrium of a community, and the degree of effectiveness of organizations as rated by people in the disaster area. Moore observes of the latter (1958: 177):

Through the effort to imprint on the public mind that "when disaster strikes, the Red Cross is there," the idea is perhaps created that the Red Cross will repair all damage and heal all wounds, no matter how great the disaster. Such expectations can lead only to frustration.

DISASTER PREPARATION The effectiveness of any organized effort after a disaster depends on how well a community has prepared for the crisis. Preparation requires an effective *warning system*, the first step in launching *standard emergency plans*. By such acts as moving people to safe places and sandbagging buildings while there is still time, as well as having trained persons prepare for disaster and relief, a community can reduce the number of injuries and the amount of damage.

How preparation can help before, during, and after impact is illustrated by the system in effect during the 1964 Nugata, Japan, earthquake. Researchers reported these systematic developments (adapted from Dynes, Haas, and Quarantelli, 1969: 180–182):

1. An elaborate multilevel disaster plan provided a framework to guide group reactions.

2. The plan was put in use, and organizations mobilized and operated within the general framework; the plan was operative at all levels. Copies of the disaster manual were readily available.

3. The plan specified organizational division of labor, functions of government agencies, public utilities, and various private organizations.

Table 9-2 Ranking by Informants of Adequacy of Performance of Participating Institutional Organizations in the 1953 Waco and San Angelo, Texas, Tornado*

Institutional organization	Rank	
	Waco	San Angelo
United States Army	1	6
United States Air Force	2	1
National Guard	3	3
State and city police	4	1
Local churches	5	5
Salvation army	6	4
Municipal government	7	7
State government	8	9
Local relief fund	9	8
Federal government	10	12
Various local agencies	11	10
American Red Cross	12	11

* Adapted from Harry E. Moore, *Tornadoes Over Texas* (Austin: University of Texas Press, 1958), p. 101. © 1958 by the Hogg Foundation for Mental Health.

Organized community responses are visible soon after the shock of a disaster. SOURCE: Martin Steingesser/Photo Researchers.

4. The planned organizational division of labor was maintained, with minor exceptions for some expanded operations, after the earthquake.

5. The plan was detailed and specific but contained unique features for various types of disasters. Lists of supplies and equipment and sources of supply were included. Without the list it is unlikely that several hundred desperately needed water trucks could have been assembled as soon as they were.

6. There was adaptive deviation from the master plan, such as developing refugee centers where the evacuees congregated, but for the most part, the plan was followed.

The number and effectiveness of such recovery organizations is related to both the frequency of disasters (see also the discussion of *sequential effects*, pages 288-289) and the size of the population involved. In the United States, there is an increasing awareness of the need to organize against disaster. An indication of the effects of this organizing process is that, while the American population has more than doubled since the 1920s, thereby making more people vulnerable to disaster-related injuries, there has been a steady decline in the number of lives lost in disasters (Dacy and Kunreuther, 1969: 6; CBS News Almanac, 1976: 904–915). It is difficult to rebuild after a disaster, but doing so usually results in community rehabilitation and a return to normal living (Moore, 1956: 737).

WARNING SYSTEMS

COMMUNICATING DANGER SIGNS In the event of a hurricane, flood, or other catastrophe, the first order of business is to warn the people in the area. The effectiveness of this warning can influence the extent of the damage, both to property and to life. The warning system of a community is thus its initial organized response to a disaster.

One type of warning system is the prior planning taken in high-risk areas. For example, while there is rarely specific warning of an earthquake, certain preparatory steps are possible; San Francisco and other communities particularly vulnerable to earthquakes have special building codes. Preparation of this nature, like a warning system, reduces damage once disaster strikes.

Aside from such prior preparation, clearly the best way to reduce injuries in a disaster is to warn people in enough time for them to protect themselves. Some disasters, such as hurricanes and floods, are preceded by clear danger signs long in advance. Hurricanes are often observed building up over ocean waters days before they strike a coastal community. Floods are often preceded by heavy rains and the buildup of water in rivers and tributaries. Our rapidly growing, sophisticated technology provides early and accurate forecasting of other potential disasters such as earthquakes and tornadoes (see *Earthquake Prediction and Public Policy*, 1975: 20–34). The National Weather Service uses a network of mini-computers and television displays in place of an old system based on teletype and facsimile machines. Under the new system more data can be analyzed more quickly and more accurately. How the new system will give earlier warning of potential disasters, here in the case of tornadoes, is summarized in a *Science News* article, "Weather Forecasts Enter the Computer Age" (1974: 120):

AUTOMATION AND DISASTER WARNING
Old System

1. The forecaster receives a message via teletypewriter from the National Severe Storms Forecast Center in Kansas City indicating a potential for tornadoes exists in his locality and delineating a box-shaped area for a tornado watch. The same message goes by NOAA Weather wire to those local media outlets and public-safety agencies which subscribe to this service.

2. Soon thereafter the forecaster receives by teletypewriter a redefining message from his State Forecast Office listing the counties involved in the tornado watch. This is transmitted on the Weather Wire.

3. He relays this information by individual telephone calls to local broadcasters and public-safety officials who are not subscribers to the NOAA Weather Wire.

4. He records a tornado watch message for dissemination via the NOAA Weather Radio and by automatic telephone-answering equipment.

5. He alerts spotter networks by phone.

6. He amends his local forecast to include a tornado watch.

7. He calls in a third man to help, while an observer is glued to the radarscope.

8. Together, the three men continuously monitor incoming teletypewriter reports and radar echoes of clouds.

New System

1. A watch message indicating a tornado threat exists and indicating the counties affected is placed in the stations' memory bank.

2. This information is automatically displayed for the forecaster on a TV screen.

3. The forecaster presses an appropriate function key and the watch goes out over teletypewriter circuits to most news media and public-safety officials.

4. He records the message on a tape cartridge and inserts this in a dial-out device which automatically and simultaneously (a) transmits the message by phone to selected recipients, (b) places the message on the station's NOAA Weather Radio, and (c) puts it on a telephone-answering device.

5. He alerts spotter networks using the same dial-out technique.

6. The forecaster and the radar observer continuously monitor their TV screens and radarscope.

VARIED COMMUNITY PREPAREDNESS Communities obviously vary widely in the sophistication of their warning systems. At one extreme are those which have taken few or no special measures. Given the infrequency of major disasters, this is probably the condition of most communities in the nation. Even so, every town or suburb has some way of warning its citizens of impending disaster. Consider the disastrous flood in Scottsdale, Arizona, a community with no experience of floods, on June 22, 1972. In this dry area, the community naturally had no special mechanisms of warning such as exist in some communities in Florida which in the last few decades have experienced twenty or more hurricanes, killing several thousands (Williams, 1964).

Even though there was no warning system in Scottsdale, there were some adaptations to the situation. Once the weather bureau determined the possible extent of the danger, the information was broadcast to the community several hours in advance by radio, television, and the local press. Public officials working in the areas that would be affected began to direct activities. Schoolteachers canceled classes so that students could get home before the flood, and police began to move into residential areas adjacent to the canal to evacuate the people.

Such steps as these illustrate that communities can respond to impending disaster even when they have had little or no experience and few if any institutionalized devices set up specifically for that purpose. In such situations the warning is likely to be shorter and less effective than in communities — such as those in Florida where hurricanes are common, Arkansas affected by floods, and Kansas by tornadoes — that have had such experiences often enough to have developed trained personnel to detect, warn, and direct responses to a disaster before it strikes.

CRESCENT CITY AND HILO A study of two communities experiencing similar disasters but reacting differently illustrates the difference between *ad hoc* and planned warning systems. Both Crescent City, California, and Hilo, Hawaii, were struck by a *tsunami* (tidal wave) after the March 27, 1964, Alaska earthquake. Crescent City, like Scottsdale, had no warning techniques and procedures, but the city of Hilo did. In Hilo a written plan included steps to be taken before, during, and after a disaster. In the before section were such spelled-out warning procedures as transmitting a warning to the community by fixed public sirens and dispatching police to critical areas to speed the warning and to supervise evacuation. Local radio stations were instructed to broadcast critical information on a twenty-four-hour basis.

Anderson (1969) documents that, even considering the lesser impact of the wave at Hilo, the fact that no lives were lost there (whereas there were eleven deaths in Crescent City) can be attributed largely to the different warning procedures. It is worth noting that if Crescent City officials and residents had not improvised warning procedures, the loss of life would probably have been much greater.

The cases of Hilo and Crescent City exemplify a larger pattern. Where there is a planned, organized warning system, it is likely that loss of life and general damage will be less severe than in communities without such planning (Anderson, 1969: 94; Barton, 1970: 140–141).

EFFECT OF DISUSE OF WARNING SYSTEMS   A recurring problem confronting even communities with established warning systems is that such systems are likely to deteriorate after prolonged disuse. A common experience is the designation of fire wardens in schools and office buildings where none of the supposedly prepared officials know what they should do. The deterioration of the Civil Defense warning system against nuclear attacks across the nation is a classic case, especially as the potential of nuclear attack has not been shown to have decreased since the systems went into effect in the 1950s. Growing public awareness of potential natural disasters and manmade catastrophes has stimulated some Civil Defense systems to partial reactivation (see "What Role for Civil Defense in Peacetime Society?" 1973: 104), but we are still far from ready.

SEQUENTIAL EFFECTS   Why do some communities develop more effective warning systems than others? The old adage that experience is the best teacher seems to be at work here. It is generally true that communities and groups that have experienced disaster manage better than those that have not (Barton, 1970: 142). The fact that there was a written set of disaster instructions in Hilo, Hawaii, was the result of earlier experience. As Anderson reports (1969: 100):

On May 23, 1960, a tsunami generated by an earthquake in Chile took the lives of 61 persons in Hilo and injured 282 others. This disaster *resulted in* [emphasis added] a number of improvements in tsunami warning and evacuation procedures utilized in the community. Another *consequence* [emphasis added] of the 1960 disaster was an increased willingness on the part of local officials and residents to take protective measures when information was received that tsunamis threatened the community. This was demonstrated by the response to the 1964 emergency.

After a disaster, local officials get *feedback* from the community. They learn how effectively public agencies and other organizations performed, the response of the general public, and criticisms and recommendations for improvement (Anderson, 1969: 102). This feedback process "may and does result in changes in official warning systems and in other systems involved in the presumed effectiveness or ineffectiveness of the warning" (Williams, 1964: 96).

People in a community where disaster has already struck are sensitive to signs of another and are more responsive in preparing for it. Five months after the June 1972 flood in Scottsdale, threat of another flood developed. This time, the response was more efficient on all levels. City officials immediately sent police into residential areas to warn people; sandbags were set up at a central distribution point, and people sandbagged their homes and took other protective steps; the local power company released more controlled water into canals to enable them to handle more of the flows building up. As a result, there was less damage than in the earlier flood, which had not been preceded by an effective warning (Scottsdale *Progress,* series of articles in November and December, 1972).

This sensitivity on the part of the people in communities with experience of disasters is found in many case studies. Fritz summarized a number of them (1961: 664):

Two days after the severe flood of 1955, in Port Jarvis, New York ... residents heard a false report that a dam above the city had broken under the weight of flood waters. About one-quarter of the city's inhabitants evacuated to high ground surrounding the city within an hour after the report circulated; but of these, *almost 90 per cent were residents of the previously flooded area* [emphasis added]. In 1957, a similarly high proportion of the population of Cameron Parish, Louisiana, evacuated when a second hurricane threatened the area *where six weeks before* [emphasis added] Hurricane Audrey had killed over 400 people and devastated several communities. This kind of hypersensitivity has been found in virtually every disaster-stricken community or group.

HYPERSENSITIVITY *Hypersensitivity* is a term that Fritz applies to people who have gone through a disaster. It is defined in *Webster's New International Dictionary* as being "abnormally and excessively susceptible to the action of a given agent." When such an agent is news of an impending disaster, a community that is excessively susceptible may find both its local government and its people overreacting to potential danger signs. The overreaction may lead to such dysfunctional responses as mass panic or mass apathy in the face of disaster.

TIMING THE WARNING Public officials must make a difficult decision: to warn or not to warn their community of a possible disaster. If they set off an alert in a community that has previously experienced a disaster or has reason to expect one (as when reports have circulated about a weakened dam or a potential accident at a nearby nuclear plant), then panic may result. Yet, if officials warn too often of possible disasters that do not occur, they may induce apathy. The care with which responsible officials inform the community may make a crucial difference in initial responses when disaster strikes.

Hypersensitivity leading to apathy is analogous to the childhood tale of crying wolf. People may fail to respond when there really is a wolf. A classic example of an apathetic response to a warning of disaster is the Japanese attack on Pearl Harbor, December 7, 1941. The Japanese military inflicted over 3,000 casualties and destroyed a large portion of the United States' Pacific fleet ("Killed in Action": 1941: 22-23). Yet days in advance of this disaster, the Japanese code had been broken and the plan for an attack was relayed to commanders on the scene. Furthermore, hours in advance of the attack, radar and naval patrol vessels had detected the approaching Japanese aircraft and submarines (Lord, 1957: 27-63).

Why didn't the military commanders and personnel respond to the warnings? Certainly, if they had done so, they could have reduced the damage substantially. Many of the commanders were combat veterans of World War I; their experience should have told them how to respond. In addition, war had broken out in Europe and in Asia, and in 1940, the United States had begun drafting men into the armed services, thereby giving national warning of impending disaster.

A good part of the apathetic reaction can be attributed to hypersensitivity. For several years before December 7, 1941, the domestic and international situations had been extremely tense: economic depression, armed conflict, Germany's domination of Europe, Japanese expansion in the Far East. Just how hypersensitive Americans were was indicated by the hysterical public reaction to Orson Welles's radio broadcast of a version of H. G. Wells's science fiction tale about an invasion from Mars. The broadcast was made in late 1939, when there were clear signs of an impending world war. It had this effect (Cantril, 1947: 210):

Long before the broadcast ended, people all over the United States were praying, crying, fleeing, frantically to escape death from the Martians. Some ran to rescue loved ones. Others telephoned farewells or warnings, hurried to inform neighbors, sought information from newspapers or radio stations, summoned ambulances and police cars. At least six million people heard the broadcast. At least a million of them were frightened or disturbed.

FALSE ALARMS   The panic that accompanied the broadcast had effects later. People became skeptical about threats of disaster. There had been a number of false alerts before the attack on Pearl Harbor actually took place. People had begun to take these warnings with a grain of salt. Military officials, thus, interpreted the situation optimistically and concluded that no disaster was going to occur, warning signs notwithstanding (Fritz, 1961: 670).

It is surprising that such a reaction occurred in a military situation, where preparedness is the rule and danger was known to exist. Communication, then, is not the crucial factor in the effectiveness of a warning system. Warnings of disasters that do not occur appear to have dysfunctional consequences for a community that are as great as lack of communication. What is needed is an effectively measured approach to warning the community, coupled with other preparations.

A number of ideas related to the development of patterns in disasters have been offered in this chapter. It should be remembered that disaster disrupts the stable patterns of society. The durability of the pre-disaster social structure can be seen after recovery and reconstruction, where the emergent social system retains many of the original features of organization.

It is not accurate to call disaster a truly disorganizing event, except in the short run. The search for order and meaning begins quickly; the search is directed largely by voices from the past.

SUMMARY

Natural and manmade disasters are fortunately not frequent. Yet, most people experience or have family or friends who experience the damaging effects of a disaster. Disasters are so widespread and unpredictable that nearly everyone is a potential victim — young, old, rich, poor, conservative, and liberal alike. Here are some findings on the effects of and social responses to disasters.

The severity of a disaster gives insight into the nature of social organization under stress. The popular view we hold of people in pervasive shock and panic, and of communities in a state of total social disorganization, is misleading. In fact, research has disproved many such myths. After disaster strikes, communities generally do experience an initial but brief state of *community disorganization** in which normal supplies of food, medicine, and other needs are disrupted. Within hours, though, communities generally begin to regain a state of *community organization** in which the necessities of life for physical and social survival are provided.

Communities go through three general stages after a disaster. The first is characterized by informal, sporadic, and individualized relief and rescue efforts. The second stage is more organized but still consists largely of volunteer efforts. It is in this second period that adaptive *voluntary associations** such as church groups and civic organizations begin to fill some essential relief functions. In the third stage, the efforts of formal government and relief agencies emerge.

The recovery and reconstruction that occur within a community following a disaster is facilitated by a sense of *community* cohesion, a *utopian* period, in which many people identify with each other in their mutually deprived condition and cooperate in efforts at reconstruction. A variety of public and private organizations set to work after the crisis. People in the area usually rate outside help, such as the army, and voluntary organizations, such as church groups, more effective than local government and private relief agencies. Most people expect more than they should of local organizations that have also been affected by the disaster.

Ultimately the rate of recovery and reconstruction depends on local government and private relief agencies. The efficiency of such local units depends on how advanced are the community's preparations before the disaster. Initial damage is lessened and recovery is speeded when there is a local body of people who are expert in handling disasters. In American society, there is wide variation in the degree of community preparedness. Some communities have detailed master plans, but many others have few or no plans. The systematic reduction in disaster-related fatalities over the past half century indicates a generally increasing awareness of the consequences of disasters and of increasingly effective organized preparation for them.

Factors related to the rate and effectiveness of disaster control are the *sequential* or *random* nature of a disaster. Communities that have experienced sequential disasters tend to be more sensitive to the need to develop *warning systems* and to have disaster plans. Communities in which the impact of a disaster is widespread rather than localized tend to experience more rapid and effective relief and reconstruction. A cautionary finding on communities with warning systems but infrequent disasters is that people may overreact to danger signals or may allow their warning system to deteriorate through disuse. Too frequent warnings when nothing happens can result in community *hypersensitivity* and lack of response to a warning even before an actual disaster.

QUESTIONS FOR DISCUSSION

1. Consider some disaster, natural or manmade, which has occurred in your community within your lifetime. What kind of *community organization** took place? What part did voluntary associations play? Did the community return to normal, or did significant changes take place over time?

2. During times of community disaster, how does the wearing of insignia or a uniform facilitate performance of particular roles and responsibilities? How may it hinder a fireman, for example, in the execution of personal rather than public duties? Which do you believe should come first?

3. What reasons can you give for the lack of initiative and organization generally found among adolescents during community crises?

4. Why are voluntary associations so often able to act in the early stages of disaster more rapidly than government agencies or formal private agencies?

5. What circumstances may have led to an increased public awareness of disasters, as evidenced by the increasing establishment of more effective warning systems around the nation? Name some important elements of a useful warning system.

6. Is a disaster a social problem? Give reasons for or against viewing a disaster in this way. Would you view natural and manmade disasters differently for purposes of this question? Why or why not?

7. What kinds of disasters are likely to produce widespread *anomie** and a sense of *relative deprivation**?

8. What role can the mass media play in changing the effects of a localized specific disaster into those of a random, generalized disaster?

9. Review your understanding of the following terms and concepts:

disaster

collective stress

community organization

community disorganization

community cohesion

discriminating disaster

voluntary associations

warning systems

standard emergency plans

role conflict in disaster

sequential effects

REFERENCES

Anderson, William
    1969   "Disaster warning and communication processes in two communities." The Journal of Communication 19: 92–104.

Brown, Michael and Amy Goldin
    1973   Collective Behavior: A Review and Reinterpretation of the Literature. Pacific Palisades, California: Goodyear.

Barton, Allen
    1970   Communities in Disaster. New York: Doubleday.

Bates, Frederick with C. W. Fogelman, V. D. Parenton, and R. H. Pittman
    1963   The Social and Psychological Consequences of a Natural Disaster: A Longitudinal Study of Hurricane Audrey. Disaster Study Number 18. Washington, D.C.: National Academy of Sciences — National Research Council.

Cantril, Hadley
    1947   "The invasion from Mars." W. Leary and J. Smith (eds.), Think Before You Write. New York: Harcourt, Brace: 209–217.

    1975   CBS News Almanac, 1976. Maplewood, N.J.: Hammond Almanac.

Cohen, Albert
    1959   "The study of social disorganization and deviant behavior." R. Merton, L. Broom, and L. Cottrell (eds.), Sociology Today: Problems and Prospects. New York: Basic Books: 461–484.

Coleman, James
    1971   "Community disorganization and conflict." R. Merton and R. Nisbet (eds.), Contemporary Social Problems. New York: Harcourt Brace Jovanovich: 657–708.

Conot, Robert
    1965   Rivers of Blood, Years of Darkness. New York: Bantam.

Dacy, Douglas and Howard Kunreuther
    1969   The Economics of Disaster. New York: The Free Press.

Danzig, Elliott et al.
    1958   The Effects of a Threatening Rumor on a Disaster-Stricken Community. Washington, D.C.: National Academy of Sciences — National Research Council, Disaster Research Group, Report No. 10, Publication 517.

1974 Disasters/Catastrophes. The Official Associated Press Almanac: 1974. Maplewood, N.J.: Hammond Almanac: 904–915.

Downey, Fred
1938 Disaster Fighters. New York: Putnam and Sons.

Dynes, Russell
1970 Organized Behavior in Disasters. Lexington, Mass.: D. C. Heath.

Dynes, Russell with J. Haas and E. Quarantelli
1969 "Some preliminary observations on organizational responses in the emergency period after the Nugata, Japan, Earthquake of June 16, 1964." Excerpted summary. A. Barton, Communities in Disaster. New York: Doubleday: 180–182.

1975 Earthquake Prediction and Public Policy. Washington, D.C.: National Academy of Sciences.

Form, William and Charles Loomis
1956 "The persistence and emergency of social and cultural systems in disasters." American Sociological Review 21: 180–185.

Form, William and Sigmond Nosow
1958 Community in Disaster. New York: Harper and Row.

Forrest, Thomas
1971 "Emergent communal response." L. Gordon (ed.), A City in Racial Crisis: Detroit Pre and Post the 1967 Riot. Dubuque, Iowa: Wm. C. Brown: 86–103.

Fritz, Charles
1961 Disaster. R. Merton and R. Nisbet (eds.), Contemporary Social Problems. New York: Harcourt, Brace and World: 651–694.

Garb, Solomon and Evelyn Eng
1969 Disaster Handbook. New York: Springer Publishing Company.

Gordon, Leonard
1967 "Field report on the racial riots in Detroit of July 23 to 27, 1967." Unpublished report to the national office of the American Jewish Committee's Institute of Human Relations (August 8). New York: Institute of Human Relations.
1971 A City in Racial Crisis: Detroit Pre and Post the 1967 Riot. Dubuque, Iowa: Wm. C. Brown.

Hachiya, Michihiko
1955 Hiroshima Diary. Chapel Hill, N.C.: University of North Carolina Press.

Heer, David
1965 After Nuclear Attack: A Demographic Inquiry. New York: Praeger.

Hersey, John
1959 Hiroshima. New York: Bantam.

Johnson, Rudy
1973 "Black groups here seek aid for drought victims in Africa." The New York Times (July 15): 20.

Jungk, Robert
1961 Children of the Ashes. New York: Harcourt, Brace and World.

Kalichman, Betty
1967 "This crucial summer: the Interfaith Emergency Center." Update. Detroit: Detroit Chapter, American Jewish Committee Newsletter (December): 1.

Keene, Donald
1959 Living Japan. New York: Doubleday.

Kentfield, Calvin
1973 "The river did not stay away." The New York Times Magazine (July 15): 14–19.

1941 "Killed in action." Life (December 22): 22–23.

Killian, Lewis
   1952   "The significance of multiple-group membership in disaster." American Journal of Sociology 57: 309–314.

Lang, Kurt and Gladys Engel Lang
   1964   "Collective responses to the threat of disaster." The Threat of Impending Disasters: Contributions to the Psychology of Stress. G. H. Gross, H. Wechsler, and M. Greeblatt (eds.), Cambridge, Massachusetts: M. I. T. Press.

Lord, Walter
   1955   A Night to Remember. New York: Holt.
   1957   Day of Infamy. New York: Bantam.

Marks, Edward and Charles Fritz
   1954   Human Reactions in Disaster Situations. Unpublished report, National Opinion Research Center. Chicago: University of Chicago Press.

Merton, Robert
   1961   "Social problems and sociological theory." R. Merton and R. Nisbet (eds.), Contemporary Social Problems. New York: Harcourt, Brace and World: 697–737.
   1970   Foreward. A. Barton, Communities in Disaster. New York: Doubleday: vii–xxxvii.

Moore, Harry
   1956   "Toward a theory of disaster." American Sociological Review 21: 733–737.
   1958   Tornadoes Over Texas. Austin: University of Texas Press.

Moore, Harry, Frederick Bates, Marvin Layman, and Vernon Parenton
   1963   Before the Wind: A Study of the Response to Hurricane Carla, Disaster Research Group. National Academy of Sciences – National Research Council, No. 19.

Quarantelli, Enrico
   1973   Human Behavior in Disaster. In Conference: Designing to Survive Disaster, Chicago: IIT Research Institute: 53–74.

Quarantelli, Enrico and Russell Dynes
   1966   "Organizations under stress." R. Brictson (ed.), Symposium on Emergency Operations. Santa Monica, Cal.: Systems Development Corporation: 3–19.
   1970   "Property norms and looting: their patterns in community crisis." Phylon 31: 168–182.

   1941   "Remember Pearl Harbor." Life (December 22): 15–23.

   1968   Report of the National Advisory Commission on Civil Disorders. Washington, D.C.: Government Printing Office.

Sills, David
   1968   "Voluntary associations: sociological aspects." International Encyclopedia of the Social Sciences, vol. 16. New York: Macmillan: 362–376.

Sisson, George
   1973   Survival in a Disaster Environment. In Conference: Designing to Survive Disaster. Chicago: IIT Research Institute: 53–74.

Stern, Richard
   1974   The Tower. New York: Warner.

Taylor, James B., Luis A. Zurcher, and William H. Key
   1970   Tornado: A Community Responds to Disaster. Seattle: University of Washington Press.

Trumbull, Robert
   1957   Nine Who Survived Hiroshima and Nagasaki. New York: Dutton.

Turner, Ralph and James Killian
   1972   Collective Behavior. Englewood Cliffs, N.J.: Prentice-Hall.

1974 "Weather forecasts enter computer age." Science News, vol. 106 (August 24 and 31): 120.

1973 "What role for civil defense in peacetime society?" American City 88 (October): 104.

Williams, Harry
1964 "Human factors in warning-and-response systems." G. Grosser et al. (eds.), The Threat of Impending Disaster: Contributions to the Psychology of Stress. Cambridge, Mass.: M. I. T. Press: 80–96.

Chapter 10

HUMAN ECOLOGY AND THE CRISIS OF THE CITIES

Why are the mayors all quitting?
Why are the cities all broke?
Why are the people all angry?
Why are we dying of smoke?
Why are the streets unprotected?
Why are the schools in distress?
Why is the trash uncollected?
How did we make such a mess?

Anonymous

THE MODERN URBAN CONDITION

The United States, indeed the world, is experiencing unprecedented urban expansion. This expansion, a consequence of industrialization, has involved a great movement of people from the country and small towns to the cities and their suburbs. Thus, the cities, the largest concentrated human settlements, are of particular interest in any analysis of social issues, for it is increasingly evident that it is in the cities that most of our social problems are concentrated.

This chapter will assess some of the social implications for America, present and future, of rapid *urbanization**. Why have so many people moved to metropolitan areas? How does our rural, small-town heritage affect the way we deal with the problems of the cities? What are the implications of the movement of large numbers of the middle and upper classes out of the cities to the suburbs? What can be done to redevelop major cities?

These and related questions imply that most major urban problems exist within the old city boundaries. This is true for a wide range of problems, including those listed by our anonymous poet at the beginning of the chapter. Concentrated in the cities are the problems of increasing racial and economic segregation, of schools with increasing needs and a declining tax base to meet those needs, of traffic congestion, air pollution, and rising rates of violent crime. Yet the picture is not all bleak. The cities remain the centers of commercial development, the home of many great universities, the setting for much of our art, theater, and music, and the place where citizens of different cultural heritage can interact.

CITIES AND SUBURBS While the cities are the focus of study, they cannot be considered apart from their relatively affluent and less troubled suburbs. Together they constitute the great metropolitan urban centers. Because of the concentration of economic resources in the metropolitan areas, the suburbs play an important role in determining what can be done in the cities. As the suburbs have developed, they have tended to concentrate their resources on their own development, not offering support for redeveloping the cities. As Bennett Harrison remarks, "Many responsible academic economists — and a growing number of congressmen and editorial writers — clearly believe that suburbanization is one of the principal underlying causes of the 'urban crisis' " (Harrison, 1974: 4–5). He observes that changes in urban form have created disequilibria in urban systems that require the reallocation of resources. With the proliferation of new suburban governments, each is individually less able to manage problems spilling over from neighboring jurisdictions, for example, pollution and neighborhood blight. Central cities lose the power to annex new resources; other areas pursue their separate interests (Harrison, 1974: 6).

The reluctance of suburbanites to aid the cities has been a factor in the racial and economic polarization separating the people of the cities from those of the suburbs (see *Report of the National Advisory Commission on Civil Disorders*, 1968: 398–400). The isolationist attitude of many suburbs calls for examination. As Michael Harrington noted in *The Other America* (1962)[1], we may be creating different social worlds by concentrating the middle and upper classes in the suburbs and the lower classes in the cities, each ignorant of and hostile to the other. Ira Mothner graphically describes the city-suburban polarization in many of the nation's great urban centers (1968: 27):

Suburbs defy their metropolitan nature. They're not little cities, but anti-cities. Against the urban disarray, the clash of class and the more touchy confrontation of race, they set up ordered streets and rows of similarity. His family tucked behind the hedge stockade, safe from rude encounters, crime and miseducation, Daddy braves the urban wilds to bring back the sirloin.

Who comes to town and stays? Mostly those who can't get out — usually Negroes. More than a million black people moved into central cities between 1960 and 1966, while better than four times as many whites left. (The Negro population of our 25 largest cities doubled between 1950 and 1966.)

Negroes are not only pushed off the farm toward town, they've quit the South for the North and West. They come for jobs, but without skills or the kind of education it takes to get work. And they come with black faces that make the difference.

The city can't help most of them over the big hump into middle-class America. Black unemployment in big cities is now four times greater than white and the cities are strapped to meet Negro needs. Just about all local costs doubled between 1955 and 1966, education went up one-and-a-half times. (New York's welfare bills have jumped from $900 million to $1.4 billion in the past two years alone.) The cities are almost bankrupt, yet they haven't even started on the job that has got to be done.

---

[1] Harrington's book was a strong influence on President Kennedy, who discovered through it the extent of poverty and its attendant problems. After adopting a new view of problems of the poor, often urban and minority poor, Kennedy began implementing New Frontier programs for social reform.

"The Negro is the city problem" is too easy an answer. He's the latest, the most urgent, but he sits under the whole pile of urban inadequacies. The urban crisis is continual, but it doesn't stop the music, the excitement, the opportunity that pull the eager young to big towns each year. Most leave in time, but there will always be those who, knowing the problems, choose to remain.

A number of useful terms and concepts have been developed for dealing with urban and suburban problems. The emerging field of *human ecology** studies people in the (particularly urban) setting in which they live. The basic processes of *urbanism** and *suburbanism** are population movements that have changed the nation in this century. Within the cities have developed areas commonly called *ghettos**, concentrations of the minorities and the poor. *Community power**, particularly who tends to have it and how it is exercised, is an important topic. And there has been great interest in the development of the *megalopolis**, a densely populated urban area that comprises many cities and their suburbs, such as the cluster that runs south from Boston to Washington, D.C. These concepts and others are useful in developing new community-wide urban planning in America.

THE URBAN TRANSFORMATION

The extent and speed of the urban movement is summarized in the decennial U.S. Census statistics. Of the nineteen censuses taken since 1790, in the first thirteen (or until 1910), most of the American population was rural. Only since 1920 have the majority of Americans been recorded as urban. By 1970, approximately three of every four were classified as urban dwellers.

RURAL AND URBAN DISTINCTIONS Since the distinction between rural and urban is an important one, we should begin by understanding what sociologists mean by the two terms. A good way to begin is to consider them in the light of Ferdinand Tonnies' *Gemeinschaft–Gesellschaft** continuum (1887). Recall that *Gemeinschaft* (rural) community life is characterized by primary relations in daily social activities. Family and other community members have a kinship feeling; they belong together. In *Gemeinschaft* communities, one is generally born into an *ascribed status** that determines one's roles throughout life. In contrast, *Gesellschaft* (urban) community life is characterized by purposive and *voluntary associations**, and is found wherever societies are large and complex. While family and primary relations may remain important, the majority of social bonds is based on the rational pursuit of self-interest, perhaps most clearly evidenced in economic behavior. *Achieved status** regulates many of the roles one plays. (See Table 2-2.)

The differences between rural and urban life and the nature of the urban trend are clear enough. The question is, why have so many Americans moved to large cities and their suburbs? What major advantages do so many people see in urban as compared to rural living? Given the popular idealization of small-town and rural life, the reasons must be compelling.

THE PUSH-PULL COMPLEX The movement toward the cities can be seen as part of a larger push–pull complex from the farms to the cities — the push away from the farms and the pull toward the industrialized cities. The economic consequences of increasing industrialization affected farming even before the middle of the nineteenth century. Like the increasingly efficient factory system, those farms that were most successful were those that became specialized in crops, manpower, and equipment. Specialization had distinct advantages (Olmstead and Smolensky, 1973: 3):

First, by concentrating on a limited number of tasks a worker could increase his knowledge of the job and develop the dexterity needed to become more efficient. Second, the worker would not have to waste

300   ISSUES FACING AMERICAN GROUPS

WHERE WE'RE GOING. The most consequential changes of location are movements from rural areas and small towns and cities to metropolitan areas.

WHERE WE ARE.

time moving from one activity to another. Third, many tasks either require special tools or can be performed much more efficiently with such tools. By specializing a worker can utilize his costly tools . . . a greater part of the time and thus significantly reduce his average cost of production. A fourth important point . . . is that by specializing, a worker with particular physical attributes, skills, or tastes can concentrate on what suits him best.

Specialization of crops and machinery enabled farmers to increase production, to the disadvantage of the more numerous but less efficient small farms. Thus, while a minority of farm enterprises were able to adapt and grow, most could not successfully compete in this new system. The larger corporate farms could more efficiently produce, ship, and distribute farm goods at a profit. However individualistic the small farmers were, most could not survive the new commercialization of agriculture; they moved by the tens of millions with their families to the cities.

SPECIALIZATION AND TECHNOLOGY Meanwhile, specialization was operating even more intensely in the industrial cities, with an increasing demand for workers and a resulting concentration of population. Nonagricultural economic activities since they use less land than farms do, make a more economical use of land, thus increasing profit. Farmers, competing unsuccessfully with larger enterprises, were attracted to the cities by higher wages (Davis, 1965: 46).

The urban trend in America was at first concentrated in the industrial Northeast, which was predominantly urban by the late nineteenth century. As Table 10-1 shows, by the 1920s, the north central area and the West were also predominantly urban. While the South, at present the most rapidly urbanizing section of the nation, took much longer, it became chiefly urban by the 1960s, and by the mid 1970s was approximately two-thirds urban.

Figure 10-1 The general rural to urban population shift in the United States. SOURCE: *Inquiries in Sociology* (Boston: Allyn and Bacon, 1972), pp. 252–253. Copyright © 1972 the American Sociological Association.

URBANISM AND SUBURBANISM

From: Louis Wirth, "Urbanism As a Way of Life," *American Journal of Sociology* XLIV (July, 1938), pp. 8, 10, 20, 22.

When Louis Wirth was developing his theory of urbanism in the 1920s and 1930s (as part of the Chicago School studies), the great population expansion into the suburbs beyond city limits had not yet occurred.

Louis Wirth, one of the leading analysts of the Chicago School. SOURCE: University of Chicago Library.

The excerpt from an article of Herbert Gans's draws on Wirth's earlier perceptions and extends the analysis of urbanism based on additional existing knowledge since Wirth's day (Wirth, 1938):

For sociological purposes a city may be defined as a relatively large, dense, and permanent settlement of socially heterogeneous individuals. On the basis of the postulates which this minimal definition suggests, a theory of urbanism may be formulated in the light of existing knowledge concerning social groups....

The city has ... historically been the melting pot of races, peoples, and cultures, and a most favorable breeding-ground of new biological and cultural hybrids. It has not only tolerated but rewarded individual differences. It has brought together people from the ends of the earth *because* they are different and thus useful to one another, rather than because they are homogeneous and like-minded.

From: Herbert Gans, "Urbanism and Suburbanism as Ways of Life," in A. Rose (ed.), *Human Behavior and Social Processes* (Boston: Houghton Mifflin, 1962), pp. 625–626.

The contemporary sociological conception of cities and of urban life is based largely on the work of the Chicago School, and its summary statement in Louis Wirth's essay "Urbanism as a Way of Life." In that paper, Wirth developed a "minimum sociological definition of the city" as "a relatively large, dense and permanent settlement of socially heterogeneous individuals." From these prerequisites, he then deduced the major outlines of the urban way of life. As he saw it, number, density, and heterogeneity created a social structure in which primary-group relationships were inevitably replaced by secondary contacts that were impersonal, segmental, superficial, transitory, and often predatory in nature. As a result, the city dweller became anonymous, isolated, secular, relativistic, rational, and sophisticated. In order to function in the urban society, he was forced to combine with others to organize corporations, voluntary associations, representative forms of government, and the impersonal mass media of communications. These replaced the primary groups and the integrated way of life found in rural and other pre-industrial settlements.

Wirth's paper has become a classic in urban sociology, and most texts have followed his definition and description faithfully. In recent years, however, a considerable number of studies and essays have questioned his formulations. In addition, a number of changes have taken place in cities since the article was published in 1938, notably the exodus of white residents to low- and medium-priced houses in the suburbs, and the decentralization of industry. The evidence from these studies and the changes in American cities suggest that Wirth's statement must be revised.

There is yet another, and more important reason for such a revision. Despite its title and intent, Wirth's paper deals with urban-industrial society, rather than with the city. This is evident from his approach. Like other urban sociologists, Wirth based his analysis on a comparison of settlement types, but unlike his colleagues, who pursued urban-rural comparisons, Wirth contrasted the city to the folk society. Thus, he compared settlement types of pre-industrial and industrial society. This allowed him to include in his theory of urbanism the entire range of modern institutions which are not found in the folk society, even though many such groups (e.g., voluntary associations) are by no means exclusively urban. Moreover, Wirth's conception of the city dweller as depersonalized, atomized, and susceptible to mass movements suggests that his paper is based on, and contributes to, the theory of mass society.

Many of Wirth's conclusions may be relevant to the understanding of ways of life in modern society. However, since the theory argues that all of society is now urban, his analysis does not distinguish ways of life in the city from those in other settlements within modern society. In Wirth's time, the comparison of urban and pre-urban settlement types was still fruitful, but today, the primary task for urban (or community) sociology seems to me to be the analysis of the similarities and differences between contemporary settlement types [in particular] . . . the inner city, the outer city, and the suburbs.

In short, urbanism has become the American way of life. The concept encompasses the whole range of living in cities, including the high degree of cultural heterogeneity, the predominance of secular values, and the extreme division of labor. Urbanism induces more rapid change than rural living. In consequence, urbanologists are constantly revising their theories. (See Herbert Gans's 1962 statement about urbanism and suburbanism as a way of life in the selection on the subject.) Gans saw the social implications of the great shift

Table 10-1   U.S. Urban Population as a Percentage of Total Population by Regions, 1790–1970

	U.S. Total	Northeast	North Central	South	West
Current SMSA[a] urban definition:					
1970	73.5	80.4	71.6	64.6	82.9
1960	69.9	80.2	68.7	58.5	77.7
1950	64.0	79.5	64.1	48.6	69.5
Previous urban definition:					
1960	63.0	72.8	63.9	52.7	66.1
1950	59.6	75.4	61.1	44.6	59.9
1940	56.5	76.6	58.4	36.7	58.5
1930	56.1	77.6	57.9	34.1	58.4
1920	51.2	75.5	52.3	28.1	51.8
1910	45.6	71.8	45.1	22.5	47.9
1900	39.6	66.1	38.6	18.0	39.9
1890	35.1	59.0	33.1	16.3	37.0
1880	28.2	50.8	24.2	12.2	30.2
1870	25.7	44.3	20.8	12.2	25.8
1860	19.8	35.7	13.9	9.6	16.0
1850	15.3	26.5	9.2	8.3	6.4
1840	10.8	18.5	3.9	6.7	[b]
1830	8.8	14.2	2.6	5.3	[b]
1820	7.2	11.0	1.1	4.6	[b]
1810	7.3	10.9	0.9	4.1	[b]
1800	6.1	9.3	[b]	3.0	[b]
1790	5.1	8.1	[b]	2.1	[b]

[a] Standard Metropolitan Statistical Area (includes suburbs around central cities).
[b] Too sparse settlement and too few states for statistical summary in these years.

SOURCE: *Number of Inhabitants, United States Summary* (Washington, D.C.: Government Printing Office, 1970) PC(1)-A1: Table 18.

in population from the central cities to the suburbs reported in the last three decennial censuses, as Wirth could not.

RURAL AND URBAN DEFINED How is it determined whether people live in rural or in urban areas? The Bureau of the Census has attempted to establish statistical and geographic criteria of the extent of urbanization in any given year or longer. In 1950, the Bureau officially adopted the designation Standard Metropolitan Area (SMA) to replace *metropolitan district,* which was restricted mainly to the legal limits of incorporated cities. The Standard Metropolitan Area was then changed to the current *Standard Metropolitan Statistical Area** (SMSA) in 1960. The intent was the same — to measure the growth of urban living beyond the legal limits of cities. A city was defined as having 2,500 inhabitants or more, and the category *urbanized areas* was added. By definition, an urbanized area consists of one or more cities of 50,000 or more and all the nearby closely settled suburban territory, or urban fringe (*U.S. Census of Population:* 1960).

ECOLOGICAL CITIES Urban sociologists describe the SMSA as an *ecological city** and use it for drawing a geographic line between city and noncity. Figure 10-2 illustrates the usefulness of the ecological city concept using a representative state, Georgia, as an example. The major city in the state, Atlanta, is part of an urban complex that includes several populous suburbs. The ecological city not only extends beyond the legal city limits but may cross state boundaries as does Chattanooga, Tennessee, whose urbanized population base includes Walker County in northern Georgia. Our larger ecological cities contain several legal cities. Thus, the ecological city of New York includes Yonkers, Jersey City, and Newark. Ecological cities may even be international, like greater Detroit, which includes Windsor, Ontario, Canada.

Using the ecological city concept, Olmstead and Smolensky recomputed the 70 percent reported as urban by SMSA criteria in the 1960 Census, and came up with a figure of 87 percent urban (1973: 20). The concepts *SMSA, urbanized area,* and *ecological city* all recognize recent developments. From the 1920 Census, when a majority of the population was first recorded in urban areas, until the 1950 Census, most population growth took place within the legal limits of the older established cities. Since 1950, when the SMA concept was first developed, most population growth has occurred close to but outside legal city limits. The new criteria enable analysts to measure and evaluate the overall urban growth trend more precisely. However, other measures are needed for evaluation of quality of life.

IMAGES OF THE CITY

American society is now predominantly urban, and most people live in large cities or their suburbs. Yet most Americans do not show the kind of deep and strong identification with their cities as the English feel for London, the French for Paris, or the Italians for Rome. Why not? In population, industrial productivity, and artistic achievement, New York, Chicago, and Los Angeles are comparable to these great capitals; but most American cities have grown up in the past century or less, while their European counterparts have been cultural centers for many centuries. The lack of tradition in most American cities is not surprising when one considers Scott Greer's point that American cities "were built on land which had no history and no hallowed memories" (1962: 17). American cities recall no royal strongholds, medieval cathedrals, or ancient Roman camps. Most of them have no past.

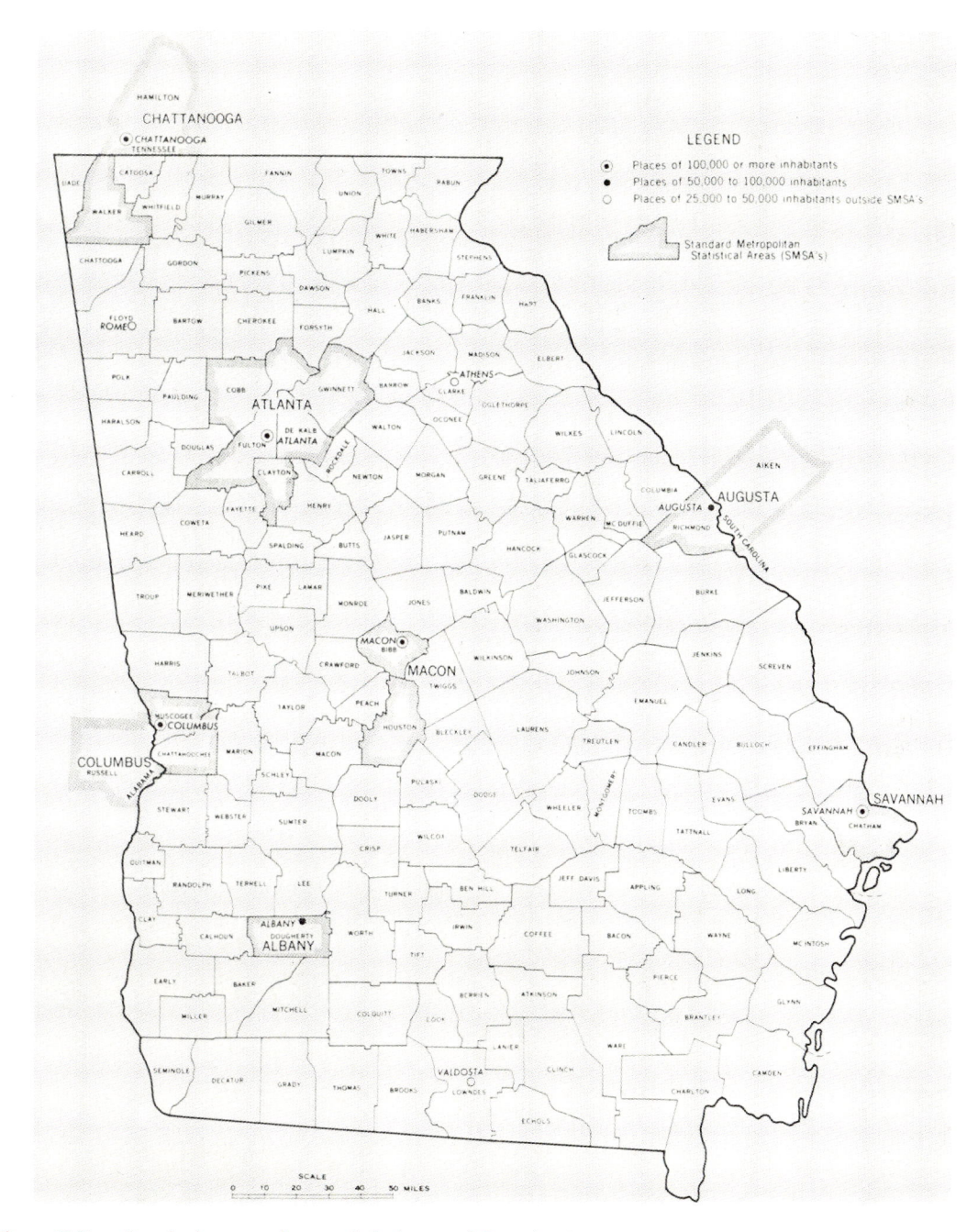

Figure 10-2 Standard metropolitan statistical areas of Georgia, 1970.

THE RURAL HERITAGE When the American republic was established, nineteen out of every twenty people lived in the country. Historic sites such as Bunker Hill and Valley Forge were then located in the country or in small towns. Moreover, most early Americans distrusted large cities. As Thomas Jefferson put it, "I view great cities as pestilence to the morals, the health and the liberties of man. True, they nourish some of the elegant arts, but the useful ones can thrive elsewhere, and less perfection in the others, with more health, virtue and freedom, would be my choice" (Bloomberg, 1967: 359).

Jefferson's belief that the city was evil and the country good was widely shared in his day, in Europe as well as in America. Still prevailing in much of the world today is the view held in the fifth century B.C., in the era of the Greek city–states. Plato held that the ideal size for a city was 5,000 inhabitants (Hoyt, 1964: 200), and that when that size was reached, a new city should be founded. In modern times, a defense minister of China, Lin Piao, viewed cities, whether in a democratic or a communist society, much as Jefferson did. In the *Peking Review* in 1965, Lin wrote that, while the city is the seat of imperialists,

[t]he countryside is the seat of the real people who protect them, i.e., the people in the cities.... Taking the entire globe, if North America and Western Europe can be called the "cities of the world," then Asia, Africa and Latin America constitute the "rural areas of the world".... In a sense, the contemporary world revolution also presents a picture of the encirclement of cities by rural areas.

GEMEINSCHAFT IDEALS AND GESELLSCHAFT REALITY This idealization of the Gemeinschaft or rural life does not in all ways match the realities. Plato himself was the product of a Gesellschaft Athens of 250,000 inhabitants. While Jefferson decried large cities, much of the momentum and leadership for democratic revolution he so strongly supported was generated in the three largest cities of the day – Philadelphia, New York and Boston – and the movement toward parliamentary reform in Great Britain was centered in London. And Lin Piao's view of the encirclement of cities by rural areas is contrary to the worldwide process of urbanization which is now taking place among the agrarian three-fourths of humanity (Davis 1965: 41–53).

NOSTALGIA FOR THE RURAL IDEA Yet, even in modern *Gesellschaft* America, tradition can run strong, and our tradition is heavily weighted toward the rural. Daily, city dwellers get fed up and seek alternatives. The hippie movement spawned many rural communes. Thoreau's *Walden (Or Life In the Woods)* still sells very well. Makers of films about returning to the wilderness have found Americans eager for such movies. Jefferson's agrarian ideal and his dislike of mass urban centers is still evident today. We look back with nostalgia to the opening of the frontier, to breathing room, limited regulation of our lives by others, clean air and water. The city is viewed as the opposite of these desired goals: the absence of freedom, health, and opportunity.

The West, of course, was open country where farms could be started and small towns settled. Urbanization in the United States has happened so fast that life in the revered small town has been a vivid and positive memory for many, who recall for their children, grandchildren, and friends a time of apparent simplicity, stability, and warmth. Sociologists Robert and Helen Lynd reported the recollections of a physician in Muncie, Indiana, which in the nineteenth century was still considered the West (1929: 11–17):

HUMAN ECOLOGY AND THE CRISIS OF THE CITIES **307**

The ideal of small town agrarian living is still an attractive one for many Americans a generation after most find themselves living in the city. Nonetheless, many Americans find city living agreeable. SOURCE: (a) Eva Demjen/Stock Boston; (b) Grant Heilman.

The log farmhouse of his father was ceiled inside without plaster, the walls bare save for three prized pictures of Washington, Jackson, and Clay. All meals were cooked before the great kitchen fireplace, corn pones and "cracklings" and bread being baked in the glare of a large reflector set before the open fire. At night the rooms were lighted by the open fire and by tallow dips; there was great excitement later when the first candle mold appeared in the neighborhood. Standard time was unknown; few owned watches, and sun time was good enough during the day.... When the fire went out on the family hearth the boy ran to a neighbor's to bring home fire between two boards; it was not until later that the first box of little sticks tipped with sulfur startled the neighborhood....

Social calls were unknown, but all-day visits were the rule, a family going to visit by horseback.... Social intercourse provided a highly important service; there were no daily papers in the region, and much news traveled by word of mouth.

MYTH AND REALITY IN THE FRONTIER
The charming homelife pictured here was not the total story of Western development, of course. Griffin attributes some current urban problems to the frontier approach to keeping up the town (Griffin, 1974: 4–5):

The trash-littered streets of American cities are another expression, albeit a less lethal one, of frontier freedom. But this still potent American talent for fouling the urban environment is merely a pallid vestige of the frontiersman's talent. Everett Dick's book *The Sodhouse Frontier: 1854-1890,* depicts the stark historical facts. In the typical frontier town of Wichita, Kansas, the ground at the hitching post was a fly-infested cesspool. Superimposed on its heady odor was the stench of outhouses, pigpens, and garbage tossed freely into the street or left at the doorstep by these pristine rugged individualists. . . .

The price paid for these filthy freedoms only began with the stench. Spread by disease-bearing flies that fed on the filth of the outhouses and streets, typhoid epidemics sometimes swept through entire towns, as did cholera, smallpox and diphtheria. . . . The primitive technology of that time and place made adequate sanitation a difficult achievement, and frontier medicine was just this side of witchcraft. But the mentally musclebound individualism of the frontier, with its contempt for public sanitation, helped to extort a graver price than was necessary from the health of frontier townsmen.

Such observations are not typical of views about the virtues of small-town living. As Arthur Vidich and Joseph Bensman found in their study of Springdale, in upper New York State, within twenty-five miles of three different commercial-industrial centers, the values of small-town America are tenaciously held by the townspeople, who refer to themselves as "just plain folks." The term *folks* means to these people (1958: 30–31):

First and foremost, the term serves to distinguish Springdalers from urban dwellers, who are called "city people," an expression which by the tone in which it is used implies the less fortunate, those who are denied the wholesome virtues of rural life. City people are separated from nature and soil, from field and stream, and are caught up in the inexorable web of impersonality and loneliness, of which the public statement in Springdale is: "How can people stand to live in cities?"

THE POPULARITY OF SMALL TOWNS
People in cities, when asked where they prefer to live, also show pronounced preferences for small towns and rural areas. While over half the people sampled in a national public opinion survey lived in medium-sized or large cities or suburbs (Table 10-2), almost two-thirds reported that they would prefer living in the open country or small towns. Perhaps most telling is that while only 12 percent lived in open country, 34 percent said they would prefer to do so.

THE REALITY OF SMALL TOWN–BIG CITY INTERDEPENDENCE Just how accurate is this image of country versus city? We are dealing here with qualitative values about the good life in a good community, and cannot be precise. Nevertheless, it appears that both views are exaggerated and do not reflect the social realities. Furthermore, these views do not touch the importance of the close interdependence between cities and small towns. The city depends on surrounding areas for workers, consumers, and suppliers of essential items such as its food supply. Smalltowners may work in the city, but even staying home, they still depend upon the city and its products. The Springdaler who dislikes New York City may confirm his opinion by reading the New York *Times*, which he also scans for advertisements of products that may be unavailable in Springdale.

INTEREST GROUPS AND SOCIAL STATUS ON MAIN STREET One way to get at the realities of rural and urban living is to seek out the basic concerns of those faced with the impersonality and loneliness of the city. It is clear that blacks, Chicanos, and other minorities are often excluded from many opportunities available to whites in cities, but small towns also have their out-groups. Vidich and Bensman found that farmers of Polish background, and small farmers more generally, were excluded from much of the township decisionmaking process, and their interests were underrepresented (157):

> The political biases of the [township board] are revealed in the condition of specific roads and in the location of good roads. These biases reflect those forces in the community, the prosperous farmers, who can make the board act.

The warmth of small-town life does not always envelop those who do not fit the pattern. Nobel prizewinning novelist Sinclair Lewis made this point in his novel *Main Street* (1920). The protagonist, Carol Milford, is conversing with Maud Dyer, a community social leader. Mrs. Dyer is critical of Mrs. Mott, wife of the superintendent of schools, who wishes to improve the old schoolhouse and upgrade the quality of schooling (1920: 133):

> Oh, so Mrs. Mott has got you going on her school craze! She's been dinging at that till everybody's sick and tired. What she really wants is a big office for her dear bald-headed Gawge to sit around and look important in. Of course I admire Mrs. Mott, and I'm very fond of her, she's so brainy, even if she does try to butt in and run The Thanatopsis [ladies' book discussion club], but I must say we're sick of her nagging. The old build-

Table 10-2   Actual and Preferred Community Settings

	Where do you live now? (percent)	Where would you prefer to live? (percent)
Open country	12	34
Small town or city	33	30
Medium-sized city or suburb	28	22
Larger city or suburb	27	14
	100	100

SOURCE: Based on a national public opinion survey by the Opinion Research Corporation in 1971 conducted for the Commission on Population Growth and the American Future, as reported in *Population and the American Future* (New York: New American Library, 1972), p. 36.

ing was good enough for us when we were kids! I hate these would-be women politicians, don't you?

The year 1920 was one of profound changes in the society. That year the U.S. Census first found that a majority of Americans were living in cities. And that year Lewis found a new urban audience that was beginning to identify with life in cities and question their former ways.

MALADJUSTMENTS IN THE COMMONS Social life in urban societies requires a high degree of social cooperation. Without it, an urban society may experience the "tragedy of the commons," as C. W. Griffin notes (1974: 14–15):

> Pollution and many other wasteful evils associated with urban growth and industrialization stem from the persistence of the frontier ethic in a drastically altered world totally unsuited for it. The inexorable mechanism at work is called *The Tragedy of the Commons* by biochemist Garrett Hardin. Consider a pasture open to

all — the commons. At a primitive, sparsely settled frontier stage of civilization, while the pasture or range offers a relatively bountiful feed supply, the community's herdsmen can use it freely without social distress. But once the grazing herds reach the critical number corresponding to the commons' food-supplying capacity, an inexorable process of deterioration sets in, unless the rules for the commons' use change drastically.

The reason the rules must change derives from a basic conflict between *individual* vs. *social* interests. To the individual herdsman, the addition of one animal to the herd represents a potential gain of plus 1, since he alone profits from the sale of an additional animal. The cost to the herdsman, however, is only a trivial fraction of minus 1, since all the herdsmen on the commons share the costs of one additional animal's grazing. Thus each herdsman, acting in his own self-interest, like Adam Smith's rational economic man, adds another, and another animal to his herd. There is an incentive to increase one's herd without limitation in a world of limited resources. . . .

Illustrations of the tragedy of the commons are ubiquitous. Public resources — water, air, and, to a lesser degree, land — are prime examples of a fixed, limited commons subjected to growing demand by a growing population. In a more restricted sense, privately distributed energy resources — electrical power, fuel oil, natural gas, and gasoline — each represent a commons. With the widening gap between supply and demand for our diminishing fossil-fuel reserves, we confront a tragedy of the commons that requires more efficient ways of reducing consumption and apportioning the use of these increasingly scarce resources. According to a recent federal study of apartment energy use, tenants in master-metered buildings consume 35% more electrical energy than tenants in individually metered buildings, where instead of sharing your waste with other tenants and the landlord, you pay for your own personal consumption. Master metering creates an energy commons, encouraging profligate waste.

Any exhaustible resource or service whose use is not economically regulated tends inevitably toward the tragedy of the commons. Free parking spaces, free use of crowded streets and highways promote congestion, air pollution and general inefficiency. New York's unmetered water supply encourages energy waste. It is never in an individual's economic interest to replace the washer in a dripping faucet; it is cheaper to share the cost of leakage with millions of other taxpayers.

ADJUSTING TO URBAN LIVING The anomie built into urban life theorized by Park, Burgess, Wirth, and others of the Chicago School may have been a characteristic of early urbanization, including the immigrants' quest for new roots as ghettos formed. By mid century, analysts began to find that most city people were not in an anomic state generally characterized by impersonality, anonymity, and secondary social relations (see Axelrod, 1956; Rogers, 1961). Most people did have informal relationships that were likely to be personal, close, and intimate. Typical was the report of Bell and Boat on four neighborhoods of different social types in San Francisco. In all four neighborhoods, whether of high or low income and many or few family ties, most people participated in informal social relations at least once a week. (Bell and Boat, 1957: 392.)

Urban living does not seem to breed alienation or to be as destructive as our stereotypes suggest. As we consider the pressing problems of cities, it will be useful to keep clear the realities of urban living. In part, such city problems as poverty, intergroup conflict, and the powerlessness of some individuals and groups are found in all communities, small or large. We associate them chiefly with cities only because most people live in metropolitan areas. Other problems, such as air pollution and traffic congestion, appear to be native to urban living.

EFFECTS OF ANTI-CITY BIAS The effects of our prejudice against cities still have to be taken into account. Urban problems are intense at least in part because of our agrarian heritage. There has been no consistent short- or long-range planning to handle them. Since most Americans now live in cities, it has become increasingly important that the nature of urban living be more fully understood. As the Protestant theologian Harvey Cox noted in *The Secular City* (1965), Americans and their institutions, including the churches, must come to terms with the reality that American society is urban. Only then can people individually and collectively manage the hard parts of urban living.

THEORIES OF ECOLOGICAL CONCENTRATION

The different kinds of population groups in urban areas are so unevenly distributed that a number of theories have been developed to help explain how and why income, racial, and other identifiable groups are concentrated where they are and participate in urban life as they do. One fruitful approach has been the development of urban ecology as part of the general field of human ecology. The main concern of human ecologists is to determine how human populations adapt to their natural environment[2] and how in the process social groups and institutions develop specific territorial arrangements, particularly in cities.

---

[2] Ecologists in the biological sciences have long employed the concept of natural environments to study how other species adapt to their spatial territorial settings. While sociologists have often borrowed the term *natural*, it is useful to keep in mind that human environments are heavily influenced by values and the cultural capability of controlling the physical environment in ways that other species' environments are not.

HUMAN ECOLOGY

From: Robert Park, "Human Ecology," *American Journal of Sociology* XLII (July, 1936), pp. 12, 33.

Like other Chicago School studies, plant and animal ecology provide the basis for theoretical development of urban analysis.

In recent years the plant geographers have been the first to revive something of the earlier field naturalists' interest in the interrelations of species. Haeckel, in 1878, was the first to give to these studies a name, "ecology," and by so doing gave them the character of a distinct and separate science....

The interrelation and interdependence of the species are naturally more obvious and more intimate within the common habitat than elsewhere. Furthermore, as correlations have multiplied and competition has decreased, in consequence of mutual adaptations of the competing species, the habitat and habitants have tended to assume the character of a more or less completely closed system.

Within the limits of this system the individual units of the population are involved in a process of competitive cooperation, which has given to their interrelations the character of a natural economy. To such a habitat and its inhabitants — whether plant, animal, or human — the ecologists have applied the term "community."

The essential characteristics of a community, so conceived, are those of: (1) a population, territorially organized, (2) more or less completely rooted in the soil it occupies, (3) its individual units living in a relationship of mutual interdependence....

Human ecology ... differs ... in important respects from plant and animal ecology. The interrelations of human beings and interactions of man and his habitat are comparable but not identical with interrelations of other forms of life that live together and carry on a kind of "biological economy" within the limits of a common habitat.

For one thing man is not so immediately dependent upon his physical environment as other animals. As a result of the existing world-wide division of labor, man's relation to his physical environment has been mediated through the intervention of other men. The exchange of goods and services has cooperated to emancipate him from dependence upon his local habitat.

Furthermore man has, by means of inventions and technical devices of the most diverse sorts, enormously increased his capacity for reacting upon and remaking, not only his habitat but his world. Finally, man has erected upon the basis of the biotic community an institutional structure rooted in custom and tradition.

THE CONCENTRIC ZONE THEORY Ecological models provide insight into the stages of urban development in America. During the 1920s, Ernest Burgess of the Chicago School advanced his *concentric zone theory**. This was at a time when the urban population of the United States was heavily concentrated within the legal limits of cities. Using Chicago as a model, Burgess observed that (1925: 50)

the typical processes of the expansion of the city can best be illustrated, perhaps, by a series of concentric circles, which may be numbered to designate both the successive zones of urban extension and the types of areas differentiated in the process of expansion.

As Figure 10-3 indicates, Burgess noted that the city population was most concentrated around the Loop, or downtown area (Zone I, with the poorest, the slum, next (Zone II), then second generation, or workingmen (Zone III). The outer zones (IV and V) contained the residences of the middle and upper socioeconomic groups. In attempting to test his model with empirical data, Burgess showed that from the Loop to the outer limit, the delinquency rates, ratio of males (many males indicates the absence of stabilizing values of family living), and percentage of foreign-born tended to decrease, while home ownership increased (1927: 178-184).

The north-south line in this circular concentric diagram has a specific and a general meaning. The specific meaning is that Chicago, which served as the prototype of Burgess's theory, is bordered on the east by Lake Michigan, which prevented Chicago's concentric zone expansion in that direction. The general meaning is that every American city of a million or more is bordered in at least one direction by water, which prevents total circular zone expansion.

The area with most problems was Zone II, which housed people in transition. Here lived first generation racial and ethnic minorities and low-income people generally. As Burgess described it (1925: 54-56):

In the zone of deterioration [Zone II in Figure 10-3] encircling the central business section are always to be found the so-called "slums" and "bad lands," with their submerged regions of poverty, degradation, and disease, and their underworlds of crime and vice. Within a deteriorating area are rooming-house districts, the purgatory of "lost souls".... The slums are also crowded to overflowing with immigrant colonies — the ghetto Little Sicily, Greektown, Chinatown — fascinatingly combining old world heritages and American adaptations. Wedging out from here is the Black Belt, with its free and disorderly life. The area of deterioration, while essentially one of decay, of stationary or declining population, is also one of regeneration... — all [are] obsessed with the vision of a new and better world.

GHETTOS This zone of deterioration houses the ghettos, originally Jewish settlements but now any segregated racial or cultural group. In a classic analysis, Louis Wirth described ghettos in the following terms (1928: ix-x):

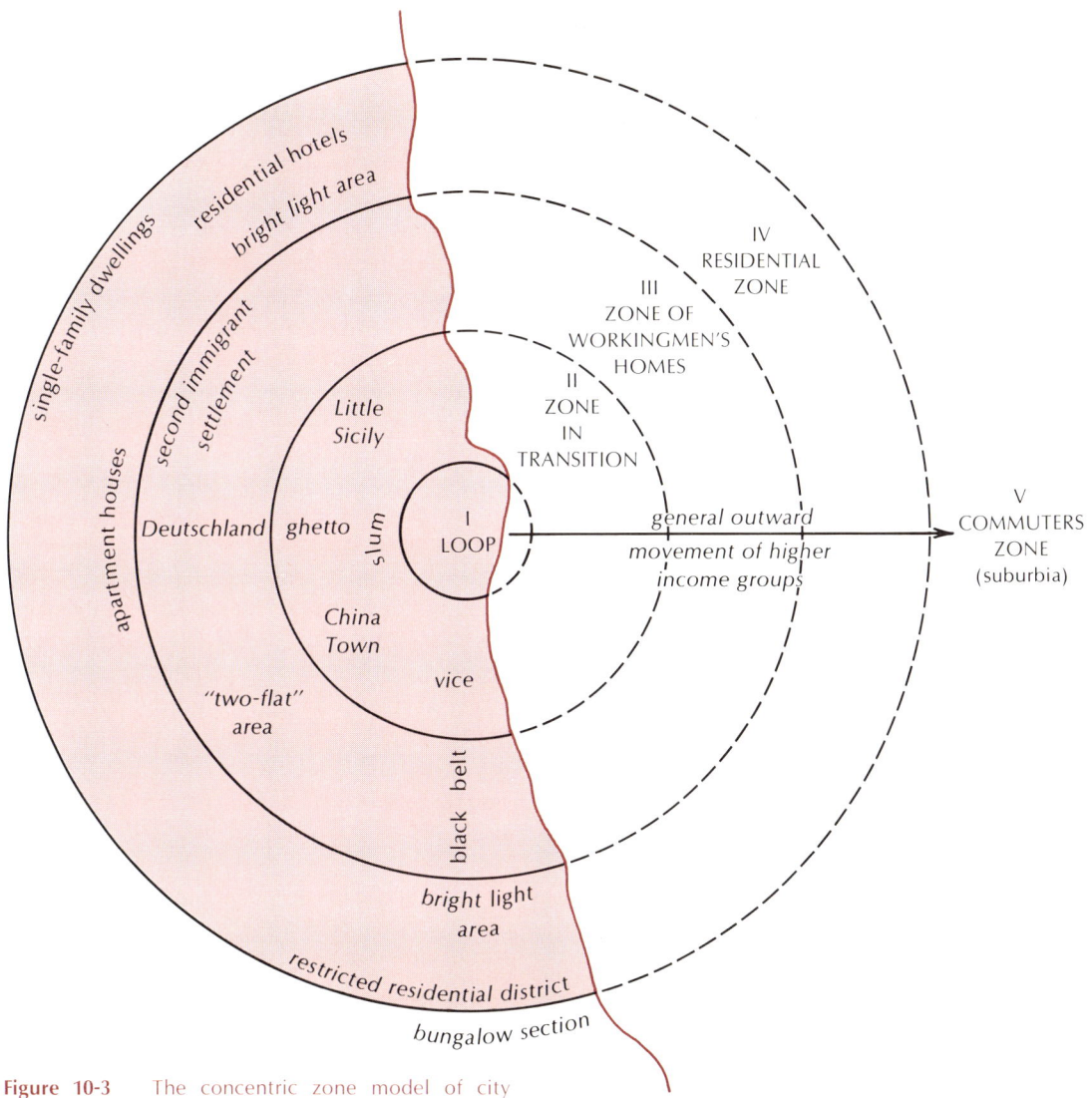

Figure 10-3 The concentric zone model of city growth. SOURCE: Adapted from "The Growth of the City," in R. Park and E. Burgess (eds.), *The City* (Chicago: University of Chicago Press, 1925), p. 55.

The ghetto seems to have been originally a place in Venice, a quarter of the city in which the first Jewish settlement was located. It became, in the course of time, an institution recognized in custom and defined in law. It became, in short, not merely the place in which Jews lived, but the place in which they were compelled to live. The walls of that ghetto have long since crumbled, but the ghost of the ancient institution lingers. It is still a place of refuge for the masses of the Jewish people and still imposes upon them, for good or ill, something of the ancient isolation.

Meanwhile other alien peoples have come among us who have sought, or had imposed upon them, the same sort of isolation. Our great cities turn out, upon examination, to be a mosaic of segregated peoples — differing in race, in culture, or merely in cult — each seeking to preserve its peculiar cultural forms and to maintain its individual and unique conceptions of life. Every one of these segregated groups inevitably seeks, in order to maintain the integrity of its own group life, to impose upon its members some kind of moral isolation. So far as segregation becomes for them a means to that end, every people and every cultural group may be said to create and maintain its own ghetto. In this way the ghetto becomes the physical symbol for that sort of moral isolation which the "assimilationists," so called, are seeking to break down. . . .

"Ghetto," as it is here conceived, is no longer a term that is limited in its application to the Jewish people. It has come into use in recent times as a common noun — a term which applies to any segregated racial or cultural group.[3]

Given the social, and often legal, pressures to force racial, religious or ethnic minority groups to segregate into ghettos by more dominant groups, this proposition of Wirth's calls for modification. Much of the motivating force in the creation and maintenance of ghettos was a response to hostile pressures from others in the urban communities. Evidence of this is clear from recent civil rights pressures to break down black and Chicano ghettos, as well as the earlier breakup of Jewish, Polish, Italian, and other tightly knit ghettos which existed in American cities at the time Wirth wrote his analysis in the 1920s. His point is well-taken, however, that the development of a ghetto is in part voluntary, to serve the interests of preservation of a common culture. For example, Jewish ghettos developed in part because of that religion's belief that one should walk to synagogue.

So many inner-city (that is, Zone II) ethnic and racial groupings have been evident in major American cities, that ghettos were viewed by the Chicago School ecologists as primary *natural areas* (McKenzie, 1925: 77). That is, distributions of population occur in a natural manner rather than through deliberate manipulations. Not all urbanologists, however, agree that such developments occur in a spontaneous, natural manner.

Whether natural or not, ghettos do exist. Indeed, this inner-city zone tends to experience successive ecological invasions of new poor groups which displace older ones in a process that ecologists call *succession* (Gist and Fava, 1969: 107). This process is analogous to plant and animal ecology, in which new species force others out of areas through success in competition for space and resources. Ghettos are unstable places, as evidenced by both internal deterioration and the outward movement of their inhabitants whenever possible.

As the population of urban areas spilled beyond the legal limits of cities into the suburbs to form larger ecological cities, new efforts were made to understand the evolving nature of urban social organization. In an updating of the concentric zone theory, Burgess, with Harvey Locke, extended the concentric model to include a suburban zone (1953: 101).

THE SECTOR THEORY The *sector theory**, developed by Homer Hoyt (1943: 475–492), challenged the concentric zone theory. Rather than focusing on one major city as Burgess did in Chicago, Hoyt gathered data from 142 American cities. The pattern he saw is illustrated in Figure 10-4. Automobile transportation and the new expressways and other roads resulted, by the late 1930s and 1940s, in a pattern of outward population movement along available transportation routes, or *sectors*, rather than in ever widening adjacent and concentric circles. Hoyt likened the growing American city to an

---

[3] From the foreword to Louis Wirth, *The Ghetto* (Chicago: University of Chicago Press, 1928), pp. ix-x. © 1928 by The University of Chicago. All rights reserved.

sector theory

multiple nuclei

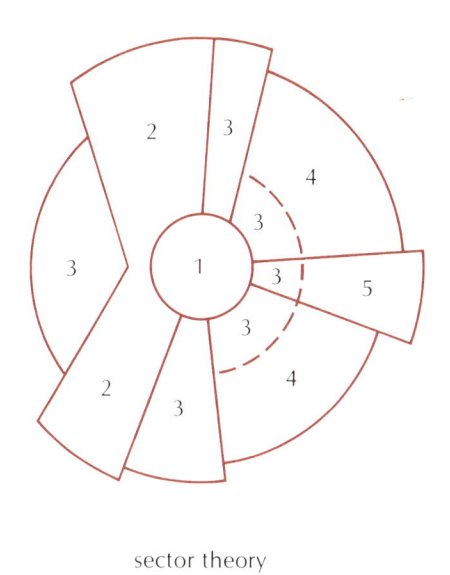

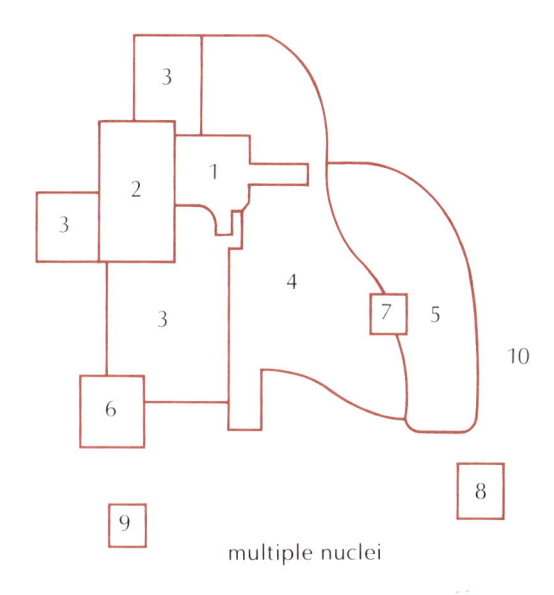

TWO GENERALIZATIONS OF THE
INTERNAL STRUCTURE OF CITIES

DISTRICT

1. central business district
2. wholesale light manufacturing
3. low-class residential
4. medium-class residential
5. high-class residential
6. heavy manufacturing
7. outlying business district
8. residential suburb
9. industrial suburb
10. commuters' zone

Figure 10-4 The sector and multiple nuclei models of urban development. SOURCE: Reprinted from "The Nature of the Cities" by C. D. Harris and E. L. Ullman in volume no. 242 of *The Annals of the American Academy of Political and Social Science*. Copyright 1945 by the American Academy of Political and Social Science.

octopus with tentacles extending in different directions along transportation lines.

THE MULTIPLE NUCLEI THEORY The next development in urban ecology was the *multiple nuclei theory** of Chauncey Harris and Edward Ullman (1954: 7–17). With expansion beyond city limits, Harris and Ullman observed the pattern illustrated in Figure 10-4. The multiple nuclei theory held that advanced metropolitan, urban–suburban development resulted in not one center in the city but several. According to this theory, as population density increases, subnuclei are formed. Note in Figure 10-4 that, in addition to the original central business district (Zone 1), there is an outlying business district (Zone 7). In this model, several Zone 7s emerge around new suburban residential areas.

SOCIAL AREA ANALYSIS A more sophisticated urban model, *social area analysis**, was developed by Shevky and Williams and by Bell (Shevky and Williams, 1949; Bell, 1959: 61–92). Using Los

Angeles, they added other social indicators to the methods of human ecology used by Burgess, Hoyt, and Harris and Ullman. The three major indices employed by Shevky and Williams and Bell were social rank, based on measures of occupation and education; urbanization, based primarily on measures of fertility and single versus multiple-dwelling residences; and segregation, based on measures of ecological segregation of ethnic or racial groups, a criterion of particular interest. The measures assume that persons who are disadvantaged are likely to have low social rank since they have no occupation or a low status occupation and inferior education; that persons of low status (and low income) are less likely than others to own their own homes, are more likely to have large families, and are more likely to be segregated from higher status persons into less desirable locations, such as the inner city. These assumptions are compatible with the development of immigrant communities in urban areas.

Shevky and Williams and Bell constructed an index which showed how much greater the concentration (segregation) of a group is than the group's proportional representation in the total urban area. If all individuals in a group were evenly distributed in all census tracts, the index would be 1. Since no groups were in fact so evenly distributed, all had an index of greater than 1, but few were so highly segregated as to reach an index of 3 or more (which would mean that their average concentration was 3 or more times what it would be if their distribution over the whole area were entirely *random**). It was found that blacks and Mexicans were particularly concentrated and that they tended to be quartered close to each other and near other highly concentrated groups such as Orientals and Italians. Similar concentrations were found in most American cities (Bell, 1959: 91–92).

It is interesting to note that one strong trend is reflected in all our urban models: all reflect major differences in social rank from lower to higher as the population moved toward the city limits and beyond. Thus, the ghetto areas observed by Burgess in the 1920s as concentrations of "submerged regions of poverty, degradation, and disease, and ... underworlds of crime and vice" continue at this writing. While earlier ghettos were primarily ethnic, the current ones are composed mainly of racial groups against whom there is long-standing *prejudice**.

POWER IN THE URBAN SETTING

The suburbs surrounding major cities are now statistically the most frequent American community setting. By 1980, over 60 million people are expected to be living in metropolitan areas (Banfield, 1970: 3), most of them in the suburban fringes. Why have so many Americans moved to the suburbs instead of remaining in the cities? A good deal of this population shift can be explained in terms of imperative ecological processes. Urban ecologists have generally held that there appears to be a natural movement toward the periphery of the city and beyond as a consequence of in-migration and natural population growth. Yet, when one reviews the research, it becomes evident that there is more in the appeal of suburbia than an inevitable outward thrust. Again, the small-town heritage has had its effect, enticing people away from central cities to the smaller and politically separate suburbs.

THE IMPACT OF THE MOVEMENT TO THE SUBURBS
The impact of this outward movement can be measured in a variety of ways. The suburbs draw people with high incomes and the most education. They contain the newer and more spacious housing and most of the middle- and upper-class whites, whereas most blacks of all social classes have remained in the cities. All these characteristics

bear on the overall crisis of the cities. Cities have sharply declining tax resources to handle growing needs for more and better schools, mass transit, fire and police protection, and a multitude of other normal needs. Note in Figure 10-5 how rapid has been the outward movement of whites who, with higher-paying jobs, are most capable of generating the tax base needed in cities. The overall effect is that, while blacks were one-quarter to one-half of most large city populations by 1970, they constituted less than 10 percent of the suburban population.

COMMUNITY POWER An overriding problem for people in the cities is that community power has moved to the suburbs. *Community power** is the ability of some individuals and groups to influence what will be done in a community by government and through private means (see the selection on this subject). Such power may be exercised by well-known and long-established local influentials or by cosmopolitan influentials (those whose influence reaches to other communities), who have an achieved status that gives them influence in a community (Merton, 1957: 400). A long-established metropolitan newspaper may serve as a local influential. A national political leader such as a senator may become a cosmopolitan influential.

METHODS OF MEASURING COMMUNITY POWER Various methods have been devised to study community power and who exercises it. Floyd Hunter, in his analysis of Atlanta, Georgia, used a *reputational* method (1953). After asking various elected and organization leaders who they thought were the community influentials, Hunter reported the existence of a power structure composed mostly of wealthy businessmen who did not

Figure 10-5 Center lines of white population and of Negro population, Detroit area, 1940, 1950, and 1960. SOURCE: Albert Mayer and Thomas Hoult, *Race and Residence in Detroit* (Detroit: Wayne State University Press, 1962), pp. 10-11.

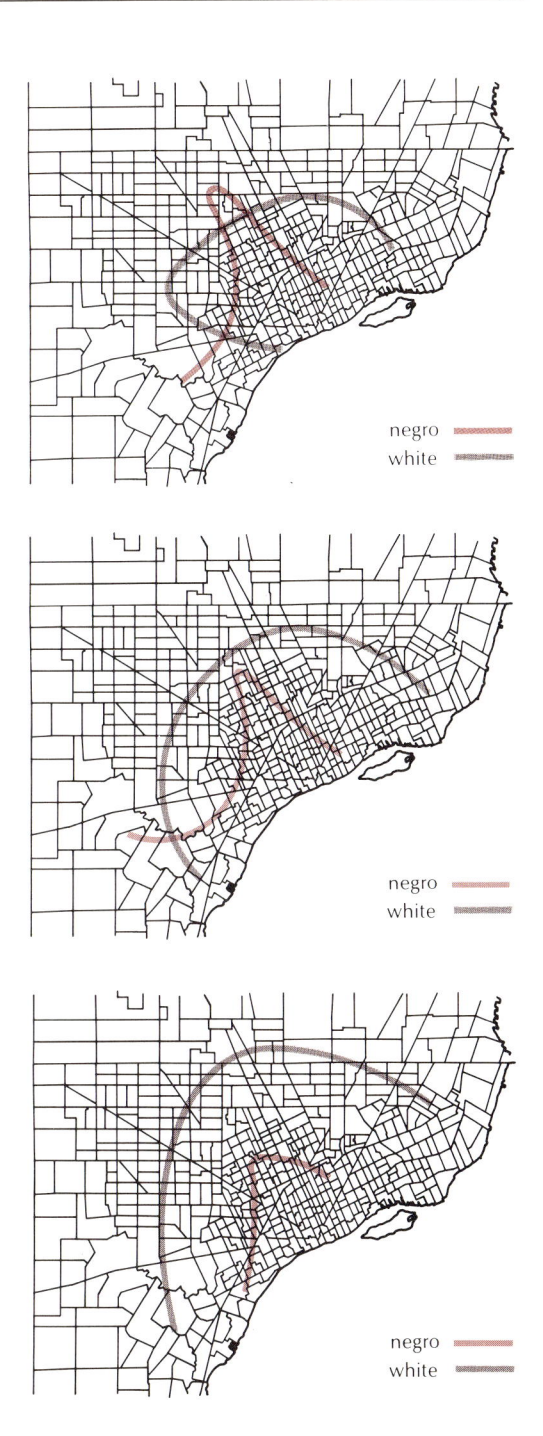

hold formal political positions but who had a determining influence in nearly all important community decisions. Helen and Robert Lynd, in their analysis of Muncie, Indiana, used a *positional* method (1937). They identified the power elite by such characteristics as their family wealth, their key positions in local government or private industry, and their leadership in such community organizations as the community fund and church groups. Nelson Polsby, in his analysis of New Haven, Connecticut, used a *functional* method (1959). He identified the community power elite by their functions in decision-making on such public issues as political nominations, school millage proposals (operating expenses), and urban redevelopment. All these studies and others (see Grimes, Bonjean, Lyon, and Lineberry, 1976; Bonjean and Olson, 1964) show that the distribution of power in American communities is characterized by a wide variety of types and arrangements.

COMMUNITY POWER

From: Floyd Hunter, *Community Power Structure* (New York: Anchor Books, 1953), pp. 2, 4, 5.

... The community is a primary power center ... it is a place in which power relations can be most easily observed ... power is defined in terms of men and their actions in relation to one another. ... Power is a word ... used to describe the acts of men going about the business of moving other men to act in relation to themselves or in relation to organic or inorganic things.

The men in the city who influence others in power relationships are cognizant of values. They, as well as the men of lesser power, recognize that power-wielding is functional in the society of which they are a part. Most men in the city apparently believe that goods and services must be moved toward definite objectives. The observable "business" of the city would indicate that this activity is deemed valuable. The real question of conflicting values in the situation arises over who is to derive the most benefit from the composite activity.

COMMUNITY POWER REVISITED

From: Taylor Branch, "Who's in Charge Now?" *Harper's Weekly*, vol. LXIV (May 16, 1975): 13. Copyright © 1975 by Harper's Magazine Co. Reprinted from the May 16, 1975, issue of Harper's Weekly by special permission.

Hunter documented the Atlanta power structure in 1953. In the following article, a current resident of Atlanta comments on the changes that have occurred. This narrative reminds us of the power of the electoral process as a vehicle for change.

Atlanta is the only city I know where everyone speaks openly, and often fondly, of "the power structure."

Back in the Eisenhower era, sociologist Floyd Hunter made the first relatively scientific attempt to determine exactly who held what political power in an urban area. Atlanta was his laboratory, and he concluded to no one's surprise that a small and well-defined circle of businessmen made virtually every important decision in the city.

He masked the leaders with pseudonyms, but their identities were no secret to the natives: Ivan Allen, Jr., president of the Chamber of Commerce; Robert Woodruff, president of Coca Cola; Richard Rich, president of Atlanta's largest department store; Mills Lane, president of the C & S bank; Jack Tarver, president of the company owning the city's two newspapers.

These men and a few others were the power structure, or the "Chamber crowd." It was believed that they planned highways at lunch, elections at the club, new museums and airports at board meetings of the elite civic groups to which they all belonged. They all came from old families in a rather *nouveau* city, and they provided leadership in keeping with the loftiest fantasies of liberal Republicans elsewhere.

These men were too smart to be reactionary, too honorable and genteel to be corrupt, too refined to be hard bigots, and too well established to become shortsighted or trapped in the demands of the moment. When other Southern cities pulled out their cattle prods and fire hoses to meet the civil rights movement, Atlanta's power structure advertised its collective decision to rise above that sort of thing. Atlanta would keep a progressive eye on the future, they said, and the path to growth and harmony was declared to be one of racial progress.

In 1964, the power structure was at the height of both its power and its vision. Ivan Allen, Jr., had moved smoothly from the Chamber to the mayor's chair, and he was the only city official in the South to testify in favor of the 1964 Civil Rights Act.

The Chamber of Commerce was following through on Allen's idea to launch a "Forward Atlanta" campaign — a multimilliondollar national advertising blitz promoting Atlanta as "a city too busy to hate." The city was pictured as the next American Mecca, free of Southern lassitude and Northern decay, and to some extent it was true. With buoyant optimism, Mayor Allen and the Chamber started a building program designed to make Atlanta the South's first "big league city."

It worked. The metropolitan population doubled within five years, and the downtown skyline became impressive enough for the Chamber to use aerial photographs in its ads in the *New Yorker*. Atlanta acquired a national reputation as the "Camelot of the South," and Ralph McGill, editor of the Atlanta *Constitution*, was widely admired for his long crusade in favor of civil rights.

Now, ten years later, everything seems turned on its head, the power structure definitely evicted. Maynard Jackson, Atlanta's first black mayor, has led a whole group of black politicians into city offices, and the old white business leaders gather at the club mostly for bitter nostalgia. The power structure lost its first city election in 1969, and its members can no longer make even their traditional private arrangements for city improvements.

Meanwhile, American urban blight caught up with Camelot. Whites have fled to the suburbs in droves, leaving the city's public schools more than 80 percent black. Atlanta leads the nation in several grisly crime categories. Businesses have moved to the suburbs, and several white leaders see Newark down the road. Unemployment has grown almost tenfold in the last four years.

The optimistic Chamber has sunk so deep in gloom that it replaced the "Forward Atlanta" slogan with "Look Up, Atlanta," a Bunyanesque phrase exhorting the city's residents to lift their eyes from the muck.

At the *Constitution*, even the spirit of the late McGill has expired. Last month, the paper ran a series of articles called "City in Crisis," which was basically a requiem for the old power structure and a blast at Maynard Jackson. Writers and editors strung together snide, bilious comments about the city, laying out their "diagnosis" of Atlanta's ills. The series fit comfortably in the country's cynical mood, but it was filled with a negativism new to the self-confident Atlanta.

Last week, *Harper's Weekly* interviewed several of Atlanta's leaders, old and new, seeking their comments on what has happened to the city's political structure. Almost unanimously, they expressed positive feelings about the city's direction, and they were disappointed with the tone and the quality of the newspapers. I found their optimism reflected in the city streets, but not in the *Constitution* or in the white suburbs.

Not all urban areas can be evaluated simply in terms of a power elite; they may have a pluralistic power structure made up of diverse power groups. The community may include conflicting special interest groups and coalitions put together to secure common goals. The more centers of power there are in a community, the higher the probability of innovative community action (Urofsky, 1973: 20–21).

The members of a community power elite, whether or not they are widely known in the community, hold influential positions in its institutions and associations. Thus, a project may be developed to remove slum housing or to build a new expressway or to determine the location of a new community college. All studies show that influentials and influential groups often press for their own particular needs without regard for the needs of others in the community. Thus, low-cost slum housing may be replaced by high-cost high-rise apartments or commercial enterprises. This may meet the felt needs of many in the upper-middle and upper classes but may leave those who had occupied the low-cost housing worse off than before urban renewal began in their neighborhood. The degree to which pressure groups and coalitions exist to combat the decisions of the elite becomes visible in legal actions and demonstrations to protest them. Such groups are most likely to be formed where people live close to each other and interact with each other; congested urban areas are naturally conducive to such development.

Where does the operation of the community power structure leave those in the central cities, particularly the ghettos? In the black and Chicano sections of Los Angeles, the population density ranges between 10,000 and 15,000 per square mile, while in the outer parts of the city and the suburbs the average density is less than 2,000 per square mile. In black Harlem, the population density is so great that if it were the same in all five boroughs of New York City, the city's population would equal the entire U.S. population of over 200 million. The human consequences of such close living were graphically described by a Los Angeles real estate expert after the racial rioting of 1965 (Jacobs, 1967: 147):

... when you go and look at the riots in the country, you'll see areas where a house is housing probably three families where there ought to be one.... Maybe those places are housing even five or six times more people than they should. Then you get hot, muggy weather and you've got two or three people in a single bedroom. So what do you do if you're living like that? You go out on the streets. You get some relief out there, and you know if you go back to that house, it's going to be noisy and you're going to have all those people around. You can't even get any rest, so why not stay out on the streets or go over to the park?

And you do that two or three nights in a row and you're losing sleep. You're getting irritated. And no one is doing anything to improve the conditions. So, if you get a chance, you riot.

The testimony of a minister from the Hough area in Cleveland points up some of the consequences of life in ghettos for many individuals and their families (Testimony, 1968: 15):

I find it very difficult when I talk to a man who is out of work who has been trying very hard to get work and who says to me, "I think I am going to leave my family so that they can get on ADC."[4] I find it very difficult to advise him not to because it is life and death that we are talking about. It is hunger and some of our people are so hungry for a day before they will come to the church and ask as a last-ditch desperate attempt to get help for food.

CONSEQUENCES OF GHETTO CONDITIONS People locked into such conditions commit crimes against persons and property in the deteriorating sections of cities. Even allowing for the unreliability of crime statistics, urban murder and robbery rates run to several times the rates found in the suburbs (FBI, Uniform Crime Reports, 1971: 127). Although looting is not found by researchers to be generally common in disasters, it was a serious problem in the rioting that occurred in Los Angeles (1965), Cleveland (1966), Detroit (1967), and elsewhere (*Report of the National Advisory Commission*, 1968: 113). In fact, it was so extensive that the disorders can be viewed as commodity riots. A careful review of dozens of urban riots shows that they

---

[4] ADC is Aid to Dependent Children, provided by the federal welfare system, which until recently has generally excluded aid to households in which a healthy adult male resides.

were less a direct interracial conflict than a venting by ghetto residents of their collective rage against the deteriorating conditions in their neighborhoods (see Fogelson and Hill, 1968). Furthermore, the rioting cut across racial lines. As Warren reported of the Detroit riot (1971: 121):

Both white and Negro looters were present in riot areas and were often described as "buddy-buddy" by Negro residents.... Spontaneous white hostility or retaliation against Negroes, as reported in [the] 1943 [riots], was absent.

The strong consensus in all social classes of the black community that conditions are deteriorating is clear from other research findings. Note in Table 10-3 that in Detroit both low-income blacks in the riot area and middle-income blacks beyond the riot area saw the causes of the rioting in precisely the same way: poor housing, lack of jobs, poverty, and police brutality. Research in other cities where there was rioting confirmed the disenchantment of middle-class blacks with conditions of city life. In all the riots, counterrioters, largely middle-class blacks, attempted to end the conflict. In a study of counterrioters in Columbus, Ohio, Indianapolis, Indiana, and Youngstown, Ohio, it was found that (Anderson, Dynes, Quarantelli, 1974: 55):

Counterrioters do not necessarily support the status quo ... [their] activities [often] reflect[ed] their considerable involvement in the black protest movement of which urban disturbances have come to be an integral part ... counterrioters ... generally support the ends toward which the protest is directed, if not always the means....

Rioting and other responses to deteriorating conditions reflect the powerlessness felt by many in cities, particularly those in the ghettos. Lack of jobs, humiliating welfare applications, confinement to inferior housing, all are seen as a result of

Table 10-3 Selected Riot Causes as Perceived by Detroit Area Blacks Following the July 1967 Riot — Rank Ordered

Low-income riot area sample[a]	Upper-income northwest area sample[b]	Middle-income Detroit-wide sample[c]
Police brutality	Poor housing	Police brutality
Poor housing	Lack of jobs	Poor housing
Lack of jobs	Poverty	Lack of jobs
Poverty	Police brutality	Poverty
Disappointment with white public officials	Disappointment with white public officials	Disappointment with white public officials
Teen-agers	Teen-agers	Teen-agers
Black nationalism	Black nationalism	Black nationalism
[d]	Too much welfare	Too much welfare

[a] 437 respondents
[b] 188 respondents
[c] 392 respondents
[d] "Too much welfare" not listed in this survey.

SOURCE: Donald Warren, "Community Dissensus," in L. Gordon (ed.), *A City in Racial Crisis* (Dubuque, Iowa: Wm. C. Brown Company, 1971), p. 145.

the Man having the power to take the best for himself. The phrase used by blacks, having the Man's foot on one's neck, symbolizes the sense of powerlessness felt by many. A study of Chicago, where the black population is almost one-third of the total, found that blacks were systematically excluded from important policymaking positions both in local government and in private organizations (Barron, 1968). This lack of community power has been a driving force in the emergence of Black

Power, Chicano Power, Red Power, and other organized social movements in recent years. Like the civil disorders, some of the "power" rhetoric has been alarming to many whites, as when Stokely Carmichael and Charles Hamilton stated in *Black Power* that (1967: 53):

Those of us who advocate Black Power are quite clear in our own minds that a "non-violent" approach to civil rights is an approach black people cannot afford and a luxury white people do not deserve. It is crystal clear to us — and it must become so with the white society — *that there can be no social order without social justice.* White people must be made to understand that they must stop messing with black people, or the blacks *will* fight back!

ALIENATION AND ORGANIZATION   Most blacks and members of other alienated groups appear to agree with Carmichael and Hamilton that organized power is necessary and that change is needed now, not in some distant future; but most appear to want to work within the system and without violence. Bayard Rustin has noted that there is a movement toward organized political coalitions to improve the conditions of life in the cities. He observed and advocated the merger of Black Power and coalition politics with other minorities and with whites who support redevelopment of the deteriorating cities (1966: 334–40).

The emergence of legitimized political influence of urban blacks is evident by the election of black mayors, for the first time, in Cleveland, Detroit, Los Angeles, and Washington, D.C. These mayors, like everyone else in America's big cities, confront the long-term task of reconstruction and redevelopment. Given the economic interrelationship of so many suburbanites with the cities, the health and welfare of entire metropolitan areas, and thus of American society itself, is affected by the successes and failures of the big cities. The federal assistance in 1975 from a reluctant President Ford for a nearly bankrupt New York City is indicative of wide recognition of this hard reality.

NEW YORK AS EVERYCITY   The problems of New York City are widely publicized. That they are not yet over and that there are still many outstanding debts is less well-known. Short-run federal assistance helped with only the most immediate fiscal problems of the city and was tied to promises of internal reforms. Other problems remain. For a number of years, the city spent more money than it had and borrowed to balance the budget until deficits reached over $3.3 billion. In 1975, the city's short-term debt reached $6.2 billion, and the city borrows about $500 million a month to convert old maturing debts to new loans (Lalli, 1975: 8). It is not surprising that banks and other lending institutions become leery of extending more credit, nor that federal government officials are loath to add such debts to their responsibilities. But the bills keep increasing, and must be paid, in part by federal taxation of suburbanites who are still economically connected to the big cities.

With shrinking tax bases, inefficient city government, increasing wage demands from city workers, and accelerating indebtedness, New York City is an unfortunate model for the financial woes of major American cities. Money troubles mean reduced services or more indebtedness; reduced services mean continuation of denied opportunities in jobs, in school, in housing.

URBAN PLANNING

What needs to be done in the cities is increasingly clear to most Americans. The most highly visible problems are the need for better schools, housing, job opportunities, transportation systems, and intergroup relations. The question facing us, then, is not *what* needs to be done but *how* it is to be done. The problems of the cities have been increasing throughout this century, and there have been growing efforts to deal with them. Indeed, the developing concern with the nature of urbanism, with ghettos, and with community power is symptomatic of this interest in developing a constructive approach to city living.

The history of private, unplanned growth in American cities has increasingly led to government programs to relieve the worst features of city life. These programs have developed, particularly since the New Deal of the 1930s, as aspects of urban renewal (Greer, 1965: 13). Because of American society's Gemeinschaft, small-town heritage, large-scale coordinated urban planning was not part of the urban renewal process until well into the 1960s. Private economic interests have seldom participated in community-wide planning, nor, until recently, have local or federal governments. The programming that did develop tended to be isolated. Some federal and local funding programs were developed for schools, others for building expressways (as noted in Hoyt's sector theory), and still others to offer welfare assistance to the unemployed and the unskilled urban poor.

SLUM CLEARANCE AND HOUSING PROJECTS Efforts at urban renewal have centered on slum clearance and housing. The goals of the Urban Renewal Agency (URA), which was set up in the 1930s, were stated in the Housing Act of 1949 (Section 2, 1961):

The Congress hereby declares that the general welfare and security of the nation and the health and living standards of its people require housing production and related community development sufficient to remedy the serious housing shortage, the elimination of substandard and other inadequate housing through the clearance of slums and blighted areas, and the realization as soon as feasible of the goal of a decent home and a suitable living environment for every American family, thus contributing to the development and redevelopment of communities and the advancement of the growth, wealth, and security of the nation.

The wish to include all individuals and groups is made explicit in the act, which further states that (Section 3)

appropriate local bodies shall be encouraged and assisted to undertake positive programs of encouraging and assisting the development of well-planned, integrated, residential neighborhoods, the development and redevelopment of communities and the production, at lower costs, of housing of sound standards of design, construction, livability, and size for adequate family life....

The statement of such national goals is tacit recognition that, for many within the cities, life is very difficult. While the term *ghetto* is not used, the terms *slums* and *blighted areas* are. The goal of developing "well-planned, integrated residential neighborhoods" recognizes that many neighborhoods have had little or poor planning and are racially segregated. The references to the American family and family life highlight the difficulties of establishing and maintaining a family in a deteriorating urban neighborhood.

It is clear, then, that the problem has been recognized at the highest governmental level; but what has been the result of these fragmented efforts to do something about urban deterioration? For those in greatest need of genuine urban renewal, the consequences of the programs have often been social disaster. As Scott Greer succinctly observed in 1965 (3):

At a cost of more than three billion dollars the Urban Renewal Agency (URA) has succeeded in materially reducing the supply of low-cost housing in American cities. Like highways and streets, the program has ripped through the neighborhoods of the poor, powered by the right of eminent domain.[5] From Boston to San Francisco, from Portland, Oregon to Portland, Maine, hundreds of American cities and their citizens are involved.

MEGALOPOLIS AS A FOCUS OF PLANNING There is a pressing need for organized community-wide efforts to formulate more effective urban renewal planning and renewal programs. Such planning must take account of the new urban reality. No longer, as in the days of Wirth's and Burgess's analyses of urban life in the 1920s and 1930s, does the overwhelming majority of urban residents reside in central cities. Some communities have even moved beyond the metropolitan city-suburban SMSAs designated by the Census Bureau as urban areas in the 1950s and 1960s.

An increasing number of Americans are concentrated in a type of urban entity known as *megalopolis**. The term was originally used by the ancient Greeks, who planned a great new city-state in the Peloponnesus. Today, it is used to describe a unit

---

[5] Eminent domain is the legal authority for government to appropriate, with compensation, land and property deemed necessary for public use.

A partial view of urban concentration, described by Jean Gottmann in his analysis of the megalopolis phenomenon. SOURCE: Elliott Erwitt/Magnum.

of two or more cities, once separated by broad expanses of open country but now joined by continuous strips of urban or semiurban settlement. The northeastern seaboard, with a population of about 40 million people in 1970, encompassing an almost continuous stretch of urban and suburban areas from north of Boston to south of Washington, D.C., is a megalopolis. The makings of other megalopolis settlements are discernible in the Chicago-Cleveland and the San Diego-San Francisco corridors. Jean Gottmann, who revived the term, makes this observation about the phenomenon (1961: 4–5; 8):

As one follows the main highways or railroads between Boston and Washington, D.C., one hardly loses sight of built-up areas, tightly woven residential communities, or powerful concentrations of manufacturing plants. Flying this same route one discovers, on the other hand, that behind the ribbons of densely occupied land along the principal arteries of traffic, and in between the clusters of suburbs around the old urban centers, there still remain large areas covered with woods and brush alternating with some carefully cultivated patches of farmland. These green spaces, however, when inspected at closer range, appear stuffed with a loose but immense scattering of buildings, most of them residential but some of industrial character. That is, many of these sections that look rural actually function largely as suburbs in the orbit of some city's downtown. Even the farms, which occupy the larger tilled patches, are seldom worked by people whose only occupation and income are properly agricultural. And yet these farm areas produce large quantities of farm goods!

Thus the old distinctions between rural and urban do not apply here anymore. Even a quick look at the vast area of Megalopolis reveals a revolution in hard use. Most of the people living in the so-called rural areas, and still classified as "rural population" by recent censuses, have very little, if anything, to do with agriculture. In terms of their interests and work they are what used to be classified as "city folks"....

Megalopolis provides the whole of America with so many essential services, of the sort a community used to obtain in its "downtown" section, that it may well deserve the nickname of "Main Street of the nation."

This Main Street is getting longer and making the urban planning process more complex. As early as 1950, at the very beginning of the suburban movement, the need for more and better transportation was obvious. Figure 10-6 shows that the daytime population of major cities tends to increase by the tens of thousands. Since many suburbanites continue to work and enjoy recreation in the central cities, or simply pass through them, the problem of planning roads or mass transit systems to move people efficiently in and out of cities cannot be solved by any city or suburb alone. While many suburbanites feel the need for improved transportation, they are not so quick to see the need for good housing, schools, and jobs in the cities where they no longer reside. Indeed, by the 1970s, most young suburbanites had never resided in central cities.

The suburban movement also has materially reduced the local tax resources of the central cities. Even though city population has remained substantial, it is made up of larger proportions of low-income individuals — the aged, the very young, and racial minorities — who especially need better jobs, housing, schools, and other elements of stable living. Thus, while the tax-related needs of people in the cities have been rising, the taxing ability of cities has been declining, leaving many in a depressed state with no apparent hope for development.

Figure 10-6 Increase of daytime over resident population. SOURCE: Wilfred Owen, *The Metropolitan Transportation Problem* (New York: Anchor Books, 1966), p. 11. Copyright © 1966 by the Brookings Institution, Washington, D.C.

URBAN RENEWAL: PROBLEMS AND PROSPECTS Can we save our cities? This is the title of a public affairs pamphlet by Maxwell Stewart (1966), who stressed the need for community-wide involvement in urban renewal designed to stabilize life in the central cities. Past efforts met the needs of higher-income city dwellers, whose cause was often advanced by special-interest groups, particularly local business and labor organizations. This process contributed to the concentration of blacks and generally low-income groups in ghettos. The largely urban civil rights movement of the late 1950s and early 1960s, and the subsequent racial rioting, made it abundantly clear that a new approach to urban renewal was needed. The conditions which make urban rioting and protest likely are not alleviated by the destruction of existing homes and work sites. Opportunities do not spring phoenix-like from their ashes. One can add any number of variations to this observation, including the danger to local, and ultimately national, democracy unless a new communal equilibrium is reached.

THE DEMONSTRATION CITIES PROGRAM   Aware of the need, Congress in 1963 enacted the Demonstration Cities program (generally known as the Model Cities program), beginning with a two-year appropriation of approximately $1 billion (Stewart, 1966: 11). This program was meant to stimulate local governments and private individuals and groups to develop a model city plan to halt deterioration. Once a plan was developed by a wide variety of city-based and suburban citizens and organizations, funding could then be secured from the federal government. To qualify, a city administration had to document the involvement of different local citizen interests. This meant that spokesmen for a variety of business, labor, civil rights, and other organizations had to have a chance to express their views about what was needed. Here, in order of priority, is a list of needed programs developed by this process in Detroit (Gordon, 1965):

1. slum clearance of dilapidated buildings in the inner city

2. development of low-cost housing for people displaced by slum clearance

3. development of improved public schooling in poverty impacted neighborhoods

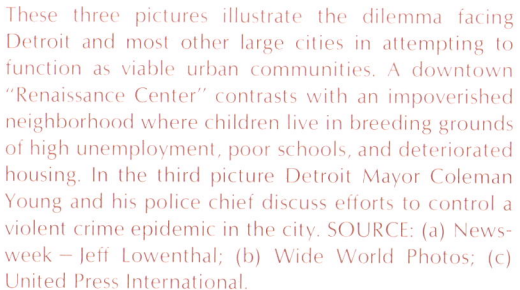

These three pictures illustrate the dilemma facing Detroit and most other large cities in attempting to function as viable urban communities. A downtown "Renaissance Center" contrasts with an impoverished neighborhood where children live in breeding grounds of high unemployment, poor schools, and deteriorated housing. In the third picture Detroit Mayor Coleman Young and his police chief discuss efforts to control a violent crime epidemic in the city. SOURCE: (a) Newsweek — Jeff Lowenthal; (b) Wide World Photos; (c) United Press International.

4. development of job training programs for unskilled adults

5. development of low-cost metropolitan mass transit to enable inner-city dwellers to work in the suburbs and ease the mobility of suburbanites into the central city

6. stimulation through zone variances and tax incentives for new commercial construction within the central city, particularly in the downtown area

7. encouragement of public officials to build within the older sections of the city new county (or state) and local government offices

8. development of middle- and high-cost apartments and housing units to attract back into the city some of those who had moved to the suburbs

9. construction of new expressways to reduce the congestion of auto traffic

Was this broad range of programs and priorities comprehensively carried out in Detroit? If you live in Detroit, you know the answer. Indeed, for Detroit, and for every other city in the nation, the answer has been No. It was one thing for cities to develop the many proposals necessary to meet the needs. It was, and is, quite a different matter to get the programs implemented in a coordinated and effective manner. If there is to be a stable and promising future for American cities, there must be a radical reshaping of urban community life. The difficulties in achieving this goal stem from the cities and from American society as a whole. Practical limitations on funding are obvious. Just as power groups within cities vie for funds, so cities vie with each other. Within a year after the Demonstration Cities bill was passed, over 800 towns and cities had developed projects that were funded to some extent (Stewart, 1966: 14). Then, through the late 1960s and into the early 1970s, American involvement in the Vietnam War drew away billions of tax dollars that had been projected for use in the Demonstration Cities program.

The result was that no city or metropolitan area was able to carry out at one time all the projects detailed in the various proposals. The traditional community power factors generally came into play. As a result, many projects of interest to less influential and poor citizens were delayed while projects favored by more influential interests were developed. Thus, in terms of the nine-point program listed above, after slum clearance (1), the next steps Detroit took related to expressway construction (9), the development of high-cost apartments (8), the construction of new government buildings (7), and the stimulation of new downtown commercial enterprises (6). In short, the priority list was reversed as soon as the local community power structure began to influence the model city plan. The general result is that life in the ghettos of America's cities has continued to deteriorate.

BENEFACTORS OF URBAN RENEWAL Harrison charges that professional planners support a class-biased use of urban renewal by accepting an elitist conception of what constitutes a slum — an older neighborhood, a neighborhood of mixed land use, a politically powerless neighborhood (Harrison, 1974: 144). These characteristics do not necessarily mean that the area should be destroyed, but demands by whites for central city space may push decisions in that direction. Displacement leaves minorities and the poor at an increasing disadvantage. As Harrison notes (1974: 144–145):

urban renewal programs almost invariably *reduce* the welfare of the poor, who are displaced from the city, find it almost impossible to afford the new housing constructed on the old sites, and — because of racial and class segregation in the non-ghetto housing market — find it difficult to obtain housing elsewhere to replace what they have lost. As a result, they move in with friends and relatives in the ghetto, increasing congestion and consequent pathologies even further. [If housing does open up outside the ghetto, whites may panic; then the ghetto can expand by blockbusting. Integration still doesn't occur.]

The damage done by urban renewal goes beyond the forcible eviction of households, although it is surely because of this that the disadvantaged (especially blacks) have a low opinion of urban renewal (hence the cynical expression, "Urban renewal means Negro removal"). The uprooted residents are seldom adequately compensated for their property. Moreover, small businesses are also uprooted, as are political-cultural institutions such as churches and community centers — the "glue" of the neighborhood. These commercial and institutional linkages are especially fragile and difficult to reproduce in the new areas into which the dislocated citizens are forced. Finally, by increasing land values in the renewal area (indeed, speculators have been known to pay enormous bribes to city officials for advance information on the location of future renewal sites), spillovers are generated which may worsen the economic welfare of ghetto residents living *outside* the renewal area. To protect values within the original renewal zone, there is pressure to bring its borders under renewal as well.

Harrison's characterization of renewal problems makes a telling point. The city is not renewed for its inhabitants but for those who see material capital as more important than human capital. For the profiteer, human community for others is expendable.

The urban issues in American society in the 1970s raise the question of whether comprehensive solutions are possible. The most likely solutions appear to lie increasingly in the combination of what Alan Shank calls political power and the urban crisis (1970). The Urban Coalition was formed in 1967 to counter the political weakness of racial minorities and others with great needs. Stimulated by such traditional civil rights groups as the NAACP and the Urban League, this coalition secured the public support of a variety of business, labor, and religious leaders as well as the open support of the mayors of New York, Chicago, Philadelphia, Detroit, Boston, Atlanta, and Phoenix (Urban America, Inc., 1967: 1). Noting both the difficulty and the urgency of restructuring the programs, and their priorities within the cities, Martin Luther King, Jr., gave this testimony before Senator Abraham Ribicoff's subcommittee dealing with urban problems (1966: 2979):

It will be necessary to form on a national scale some type of union of slum dwellers. A quality of leadership and organization that is rooted in the slums and designs the techniques of struggles uniquely suited for action there ... the racial minorities and urban poor generally ... will not do it alone, but they will not permit it to be done without them. This should be a basis for constructive collaboration between white and Negro, government and citizen, not in some distant time, but in the immediate present with all its emergencies that urgently call for creative statesmanship, risks of radical action and confidence that the bonds uniting humanity are stronger than the hostilities separating them.

In this testimony, Dr. King presented a visionary prospect for the reconstruction of the cities. The hard reality that followed has not yet provided the basis for reversing the deterioration of community and quality of life of the inner city.

COMMUNITY POWER AND URBAN RENEWAL
Effective community power mechanisms for bringing programs to the deteriorating core of America's cities will not alone solve the problem of urban redevelopment. It is, nevertheless, a necessary precondition before the many problems spelled out in the Demonstration Cities program can be faced. Even with universal commitment to urban planning and development, major controversies will surely persist. There will be those who, like Jane Jacobs, challenge the total destruction and clearance of slum districts rather than redeveloping them (see *The Death and Life of Great American Cities*, 1961). There will be conflicts among the urban poor about whether to press for low-cost housing and other needs in their slum neighborhoods or for resettlement in other parts of the city or in the suburbs.

Yet, these are issues that can be dealt with once there are resources and commitment for urban planning and city reconstruction. The internationally known urban planner C. A. Doxiadis stated the issue well when he observed (1967: 14):

Personally, I am convinced that the root of all problems in our cities lies in our minds, in our loss of belief in man and in his ability to set goals and to implement them.

We can never solve problems and tackle diseases unless we conceive the whole. We cannot build a cathedral by carving stones but only by dreaming of it, conceiving it as a whole, developing a systematic approach, and then working out the details. But dreaming and conceiving are not enough.

Quite simply — and complexly — the cities in American society cannot be revived as viable communities until there is a shift in national priorities and a shift in government and private resources. Since the cities are strategically located, their vitality is closely linked to the health and welfare of the entire society.

SUMMARY

Urbanization* is a recent historical trend and has been rapidly expanding. The many problems of large cities are studied in terms of *human ecology** and other concepts in the field.

The transformation of American society from *Gemeinschaft** (rural) to *Gesellschaft** (urban) community life has occurred within the last century. In order to assess the urbanization more accurately, the Census Bureau has developed the measurement called the *Standard Metropolitan Statistical Area** (SMSA), which enables the bureau to determine population trends in cities and their suburbs, which together are considered *ecological cities**. Life in cities is so different from life in suburbs that the concept of urbanism, as defined by Louis Wirth, is differentiated from the concept of suburbanism, as defined by Herbert Gans.

Human ecology as a field in sociology developed as a way of discovering why particular economic, ethnic, age, and other social groupings were concentrated as they are in urban areas. It has long been evident that poor, often minority groups, were located in *ghetto** areas near the deteriorating inner core of large cities, and that more affluent groups lived near the periphery of the cities, or in the suburbs. To explain this phenomenon, a number of ecological theories were developed. Some of the more prominent were the *concentric zone theory**, the *sector theory**, the *multiple nuclei theory**, and *social area analysis**, based on patterns of land use and population characteristics.

A number of problems facing large cities stem from the continuing effects of a small-town ideology in the American value structure. The lack of age or tradition in American cities and of allegiance to large cities, and the continued longing for small-town life by people who live in metropolitan areas, still limit our willingness to aid cities.

The population shifts from country to city to suburb have had profound effects. Racial minorities and lower-income people are now concentrated in the inner city; ethnic nationality groups and blue-collar workers tend to be located in the outer rim of cities; and upper-middle and upper socioeconomic groups occupy the suburbs. The varied abilities of these groups to attain their political and private interests reflects the framework of *community power** and its use by particular individual and group interests. Lack of power even to save one's community is seen in the plight of victims of urban renewal projects — minorities and the poor.

There is no tradition of consistent, community-wide planning in American society. Among issues calling for comprehensive, planned management are traffic congestion, air pollution, education, housing, and jobs, and these needs are felt most intensely among low-income groups in the cities. The emergence of suburbia and of the *megalopolis** point to the need for metropolitan planning efforts. A step in this direction is the Demonstration Cities concept, which has been developed in the past decade. The importance of working with the whole in dealing with problems of the cities has not been appreciated in urban planning; it is time for a change.

QUESTIONS FOR DISCUSSION

1. What differences in value orientation exist between suburbanites and city dwellers? Do you believe greater integration of housing in urban and/or suburban areas would alter these differences?

2. Early ecological theories of Ernest Burgess, Robert Park, and others identified population concentrations of various ethnic groups in cities as *natural areas*. Why might a current analyst reject this concept?

3. What social problems are found within cities because they are found in all community settings, and what social problems appear to be native to big cities?

4. Why is it unlikely that suburbs can be insulated from the deterioration of central cities? Do you believe suburbanites are aware of their relationship to the city?

5. According to Table 10-3, suburban whites, unlike urban whites, tended to agree with blacks about the causes of the 1967 Detroit riots. What explanation can you provide for this difference in viewpoint among whites?

6. Jane Jacobs argues that it is best for cities not to clear out slum areas but to redevelop them, keeping many of the same residents and buildings. Discuss the merits and disadvantages of this idea in terms of the Demonstration Cities proposal.

7. How might you use social-area analysis to support or deny the allegation that urban housing is still restricted, even though restrictive covenants are no longer legal?

8. Explain how invasion and succession as an ecological explanation might be used to describe ghetto expansion.

9. Review your understanding of the following terms and concepts:

urbanism

suburbanism

human ecology

ghetto

concentric zone theory

sector theory

multiple nuclei theory

social area analysis

Demonstration Cities program

community power

megalopolis

reputational, positional, functional analyses of power

REFERENCES

Anderson, William with R. Dynes and E. Quarantelli
   1974   "Urban counterrioters." Society 11 (March/April): 50–55.

Axelrod, Morris
   1956   "Urban structure and social participation." American Sociological Review 21 (February): 13–18.

Banfield, Edward
1970 The Un-heavenly City: The Nature and Future of Our Urban Crisis. Boston: Little, Brown.

Barron, Milton
1968 Minorities in a Changing World. New York: Knopf.

Bell, Wendell
1959 "Social areas: typology of urban neighborhoods." M. Sussman (ed.), Community Structure and Analysis. New York: Thomas Y. Crowell: 61-92.

Bell, Wendell and Marion Boat
1957 Urban neighborhoods and informal social relations. American Journal of Sociology LXII (January, 1957): 391-398.

Bloomberg, Warner
1967 "Community organization." H. Becker (ed.), Social Problems. New York: John Wiley and Sons: 259-425.

Bonjean, Charles and David Olson
1964 "Community Leadership: Directions of Research." Administrative Science Quarterly 9: 278-300.

Branch, Taylor
1975 "Who's in charge now?" Harper's Weekly (May 16): 13.

Burgess, Ernest
1925 "The growth of the city." R. Park and E. Burgess (eds.), The City. Chicago: University of Chicago Press: 47-62.
1927 "The determination of gradients in the growth of the city." Washington, D.C.: Publications of the American Sociological Society 21: 178-184.
1953 The Family. New York: American Book Company.

Carmichael, Stokely and Charles Hamilton
1967 Black Power: The Politics of Liberation in American Society. New York: Vintage.

Cox, Harvey
1965 The Secular City: Secularization and Urbanization in Theological Perspective. New York: Macmillan.

Davis, Kingsley
1965 "The urbanization of the human population." Scientific American (September) : 41-53.

Doxiadis, C.A.
1967 "The coming era of ecumenopolis." Saturday Review (March 18): 11-14.

FBI Report
1971 FBI, Uniform Crime Reports. Washington, D.C.: Government Printing Office.

Fogelson, Robert and Robert Hill
1968 "Who riots? A study of participation in the 1967 riots." Supplemental Studies for the National Advisory Commission on Civil Disorders. Washington, D.C.: Government Printing Office: 221-243.

Gans, Herbert
1962 "Urbanism and suburbanism as ways of life." A. Rose (ed.), Human Behavior and Social Processes. Boston: Houghton Mifflin: 625-648.

Gist, Noel and Sylvia Fava
1969 Urban Society. New York: Thomas Y. Crowell.

Gordon, Leonard
1965 Notes by the co-secretary of the Metropolitan Detroit Religion and Race Conference.

Gottmann, Jean
1961 Megalopolis: The Urbanized Northeastern Seaboard of the United States. Cambridge: M.I.T. Press.

Greer, Scott
1962 Governing the Metropolis. New York: John Wiley and Sons.
1965 Urban Renewal and American Cities. New York: Bobbs-Merrill.

Griffin, Jr., C. W.
　1974　Taming the Last Frontier: A Prescription for the Urban Crisis. New York: Pitman.

Grimes, Michael, Charles Bonjean, J. Larry Lyon, and Robert Lineberry
　1976　"Community structure and leadership arrangements: A multi-dimensional analysis." American Sociological Review 41: 706–725.

Harris, Chauncey and Edward Ullman
　1945　"The nature of cities." The Annals 242 (November): 7–17.

Housing Act
　1961　The Housing Act of 1949, As Amended Through June, 1961 (Public Law 171, 81st Congress). Washington, D.C.: Government Printing Office.

Harrison, Bennett
　1974　Urban Economic Development: Suburbanization, Minority Opportunity and the Condition of the Central City. Washington, D.C.: The Urban Institute.

Hoyt, Homer
　1943　"The structure of American cities in the post-war era." American Journal of Sociology 48 (January): 475–492.
　1964　"Evolution of the ecology of United States cities." Land Economics XL (May): 199–212.

Hunter, Floyd
　1953　Community Power Structure. Chapel Hill: University of North Carolina Press.

Jacobs, Jane
　1961　The Death and Life of Great American Cities. New York: Random House.

Jacobs, Paul
　1967　Prelude to a Riot. New York: Vintage.

King, Jr., Martin Luther
　1966　Testimony before Senator Ribicoff's Senate subcommittee. Federal Role in Urban Affairs, Part 14. Washington, D.C.: Government Printing Office (December 14–15): 2967–2979.

Lalli, Frank
　1975　"A defense of the big banks." Harper's Weekly. vol. LXIV (September 29): 8.

Lewis, Sinclair
　1920　Main Street. New York: Harcourt, Brace.

Lynd, Robert and Helen Lynd
　1929　Middletown. New York: Harcourt Brace Jovanovich.
　1937　Middletown in Transition. New York: Harcourt, Brace.

Mayer, Albert J. and Thomas Ford Hoult
　1962　Race and Residence in Detroit. Detroit: Wayne State University Institute of Regional and Urban Studies.

McKenzie, R.D.
　1925　"The ecological approach." R. Park and E. Burgess (eds.), The City, Chicago: University of Chicago Press: 63–79.

Merton, Robert
　1957　Social Theory and Social Structure, Glencoe, Ill.: The Free Press.

Mothner, Ira
　1968　"Our cities: the uptight life." Look (June 11): 27.

Olmstead, Alan and Eugene Smolensky
　1973　The Urbanization of the United States. Morristown, N.J.: General Learning Press Module.

Owen, Wilfred
　1966　The Metropolitan Transportation Problem. New York: Anchor Books.

Park, Robert
　1936　"Human ecology." American Journal of Sociology 42 (July 1936): 1–15.

Polsby, Nelson
1959 "Three problems in the analysis of community power." American Sociological Review 24: 796–803.

1968 Report of the National Advisory Commission on Civil Disorders. New York: Bantam.

Rogers, William
1961 Voluntary associations and urban community development. International Review of Community Development no. 7: 140–141.

Rustin, Bayard
1966 Black power and coalition politics. Commentary 41 (September): 35–40.

Shank, Alan
1970 Political Power and the Urban Crisis. Boston: Holbrook Press.

Shevky, Eshert and Marilyn Williams
1949 The Social Areas of Los Angeles. Berkeley: University of California Press.

Stewart, Maxwell
1966 Can we save our cities? The story of urban renewal. Public Affairs Pamphlet no. 374 (November): 28 pp.

1968 Testimony before the U.S. Commission on Civil Rights. City 2 (January): 14–15.

Tönnies, Ferdinand
1887 Gemeinshaft and Gesellschaft. C. Loomis (trans.), Community and Society. New York: Harper and Row, 1968.

1961 United States Census of the Population, 1060 Number of Inhabitants, United States Summary. Final Report PC (1)-A1. Washington, D.C.: Government Printing Office, 1961.

1970 United States Census of the Population. General Population Characteristics Final Report PC (1)-A12. Washington, D.C.: Government Printing Office, 1970.

Urofsky, Melvin I. (ed.)
1973 Perspectives on Urban America. Garden City: Doubleday Anchor Books.

Venetoulis, Ted and Ward Eisenhauer (eds.)
1971 Up Against the Urban Wall. Englewood Cliffs, New Jersey: Prentice-Hall.

Vidich, Arthur and Joseph Bensman
1958 Small Town in Mass Society. New York: Anchor.

Warren, Donald
1971 "Community dissensus." L. Gordon (ed.), A City in Racial Crisis. Dubuque, Iowa: Wm. C. Brown: 129–145.

Wirth, Louis
1928 The Ghetto. Chicago: University of Chicago Press.
1938 "Urbanism as a way of life." American Journal of Sociology 44: 1–24.

Wright, Jr., Nathan
1967 Black Power and Urban Unrest: Creative Possibilities. New York: Hawthorn Books.

Part 4

ISSUES FACING AMERICANS ON A GLOBAL SCALE

Rich nations and poor alike have grossly misused the world's resources, both material and intellectual; neglected them, wasted them, and fought each other over how to share them. Thus the basic question is not how many people can share the earth, but whether they can devise the means of sharing it at all.

Otto Fredrich

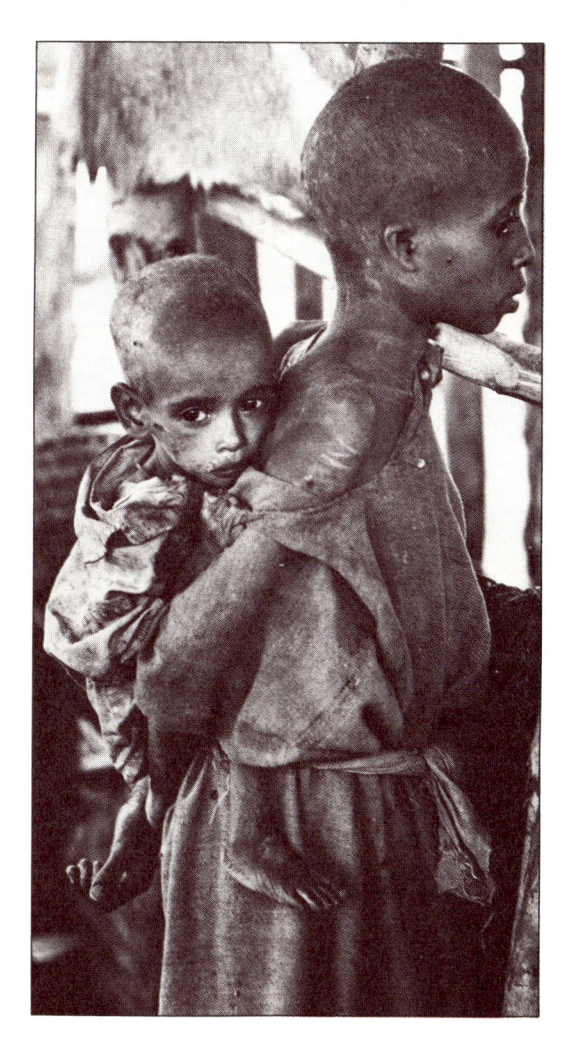

Chapter 11

DEMOGRAPHY AND THE POPULATION EXPLOSION

Long-range projections of current rates of population growth simply run off the chart and beyond the range of agricultural solutions that are either possible or conceivable.

Kenneth R. Farrell, Deputy Administrator, Economic Research Service, 1974

DEMOGRAPHY AS A FIELD OF STUDY

As you read this book, are you hungry? Did you ride to school or work today on a crowded freeway? If you live in a big city like Los Angeles, did you have a smog alert today? Did you go camping recently amid wall-to-wall campers, making it hard to find a spot of your own? If so, you are probably aware of the problems we shall discuss in this chapter. Problems of hunger, pollution, and congestion may have several sources; one is population pressure — too many people living in too little space with too few resources.

The population of a society is the total number of human beings in it. People can be counted and classified by such *demographic* (Greek *demos* = people) characteristics as age, race, sex, occupation, and in other useful ways, as is done by the United States Census. The study of populations has given rise to the field of *demography**. Demographic analysis is performed not only by sociologists but also by such practitioners as market analysts in business, insurance researchers developing actuarial (life expectancy) tables, and government census-takers. The findings of all these and others are used in the analysis of population.

Demography is a broad field and is worldwide in scope. Partly because of its findings, there is growing recognition that the total number of people, or number of people with given characteristics within a society, can create a social problem. (See the selection on People, Pressures, and Pollution.) As the American population grows, it must rely more and more on foreign resources and markets. And as the world population grows, there are more and more pressures on American society.

PEOPLE, PRESSURES, AND POLLUTION

From: "The World's Population Crisis" by Kingsley Davis in *Contemporary Social Problems,* fourth edition, pp. 282-283, Robert K. Merton and Robert Nisbet, eds. Copyright © 1961, 1966, 1971, 1976 by Harcourt Brace Jovanovich, Inc., and reprinted with their permission.

While for poorer countries population growth brings problems because of poverty, for richer ones it brings troubles because of affluence. As individual consumption mounts and population multiplies, two exponentials are added to produce an extremely high rate of total consumption. Between 1960 and 1975 in the United States, for example, the population increased 1.1 percent per year, and per capita consumption of energy increased 2.8 percent per year. Accordingly, total consumption of energy increased as the sum (3.9 percent) of these two rates, doubling in 15 years and adding the equivalent of 1.2 billion tons of coal to the nation's annual energy consumption.

The congestion of people and possessions tends to be self-defeating. An ever-higher proportion of effort and energy is expended simply to mitigate the effects of a high level of effort and energy. As the giant urban aggregates grow larger, for example, the congestion becomes more costly and frustrating. Automobiles, radios, television antennae, boats, houses, freezers, and myriad other possessions multiply relentlessly. To enjoy and store their goods and to escape the noise and pollution of the central city, families move to the suburbs, but the costs are enormous. Freeways and mass transit systems, shopping centers, schools, water systems, and sewage plants must be built, and land is removed from agriculture. Yet the problem of urban crowding is not solved. The escape from congestion simply creates more congestion. As the urban population grows, the quest for space moves the suburbs farther out and multiplies the connecting links. The home that was once "in the country" or "in a pleasant little suburb" becomes a dot in a continuous sea of housing developments and shopping centers. The freeway that was so spacious and convenient when finished soon becomes an exasperating trap at rush hours. The industries that supply the material wealth, the automobiles and buses that travel greater distances between home and work, the dumps where growing mountains of refuse are burned — all combine to create an environmental blight, smog. The air pollution extends far beyond the cities themselves, injuring crops and forests. In their unquenchable thirst for water, the cities go hundreds of miles, altering the topography and damaging the economy of rural areas. Many metropolitan areas expand spatially until they collide, thus creating what have been called megalopolises and making escape all the more difficult.

As is well known, cities generate heat. When summer comes, millions of air conditioners are switched on, not simply to modify natural heat but also to cancel the extra heat of the city. Air conditioners, however, use energy at a prodigious rate. The power plants required to run them pollute the air further and generate still more heat, in turn requiring the air conditioners to work harder.

An example of a natural paradise despoiled by population growth and a high level of living is California. It added 5 million people to its population between 1960 and 1975, making it the twelfth most densely settled state in the union. Most of its population is concentrated in a semi-desert running from Santa Barbara to San Diego, which contained more than 12 million people in 1975. Air pollution from this urban belt is damaging forests in the coastal range and the Sierra and injuring crops in the Central Valley, the world's richest agricultural region. The largest city, Los Angeles, has more than 30 times the population that could be supplied with the scant local rainfall. Long ago (in 1913) Los Angeles took all the water from the Owens Valley, 250 miles away, making a wasteland of the valley. Later it took water from the Mono Basin and next from the Colorado River, depriving Nevada, Arizona, and Mexico of their rightful supply. Finally it used its overwhelming concentration of votes to pass in the state legislature the "California Water Plan," a scheme to dam the rivers of the northern part of the state and transport their water several hundred miles to Los Angeles. The canals, pipes, and tunnels required are 6,265 miles long; when the system is fully operative, the total energy required to pump the water, which must go over high mountains, is scheduled to use 10.6 percent of the state's production of electricity. The northern part of the state considers the damage to its agriculture and environment incalculable. Nevertheless, in the Los Angeles area the herculean effort is justified in the name of growth. As one progress report said, it "will stimulate the development of industry, population growth, and in-migration."

THE POPULATION EXPLOSION Just how rapidly is world population growing? The term *population explosion* is no exaggeration. Over the past several centuries, advances in agricultural technology and medical science and other factors have dramatically reduced the death rate and lengthened the life span of people in most parts of the world. It is estimated that in the mid-seventeenth century, there were .5 billion people on earth, and that this number had doubled by early in the eighteenth century (Carr-Sanders, 1936: 42). In another century and a half, or by the mid-twentieth century, the number had tripled to about 3 billion, and it is estimated that the number will pass 7 billion by the year 2000. This will occur within the life span of most people now living (see Figure 11-1). For over 99 percent of the time span of human evolution, population growth was slow; during the remaining one percent, it has already increased fivefold. If the rate of increase in 1970 (about 2 percent per year) holds steady, the earth's population will double in thirty-five years. (Petersen, 1975: 9–10).

American society has been an important part of this expansion. Table 11-1 shows just how rapid its growth has been. A nation of fewer than 4 million in 1790, we are now over 200 million, and the low estimate for early in the twenty-first century is over 300 million (*Population,* 1972: 9).

Figure 11-1 illustrates graphically the world population explosion in recent history. The implications for human life are profound and affect the functioning of all institutions from the primary family level to the larger secondary economic and government levels.

Demographic analysis has developed a number of testable concepts in attempting to understand the effects of massive population growth on human behavior. One concept is Thomas Malthus's famous natural law (1798) that population tends to

Table 11-1 Growth of the United States Population: Selected Years from 1790 to 1970 (Projected to 2015)

Census year	Total population (in thousands)
1790	3,929
1850	23,191
1920	106,466
1970	203,211
2015 (projected)	300,000

SOURCES: *Historical Statistics of the United States: Colonial Times to 1957.* U.S. Bureau of the Census (1961), Table 3, 1-42; *Number of Inhabitants. United States Summary,* U.S. Department of Commerce (December 1971), Table B, VIII; *Population. The U.S. Problem. The World Crisis,* the New York *Times* (April 30, 1972), p. 9.

340 ISSUES FACING AMERICANS ON A GLOBAL SCALE

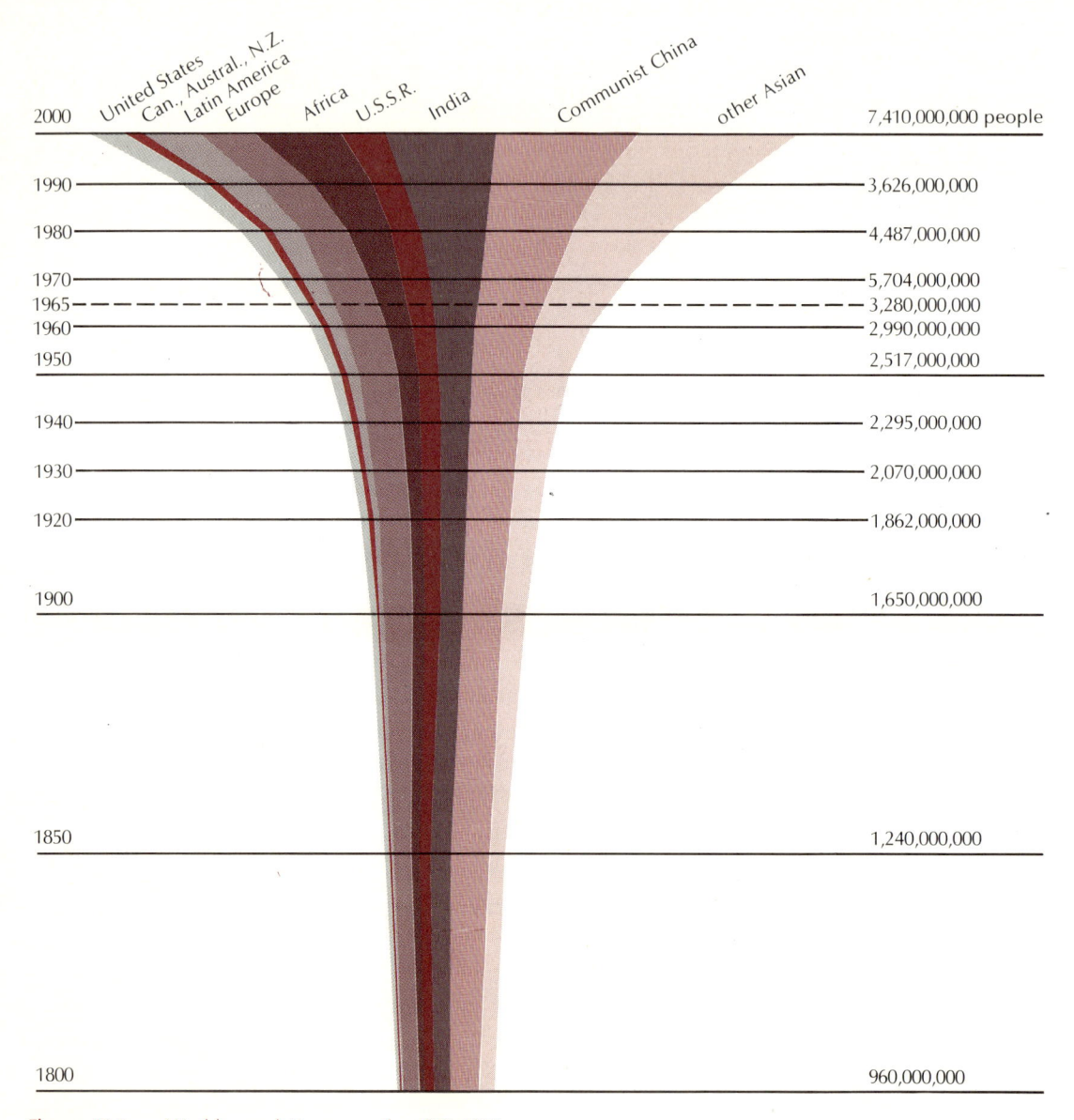

Figure 11-1 World population growth, 1800–1965 (projected to 2000). SOURCE: Alexander Semenoick, *Fortune* Magazine, June 1966, p. 110.

DEMOGRAPHY AND THE POPULATION EXPLOSION   341

Some members of the global population explosion. SOURCE: (a) Bernard Pierre Wolff/Photo Researchers; (b) Sepp Seitz/Magnum.

grow faster than the supply of food. Other concepts we shall discuss in this chapter are *cultural evolution** and its effect on population growth; *demographic transition**, a hypothesis about the population stages through which societies pass; and *cultural lag**, the hypothesis that technology changes faster (but not always for the better) than the values and ways of life rooted in earlier cultural experience.

POPULATION GROWTH AND DEMOGRAPHIC ANALYSIS

Cultural evolution* (see the selection on this subject), which gave humankind tools, agriculture, and industrialization, was also the stimulus for the population explosion. The recent enormous growth in world population has meant that most societies now have too many people to know how many they have altogether or how many there are in any group within the society. Without the information gathered by demographers, a nation cannot develop clear plans to meet the changing needs of its people for jobs, housing, education, and so on. Through such summaries as the decennial Census reports and the United Nations demographic yearbooks, it is possible to determine the extent of national and world populations, as well as the rate of changes that have occurred and are likely to occur.

CULTURAL EVOLUTION

From: Ralph Thomlinson, *Population Dynamics: Causes and Consequences of World Demographic Change* (New York: Random House, 1965), pp. 11–12.

World wide cultural evolution has resulted in the following: Three revolutional changes in man's ability to adjust to and control his environment have had profound demographic consequences. The first of these cultural accomplishments was the acquisition of tools some millions of years ago. The tool-using revolution antedates man; use of tools by prehuman primates may even have been the major impetus giving rise to the initial differentiation of *Homo Sapiens* from apes. By increasing primate ability to cope with his environment, tools probably increased the density of habitation.

Second came the agricultural revolution about 10,000 years ago, changing man from a hunting-gathering-scavenging nomad to a villager with domesticated animals and cultivated fields of wheat and barley. Without settled farming, congregation into cities would have been impossible. This great achievement of our species took place initially in the fertile crescent of southwest Asia and later (possibly independently) in China and (certainly independently) in the Western Hemisphere. In the million or more years intervening between these two revolutions, men and other primates must have devoted their days to the search for their next meal — and when they made a kill, they gorged on it. Not until man learned to produce his own food (and store it against hard times) instead of collecting it subject to the vicissitudes of his environs did his horizon expand. He could then look forward confidently to eating next week, and his energies and preoccupations were released for a wide spectrum of new endeavors and inventions.

The third of these technological revolutions was industrialization.

Each of these periods is a stage in demographic history. Achievement of a new technological level was accompanied by a surge in population. . . .

Cultural evolution makes possible (though not inevitable) demographic evolution. Population expands when enabled to do so by new technological weapons in the battle against environment. For nearly the entirety of man's existence, we were forced to concede the upper hand to nonhuman forces, a balance of power reversed only by the technological skills acquired during the last quarter millennium.

DEMOGRAPHERS' ASSESSMENTS Population statistics have led demographers to an unusual degree of consensus about the need to control and limit future population growth. As we shall see later in this chapter, there is considerable controversy among nondemographers about birth control and other methods of limiting population growth, but there is little controversy among demographers themselves. As Ralph Thomlinson, a well known demographer, put it (1967: 112):

Professional demographers almost unanimously favor controlling fertility by whatever techniques science can offer. This unanimity has reached the point where, when a television network wants to stage a pro-con discussion of birth control, it is easy to find debaters for the affirmative but extremely difficult to locate qualified experts willing to take the negative.

Demographers are not so much concerned with the total population growth, formidable as this is (see Table 11-2); rather, they worry about the *rate* of growth and how it is distributed. Of the large current and larger projected total human population, one expert, Lord Boyd-Orr, holds that (1970: 47):

The only practical limit to food production is the effort governments devote to it. Sufficient food could be produced to support three or four times the present world population.

Not all experts would agree with Boyd-Orr. He is suggesting that there is a technological solution for problems, that with the right technology, the resource base can expand to accommodate increasing population. (For another technological view, see Petersen, 1975: 168–178).

Opponents of this view have sometimes been called *prophets of doom* because of their belief that, even with the best efforts now available and with whatever technology can provide, expanding population will eat up these gains and reduce quality of life. (For an attack upon the antitechnological approach of Paul Ehrlich and others, see Endres, 1975: 31–34.)

A third, cautiously optimistic view is that with a combination of technological achievement and determined planning to bring population growth under control, population pressures on the environment and quality of life will be reduced, or at least made no worse. The practical limit on food production to which Lord Boyd-Orr refers means disaster for millions now and in the near future. While the world population is growing, the rate of growth varies markedly by nation and by region. Industrial nations such as the United States, Australia, the countries of Western Europe, and increasingly the Soviet Union and China, tend to be

Table 11-2 Billion-Fold Increases in the World's Population

Number of people	Approximate date of achievement	Approximate time taken to add another billion
One billion	1820	hundreds of thousands of years
Two billion	1930	110 years
Three billion	1965	35 years
Four billion*	1980	15 years
Five billion	1990	10 years

* Note that these projections have proven too conservative. United Nations Monthly Bulletins of Statistics noted that the world population passed the 4 billion mark in 1976, four years prior to the projection on this table. This table was developed on the basis of trends evident in the mid 1960s.

SOURCE: Ralph Thomlinson, *Population Dynamics: Causes and Consequences of World Demographic Change* (New York: Random House, 1965), p. 10.

self-sufficient or to produce more food than they need. These nations also tend to have the lowest rates of population growth, while those least developed industrially tend to have the highest (Figure 11-2). By the mid 1970s, there was not enough food in large parts of Latin America, Africa, and India. Famine struck across north central Africa, in central India, and in Bangladesh. Experts held that, in the mid 1970s, close to .5 billion people were threatened with starvation (Special Report, 1974: 56).

POPULATION COMPOSITION The demographic boundaries of the population problem can be seen in the composition of populations by types within a given society or worldwide. Such types include the sex ratio, age distribution, levels of education, and

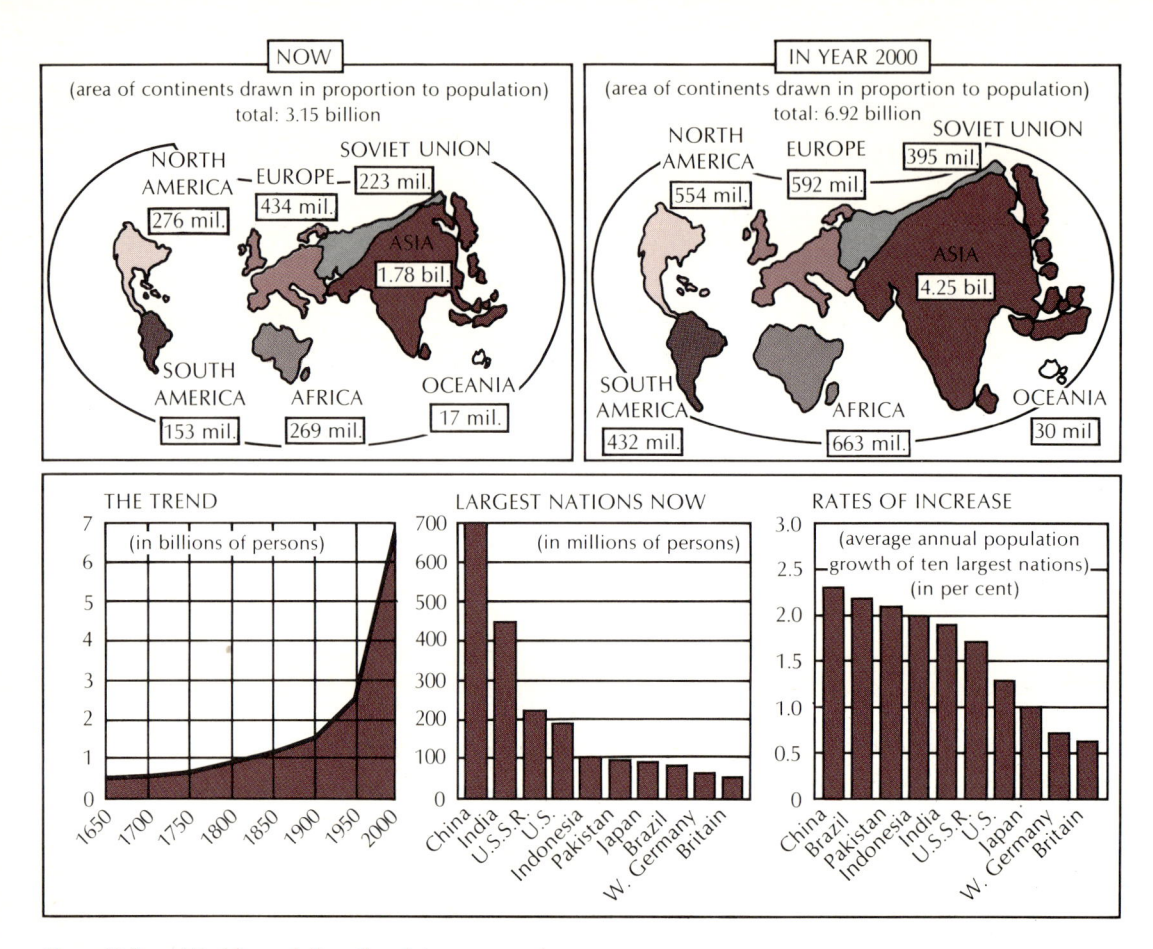

Figure 11-2 World population: the picture now and a look toward 2000. SOURCE: © 1963 by the New York Times Company. Reprinted by permission.

economic status. In American society, such classification can pinpoint a problem in the area of changing age composition. Between 1950 and 1970, the youngest (under twenty) and oldest (over sixty-four) age groups grew five times faster than the group between twenty and sixty-four. We saw in Chapters 5 and 7 that familial, educational, and economic institutions are not meeting the needs of many young and old people. When we add the growth rate of these age groups to other known complications, the dimensions of the problem become clearer.

Knowing the makeup of population types worldwide helps in similar ways. Thus, by grouping industrialized and nonindustrialized populations, we see (Figures 11-2 and 11-3) that the most rapidly growing populations are in nonindustrialized societies, and there we find barely adequate food supplies or famine.

We already know that within a decade after Paul Ehrlich wrote in the 1960s of the coming famine, 10 million people a year were starving to death. As the world economy has become increasingly interdependent, it has become clear that the resolution of

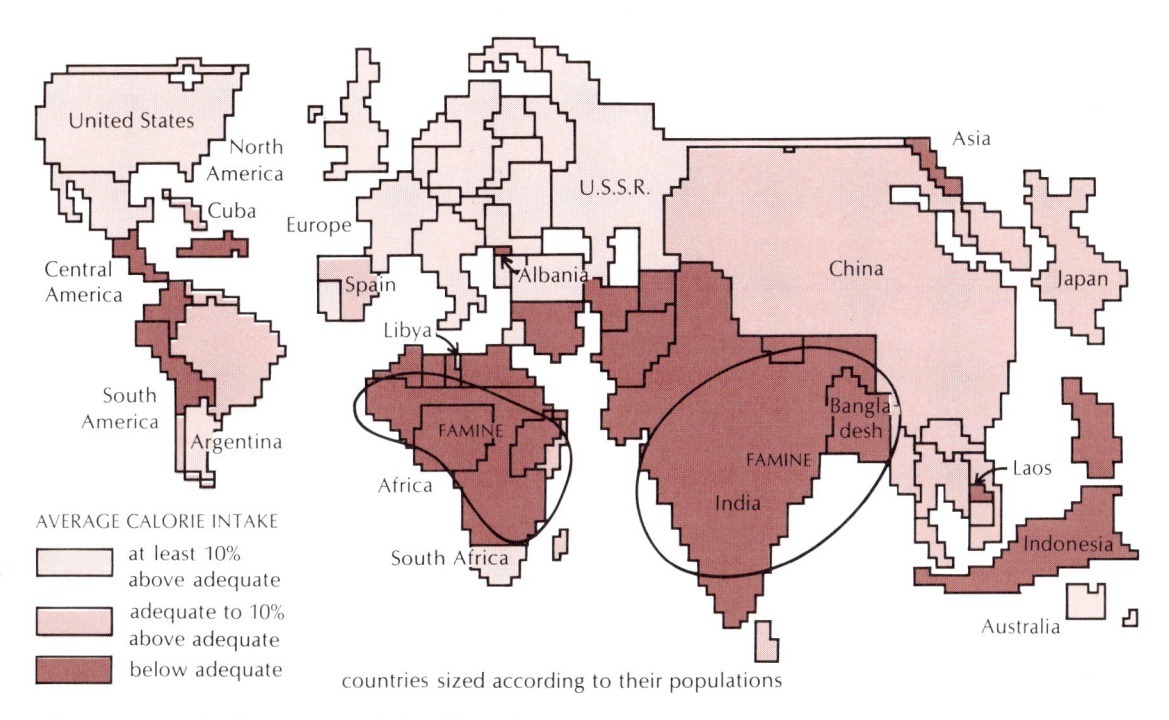

Figure 11-3 The fat nations and the thin nations. SOURCE: Reprinted by permission of Scholastic Magazines, Inc. from Headline Focus Map, © 1974 by Scholastic Magazines, Inc.

the world population crisis is as much a bread-and-butter issue for Americans as for those people caught in the crisis. It is, therefore, time for us to consider the demographic mechanisms responsible for the population pressures we are now experiencing. (See also *Population: The U.S. Problem — The World Crisis,* New York Times Publication, 1972.)

THE CONTROLLING TRIAD: MIGRATION, FERTILITY, AND MORTALITY

The population explosion has been so vast, so rapid, and so steady that it is tempting to take Charlie Brown's view that no problem is so pressing or so important that it can't be avoided. As we shall see, Malthus's gloomy prediction lends weight to this position. Americans may well tend to focus on their own problem and ignore the crisis in the rest of the world; but avoiding the issue can turn the American problem into an international crisis, even though there are ways of viewing the current dilemma as one that can be managed realistically and humanely.[1] To solve any problem, we must first know the facts. Although demographic

---

[1] We shall make the point in Chapter 12 that the newly independent and industrializing societies growing fastest are now also experiencing a *revolution of rising expectations* (see Davies, 1962). This phenomenon increases international tensions and conflict with the richer societies (see Ward, 1962).

knowledge is not totally precise, population statistics are in general among the most accurate measurements taken with respect to human beings (Thomlinson, 1967: 16).[2]

Population is a function of three variables: people may move into or out of a society (the *migration** variable); they are born into every society (the *fertility** variable); and they die in every society (the *mortality** variable).

---

[2] For a discussion of some measuring problems, particularly for racial minorities in the United States Census, see Chapter 4.

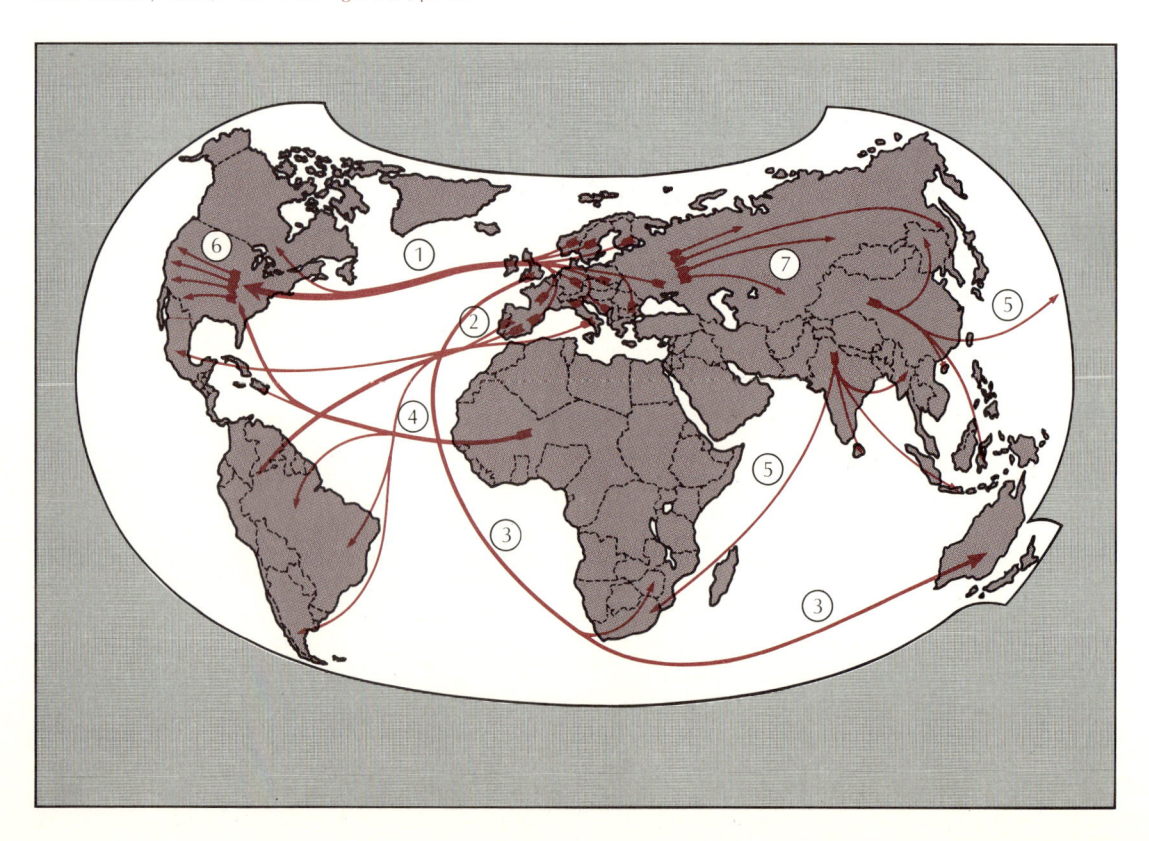

Figure 11-4 International migration since 1500. SOURCE: W. S. Woytinsky and E. S. Woytinsky, *World Population: Trends and Outlook*, © 1953 by the Twentieth Century Fund, New York. Figure 27, p. 68.

MIGRATION From the age of exploration in the sixteenth century until the mass settlement of all continents early in the twentieth century, international migration was a major factor in the stability or change of populations around the world. People generally moved out of old settled societies *(emigration*)* into new societies or other old ones in which there were greater opportunities *(immigration*)*. The population of most nations today cannot be understood without reference to this process. This is particularly true for the United States, which has been peopled by a higher proportion of immigrants than any other nation today, with the possible exception of the renewed contemporary state of Israel. The global pattern can be seen in Figure 11-4. The main flows of international migration since the beginning of the sixteenth century have been: (1) from all parts of Europe to

North America; (2) from Latin countries of Europe to Central and South America; (3) from Great Britain to southern Africa and Australia; (4) from Africa to America (as part of the slave trade); and the largely intracontinental flows (5) in China and India; (6) westward in the United States; and (7) eastward in Russia.

THE INDUSTRIAL REVOLUTION AND MASS MIGRATION This global migration pattern affected all continents in the 1500s, 1600s, and 1700s, but it was the industrial revolution in Britain and Europe that stimulated the greatest wave. In the century between 1820 (the first year in which the United States government kept immigration records) and 1920 (the year before Congress passed the first restrictive immigration act), approximately 35 million Europeans migrated into the United States (Carr-Saunders, 1936: 49). The records of other countries were rarely as precise as those of the United States in that period, but this was perhaps half the total European exodus, triggered by (Fairchild, 1925: 69):

> ... the expectation of a higher level of living.... In much of rural Europe land was scarce and was becoming more scarce as population growth accelerated under the impetus of declining mortality. Wages in European cities were relatively low and periods of unemployment frequent ... the development of manufactures and commerce was not rapid enough to match the increase of the labour supply brought about by the excess of births over deaths and by migration from rural areas.

The consequences of an imbalance of birth and death rates will be taken up in our discussion of demographic transition theory.

The people who came to America's shores were generally poor, and the conditions under which they came demonstrate their great desire for a new start. (Recall the discussion of immigration in Chapter 8.) In the nineteenth century, the average mortality rate on the crowded ships bringing immigrants was about 10 percent. On one occasion in 1847, on Gross Isle near New England, ten thousand Irish immigrants died, "three thousand so alone that their names were never known" (Handlin, 1951: 55). These immigrants had been stranded with insufficient supplies in severe weather, far from help from the mainland, and cut off from other ships for months.

DECLINING AVAILABLE SPACE By the early twentieth century, the cheap land and plentiful jobs that had attracted immigrants into the New World became subject to the same pressures that had previously affected the older societies.[3] The United States, as the largest recipient of this immigration, began to pass restrictive laws to slow it down. The first comprehensive acts, passed in 1921 and 1924, were amended in 1952 and 1965. The latter act was designed to end discriminatory provisions of the earlier acts while keeping a ceiling of 290,000 on immigration annually.[4] Just how low is this ceiling compared to past patterns is indicated by the average annual immigration rates into the United States. Even with quota exceptions resulting from special situations (such as allowing more Cubans into the United States after the Castro revolution in

---

[3] The New World was of course populated, if sparsely, by native American Indians who were overwhelmed by the mass of immigrants into their former lands. This problem was the basis of another contemporary social issue (Chapter 8).

[4] Until the passage of the Immigration Act of 1965, the United States' control of immigration was highly discriminatory against Africans, Asiatics, and southern and eastern Europeans, and was biased in favor of British and northern Europeans (see Chapter 8).

the 1960s, and letting in Vietnamese refugees after the collapse of the South Vietnamese government in 1975), the average annual immigration is less than 400,000. This is about half the average at the turn of the century (Annual Reports, 1974).[5]

This slowing of immigration into the United States also reflects a general slowing of migration from society to society. Population growth in twentieth-century societies throughout the world has been influenced far more by the internally generated population explosion, which is related to the variables of fertility and mortality.

FERTILITY   Knowing the number of women in a society who can bear children — generally treated statistically as the age group from fifteen to forty-four — makes it possible to determine the *fecundity** level of the society, or its total ability to reproduce. No society has ever achieved the maximum possible fecundity, and if women have anything to say about it, as they increasingly do, this is not ever likely to happen, for it would mean an average of over twenty children for each woman in her lifetime.

FERTILITY TRENDS   Fertility trends are more useful in analyzing population growth. *Fertility** refers to the actual rather than the potential number of births. While the total number of births is limited by the number of fecund women, the total fertility rate for a society is usually figured on the basis of the number of live births per year per 1000 people. The formula for what is called the crude birth rate[6] (CBR) is:

$$\frac{\text{births in a year}}{\text{annual (midyear) population}} \times 1000$$

= crude birth rate (CBR)

Using census figures, the formula would have resulted in the following crude birth rate for the United States in 1970:

$$\frac{3{,}718{,}000 \text{ live births}}{203{,}185{,}000 \text{ total (midyear) population}} \times 1000$$

= a CBR of 18.3

Using the same formula with 1973 data (Indonesia, 1974: 547), the newly industrializing but still largely agrarian nation of Indonesia has the following crude birth rate:

$$\frac{6{,}362{,}000 \text{ live births}}{131{,}712{,}500 \text{ total (midyear) population}} \times 1000$$

= a CBR of 48.3

The current birth rate in the United States is about half what it was at the turn of the century and is now similar to that of other industrialized societies. Newly industrializing societies, such as Indonesia, reflect the high birth rates characteristic of agrarian societies.

THE INFLUENCE OF SOCIAL NORMS   The fertility rate is heavily influenced by the social norms operating within a society. While norms differ from one society to another and are not equally supported by all groups, particular norms appear to be very important in determining fertility. First, there are religious norms, such as the biblical admonition to be fruitful and multiply; there are Jewish regulations regarding frequency of sexual intercourse;

---

[5] Excluded from official immigration figures for both the current and the earlier immigrants are the number of illegal aliens from Canada, Mexico, and other nations for which no reliable data are available.

[6] The birth rate, or the reported number of births per year, is widely used as a measure of fertility. For a discussion of some of its limitations (such as the requirement that all births be registered, which is not the case in every society), see Thomlinson, *Population Dynamics*, pp. 159–164.

and there are the Catholic views that the principal purpose of sexual intercourse is procreation, and that abortion and various forms of birth control are sins, as some Fundamentalist Protestants hold.

There are also numerous secular norms, such as the idea that marriage is complete only when children are born, which translates into normative pressures to prove the solidity of one's marriage by having a family. Many people believe that failure to have children means that a couple are selfish, unwilling to give of their time, love, and material wealth to children. Sterile men and women may be made to feel that they are sexually inadequate. The *macho* syndrome often attributed to men of other cultures (proving one's sexuality by siring children) is more common in American culture than some people would like to think. Men may find that having a wife and child(ren) influences employers to regard them as stable or mature. Such beliefs subtly or not so subtly communicate the message that it is *normal* to have children, *abnormal* to be childless.

Only recently have people begun to evaluate norms in favor of childrearing and to offer opposing norms. Organized groups have formed to publicize the value of alternative (that is, childless) lifestyles. Still other groups (such as Zero Population Growth) advocate limiting the number of children to two per family, adopting children rather than bearing one's own, and using permanent sterilization procedures such as vasectomies. Nonetheless, our cultural view of the desirability of having children is long standing and not quickly put aside.

Note in Figure 11-5 that in the nineteenth century, an agrarian period in American history, the average number of children per woman ranged between four and six, compared to an average of two to three in the urbanized, nuclear-family period of the twentieth century. Social norms tend to continue for a period of time even when conditions change. For example, in the section on *migration**, we noted that in the early nineteenth century,

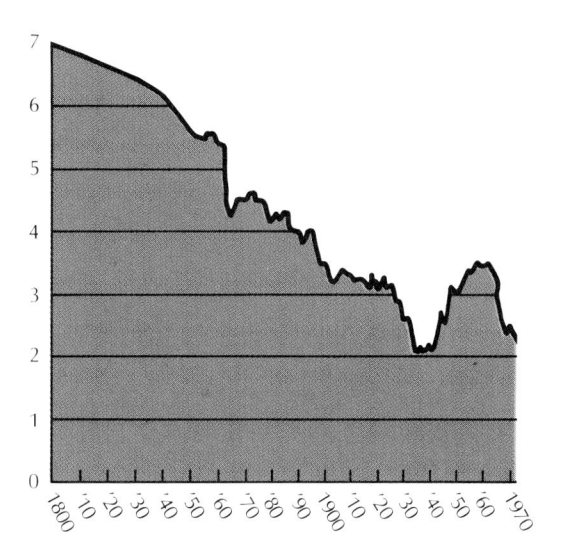

Figure 11-5 Total fertility rate in the United States, 1800–1970 (prior to 1917 data available only for white population; after 1917 for total population). SOURCE: *Population and the American Future*, The Report of the Commission on Population and the American Future (New York: New American Library, 1972), p. 13.

over 70 million Europeans came to the New World, partly in response to European population growth pressures. What had happened, along with a decline in the death rate (which will be considered in the next section), was that the high fertility rates in European societies continued into the twentieth century, when families in all European countries began to shrink to three or fewer children.

THE CULTURAL LAG THESIS The tendency for one part of a culture to change more rapidly than another is referred to as *cultural lag**. William Ogburn described the cultural lag process in the following terms (1922: 200–201):

The thesis [of cultural lag] is that various parts of modern culture are not changing at the same rate, some parts are changing more rapidly than others; and that since there is a correlation and interdependence of parts, a rapid change in one part of our culture requires readjustments through other changes in the various correlated parts of culture. For instance, industry and education are correlated, hence a change in industry makes adjustments necessary through changes in the educational system. Industry and education are two variables, and if the change in industry occurs first and the adjustment through education follows, industry may be referred to as the independent variable and education as the dependent variable.[7] Where one part of culture changes first, through some discovery or invention, and occasions changes in some part of culture dependent upon it, there frequently is a delay in the changes occasioned in the dependent part of culture. The extent of this lag will vary according to the nature of the culture material, but may exist for a considerable number of years, during which time there may be said to be a maladjustment. It is desirable to reduce the period of maladjustment, to make the cultural adjustments as quickly as possible.

As Ogburn notes, cultural lag usually means that the material culture of a society is changing more rapidly than the nonmaterial culture (although the reverse can occur). Whenever industrialization occurs, the fertility rate eventually declines, but it may not do so for a generation or more. As noted in the crude birth rate computation, in the United States, the birth rate in 1970 was 18 per 1000 compared to 32 per 1000 in 1900 (*Population and the American Future*, 1972: 11). The shift downward in fertility took more than one generation.

A high fertility rate is a consequence of specific components of the nonmaterial culture, such as a high value placed on having children, which may outweigh other values such as approval of using contraceptive techniques or waiting until one is able to provide financially for children. The term *cultural lag* connotes no value judgment between sets of values but refers simply to a disjuncture or discontinuity of values owing to different rates of change.

The eventual decline in fertility rates in industrializing societies is due partly to the rise of new values as new functional needs are created. For example, in modern society, prolonged education, among other pressures, delays marriage, resulting in couples having fewer children.

Reasons for this sort of cultural lag are not hard to find. Until modern times, rural agrarian societies had high infant mortality rates. With limited economic specialization, they also had a great need for cheap labor. Moreover, the care of the elderly in such societies depended largely upon younger kin, which further increased the desire of parents to have many children on whom they could rely in old age. High infant mortality rates and dependence on children by the elderly continued for a time after industrialization and urbanization began. An *empirical** consequence was that, even in the 1920s, when most Americans were urbanized, the birth rate was closer to the levels of 1900 and earlier than to more recent levels.

This process can be seen again in contemporary agrarian societies that are moving from rural to urban living. We noted that Indonesia has a birth rate of 48 per 1000. Like European societies of the nineteenth century, Indonesia and other developing countries are having great difficulty adjusting economic, educational, familial, and other institutions to meet the changing conditions created by a rapidly changing material culture.

THE CRUDE BIRTH RATE-CRUDE DEATH RATE EQUATION   The birth rate itself, no matter how high it is, is not the only determinant of population growth. The death rate is also an important factor. The total natural increase in population aside from

---

[7] For a discussion of independent and dependent variables see Appendix B on the scientific method.

the factors of immigration and emigration is determined by subtracting the death rate from the birth rate. Like the crude birth rate (CBR), the crude death rate (CDR) is generally determined annually on a per 1000 population basis.

Thus, in 1973, Indonesia had a CBR of 48.3 and a CDR of 19.4, so the crude rate of natural increase (CRNI) was 28.9 per 1000 (Indonesia, 1974: 547). For the same year, the United States had a CBR of 17.3 and a CDR of 9.3, for a CRNI of 8.0 per 1000 (United States, 1974: 641). The contrast between these figures reflects different stages of demographic development in these two nations. Neither is experiencing much migration, while both are feeling the effects of their differing birth and death rates. This mortality factor is particularly important in understanding the rapid growth of population.

MORTALITY The most dramatic factor in the explosive rise in population is a worldwide decline in *mortality**. While birth rates have been decreasing slowly, death rates have been decreasing rapidly. The gap between these two rates has resulted in the global population explosion (Freedman and Berelson, 1974: 32). The age-old goal of achieving the biblical span of three-score years and ten is being reached by more people than ever before in human history.

CLOSING THE MEDICAL CULTURE LAG   What has occurred recently is the closing of what Ralph Thomlinson refers to as the medical culture lag (1967: 67). For centuries after the decline of Greco-Roman culture, during the medieval period, scientific research was generally discouraged as a sacrilegious challenge to the divine order of things. Even during the Age of Reason in the eighteenth century, when Galileo and others were experimenting with new concepts in physics and astronomy, the social norms of the period would not allow objective research on the human body. Medical science did not begin to develop the idea of sanitation until well into the nineteenth century, and many of the diagnostic tools and miracle drugs that have sharply reduced the death rate are products of the last few decades. Until the last century, along with advancing commercial development and urbanization came frequent plagues that killed thousands in short periods. Samuel Pepys left notes in his diary on the great plague that struck London in 1665 (1946: 155):

August 12th. The people die so that now it seems that they are fain to carry the dead to be buried by day-light, the nights not sufficing to do it in. And my Lord Mayor commands people to be within at nine at night all, as they say, that the sick may have liberty to go abroad for ayre.

August 31st. In the City died this week 7,496, and of them 6,102 of the plague. But it is feared that the true number of the dead this week is near 10,000; partly from the poor that cannot be taken notice of (through the greatness of their number) and partly from the Quakers and others that will not have any bell ring for them.

It is unlikely that such epidemics could occur in modern societies; but what of societies in the early stages of modernization? Given the state of medical knowledge and the ability of nations such as the United States acting alone or in concert with the United Nations, epidemics can usually be stopped before widespread death occurs. However, this does not always happen. Consider the hundreds of thousands who died of disease brought on by famine in north central Africa and in northeast India and Bangladesh in 1974 (Special Report, 1974: 56–58). There are many causes for such disasters, including international political conflicts, racism, and economic disruptions in modern societies. One underlying factor is the sharply declining death rates and consequently rapid population growth.

CONSEQUENCES OF A SHARPLY REDUCED MORTALITY RATE   In American society, a lower death rate puts strain on the social system. As more people reach the age at which social security benefits are available, funds may become insufficient. As more people live beyond the years designated as productive work years, they are forced, often unwillingly, into retirement. As more of our population ages, nursing homes and retirement communities develop to fill the need to find places for the elderly (see Chapter 7). New problems thus develop. Expanded demand for goods and services invites abuse. Where births exceed deaths, population grows, often faster than support services and goods can be supplied.

THE DEMOGRAPHIC TRANSITION THEORY   Demographers have long held that explosive population growth is a consequence of *demographic transition** (see Figure 11-6). This theory holds that, as societies become technologically modern and urbanized, they go through three periods: (1) the traditional past pattern of a high birth rate and a high death rate, (2) a period of continuing high birth rate but low death rate, and (3) a stable period with low birth rate and low death rate (Thompson, 1929: 959–975). The second period (Figure 11-6) is the one of greatest natural increase. The mortality rate comes under greater control, but cultural lag delays a drop in the birth rate, reflecting the former need for many births to sustain the society.

The fact that there is a relatively stable population base in Europe and North America is no guarantee that the process will occur in the same way for other societies in the future. Advanced technology through automation and cybernation has, since mid century, brought about a decline in the need for unskilled labor in rural areas. Past labor needs were made up by migration from farms to cities and immigration from Europe. Yet, the European population shift occurred more slowly than the recent shift in the newly modernizing societies. For example, in industrially developing France in 1865, although only 10.7 percent of the population lived in urban areas, 29 percent worked in industry, which then was less concentrated and needed relatively more unskilled labor. A century later, in the developing former French colony of Tunisia in North Africa, a United Nations survey showed that 17.5 percent of the people lived in cities but only 6.8 percent of the labor force was working in industry (Power, 1972).

In light of changing conditions, Kingsley Davis, a prominent demographer, described several possibilities for developing societies as they pass through a demographic transition (Davis, 1949: 18–21). One is gradual industrialization and modernization, resulting in rapidly declining mortality rates, closely followed by declining fertility rates, as occurred in the industrialized countries. A second possibility is that the changing conditions may result in such a slow transition to declining fertility rates and a stable and limited population growth that there may be a sharp rise in the global death rate during the last quarter of the twentieth century. There would be insufficient economic capability to sustain minimum life. A third and more hopeful possibility is that fertility will decline even before industrialization and modernization are complete. Of these alternatives, the first two cast grave doubt on the future stability of human society.

It is unlikely that, at the current rate of demo-

Figure 11-6   The demographic transition. SOURCE: Ralph Thomlinson, *Population Dynamics* (New York: Random House, 1965), p. 18.

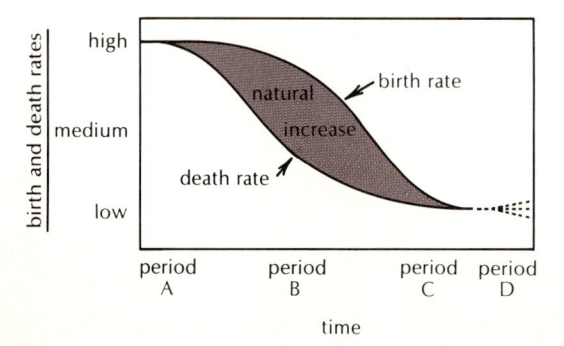

graphic transition, developing societies can stave off widespread famine and a rising death rate. While high death rates may provide one answer to population pressure, in the humanitarian view, this is an unacceptable solution. The transition might be accomplished without disaster with the third alternative, a decline in fertility before modernization is complete. This has never happened, but the present level of natural increase in agrarian societies has never yet occurred either.

POPULATION AND THE AMERICAN FUTURE

While the most pressing population problems have arisen in less developed societies, population growth in the United States has been receiving increasing attention. The United States is not in immediate danger of becoming unable to sustain a large population, but a number of social issues have arisen as a result of population growth. Is widespread acceptance of birth control, contraception, and abortion a sign of moral deterioration? Are the warnings about population growth a ploy by privileged economic groups to control the numbers of the less advantaged, who are often non-white? Is population planning sexist? The implications of expanding age groups in American society were discussed in Chapter 5 on adolescence, and in Chapter 7 on the elderly. More generally, the rapid growth of the American population in recent decades has placed considerable strain on various institutions, including public education, public and private colleges, and places of business as they attempt to absorb much larger numbers of people.

The immediate and the long-range prospects for increasing or decreasing strains on such institutions depend on many things. One general consideration is the nature of the demographic transition in American society, which is affected by long held, often religiously based values. There is also a growing wish to preserve our natural environment, as well as new concerns about the impact of mass

In a world of rising expectations, mass poverty in societies that have not yet experienced a demographic transition produces international tensions that affect everyone. SOURCE: Woodfin Camp and Assoc./Thomas Hopker.

living conditions on the quality of life. There is bound to be an increase in problems of adjustment as our population expands.

THE AMERICAN DEMOGRAPHIC TRANSITION AND ITS LIMITATIONS In terms of fertility and mortality, the United States appears to have entered the third, relatively low and stable period of the *demographic transition** (Figure 11-6). Since the 1920s and the urbanization of American society, the average annual population increase has been about 1.5 percent, less than half of what it was at the turn of the century and about half that in developing nations. Furthermore, in the past decade, the rate has dropped to about one percent. Thus, the American birth rate has been declining, as has the death rate. These declines have been accompanied by a reduction in immigration. Immigration rates averaged over 800,000 per year in the first decade of the twentieth century, when the American population was under 100 million, compared to an average of less than 400,000 per year with a population of over 200 million in the decade from 1965 to 1974 (*Annual Report,* 1974).

An analysis of the age composition of the American population illustrates these changes. The age–sex pyramids shown in Figure 11-7 show the change from high birth rates, high death rates, and immigration of mostly young people in the agrarian nineteenth century, to the lower birth rates, lower death rates, and limited immigration of the urbanized mid-twentieth century. Such an age–sex pyramid reflects the consequences of a number of factors. Note that by 1970, the age–sex groups between thirty and fifty were relatively smaller than those under thirty or over fifty. This smaller proportion in the middle was a result of comparatively low fertility during the Depression and war years of the 1930s and early 1940s. Even after the mid 1940s, with the general advent of peace and prosperity, the secular values developing in urban life kept the birth rate well under 32 per 1000 at the turn of the century.

ZERO-POPULATION GROWTH Age–sex pyramids give useful clues as to whether the United States is approaching a stable, zero-growth population base. With less immigration, lower fertility, and lower mortality, the 1940 pyramid appeared to reflect a movement toward stability. By 1970, the fertility rate of about 18 per 1000 suggested a continued trend toward stability. However, the relatively large age cohorts between ten and fourteen, fifteen and nineteen, and twenty and twenty-four (Figure 11-7) suggest a different prospect. The large number of babies born from the mid 1940s to the 1960s will have a considerable effect on the fertility rate in the late 1970s and 1980s. As the National Commission on Population Growth and the American Future put it in their final report (1972: 18-19):

> The boom generation will continue to exert a heavy impact on our society as they move up the age ladder ... it should be evident that, even if the recent ... drop in the birthrate should develop into a sustained trend, there is little cause for complacency. Whether we see it or not — whether we like it or not — we are in for a long period of growth, and we had best prepare for it.

The population will continue to grow substantially even if the fertility rate drops still further. Note in Figure 11-8 that our population passed 100 million in 1915 and reached 200 million in 1968. If families average two children in the future, growth rates will slow, and the population will reach 300 million in 2015. If families average three children, the population will reach 300 million in this century and 400 million in 2013. Indeed, the large generation soon to reach child-bearing age makes this projection conservative. These projections assume small future reductions in mortality and assume also that future rates of immigration will remain at present levels.

EFFECTS OF POPULATION DISTRIBUTION Any change in the distribution of a society's population brings with it a change in the kinds of institutions it

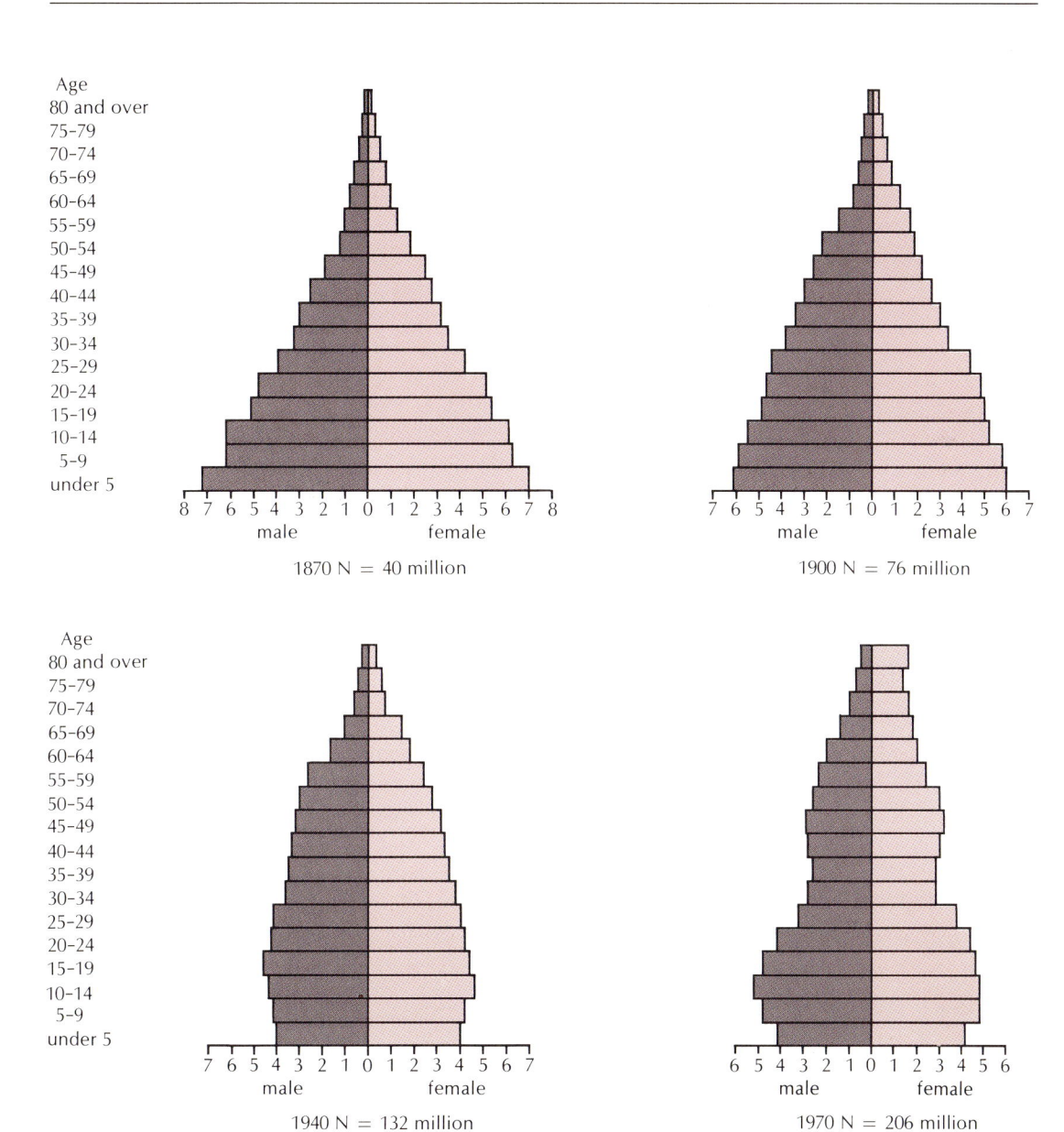

Figure 11-7 Age-sex population pyramids for the United States, 1870, 1900, 1940, and 1970.

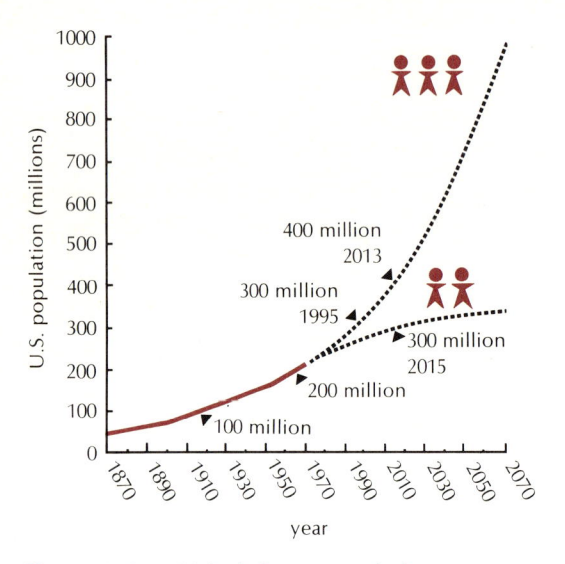

Figure 11-8 United States population: two vs. three-child family. SOURCE: *The Report of the Commission on Population Growth and the American Future* (New York: New American Library, 1972), p. 19.

needs. The capacity of the social system to meet the basic needs of the people is placed under a strain. New concentrations of population create a demand for new housing, schools, and roads. Meanwhile, areas losing population become underutilized. As we saw in Chapter 10 on urban problems, just such a shift of population from cities to suburbs is taking place in America today (see Table 11-3).

Table 11-3 The Growth of U.S. Urban Areas of One Million or More: 1940 and 1960 Projected to 1980 and 2000

Year	Number of such areas	Percent of total population
1940	12	28%
1960	23	38
1980	39	54
2000	44+	63

SOURCE: *Population and the American Future: The Report of the Commission on Population Growth and the American Future* (New York: The American Library, 1972), p. 299. (Data and projections based on U.S. Census reports.)

The prospect of continued population growth and denser concentration in urban centers has raised widespread concern. It was this concern that led the president and the Congress to establish the Commission on Population Growth and the American Future in 1970 (some of their findings were cited earlier). The Commission concluded that, for the future health and stability of American society, it is necessary to pursue a policy, with government support, that will result in a significant slowing and eventual stabilization of the size of the American population.

The Commission's conclusions were not universally applauded. Opposition to any concerted effort to control American population growth takes two forms, one based on religious grounds and the other on racial grounds. Both these sources of opposition are international and thus have an effect well beyond the boundaries of American society.

BIRTH CONTROL AND RELIGION Be fruitful and multiply is an ancient Judaeo-Christian moral imperative. From the time of the Puritans of New England until quite recently, many Americans took this dictum literally. Despite secular influences on modern urban society and the wide use of birth control devices, the effects of such established values still continue. There is still no consensus on birth control. This is particularly evident whenever any population-control policies are urged. Not only do such policies sharpen value conflicts; they also bring strong reactions from certain racial, economic, and other groups. So there remains considerable controversy over the issue of population control.

The extent of the opposition can be seen in legal developments on birth control in America. Wide acceptance of the procreation doctrine enabled Anthony Comstock and his associates in the Society for the Suppression of Vice to advance both state and federal laws in the 1870s making it illegal for a physician or anyone else to manufacture, sell, or disseminate birth control devices or information

SOURCE: (a) Ellis Herwig/Stock Boston; (b) Charles Gatewood.

(Thomlinson, 1967: 59). It was not until 1965, when the Supreme Court struck down the Connecticut law banning the use of contraceptives by anyone, including married couples, that the Comstock laws lost most of their legal underpinning.

Religious leaders still object to proposals for individuals or government to encourage conscious limitation of births. Although some Protestant and Jewish theologians oppose birth control, the main theological opposition comes from the Catholic church, which has long adhered to the dictum of St. Augustine that procreation should be restricted to marriage and that all sex acts must have that purpose. Catholic opposition to contraception was designed to influence not only the 50 million American Catholics and the 500 million Catholics worldwide but others as well. As Monsignor George A. Kelly put it, "Many persons think that contraception is a sin only for Catholics. Contraception is a sin for everyone." (1963: 81). Position statements by Pope Paul VI following Vatican II in 1965 indicate that, though the church now puts emphasis on the affectional as well as the procreational values of marital sex, their basic position has not changed. Arguing that rapid population growth is not a crucial issue, Reverend Theodore

Hesburgh, president of Notre Dame University, noted in 1972 (*Population:* 11):

> We are, especially in developed and affluent countries, facing a crisis of values and priorities that will destroy us much more quickly and far more efficiently than a crisis in population.

Dr. Hesburgh also observed that "conscience must do what it can to meet obligations that often seem to work at cross purposes." This statement recognizes implicitly the widespread use of birth control among Catholics (as among others) in response to the social effects of urbanization — prolonged schooling and specialized occupations. It has long been known that most urban Catholics practice birth control as do Protestants, Jews, and others.[8]

BIRTH CONTROL AND RACE This comment about abortion could have been made on religious grounds:

> ... the more militant of my colleagues refer to the total policy as the initial step to legitimizing genocide. ...

Actually, it was made by the black Protestant minister Reverend Jesse Jackson about birth control as it affects the issue of race. A former close associate of Dr. Martin Luther King, Jr., the Reverend Mr. Jackson summarized the concern of many blacks who have long faced arbitrary and capricious discrimination in America and Europe (*Population,* 1972: 12):

> That this issue of population control should surface simultaneously with the emergence of blacks and other non-whites as a meaningful force in the nation and the world appears more than coincidental.

It is not that Reverend Jackson fails to recognize population growth as a major problem; but he holds that, until there is an end to the unequal opportunity based on race that has resulted in "a basic maldistribution of the resources," then "population control is subordinate to wealth control."

This cautionary view toward the general society is also reflected in the positions of moderate black leaders. For example, Roy Wilkins, speaking as executive director of the NAACP, wants any birth control decisions left entirely to the individual; he argues that "minority group families ... shall not be denied access to family-planning help by reason of their racial and economic deprivations" (*Population,* 1972: 13). Black Congresswoman Shirley Chisholm reflected a similar position when she said (*Population,* 1972: 13):

> There is a difference between making information and services available and coercion. It is a very important difference that we must jealously guard and respect. Women should neither be forced into having children they don't want nor restricted from having children they do want.

(See also the selection on Population Planning: A Feminist View, page 367.)

PRESSURES TO CONTROL POPULATION GROWTH Controversies over birth control are symptomatic of the new phenomenon of growing pressure to control the American population. Some of these pressures come from large urban communities, where population is increasing faster than in

---

[8] In a national sample in the late 1950s, before the liberalizing effects of Vatican II in the 1960s, it was found that 70 percent of fecund Catholics practiced some means of artificial birth control. See Ronald Freedman, Pascal Whelpton, and Arthur Campbell, *Family Planning, Sterility, and Population Growth* (New York: McGraw-Hill, 1959), p. 65.

the country as a whole. Private economic interests and government policymakers continually face problems arising from a changing labor force, altering market needs, and rising pressures on the public schools to absorb a rapidly growing or shrinking school-age population with new educational needs.

Also, a growing number of people consider rapid population growth to be a major factor in environmental pollution. These and related developments have created new pressures to control population in order to preserve the quality of life. In response to these growing pressures, the national Commission on Population Growth and the American Future was enacted in 1969 by a conservative Republican administration and established in 1970 by a liberal Democratic Congress. A federal Environmental Protection Agency was created in 1970 to preserve the environment. Public interest in conserving clean air, water, and the natural environment inspired a social movement in the 1960s. Established conservation groups such as the Audubon Society and the Sierra Club found a mass following for their ideas; over 10 million people participated in Earth Day demonstrations on April 22, 1970.

What the leaders of the environmental movement have in common with demographers such as Kingsley Davis and Ralph Thomlinson is that both urge a decline in the American and world population growth rates. The name of one prominent ecological organization – Zero Population Growth, Incorporated – epitomizes the relationship of the environmental movement to the movement to lower and control fertility. As American industry and technology expand to meet the needs of a rapidly growing population, the lakes and rivers – including the Mississippi and the Great Lakes – become polluted. The cities face similar pollution problems. The environmentalists and their supporters increasingly argue that the quality of American life is being threatened by its increased quantity. As one environmentalist put it (Stockwell, 1968: 199):

the quality of American life shows signs of deteriorating. Continued increases in the size of the population will make it increasingly necessary to spend more and more on every conceivable kind of public service; and as maintenance costs rise, it will become less and less possible to achieve further progress in raising the standard of living.

JOHN STUART MILL ON FREEDOM AND ENVIRONMENT This concern about the ability to sustain a free and wholesome environment in the face of an indefinitely expanding population is reminiscent of observations made in the nineteenth century by John Stuart Mill, author of the classic essay *On Liberty* ([1859] 1917: 748):

A population may be too crowded, though all be amply supplied with food and raiment. It is not good for man to be kept perforce at all times in the presence of his species. A world from which solitude is extirpated is a very poor ideal. Solitude, in a sense of being often alone, is essential to any depth of meditation or of character; and solitude in the presence of natural beauty and grandeur, is the cradle of thoughts and aspirations which are not only good for the individual, but which society could ill do without. Nor is there much satisfaction in contemplating the world with nothing left to the spontaneous activity of nature; with every rod of land brought into cultivation, which is capable of growing food for human beings; every flowery waste or natural pasture ploughed up, all quadrupeds or birds which are not domesticated for man's use exterminated as his rivals for food, every hedgerow or superfluous tree rooted out, and scarcely a place left where a wild shrub or flower could grow without being eradicated as a weed in the name of improved agriculture.

Like those of the Audubon Society and the Sierra Club, Mill's views are not novel. What is new is the support that such opinions have been gaining.

THE COMMISSION ON POPULATION AND THE AMERICAN FUTURE The Commission on Population Growth and the American Future was created in a social context in which the developing countries' pressing need for sustenance was less a direct issue than was a concern for the quality of life beyond mere survival. The commission noted the enormous strain on family, education, and other institutions trying to contend with the effects of the post-World War II baby boom coupled with a continued declining mortality rate. The demographic result, between 1950 and 1970, was a rate of increase among both the oldest and the youngest groups five times the rate for those between twenty and sixty-four. The commission concluded, in a summary statement to the president and the Congress by its chairman John D. Rockefeller, that stabilization of population would significantly help the nation solve its problems. (*Population and the American Future*, 1972: iii). The commission recommended that (*Population*, 1972: 9):

In order better to prepare present and future generations to meet the challenges arising from population change, the federal government should enact a Population Education Act to offer assistance to school systems in establishing well-planned population education programs.

In order to maximize information and knowledge about human sexuality and its implications for the family, sex education should be made available through responsible community organizations, the media, and especially the schools; and similarly we should seek to improve the quality of education for parenthood throughout society.

In order to enable all Americans, regardless of age, marital status, or income, to avoid unwanted births and enhance their capacity to realize their own preferences in childbearing and family size, there should be:

Increased investment in the search for improved means by which individuals may control their own fertility.

Extending of family planning programs.

Liberalized access to abortion services with the admonition that abortion not be considered a primary means of fertility control.

Extended and improved delivery of health services related to fertility — including prenatal and pediatric care, contraceptive services, voluntary sterilization, abortion, and the treatment of infertility — through public and private financing mechanisms.

In order to regulate the impact on population migration from outside this country, present levels of legal immigration should not be increased and illegal immigration should be stopped.

These are tough, sometimes radical, proposals. Just how rapidly the climate of opinion on population control has been changing is reflected in Figure 11-9, showing new general acceptance of government policies to encourage birth control. Symptomatic of this view was the change in perspective of Dwight Eisenhower. In 1959, President Eisenhower rejected the proposal that the government involve itself directly in the issue of population control. However, on June 22, 1965, Eisenhower prepared a statement for the senate subcommittee that was considering legislation permitting government distribution of birth control information. In this statement, Eisenhower urged that the government develop programs looking to population stabilization.[9]

---

[9] In that statement, Eisenhower held that, unless fertility control action was taken by the government, the nation "will find itself in the curious position of spending money...and...providing financial incentive for increased reproduction by the ignorant, feeble-minded, or lazy." This statement brought sharp criticism from civil rights advocates, many of whom supported birth control but not on the grounds that any group in the society was generally "ignorant, feeble-minded, or lazy."

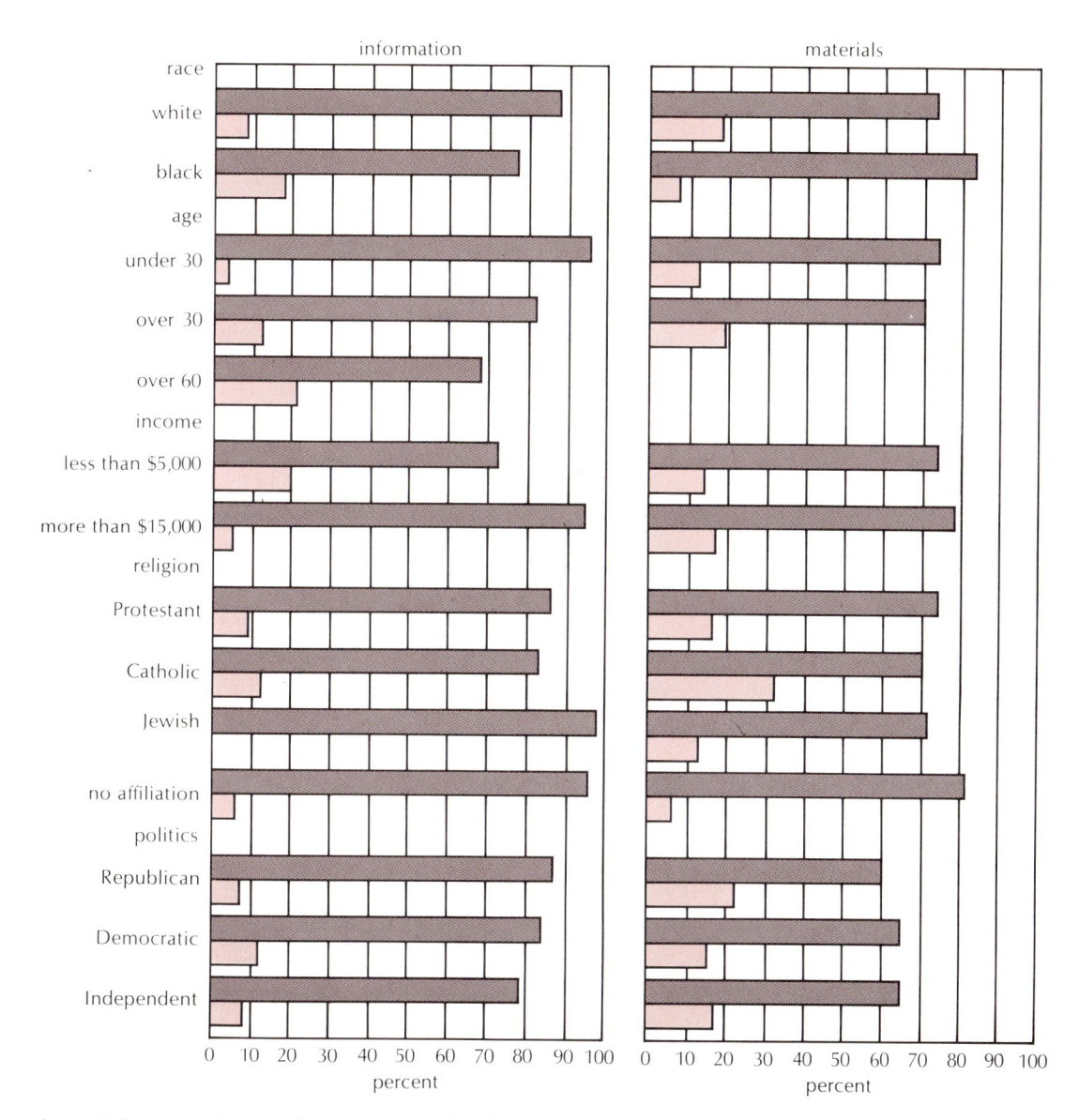

Figure 11-9 American public opinion on the dispensing of birth control information and materials by the government, 1971. SOURCE: From Frederick S. Jaffee, "Results of Polls Taken in 1971. . ." in "Public Policy on Fertility Control," *Scientific American* (July 1973), p. 19. Copyright © 1973 by Scientific American, Inc. All rights reserved.

TRUMAN AND EISENHOWER ON POPULATION CONTROL That year, former presidents Eisenhower and Truman became honorary cochairmen of the Planned Parenthood Federation of America. Furthermore, three days after Eisenhower's testimony, then President Lyndon Johnson took a public stand in favor of government involvement in birth control by stating, "Let us act on the fact that less than $5 invested in population control is worth $100 invested in economic growth." Johnson was also drawing on the presidential leadership of John Kennedy, who had favored a government role in birth control (surprising to some Catholic leaders) and observed in a message to Congress on March 22, 1961, that in developing countries, "population growth is already threatening to outpace economic growth."

Figure 11-9 shows the results of a poll taken in 1971 by the Opinion Research Corporation for the U.S. Commission on Population Growth and the American Future. The chart shows the percentage of people in each category responding affirmatively (dark gray) and negatively (light gray) to a question about birth control information and a question about birth control materials. One question asked, "Do you think that information about birth control should or should not be made available by the government to all men and women who want it?" The other asked whether or not the government should make birth control materials available.

SOME ONGOING POPULATION ISSUES Though the climate of opinion has been changing, many of the recommendations of the Commission on Population Growth remain controversial. For example, though the Supreme Court has held that it is constitutional for abortions to be made available, some Roman Catholic and other religious leaders believe that abortion amounts to infanticide.

While immigration is restricted by federal law, this limitation is at odds with the American heritage. Most of our ancestors came to these shores under an open-door policy epitomized in the inscription on the Statue of Liberty: "Give me your tired, your poor, your huddled masses yearning to breathe free."

These and other population issues will surely continue, given the radical shift not only in public policy but in the mores of our society which, until recently, idealized the large family.

MALTHUSIAN GLOOM REVISITED

As we have seen, the first comprehensive theory of population was developed by Thomas Malthus, an English clergyman with an interest in economics and mathematics. In 1798, he published his *Essay on the Principle of Population* (Malthus, 1971 edition), in which he saw the world population of his day (nearly a billion) growing unchecked in geometric progression (2,4,8,16,32,64,128,256 . . .), whereas the food supply would increase only in arithmetical progression (1,2,3,4,5,6,7,8 . . .) (1963: 6).

One consequence of rapid population growth would be a sharp rise in the death rate. Malthus held that two *preventive checks* could decrease the birth rate and thus hold down the death rate. One was delaying marriage and the other was celibacy (no sexual activity), though Malthus realized that neither was likely to be widely practiced. Reflecting the social norms of his day, Malthus himself regarded the use of contraceptives as a vice that permitted men and women to escape the consequences of sexual intercourse. Malthus also believed that certain *positive checks* would hold down future population growth: hunger, disease, war, and vice — a minor factor (Malthus, 1971: 36–39). In effect, Malthus's population theory postulated increasing misery.

MALTHUS AND CONTEMPORARY SOCIETY How likely is it that Malthus's apocalyptic vision will in fact occur? A more precise and sociologically useful way to ask the same question is, under what conditions is Malthus's population theory valid? We know that his projections of population growth

have not been borne out in the twentieth century. As an example of his miscalculations, at a rate of geometric growth, the United States population would have reached 494 million by 1970; in fact, it was recorded by the Census as 203 million, or less than half (see Figure 11-10). On world population growth, Malthus was similarly off the mark, for, by his calculation, there would now be well over 10 billion people on earth, whereas there is actually less than half that number.

What made Malthus's original projection so wrong? First, he was unaware that the industrial revolution would give us new ways to sustain life, including improved means of producing food. By the 1820s in North America and Western Europe, horse-drawn hay rakes did as much work as six to ten men using the age-old hand rakes of Malthus's time (Carman and Syrett, 1954: 397). Technology made possible canals, steamboats, and railways, which enabled millions to settle and develop land in the New World, relieving population pressures in Europe while increasing international trade and improving standards of living. One consequence of all this was a shift in social norms. The belief in the immorality of contraception weakened as urban living caused people to adopt secular values. These changed values led to a reduction in the birth rate.

The conditions in Europe and America that made possible a successful demographic transition over more than a century are not operating in the same way for those nations now undergoing modernization. Two major differences are that today's advanced technology reduces rather than increases the need for unskilled labor and that there are no longer the vast unsettled lands that existed in the nineteenth century to relieve internal population pressures. Global overpopulation may yet lead to an insufficiency of the world's resources.

Consider our neighbor Mexico. Mexico, like other Latin American nations, has a natural rate of population increase of over 3 percent, which is more than double that of the United States, Canada, and Western Europe. Until the mid-twentieth century, the population of Mexico rose at a slower

Thomas Malthus. SOURCE: The Bettmann Archive.

rate because of two of Malthus's positive checks, war and disease. Since the revolutionary period of social reform, 1910 to 1920, when more than one million lost their lives, Mexico has enjoyed a stable peacetime development, even during the two world wars. Still, until mass inoculations ended them around 1950, smallpox and diphtheria killed tens of thousands each year. With these diseases under control, the average life expectancy rose from forty-eight years in 1950 to sixty-four years in 1970 (Alisky, 1974: 200). Over half the Mexican population is under twenty years of age and just now coming into the child-bearing stage, thus providing the basis for a new population explosion even if the fertility rate is reduced.

It is just this kind of population explosion in Mexico and other developing countries that can prove Malthus right: population might increase faster than the food supply. Even if the demo-

Figure 11-10 The actual and Malthusian projected United States population.

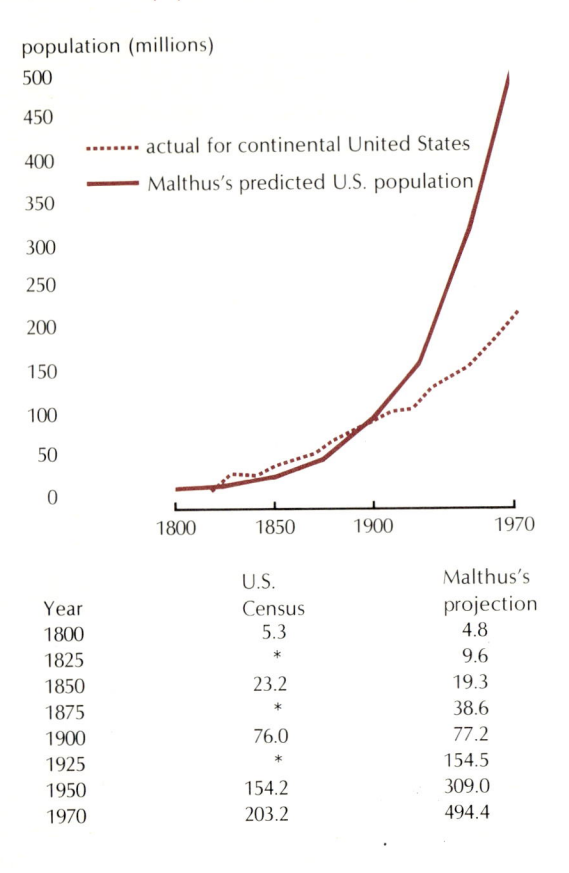

population (millions)

······· actual for continental United States
——— Malthus's predicted U.S. population

Year	U.S. Census	Malthus's projection
1800	5.3	4.8
1825	*	9.6
1850	23.2	19.3
1875	*	38.6
1900	76.0	77.2
1925	*	154.5
1950	154.2	309.0
1970	203.2	494.4

graphic transition does occur in developing nations, the natural increase may not drop in time to prevent the worst of consequences for millions now living and soon to be born.

A GLOBAL POPULATION STRATEGY

We now come back to the quotation with which this chapter began:

Long-range projections of current rates of population growth simply run off the chart and beyond the range of agricultural solutions that are either possessed or conceivable.

When he made this statement, Kenneth R. Farrell had taken a look at the lowest projections for stabilizing world population in the next generation (see Figure 11-11) and the highest estimates of his economic development research service and concluded that there was little chance of sustaining population and development at a minimal level. This view is a prophecy of doom.

Given the economic and military interdependence of nations, ecologists Barry Commoner in his *The Closing Circle* (1971) and Paul Ehrlich in his *Population Bomb* (1968) foresee the death of the world unless drastic steps are taken to cut population growth and to preserve environmental resources. Such observations have rekindled interest not only in the gloomy Malthusian prognostications but in a recent book by William and Paul Paddock entitled *Famine — 1975!* The Paddocks' book appeared in 1967 and was treated lightly at the time. The *green revolution* of miracle rice, wheat, and other grains then promised to solve the problem of famine. This, in effect, is what Amitai Etzioni (1972) identifies as technological shortcuts to social change. Yet, by 1974, the most conservative estimates of worldwide famine given at the United Nations World Food Conference in Rome were that 10 million people had died of starvation that year and at least another 460 million were threatened by starvation (Special Report, 1974: 56).

POPULATION PROJECTIONS Figure 11-11 projects future population growth for the developing countries, which include most nations outside of

Europe, North America, and Japan. The total population of these developing countries in 1970 was about 2.5 billion. If families in these countries average two children in the future, which is less than their current rate, by the year 2000, they will have a total population of almost 7 billion, and by the middle of the twenty-first century, about 14 billion.

THE TRIAGE THESIS   The Paddocks theorized that the United States and other leading agricultural nations would soon be forced to consider food triage. The term *triage* is derived from the French verb *trier*, to sort. As Wade Greene explains it (1975: 9):

During the trench-warfare slaughter of World War I, a system for separating the wounded into three groups was practiced in Allied medical tents. The groups consisted of those likely to die no matter what was done for them, those who would probably recover even if untreated, and those who could survive only if cared for immediately. With supplies and manpower limited, the third group alone received attention. Such a practice was called *triage* [emphasis added].... While it is still little discussed, triage has become standard wartime procedure for making the most efficient use of scarce medical resources.

The principle of triage has been applied to the limited ability to produce food to meet the needs of growing populations. The thesis advanced by the Paddocks — and some others such as the biologist-ecologist Garrett Hardin and Jay Forrester, a management professor at the Massachusetts Institute of Technology — holds that nations in which population growth has already passed agricultural potential should be denied food aid from the agriculturally overproducing nations such as the

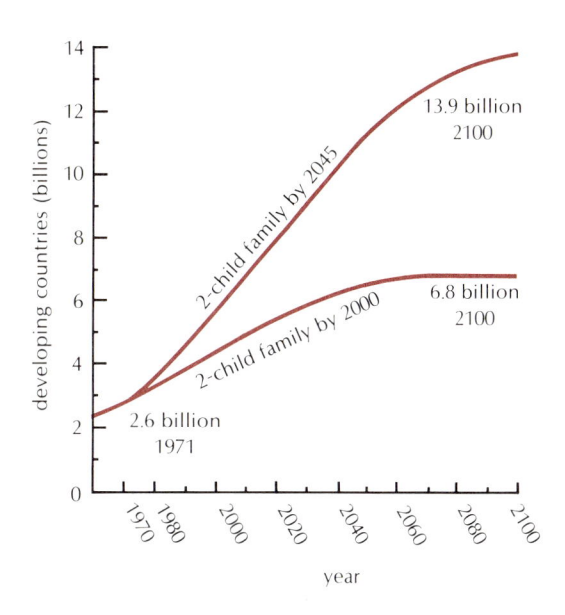

Figure 11-11   Alternatives of population growth for the developing countries. SOURCE: From "Alternatives of Population Growth for the Developing Countries," April 30, 1972 by Thomas Frejka. Copyright © 1972 by the New York Times Company. Reprinted by permission.

United States and Canada. The triagists thus propose a *lifeboat ethic*, reasoning that, if everyone tries to climb aboard a lifeboat in open seas, then all will drown. It is best for the future of human civilization, they argue, to save some by the rational process of triage — selection of some and disposal of others.

SOME MORAL AND PRACTICAL ISSUES   To those in developing countries such as India, most nations in Africa, and western South America (see Figure 11-3), which are having trouble sustaining their people, the triage proposal may sound reminiscent of the eighteenth-century Irish clergyman Jonathan Swift's satiric "Modest Proposal" to use excess Irish babies as food. As Swift put it, the infants would (1928: 498):

be offered in sale to the persons of quality and fortune throughout the kingdom; always advising the mother to let them suck plentifully in the last month, so as to render them plump and fat for a good table. A child will make two dishes at an entertainment for friends; and when the family dines alone, the fore or hind quarter will make a reasonable dish, and seasoned with a little pepper or salt will be very good boiled on the fourth day, especially in winter. . . .

Perhaps the fundamental defect of triage is the dubious assumption that the United States and other developed nations are now in safe lifeboats and everyone else is trying to swim about in open seas. A more accurate analogy is that all peoples, including Americans, are adrift in ships of limited capacity, each of which needs some assistance from others to make it safely ashore. The developing societies, with the greatest population growth, possess most of the untapped natural resources from aluminum to petroleum to zinc, all of which the developed nations need in great quantities for their industries. In addition, like Dean Swift's Irish, the poor and starving are not likely to acquiesce quietly to their own demise.

After reflecting on the global facts of life, bolstered by humanitarian and ethical considerations, a growing number of American and world leaders are proposing active programs to meet the population explosion.

THE GLOBAL PERSPECTIVE The rapidity of population growth through declining mortality rates in the developing nations has stimulated a great shift in government policies. Between the early 1960s and the early 1970s, more government support for population control was initiated worldwide than ever before (Davis, 1974; *Population*, 1972). When, in 1965, President Johnson announced an American policy to assist family planning programs in nations that request help, the offer was taken up by India, Taiwan, Korea, the Republic of Singapore, and a number of other developing nations. By the 1970s, Mexico and some other predominantly Catholic Latin American nations had instituted population-control policies, as had such African nations as Ghana, Kenya, Mauritius, and the North African and Mideast nations of Egypt, Morocco, and Tunisia. In 1976, India announced a compulsory sterilization program for fathers after voluntary and incentive programs had fallen short of desired results, to enforce limits to family size. The central impetus behind all these measures was stated by Alberto Llaras Camargo, a United Nations spokesman from Colombia (*Population*, 1972: 18–19):

Population, the traditional principal resource and ultimate objective of development, is now a restraint to progress. . . . Obviously, each Latin American government should recognize the right of the citizen to plan the size of his family and should provide the services indispensable to civilized society.

Given these developments, some writers such as the British political economist Wilfred Beckerman (1974) have argued that world society is about to enter a period of successful demographic transition that will prove the modern triagists as wrong as were the Malthusians of the nineteenth century. Yet, it is not easy to forget the famines in Africa and Bangladesh in the early 1970s. The cultural lag during the transition will probably continue for some years. As Kingsley Davis put it (1974: 375):

the relief that "at last something is being done" is no guarantee that what is being done is adequate. On the face of it, one could hardly expect such a fundamental reorientation to be quickly and successfully implemented.

Davis went on to note that within the population policy movement, there had been little explicit discussion of long-range goals. Ralph Thomlinson recommends adopting three such goals (1965: 329): a slowing of the rate of population growth, an increase in the world's food supply, and the development of higher real income and general well-being in technologically developing as well as developed societies.[10]

THE FIRST WORLD POPULATION CONFERENCE All three goals were on the agenda when the United Nations convened the World Population Conference in Bucharest in 1974. Representatives of 113 nations, including the United States, all agreed that there is a population problem but not on what to do about it. The predominantly white developed countries stressed the need for lower fertility, while the predominantly nonwhite developing countries stressed the need for increasing the world's food supply and raising the general standard of living. Another divisive factor is the alleged sexism of population planning (see the selection, Population Planning: A Feminist View).

POPULATION PLANNING: A FEMINIST VIEW

From: Gloria Steinem in Dom Moraes (ed.), *Voices for Life* (New York: Praeger, 1975), 241–243. Published in cooperation with the United Nations Fund for Population Activities.

Gloria Steinem, writer and editor, born 1934 in the United States, an editor and founder of *Ms.* magazine and a convenor of the National Women's Political Caucus, is one of the best-known feminists in America. She has been a free-lance writer for publications in the United States and Europe since 1962.

Yes, there is a feminist view of what is now referred to as "the population problem." And most of the solutions practiced or proposed so far — especially those advocated by the almost totally male councils of religions, national governments, and some international organizations — seem doomed to substantial failure precisely because they ignore that view or simply don't know that it exists.

How can a powerful, decisive female presence be excluded from any representative council? Or from any group, with or without democratic pretensions, discussing a process that takes place largely in the bodies of women? If our cultures, East or West, were less patriarchal, this exclusion would seem foolish — and self-defeating to men as well. As it is, even our small understanding of racism surpasses our consciousness of sexism and the political uses of sex-as-caste. It may now seem immoral, or at least impractical, for a white, Europeanized minority of the world to make decisions for a nonwhite Third World majority, for instance, but it still seems moral, practical, and even "natural" for men of every race to make decisions for the half of the world that is women.

So natural, in fact, that many people, some women as well as men, are sure that females in power would either duplicate the male population planners' ideas exactly (though perhaps with less skill, since we have fewer "experts" among us), or express our natural differentness and purpose by disastrous, uncontrolled production of children.

But both these predictions are based on male-supremacist values: In the first, male culture is seen as the model or even the only choice; in the second, women's primary impulse and value is assumed to be breeding. The truth is that, whenever we have been allowed the ability to enforce it, women have turned out to have an effective and culturally distinct solution to "the population problem." Its essentials are as old as the women of ancient Greece and pre-Christian Rome,

---

[10] An interesting assumption by Thomlinson and other demographers is that the world's population is now so vast that only through further technological development and output can a higher standard of living be achieved. In this sense, they see no possibility for a successful return to an agrarian existence for most peoples.

or even the gynocracies of prehistory, if mythology and archaeology are any guide. Its current extensions sound similar, whether the feminists advocating them are in India or France or the United States.

Of course, modern patriarchal governments and religions won't like this solution very much, for it requires free and powerful women. Population planners will mistrust it for the same reason, as well as for its vesting of decision-making power in nonexperts, men as well as women, without a centralized control. But in modern dress, the prescription would go like this:

1. *Establish reproductive freedom as a fundamental human right, never to be denied by government or by other individuals.* This means, for instance, no forced sterilization — of men or women. It also means an end to forced motherhood — no restriction, whether by husband or state, of a woman's right to abortion, contraception, and the control of her own body.

2. *Make the provision of free and safe contraception and abortion a major responsibility of government.* Easy access to information and to a full range of contraceptive methods, with research on improvements for men as well as for women, should be close in priority to the provision of food and shelter.

3. *Allow women and men equal political power, human value, and opportunity to develop as individuals.* This not only gives women — and men — choices of rewards other than parenthood, but it will eventually remove a patriarchal motive for overpopulation: the need to continue procreating until there are one or many sons. Social equality also leads to equal responsibility for children, an emphasis on parenthood rather than motherhood, which increases men's stake in family planning.

4. *Advocate free choice, not impossible and oppressive conformity.* Even phrases like "population control" betray their elitist origins and tend to make the least powerful groups fearful that they will be restricted the most. "Reproductive freedom," both as phrase and reality, does not. "Two or Three Children Are Enough," for instance, has been an unsuccessful slogan, whether used by Plato or the modern planners of India. It manages simultaneously to alienate the person who wants four, five, or six children and to suggest that someone who doesn't want to be a parent at all is abnormal. "Children Are a Choice" accommodates both — and the average number of births is the same.

The first world population conference produced no plan of action. Formidable stumbling blocks included the problem of how to agree upon a global population limit in a world in which many religious and economic values urge continued population expansion and each nation still holds to its absolute sovereignty, whatever the resolutions of the United Nations or any other international body. Representatives passed a policy resolution holding that nations should "encourage appropriate education concerning responsible parenthood and make available to persons who so desire advice and means of achieving it" (the New York *Times*, August 28, 1974: 7C). The conference ended on an encouraging note. Neither officials nor delegates seemed unhappy with the conference's limited goals. That population problems were no longer being ignored and that study and debate were occurring, even that a conference took place, indicated hope for the future (Hill, 1974).

The trouble with this optimistic assessment was pointed out at the world food conference sponsored by the United Nations in Rome in 1974. At a hearing of the nutrition committee, Nobel laureate Norman Borlaug warned that (1974: 1)

... 50 million people, perhaps more, could perish from famine ... it will probably take a disaster — perhaps the death of tens of millions — before we will come to grips with this.

The general and unspecific nature of the World Population Conference resolutions bring to mind Kingsley Davis's warning that "the world's population problems cannot be solved by pretense and wishful thinking" (1974: 388). Michael Endres has suggested that population control policy be based on relative priorities assigned to survival goals, quality of life, and values involved with relating means to ends. He takes the view that we must rationally order and reconcile value-oriented choices. Policies based on conflicting or inconsistent values or policies that ignore important values or that favor unacceptable means should be changed. He defines a pragmatic or workable policy as one that meets two criteria: its actions complement values of the society in fulfilling its most important goals, and the means are both practical and morally acceptable (Endres, 1975: 166–167). This is a *functionalist* view of population planning.

While there is global recognition of the need to adopt population policies, only about a quarter of the nations of the earth had moved to do so by the mid 1970s. As United Nations Secretary-General Kurt Waldheim observed, the other three-quarters of the nations must also adopt population policies if the world is to avoid "constraints that past ages never knew and that we violate at our peril" (*Population*, 1972: 14).

There have been some signs of a tapering off of global population growth. Lester Brown, director of Worldwide Institute, reported that the world growth rate fell from 1.9 percent in 1970 to 1.64 percent in 1975 (Panati, 1976: 58). If this constitutes a trend, then governments may have more time to adjust — but not much more time.

SUMMARY

The population explosion has led to popular interest in *demography**, the specialized study of populations. Demographic analysis has documented the rapid population growth in the past century. Demographers analyze population size, population distribution, and population composition. We compared population characteristics of different groups within American society and other societies.

Three main factors influencing population stability, growth, or decline are *fertility** (number of children born), which is related to such factors as social class and rural or urban residency; *mortality** (deaths in a society), the most dynamic influence on recent population growth, as death rates have declined sharply in the past century; and *migration** (movement into or out of a society), which is at present less important to population growth than it has been in the past.

We examined important demographic characteristics of the American population, noting the relative slowing of the population growth rate that has accompanied the trend toward urbanization and the decline of immigration rates. We discussed the implications of internal migration of population from rural to urban to suburban areas. Population growth has brought about problems of pollution, congestion, and strain on resources and services. Disagreement exists as to who should make policy to avoid moral decay, elitism, sexism, and ageism. The changing balance of young and old citizens creates other problems, such as availability of support services and exploitation of need.

We introduced the Malthusian theory of positive and preventive checks on population, which projects a law of increasing misery based on geometrically accelerating population growth and declining capability to feed and otherwise sustain people. By examining the concepts of *cultural evolution** and the *demographic transition** hypothesis regarding alterations of the relationship between birth and death rates, we discovered that the Malthusian thesis has not been borne out. Malthus failed to foresee technological developments and changes in social norms. Recent famines in Africa and Bangladesh have rekindled interest in Malthus's theories and in contemporary prophecies of doom, such as the idea of *triage*.

The World Population Conference of 1974, advanced various proposals to meet the challenge of continued population growth.

Cultural lag* is a concept that refers to differential rates of social change in the material and nonmaterial segments of culture. The need for population planning using acceptable means to achieve an agreed-upon end is constantly increasing.

QUESTIONS FOR DISCUSSION

1. Why does the population of a society continue to grow even when the birth rate falls?

2. What problems preclude mass migration from overcrowded countries to other countries, a regular phenomenon until the twentieth century?

3. Why did Malthus not advocate keeping the population in check by widespread use of contraceptive devices? Is this view still important?

4. What factors are involved in the recent drop in the birth rate in the United States? Is the drop likely to continue?

5. Even if the theory ultimately proves to be valid, what are some of the adjustment problems society faces during the demographic transition?

6. Is triage, in effect, already in operation? If not, is it likely to be supported?

7. Why might terms such as *cultural disjuncture* or *cultural discontinuity* be more accurate than the widely used *cultural lag*?

8. What consequences for the society do you see if the proposed zero-population-growth policy advocated by the Commission on Population Growth and the American Future is achieved?

9. In your opinion would widespread use of birth control measures ultimately lead to the moral decay feared by some?

10. Review your understanding of the following terms and concepts:

demography

cultural evolution

migration

fertility

mortality

population pyramid

age composition

cultural lag

demographic transition

Malthus's principle of population

triage thesis

REFERENCES

Alisky, Marvin
    1974   "Mexico versus Malthus: national trends." Current History 66 (May): 200–203; 227–230.

    1974   Annual Report of the Immigration and Naturalization Service: 1973. Washington, D.C.: Government Printing Office.

Beckerman, Wilfred
    1974   In Defense of Economic Growth. London: Jonathan Cape.

Borlaug, Norman
    1974   From a report based upon Rabbi Marc Tannenbaum's testimony before the Ad Hoc Senate Committee Hearings on World Hunger, December 18, 1974. New York: Institute of Human Relations. 2 pp.

Boyd-Orr, Lord
1970 Quoted in the New York Times (December 17): 17.

Carman, Harry and Harold Syrett
1954 A History of the American People, vol. I. New York: Knopf.

Carr-Sanders, A. M.
1936 World Population. Oxford: Clarendon Press.

Commoner, Barry
1971 The Closing Circle. New York: Knopf.

Davies, James
1962 "Toward a theory of revolution." American Sociological Review 27 (February): 5–19.

Davis, Kingsley
1949 Future Population Trends and Their Significance in Human Society. New York: Macmillan.
1974 "World population crisis." L. Rainwater (ed.), Inequality and Justice. Chicago: Aldine: 375–388.
1976 "The world's population crisis." Chapter 6, R. Merton and R. Nisbet (eds.), Contemporary Social Problems. New York: Harcourt Brace Jovanovich.

Ehrlich, Paul
1968 The Population Bomb. New York: Ballantine.

Ehrlich, Paul and Anne Ehrlich
1970 Population, Resources, Environment: Issues in Human Ecology. San Francisco: W. H. Freeman.

Endres, Michael E.
1975 On Defusing the Political Bomb. New York: Halstead.

Etzioni, Amitai
1972 Technological Shortcuts to Social Change. New York: Russell Sage Foundation.

Fairchild, Henry
1925 Immigration. New York: Macmillan.

Farrell, Kenneth
1974 Quoted in the New York Times (August 25): 48.

Freedman, Ronald and Bernard Berelson
1974 "The human population." Scientific American 231 (September): 31–39.

Greene, Wade
1975 "Triage: who shall be fed? who shall starve?" The New York Times Magazine (January 5): 9–11; 44–45; 51.

Handlin, Oscar
1951 The Uprooted. Boston: Little, Brown.

Hill, Gladwin
1974 "Slow going in population talks." The New York Times (August 29): 6C.

Indonesia
1974 The Official Associated Press Almanac. Maplewood, N.J.: Hammond Almanac: 547.

Jaffee, Frederick
1973 Public Policy on Fertility Control. New York: Scientific American.

Joyce, James
1971 "The population bomb: can the U.N. defuse it?" War/Peace (April): 10–11.

Kelly, George
1963 Birth Control and Catholics. New York: Doubleday.

Malthus, Thomas
1963 An Essay on the Principle of Population (originally published in 1798). Ann Arbor: University of Michigan Press.
1971 An Essay on the Principle of Population (1803 revised version). Homewood, Ill.: Richard D. Irwin.

Mill, John Stuart
1917 Principles of Political Economy. Book IV. London: Longmans, Green.

Moraes, Dom
1975 Voices for Life: Reflections on the Human Condition. New York: Praeger.

Ogburn, William
1922 Social Change. New York: Viking.

Paddock, William and Paul Paddock
1967 Famine — 1975! Boston: Little, Brown.

Panati, Charles
1976 "Population implosion." Newsweek (December 6): 58.

Pepys, Samuel
1946 The Diary of Samuel Pepys: 1660–1669. Eau Claire, Wis.: E.M. Hale.

Peterson, William
1975 Population. New York: Macmillan.

1972 The U.S. problem — the world crisis. A New York Times supplement (April 30): 28 pp.

1972 The Report of the Commission on Population Growth and the American Future. New York: New American Library.

Power, Jonathan
1972 "The city in Africa." Commonweal (April 28): 189–190.

1974 "Running out of food?" Newsweek (November 11): 56–68.

Stockwell, Edward
1968 Population and People. Chicago: Quadrangle.

Swift, Jonathan
1928 A Modest Proposal for Preventing the Children of Poor People in Ireland from Being a Burden to Their Parents or Country, and for Making Them Beneficial to the Public (1729). P. Lieder, R. Lowett, and M. Root (eds.), British Poetry and Prose. Boston: Houghton Mifflin.

Thomlinson, Ralph
1965 Population Dynamics. New York: Random House.
1967 Demographic Problems. Belmont, Cal.: Dickenson.

Thompson, Warren
1929 "Recent trends in world population." American Journal of Sociology 34 (May): 959–975.
1953 Population Problems. New York: McGraw-Hill.

Ward, Barbara
1962 The Rich Nations and the Poor Nations. New York: W.W. Norton.

Woytinsky, Wladimir and Emma Woytinsky
1953 World Population and Production. New York: Twentieth Century Fund.

Chapter 12

SOCIAL COHESION IN COLD AND HOT WARS

Would we now keep the peace by leaving the levers of power largely in the hands of vast imperial systems whose ideological aim is to dominate the world? And at what point should we cry "halt" — and probably confront a nuclear holocaust?

What we must attempt today is to extend to the whole society of men the techniques, the methods, the habits — if you will the courtesies — upon which our own sense of citizenship is based. In our free society, we ask that all citizens participate as equals. We accept their views and interests as significant. We struggle for unforced consensus. We tolerate conflict and accept dissent. But we believe that because each citizen knows he is valued and has his chance for comment and influence, his final loyalty to the social order will be more deeply rooted and secure.

Adlai Stevenson[1]
Two-time presidential candidate and former American ambassador to the United Nations.

---

[1] From "Outline for a New American Policy," *Look* (August 24, 1965), p. 71.

THE UNITED STATES AS A MILITARY POWER

This statement by a perceptive analyst points up reasons for concern about the effect of international conflict on the nature of American society. Today we must find answers to questions about the relative influence of the average citizen and the managerial power brokers who strongly influence our national policy. Have basic tensions between these groups affected our ability to wage peace? The response to this question takes many forms. We must consider the mass horrors of modern war and the historical, economic, and political dimensions of international conflict. While we shall note these areas of concern, our primary focus in this chapter is a sociological one: What are the problematical consequences for American society of the Cold War and continuing international tensions? What policy choices are available in the face of these consequences?

World War II ended in 1945, but there has been no real peace since. The Cold War, involving the United States, the Soviet Union, and China and their allies may not have brought direct worldwide confrontation, but it has involved American forces in two limited hot wars, in Korea and Vietnam. The American responses to these conflicts are of sociological interest because they have had widespread social consequences. Continuing tensions in the Middle East and among African nations such as

Angola, Uganda, and South Africa threaten international peace. American foreign policy is undergoing revision to allow for conditions under which direct confrontation may occur.

RECENT EMERGENCE OF A LARGE STANDING MILITARY Except during the Civil War and World Wars I and II, the United States did not maintain a large military establishment until a few years after the end of World War II. In response first to Russian military occupation of once independent nations in Eastern Europe and to an international revolutionary doctrine proposed to subvert western capitalist societies, by 1948, the United States had begun a peacetime draft and entered into the North Atlantic Treaty Organization (NATO), an alliance with Canada, Great Britain, and most of the Western European nations (Carman and Syrett, 1955: 649–659). American troops intervened in South Korea after it was invaded by North Korean communist forces in 1950. The result is that, in the past quarter century, the United States has maintained a large defense establishment. Into the 1970s, the defense effort of the United States has been greater than at any other time in history except during the late years of World War II (Melman, 1972: 273–274).

The defense establishment is clearly designed to protect the nation, its people, and their institutions. Yet, as more and more analysts are noting, such a prolonged military effort has serious latent consequences for our economic, political, and social life. In addition to setting up a possible challenge to our nonmilitaristic tradition, it has had purely practical implications. The large and continuous defense effort sets limits on the amount of money the government can spend in other areas such as schooling, social security benefits to match increasing costs of living, and mass transit. A large military establishment also distorts traditional economic practices in the private sector of the economy. The American capitalist system is based on competition and profit, but the military procurement system limits competition to favored industries, and the goods produced are not designed for profit and use. Indeed, it is hoped that they will become obsolete without ever being put to use.

As the columnist and political analyst Walter Lippmann noted in 1920, the oceans that were once protective barriers for American society are now highways for commerce, war, and other purposes, both good and bad. Americans no longer have a choice — if indeed we ever did — between isolation and world involvement. The only question is *how* we will become involved and what will be the impact on our society.

TECHNOLOGICAL MILITARISM AND THE COSTS OF DETERRENCE A group of thirty-two social critics met in Washington, D.C., in March 1964, to evaluate certain issues facing America and the world in this era of great social change. This ad hoc committee produced a policy statement that identified technological militarism as one component of a worldwide triple revolution.[2] How could anything military be revolutionary in the sense of being new? For thousands of years warfare has involved increasingly sophisticated weapons. Even the two world wars in this century did not destroy the civilized world, and the United States came out of both not only intact but stronger than before. What is different is the new technology.

The end of World War II, with the United States in possession of the atomic bomb, ushered in the new era of technological militarism that has already had profound effects on the strategy of defense. The United States had shown that a small number of technological specialists and military personnel could activate the most destructive weaponry in

---

[2] The other two components were human rights and cybernation. The first of these was the national and international *social movement** of blacks, women and other minorities toward equal *status**. The second dealt with the effects of computerized automation in modern industry, which is fundamentally altering the occupational pattern of all societies. These two revolutionary social changes are taken up in parts 2 and 3 of this book.

world history. Given the United States and the Soviet Union's suspicions of each other, a new potential confrontation soon became a reality.[3] Former secretary of state Henry Stimson described this confrontation as "a great armament race of a rather desperate character" (Williams, 1972: 265). This race became known as the Cold War, since it consisted in developing nuclear armaments rather than using them.

THE BALANCE OF TERROR   Nuclear weapons systems are so destructive that neither the United States, the Soviet Union, nor any of the other nations that developed nuclear arsenals, such as the British, the Chinese, and the French, have been willing to use them for fear of retaliation. In effect, the new military technology had ushered in what Adlai Stevenson called a balance of terror (1965: 81). No longer was Karl von Clausewitz's classic nineteenth-century treatise *On War* considered a tenable view of warfare. Clausewitz had described civilized war as a means to a political or diplomatic end, such as territorial gain or the prevention of such gain by an adversary. In a book also titled *On War*, Midlarsky refutes Clausewitz's view of war as a continuation of politics through other means. He regards war as being more akin to coercive application of force, and therefore more a failure of than an extension of political relations (1975: 1-2). However one interprets Clausewitz, nuclear warfare is so devastating as to render his traditional view obsolete. The destructiveness of nuclear weapons and what their use means was made demonstrably clear when atomic bombs destroyed the cities of Hiroshima and Nagasaki at the end of World War II.

The effects of the bombs dropped on the two Japanese cities and the study of post-war testing by the United States up to the signing of the test ban treaty with the Soviet Union in 1962 (Schlesinger, 1967: 834) have shown in some detail what destruction a bomb of any given size could cause. For example, a committee of scientists (1962: 24-32) described what would happen if a single twenty-megaton bomb hit Columbus Circle in midtown Manhattan (26):

On a clear day, a 20-megaton (MT) low air burst would produce these injuries to exposed skin:
Third-degree burns (12 cal/cm^2) 27 miles from the explosion[4]
Second-degree burns (10 cal/cm^2) 35 miles away
First-degree burns (4 cal/cm^2) 54 miles away

How the destructiveness of a nuclear attack translates into loss of life city by city can be seen in

---

[3] Toward the end of World War I, after the Communist Revolution in Russia, an American expeditionary force was sent to Siberia to help overthrow the Communist regime — an act the Soviets never forgot (see: George Kennan, *Russia and the West* (Boston: Little, Brown, 1961), pp. 105-119). Then, after World War II, the Russian military moved in and broke agreements in Poland and in other Eastern European nations that would have enabled those countries to reestablish their independence (see: Arthur Link, *An American Epoch* (New York: Knopf, 1955), pp. 649-659). Americans, British, and Western Europeans were generally suspicious that the Soviet Union meant to dominate all of Europe and do injury to American economic and military interests.

[4] The extent of heat damage was predicted by determining the number of calories (unit of heat) per square centimeter of surface a given object would receive if exposed to the flash of the bomb. To help lay readers gauge the level of destructiveness for a twenty-megaton bomb, the committee noted that the heat varied with distance and that about seven calories per square centimeter (cal/cm^2) will ignite shredded newspaper, and thirteen cal/cm^2 will ignite deciduous leaves.

Table 12-1. Note that one consequence of *urbanization** in America is that even one ten-megaton weapon would probably kill or seriously injure most of the people in almost any metropolitan area.

WAR GAMES ANALYSIS Given the ability of the Soviet Union to inflict heavy damage in a nuclear war, whatever similar damage the United States might inflict in return, there developed within the United States a simulated war games analysis industry. The RAND (Research and Development) Corporation was established by the Air Force in California after World War II to simulate models demonstrating the United States' ability to sustain itself during and after a nuclear war. The calculations in Table 12-1 illustrate this approach. One of

Table 12-1   Projected Casualties in a Nuclear Attack on the United States

Target area and weapons	Population	Number killed first day	Fatally injured	Nonfatally injured
Two 10-megaton weapons each				
Boston	2,875,000	1,052,000	1,084,000	467,000
Chicago	5,498,000	545,000	447,000	648,000
Detroit	3,017,000	820,000	593,000	557,000
Los Angeles	4,367,000	698,000	2,136,000	814,000
New York	12,904,000	3,464,000	2,634,000	2,278,000
Philadelphia	3,671,000	1,309,000	989,000	777,000
One 10- and one 8-megaton weapon each				
Baltimore	1,338,000	591,000	466,000	174,000
Cleveland	1,466,000	394,000	298,000	316,000
Pittsburgh	2,214,000	597,000	659,000	43,000
St. Louis	1,292,000	563,000	370,000	161,000
San Francisco	2,241,000	734,000	769,000	301,000
Washington, D.C.	1,465,000	579,000	433,000	228,000
One 10-megaton weapon each				
Atlanta	672,000	155,000	206,000	160,000
Buffalo	1,089,000	253,000	140,000	158,000
Cincinnati	904,000	461,000	261,000	93,000
Dallas	614,000	130,000	314,000	124,000
Houston	807,000	81,000	57,000	114,000
Kansas City	814,000	265,000	230,000	144,000
Milwaukee	872,000	151,000	112,000	189,000
Minneapolis	1,117,000	201,000	92,000	97,000
New Orleans	685,000	319,000	226,000	74,000
Portland	705,000	156,000	103,000	131,000
Providence	682,000	210,000	263,000	144,000
Seattle	732,000	168,000	99,000	126,000

SOURCE: *Fallout: A Study of Superbombs, Strontium 90 and Survival,* John M. Fowler (ed.), pp. 211-213. © 1960 by Basic Books, Inc., Publishers, New York.

The atomic bombing of Hiroshima ushered in the international balance of terror that has produced new kinds of domestic strains on society. SOURCE: Los Alamos Scientific Library.

the RAND analysts, Herman Kahn (1960: 82–85), summarized the economic costs of an attack in which 45 percent of the American population is killed and all military and metropolitan targets are obliterated. He estimated that two-thirds to three-quarters of the productive capacity of the nation would be destroyed.

This range of destruction would affect such basic industries as general machinery, petroleum and coal, printing and publishing, and transportation equipment. If the country were not attacked further, it would have to get the economy going again quickly or it would not rebound within a generation. To accomplish this, the RAND analysts noted, the country would have to restore, at a minimum, a usable transportation system, power and communication apparatus, and long-term shelter, food, and clothing for the working population. If this were accomplished, and there were no further attacks, economic recovery would be complete within ten years.

The RAND study concludes: "Disaster studies show that human societies have enormous resilience and recuperative power" (Kahn, 1960: 85).[5]

---

[5] Chapter 9 on community organization and disasters supports this general evaluation of human response to various types of disasters, including wars; but in nearly all the cases noted in that chapter, there was significant outside help on local, national, and international levels. In a nuclear war, this key element might not exist.

This kind of recovery did in fact occur in Japan and in Germany after World War II; but at that time, the American economy was strong and growing, and much of the Japanese and German recovery was stimulated by extensive American aid provided under the Marshall Plan. A moot question here is: What nation would be in a position to offer such aid to the United States after the widespread destruction of a nuclear war?

While the RAND analysts and others try to estimate the general destruction and economic cost of a nuclear war, we know what nuclear technology has already cost American taxpayers. As we have seen, the long tradition of a low military budget except in wartime was broken after World War II. Note in Figure 12-1 that, in the years between American involvement in World Wars I and II, the defense budget was well under 10 percent of the total federal budget. With the advent of nuclear capability at the end of World War II, even before we entered the Korean War in 1950, defense costs had grown to over a third of the total budget. With the increasing spread of nuclear weapons in the Soviet Union and among other nations, the defense budget continued to grow well into the 1970s. There has been pressure to expand military expenditures not only for nuclear weapons systems but also for a large standing army and other conventional forces.

THE STRATEGY OF DETERRENCE Since the late 1940s, American defense has been based on the strategy of *deterrence*, that is, on the assumption that nuclear warfare is so destructive that the best defense is the power of overwhelming retaliation. Until then, the United States had armed only when it planned to actually use its weapons; from

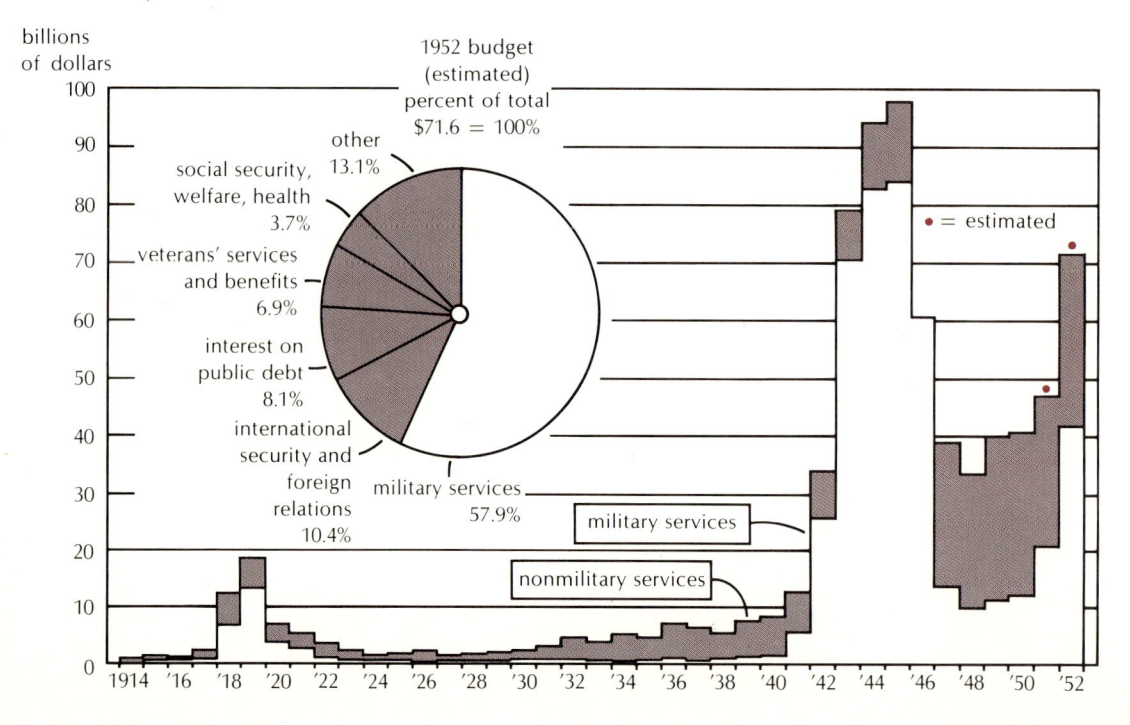

Figure 12-1   Military and nonmilitary expenditures of the United States government, 1914–1952. SOURCE: From *American Epoch*, by Arthur S. Link. Copyright © 1955 by Arthur S. Link. Reprinted by permission of Alfred A. Knopf, Inc.

repeater rifles to Flying Fortresses, the idea was to build weapons to be used for total victory. The contrasting idea of deterrence was put into words by Henry Kissinger in the 1950s, long before he became secretary of state. Kissinger summarized deterrence as a policy designed to prevent general war by demonstrating to potential adversaries the ability and the willingness to fight a conventional or a nuclear war. It was believed that the existence of nuclear power would prevent any challenge to its use, and the existence of an effective conventional force would limit any armed engagement to a point far short of total war. The defense budgets from the Truman to the Ford administration all reflected this policy of deterrence.

Deterrence, however, requires an immense annual defense expenditure. The rationale for this enormous outlay is the belief that it is necessary to be stronger than any potential military adversary. This theory leads one to wonder how much defense in relation to the Soviet Union, China, and the general enemy bloc is enough. Should the United States spend more, and if so, how much more? From the late 1940s to the early 1970s, the United States spent over twice as much on defense as did the Soviet Union. This ratio also held in the total combined spending by the United States and its NATO allies. A typical breakdown for those years is given in Table 12-2 for 1966 to 1968.

Other societal pressures and needs began to change this pattern. By the mid 1970s, a number of international and domestic factors led to parity in American and Soviet defense spending. Among the factors influencing the American defense budget were the widespread negative reaction to the involvement in the Vietnam War, the sharp rise in defense costs following the Arab oil consortium's price escalation, increasing public pressures to fund domestic health and welfare programs, and the growing strength of the Soviet and Chinese economies. By 1975, the Defense Department estimated that the Soviet Union was for the first time outspending the United States on defense by approximately 20 percent (Matthews and Norman, 1975: 45).

Table 12-2 Defense Spending and the Gross National Product of the Major Military Blocs, 1966–1968

	Gross national product (1966)	Defense spending (1967–1968)	Defense spending as a percentage of the GNP
Soviet Union and allies			
Country			
Soviet Union	$357 billion	$32 billion	9 percent
China	74 billion	7 billion	9.5
Communist bloc countries of Eastern Europe	115 billion	5 billion	4.5
Total	$546 billion	$44 billion	8 percent
United States and allies			
United States	$743 billion	$73 billion	10 percent
Other NATO countries	481 billion	21 billion	4.5
Total	$1,224 billion	$94 billion	7.5 percent

SOURCE: Based upon Library of Congress sources as reported in Morris K. Udall's *Congressman's Report*, "The Tough Problem of Priorities," May 15, 1969 (Washington, D.C.: House Office Building), p. 1, 2.

STRATEGIC REASSESSMENTS In part, this shift resulted from new assessments of the nature of nuclear power. By the 1960s, both the United States and the Soviet Union were able to launch thousands of nuclear missiles at each other, resulting in far more extensive damage than that suggested by Table 12-1. Robert McNamara, secretary of defense in the Kennedy and Johnson administrations, moved to cut back on some domestic military facilities (Halberstam, 1973: 302). Henry Kissinger as secretary of state in the Nixon and Ford administrations continued this policy and stressed the concept of *sufficiency*, by which he meant the ability to destroy the opposition, whatever its level of defense.

Those who have power to start a war may well lack power to end it (Ikle, 1971: 106). It was the fear of the inability of leaders to withdraw from conflict that led Soviet Premier Nikita Khrushchev to back down at President John Kennedy's insistence that Russian missiles be removed from Cuba in 1962. Most leaders are aware that the use of violence sharpens feelings of hostility and makes compromise more difficult. As Ikle notes, with nuclear armaments, the need to prevent war is particularly compelling (Ikle, 1971: 107). He suggests two ways to do so: by eliminating the sources of conflict that would lead nations to resort to war and by rendering the use of arms so unattractive that nations would prefer to live with tension (108). The latter form is the basis of the strategy of deterrence. While deterrence requires sufficiency of arms, leaders have been seeking limitations to arms. The partially successful Helsinki Strategic Arms Limitation Treaty (SALT) was concluded in 1976.

By the mid 1970s, these developments had led to a leveling off of American defense spending. It was still substantial — between 1970 and 1975 approximately $100 billion in an annual budget of approximately $300 billion — and by then the total American defense investment since World War II had come to well over one trillion dollars, more than the value of all houses and office buildings in the United States (Melman, 1970b: 184). Even excluding the cost of the Vietnam War, most of this expenditure occurred in the 1960s and 1970s. The economic impact is evident quite apart from the costs of actual combat. For example, the military economic analyst Seymour Melman noted in 1965, before our involvement in Vietnam intensified the trend (1970b: 185):

The competence of the industrial system is being eroded at its base. Entire industries are falling into technical disrepair, and there is massive loss of productive employment because of inability to hold even domestic markets against foreign competition. Such depletion in economic life produces wide-ranging human deterioration at home. The wealthiest nation on earth has been unable to rally the resources necessary to raise one fifth of its own people from poverty.

Thus, the cost of modern military technology is both direct and indirect. Its economic impact has been analyzed in depth within the framework of the military–industrial complex. This complex, or close working relationship between private industry and the government defense system, has been growing for more than a quarter century. It is now so vast that it bears special consideration.

THE MILITARY-INDUSTRIAL COMPLEX

In Chapter 1, we discussed manifest aims and latent consequences. It often happens that in trying openly to reach a particular goal, we produce some quite unexpected latent, or hidden, results. This appears to have happened with the emergence of the enormous military defense industry in response to the Cold War conflict with the Soviet Union. It is instructive to consider the very different emphasis on American policy needs made by Dwight Eisenhower, first as chief of staff of the Army in 1946, and then as president in 1961. In both years, he considered the Soviet Union a serious military threat, but by 1961, he had come to feel that continuous and large defense efforts raise new dangers for American society quite apart from the dangers inherent in foreign military challenges.

In his 1946 memorandum to the directors and chiefs of the War Department, General Eisenhower advocated a close working relationship among all branches of the armed forces and civilian scientists, private industry, technologists, and the universities.[6] This statement, titled "Scientific and Technological Resources as Military Assets," outlined five proposals for effectively welding private industry, civilian research, and military technological needs, including separating responsibility for research and development in the Army from other functions and increasing military officers' awareness of the advantages to be derived from close integration of civilian talent with military plans and development. (Melman, 1970b: 231–234.)

The statement set out a basic policy of interdependence between the civilian industrial economy and the military establishment. How vigorously this policy was followed is reflected in annual federal budgets since the late 1940s, in which expenditures for defense average over one-third of the total every year.

In his last address as president in 1961, Eisenhower reevaluated American policy and warned of the great danger of the *military–industrial complex* to the democratic social order of American society, a social order that this complex was supposedly designed to protect. See the selection on this subject for the points made by Eisenhower as well as related ideas of C. Wright Mills, who thought of this complex as the location of the leaders of the *power elite*. Mills held that the American tradition of civilian checks on military power was being challenged (1956). Rejecting the Marxian analysis of a capitalist ruling class, Mills believed that civilian and military personnel in the military–industrial complex were joined by new mutual interests engendered by the crisis nature of modern military technology. In the past, there had been industrial profiteering during war, but no evidence was found that businessmen were a major influence on American defense policy, and in times of peace there had been no close link between civilian industrialists and military strategists. But Mills saw the post-World War II situation in a different light.

THE MILITARY-INDUSTRIAL COMPLEX

From: Dwight Eisenhower, "Farewell Address." The New York *Times* (January 17, 1961): p. 22. C. Wright Mills, *The Power Elite*. (New York: Oxford University Press, 1956), p. 278.

The Eisenhower statement:

This conjunction of an immense Military Establishment and a large arms industry is new in the American experience. The total influence — economic, political, even spiritual — is felt in every city, every statehouse, every office of the Federal Government. We recognize the imperative need for this development. Yet we must not fail to comprehend its grave implications. Our toil, resources, and livelihood are all involved; so is the very structure of our society.

In the councils of government we must guard against the acquisition of unwarranted influence whether sought or unsought, by the military-industrial complex. The potential for the disastrous rise of misplaced power exists and will persist.

We must never let the weight of this combination endanger our liberties or democratic processes. We

---

[6] Upon his retirement from the Army in 1947, Eisenhower became president of Columbia University, where he continued to encourage a liaison of university research and defense efforts. He served as president of the United States from January 20, 1953, through January 19, 1961.

should take nothing for granted. Only an alert and knowledgeable citizenry can compel the proper meshing of the huge industrial and military machinery of defense with our peaceful methods and goals so that security and liberty may prosper together.

The Mills statement:

> The power elite ... take(s) its current shape from the decisive entrance into it of the military. Their presence and their ideology are its major legitimations ... what is called the "Washington military clique" is not composed merely of military men, and it does not prevail merely in Washington. Its members exist all over the country, and it is a coalition of generals in the roles of corporation executives, of politicians masquerading as admirals, of corporation executives acting like politicians, of civil servants who become majors, of vice-admirals who are also the assistants to a cabinet officer, who is himself, by the way, really a member of the managerial elite.

EVIDENCE OF THE MILITARY-INDUSTRIAL COMPLEX What evidence is there that a substantial part of the civilian economy is now devoted to military production rather than civilian supply and demand or domestic needs created by social security and unemployment compensation? The existence of *institutional interpenetration* between private industry and the defense establishment is pervasive. As Seymour Melman reports in *Pentagon Capitalism*, a substantial part of the business of the largest corporations is directly related to defense contracts paid for by federal tax sources. Using Department of Defense and private corporation data, Melman lists the ten prime defense contracts with American companies from 1960 to 1967 and the percentage of the companies' total business those contracts represented (1970b: 77):

	7-year total (in millions of dollars)	Percent of total sales
1. Lockheed Aircraft	$10,619	88%
2. General Dynamics	8,824	67
3. McDonnell-Douglas	7,681	75
4. Boeing Company	7,183	54
5. General Electric	7,066	19
6. North American-Rockwell	6,265	57
7. United Aircraft	5,311	57
8. American Telephone & Telegraph	4,167	9
9. Martin-Marietta	3,682	62
10. Sperry-Rand	2,923	35

Such continuous expenditures over the past quarter century have affected the basic economic structure of the society. As Fred Cook (1962: 24) observed in his warfare state analysis, between 20 and 30 percent of all manufacturing jobs in the states of California, Connecticut, Kansas, New Mexico, and Washington are accounted for by defense contracts. Contracts in some cities, such as San Diego, Wichita, and Seattle, account for over half the manufacturing jobs. Has American society come to the point in industrial-military interdependence where Parkinson's law is coming into play? C. Northcote Parkinson has argued, not altogether facetiously, that there is a human tendency to continue complex organizational tasks which are profitable or rewarding to individuals in the organization, even after the tasks have been accomplished or are no longer needed.

PARKINSON'S LAW

From: C. Northcote Parkinson, *Parkinson's Law and Other Studies in Administration* (Boston: Houghton Mifflin, 1957), pp. 2–4. Also used by permission of John Murray (Publishers) Ltd.

The military-industrial complex is evident in the mass production lines used for war material as well as consumer products. SOURCE: (a) Courtesy of Chrysler Corporation; (b) Courtesy of Ford Motor Company.

Work expands so as to fill the time available for its completion. General recognition of this fact is shown in the proverbial phrase "it is the busiest man who has time to spare." Thus, an elderly lady of leisure can spend the entire day in writing and dispatching a postcard to her niece at Bognor Regis. An hour will be spent in finding the postcard, another in hunting for spectacles, half an hour in a search for the address, an hour and a quarter in composition, and twenty minutes in deciding whether or not to take an umbrella when going to the mailbox in the next street. The total effort that would occupy a busy man for three minutes all told may in this fashion leave another person prostrate after a day of doubt, anxiety, and toil.

Granted that work (and especially paperwork) is thus elastic in its demands on time, it is manifest that there need be little or no relationship between the work to be done and the size of the staff to which it may be assigned. A lack of real activity does not, of necessity, result in leisure. A lack of occupation is not necessarily revealed by a manifest idleness. The thing to be done swells in importance and complexity in a direct ratio with the time to be spent. This fact is widely recognized, but less attention has been paid to its wider implications, more especially in the field of public administration. Politicians and taxpayers have assumed (with occasional phases of doubt) that a rising total in the number of civil servants must reflect a growing volume of work to be done. Cynics, in questioning this belief, have imagined that the multiplication of officials must have left some of them idle or all of them able to work for shorter hours. But this is a matter in which faith and doubt seem equally misplaced. The fact is that the number of the officials and the quantity of the work are not related to each other at all. The rise in the total of those employed is governed by Parkinson's Law and would be much the same whether the volume of the work were to increase, diminish, or even disappear. The importance of Parkinson's Law lies in the fact that it is a law of growth based upon an analysis of the factors by which that growth is controlled.

The validity of [this law rests on] two motive forces. They can be represented . . . by two almost axiomatic statements, thus: (1) "An official wants to multiply subordinates, not rivals" and (2) "Officials make work for each other."

Whether fully functional or not, the wedding of private industry and military procurement has become part of the American economic structure. The processes have been characterized as *convergence* and *institutional interpenetration;* they produce a *technostructure.* These terms refer to the high degree to which private industry and government, particularly the military, have become intertwined. It has not been proven that a secret group of political conspirators has become a power elite. Mills suggested instead that (275) it is "not the politicians, but corporate executives [who] sit with the military

and plan the organization of the war effort". Observers of interaction among government, industry, and the military see strong potential for dysfunctional consequences for the society. Decisions may be made that will benefit the participants at the expense of the general society. As Vietnam War protesters proclaimed sarcastically, "War is good business, so invest your son."

This interaction is part of a larger trend in American society. The economist John Kenneth Galbraith has observed that, over time, the line between the mature corporation and the administrative complex associated with the state will disappear (Galbraith, 1967: 393).

POTENTIAL CONSEQUENCES OF THE MILITARY-INDUSTRIAL COMPLEX The economic and political process of *centralization** (see the selection on this subject) is closely related to the new military technology. Serious questions have been raised about whether the policy first laid out by General Eisenhower in 1946 has already led to the consequences that President Eisenhower warned against in 1961. One writer wrote a satire concerning a special study group, set up in Iron Mountain, New York, during the Kennedy administration, that came to the conclusion that a war economy was necessary. The study group was composed of fifteen analysts in economics, history, industry, literature, physics, psychiatry, and sociology. It was charged with outlining the process by which American society could make the transition from a wartime to a peacetime economy if an international accord with the Soviet Union and other adversaries could be reached. The conclusions of the imaginary group were so disturbing that their report was never officially released by the government. The report finally "surfaced" when one of the group's members, using the pseudonym "John Doe," released it in full to the book's author, Leonard Lewin, under the title *Report from Iron Mountain* (1967).

What made this fictional report so disturbing? The answer can be found in its evaluation of the nature of preparation for modern warfare (79):

War is not, as is widely assumed, primarily an instrument of policy utilized by nations to extend or defend their expressed political values or their economic interests. On the contrary, it is itself the principal basis of organization on which all modern societies are constructed.

The special study group presented the thesis that the United States — like the Soviet Union and other modern military powers — had for so long constructed so much of its economic life and political authority around military defense, that to stop it would disrupt the society. As Leonard Lewin put it in his foreword (p. X): "they [the Study Group] concluded [that] lasting peace, while not theoretically impossible, is probably unattainable; even if it could be achieved it would almost certainly not be in the best interests of a stable society to achieve it...." Thus, maintaining conflict, although dysfunctional for human life and property, is functional for stability, that is, economic stability.

Report from Iron Mountain says, in effect, that a policy designed to keep the American society out of war instead creates conditions that produce the need to maintain a state of readiness for war. This fictionalized report so resembled real ones that a New York *Times* book reviewer, Robert Lekachman, wrote: "without accepting every detail of the author's somber speculations, there is, I freely concede, a certain nasty plausibility about his conclusion" (1967: 70).

SUBVERSION OF DEMOCRATIC PROCESSES
Other analysts have seen subversion of democratic institutions under the pressure of continuous international tensions. Fred Neal, writing for the Center for the Study of Democratic Institutions, advanced the view that the Cold War, under the wartime concept of national security, led directly to the Watergate scandal of the Nixon administration. Neal argued that the illegal 1972 break-in at Democratic party headquarters in the Watergate complex had the approval of presidential aides — including personnel from the Attorney General's office, the FBI, and the CIA — because of the long-term moral effects of living in a state of warfare. The nature of warfare and war preparation increases the national security power of the administration. Since national security involves confidentiality and secrecy, the potential for misuse and abuse of power is considerable. Such unconstitutional abuse of power had in fact been occurring before Carl Bernstein and Bob Woodward of the Washington *Post* and other members of the mass media (sometimes referred to as the fourth branch of government) exposed the Watergate break-in; Watergate was only a small part of the attempt to harass a political party in its legitimate operations. As Neal noted in a publication of the Center for the Study of Democratic Institutions (1973: 19):

What is of such frightening significance is the deep, extensive, and continuing misuse of Presidential authority in ways, both illegal and semilegal, that could have altered the very nature of the democratic system.

CENTRALIZATION VERSUS DECENTRALIZATION
*Decentralization** of authority as a counter to these developments would be inefficient and would put American society in a vulnerable economic and military position. Yet, the intensive industrial and political *centralization** of the military–industrial complex has both direct and indirect costs. The direct economic costs can be measured in the

impact on our competitive efficiency in domestic and world markets. These costs are a measurable symptom of other social and psychological effects of the nuclear age.

CENTRALIZATION AND DECENTRALIZATION OF STATE AUTHORITY

From: Robert MacIver, *Politics and Society*, a collection of Robert MacIver's work edited by D. Spitz (Chicago: Aldine, 1968), p. 237.

As a general rule... centralization and decentralization, both within and beyond the limits of the state... must go hand in hand.... the two being not antagonistic but complementary principles. Most empires have been failures because they pursued the principles of centralization alone — the Roman empire in particular, when at the last it became a world-state and not simply an aggregation of states around one central state, showed how impossible it was for a completely centralized system to meet the needs of peoples of different temperaments and living under very different physical and social conditions. If centralization is necessary for peace and order, decentralization is equally necessary for development and life.... It is only by keeping this distinction in mind that we can hope to understand the difficult relations of political and economic forces.

DEHUMANIZATION AND DESTRUCTION

LEGITIMIZING BUREAUCRATIC AUTHORITY

There is a pre-World War II tale about Germany, a nation not allowed to rearm under the terms of the Versailles Peace Treaty ending World War I. According to the story which circulated in the United States during the Second World War, several German workers in an alleged typewriter factory decided to assemble the individual parts they handled and make their own typewriter; but after assembling all the different parts, they ended up with a submachine gun.

While this tale may be apocryphal, it does illustrate a real point: in modern complex organizations, people may become removed from the purposes of the organization developed by technical experts and policymakers. Specifically, most citizens have very little actual involvement with preparation for modern warfare or policy implementation. The analysis of and preparation for a hypothetical nuclear attack are largely in the hands of war games experts and are carried out by large, impersonal industrial and military bureaucracies. Except for the people directly engaged in a limited war, it is also a highly impersonal process. What direct influence did most citizens have on the American B–52 bombings in Vietnam?

FORMS OF AUTHORITY   In theory, decisions on how to avoid or engage in war are made by the elected representatives of the American people; but the nature of authority in modern society is such that other powerful forces are in operation. Max Weber, the German social analyst, noted early in this century the importance of expert authority in modern states. Recall from Chapter 3, on government, Weber's model of three ideal types of authority: *traditional authority*, in which the rules are based on long-held values and social practices over generations; *charismatic authority*, in which a leader of great mass appeal, whether authoritarian like Hitler and Stalin, or democratic like Churchill and Roosevelt, is followed because of mass faith in his leadership; and *rational–legal authority*, the type found in most modern societies, consisting of clear division of labor in which everyone is subject to rules and where work and decision-making are generally systematic and routine.

It is in the rational–legal type of authority that bureaucratic and technical expertise becomes a major, if not the dominant, source of legitimate authority. With respect to the defense effort, one danger for a democratic society lies in the ivory tower effect, the distance of the experts from most people, even from the president. As Harlan Cleveland observed from his vantage point in the State Department (1973: 11):

In an antiballistic missile system ... experts have to program into computers the possible characteristics of incoming missiles, so the machine can identify, track, and fire at them before they appear over the horizon. With such a system, the decision to fire is no longer the Commander-in-Chief's; that decision has been predelegated, with instructions, to the computer. The President's responsibility is exercised, if at all, much earlier in the process, by trying to make sure the experts who programmed the computer knew what they were doing. And how does he make sure of that?

Thus, the continued existence of society may rest on the activities of the experts and of the industrial and defense bureaucracies.

GAMING EXPERTS AND THE PUBLIC As if the technical world of nuclear physics were not complex enough, there is also a communication problem between the social science *gaming* experts and most others in the society. Their language is so technical that the theories advanced about international conflict are not easily understood by untrained specialists. Consider the introduction to a series of theoretical articles from *The Journal of Conflict Resolution*, which specializes in the analysis of peace and war research (Rapaport, 1970: 66–67):

For the following theoretical articles it should be pointed out that the predictive power of a theory depends not only on the fraction of choices predicted but also on the "entropy" of choices. In games where "lock-ins" are common any rule which favors the response locked-in will predict well. Hence, there will be many rules that predict "accurately" and the predictive power of each will be diminished. On the other hand, if the "entropy" of a protocol of a single player is maximal, that is, one bit per play in 2×2 games, then the rule that predicts 80 per cent of the choices would be much more impressive. A good measure of the predictive power of a rule is the reduction of uncertainty of responses effected by it. Thus, if a 2×2 game could be found in which the complete protocol (of both players' choices), considered as a stochastic process, had an entropy approaching the maximal (two bits per play), it would offer the best opportunity for testing the predictive power of several models.

If you figured that out on first reading, you are indeed a budding games analyst. If you are not familiar with the term *entropy*, involving the measure of unavailable and available energy in closed thermodynamic systems (which is here applied to social systems), then all else becomes unintelligible. Then there is the problem of understanding the deceptively simple methods of analyzing nation-state interactions (the 2×2 *stochastic process*) to determine the probability of accurately analyzing conflicting power groups.[7] After deciphering all the jargon, we discover that the point the authors want to make is that an 80 percent chance of making a successful prediction is impressive. In the age of potential nuclear holocaust, one may reasonably feel that any war-games model that falls below 100 percent accuracy in making predictions is disquieting. While probability statistics are not by their nature likely to provide 100 percent predictability (recall Chapter 4), a 20 percent chance of failure, or one chance in five, is unsettling, given the nature of the problem.

---

[7] Not to mention the major complication in games analysis of team members changing sides or deciding to withhold their services. For example, Yugoslavia left the Soviet alliance system in the late 1940s and the French forced the United States and NATO headquarters out of France in the early 1960s.

Where does all this leave most people? At the very least, it leaves them with the problem of not losing their own sense of judgment in face of a complex defense system that very much affects their lives. Foretelling Parkinson's law in 1909, Max Weber, while arguing for the necessity of large bureaucracies in modern society, warned of the possible dangers in bureaucratic operations (Mayer, 1943: 127-128):

This passion for bureaucracy . . . is enough to drive one to despair. It is as if in politics the spectre of timidity . . . were to stand alone at the helm; as if we were deliberately to become men who need "order" nothing but order, who become nervous and cowardly if for one moment this order wavers, and helpless if they are torn away from their total incorporation in it.

POWERFUL VESTED INTERESTS Even the assertive, activist President Kennedy publicly obscured his own strong personal views about the necessity for challenging the vested interests of large defense-oriented industries. When his brother Edward, as senator from Massachusetts, expressed concern over a Massachusetts defense industry and its workers, saying, "when the Army gets that new rifle, there's another 600 men out of work in Springfield," the President replied "tough shit" (Bradlee, 1975: 176), then told his personal biographer on the scene, Benjamin Bradlee, not to report his views — literally or in any other manner — until at least five years after he left office. All the presidents since World War II, not just Kennedy, have been cautious in publicly challenging the institutionalized interests created by the military-industrial complex.

There has been a corrosive effect from depending on the various forms of bureaucratic order against which Weber warned. Those in authoritative positions have difficulty challenging dysfunctional aspects of the system such as red tape, cost overruns, and contract frauds. Consider all those whose self-interest would suffer if it were possible to have world stability and a smaller defense establishment.[8] As Seymour Melman noted, there are millions in American society, including managerial personnel, industrial workers, and technical experts, who depend for their livelihood upon the defense effort.

The short-term benefits of this system produce psychological and social mechanisms that interfere with the long-range goals of more peaceful international relations. In this maze of complicated expertise, bureaucratic routine, and vested interests, it is not hard to see how the human side of modern warfare can get lost.

DEHUMANIZING THE OPPOSITION Through urbanization and the expansion of secondary interpersonal relations, American society has already moved a long way toward dehumanization. When the military-industrial complex relies on technical expertise and implements policy through huge bureaucracies, the tendency to view outsiders impersonally becomes a habit. People interact without knowing each other as individuals. In the era of modern warfare, with its collective destructiveness, it is a short step from depersonalization to dehumanization.

Dehumanization is a concept that has come to be associated with the terror engendered by modern military technology. Three social psychologists make this association explicit (Bernard, Ottenberg, and Redl, 1970: 64):

We conceive of dehumanization as a particular type of psychic defense mechanism and consider its increasing prevalence to be a consequence of the nuclear age. . . . Dehumanization as a defense against painful or overwhelming emotions entails a decrease in a person's sense of his own individuality and in his perception of the humanness of other people. The misperceiving of

---

[8] Recall here the all too plausible Swiftian satire of *Report from Iron Mountain.*

others ranges from viewing them *en bloc* as "subhuman" or "bad human" (a long-familiar component of group prejudice) to viewing them as "nonhuman," as though they were inanimate items of "dispensable supplies." As such, their maltreatment or even their destruction may be carried out or acquiesced in with relative freedom from restraints of conscience or feelings of brotherhood.

LEGITIMIZING PROCESSES Once the mass psychology of dehumanization takes effect, then processes of social authorization and legitimization begin to occur. The perception of the enemy as being less than human enables legitimizing agencies such as industrial bureaucracies and the Army to engage in massive human destruction. As Nevitt Sanford observes, once the agencies of the society are involved in a conflict in which dehumanization of the opposition has occurred, then one group murders, tortures, enslaves, or otherwise assaults the dignity of others, believing that the actions are necessary or right and that the victims are not human (1971: 26-27).

This combination of mass psychological dehumanization with agencies of the state legitimizing actions toward an enemy group reached a high peak of efficiency in Nazi Germany, where the government organized the systematic extermination of over 6 million Jews. Similarly, the Communist regime in the Soviet Union organized the forced migration and killing of over 10 million kulaks (independent farmers) between 1928 and 1933 once they had been officially identified as enemies of the people.

PAST CHALLENGES TO THE HUMANITARIAN TRADITION American society, with its strong democratic and humanitarian traditions, might be considered unlikely to develop such dehumanizing behavior with official sanction. Yet, elements of the dehumanization process can be seen in the American experience. The enslavement of blacks and their legally sanctioned segregation in the century following the Civil War is an example of the acquiescence of most white Americans in mass dehumanization. Much the same thing was true of the early official relations of the new republic with the American Indians. Such relations were centered in the Department of War. The policy carried out toward the various tribes came so close to genocide — the total destruction of a people — that by the mid-twentieth century, there were fewer than one million Native Americans in the United States; there had been more when Columbus first landed off American shores nearly four hundred years earlier (Vander Zanden, 1966: 25).

The ability to put such mass destructive behavior into official practice rests in good measure on the general view of a group toward which opposition is expressed. An illustration of the dehumanized image of Native Americans can be found in a mid-nineteenth century news item from the *San Francisco Bulletin* (Sanford, 1971: 28):

Some citizens of this city, while hunting in Marin County yesterday, came upon a large group of miserable Digger Indians. They managed to dispatch 30 of the creatures before the others ran away.

It is noteworthy that, by the first decade of the twentieth century, only one member of the northern California Yahi tribe was known to be alive, and he died in captivity in 1911 (Kroeber, 1961).

The same *en bloc* labeling of enemies can be seen in the 1970 killing of radical black students at Jackson State College by police, and of radical white students at Kent State University by national guardsmen. The students were protesting American involvement in the Vietnam War, and they posed no threat to authorities at either institution at the time they were shot (Scranton Report, 1970). In the same way, loyal American citizens of Japanese ancestry were viewed as aliens during World War II. Once Japanese-Americans were so labeled, the liberal Roosevelt administration could and did sanction the rounding up of over 100,000 of them by armed force. Their property was confiscated, and they were placed in internment (or concentration) camps for three years (Bloom and Riemer, 1949).

A particularly disquieting action by regular American forces in the era of modern warfare was the My Lai massacre in Vietnam on March 16, 1968. Both the Johnson and the Nixon administrations tried to cover up knowledge of this military action, in which a company of soldiers systematically corralled and shot dozens of unarmed men, women, and children because they were defined as enemies in an enemy village. It was not until a year later that hard investigative reporting by free-lance reporter Seymour Hersh (1970) uncovered evidence of the massacre. Even after public pressure was brought to bear, only one combat soldier, Lieutenant William Calley, was indicted, tried, convicted, and imprisoned. He served only forty months of a ten-year prison term. Calley's own evaluation of his and other soldiers' actions helps us to see how the Vietnamese Communist opposition was dehumanized in combat. Speaking of the killing of infants and children at My Lai, Calley said: "It was not a matter of questioning [orders].... I was in a vacuum, I knew nothing about myself because that's the way the Army trains you" (Calley, 1975). Is it only the Army that trains people not to ask questions?

INTERNATIONAL LAW AND AMERICAN IDEALS
There are fundamental reasons why the trend toward dehumanization should be challenged. One immediate problem is the dilemma of American policymakers if the United States is to maintain its support of international treaty principles on human rights. For instance, the United States was a leader in bringing to trial a number of Nazi leaders who ordered the killing of noncombatants during World War II. A number of Nazis were found guilty and executed, as was Japanese General Yamashita for ordering the killing of civilian Filipinos toward the end of the war. The implications of My Lai in relation to American officers and policymakers are seen in the words of Associate Justice Robert Jackson, chief prosecutor at the Nuremberg trials (Reston, 1970: 14):

If certain acts in violation of treaties are crimes, they are crimes whether the United States does them or whether Germany does them, and we are not prepared to lay down a rule of criminal conduct against others which we would be unwilling to invoke against ourselves.

In addition to this fundamental moral problem, Americans face the pragmatic problem that, as a response to international conflict, the dehumanization process is ineffective. While dehumanization is often used as a psychological defense against painful facts, it prevents people from coming to terms with the realities of war. The result is that (Bernard, Ottenberg, and Redl, 1970: 65):

dehumanization facilitates the tolerating of mass destruction through by-passing those psychic inhibitions against the taking of human life that have become part of civilized man. Such inhibitions cannot be called into play when those who are to be destroyed have been divested of their humanness ... the freedom from fear which dehumanization achieves by apathy or blindness to implications of the threat of nuclear warfare increases the actuality of the threat....

There are also clear moral issues to face. As James Reston, Jr., observed about the implications of the My Lai massacre (1970: 61):

Will we...reclaim our original ideals? My Lai could lead to a new maturity in our recognition that Americans are humans like everyone else, capable of nobility, but also capable of bestiality, and that when our technology places upon us the highest responsibility in the world we must work toward a climate where the nobler instincts can flourish once again.

In this era of the military–industrial complex and a balance of terror between American and Soviet superpowers, achieving a climate in which nobler ideals can flourish is clearly a necessity, but it will not be an easy process.

COHESION AND MORALE

The development of *social cohesion** in American society was generally advanced by involvement in wars from the time of the American Revolution to World War II. Recall from Chapter 9 on disasters the discussion of disaster utopias. As people put together a workable social order to accomplish important ends, there is a great feeling of camaraderie and enthusiasm. Turner and Killian suggest that social cohesion in social movements is characterized by feelings of new-found spontaneity, a sense of power, and a vision of enthusiastic consensus, particularly in the early stages or in the face of confrontation between the movement and its enemies (in-group versus out-group). A sense of vitality rather than of being manipulated to conform to a script encourages people to maintain the movement experience, shutting out or distorting unacceptable reality (Turner and Killian, 1972: 366–367). Thus, as people rally to a war effort, it is likely that they will interpret the situation to conform to beliefs that sustain the war effort.

GROUP COMMITMENT AND UNITY IN THE MODERN WAR ERA   Group commitment and unity, the components of social cohesion, had long been typical of American behavior in wartime. It had become an American tradition either to stay out of wars or, once in them, to go all out for victory. Past American involvement in war often took on the characteristics of a goal-oriented social movement, even a crusade. The Civil War marshaled most Northerners to save the Union, and most Southerners to save the Confederacy. World Wars I and II saw Americans pulling together to save the world for democracy.

In contrast, the effects on American unity and morale of the post-World War II era of international conflict have been negative. The complexity of war in the nuclear age goes far beyond all past concerns with the probable costs of war. The difficult decision — whether or not to wage war — creates great national unease. Not to respond to military expansion of the Soviet Union or China, for example, is to court the disaster of the 1930s. At that time, our failure to respond early to German and Japanese military aggression resulted in our eventually being forced to go to war in a weaker position than if we had acted earlier. On the other hand, total response to foreign military expansion would court nuclear war, in which victors would face as much destruction as losers. Some Americans have called for a pacifist solution in which war would be abolished; no known practical means to accomplish this end have been advanced (see Etzioni, 1962). There has been a reversal of the socialization process which used to accompany our war efforts. As Keith Nelson put it in *The Impact of War on American Life,* instead of unity there has developed in the modern war era growing political polarization, weakening of traditional standards, and loss of confidence (Nelson, 1971: 6).

FEAR AND RETREATISM   Americans have exhibited a good deal of fear and retreatism in attempting to meet the demands of international conflict in the nuclear era. In the early years of the Cold War, in the late 1940s and during the Korean War in the early 1950s, this widespread fear turned into divisive suspicion and attacks on the loyalty of many Americans. The revelation that Soviet spying on the American war effort, including ultrasecret atomic research, had been assisted by a small number of Americans frightened many into irrational attacks on their fellow citizens.

McCARTHYISM It was in this period of fear and uncertainty that we experienced the phenomenon known as McCarthyism. Senator Joseph McCarthy of Wisconsin was able to build a national power base in this climate of apprehension. He charged that the growing nuclear strength of the Soviet Union and the communist successes in China and elsewhere came not through general technological knowledge and growing nationalist movements but through the efforts of disloyal American citizens who were Communists. Starting early in 1950, McCarthy charged that he had the names of 205 Communists in the State Department — though he never documented the existence of a single one — and successfully played on the growing frustrations and fears of the American people. The American historian Arthur Link observed that McCarthy, through his indiscriminate and reckless attacks, did more than any other living American to confuse and divide people (1955: 645).

Millions of Americans were willing to believe McCarthy, even after he accused such war heroes as Generals George Marshall and Dwight Eisenhower of being supporters of a communist drive to destroy American society. Not surprisingly, Americans began to stress the virtues of conforming to established authority and conventional wisdom. Many respected Americans in the arts, sciences, and business were blacklisted by potential employers, and their careers were ruined or nearly so. It is not surprising that the decade of the fifties produced the apathetic generation.

While young people generally pose the greatest challenge to the status quo, in the mid and late 1950s, the dark-clothed, poetry-reciting beat generation represented primarily a rebellion against responsibility. Unlike the lost generation that followed World War I, the Beats produced no large number of first-rate writers, artists, or musicians, and their style of life appeared to be another kind of conformism (Polsky, 1961: 339–359). They were only a somewhat more visibly alienated group in a generally alienated society, to be replaced in the 1960s by the even more visible hippie movement (see the selection on hippies in Chapter 5).

DIVISIVE REACTIONS TO WAR The sense of national purpose and self-confidence that characterized American involvement in World Wars I and II was dissipated in the tensions and incongruities of the Cold War. The relatively cohesive civil rights movement of the early 1960s (see Chapter 8) was a collective counter to the McCarthy era of fear and alienation. Yet the divisive reaction to America's entry into Vietnam on a large scale in the mid 1960s showed that military conflict in the nuclear age still brought on the growing polarization noted by Nelson.

Organized opposition to the Vietnam War was grounded on such issues as the indiscriminate bombing of whole villages and the propping up of the corrupt, authoritarian Diem and Thieu regimes (Halberstam, 1973). Furthermore, the Vietnam War heated up in the mid 1960s, just as the civil rights movement seemed near to achieving its goals. Resources for such programs as reconstructing slums and providing equal educational opportunity for minorities fell into short supply. As Bayard Rustin observed (1966: 36):

> ...the war in Vietnam...poses many ironies for the Negro community. On the one hand, Negroes are bitterly aware of the fact that more and more money is being spent on the war, while the antipoverty program is being cut; on the other hand, Negro youths are enlisting in great numbers, as though to say that it is worth the risk of being killed to learn a trade, to leave a dead-end situation, and to join the only institution [the Army] in this society which seems to be integrated.

Martin Luther King, Jr., concluded that "the promises of the Great Society have been shot down on the battlefield of Vietnam" (1968: 152).

Yet there is strong evidence that opposition to the Vietnam War sprang from America's unease at a limited and indecisive hot war, whatever its merits. American policy precluded an all-out effort to defeat the communist field forces because of the risk of setting off a nuclear confrontation with the Soviets and Chinese who supplied the Northern forces. This divided reaction was much like that to the Korean War, even though the two conflicts were very different in many ways. Some of these differences are noted below (based on Link, 1955: 681–696; Schlesinger, 1967: 495–499, Halberstam, 1973: 157):

HERBLOCK'S CARTOON
"Uncouth Little Beggars!"

© 1970 by Herblock in The Washington Post.

SOURCE: from Herblock's *State of the Union*. (Simon and Schuster, 1972).

South Korea	Vietnam
Americans identified with independence movement, having liberated South Korea from Japan after World War II.	Reoccupied by France as part of its colonial empire; Americans could identify with revolutionaries fighting for independence from foreign control.
Elections held after World War II had U.S. and U.N. cooperation; North Korea had no free elections under Russian control.	U.S. refused to sign Geneva Peace agreement guaranteeing free elections: U.S. backed Diem regime, thinking communist Ho Chi Minh would win free election.
International community saw communist invasion in June, 1950 as aggression; UN sent over a dozen nations to aid U.S. troops to repel invasion.	Until mid 1960s, native communists and nationalists were fighting a civil war against an unpopular regime. U.S. entered war without support from U.N.

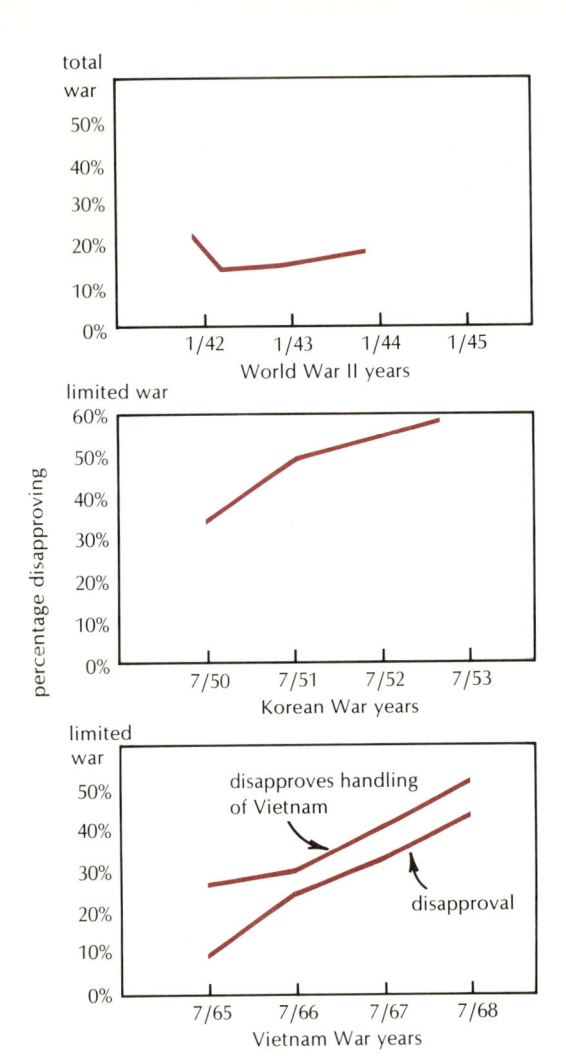

Figure 12-2 Disapproval of the president during three wars. SOURCE: These figures are drawn from "Disaffection, Delegitimation and Consequences: Aggregate Trends for World War II, Korea, and Viet Nam" by Robert B. Smith and reprinted from *Public Opinion and the Military Establishment*, Charles C. Moskos, Jr. (editor) © 1971, pp. 230–238 by permission of the publishers, Sage Publications, Inc.

DISAFFECTION FROM THE GOVERNMENT For all the differences between the conflicts in Korea and Vietnam, there was one great similarity. In neither one did the administration in power move to attack the Soviet or Chinese suppliers of the communist forces in the field. When General Douglas MacArthur proposed to send his American and United Nations forces into Chinese Manchuria during the Korean War, President Truman replaced him with another general, and President Eisenhower continued the policy of military restraint to avoid precipitating another world war in which nuclear weapons could be used (Link, 1955: 692–696). Similarly, the Nixon administration continued the negotiations with the North Vietnamese that were begun in the Johnson administration.

CHANGING LEVELS OF SOCIAL SUPPORT DURING WARFARE The bipartisan policy of military restraint in both Korea and Vietnam meant a frustrating and indecisive war with many American casualties. It is hard otherwise to explain the negative public reaction to both wars. In contrast to increasing social support during the three years of heavy fighting in World War II, for similar periods in both Korea and Vietnam there was decreasing social support. In an analysis of this phenomenon, Robert Smith (1970, Figure 1) outlines his formula of disaffection and delegitimation of American society in limited hot wars:

Protracted Limited Wars (leads to) .... → Mass Restlessness and Disaffection from the Goals of the War (which leads to) .... → Delegitimation of National Authority (which leads to) .... → Divisive Social Consequences Including Political Polarization, Protest Movements, and Electoral Punishment for the Incumbent Party in Office.

Smith provides extensive documentation to illustrate that the growing opposition to active American involvement in Korea and in Vietnam followed similar patterns, whereas, in the total war effort of World War II, there was growing support over a similar period (Figure 12-2). As a measure of American support for the legitimacy of the war effort, consider the similar findings reported in Figure 12-3. At the beginning of World War II, approximately thirty men per 10,000 appealed their first-class military draft status (1-A), but by the end of the war three years later, this ratio had declined to fewer than five per 10,000. Just the opposite happened during both the Korean and Vietnam wars.

The divisiveness engendered by the limited wars in Korea and Vietnam brought to the surface existing tensions. We had entered a period in which a dramatic and crucial decision has to be made: whether thermonuclear power would be used peacefully or merely as a new instrument of mass destruction. The stable future of American society is intimately wedded to that of the world community. The degree of social cohesion Americans can muster will affect the outcome.

REFLECTIONS ON DOMESTIC AND INTERNATIONAL STABILITY

If American society is not to move toward perpetual warfare, as envisioned in the satiric *Report from Iron Mountain*, then certain traditional views and processes will have to be changed within the society and throughout the world. Most fundamental is the need to repudiate Clausewitz's proposition that war is a rational way of settling international conflicts. An all-out war would end American society and world civilization in any recognizable form. It is a matter of national self-interest, even of survival, to create conditions in which American society can be secure from warfare and international conflicts can be resolved by means other than war. Only then can there be a reduction of the powerful bureaucracies and economic forces that sustain the military–industrial complex. While such choices may be economically dysfunctional for some

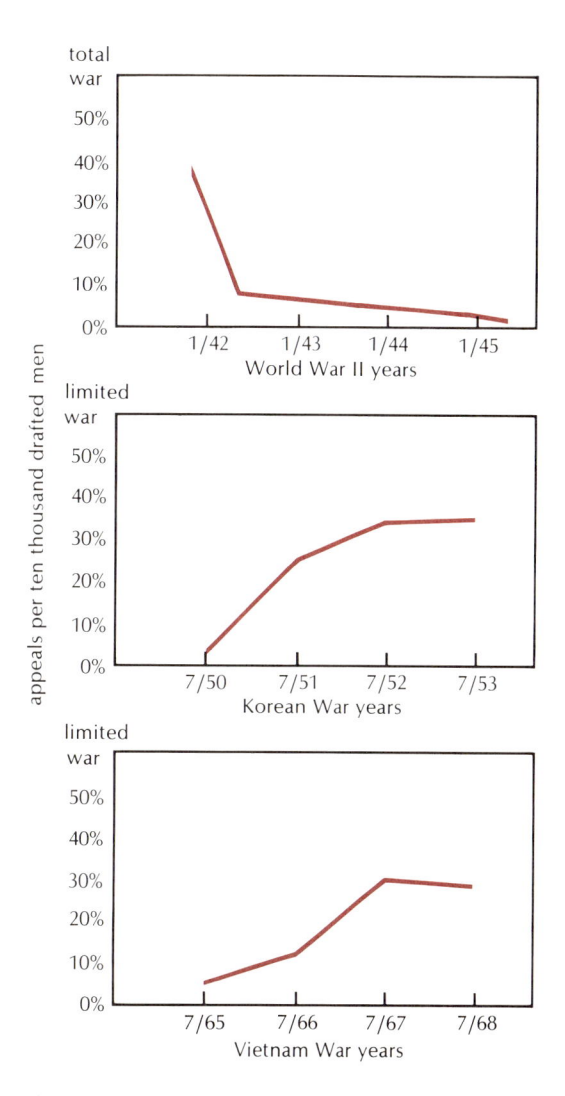

Figure 12-3 Delegitimation during three wars. SOURCE: "Disaffection, Delegitimation and Consequences: Aggregate Trends for World War II, Korea, and Viet Nam" by Robert B. Smith and reprinted from *Public Opinion and the Military Establishment*, Charles C. Moskos, Jr. (editor) © 1971, pp. 230–238 by permission of the publishers, Sage Publications, Inc.

groups in the short run, we must consider the greater functionality for human life and quality of life in the long run.

ADJUSTING TO THE REALITY OF GLOBAL CONFLICT Ironically, attempts to end international conflict would not be likely to ensure American security or world stability. There are differences in the ideology, economic productivity, and overall social stability of peoples in different societies. Such differences are bound to persist between nations and groups of nations. It is useful to keep in mind Lewis Coser's dictum that conflict is far from being dysfunctional (1956: 31) and that, like cooperation, it is one of the social processes by which people attempt to solve their problems. Social forces exist that make it impossible to avoid international conflict altogether. The British socioeconomist Barbara Ward (1962) has said that the worldwide revolutionary idea of social progress characterizes the modern era. However one defines social progress — equal rights for all, widespread economic growth, general improvement of health and welfare — there is a global movement to achieve better socioeconomic conditions. Inevitably, such efforts, whether by minorities within American society (see Chapter 8) or by *have not* nations, create stress and social conflict.

CONFLICT RESOLUTION WITHOUT WAR The problem facing Americans, then, is not the vain task of trying to end conflict but rather the necessary task of resolving conflict without war. The task is a formidable one, and social scientists, among others, have increasingly turned their attention to it. The statement of purposes in the first issue of the *International Journal of Group Tensions* (1971: 5) noted:

Certainly, the law of the jungle is the oldest law — but is this the law we want to abide by? Must human beings renounce humanity and go all the way back to a jungle? Is there no other solution for conflict but fratricidal and suicidal wars? Must mankind perish in self-destruction?

In the light of that last query, consider Quincy Wright's observation in his classic *A Study of War* (1942: 1148):

There is no natural law which decrees that the human population must be subdivided in any particular way and that the members of one subdivision must compete and perhaps conflict only with members of another. Populations of any size may cooperate or unite and become one "people."

COMING TO TERMS WITH GLOBAL INTERDEPENDENCE One point of consensus to be found in journals on the nature of war and peace, such as the *Journal of Conflict Resolution*, is that the nations of the world are now so interdependent economically and militarily that no one of them can safely exist in isolation from the others. This interdependency harbors the seeds of either increasing global conflict or increasing global peace with resolution of conflict. In facing the threat of nuclear attack by the Soviet Union and China, or the economic impact of the Arab oil cartel, American policymakers must respond in such a way that both American stability and the stability of its adversaries are protected. It is for this reason that efforts at détente with the Soviet Union proceed, with such agreements as the Test Ban Treaty of 1962 and the Strategic Arms Limitation Treaty (SALT) negotiations begun in 1971, even as open conflict occurred in Vietnam and elsewhere. The fact that the Soviet Union enters into such agreements reflects their vulnerability to the same forces. No longer is the United States, the Soviet Union, or anybody else in a position to dominate their friends or their foes totally.

The uneven peacekeeping record of America and its allies and of the United Nations since the end of World War II points up how fragile is the peace of the world. Yet, the fact that World War III has not broken out (at least not as this is written, over thirty years after World War II) suggests that there is a growing world consensus that conflicts must be resolved by means other than all-out war.

The future stability of international relations rests on how livable life is around the globe. We must come to terms with the global revolution toward social progress referred to by Barbara Ward. Solutions to such problems as the population explosion and the need to raise the standard of living of millions everywhere cannot be found unless institutions are created through which the solutions can be implemented. It is difficult enough, for example, to establish a workable mechanism for typhoid control, an issue on which there is wide international consensus; imagine how formidable a task it will be to institute peaceful development and resolution of conflict worldwide.

This last point reveals a profound irony in the business of achieving a stable peace. Much of this chapter has dealt with the potential danger to American institutions of centralization and the huge, bureaucratic, Parkinsonian forces of the military–industrial complex. Yet, peaceful policies cannot be implemented without effective establishment or continuation of complex organizations. The nature of modern mass society is such that very large, complex organizations are necessary until or unless some better vehicle is devised. As former Assistant Secretary of State Harlan Cleveland said of the future operation of institutions at the national and international levels (1973: 11):

The first thing to be said about the coming administrative environment is that organizations will have to be bigger, more inclusive, than ever before. This may sadden both the reactionaries and the radicals who pine for the corner grocery, the one-room school house, and the municipal telephone company. But if we are to take hold of our future, we are going to require more comprehensive systems, not simpler ones.... What the Communists call "collective leadership" and we call committee work ... are imperatives of bigness and complexity.

The implications of this observation are clear. Even should we achieve rational global agreement on the need to resolve conflicts peacefully, the necessary institutional machinery will have to be large and bureaucratically complex. This is true in a limited case such as an American economic assistance program to an underdeveloped nation or in a larger cooperative effort of the United Nations to establish population control measures and increase crop production. As an E. B. White character once observed in the *New Yorker*, "I'll predict a bright future for complexity.... Have you ever considered how complicated things can get what with one thing always leading to another?"

How likely is it that a stable peace can be achieved in which American democratic institutions are preserved and advanced? Perhaps the best answer is the response of an Israeli official to a query about chances of achieving a stable peace with Israel's Arab neighbors: "No alternative."

SUMMARY

We have explored the consequences of international conflict on the social cohesiveness of American society. World-wide technology has brought about a close interdependence between this society and others in all parts of the world. These interrelationships have raised a number of problems, including the need to maintain a strong military establishment and at the same time sustain democratic institutions.

The chief defense policy of the United States since the end of World War II has been one of *deterrence*, based on the possibility of nuclear warfare. A latent consequence of the need for a large military defense is the emergence of what President

Eisenhower called a *military–industrial complex*. The danger to the stability of democratic institutions from military–civilian interpenetration is shown in Parkinson's law — as work expands to fill the time available, so bureaucracies tend to sustain themselves long after their original functions cease, or artificially maintain such functions.

The routinization of bureaucratic behavior in a large military establishment has its dangers. The military, like other institutionalized bureaucracies, is a legitimizing agency. There is increasing concern about the relationship between a large, long-term military establishment, the routinization of war measures, and such events as the indiscriminate bombing in Vietnam and the massacre of civilians at My Lai. One consequence of a large, active military is the pressure to use a military approach to international conflict.

Strain in the social cohesiveness of American society emanates from the general Cold War and continuing international tensions and limited, indecisive wars. Comparison of public responses to World War II and the limited Korean and Vietnam wars suggests that limited war efforts in the nuclear era result in divisive domestic conflicts.

In the past quarter century, there has been a shift in the American attitude toward George Washington's dictum that we remain clear of entangling alliances. Dramatic evidence from limited wars and international boycotts on needed raw materials shows modern America's interdependence with other societies. One consequence is the growth of national and international pressures toward the resolution of global conflict. Forces behind these pressures are continuing large military expenditures and growing nuclear capabilities on a global scale and increasing pressures within America and elsewhere caused by rising expectations for higher standards of living and general economic and social security. If such social progress is to occur, institutions must be created to implement solutions to problems that impede such progress. In such pursuits, we ironically face the problems of a military–industrial complex as well as the need for effective complex organizations.

QUESTIONS FOR DISCUSSION

1. Why has technological militarism been cited as part of a world-wide triple revolution?

2. Why is Clausewitz's concept of civilized wars unlikely to be accepted now as a justification for war? Do you think it was a reasonable belief in earlier times?

3. On what assumption(s) is the strategy of deterrence based? Is it the current American policy? Do you believe it should be?

4. What problems might the military–industrial complex encounter should peace become a normative pattern in international relations?

5. To what extent is the dehumanization process that becomes apparent in war a general characteristic of modern society?

6. How might technology be employed to induce more humanization rather than dehumanization? Can war technology be developed toward such an end?

7. If America became involved in another limited war, what policies might induce more approval for the war?

8. To what extent is Quincy Wright's observation that populations of any size may cooperate or unite and become one people a practical goal for Americans to pursue?

9. Review your understanding of the following terms and concepts:

military–industrial complex

Parkinson's law

centralization and decentralization

Report from Iron Mountain

dehumanization

traditional, charismatic, legal authority

social cohesion

REFERENCES

Ad Hoc Committee
    1964   "The triple revolution." Liberation (April): 1–7.

Bernard, Viola, Perry Ottenberg, and Fritz Redl
    1970   "Dehumanization: a composite psychological defense in relation to modern war." M. Schwebel (ed.), Behavioral Science and Human Survival. Palo Alto, Cal.: Science and Behavior Books: 64–82.

Bloom, Leonard and Ruth Riemer
    1949   Removal and Return. Berkeley: University of California Press.

Bradlee, Benjamin
    1975   "Conversations with Kennedy." Playboy (April): 81–82; 170–177; 182–186.

Calley, William
    1975   UPI interview. The Arizona Republic (March 8): 2.

Carman, Harry and Harold Syrett
    1955   A History of the American People, vol. II. New York: Knopf.

Clausewitz, Karl von
    1968   On War (translation of 1908 version). New York: Pelican.

Cleveland, Harlan
    1973   "The decision makers." The Center Magazine VI (September/October): 9–18.

Cook, Fred
    1962   The Warfare State. New York: Macmillan.

Coser, Lewis
    1956   The Functions of Social Conflict. Glencoe, Ill.: The Free Press.

Eisenhower, Dwight
    1961   Farewell address. The New York Times (January 17): 22.

Etzioni, Amitai
    1962   The Hard Way to Peace. New York: Crowell-Collier.

Fowler, John
    1960   Fallout: A Study in Superbombs, Strontium 90 and Survival. New York: Basic Books.

Galbraith, John Kenneth
    1967   The New Industrial State. Boston: Houghton Mifflin.

Halberstam, David
    1973   The Best and the Brightest. New York: Fawcett Crest.

Hersh, Seymour
    1970   My Lai 4: A Report on the Massacre and Its Aftermath. New York: Random House.

Ikle, Fred Charles
    1971   Every War Must End. New York: Columbia University Press.

Kahn, Herman
    1960   On Thermonuclear War. Princeton: Princeton University Press.
    1965   On Escalation. New York: Praeger.

Kennan, George
    1961   Russia and the West. Boston: Little, Brown.

King, Jr., Martin Luther
    1968   I Have a Dream: The Quotations of Martin Luther King, Jr. New York: Grosset and Dunlap.

Kissinger, Henry
   1957   Nuclear Weapons and Foreign Policy. New York: Harper and Brothers.

Kroeber, Theodora
   1961   Ishi in Two Worlds: A Biography of the Last Wild Indian in North America. Berkeley: University of California Press.

Lekachman, Robert
   1967   Book review of Report from Iron Mountain. The New York Times Book Review (November 26): 70.

Lewin, Leonard
   1967   Report from Iron Mountain on the Possibility and Desirability of Peace. New York: Dial.

Link, Arthur
   1955   American Epoch. New York: Knopf.

Lippmann, Walter
   1922   Public Opinion. New York: Harcourt, Brace.

MacIver, Robert
   1969   Politics and Society. A collection of Robert MacIver's writings. D. Spitz (ed.). New York: Atherton.

Matthews, Tom and Lloyd Norman
   1975   "U.S. arms: are our defenses down?" Newsweek (March 17): 45–53.

Mayer, J. P.
   1943   Max Weber and German Politics. London: Faber.

Melman, Seymour
   1970a   Conversion From a Military to Civilian Economy. New York: Praeger.
   1970b   Pentagon Capitalism: The Political Economy of War. New York: McGraw-Hill.

Midlarsky, Manus
   1975   On War. New York: The Free Press.

Mills, C. Wright
   1956   The Power Elite. New York: Oxford University Press.

Moore, Dumas and Basil Rauch
   1965   America and World Leadership. New York: Appleton-Century-Crofts.

Neal, Fred
   1973   "The Cold War: road to Watergate." The Center Magazine VI (September/October): 19–23.

Nelson, Keith
   1971   The Impact of War on American Life. New York: Holt, Rinehart and Winston.

Parkinson, C. Northcote
   1957   Parkinson's Law and Other Studies in Administration. Boston: Houghton Mifflin.

Pilisuk, Marc and Thomas Hayden
   1965   "Is there a military industrial–complex which prevents peace? consensus and countervailing power in pluralistic systems." Journal of Social Issues XXI, no. 3: 67–68; 87–99.

Polsky, Ned
   1961   "The village beat scene." Dissent 8: 339–359.

Rapaport, Anatol
   1970   Gaming. The Journal of Conflict Resolution XIV.

Reston, Jr., James
   1970   "Is Nuremberg coming back to haunt us?" Saturday Review (July 18): 14–17; 61.

Rustin, Bayard
   1966   "Black power and coalition politics." Commentary 42 (September): 35–38.

Sanford, Nevitt
   1971   "Dehumanization and collective destructiveness." International Journal of Group Tensions 1 (January–March): 26–41.

Schlesinger, Jr., Arthur
   1967   A Thousand Days. New York: Fawcett Crest.

Scientists' Committee for Radiation Information
   1962   The effects of a 20-megaton bomb. New University Thought (Spring): 24–32.

Scranton Report
   1970   President's Commission on Campus Unrest. Washington, D.C.: Government Printing Office.

Smith, Robert
   1971   "Disaffection, delegitimation and consequences: aggregate trends for World War II, Korea and Vietnam." C. Moskos (ed.), Public Opinion and the Military Establishment. Beverly Hills, Cal.: Sage: 230–238.

   1973   A special report prepared by the staff of the Center for the Study of Democratic Institutions respecting the Center's national Convocation Pacem in Terris III, held in Washington, D.C., October 9–11, 1973. Center Report (December): 15–24.

Stevenson, Adlai
   1965   "Outline for a new American policy." Look (August 24): 71–72; 74; 76; 78; 81.

Turner, Ralph and James Killian.
   1972   Collective Behavior. Englewood Cliffs, N.J.: Prentice-Hall.

Udall, Morris
   1969   "The tough problem of priorities." Congressman's Report. Washington, D.C.: House Office Building.

Vander Zanden, James
   1966   American Minority Relations. New York: The Ronald Press.

Ward, Barbara
   1962   The Rich Nations and the Poor Nations. New York: W.W. Norton.

Weber, Max
   1947   The Theory of Social and Economic Organization. A. M. Henderson and T. Parsons (trans.). New York: Oxford University Press.

Williams, William
   1972   The Tragedy of American Diplomacy. New York: Dell.

Wright, Quincy
   1942   A Study of War. Chicago: University of Chicago Press.

Part 5

SOCIAL CHANGE AND THE FUTURE

...change can occur only through mechanisms for overcoming the resistance based on vested interests.

Robin Williams

Chapter 13

THE SOCIOLOGICAL IMAGINATION

Things are seldom what they seem.

an old sociological caution

IMAGINATION AND SCIENCE

In 1959, when C. Wright Mills coined the term *the sociological imagination*, it may have seemed to some a contradiction in terms. How could sociology involve imagination? After all, when Auguste Comte coined the term *sociology* in 1837, he meant literally *the science of society*. The term *science* brings to mind a laborious set of procedures for empirically checking carefully developed propositions. In contrast, the term imagination suggests images and thoughts akin to poetry and art.

Yet, there is no contradiction in terms. Comte himself saw sociology as having a dual purpose. One purpose was *voir pour prévoir,* to see in order to foresee. The other was *prévoir pour pouvoir,* to foresee in order to control. This Comtean legacy was meant to build a science and to use scientific understanding toward solving social problems. But to see and to foresee require imagination, however solidly grounded one is in scientific propositions about society. Control — whether by individuals, groups, or society as a whole — also involves the use of imagination, particularly in a democratic society, in which arbitrary controls are few.

CRITICAL CONSCIOUSNESS The very development and use of sociological concepts can lead to what Peter Berger (1963) calls "a form of critical consciousness" of how the system works. For

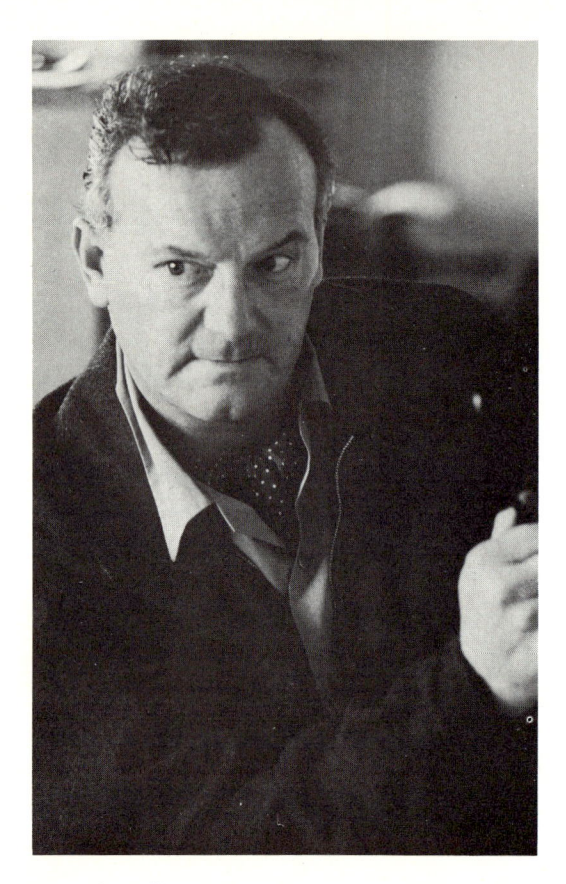

C. Wright Mills. SOURCE: Courtesy of Yaroslava Mills.

and other social realities. We know that values change over time and that different religious and ethnic groups in a community often hold widely differing normative values. Yet, by stimulating the sociological imagination, a new angle of vision, in Comte's terms, can be gained on how and why changes occur or do not occur.

SOCIOLOGICAL THEORIZING How can sociological theorizing influence the angle of vision? In this chapter, we shall examine five perspectives from which social problems may be viewed, and we shall see that people may draw different conclusions from these perspectives. Each perspective has a unique focus on problems. For example, on such specific issues as homosexuality or the use of drugs, the applied social remedies that flow out of the *theory of deviant means* are quite different from those drawn from *labeling theory*. The former considers deviance to be a rational response to socially structured obstacles, and suggests that by changing the social structure, we reduce the amount of deviant behavior. The latter theory suggests that general normative standards should be made more flexible to allow for wider acceptance of deviance rather than trying to end it. Although the five perspectives developed from research were not necessarily designed to solve social problems, creative sociologists and others have been quick to see their possibilities for practical application.

Developing and using different theoretical perspectives is an exercise in the sociological imagination. They illustrate the old caution cited at the beginning of this chapter — that things are seldom what they seem. Each of the many research-based perspectives adds new dimensions to our understanding of social realities. As soon as sociologists believe that they have attained new insights into

instance, merely knowing that there are changes in the notion of what is normative and deviant can lead one to ask questions: Why is it that behavior such as divorce or the use of alcohol is considered unacceptable, or deviant, at one time and acceptably normal at another time? Why is it that at any given time in a community, the active sexual behavior of teenagers is tacitly accepted by some adults and disapproved of by others? We have already considered some of the reasons for these the social system, they ask new questions in order to test the validity of their assumptions. This process illustrates the marriage of imagination and science. As Max Weber observed (Selltiz: 40), "Every scientific fulfillment raises new questions; it asks to be surpassed and outdated."

THE PROBING NATURE OF SOCIOLOGY One of the points made in Chapter 1 was that we need to look beyond the manifest, or planned, patterns of social life in order to see those that are latent, or unintended. Chapters 5 to 12, on different social issues, give examples of latent consequences. For example, the development of a technologically advanced society, calling for increased formal education, has unintentionally lengthened the period of adolescent dependency. The movement of the middle class to the suburbs has left many cities in a destitute condition that threatens whole metropolitan areas. The development of a large defense establishment in the nuclear era has unintentionally produced a military–industrial complex that many respected leaders feel could threaten democratic institutions.

In Chapter 1, we discussed the difference between basic and applied research. It is appropriate in this context to mention that researchers have in recent years become aware of the consequences not only of applied research, which can be seen soon after application, but in the potential consequences of basic research for future application. The consequences of nuclear research have been more far-reaching than was at first predicted; genetic research might have larger social consequence than we can now foresee (see Cloning and Social Living, Chapter 14). In social research, the sociologist must use sociological imagination to see more clearly not only the relationships among different patterns of social behavior but also the potential positive and negative consequences of this new knowledge.

In this chapter, we shall explore how the sociological perspective can advance one's insights into what is happening and what can happen in our world.

SOCIOLOGY AS A FORM OF CONSCIOUSNESS

The sociological perspective aims to provide a Comtean angle of vision or Weberian sense of *Verstehen* (subjective understanding) about modern society with its masses of individuals and subgroups. Sociologists generally approach this task as members of the establishment, since sociology is one of about twenty respected academic disciplines in our universities.

Yet, if sociology is part of the establishment, it is a peculiar part, for a good deal of sociological analysis takes a critical and often highly nonestablishmentarian view of society. This is so in good measure because sociological method stresses objective and accurate assessment of social behavior.[1] The fact is that those in established and respected positions project an image that does not always reflect reality. Thus, if sociologists effectively analyze and document social behavior, it is to be expected that they will provide a critique of the society.

FOUR SOCIOLOGICAL MOTIFS Through the sociological perspective, and the imagination to use it, we view the whole of society. This includes those within its accepted structure and *deviants* outside the accepted structure. As noted, Peter Berger (1963) explains this process by calling sociology a form of consciousness. He further describes the sociological consciousness as having four components, or motifs, often functioning within the

---

[1] For a discussion of sociological research methods, see Chapter 4 on methods of inquiry and Appendix B on the sociological use of the scientific method.

establishment: the debunking motif, the theme of unrespectability, the idea of relativism, and the cosmopolitan motif. Each of these is a means of seeing through the façades of social structures. Let us consider their implications.

THE DEBUNKING MOTIF Ann and Scott Greer make this telling point about how sociologists advance the sociological perspective (1974: 1):

> ... sociologists make social life *problematic*. They do not assume that black and white, male and female, young and old, are automatically different in the ways that our friends think they are. Nor do they assume knowledge of *why* they are different; instead, they question. Such questioning may easily appear to be an insult to the good, the true, the beautiful.

The process of questioning what people say and do is the beginning of the debunking process. When a white southern segregationist talks about how he "loves our nigras," the documentation of forced segregation into inferior schools and periodic violence toward blacks gives the lie to this expression of love. When a white northern suburbanite admonishes those racist southerners, the fact of greater northern racial segregation in housing and in schools reveals the hypocrisy.

In this sense, sociological analysis can be compared to news reporting that challenges the official version of a story. In the mid 1960s, while President Lyndon Johnson was telling the American people that the Vietnam War was being won and we were coming to the "light at the end of the tunnel," many news sources in Vietnam were reporting the reality — that no victory was in sight. Sociological analysis often debunks official or widely held views that do not hold up under objective examination.

Much of what we create for a manifest purpose has latent consequences we dislike. When Thorstein Veblen analyzed the growing and prospering American middle and upper classes in *Theory of the Leisure Class,* he perceptively noted pressures to keep up with the Joneses. Looking at the "outs" who apparently made it "in" to respectable society, E. Franklin Frazier, in *Black Bourgeosie* (1957), documents the sham of "high society" in a black community that is still excluded from white society.[2]

There is thus an element of the exposé in much sociological analysis. Such a book as Upton Sinclair's muckraking classic, *The Jungle* (1906), which exposed the unsanitary and dangerous conditions in meat-processing plants at the turn of the century, can serve a useful social purpose. Since Sinclair's day, public pressure has led to more sanitary preparation of meat. Debunking carries no guarantee that people will be moved to constructive reforms, but it can often provide an informed basis for individual or social action.

THE UNRESPECTABILITY MOTIF From the start, American sociology has been fascinated by the seamy side of life, as seen in the titles of works from the Chicago school a half century ago. In Nels Anderson's *The Hobo* (1923), down-and-outers look for a cheap "flop" and a cheap glass of wine in the city. In Frederic Thrasher's *The Gang* (1927), the 1,313 boy gangs studied reflect other problems of Burgess's same zone in transition described in his concentric zone theory. In Harvey Zorbaugh's *The Gold Coast and the Slum* (1929), ethnic, racial, and social class divisions are shown to result in a sense of anomie among slum-dwellers.

The works of Howard S. Becker, such as *Outsiders* (1963) and *The Other Side* (1964), show the continuing interest in the unrespectable — the narcotics addict, the life style of popular musicians, who are often stigmatized and afflicted. Such works

---

[2] In 1948, E. Franklin Frazier became the first black president of the American Sociological Association.

as Liebow's *Tally's Corner* (1967), about poor blacks in Washington, D.C., and Gittlin and Hollander's *Uptown* (1970), about poor whites in Chicago, focus on the other America that exists "wherever people are excluded, or exclude themselves, from the world of middle-class propriety" (Berger, 1963: 12). Sherri Cavan's *Hippies of the Haight* (1972) offers contrasts between hippies and straights in San Francisco, but also shows how deviance is regulated within the hippie movement. Such internal regulation among deviant groups is not uncommon.

The interest in the unrespectable expressed by sociologists suggests a relationship between sociology and democracy. To analyze and report freely on the unrespectable is an academic freedom not tolerated by totalitarian regimes. Sociology was not allowed in Soviet Russia under Stalin. There was research in the 1920s, in the democratic Weimar Republic in Germany, but when the Nazis came to power, it ceased. It was viewed as a danger to the perfectionist image of Germany that the regime wanted to protect. Pursuing the unrespectable in sociology is one of the continuing tests of democracy.

THE RELATIVISM MOTIF A number of social forces have made us aware of the great variety of human behavior acceptable to different people and groups. Urbanization in America has brought together in a small space people of widely differing ethnic and class backgrounds. The mass media, particularly television, have brought into the American home images of different ways of life within American society and around the globe.

Sociology has come to maturity as these changes have occurred. Hence, the sociological focus has become part of our growing awareness that the rightness of certain values and behavior patterns is relative. Recall the discussion of *cultural relativism** in Chapter 2, in which we noted that the rightness or wrongness of ideals of beauty, forms of religious belief, expressions of sexuality, taste in food, and virtually everything else depends on the standards that prevail in any given culture. The sociological consciousness expands this social truism both in terms of cross-cultural analysis and of cultural variety in American society.

Relativism challenges the intolerance of many Americans. Respectable middle-class society often ignores the fact that the United States includes many subcultural groups and discernibly changing patterns of life. In *Middletown in Transition* (1937), Robert and Helen Lynd described intolerance as the *of course syndrome*, in which the consensus is so strong that the answer to a question elicits the answer, "Of course." Is our economy one of free enterprise? Of course! Are all our important decisions made through the democratic process? Of course! Is monogamy the natural form of marriage? Of course! Yet in Chapter 3 on the basic institutions of society — including the family, religion, education, government, and the economy — we saw how many overgeneralized beliefs are so common that they are often taken for granted.

Relativism can give us realistic bench marks not only about other cultures but about changes in our own. Even while the Lynd study was under way in the mid 1930s, the passage of the Social Security Act, the recognition of collective bargaining, and the establishment of minimum wage laws had injected significant socialistic features into the mixed American economy, now less characterized by free enterprise than it once was. Given powerful vested interests such as big business and big labor, democratic processes have seldom been fully realized in all important governmental decisionmaking in our society. As for monogamy, the successful Mormon polygamy of the nineteenth century, communal living arrangements, and the high rate of divorce and remarriage all challenge the naturalness of the monogamous state.

THE COSMOPOLITAN MOTIF Recognition of the many ways there are to solve problems in different cultures gives rise to Peter Berger's final motif: cosmopolitanism. The sociological consciousness attempts to avoid narrow provincialism and to stress a worldwide perspective. As Berger notes, such a perspective has often been a characteristic of city cultures. This was true in ancient Athens and Alexandria, in medieval Paris, in Renaissance Florence, and in the great modern cities where sociologists now do much of their research.

In an early text (1936) Ralph Linton, still one of the most widely cited cultural anthropologists (Oromoner, 1968: 125), discussed *cultural diffusion**, by which one culture borrows tools, techniques, values, and so on from another culture. Linton highlighted the need for a sense of cosmopolitanism for the "100 percent American". In his now-classic example of the enrichment of American culture by its acceptance of concepts and material objects from other cultures, Linton not only showed how the contents of culture are "diffused" from one place to another but also demonstrated the irony of the individual who is fully endowed with these benefits but lacks the cosmopolitan viewpoint to recognize the debt to others. (See the selection Cultural Diffusion and the Cosmopolitan Viewpoint.)

CULTURAL DIFFUSION AND THE COSMOPOLITAN VIEWPOINT

From: Ralph Linton, *The Study of Man: An Introduction*, © 1964, pp. 326–327. Reprinted by permission of Prentice-Hall, Inc. Englewood Cliffs, New Jersey.

Our solid American citizen awakens in a bed built on a pattern which originated in the Near East but which was modified in Northern Europe before it was transmitted to America. He throws back covers made from cotton, domesticated in India, or linen, domesticated in the Near East, or silk, the use of which was discovered in China. All of these materials have been spun and woven by processes invented in the Near East. He slips into his moccasins, invented by the Indians of the Eastern woodlands, and goes to the bathroom, whose fixtures are a mixture of European and American inventions, both of recent date. He takes off his pajamas, a garment invented in India, and washes with soap invented by the ancient Gauls. He then shaves, a masochistic rite which seems to have been derived from either Sumer or ancient Egypt.

Returning to the bedroom, he removes his clothes from a chair of southern European type and proceeds to dress. He puts on garments whose form originally derived from the skin clothing of the nomads of the Asiatic steppes, puts on shoes made from skins tanned by a process invented in ancient Egypt and cut to a pattern derived from the classical civilizations of the Mediterranean, and ties around his neck a strip of bright-colored cloth which is a vestigial survival of the shoulder shawls worn by the seventeenth-century Croatians. Before going out for breakfast he glances through the window, made of glass invented in Egypt, and if it is raining puts on overshoes made of rubber discovered by the Central American Indians and takes an umbrella, invented in southeastern Asia. Upon his head he puts a hat made of felt, a material invented in the Asiatic steppes.

On his way to breakfast he stops to buy a paper, paying for it with coins, an ancient Lydian invention. At the restaurant a whole new series of borrowed elements confronts him. His plate is made of a form of pottery invented in China. His knife is of steel, an alloy first made in southern India, his fork a medieval Italian invention, and his spoon a derivation of a Roman original. He begins breakfast with an orange, from the eastern Mediterranean, and a canteloupe from Persia, or perhaps a piece of African watermelon. With this he has coffee, an Abyssinian plant, with cream and sugar. Both the domestication of cows and the idea of milking them originated in the Near East, while sugar was first made in India. After his fruit and first coffee he goes on to waffles, cakes made by a Scandinavian technique from wheat domesticated in Asia Minor. Over these he pours maple syrup, invented by the Indians of the Eastern woodlands. As a side dish he may have the egg of a species of bird domesticated in Indochina, or thin strips of the flesh of an animal domesticated in Eastern Asia which have been salted and smoked by a process developed in Northern Europe.

When our friend has finished eating he settles back to smoke, an American Indian habit; consuming a plant domesticated in Brazil in either a pipe, derived from the Indians of Virginia, or a cigarette, derived from Mexico. If he is hardy enough he may even attempt a cigar, transmitted to us from the Antilles by way of Spain. While smoking he reads the news of the day, imprinted in characters invented by the ancient Semites upon a material invented in China by a process invented in Germany. As he absorbs the accounts of foreign troubles he will, if he is a good conservative citizen, thank a Hebrew deity in an Indo-European language that he is 100 percent American.

As the world becomes increasingly interdependent politically, economically, and ecologically, the need for a more cosmopolitan and less ethnocentric sociology becomes evident. To stress cosmopolitanism is to stress a value; but isn't the science of society expected to be value free? Here again Peter Berger has something useful to say. He distinguishes between the methods of sociology and the values of the sociologist. Berger notes that the methods of sociological research must be value free, that is, they must report findings objectively whether the researcher likes those findings or not; but he also notes that sociologists must not be value free if they are to retain their humanity (1971: 5).

Sociology is too much linked to the organizing dilemmas of our time to permit most of its practitioners to pursue their theoretical interests in detachment from the struggles of their fellow-men.

Alvin Gouldner offers a modification of this viewpoint. He believes that values are found even within the methods of sociologists, and that wherever values exist, they must be recognized and considered. In his argument for a *reflexive sociology*, in which the sociologist takes a hard look inward, Gouldner sees the potential for the sociologist to improve scholarly work and accept greater responsibility as well for his or her humanness. (See the selection Value Unfreedom and Reflexive Sociology.)

VALUE UNFREEDOM AND REFLEXIVE SOCIOLOGY

From: Alvin W. Gouldner, *The Coming Crisis of Western Sociology*, © 1970 by Alvin W. Gouldner, Basic Books, Inc., Publishers, New York, pp. 499 and 511. Also used by permission of Heinemann Educational Books Ltd.

A Reflexive Sociology can grasp this hostile information: *all the powers-that-be are inimical to the highest ideals of sociology.* At the same time, it further recognizes that most often these are not external dangers, for they produce their most powerful effect when allied with the dispositions and career interests internal to sociologists themselves. A Reflexive Sociology is fully aware that sociology is most deeply distorted because and when the sociologist himself is a willing party to this. A Reflexive Sociology therefore prefers the seeming naivete of "soul-searching" to the genuine vulgarity of "soul-selling."

Insofar as a Reflexive Sociology focuses on the problem of dealing with hostile information, it confronts the problem of a "value-free" sociology from two directions. On the one hand, it denies the possibility and, indeed, questions the worth of a value-free sociology. On the other hand, it also sees the dangers, no less than the gains, of a value-committed sociology; for men may and do reject information discrepant with the things they value. It recognizes that men's highest values, no less than their basest impulses, may make liars of them. Nonetheless, a Reflexive Sociology accepts the dangers of a value commitment, for it prefers the risk of ending in distortion to beginning in it, as does a dogmatic and arid value-free sociology.

Again, insofar as a Reflexive Sociology centers on the problem of hostile information, it has a distinctive awareness of the ideological implications and political resonance of sociological work. It recognizes that under different conditions an ideology may have different effects upon awareness; it may be liberating or repressive, may increase or inhibit awareness. Moreover, the specific problems or aspects of the social world that an ideology can make us aware of also change over time. A Reflexive Sociology must, therefore, have an *historical* sensitivity that alerts it to the possibility that yesterday's ideologies may no longer enlighten but may now blind us....

Why does such an effort emerge today? What are the conditions under which there now emerges an expressed need for a reconstruction of sociology — for both a critique and a reconstruction of conventional Academic Sociology are implicit in the movement toward a sociology of sociology. Can a sociology of sociology, or a Reflexive Sociology as one version of this, account for itself?

While, at this juncture, I can do no more than venture a guess about this, I suspect that these new trends in sociology imply a growing detachment from the sociology once conventional in the United States. What is it that fosters such a detachment? It derives partly, I suspect, from the growing detachment of sociologists and others from the *larger* society in which they work and live, *and,* at the same time, from their mounting awareness of the ways in which their sociology is becoming inextricably integrated into this very society. That is, alienation from the larger society would not, of itself, have disposed sociologists to a critique of their own discipline and its establishments, did they not feel that the latter were entangled with the larger society. But as their discipline and its establishments become increasingly supported by and openly involved with the Welfare State; as sociologists wing their way back and forth between their universities and the centers of power; as they are heard ever more frequently in the councils of power; and as their most immediate work environments — the universities themselves — become drawn into the coalescing military-industrial-welfare complex, it becomes unblinkingly evident that sociology has become dangerously dependent upon the very world it has pledged to study objectively.

This dependence is dissonant with the ideal of objectivity. It becomes ever more difficult for the sociologist to conceal from himself that he is not performing as he had pledged, that he is not who he claimed he was, and that he is becoming more closely bound to the system from which he had promised to maintain his distance. A crisis is emerging in sociology today, not merely because of larger changes in society, but because these changes are transforming the sociologist's *home* territory, his own university base. "Corruption" is now not something that one can pretend is going on only "out there" in the base world surrounding the university, or something that one reads about only in the newspapers; it has become all too evident in the eye-to-eye encounter of daily life in the college corridor. A man may begin to move away from others of his own kind when he no longer takes pride in his likeness to them.

THEORETICAL PERSPECTIVES AND THE DEFINITION OF PROBLEMS

There is an implicit link between C. Wright Mills's sociological imagination and sociological theorizing. The sociological imagination tries to make sense out of the complexities of social life. That is precisely what theoretical concepts try to do in a more sharply focused way. Since much of the emphasis of this text has been on the analysis of social problems to illustrate basic sociological principles, we should illustrate here how theoretical perspectives both expand and limit our understanding of and ability to deal with social reality.

PERSPECTIVES IN PROBLEMS THEORY   In twentieth-century sociology, there have emerged five major perspectives on the causes of social problems. These have been usefully delineated in two works (1971 and 1973) by Earl Rubington and Martin Weinberg, who identify these perspectives as: social pathology, social disorganization, value conflict, deviant behavior, and labeling. Each of these locates the causes of social problems in a different part of the social system. The result is that each perspective differently influences what is considered to be a social problem and what we think can or should be done about it. We shall discuss these perspectives in the order in which they emerged, from the early 1900s to the 1970s. In a sense, each was meant to replace an earlier perspective, but each provides some insight, and all still have some influence — though the deviance and labeling perspectives have been most influential in recent decades.

It will be evident that each theoretical perspective enables us to expand our angle of vision into complex social phenomena and, at the same time, limits our ability to see certain social realities operating at the same time and in the same place. The review of these perspectives underlines the need to sustain our imaginative power so that we may continue to have fresh perspectives and insights.

SOCIAL PATHOLOGY THEORY   The social pathology theory is rooted in the early development of sociology at the turn of the century. Three quarters of a century after Comte coined the term *sociology*, the field was still in its developmental stage. Early theoretical propositions often borrowed from other, more developed fields. This was particularly true of the pathological perspective. In medicine, organic theories had brought major breakthroughs on the causes, identification, and cure of many diseases. Freudian psychoanalysis had identified emotional disabilities that could be cured. Darwin's theory of biological evolution produced Social Darwinism, which simply took over the theory of the survival of the fittest and applied it to social systems. Darwin noted an empirical discrepancy, however, when he observed that in saving their weak and afflicted and in sacrificing their bravest men in war, societies operate against the principle of survival of the fittest (Darwin, 1880: 130–135).

THE FOCUS ON THE INDIVIDUAL   All these influences led many sociologists early in the century to turn their attention directly upon the individual, to find to what degree he or she was adjusted or maladjusted to society. In this view, people create problems for the society rather than vice versa. In the pathological perspective, such persons — whether they engage in criminal behavior, are mentally ill, fail to be productive occupationally, or exhibit other behavior generally considered to be a problem — are often considered sick or immoral. Early social pathologists such as Charles Henderson (1909) and Samuel Smith (1911) saw most social problems as the result of the maladjustment of some individuals to the social organism, society. The title of Henderson's work, *Introduction to the Study of the Dependent, Defective, and Delinquent Classes and of their Treatment,* is revealing. He thought it possible to cure the individual who had an identifiable social disease such as delinquency or alcoholism.

MODERN SOCIAL PATHOLOGY   Modern social pathologists, considerably more sociologically oriented than their early predecessors, agree with them that elements of a society can be sick or immoral; but they have shifted the focus from the individual to social institutions, a perspective that draws upon the widely employed *structural functional** analysis of society discussed in Chapter 1. The reference in Chapter 12 to Viola Bernard, Perry

Ottenberg, and Fritz Redl's analysis of dehumanization in modern warfare is an example of modern social pathological analysis. To these moderns, such destructiveness is a sign of social sickness. They cite as examples the mass extermination of Jews in Nazi Germany and the elimination of millions of Kulaks in the Soviet Union, and in recent American experience, the destruction of the civilians in the Vietnamese village of My Lai.

What the moderns have in common with earlier pathologists is that both believe that the remedy to social problems remains with the individual. If enough individuals can recapture their humanness and counteract the depersonalization of modern society, then society can again be made healthy and social problems can be successfully resolved. Rubington and Weinberg note that (1973: 303) the major theme of current social pathology is the development of humanism. That may be, but the independent impact of social structure and of social conditions on individual human behavior is not a primary focus of the social pathologists. Most other sociologists view this as a failing.

SOCIAL DISORGANIZATION THEORY The social disorganization theory reflected the independent growth of sociology. Its advocates, like the social pathologists, sought to regulate human behavior, but they located social problems primarily in the social structure, not in individual behavior. Society was seen as an organic whole.

The social disorganizationists considered the fundamental problems of society to be the results of breakdowns in the norms of behavior. Such breakdowns, they felt, were caused by the clash of cultures within society and the shift in aspects of the culture. Recall the discussion of William Ogburn's (1922) concept of *cultural lag**, which postulates that technological change often outruns the ability of groups and institutions to keep up and adapt. The result is a disorganizing effect on social rules and a period of normlessness (anomie), which produces many problems.

DISORGANIZATION AND MECHANICAL BALANCE Rubington and Weinberg conclude (1973: 303) that "the major theme of any solution derived from this perspective is *mechanics*." The cure is to restore the balance between the social and the technological, or to bring together and resolve the cultural differences between subgroups. Erich Fromm has written extensively on this theme, describing the gap between human needs and the institutions set up to serve them. In *The Revolution of Hope: Toward A Humanized Technology* (1968), he asks whether people can be mobilized to regain control of their lives and restore the balance. The alleviation of social problems will bring society into a new state of effective formal and informal organization. One problem with this approach is the assumption that social disorganization is a necessary characteristic of individuals and groups with problems. Studies such as Thrasher's *The Gang* (1927), dealing with boys' gangs, Whyte's *Street Corner Society* (1943) describing a gang of unemployed young men, Liebow's *Tally's Corner* (1967), concerned with poor black men of Washington, D.C., and Cavan's *Hippies of the Haight* (1972) demonstrated that the alleged disorganized elements in society are often highly, if differently, organized. The effect of such empirical evidence was to open still other perspectives.

VALUE CONFLICT THEORY The emergence of the value conflict theory shifted the focus to the cultural values of a society or a group within a society. Richard Fuller and Richard Myers, in their classic article, "The Natural History of a Social Problem" (1941), stressed the importance of values in identifying social problems.

OBJECTIVE CONDITIONS AND SUBJECTIVE BELIEFS They noted that subjective cultural values may lead us to identify a problem where none exists. As an example, they state that, in seventeenth-century Salem, Massachusetts, the belief in witches was in itself enough to create a social problem. The hanging of nineteen women accused of being witches was an attempt to solve it. Values can identify objective phenomena such as murder or racism, which cause injury to others, as problems also. In either case, the source of problems in society is not the individual but groups and their values.

According to the value conflict perspective, social problems are resolved when conflicting values are reconciled. As Rubington and Weinberg

Identity confusion results when a black member of the Ku Klux Klan addresses a crowd in a scene from the motion picture *Shock Corridor* (1963). SOURCE: Copyright © 1963, Allied Artists Pictures Corporation.

note (1973: 303), "The theme of value conflict solutions is solidarity." Two common approaches to achieving such social solidarity, are resolving contradictory principles by reconciling (integrating) values and resolving intergroup value conflicts by maintaining the conflicting values but separating the groups.

An example of the integrative approach is Gunnar Myrdal's proposal in *An American Dilemma* (1944). Here, two groups have opposing values: the black value of desegregation opposed to white segregationist values leads to conflicting values for white individuals. Myrdal noted that interracial tensions cause whites to have allegiance to two contradictory values: that all people are created equal and that whites are genetically superior to blacks. Myrdal proposed as a solution to this value conflict the need to adopt the first value, which he identified as the American creed, exclusively. An example of the group separationist proposal is the thesis of Stokely Carmichael and Charles Hamilton in *Black Power* (1967) that only when blacks take over political power in black ghettos will they be able to develop programs that meet their needs.

Given the focus on different groups and different values, the value conflict perspective introduces *cultural relativism* to the task of understanding and resolving social problems. (In this respect, it is akin to the labeling perspective, which also emphasizes the existence of different values in society.)

DEVIANCE AND FUNCTIONAL THEORY The deviance theory, like the social disorganization theory, assumes that there is a desirable normative social structure. The deviance perspective focuses on the predominant normative social structure and how those outside its acceptable norms can be brought into it. As Talcott Parsons said, in discussing social systems (1961: 325):

Every such system must by definition have an environment which is external to it, vis-a-vis which there is a boundary . . . and relative to which there is a problem of "control," i.e., of maintenance of the pattern of the system vis-a-vis the fluctuating features of the environment.

MERTON'S THEORY OF DEVIANT MEANS The theory of deviant means, the classic statement of the deviance perspective, was made by Robert Merton in his 1938 article on social structure and anomie. Merton noted that certain widely held goals such as material success and respected status could not be achieved by all through the legitimate institutional structures of the society. When large segments of the population face institutional blocks such as poor schools or a shortage of good jobs, then a high degree of delinquency and other problem behavior can be expected. Rubington and Weinberg note (1973: 304), "The central theme of the deviant behavior solution is opportunity." Lack of opportunity leads to seeking of alternative means to goals, sometimes criminal in nature.

The deviance theory holds that the social structure must be changed in order to bring deviant behavior within acceptable boundaries. If there are many school dropouts in a community, then the solution is to improve education. If people cannot find work because they lack skills, then private and/or government programs should be developed to increase people's skills. (See Table 13-1.)

LABELING THEORY Labeling theorists offer a different perspective, particularly in the area of moral deviance. The labeling theorists hold that the social power of one group to call the behavior of another group a problem is the most important element in determining what is a social problem. Howard Becker explains the process by which this occurs (1963: 9):

Social groups create deviance by making the rules whose infraction constitutes deviance, and by applying those rules to particular people and labeling them as outsiders. From this point of view, deviance is not a quality of the act the person commits, but rather a consequence of the application by others of rules and sanctions to an "offender." The deviant is one to whom that label has successfully been applied; deviant behavior is behavior that people so label.

John Lofland observes (1969: 19):

It is in the situation of a very powerful party opposing a very weak one that the powerful party sponsors the *idea* that the weak party is breaking the rules of society. The very concepts of "society" and its "rules" are appropriated by powerful parties and made synonymous with their interests.

These are rather extreme statements of the labeling perspective. The implications of Becker's and Lofland's position would appear to be that any form of deviance exists simply because some people have the power to say so and to enforce what they say. In fact, however, Becker, Lofland, and other labeling theorists make a distinction between types of deviance. Edwin Schur, in *Crimes Without Victims* (1965), suggests that there are forms of deviance such as murder and robbery that are demonstrably injurious to someone while other forms of deviance, such as sex relations between unmarried consenting adults or the use of nonaddictive drugs, cause no demonstrable injury to anyone. Erving Goffman, in *Stigma* (1963), noted that inherently harmless characteristics such as being ugly or being black are labeled deviant even when no overt acts are involved. When society treats certain characteristics or conduct in a degrading and isolating manner, then the life and identity of the individual in the stigmatized group become organized around the facts of deviance (Lemert, 1967: 41).

The practical implications of labeling were shown in the British Wolfenden report, which advocated the termination of laws in Great Britain that classified homosexual acts between consenting adults as criminal. As Rubington and Weinberg point out (1973: 304), according to the labeling perspective, the solution to many social problems is *redefinition*. For some acts and in some circumstances, this approach is akin to Senator George Aiken's advice about the American involvement in the Vietnam War: "We should declare victory and get out." American society moved in this direction when Prohibition ended in 1933. It had become evident that more problems were created by the law than by alcohol.

Table 13-1   Merton's Typology of Modes of Individual Adaptation

Modes of adaptation	Culture goals	Institutionalized means
I. Conformity	+	+
II. Innovation	+	−
III. Ritualism	−	+
IV. Retreatism	−	−
V. Rebellion[1]	±	±

[1] Merton notes: "This fifth alternative is on a plane clearly different from that of the others. It represents a transitional response seeking to *institutionalize* new goals and new procedures to be shared by other members of the society. It thus refers to efforts to *change* the existing cultural and social structure rather than to accommodate efforts *within* this structure."

SOURCE: Robert K. Merton, *Social Theory and Social Structure* (New York: The Free Press, 1959), p. 140. Copyright 1957 by The Free Press, a Corporation.

More homosexuals now make public their sexual preferences and lifestyles, but discrimination and negative labeling are still widespread. SOURCE: Jim Scherer.

Adherents of the labeling perspective feel that ending the legal and informal prohibitions against victimless crimes would help stabilize society. They argue that if those with power concentrated on such problems as violent crime and poverty, which cause objective injury, they would better serve society.

In summary, it is likely that each of these perspectives has tapped some dimension of social reality and its remedy; but, the problem remains of determining which gives the most useful insights into the causes of problems and their solutions. Furthermore, additional perspectives may develop, and so may new combinations of two or more older ones. We should keep in mind Rubington and Weinberg's warning: "The source of many modern difficulties may be that proposed solutions are outrunning the number of problems rather than the reverse."

Whatever perspectives develop will influence what we see and do not see as, and what we want to do and can do about social problems.

BEHIND THE SOCIAL FAÇADE

The Comtean aim to see and to foresee implies, quite correctly, that a good many beliefs common in a society are either a distortion of social reality or simply not true at all. Such a belief may be a *social façade* instead of a recognition of social reality. Given our *socialization** into the culture by our own family in a particular neighborhood, school, and community, it is not surprising that many of us have inaccurate perceptions about much of what exists in our own society.

If one lives in an all-white suburb, how can one know much about life in a black inner-city ghetto? If one lives in a low-crime area, how can one know much about those who commit and those who are the victims of violent crimes? If one's family is puritannical, how can one know about pornography? The fact is that much of what people believe about other communities, other people, and other social practices is inaccurate, although, as W. I. Thomas noted (1931: 189): "If men define situations as real, they are real in their consequences."

PRESIDENTIAL STUDY COMMISSIONS Situations sometimes develop that make people doubt their own understanding of what is going on. When this happens, many may stimulate their sociological imagination in order to gain new understanding. Research often helps us to see more accurately and to foresee choices. Sociological research has been used more and more in recent years to develop new perspectives on social issues. While much research is performed by sociologists to test such perspectives, some research is stimulated by a general need to clear up basic misunderstandings and to help solve problems of public concern.

Three issues that were studied by presidential commissions are urban racial rioting, general violence, and pornography. The rioting in Los Angeles, Detroit, Newark, and other cities in the mid 1960s led to the National Advisory Commission on Civil Disorders (1968). The widespread concern with criminal and other violence led to the National Commission on the Causes and Prevention of Violence (1969). Concern with the alleged effects of pornography led to the National Commission on Obscenity and Pornography (1970).

These commissions were composed of prominent leaders in government, business, labor, religion, and other sectors of society. Each commission hired a staff of trained researchers, many of them sociologists, to develop research on which to base policy recommendations. The social scientists exhibited a good deal of sociological imagination. Their findings indicated that much general belief was a distortion of reality and that the distortions were part of the problem.

Let us consider each commission's findings in relation to general beliefs then operating in American society.

NATIONAL ADVISORY COMMISSION ON CIVIL DISORDERS The commission, cochaired by Illinois governor Otto Kerner and New York City mayor John Lindsay, was set up by President Johnson following a series of race riots. Over one hundred people had been killed and over $100 million in property damage had occurred in a number of disorders including the Watts riot in Los Angeles in 1965, the Hough riots in Cleveland in 1966, and the extensive Newark and Detroit riots in 1967. The Detroit riot alone resulted in forty-three deaths and over $50 million in property damage.

These events forced many whites to question the cultural assumption holding that the American creed that all people are created equal is effectively practiced in America. The civil rights movement of the late 1950s and early 1960s had produced much legislation to protect the rights of blacks and other minorities. The general belief was that inequalities between blacks and whites in terms of treatment and opportunity were being eradicated. The civil disorders gave notice that these assumptions were questionable.

The commission charged its staff with answering three questions: What happened? Why did it happen? and What can be done to prevent it from happening again? The staff's strategy was to develop carefully documented profiles of disorder. Field teams went into twenty-three cities that had experienced racial rioting and conducted extensive interviews with both black and white leaders. Rioters and nonrioters were interviewed in sections struck by disorders and in metropolitan areas outside these sections. Census and other data were compiled for each city on such characteristics as income and educational levels of blacks and whites.

Table 13-2 Income and Educational Levels of Riot Participants and Noninvolved in Detroit and Newark Civil Disorders

| | Income level |||| | Educational level ||||
| | Detroit survey || Newark survey || | Detroit survey || Newark survey ||
	Riot participants	Non-involved	Riot participants	Non-involved		Riot participants	Non-involved	Riot participants	Non-involved
Annual income	(N=44)	(N=287)	(N=104)	(N=126)	Education	(N=43)	(N=272)	(N=106)	(N=126)
Less than					Less than				
$2,000	13.6%	12.9%	4.7%	3.2%	grades 1–6	2.3%	7.7%	0.0%	3.2%
$2,000–$5,000	25.0	17.4	27.9	26.2	Grade school	4.7	20.2	1.9	11.1
$5,000–$7,500	13.6	20.6	27.9	30.1	Some high				
$7,500–$10,000	18.2	13.9	14.4	11.1	school	53.5	33.8	63.2	46.8
$10,000–$12,500	2.3	33.8	1.0	4.0	High school				
$12,500–$15,000	0.0	1.7	1.0	1.6	graduate	23.3	26.1	29.2	31.0
More than					Some college	14.0	10.3	5.7	6.3
$15,000	2.3	0.3	0.0	3.2	Graduated				
No answer	25.0	29.4	23.1	20.6	college	–	1.5	–	1.6
	100%	100%	100%	100%	Graduate work	2.2	.4	–	–
						100%	100%	100%	100%

SOURCE: *Report of the National Advisory Commission on Civil Disorders* (New York: Bantam, 1968), p. 174.

Then from an analysis of the documents compiled and field interviews, ten of the twenty-three, a fair cross section of the cities, were chosen for intensive further investigation (1968: 108).

The aim of the research as stated by President Johnson was to cut through "the thicket of ... conflicting evidence and extreme opinions" (*Report of the National Advisory Commission on Civil Disorders*, 1968: 203). The researchers attempted to do this by identifying the causes of the disorders — pervasive discrimination and segregation, black migration to the cities, white exodus to the suburbs, the creation of poor black inner city ghettos, the frustration of rising hopes for better education and job opportunities, the legitimation of violence by some whites who terrorized black and white civil rights workers, and a prevailing sense of powerlessness among blacks in their efforts to achieve equality of treatment and opportunity.

REPORTS ON RACISM The conclusions of the commission were so disturbing that there was an attempt at suppressing one reported finding, concerning the National Guard. In the civil disorders in Detroit in 1967, most deaths and damage occurred in areas under control of the National Guard rather than federal troops. The day after the rioting ended on July 27, 1967, Lieutenant General John L. Throckmorton reported that the response of local citizens to the federal troops was positive and helpful but "in areas where the National Guard tried to establish rapport with citizens, there was a *smaller* [emphasis added] response." This language was used in the summary report of the full report of the commission, sponsored by twenty-three organizations including the American Civil Liberties Union, the American Jewish Committee, the Methodist Church's Board of Christian Social Concerns, and the National Catholic Conference for Interracial Justice (see: *Summary Report*, 1968: 5). Yet, the report released by the government reads: "In areas where the National Guard tried to establish rapport with citizens there was a *similar* [emphasis added, note here the change from *smaller*] response" (see: *Report of the National Advisory Commission on Civil Disorders*, 1968: 100). There is a strong suggestion here of an official agency (in this case, the federal government) attempting to use the mass media to do what David Altheide (1976) calls *creating reality* by means of official reports released to the mass media.

Yet, in the main, the report appears to be uncensored and well documented. The conclusions of the commission were a challenge to the general belief in the operation of the American creed. The report said that (1968: 203), "White racism is essentially responsible for the explosive mixture which has been accumulating in our cities since the end of World War II." Whether whites wanted to do anything about it or not, the new findings of the National Advisory Commission highlighted what other research had long indicated: white treatment of black citizens was far from the ideals expressed in American homes, churches, and schools. One of the findings of the commission that surprised many was that those who rioted tended to have as high an income and educational level as those who were not involved in the rioting. The question about income alone (see Table 13-2), to which so many gave no response, might have led to the suspicion that differences in income did separate rioters from nonrioters. However, the higher average educational attainment of riot participants negates that likelihood, since there is a close correlation between educational and income levels.

The exposure of such distortions of reality is not unusual in the findings of social research, but the presentation of such findings by a national presidential commission was unusual. The methods used were designed for the particular circumstances being investigated and show how the sociological imagination can be used to gain new and valid insights into social reality.

NATIONAL COMMISSION ON THE CAUSES AND PREVENTION OF VIOLENCE The National Commission on the Causes and Prevention of Violence, chaired by Johns Hopkins University president emeritus Milton Eisenhower, was established by President Johnson and continued under President Nixon. The commission was set up after years of growing public concern about an apparent rise in the rate of violent crime and the use of violence both to support and to oppose civil rights, war, and other protests. The leaders of such groups as the Ku Klux Klan, the Student Non-Violent Coordinating Committee, and the Students for a Democratic Society were advocating violence to achieve their ends.[3] Black militant Rap Brown, in defending violence as a civil rights protest technique, had said, "Violence is as American as apple pie." Then the assassinations of Robert Kennedy and Martin Luther King, Jr., five years after the assassination of President Kennedy threw the nation into a period of grief and soul-searching.

REEXAMINING VIOLENCE These events induced many Americans to reexamine the nature of American society. The ideals of life, liberty, and the pursuit of happiness had seemed realities for so many Americans that certain other realities were ignored. The commission wanted to know in particular about the causes of violence in American society. Its first step was to review existing research on violence in America and elsewhere. However, the commission could find no significant work on violence in America, much less any that would relate it to other countries (1969: xv). Scholars had simply not studied this issue.

---

[3] Each of these organizations had its ironic side. The Ku Klux Klan spoke of Christian values while terrorizing their fellow Christians who were black. The Student Non-Violent Coordinating Committee was widely referred to in the late 1960s as "Student Violent Non-Coordinating Committee," and the Students for a Democratic Society used firebombing and other violent tactics that were anything but democratic.

This lack of resources affected the research strategy of the codirectors, both prominent sociologists, James Short of Washington State University and Marvin Wolfgang of the University of Pennsylvania. They decided to concentrate on historical sources that would show the extent to which violence had been employed in the growth and development of the republic since its founding in the late eighteenth century.

The research was reported to the commission by historian Hugh Davis Graham and political scientist Ted Robert Gurr (1969). After reviewing the findings of over twenty fellow social scientists, Graham and Gurr concluded (xiv):

Americans have always been given to a kind of historical amnesia that masks much of their turbulent past. Probably all nations share this tendency to sweeten memories of their past through collective repression,

Table 13-3 Number of Known Persons Killed by American Vigilante Groups

Period	Number of deaths
1760–1769	16
1770–1779	0
1780–1789	0
1790–1799	0
1800–1809	0
1810–1819	0
1820–1829	3
1830–1839	5
1840–1849	64
1850–1859	119
1860–1869	179
1870–1879	125
1880–1889	107
1890–1899	25
Total	643

SOURCE: Richard Maxwell, "The American Vigilante Tradition" in *The History of Violence in America: A Report to the National Commission on the Causes and Prevention of Violence* (New York: Bantam, 1969), p. 175.

but Americans have probably magnified this process of selective recollection, owing to our historic vision of ourselves as a latter-day chosen people, a New Jerusalem.

Given the general belief among Americans that our religious heritage is one of humane consideration for others and intrinsic virtue, it is easy for Americans to view themselves as a New Jerusalem. However, as the research staff emphasized, when such a perception keeps one from recognizing the existence of violence within the tradition, then continuing violence is likely.

The extent and nature of the violent strain in America is indicated by the titles of some articles assembled by the commission: "A 150-Year Study of Political Violence in the United States," "The American Vigilante Tradition," "Violence in American Literature and Folk Lore," "American Labor Violence," "Patterns of Collective Racial Violence," and, in an article that touches on modern urbanization, "Overcrowding and Human Aggression."

The findings of the commission punctured many myths about inherent American goodness and the ability to work out problems democratically. The violence of the American Revolution and the Civil War, the destruction of Native American tribes during the westward movement, the violent labor-management conflicts and the urban racial rioting of the twentieth century indicate that American society has seen a parade of violent attempts to solve its problems.

Why raise such unpleasant facts? If most people believe in a social façade, why not let well enough alone? Reflecting on the continuing influence of this historical pattern, John Herbers noted in the introduction to the commission's report that the commissioners (xix):

are not asking for self-condemnation, nor are they discrediting the belief that America is a land of special promise and potential. They are laying out the facts and it is the facts that cry out for a search for a non-violent tradition — one that would preserve the mobility of American classes and groups and allow for changes, reforms and political pressures without the use of violence. Perhaps there must be a new tradition before there can be a New Jerusalem.

Perhaps no more appropriate statement of the rationale behind the probing sociological perspective could be made. The sociologist must, to use Melville's metaphor in *Moby Dick*, "pierce the mask" and discover the fact behind illusion if the knowledge of social scientists and those they serve is to increase.

NATIONAL COMMISSION ON OBSCENITY AND PORNOGRAPHY The National Commission on Obscenity and Pornography, chaired by University of Minnesota dean of law William Lockhart, was set up by President Johnson and made its report during the presidency of Richard Nixon. From the late nineteenth century Comstock Laws (see Chapter 11) until the mid-twentieth century, obscene and pornographic literature and movies were widely censored in the United States. Then, in the 1950s and 1960s, the Supreme Court began to interpret the Constitution's First Amendment that "Congress shall make no law abridging the freedom of speech, or of the press" as applying to much pornographic expression previously defined as criminally offensive. The Court's decisions allowed the widespread distribution of such books of recognized literary worth as John Cleland's *Fanny Hill* and the works of Henry Miller and many works of little or no literary worth as well.

EXPLORING SEXUAL MYTHS The subsequent growth and widespread consumption of erotica in

American society has aroused much public concern. There is a strong tradition in American society that sex is a private matter between man and wife and is for procreation only. Any open interest in sex has been viewed as morally corrupt. The task of the commission was to find whether these puritannical values were still dominant and, whether they were or not, what the consequences are of exposure to erotica in literature and the mass media.

The findings of the staff and the majority report of the commission gave another jolt to general cultural beliefs by finding that most Americans oppose laws that prevent adults from having access to pornographic materials and that over three-quarters of American adults had in fact been exposed to explicit sexual materials. In addition, the commission found no causal relationship between exposure to pornography and the sex-related crime.

These conclusions contrasted with the view that widely available exposure to pornography would undermine American culture. One commissioner was so outraged that he resigned and submitted his own report on the need for continued legislation for censorship of obscene and pornographic material (1970: 578–605). Yet, the findings of the commission staff were such that two other commissioners issued a separate report arguing

A wide cross-section of Americans have seen pornographic films or read pornographic literature. SOURCE: Jan Lukas/Photo Researchers.

Table 13-4 Total Sex Crimes Reported to the Police in Copenhagen, Denmark, 1958–1969

Year	Total crimes[a]	Percent increase or decrease over previous year
1958	982	–
1959	1,018	+ 3.66
1960	899	− 11.69
1961	1,000	+ 11.23
1962	749	− 25.10
1963	895	+ 19.49
1964	732	− 18.21
1965	762	− 4.10
1966	783	+ 2.75
1967[b]	591	− 24.52
1968	515	− 12.86
1969	358	− 30.48

[a] Total reported sex crimes included rape and attempted rape, coitus with minors, "indecent interference short of rape" with both minor girls and adult women, exhibitionism, voyeurism, homosexual offenses, and verbal indecency.

[b] In 1967, the Danish parliament voted to remove erotic literature from its obscenity statute and moved to abolish legal prohibitions against the dissemination of sexually explicit materials to persons sixteen years of age or older.

SOURCE: *The Report of the Commission on Obscenity and Pornography* (New York: Bantam, 1970), p. 273.

that legal restrictions ought to be eliminated, even in the case of children, whose parents ought to be the ones to determine exposure (1970: 446–448).

THE COMMISSION'S RESEARCH PROCEDURES
The procedures employed by the commission's staff included a variety of well-established research methods. In addition to researching the historical background of the problem, the staff surveyed national probability samples of adults and young persons; made quasi-experimental studies of selected populations; conducted controlled experiments; and made studies of national rates of incidence of sex offenses and illegitimate births (1970: 26).

RESISTANCE TO THE COMMISSIONS' REPORTS

It is not surprising that President Nixon was cautious and critical about accepting the reports of the commissions on racial riots, violence, and pornography. The president is an elected official. If most deny that they hold racist beliefs, do not recognize the existence of a violent heritage, and believe that open interest in sexual expression produces moral and cultural decline, then it would take courage in an elected official to challenge those beliefs directly, however extensive the findings that pointed in another direction.

If this is to be the fate of all such commission reports, then what is the value of research strongly indicating that many common beliefs are not grounded in social reality? Those who hold to the sociological perspective can well argue that the exposure of social myths is of some value. Clive Barnes, the theater critic of The New York *Times*, in his special introduction to the pornography commission's report made the following observation, which could well apply to all these myth-puncturing reports (1970: xvii):

The Report of the Commission on Obscenity and Pornography provides all of us for the first time with data and evidence on this terribly complex subject. It seriously requires the attention of every citizen concerned with the quality of our lives. As much as any other public document it represents the United States of America, 1970. Read it. You may love it or hate it, accept it or challenge it, but you shouldn't ignore it.

PRIVATE TROUBLES AND PUBLIC ISSUES

If one function of sociology were to turn private troubles into public issues, then any private trouble would become a public issue when enough people shared it. In relation to unemployment, C. Wright Mills noted (1959: 9):

When, in a city of 100,000 only one man is unemployed, that is his personal trouble, and for its relief we properly look to the character of the man, his skills, and his immediate opportunities. But when in a nation of 50 million employees, 15 million . . . are unemployed, that is an issue, and we may not hope to find its solution within the range of opportunities open to any one individual.

THE HUMANISTIC STRAIN IN SOCIOLOGY

Mills's statement clearly suggests that we ought to be looking for ways to alleviate such troubles. Mills was tapping into the humanistic strain in sociology. A leading exponent of this view, Thomas Ford Hoult, defined *humanism* as the belief that every person has potential worth and should be given the opportunity to develop to the greatest extent possible consistent with the development of others (1974: 3).

Many of the issues taken up earlier in this text illustrate the relationship between widespread private troubles and changing social conditions. Consider age-related problems. It would not be difficult to find an adolescent who felt alienated from her or his parents or an elderly person who felt a sense of alienation from her or his children. The rapid physical and social mobility of middle-aged people has left millions of young and old without the clear social roles they once had in American society. These individual private troubles can be seen as a public issue.

Consider the personal troubles of a young black man in prison for the third or fourth time. Since educational and occupational opportunities in the inner-city ghettos have declined in the past quarter of a century, the private trouble of this young man is a typical result of deteriorating conditions of life for thousands of similarly situated young men and women.

Consider the issue of war. A permanently disabled veteran has the personal problem of working out his life. Yet the fact that he was a fighting soldier is a result of the structure of society. (This was particularly true in a limited war such as Vietnam;

the front-line fighting men were drawn largely from the lower and lower-middle classes.)

Neither social science nor any other discipline or viewpoint can totally eliminate private troubles. The founders of the American republic tacitly admitted this when they stated that a major aim of the society was to make possible for all the pursuit, but not necessarily the achievement, of happiness. The sociological perspective does hold that, for those private troubles that are related to the operation of the social structure (a public issue), it is possible to alter that structure and to reduce substantially the private troubles of many people. Whether it is the family structure, the educational system, the occupational structure, the structure of our cities and suburbs, or any other institutionalized forms of life, the sociological imagination envisioned by Mills holds that the solution to many private troubles is a new degree of institutional flexibility, or perhaps new types of social structures.

THE QUALITY OF INSTITUTIONAL FLEXIBILITY In the past, American society has exhibited a good deal of institutional flexibility. When the large extended family of the nineteenth century no longer met the needs of most people, then the mobile nuclear family became the new twentieth-century norm. When new capital was needed to finance the development of American industry, the corporation achieved the status of a legal person, so that people could invest, and even if the corporation went bankrupt, the investors were liable only to the extent of their investment. When industrial laborers needed fair wages and protection from working conditions, the union was invented. Like the corporation, the union was empowered to bargain on behalf of all its members.

How did these and other institutional innovations come about? Some arose when groups of individuals made decisions on a mass basis. Often public action was needed to modify laws, such as those on marriage and divorce; legal means were developed to achieve new forms of economic interaction, as with the National Labor Relations Act of 1935, sanctioning collective bargaining between corporations and labor unions.

The task of the sociological imagination was well stated by Ray Rist, program chairman of the Pacific Sociological Association's annual meeting in 1974. On Mills's theme of private troubles and public issues, Rist said (1974: 1):

Beyond the current morass of the political scene, there lies a more fundamental condition demanding the attention of social scientists: the ... need ... to come to grips with the interrelations of private troubles and public issues. We ... must try to ... generate either self-educating individuals or self-cultivating publics.

Mills would add to this observation, "only then might society be reasonable and free."

ADJUSTING TO RAPID SOCIAL CHANGE

The sociological imagination involves two basic assumptions about social change in modern American society. One is that individuals are faced with a continuing need to make personal adjustments. The other is that a "self-cultivating" (self-improving) public can control and direct desirable changes in the social system. Suicide, murder, unemployment, and other problems make it clear enough that many individuals and institutions do not always successfully adjust to change. It is useful at this point to explore some ways in which individuals and publics do attempt to adjust.

COPING WITH DAY-TO-DAY LIFE How do individuals successfully cope with life day after day? To answer this question is to look into what Marcello Truzzi calls the sociology of everyday life (1968). Most men, and now most women, work in a large private business or a government bureaucracy. Four topics that touch on the sociology of everyday life are the coffee break, American graffiti, discotheque dance clubs, and privacy. The four may be considered in light of what they help the individual achieve: more successful management of stress, greater personal enjoyment and fulfillment from life, opportunity for self-expression. Let us examine each one.

THE COFFEE BREAK Millions of individuals begin their work day in a large corporate or government unit. Each has specific tasks which make up a minute part of the work necessary to complete the task or the organization, whether it is producing consumer goods or offering services.

It has long been recognized that, in this setting, the function of the coffee break has little to do with coffee. In a study of workers in the Western Electric Company at its Hawthorne works in Chicago in 1927, it was discovered that ten- to fifteen-minute coffee breaks in the morning and afternoon decrease work fatigue and increase efficiency (Roethlisberger and Dickson, 1946). The actual consumption of coffee had little to do with this effect. It did not matter whether the worker drank coffee, tea, or nothing. What did matter was that the coffee break had important psychological implications. As Gary Felton points out (1966: 36):

the significance of rest pauses lies in the meaning of the respites rather than the respites themselves.... The workers were able to congregate and converse, to relax and relieve tension — normal interaction was permitted ... favorable to maintenance of individual integrity.

AMERICAN GRAFFITI During the course of the day, an individual probably sees, and perhaps writes, graffiti on bathroom walls, city billboards, or buildings. Graffiti have increasingly been studied as an aspect of modern or modernizing cultures (Stocker, et al., 1972). Graffiti have become so common in American society that they have increasingly been recognized as a means of coping with everyday life.

One function of graffiti is to serve as a personalized protest against restrictions and strains. For example, in the Philippines, where the attitude toward homosexuality is relatively tolerant, graffiti make few references to homosexuality; but in the United States, where social disapproval of homosexuality has been strong, graffiti frequently refer to homosexual requests and acts, both male and female (Stocker et al., 1972: 98–100). Besides sexual content, graffiti include sayings and drawings on other frustrating aspects of life, including racial and racist references *(All whites must die)*, drug statements *(I ain't going to sell drugs no more)*, and various social and political statements *(Sisters remember you are women and not men)* and grim political views *(Assassinate Spiro Agnew and become a national hero* and *Lee Harvey Oswald, where are you now that we need you?).*

Graffiti may seem ugly, yet they are so much a part of the American social landscape that, for

A longtime American institution, coffee breaks relieve tension, decrease worker fatigue, and increase efficiency. SOURCE: J. Berndt/Stock Boston.

thousands, they regularly serve as an outlet for the expression of frustrations. Furthermore, some researchers hold that the study of graffiti is an accurate indicator of the social attitude of a community (Stocker and others, 1972: 103). They show just how well or how poorly many people are adjusting to life.

DISCOTHEQUES   Much of modern life is restrictive in style. Whether working, walking down a crowded street, sitting in a bus or subway car, or snarled in a rush-hour traffic jam, people find themselves in physically inhibiting situations. For young people in particular, the dance fashions of the day have served to release tensions. A study by Lucille Blum (1966) of young people who frequent popular discotheque dance clubs provided some interesting evidence of this. Dances over the years have been characterized by a great deal of gyrating movement. This was true of the Charleston of the twenties, Swing of the thirties and forties, Rock and Roll of the fifties and sixties, and the more recent reggae and disco styles.

Blum notes that psychoanalysis has burgeoned as an outcome "of the numberless selves being ground up by the technological system" (366). The self-indulgence and impulse release of popular dancing can serve as a temporary stabilizer. As Blum observes (366):

The abandon which is experienced in dances such as the frug [a popular dance of the mid 1960's] appears a remedy for pent-up tension which . . . might otherwise take a course incompatible with the "world of morals."

SOURCE: Bert Glenn/Magnum.

Interestingly, Blum goes on to note of older Americans (366):

> ... it would seem that some of the findings in the study have implications with respect to persons consciously beyond the adolescent and young adult periods, who have hitched on to youth's discotheque band wagon.

In one interesting case, the Twist, a dance popular in the mid 1960s, was so easily mastered by older people that young people turned from it in order to maintain their social distance from their elders.

PRIVACY   A typical day for most Americans involves interaction with many people at home, on the job, in public transportation, in entertainment centers, and elsewhere. Privacy thus serves for many as a stabilizing influence on their lives. As Barry Schwartz observes in his article on the social psychology of privacy, "Withdrawal ... provide(s) a release from social relations when they become sufficiently intense to be irritating" (1968: 746). Given this need for a degree of privacy, it is not surprising that most Americans own their own homes. The ability to withdraw from public scrutiny is a widely felt need. The function of this desire for some degree of individual privacy is explained by Robert Merton in the following terms (1964: 343):

> Resistance to full visibility of one's behavior appears... to result from structural properties of group life. Some measure of leeway in conforming to role expectations is presupposed in all groups. To have to meet the strict requirements of a role at all times, without some degree of deviation, is to experience insufficient allowances for individual differences in capacity and training and for situational exigencies which make strict conformity difficult.

One's home comes to be seen as a haven or sanctuary from the social rules of one's occupational or other social roles among critical judges. Where a family lives in the home, detaching oneself from other institutional roles and rules does not mean full escape. The family itself requires us to adhere to certain behavior patterns. These informal, personal forms of coping, however, aid primarily in managing the tensions brought on by private problems. It remains for us to consider how the larger structure of the society adjusts to rapid social change.

SOCIETY-WIDE POLICIES

In the American democratic social system, the degree to which institutions remain rigid or reflect innovations is closely related to C. Wright Mills's reference to self-cultivating publics. By public, Mills meant a large number of people with common interests. Common interests in America have produced social decisions *not* to do certain things, such as not to allow police into a home without a search warrant and not to stop people from criticizing their government. Common interests have also produced social policies to establish and maintain schools, roads, military defense, and other structures of organized social life. The American public is often strained to develop coherent views on what needs to be done to ensure continuing stability. With the population growing by millions every year, rural–urban–suburban population shifts going on all the time, and new technology developing, it is difficult to match needs with effective institutionalized processes. It may be that management needs labor and labor needs management, but each technological development changes the economic equation of how each needs the other. It may be that good man–woman relationships occur best within a family, but with the change toward greater opportunity for women to play roles outside the family, there is a need for men to adjust to new demands within the family and for women to those outside it. Children must be socialized into the society, but parents may have a problem in socializing their children into a society fundamentally different from the one in which they were raised.

TENSION MANAGEMENT THEORY Wilbert Moore (1963) identifies the problem facing the American public as one of developing effective *tension-management systems*. According to his theory, different aspects of society don't always mesh completely with each other. The resulting strains must be brought under control if the social system is not to become seriously unbalanced. Managing the system effectively involves a good deal of directed social change, or what Robert Lauer calls *willed history* (1973: 237–257). When cybernetic changes occur, many old occupations disappear and new ones are created for a new planned or willed history. When most middle- and upper-middle-class whites leave the cities for the suburbs, those left need new planning. When the traditional school system no longer meets the educational needs of millions of young people, then a new willed history of education is called for.

COLLECTIVE BEHAVIOR AND DIRECTED CHANGE Collective change in American society has often been brought about through formal organizations. When thousands of individual laborers wanted to improve their working conditions, they organized into the American Federation of Labor and other labor organizations and thus secured the power needed to negotiate with corporations. When blacks wanted guaranteed equality of treatment, they organized the National Association for the Advancement of Colored People and other civil rights organizations that forced the passage of civil rights laws. When thousands of American consumers began to feel powerless in the face of private industry, they organized behind Ralph Nader. When government appeared unresponsive to public opinion on the issues of war and government corruption during the presidencies of Lyndon Johnson and Richard Nixon, Common Cause, an organization led by John Gardner, sought political reforms in local and national government.

ORGANIZED PUBLICS In America, there are now many organizations representing a small public within the society. These are self-cultivating, and are one way people attempt to bring about changes to meet their needs. Note the organizations listed in Table 13-5. The mere size of the American Automobile Association shows dramatically how automobile production is both good business and held to be good. The American Federation of Labor would not disagree, except to argue that union members working in the automobile and other unionized industries ought to get a larger share of the profits.

Such organizations are one means of controlling tensions in the society. It is also true that the pressures of such organizations may directly or indirectly oppose each other. The American Farm Bureau Federation may well oppose the American Automobile Association's pressures for more highway construction funds in favor of more assistance for small farms. The National Association for the Advancement of Colored People opposes the continued legality of handguns, which are generally cheap and often used in the urban ghettos where great daily frustrations exist, while the National Rifle Association strongly supports the continued private possession of all types of guns. The dilemma of these many and often conflicting pressures was expressed in an article by the nationally syndicated columnist James Reston. In

Table 13-5 Ten Organizations That Influence Social Policy in the United States

Organization	Number of members
American Association of Retired Persons	5,000,000
American Automobile Association	16,000,000
American Farm Bureau Federation	2,000,000
American Federation of Labor–Congress of Industrial Organization	13,500,000
B'nai B'rith	500,000
National Association for the Advancement of Colored People	450,000
National Education Association	1,100,000
National Grange	600,000
National Rifle Association	1,100,000
Veterans of Foreign Wars of the United States	1,800,000

SOURCE: *The CBS News Almanac* 1976 (Maplewood, N.J.: Hammond Almanac, 1975), pp. 878–882.

viewing the many needs and conflicts in our society, Reston wrote this imaginary comment by Benjamin Franklin (1975: A7):

Some people seem to think that this country can afford to fight wars, feed and police the world, send everybody to college, bring back the nickel subway fare, invade the moon, raise wages, lower prices, expand production, and stamp out inflation, pollution, cancer, and the singing commercial — all at once. But we must choose.

Choose we must. But how we choose is the issue. Reston's Franklinesque wisdom makes it clear that the pressures and counterpressures of one organization against another do not necessarily bring the best possible results.

SYSTEMS THEORY   An emerging sociological perspective on the problem of bringing about constructive change in modern society is based on *systems theory* (Buckley, 1967). Systems theory draws on earlier theoretical perspectives on how the social system works from the early organic concepts to the more recent concern with power and labeling. In essence, systems theory holds that modern urban society is an intricate, interrelated system in which balance cannot be maintained by working on only one problem at a time. We may have to choose priorities, but it is unlikely that any one priority can be worked on to the total neglect of all others.

SYSTEMS THEORY AND THE CITIES   The Demonstration Cities concept discussed in Chapter 10 offers a practical illustration for systems analysis. The civil rights movement of the late 1950s and early 1960s, forced both industry and government to develop new policies. Corporations such as the

SOURCE: Sidney Harris.

"You know as well as I do, a man is measured by the amount of pollution he creates."

Ford Motor Company and New York's Chase Manhattan Bank began for the first time to recruit employees from the poorest sections of the city. New preschool and other educational programs were begun in poverty areas, and a multitude of other programs were initiated.

These many programs were meant to create model cities and a better life for all; but after several years, it became clear that a fundamental problem with these programs was that, whether private or governmental, they were developed independently of each other, at different times and in different places. If a preschool program was begun while a city's tax support for its regular school program was declining, then quality education was not advanced. If jobs for minorities opened up in suburban industrial parks but there was no mass transportation to those jobs, then occupational opportunities were not advanced. As Mel Ravitz observed about the model cities program, "We must now attend to a comprehensive approach" (1971: 160). He was pointing to the need to view the city and the society as a single social system. Such a system requires a continuing exchange about needs between various individuals and groups (Blau, 1964).

THE POST-INDUSTRIAL PERIOD The American system that systems analysts theorize about appears to be entering a post-industrial period (see Bell, 1967a, b). This period constitutes at least as big a challenge to the management of tensions as did the transition from a pre-industrial to an industrial state between the mid-nineteenth and mid-twentieth centuries. Pre-industrial workers were mostly small farm workers, industrial workers mostly blue-collar, and post-industrial workers mostly white-collar and middle class.

According to Daniel Bell (1967a, b), the post-industrial period America is entering has five main characteristics: services will dominate economic activity as cybernated automation increases the efficiency of consumer production with less hand labor; labor will be predominantly service-oriented, white collar, and middle class; intellectual and technological knowledge will be in increasing demand in the economy and in the society at large, thus expanding the influence of scientists and highly educated specialists; computerized systems, the major technological innovation of the post-industrial period, will replace many forms of blue-collar and white-collar labor needed in the industrial age; and government is likely to employ more people, especially in the social services, the regulation of industry, and the protection of the natural environment. On this last point, the economist John Kenneth Galbraith observes in *The New Industrial State* (1967) that the government (public) and private sectors will increasingly merge.

Historians often refer to the industrial revolution; sociologists can now refer to the post-industrial revolution. One of the fundamental adjustments facing society is that these have been accidental revolutions in terms of the values and structure of the society. The term *accidental* does not apply to the multitude of scientific and technological developments that shape our world. It is, of course, no accident that scientific theories based on research have led to vast technological advances. What is accidental is the often unplanned and impromptu social adjustments made necessary by the enormous changes of the industrial age. As Michael Harrington put it (1965: 41):

... these most conscious and man made of times have lurched into the unprecedented transformation of human life without thinking about it. And in a sense, this century, this scientific, technological, and utterly competent century, has happened accidentally.

Perhaps the greatest problem in America today is that the values and social organization nurtured through generations were well designed for the pre-industrial and industrial ages; but unless self-educating individuals and self-cultivating publics can better control the vast changes from the industrial to the post-industrial age, then the American and other modern societies, are likely to be controlled by events. As C. Wright Mills put it, if people "do not make history, they tend increasingly to become the utensils of history-makers as well as the mere objects of history" (1967: 25).

There is a culture-wide debate taking place about whether or not we are making progress toward meeting our newly developed needs. It is with this question in mind that we explore in the next two chapters our fears and hopes for the future.

SUMMARY

We explored the nature of the *sociological imagination,* a term coined by C. Wright Mills. In essence, the idea of the sociological imagination draws upon the Comtean legacy of *voir pour prévoir,* to see in order to foresee, and of *prévoir pour pouvoir,* to foresee in order to control. As such, the sociological imagination is designed to use empirical knowledge about social behavior to provide practical insights on achieving more effective direction over various aspects of life in the society.

Sociology can be viewed as a form of consciousness. The angle of vision discussed by Auguste Comte and the *Verstehen,* or subjective understanding, noted by Max Weber are related to four sociological motifs observed by Peter Berger: (1) the debunking motif, (2) the theme of unrespectability, (3) the idea of relativism, and (4) the cosmopolitan motif. Berger and Gouldner offer views on values and value-freedom in sociology.

Differing theoretical explanations have developed to explain social behavior and social problems. Any given theoretical perspective influences how and what is seen as a social problem and leads to the formulation of policy for dealing with the perceived problem. Five influential social problems theories are reviewed: (1) social pathology (individual or social illness), (2) social disorganization, (3) value conflict, (4) anomic deviancy, and (5) labeling theory. An example shows how each might be employed to describe the cause of a criminal act.

The aim of all these research-based theoretical orientations is to get behind social façades. The basic task of sociological analysis is to assess accurately, analyze, and report on social situations, whether the conclusions reached are in agreement with or in conflict with popular beliefs. One consequence of such an approach is the exposure of the *Thomas theorem** in which false popular beliefs lead to real consequences. Examples of applied research designed to test popular myths are drawn from the reports of three national advisory commissions — on civil disorders, on obscenity and pornography, and on the causes and prevention of violence.

One function of the sociological imagination is to discover where particularized widespread private troubles of individuals have become public issues. Examples are unemployment and calls for sacrifice in limited international conflicts, both of which disrupt thousands of private lives and families while leaving most others unaffected.

Drawing upon the sociological imagination, we presented two assumptions about the nature of adjusting to a rapidly changing American society: that individuals *en masse* are faced with the continuing need to make personal adjustments in order to maintain a successful life pattern (self-education) and that it is possible for a self-cultivating public to control and direct desired changes in the social system. These assumptions are explored in terms of individual coping day-to-day and developing society-wide policies.

QUESTIONS FOR DISCUSSION

1. What social implications are there in Auguste Comte's view that one of the purposes of sociology is *prévoir pour pouvoir,* to foresee in order to control?

2. Insofar as they communicate effectively, why do "sociologists make social life problematic," according to Ann and Scott Greer? Are the problems created in any sense useful?

3. What sociological value is there to the study of the unrespectable, as in the case of Howard Becker's *The Outsiders* or Elliot Liebow's *Tally's Corner*?

4. Consider two social problems theories and discuss how each theory influences our angle of vision.

5. Why has the social disorganization theory of social problems been generally discounted?

6. Given your reading of American society, do you believe that the conclusions of the national advisory commissions on civil disorders, on obscenity, and on violence will or will not be generally accepted in the long run?

7. The nineteenth-century social inventions of the corporation and the labor union were a reflection of institutional flexibility and adaptation to rapid social change. Do you think some new social inventions are needed to adjust to modern social change? Can you visualize any such invention?

8. Discuss some of the latent functions of the coffee break.

9. How have formal organizations typically been used in the past to get desired social changes in modern society?

10. Review your understanding of the following terms and concepts:

voir pour prévoir

prévoir pour pouvoir

debunking motif

theme of unrespectability

relativism

private troubles, public issues

cosmopolitan motif

social pathology theory

value conflict theory

anomic deviancy theory

labeling theory

REFERENCES

Altheide, David
    1976   Creating Reality. Beverly Hills, Cal.: Sage.

Anderson, Nels
    1923   The Hobo. Chicago: University of Chicago Press.

Becker, Howard
    1963   Outsiders. New York: The Free Press.
    1964   The Other Side. New York: The Free Press.

Bell, Daniel
    1967a   "Notes on the post-industrial society (I)." The Public Interest (Winter): 24–35.
    1967b   "Notes on the post-industrial society (II)." The Public Interest (Spring): 102–118.

Berger, Peter
    1963   Invitation to Sociology. Garden City: Doubleday.
    1971   "Sociology and freedom." The American Sociologist 6: 1–5.

Blau, Peter
    1964   Exchange and Power in Social Life. New York: John Wiley and Sons.

Buckley, Walter
    1967   Sociology and Modern Systems Theory. Englewood Cliffs, N.J.: Prentice-Hall.

Carmichael, Stokely and Charles Hamilton
    1967   Black Power. New York: Random House.

Cavan, Sherri
    1972   Hippies of the Haight. New York: Dutton.

Comte, Auguste
    1915   The Positive Philosophy. Harriet Martineau (trans. and ed.). London: George Bell and Sons.

Darwin, Charles
    1880   The Descent of Man. New York: Appleton.

Felton, Gary
    1966   "Psychosocial implications of the coffee break." Journal of Human Relations 14: 434–449.

Frazier, E. Franklin
    1957   Black Bourgeoisie. New York: The Free Press.

Fromm, Erich
    1968   The Revolution of Hope: Toward a Humanized Technology. New York: Bantam.

Fuller, Richard and Richard Myers
    1941   "The natural history of a social problem." American Sociological Review 6: 320–328.

Galbraith, John Kenneth
    1967   The New Industrial State. Boston: Houghton Mifflin.

Gittlin, Todd and Nanci Hollander
    1970   Uptown: Poor Whites in Chicago. New York: Harper and Row.

Goffman, Erving
    1963   Stigma. Englewood Cliffs, N.J.: Prentice-Hall.

Gouldner, Alvin
    1970   The Coming Crisis of Western Sociology. New York: Basic Books.

Greer, Ann and Scott Greer
    1974   Understanding Sociology. Dubuque: Wm. C. Brown.

Harrington, Michael
    1965   The Accidental Century. New York: Macmillan.

Henderson, Charles
    1909   Introduction to the Study of the Dependent, Defective, and Delinquent Classes and of Their Social Treatment. Boston: D.C. Heath.

Hoult, Thomas Ford
    1974   Sociology for a New Day. New York: Random House.

Lauer, Robert
    1973   Perspectives on Social Change. Boston: Allyn and Bacon.

Lemert, Edwin
    1967   Human Deviance, Social Problems, and Social Control. Englewood Cliffs, N.J.: Prentice-Hall.

Liebow, Elliot
    1967   Tally's Corner. Boston: Little, Brown.

Linton, Ralph
    1936   The Study of Man. New York: Appleton-Century-Crofts.

Lofland, John
    1969   Deviance and Identity. Englewood Cliffs, N.J.: Prentice-Hall.

Lynd, Robert and Helen Lynd
    1937   Middletown in Transition: A Study in Cultural Conflicts. New York: Harcourt, Brace, Jovanovich.

Merton, Robert
    1938   "Social Structure and anomie." American Sociological Review 3: 672–682.
    1964   Social Theory and Social Structure. New York: The Free Press.

Mills, C. Wright
- 1959 The Sociological Imagination. New York: Oxford University Press.
- 1967 Power, Politics and People: The Collected Essays of C. Wright Mills. Irving L. Horowitz (ed.). New York: Oxford University Press.

Moore, Wilbert
- 1963 Social Change. Englewood Cliffs, N.J.: Prentice-Hall.

Myrdal, Gunnar
- 1944 An American Dilemma. New York: Harper and Brothers.

National Commission on the Causes and Prevention of Violence
- 1969 The History of Violence in America: A Report to the National Commission on the Causes and Prevention of Violence. T. Gurr and H. Davis (eds.). New York: Bantam.

National Commission on Obscenity and Pornography
- 1970 The Report of the Commission on Obscenity and Pornography. New York: Bantam.

Ogburn, William
- 1922 Social Change. New York: Viking.

Oromaner, Mark
- 1968 "The most cited sociologists: an analysis of introductory text citations." The American Sociologist 3: 124–126.

Parsons, Talcott
- 1961 "The point of view of the author." M. Black (ed.), The Social Theories of Talcott Parsons. Englewood Cliffs, N.J.: Prentice-Hall.

Ravitz, Mel
- 1971 "The crisis in our cities: an action perspective." L. Gordon (ed.), A City in Racial Crisis. Dubuque: Wm. C. Brown.

- 1968 Report of the National Advisory Commission on Civil Disorders. New York: Bantam.

Reston, James
- 1975 "The year the richest city in the world went broke." The Arizona Republic: A7.

Rist, Ray
- 1974 Call for papers for the 1974 Annual Convention of the Pacific Sociological Association on the theme of "On Private Trouble and Public Issues" in San Jose, California March 28–30, 1974.

Roethlisberger, F. J. and W. J. Dickson
- 1946 Management and the Worker. Cambridge, Mass.: Harvard University Press.

Rubington, Earl and Martin Weinberg
- 1971 The Study of Social Problems: Five Perspectives. New York: Oxford University Press.
- 1973 The Solution of Social Problems: Five Perspectives. New York: Oxford University Press.

Schur, Edwin
- 1965 Crimes Without Victims. Englewood Cliffs, N.J.: Prentice-Hall.

Selltiz, Claire et al.
- 1959 Research Methods in Social Relations. New York: Holt, Rinehart and Winston.

Sinclair, Upton
- 1906 The Jungle. New York: Jungle Publishing Company.

Smith, Samuel
    1911   Social Pathology. New York: Macmillan.

Stocker, Terrance and Linda Deutscher, Stephen Hargrove, and Edwin Cook
    1972   "Social analysis of graffiti." Journal of American Folklore 85: 356–366.

    1968   Summary Report. Report of the National Advisory Commission on Civil Disorders. New York: A. Philip Randolph Institute.

Thomas, W. I.
    1931   "The relation of research to the social process." Essays on Research in the Social Sciences. Washington, D.C.: The Brookings Institution.

Thrasher, Frederic
    1927   The Gang. Chicago: University of Chicago Press.

Truzzi, Marcello
    1968   Sociology and Everyday Life. Englewood Cliffs, N.J.: Prentice-Hall.

Veblen, Thorstein
    1934   The Theory of the Leisure Class: An Economic Study of Institutions. New York: Modern Library.

Whyte, William
    1943   Street Corner Society. Chicago: University of Chicago Press.

Zorbaugh, Harvey
    1929   The Gold Coast and the Slum. Chicago: University of Chicago Press.

Chapter 14

FEARS FOR THE FUTURE

Run to the roundhouse, Nellie — they can't corner you there.

Fred Allen

THE BASIS OF FEARFUL PERSPECTIVES

It is easy to feel cornered by the enormous problems confronting America and the world today. The pace and extent of social change are faster and broader than ever before in human history. Urbanization continues to change our environment. New technology constantly changes our occupational structure and advances our economic interdependence with other societies. The danger of nuclear holocaust grows in a world that is tense with conflict and restrained only by tenuous international controls. The depersonalization and sometimes dehumanization of foreign enemies and of members of minorities in our own society appear to be characteristic of the time. All this and more has had the effect of inducing a widespread sense of individual and group powerlessness in solving the problems of the day. As a *Mad* magazine bumper sticker once put it: "Vote — It won't do any good — but vote!"

TEXTBOOK WARNINGS OF SOCIAL PATHOLOGY Symptomatic of a perceived system-wide illness are a number of recent sociological and other analyses of the state of the society. Some recent popular textbooks in sociology have avoided the traditional phrase social problems in their titles in an attempt to stress the foreboding social conditions we face. One of these is Bernard Rosenberg, Israel Gerver, and F. William Howton's text, *Mass Society in Crisis* (1971). In this book, the authors take

440 SOCIAL CHANGE AND THE FUTURE

a

b

c

FEARS FOR THE FUTURE 441

Nationally traumatic events in the sixties and seventies. SOURCE: (a) Bob Adelman/Magnum; (b) Charles Harbutt/Magnum; (c) Charles Gatewood/Stock Boston; (d) Roger Malloch/Magnum; (e) Charles Gatewood; (f) Wide World Photos.

rather a social pathological view of modern society. They hold that our problems are so pressing that they consider not just American society but civilization to be *in extremis* (vii). At such a time, the authors feel, "he who remains in his accustomed groove could indeed find that it will be his grave" (vii).

Another such text, by Jerome Skolnick and Elliott Currie, concurs with this view but goes a bit further. Their *Crisis in American Institutions* (1973) sees a fundamental breakdown in the ability of American institutions to meet the growing challenge. Religion is unable to mitigate the problems of most people living in cities. Educational institutions at all levels, from elementary schools to colleges, fail to socialize millions of young people into adult roles. The complex American economy is increasingly vulnerable to shifting technological innovations and the need to rely on sources of raw materials from overseas.

THE DECLINE OF THE FAMILY Well, there is always the institution of the family to stabilize people's lives as they face system-wide problems. Or is there? Although not all scholars agree that the family is unstable, many fear for its future.[1] The raw census data tell us that out of every four marriages, one ends in divorce, and John Cuber and Peggy Haroff (1965) and Mirra Komarovsky's (1964) research findings suggest that, for different social class levels, a third or more of the marriages that survive are unhappy. So much is expected of the relatively isolated modern nuclear family that one analyst believes we are nearing the death of the family (Cooper, 1970).

---

[1] Because the focus of this chapter is on facts and beliefs that encourage fear of the future, the more optimistic views of the family, such as those of Margaret Mead, Alvin Toffler, and others, are not included here but are taken up in Chapter 15 on hopes for the future.

Instability in the family is evident in the high rates of divorce and marital unhappiness and is clearly related to instability in larger institutions, as noted by Rosenberg, Skolnick, and others. Perhaps we have come to what Peter Schrag called the end of the American future (1973). In the past, the collective American vision, the American dream, was optimistic about the future. The basic characteristic of this vision was the sense of possibilities (Schrag, 1973: 14). A series of nationally traumatic events in the 1960s and 1970s shook the confidence of many Americans in their society's future. The political assassinations of the Kennedys and Martin Luther King, Jr., the racial rioting in dozens of major cities, the recession following the Arab oil boycott, the Watergate scandals, and the military defeat in Vietnam all gave rise to a crisis of confidence in the ability to answer challenges effectively. These traumas accentuated the tendency toward **disorganization** and **anomie** too evident in much of society for the comfort of most Americans.

THE COMTEAN TECHNIQUE OF NARRATIVE ANALYSIS The sociological approach is to examine these pessimistic developments and attitudes quantitatively. What are the statistical trends for the population as a whole and for selected subgroups in terms of unemployment, levels of educational achievement, crime rates, and new building for cities and suburbs? These and other quantified data are useful analytical tools; we have drawn upon them earlier in this text. At this point, however, it may be more useful to shift to a narrative discussion, the simple telling of the story, to analyze a number of fearful prospects for the American future.

The narrative approach in sociology is an old Comtean technique that has had a recent rebirth. It lends itself well to an interdisciplinary approach that draws on other fields of analysis such as history, literature, and philosophy. In exploring our fears for the future of American society, we must keep in mind that there are as many, and more, hopeful signs for the future, and we shall examine many of them in Chapter 15.

THE SOCIOLOGY OF THE ABSURD

Given the many crises of modern society and the questionable ability of our institutions to meet them, it is not surprising that there should have developed in the 1960s and 1970s a sociology of the absurd. When Stanford Lyman and Marvin Scott (1970) adapted the term *absurd* to characterize an emerging influential sociological perspective, they were borrowing from the modern theater a term to describe two fundamental points about the nature of society. One is that the world is essentially without meaning (1970: 1); the other is that we strive for meaning through continual conflict. As Lyman and Scott put it, "By beginning with the assumption that social life is one of conflict, it follows that every social situation is problematic for those involved" (1970: 6).

The troubles of recent decades have greatly strengthened the feeling that all of social life, from interpersonal relations to broad clashes between classes, races, and states, is characterized by conflict. As Alvin Gouldner observes in *The Coming Crisis of Western Sociology* (1971: vii):

Social theorists work within a crumbling social matrix.... It is no exaggeration to say that ... the old order has the picks of a hundred rebellions thrust into its hide.

Gouldner goes on to note that it is not only the unsuccessful aspects of social life that this new perspective finds meaningless. A hard look at the incompetence and lack of ethics in the highest ranks of business and government also suggests a meaningless success (407). In this context, Gouldner and others correctly note that many of the radical antiestablishment movements of the 1960s and early 1970s were led by young people from the successful upper-middle class. Feeling that one's accomplishments are hollow, and being unable to find guidelines for more positive orientation, can lead to a sense of alienation not merely from others, but from oneself as well. Such feelings can lead to further estrangement from others or from oneself to a point of extreme despair.

INNER-DIRECTED STABILITY AND OTHER-DIRECTED ALIENATION This alienating sense of lost purpose has been analyzed as a consequence of changes in the American character. Years ago, David Reisman (1953) noted that, for most of American history, the social conditions of small-town life, individually owned businesses, and relatively self-supporting small farms nurtured the development of *inner-directed** people. Such people set their goals according to their own beliefs and interacted with others on the basis of their own values and desires. By contrast, in the twentieth century, Americans have moved into impersonal cities where they have become part of, in Reisman's phrase, the lonely crowd. Thus, the American character has shifted from being inner-directed to being *other-directed**. As Reisman puts it (23):

...the society... develops in its typical members a social character whose conformity is insured by their tendency to be sensitized to the expectations and preferences of others. These I shall term *other directed* people and the society in which they live one dependent on other-direction.

It is Reisman's argument that the other-directed type is particularly evident in the upper-middle class in our larger metropolitan areas (34–35). These are the people who have made it socially and economically. It is their life style to which most people presumably aspire.

THE OTHER-DIRECTED ORGANIZATION MAN William H. Whyte (1951 and 1956) further analyzes the pervasiveness of other-directedness. A successful business executive with *Fortune* magazine, Whyte casts a critical eye on the meaning of success in modern America. For the upper-middle-class managerial elite who work in large business or government bureaucracies and who live in comfortable suburban neighborhoods with wife and children, there is a real question of just how satisfying this kind of success is. Whyte, speaking as an insider, is dubious about it all. He refers to Reisman's other-directed upper-middle-class suburbanite as the organization man (1956). Since the underlying causes of other-directedness are in the nature of mass urban society, Whyte's concept also applies today to women, racial minorities, and young people as they successfully move into the system.

The other-directedness of the successful organization man is evident. In business, symbols that others recognize of *status** and prestige often become crucial in communicating just how successful one is, not only in keeping up with but in getting ahead of the Joneses. Whyte describes how far the office status game can go at all levels of the organization (1951, pp. 80–81).

... the American office is a veritable temple of status. Though they may seem almost imperceptible, the symbols are manifested everywhere. Some have a useful purpose — the memo pad "From the desk of . . ."; the routing slip (should the names on the memorandum be listed by seniority, or alphabetically?); who sits with whom in the company dining room. Others are rooted in propriety: who can call whom by nicknames; at what level people may smoke. To what grade of washroom is one entitled? Is the office carpeted or does he rate only linoleum? Some are rooted in functions only marginal: the facsimile signature stamp, for example — evidence that a man's importance is such that he must write to a great number of people, even if he doesn't use the facsimile signature in doing it. All these are favorite topics of office humor, of course, but as this fact itself is witness, the symbols *communicate*. . . . Ordinarily there is one department that is considered more aristocratic than the others. It doesn't often get as pronounced as it did at a chemical firm some years back — all employees were required to tip their hats to the chemists of the company — but with few exceptions even those in the lowest level of such departments feel superior to their counterparts elsewhere, no matter how identical their work. In the same fashion, secretaries derive . . . [prestige] from the position of their superiors, and many are the chronic if muted squabbles as to just who has the more important boss.

It is not in the symbols of status nor in codes or allegiances . . . that the trouble lies. It is in overlooking the tremendous effect they have on communication (of one's status). And while it may be a case, as the semanticists like to argue, of confusing the symbol with the reality, the distress it causes is nonetheless real. . . . Recently, for example, a large Midwestern corporation almost lost one of its most valuable V.P.'s. In a shift of offices, inadvertently he was given a metal desk instead of the mahogany variety common to his bracket. Why? He pondered and fretted, and began reading hurts, omens, and hidden meanings in every casual conversation. Eventually the matter came out in the open, for the V.P. could go on no longer; he was on the brink of a complete nervous breakdown. Silly? Ask the man who's had one.

The other-directed, status-oriented organization man Whyte describes illustrates two basic points: first, life in such a setting is arguably meaningless, with striving after internal office status taking precedence over what the organization was set up to accomplish; second, such meaning there is exists in spite of continual conflict to maintain or improve one's status. In the office setting Whyte describes, this striving for status is as true of secretaries as of their bosses. As Thorstein Veblen (1934: viz. 1899) observed early in the century, it may be as true out of the office as in the office.

Can a people becoming more and more other-directed effectively solve the many objective problems they face? Some perceptive literature raises grave doubts about their chances.

THE LITERATURE OF DESPAIR

At the 1972 annual meeting of the American Sociological Association, Robert Leighninger presented a paper entitled "Scott Fitzgerald's Theory of Anomia." He illustrated that, as Lewis Coser (1963) observed, it is possible to practice sociology through literature and, indeed, through all art forms. Modern abstract painting may appear chaotic to the uninitiated, but in a century in which there have been two world wars and a worldwide depression, as well as the potential for nuclear holocaust, such art reflects a large part of social reality. Similarly, modern music and its dancing styles, from jazz and the Charleston of the 1920s to more recent rock and roll music and dancing, serves as an index to prevailing values and attitudes. Such expression can be characterized as uninhibited and undirected — a reflection of many of the social changes that were occurring at the same time.

Leighninger's choice suggests that, of all artistic forms of expression, literature is most suitable to sociological analysis. Although it may be that in the future, as Marshall McLuhan argues (1964), the printed word will become obsolete and new forms of consciousness and communication will prevail, it is still true that literature communicates. Explicit verbal expression of ideas and feelings communicates more clearly to most people than the less explicit language of music, painting, and other forms of art. As Judith Merrill puts it, science fiction and other speculative fiction (1971: 60):

makes use of the traditional "scientific method" . . . [by] examin[ing] some . . . approximation of reality, by introducing a given set of changes — imaginary or inventive — into the common background of "known facts" creating an environment in which the responses and perceptions will reveal something about the inventions, the characters, or both.

UNCERTAINTY AND ALIENATION What a good deal of modern literature tells us about contemporary life is that it is strongly tinged with pessimism and despair. Traditional ways have been uprooted, often with considerable violence. Scott Fitzgerald, in *The Great Gatsby* (1925) and other works, became a spokesman for the rootless generation of the 1920s. The book brings a set of spoiled and dissatisfied young aristocrats who have little sense of purpose in life together with a pathetically comic *nouveau-riche* bootlegger who acquires the outward trappings of wealth and luxury without knowing how to use them. These two extremes are seen by a middle-class narrator who understands something of both but who also reflects the growing loss of purpose, the anomie, of his society. Other writers tell us that we are going from rootlessness to a new set of rules that will make the time of the other-directed organization man look like a golden age. Reflecting this view, the British author Aldous Huxley wrote after a trip to America, Europe, and around the world in the mid 1920s:

To travel is to discover that everybody is wrong. The philosophies, the civilizations . . . all prove on a close inspection to be in their way just as hopelessly imperfect.

This is a much more pessimistic view of society than Peter Berger's cosmopolitan motif noted in Chapter 13.

In *Brave New World*, one of the most powerful fictional social criticisms of the 1930s, Huxley drew a chilling picture of what the future might be like in a society in which government and all other social institutions are totally dominated by scientists. Huxley's world is one in which genetic manipulation and postnatal conditioning are used by the world controllers to develop a ruthlessly functional society in which all individuality is crushed. The functional needs and stability of the society are predetermined in this process of eugenic control. Stratification is fixed for the benefit of the elite. As Huxley describes it:

SOURCE: *Audubon,* September 1976, p. 102.

In one set of bottles biologically superior ova, fertilized by biologically superior sperm, were given the best possible pre-natal treatment and were finally decanted as Betas, Alphas and even Alpha Pluses. In another, much more numerous set of bottles, biologically inferior ova, fertilized by biologically inferior sperm, were subjected to the Bokanovsky Process (ninety-six identical twins out of a single egg) and treated pre-natally with alcohol and other protein poisons. The creatures finally decanted were almost sub-human; but they were capable of performing unskilled work. . . .

The cartoon on this page shows another instance of manifest aims leading to latent consequences. Hormonal biological research laboratories have been set up to develop new techniques to improve healthy biological reproduction. Yet, these same labs may generate air pollution which inflicts biological injury.

That the real consequences of scientific ability to produce multiple people with relative ease are nearly upon us is seen in the selection, Cloning: A Generation Made to Order, in which the author speculates on the social consequences of made-to-order people.

CLONING: A GENERATION MADE TO ORDER

From: Caryl Rivers, "Cloning: A Generation Made to Order." *Ms.* (June 1976), p. 51. Copyright Ms. Magazine Corp. 1976. Reprinted with permission.

Human reproduction begins with the merger of the sex cells, sperm and egg. Since each contains only half a set of chromosomes, the joining of sperm with the egg is the first step in the creation of a new and unique individual, with traits inherited from both parents. But this is not the only possible way for life to begin.

The other type of cells in the human body already has a full set of chromosomes. All the genetic information necessary for an organism to reproduce itself is contained in the nucleus of every cell in that organism. If body cells could be made to divide, the result would be asexual reproduction — the production of offspring with only one parent. Such a process is already being used with other species — it is called cloning. It has been tried successfully with plants, fruit flies — and more significantly, with frogs.

In 1968, J. B. Gurdon at Oxford University produced a clonal frog. He took an unfertilized egg cell from an African clawed frog and destroyed its nucleus by ultraviolet radiation. He replaced it with the nucleus of an intestinal cell of another frog of the same species. The egg, suddenly finding itself with a full set of chromosomes, began to reproduce. It was "tricked" into starting the reproductive process. The result was a tadpole that was a genetic twin of the frog that donated the cell. The "mother" frog contributed nothing to the genetic identity of the tadpole, since her potential to pass on her traits was destroyed when the nucleus of her egg was obliterated.

How would it work with human beings? Roughly the same way. A healthy egg could be removed from a woman's body.... But instead of fertilizing the egg with sperm, scientists could destroy the nucleus of the human egg and replace it with a cell taken from the arm or anywhere of a donor we'll call John X. The egg would be reimplanted in the uterus of a woman. Although its identity would be wiped out with the destruction of its nucleus, it could nonetheless start to divide, because it had received the proper signal — the presence of a full set of chromosomes. The baby that would be the result of that process would have only one parent — John X. It would, in fact, be a carbon copy of John X — his twin, a generation removed. (Or her twin, if the cell donor were female.)

In March of this year scientists announced major progress on the hunt for the substance that "switches on" the reproductive mechanisms of the cell. Gurdon's first experiments with the frog proved that such a mechanism exists and that all cells — not just sex cells — could be made to reproduce. Now, work done by Gurdon at Cambridge and by Ann Janice Brothers at the University of Indiana is moving science closer to discovering the identity of the "master switch."

Gurdon inserted the nuclei of human cancer cells into immature frogs eggs, and the human cell nuclei responded in dramatic fashion, swelling in size to as much as a hundredfold.

Brothers, working with amphibians, axolotls, has observed that a molecule identified as the 0+ factor appears to be the substance that signals the reproductive process to carry on. Eggs produced by axolotls that did not contain the 0+ factor did not develop past very rudimentary stages until they were injected with 0+ substance. Brothers and her colleagues at Indiana report that 0+ appears to be a large protein molecule that is somewhat acidic. The scientists are working to isolate and define that molecule. The identification of the "master switch" would be a giant step toward understanding cancer and would bring the day of human cloning closer.

The consequences of human cloning are almost impossible to imagine. Widespread human cloning would alter human society beyond recognition. The family would no longer exist, sexuality would have no connection with reproduction. The idea of parenthood would be completely changed. The diversity of human beings provided by sexual reproduction would vanish. One could imagine entire communities of people who looked exactly the same, whose range of potential was identical. Some scientists have suggested that "clones and clonishness" could replace our present patterns of nation and race.

The misuses of cloning are not hard to predict. Would an aging dictator try to insure the continuance of his regime by an heir apparent who was his genetic double? Would women and men project their egos into the future by producing their own "carbon copies"? Would society choose to clone our most valued citizens? Artists? Generals? Members of elite groups? The capacity of our species to change and adapt may be rooted in the diversity of the gene pool. By tampering with that process we could be limiting our own ability to survive.

There are some who believe that current work in test-tube fertilization to extract eggs is a first step in the direction of cloning. There have been some estimates that human cloning will be a reality within the decade. Who will say where we draw the line?

IT CAN'T HAPPEN HERE   At about the same time Huxley was writing, American novelist Sinclair Lewis produced *It Can't Happen Here*, which sounded the alarm to the dangers of dictatorships such as those of Hitler, Mussolini, and Stalin, and warned that unless we as a nation exercised great care, the same fate could befall us. Lewis's book appeared at a time when President Franklin D. Roosevelt was admonishing Americans, as they faced economic depression, that they had nothing to fear but fear itself. Lewis showed how mass fears could turn the American people toward a dictatorial demagogue who promised salvation even as he was securing all the power for himself. Given the efficiency of modern bureaucratic organization, the technology for surveillance and destruction, said Lewis, a dictatorship would be extremely difficult to challenge once it was established.

Some of the great power of the fascist dictatorships to which Lewis responded came from their use of business and industry; there was relatively less concern with dictatorships of a communist nature. Communist Russia was not yet as powerful or as expansionist as Germany, Italy, and Japan, and China had not yet become a communist state. Further, communist nations espoused Karl Marx's doctrine that industrialized workers should share more fully in the fruits of their labor. This had a humanistic ring to it that appealed to many in the United States and other western democracies.

In the late 1960s, some Americans, including many in the hippie movement, expressed their mistrust and dislike of the Nixon–Agnew administration and indicated their concern with what they saw as a movement toward absolute power. Rumors circulated concerning the suspension of elections by Nixon and Agnew and the ascent to the presidency by Agnew in the symbolic year 1984. While these fears were alleviated by the exposure of payoffs to Agnew and his subsequent resignation, the use of surveillance discovered in the later Watergate scandal bore out the fear of violation of civil liberties.

VISIONS OF DICTATORIAL CONTROLS   Perhaps the most influential literary analysis of the communist system was George Orwell's *1984*, which appeared shortly after World War II. Orwell sketched a dictatorial society in which individual citizens either conformed totally to the dictates of Big Brother or else they were ruthlessly destroyed. The book details the methods by which dictatorial control stamps out human thought and individuality. Winston Smith, the protagonist in *1984*, lives in a world in which those who govern purposely reverse the meaning of the human reality he sees and senses for himself. The rulers use doublethink, a language that changes the meanings of words. On the building of the Ministry of Truth are engraved the slogans:

War Is Peace
Freedom Is Slavery
Ignorance Is Strength

By substituting falsehood for truth, the system first confuses the individual, then breaks his will, and finally makes him eager to accept the dictates of the rulers. The techniques of enforcement include government television and listening devices which monitor individuals everywhere, even in their most private lives. This vision of Orwell's cannot be lightly dismissed, particularly in light of recent revelations of government bugging of private homes.

Arthur Koestler's *Darkness at Noon* (1941) was another powerful fictionalized account of how dictatorship controlled the individual. Koestler's book was based on well documented cases during the Moscow show trials of the late 1930s, in which political dissidents were forced to confess publicly their crimes against the state before being executed. The protagonist resembles Orwell's Winston Smith but represents a synthesis of a number of innocent victims of these trials. More recently, Alexander Solzhenitsyn's factual *The Gulag Archipelago* (1973), banned in the Soviet Union, exhaustively describes how millions faced similar coercion by the state in the form of imprisonment and torture.

TECHNIQUES OF CONTROL   The British novelist Anthony Burgess in *A Clockwork Orange* (1963) describes the Ludovico Technique for conditioning human behavior, a device somewhat reminiscent of Aldous Huxley's Bokanovsky Process in *Brave New World*. In Burgess's novel, deviants are reconditioned into model citizens — actually mindless pawns whose behavior is controlled by the authorities. Like Huxley's, Burgess's society of the future is an impersonal superstate in which uninhibited sensual gratification is considered harmless. When the destructive teenage hero of the book is finally reconditioned, the reader wonders whether he was a greater horror before or after.

How does such a system maintain itself? Huxley in *Brave New World Revisited* (1958) explains that "most men and women will grow to love their servitude and never dream of revolution." They will do so because the rulers will employ the well-established psychological principle of stimulus-response conditioning (as in Skinner's *Beyond Freedom*, 1971), in which all material and sensual pleasures are satisfied so long as a person is obedient to the system. In this view, if material poverty and Victorian moral rigidity led to widespread rejection of the social system in the past, just the opposite would hold people to even a totalitarian system. Floor-to-ceiling color television would be standard in all homes. Full and healthful nourishment would be given to all, and absolute sexual license would be the norm. Given these methods, Huxley concludes "there seems to be no reason why a thoroughly scientific dictatorship should ever be overthrown."

As in Ray Bradbury's *Fahrenheit 491* (1967), totalitarian rulers can destroy all books and records and invent a past that idealizes Big Brother, Little Sister, Big Mama, or whoever they choose in order to control the present and the future. In Huxley's vision of the future, the slow and painful evolution of individuality and personal autonomy in society is likely to be stamped out. Huxley's *Brave New World*, like Burgess's *A Clockwork Orange* and Bradbury's *Fahrenheit 491*, is one in which a scientific dictatorship is as ruthless as the most corrupt theological medieval societies but is much more efficient at maintaining its power. Huxley, in *Brave New World Revisited*, cites the testimony of Albert Speer, a high-ranking officer in Hitler's Nazi government, after World War II (47):

Hitler's dictatorship differed in one fundamental point from all its predecessors in history. It was the first dictatorship in the present period of modern technical development, a dictatorship which made complete use of all technical means for the domination of its own country. Through technical devices like the radio and the loudspeaker, eighty million people were deprived of independent thought. It was thereby possible to subject them to the will of one man.... Earlier dictators needed highly qualified assistants even at the

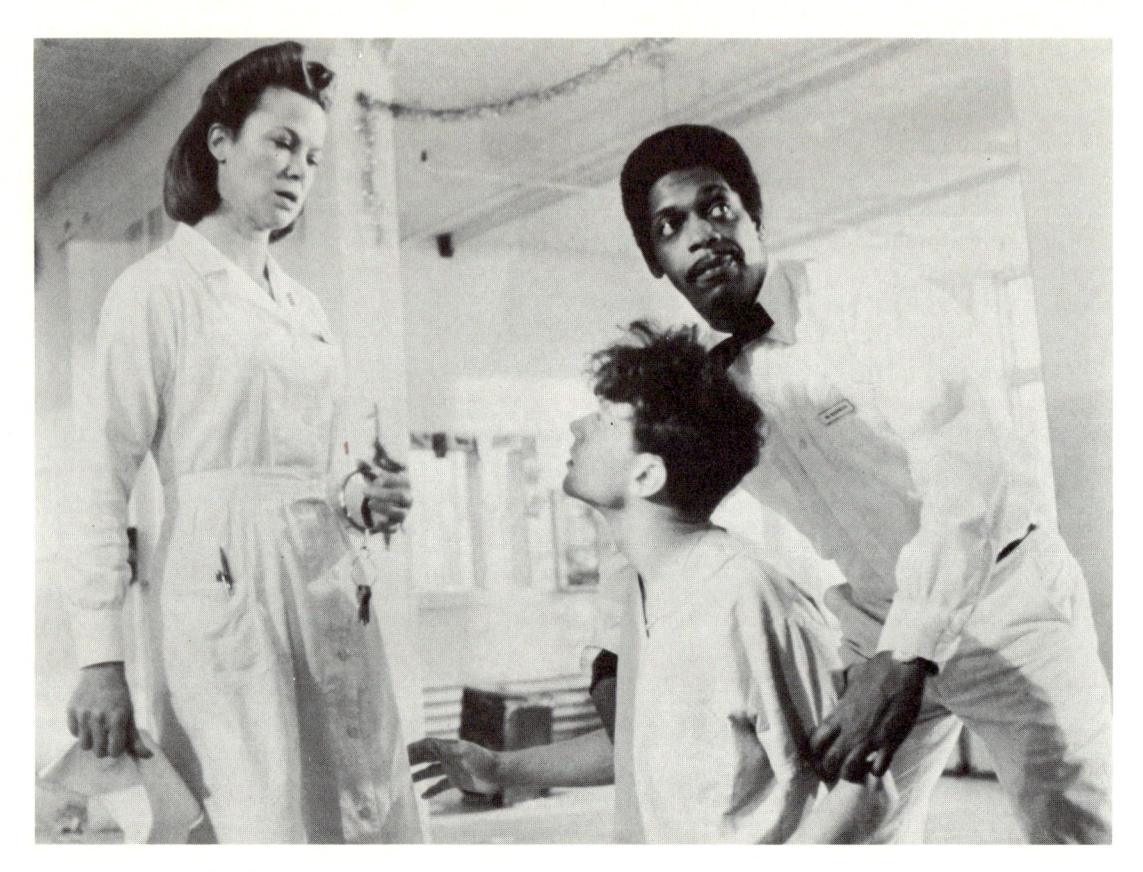

In the novel and film "One Flew Over the Cuckoo's Nest" mental patients were expected to "adjust" — or else. SOURCE: Copyright © 1975, Fantasy Films and United Artists Corporation, all rights reserved. Printed in U.S.A.

lowest level — men who could think and act independently. The totalitarian system in the period of modern technical development can dispense with such men; thanks to modern methods of communication, it is possible to mechanize the lower leadership. As a result of this there has arisen the new type of the uncritical recipient of orders.

Another extension of the theme of people's being controlled rather than allowed to proceed with autonomy is found in *One Flew Over the Cuckoo's Nest,* Ken Kesey's novel of life in a mental institution where control rather than genuine rehabilitation is paramount.

Kesey taps the problem of displaced goals — the goal of control outranks any other for the powerful Big Nurse in charge. In doing so, he dramatizes what Erving Goffman documented in his nonfiction analysis of *Asylums* (1961). Kesey describes the manipulation and demoralizing system of control found in some of our institutions (© 1962 by Ken Kesey. Reprinted by permission of The Viking Press.)

The Big Nurse tends to get real put out if something keeps her outfit from running like a smooth, accurate, precision-made machine. The slightest thing messy or out of kilter or in the way ties her into a little white knot of tight-smiled fury. She walks around with that same doll smile crimped between her chin and her nose and that same calm whir coming from her eyes, but down inside of her she's tense as steel. I know, I can feel it. And she don't relax a hair till she gets the nuisance attended to — what she calls "adjusted to surroundings."

Under her rule the ward Inside is almost completely adjusted to surroundings. But the thing is she can't be on the ward all the time. She's got to spend some time Outside. So she works with an eye to adjusting the Outside world too. Working alongside others like her who I call the "Combine," which is a huge organization that aims to adjust the Outside as well as she has the Inside, has made her a real veteran at adjusting things. She was already the Big Nurse in the old place when I came in from the Outside so long back, and she'd been dedicating herself to adjustment for God knows how long.

. . . Year by year she accumulates her ideal staff: doctors, all ages and types, come and rise up in front of her with ideas of their own about the way a ward should be run, some with backbone enough to stand behind their ideas, and she fixes these doctors with dry-ice eyes day in, day out, until they retreat with unnatural chills. "I tell you I don't know *what* it is," they tell the guy in charge of personnel. "Since I started on that ward with that woman I feel like my veins are running ammonia. I shiver all the time, my kids won't sit in my lap, my wife won't sleep with me. I *insist* on a transfer — neurology bin, the alky tank, pediatrics, I just don't *care!"*

Seven-thirty back to the day room. The Big Nurse looks out through her special glass, always polished till you can't tell it's there, and nods at what she sees, reaches up and tears a sheet off her calendar one day closer to the goal. She pushes a button for things to start. I hear the wharrup of a big sheet of tin being shook someplace. Everybody come to order. Acutes: sit on your side of the day room and wait for cards and Monopoly games to be brought out. Chronics: sit on your side and wait for puzzles from the Red Cross box. Ellis: go to your place at the wall, hands up to receive the nails and pee running down your leg. Pete: wag your head like a puppet. Scanlon: work your knobby hands on the table in front of you, constructing a make-believe bomb to blow up a make-believe world. Harding: begin talking, waving your dove hands in the air, then trap them under your armpits because grown men aren't supposed to wave their pretty hands that way. Sefelt: begin moaning about your teeth hurting and your hair falling out. Everybody: breathe in . . . and out . . . in perfect order: hearts all beating at the rate the OD cards have ordered. Sound of matched cylinders.

FROM HUMAN EXPLOITATION TO HUMAN OBSOLESCENCE The literary visions of Huxley and others have one thing in common with Speer's testimony. It is that modern society is rapidly making obsolete many of the roles people have filled in the past. This is quite clear in respect to minority groups — blacks, Spanish–Americans, women, and others — who have long been exploited as cheap unskilled labor, filling the needs of society just as effectively as if they had been through Huxley's

SOURCE: © 1968 by Boris Drucker.

"'Well, if you don't know who I am, I'll tell you who I am,' I said to him."

Bokanovsky Process or Burgess's Ludovico Technique. Now that the *cybernetic revolution** and other modern developments require less unskilled labor, minority group members have gone from being exploited to being obsolete. The wide sales of black novelist James Baldwin's books — *Another Country* (1959), *Nobody Knows My Name* (1960), and *The Fire Next Time* (1962) — made it evident that there was extensive recognition of the problems of racial minorities in finding a place for themselves in American society.

The literary works cited in this chapter suggest that modern society has made everybody — not just out-group members — obsolete and alienated, with the possible exception of a few power brokers in key government and economic positions.

The extreme to which other-direction can lead is made explicit by Charles Beaumont in his essay "The Vanishing American" (1975). The protagonist in Beaumont's tale is like *le businessman* in Saint-Exupéry's fable. He is caught up in numbers and in making sure that all is accurate on the adding machines and computers that help to run modern businesses. Indeed, the numbers and the efficiency of the system are such that this businessman comes to believe that he is totally unimportant in the social scheme. This leads to the hallucination that he cannot be seen, that he has in effect vanished. The man desperately attempts to regain human recognition and response by climbing onto a statue of a lion in a city park. The mocking attention he gets clears up his hallucination about vanishing, but not much else.

The business as usual approach to life is deeply ingrained in people, and we can understand what Walt Kelley's Pogo meant when he said, "We have met the enemy and he is us." Professor Stanley Milgram of Yale University conducted an experiment illustrating this problem and reported it in his book *Obedience to Authority* (1973). Professor Milgram requested a random sample of students to administer electric shocks to respondents when they failed to memorize nonsense syllables cor-

Conformity in a land that lauds the value of individuality. SOURCE: Charles Gatewood.

rectly. Even when the shocks were labeled dangerously severe (which they were not, though the students did not know that), most students administered the shocks anyway. This experiment gives some idea of what Huxley was getting at when he cited Albert Speer on how the Nazi system worked.

All these literary analyses create fearful visions of the future, and they are very much extensions of the kind of society we have been creating. The stories may be fantasies, but their implications are quite real. Much human interaction in modern society is impersonal and secondary. The traditional source of primary contacts, the family, shows signs of serious instability. Our great economic and government bureaucracies give people a sense of powerlessness in the face of organizations that dominate their work and leisure time. Our society is faced with the challenge of controlling and changing the conditions of life in order to allow for more individual autonomy lest these literary fantasies of an alienated and manipulated future become reality.

THE PROSPECT OF CHANGING OR PERISHING

... I had no intention of shooting the elephant — I had merely sent for the rifle to defend myself if necessary — and it is always unnerving to have a crowd following you....

But at that moment I glanced around at the crowd that had followed me. It was an immense crowd, two thousand at least and growing every minute. I looked at the sea of yellow faces.... They were watching me as they would watch a conjurer about to perform a trick.... And suddenly I realized that I would have to shoot the elephant after all. The people expected it of me and I had got to do it; I could feel their two thousand wills pressing me forward irresistibly.... Afterwards ... I often wondered whether any of the others grasped that I had done it solely to avoid looking a fool.

This passage from George Orwell's story–essay, "Shooting an Elephant" (1950), exemplifies the other-directed character of modern mass society that appeals so strongly to David Reisman in *The Lonely Crowd* and to William Whyte in *The Organization Man*. Whyte (1956) in particular notes that a new social ethic is replacing our traditional ethical system in which the individual is considered primary. In the emerging social ethic, key terms are often linked with the term *group*, as in such phrases as *group loyalty, group dynamics, group creativity,* and *group thinking.*

Social scientists have long been concerned with the impact of group pressures upon individual attitudes and behavior. George Homans (1950) summarized much early research on the tendency of most people in small groups to acquiesce to an authority figure or figures. This can be seen in the processes by which trial juries generally develop total consensus (Eakin, 1975). On a larger collective basis, leadership in mass society — whether by people in key economic or government positions or by new *charismatic** leaders — may establish what Ralph Turner and Lewis Killian call a *circular reaction** (1957: 112), involving the stimulation of unified group or crowd behavior, as often occurs in the commercial advertising of products or even candidates for office, and in other areas where group pressure operates. In circular reaction, one individual stimulates another, who, in addition to stimulating others with his response, further stimulates the first individual.

VICTIMS OF GROUPTHINK   One may ask what all this evidence of group action has to do with projections of a gloomy future. The answer lies in the domestic and international conflicts and rapid changes occurring around us. Accepting on faith what leaders or general public opinion hold to be true and sensible may lead to the most destructive consequences. Thus, in 1939, the slogan "fifty million Frenchmen can't be wrong" reflected the widespread belief that France's Maginot Line was an impregnable defense of France. Yet, the Nazi military *Blitzkrieg* broke through that line easily and defeated France in a matter of months. In 1959, Clark Kerr, chancellor of the University of California at Berkeley, said at commencement ceremonies that this generation of young people were quietly adaptable. He reported that "they are going to be easy to handle," and "there aren't going to be any riots." Kerr was unwilling or unable to see the conditions that would lead young people to become involved in the civil rights and antiwar movements — and rioting — over the next decade.

What appears to be happening is that people are engaging in what social psychologist Irving Janis of Yale University calls *groupthink* (1973), the kind of thinking people do when they are dominated by pressures to agree. Janis examines a number of historical fiascos and identifies eight symptoms of groupthink (*Punch* Sunday section, January 17, 1973):

1. an illusion of invulnerability, shared by most or all the members of the group, which creates excessive optimism and encourages taking extreme risks

2. collective efforts to rationalize in order to discount warnings that might lead the members to reconsider their assumptions before they recommit themselves to their past policy decisions

3. an unquestioned belief in the group's inherent morality, inclining the members to ignore the ethical or moral consequences of their decisions

4. stereotyped views of rivals and enemies as too evil to warrant genuine attempts to negotiate, or as too weak and stupid to counter whatever risky attempts are made to defeat their purposes

5. direct pressure on any member who expresses strong arguments against any of the group's stereotypes, illusions, or commitment, making clear that this type of dissent is contrary to what is expected of all members

6. self-censorship of deviations from the apparent group consensus, reflecting each member's inclination to minimize to himself the importance of his doubts and counterarguments

7. a shared illusion of unanimity concerning judgments conforming to the majority view (partly resulting from self-censorship of deviations, augmented by false assumption that silence means consent)

8. the emergence of self-appointed mindguards — members who protect the group from information that might shatter their shared complacency about the effectiveness and morality of their decisions

Such thinking can infect groups of the highest status and greatest influence in our society. Edward Weisband and Thomas Franck, in *Resignation in Protest* (1975), found that, of 389 people who resigned in protest from positions ranking from assistant secretary to Cabinet officer between 1900 and 1970, only thirty-four explained publicly why they resigned. Overwhelmingly, those who resigned maintained loyalty to the team. (See the selection drawing on a verse of Emily Dickinson's about dissent.)

EMILY DICKINSON ON THE SANITY OF DISSENT

From: *The Poems of Emily Dickinson.* Cambridge, Mass.: The Belknap Press of Harvard University Press, 1955. Copyright © 1955 by The President and Fellows of Harvard College. Reprinted by the permission of the President and Fellows of Harvard College.

Opposite ends of the political spectrum: members of the John Birch Society and a group from Students for a Democratic Society. SOURCE: (a) Bill Freedman/Magnum; (b) Charles Gatewood/Magnum.

In reading this verse keep in mind the processes of groupthink.

**Much Madness is divinest Sense —
To a discerning Eye —
Much Sense — the starkest Madness —
'Tis the Majority
In this, as All, prevail —
Assent — and you are sane —
Demur — you're straightway dangerous —
And handled with a Chain —**

c. 1862 (1890) no. 435, *Complete Poems*, 1960

In essence, groupthink is a process in which people put on collective blinders in order to achieve agreement even at the expense of ignoring social reality. If American society were experiencing slow social change and few conflicts or objective dangers, groupthink would not necessarily have serious consequences; but our society is facing changes and conflicts that greatly affect the realities of social life. Intergroup conflicts, rapid population growth, economic vulnerability to international cartels, environmental decay, and other problems affect us whether we ignore them or not.

HOSTILE CHALLENGES TO THE SYSTEM   The fact that American society is facing so many problems creates, on the one hand, the search for conformity and concurrence described by Irving Janis and on the other, it gives rise to groups that are willing to face conflict but do so by group activity based on emotions and directed against people in positions of authority. For example, members of the John Birch Society decry a whole range of social changes from racial integration to the acceptance and legal protection of pornography (Broyles, 1968). The Birch society's leader, Robert Welch, takes aim at all presidents since Franklin Roosevelt, calling them traitors and subversives. He described President Eisenhower as "a dedicated, conscious agent of the Communist conspiracy" (Epstein and Forster, 1967: 187). As with the John Birch Society, the reemergence of the Ku Klux Klan was based on public opposition to social change but focused mainly on changing race relations (Vander Zanden, 1960).

Other groups exhibiting a similar highly emotional and embittered view of social change hold that American society is not changing rapidly enough. Such youth organizations of the 1960s as the Students for a Democratic Society (SDS) and the Student Non-Violent Coordinating Committee (SNCC) pressed for rapid changes in the directions they desired. Some of their leaders, for example, Mark Rudd of the SDS and Rap Brown of SNCC, advocated violent confrontation with authorities to force conflict and change (Keniston, 1968). It is ironic that such organizations, which have attempted to break out of society-wide groupthink, have themselves been characterized by groupthink processes of a different sort. These groups have faced real issues but with an unquestioning belief in their own inherent morality and a negative stereotype of the opposition. Given these approaches on the one hand and, on the other, a generally uncritical acceptance of the status quo, one might wonder if there is any mechanism for challenging groupthink. It is not true that the groupthink process is inherent in every organization or among all individuals. A number of political, civil rights, civil liberties, religious, and other organizations have traditional formal and informal mechanisms, ranging from Roberts' Rules of Order to a general consensus on values, that protect individual thinking and expression of majority and minority views; but such organizations are often composed of the very cross section of the society that social critics hold are most susceptible to groupthink.

GLOOMY PROJECTIONS ABOUT RIGHTS AND RESOURCES   It is not surprising that many social analysts are pessimistic about the human capacity to adjust to the challenges now facing society. On the one hand is the general tendency to seek mass concurrence, to go along with others without taking a hard look at social reality. On the other are those fringe organizations and leaders who take a hard look at social reality and either rigidly oppose it or try to create their own *utopia**, their own ideal society.

The titles of many books reflect a deep concern with the capacity of Americans and others to become rationally flexible in adjusting institutions and individual behavior to meet the many challenges of the future. In his last book, Martin Luther King, Jr., raised a fundamental question: *Where Do We Go From Here: Community or Chaos?* (1967).

Reviewing the efforts of minorities to achieve equality of treatment in American society, Lewis Killian questioned the prospect in his *The Impossible Revolution?* (1968). Reviewing the research on inadequate American adjustment to technological change and population growth, Harrison Brown and Edward Hutchings wrote *Are Our Descendants Doomed?* (1972).

ENERGY RESOURCES AND MODERN SOCIETY
Unlike the literature of fantasy discussed earlier, these books are nonfiction but are quite as dramatically foreboding. In *Are Our Descendants Doomed?*, Brown makes this point about the United States and other relatively fortunate countries (1972: 12):

> ...the prospects for the rich countries are by no means bright. They must consume vast quantities of raw materials and energy of decreasing availability in order to produce the goods that people want, and in the process their factories excrete equally vast quantities of waste products into rivers, lakes, oceans, and the atmosphere. Technological man is changing his environment with unprecedented speed, and the ultimate effect of those changes can be only dimly perceived. As wastes are poured out, as cities become more congested, as wilderness is replaced by asphalt and concrete, and as man increasingly divorces himself from the world of nature from which he emerged, he enters an uncharted universe that offers few guidelines. Confronted on the one hand by the rebellion of poor countries which also want to be rich and on the other by a combination of the world's diminishing resources and deteriorating environment, technological man might well be a transitory phenomenon on the earth.

Modern society presses to utilize all available sources of technology to maintain and increase its level of productivity and standard of living. British nuclear physicist Sir Brian Flowers, former chairman of Britain's elite seventeen-member Royal Commission on Environmental Pollution, addressed himself to the issue of nuclear technological development, an important part of modern technology. He said, "I am not an advocate against nuclear power. I have not said stop. What I have said is certain things have not been done that should have been done" (1976). Flowers went on to observe that nuclear plant proliferation, given current inadequate controls, could result in a world glutted with plutonium, a *plutonium economy*, in which terrorists might hijack vehicles carrying the material to and from processing plants and unstable individuals, groups, or countries might use it to make weapons. These warnings come from a variety of informed sources.

There is a widely held view among professional social analysts that American and world society must change basic attitudes of individuals and performance of institutions in order to maintain a stable social system, and perhaps even to survive.

THE IMPERATIVE FOR DIRECTED CHANGE In many areas of American life, dry rot has set in. Cities find themselves constantly battling to avoid bankruptcy; environmental decay proceeds with expanding industry and urbanization. Vested political and economic interests often hinder changes needed for continued growth and development or just plain stability and maintenance of a democratic society.

MAINTAINING LIBERTIES AND OPPORTUNITIES All this adds up to a cultural imperative for directed social change to maintain individual liberties and opportunities. The first step in this direction is the development of a general awareness of the dimension of the problems facing American and world society. The dangers to American society are both from within and from outside. The combination of such problems as intergroup conflicts in the cities, the revolution of rising expectations among former colonial peoples who control vast resources, the population explosion relative to available food resources, and the spread of nuclear weapons among nations mean quite simply that the very survival of human society is threatened. Through such cultural mechanisms as daily news reports, the mass media, and reports of presidential commissions on such issues as violence and civil disorders, we become increasingly aware of the problems we face.

There is an old saying that half the problem is solved once you recognize it. That may be, but there is often a very big step between recognizing a problem and solving it. If this is true in the case of individuals' problems, it is more complexly true in our mass democratic society with tremendous problems and great technical capabilities. We must adopt a general problem-solving orientation and continuous experimentation to test old and new approaches to problems in such basic areas as family life, educational practices, planned communities, economic opportunities, and government.

PROBLEM SOLVING AND THE EXPERIMENTAL ORIENTATION   The ultimate reason for social experiment is rooted in the values and traditions of this society. In America, these values are based on maintaining a society that best permits the individual to pursue life, liberty, and happiness in his or her own way. It is increasingly recognized that today this pursuit within a secure and stable framework ironically depends upon effectively organized planning as well as upon individual initiative. There is not much personal freedom when people do not go to a library in the evening for fear of being mugged on the way. There is not much personal freedom, or very bright prospects, for young people attending a poor school torn by violence. There is not much personal freedom for industrial workers laid off for months after an international oil boycott. There is not much personal freedom for women who want a career but are expected to bear the full burden of housekeeping and child care while their male professional peers are not. There is not much personal freedom for elderly persons needing medical assistance when facilities and resources are not available.

We must go beyond recognizing problems to specifying desired and needed changes. George Fairweather, in his perceptive monograph, "Social Change: The Challenge to Survival" (1972), outlines a number of conditions necessary for bringing about change. Key terms in Fairweather's analysis are *organization, adopting group, inside group, pressure to conform,* and *probability.* Fairweather takes the very group orientation that William Whyte abhors in *The Organization Man* and attempts to point out how group action is now necessary to achieve the conditions that allow personal autonomy.

EFFECTIVE ORGANIZATION   Fairweather's stress on organization implicitly recognizes that changes that will adjust institutions to meet new challenges are unlikely to occur through the adaptation of individuals alone. There must be an adopting group to initiate and help institutionalize the changes. Such a group could be the nuclear family, adjusting to more equality for women at home and at work. It could be a business adjusting to organized group demands to monitor and control air and water pollution. The inside group is crucial to achieving long-term adaptation. Unless inside members of a government, business, or other organization are committed to hiring members of minority groups, such efforts are likely to languish, whatever the law and the courts say. The pressure to conform is a tacit recognition that many people will adapt to changes — including those designed to increase their personal freedom — once they believe them socially acceptable. The concept of probability takes into account that through even the best planned changes, based on considerable participation by citizens, we can hope to achieve only part of what we want. Fairweather is not a utopian; from Plato to Thomas More to Karl Marx, no utopia has ever fully achieved its aims.

Neither Fairweather nor anyone else foresees all the social changes that will resolve the dilemmas of our society; but Fairweather's approach shows that social scientists, drawing on many other fields, can develop comprehensive approaches that can achieve needed change. The central issue is whether any such approaches will be applied soon enough and broadly enough, with or without the help of the social sciences, to ensure a viable future.

Not all social analysts, including people from many fields besides sociology, are gloomy about prospects for constructive change. Many analysts from a variety of fields believe that American and world society can achieve short-term stability and long-term resolution of problems that will ensure the vitality and health of America and the world. In Chapter 15, we turn to these hopes for the future.

SUMMARY

Attempting to foresee possible future developments within society is an exercise in the sociological imagination. In this exercise, there is a basis for bleak predictions. The pace and nature of social change is a prime basis of value conflicts and institutional strains in the society. In addition to such powerful trends as *urbanization** and *cybernation**, there have occurred in recent decades a series of nationally traumatic events, including assassinations, corruption in government and business, and widespread civil disorders. There were also such international developments as the Vietnam War and the international OPEC oil boycott, both of which have had long-term economic consequences.

Sociological and other books evaluate these kinds of developments in despairing terms. Stanford Lyman's sociology of the absurd thesis states that the world is essentially without intrinsic meaning, and that we strive after meaning through continual conflict. These problems are fostered in part by our culture's movement from inner- to other-direction.

Literary works can be used as a source of sociological analysis. Symptoms of deeply felt anomie and despair in the society are evident in the works of such widely read authors as Aldous Huxley *(Brave New World)*, George Orwell *(1984)*, and Anthony Burgess *(A Clockwork Orange)*, who also warn of the effects of totalitarian control and loss of individual critical ability.

There is a growing consensus among analysts that there is a need for organized directed efforts to adapt to a constantly changing modern society. Both the necessity and dangers of organized directed action in mass society are explored in terms of victims of groupthink, projections of gloom and doom, and the imperative for directed social change. This last is necessary if we are to avoid the deterioration of effective institutional functioning. Fairweather suggests reasons why personal freedoms and autonomy can best be achieved through organizations which include *adopting* and *inside* groups. The underlying issue is whether changes will be instituted democratically or otherwise.

QUESTIONS FOR DISCUSSION

1. Alvin Gouldner holds that "social theorists work within a crumbling social matrix." What ongoing developments could lead him to make this point?

2. Do you agree that people appear to be "other-directed" in contemporary society? Would there be any advantage to a return to "inner-direction"?

3. In commercial advertising and in political campaigns what examples can you provide of the Orwellian "doublethink" phenomenon?

4. Robert Leighninger holds that F. Scott Fitzgerald's stories of the 1920s constituted a "theory of anomie." Assuming that this is true, what implications do you believe this holds for the future stability of American society a half century later?

5. The concept of "utopia" is usually discussed in terms of a hopeful future. Why could the utopian concept reasonably be discussed in terms of a fearful future?

6. Review your understanding of the following terms and concepts:

the sociology of the absurd

inner-directed

other-directed

circular reaction

groupthink

status symbol

organization man

REFERENCES

Baldwin, James
    1959   Another Country. New York: Dell.
    1960   Nobody Knows My Name. New York: Dell.
    1962   The Fire Next Time. New York: Dell.

Beaumont, Charles
    1975   "The vanishing American." M. Greenberg et al. (eds.), Social Problems Through Science and Fiction. New York: St. Martin's: 111-119.

Bradbury, Ray
    1967   Fahrenheit 491. New York: Simon and Schuster.

Brown, Harrison and Edward Hutchings
    1972   Are Our Descendants Doomed? New York: Viking.

Broyles, J. Allen
    1963   "The John Birch Society." The Journal of Social Issues 19: 51-62.

Burgess, Anthony
    1963   A Clockwork Orange. New York: W. W. Norton.

Cooper, David
    1970   The Death of the Family. New York: Vintage.

Coser, Lewis
    1963   Sociology Through Literature. Englewood Cliffs, N.J.: Prentice-Hall.

Cuber, John and Peggy Haroff
    1965   The Significant Americans. New York: Appleton-Century-Crofts.

Eakin, Beth
    1975   An Empirical Study of the Effect on Decision Outcomes in Different Sized Jury Panels. Unpublished Masters Thesis, Department of Sociology, Arizona State University.

Epstein, Benjamin and Arnold Forster
    1967   The Radical Right. New York: Vintage.

Fairweather, George
    1972   Social Change: The Challenge to Survival. Morristown, N.J.: General Learning Press.

Fitzgerald, F. Scott
    1925   The Great Gatsby. New York: Charles Scribner's Sons.

Flowers, Brian
    1976   Quoted in the New York Times (October 31).

Goffman, Erving
    1961   Asylums. Garden City, New York: Anchor.

Gouldner, Alvin
1971 The Coming Crisis of Western Sociology. New York: Equinox.

Homans, George
1950 The Human Group. New York: Harcourt, Brace & World.

Huxley, Aldous
1927 Jesting Pilate. New York: Harper & Row.
1932 Brave New World. New York: Harper & Row.
1958 Brave New World Revisited. New York: Harper & Row.

Janis, Irving
1973 "The groupthink follies." The San Francisco Examiner & Chronicle (January 17).
1973 Victims of Groupthink. New Haven, Conn.: Yale University Press.

Keniston, Kenneth
1968 "Youth, change and violence." The American Scholar 37: 227-245.

Kesey, Ken
1962 One Flew Over the Cuckoo's Nest. New York: Signet.

Killian, Lewis
1968 The Impossible Revolution? Black Power and the American Dream. New York: Random House.

King, Jr., Martin Luther
1967 Where Do We Go From Here: Community or Chaos? New York: Harper & Row.

Koestler, Arthur
1941 Darkness at Noon. New York: Macmillan.

Komarovsky, Mirra
1964 Blue-Collar Marriage. New York: Random House.

Leighninger, Robert
1972 "Scott Fitzgerald's theory of anomia: the novelist as sociological theorist." The Annual Proceedings of the 1972 ASA Meetings. Washington, D.C.: American Sociological Association.

Leighton, Isabel
1949 The Aspirin Age. New York: Simon and Schuster.

Lewis, Sinclair
1935 It Can't Happen Here. New York: Sun Dial.

Lyman, Stanford and Marvin Scott
1970 A Sociology of the Absurd. New York: Appleton-Century-Crofts.

McLuhan, Marshall
1964 The Extensions of Man. New York: McGraw-Hill.

Merrill, Judith
1971 "What do you mean: science? fiction?" T. Clareson (ed.), SF: The Other Side of Realism. Bowling Green, Ohio: Bowling Green University Popular Press: 53-95.

Milgram, Stanley
1974 Obedience to Authority. New York: Harper & Row.

Orwell, George
1948 1984. New York: Harcourt, Brace and World
1950 Shooting an Elephant and Other Essays. New York: Harcourt, Brace and World.

Reisman, David with Nathan Glazer and Reuel Denney
1953 The Lonely Crowd. New York: Doubleday Anchor Books.

Rivers, Caryl
1976 Cloning: A Generation Made to Order. Ms. (June): 51.

Rosenberg, Bernard with Israel Gerver and F. William Howton
   1971   Mass Society in Crisis: Social Problems and Social Pathology. New York: Macmillan.

Saint-Exupéry, Antoine de
   1946   Le Petit Prince. Boston: Houghton Mifflin.

Schrag, Peter
   1973   The End of the American Future. New York: Simon and Schuster.

Skinner, B. F.
   1971   Beyond Freedom and Dignity. New York: Knopf.

Skolnick, Jerome and Elliott Currie
   1973   Crisis in American Institutions. Boston: Little, Brown.

Solzhenitsyn, Alexander
   1973   The Gulag Archipelago. New York: Harper & Row.

Tolkien, J. R. R.
   1937   The Hobbit. London: George Allen & Unwin.
   1965   The Lord of the Rings (a trilogy). Boston: Houghton Mifflin.

Turner, Ralph and Lewis Killian
   1972   Collective Behavior. Englewood Cliffs, N.J.: Prentice-Hall.

Vander Zanden, James
   1960   "The Klan revival." The American Journal of Sociology 65: 456–462.

Veblen, Thorstein
   1934   Theory of the Leisure Class. (First edition 1899). New York: Macmillan.

Weisband, Edward and Thomas Franck
   1975   Resignation in Protest. New York: Viking.

Whyte, William H.
   1951   "Problem for the front office." Fortune Magazine (May): 78–81; 146.
   1956   The Organization Man. New York: Simon and Schuster.

Chapter 15

HOPES FOR THE FUTURE

While the sick man has life there is hope.

Cicero

THE CAUSE FOR HOPE

A useful analytical approach to many of the gloomy projections for the future is *social pathology**. Pathology, or the study of disease, is the scientific analysis of the nature, causes, and cures of illnesses and malfunctions, whether of the human body or of society. The study of social, as of physical, diseases always holds out the hope that a cure may be found while the patient still lives: like Cicero's sick man, modern sick society still has life, and while there is life, there is hope.

SOME ENCOURAGING SOCIAL REALITIES

Beyond this perhaps tenuous basis for hope is some encouraging evidence. From New York to Los Angeles, whatever deterioration America's great cities may experience, they are still functioning communities. Despite the acquisition of nuclear weapons by more and more nations, there has not been a general nuclear war. Whatever the damage to health from air and water pollution and from famine in overpopulated areas, life span continues to increase worldwide. All is not lost by any means.

While there is a consensus among social analysts that time for solving problems cannot be measured in generations, there does appear to be some time left in which to develop solutions to many pressing social problems. Some of the gloomy projections come from viewing society only in the light of immediate developments. This *ahistorical* approach is of doubtful use, whether one is optimistic or pessimistic about the future.

One example of projecting from a limited context is Arthur Waskow's optimistic thesis in *From Riot to Sit-In* (1966). Waskow held that interracial conflict had shifted away from the violent race rioting of earlier years experienced by such cities as St. Louis (1917), Chicago (1919) and Detroit (1943) and that the nonviolent approaches of the 1950s and early 1960s demonstrated that American society was gradually accepting the idea of equality for racial minorities.

The dozens of urban race riots that developed in the mid 1960s, just as Waskow's book came out, led Lewis Killian to the opposite conclusion. Reviewing the mass destruction of the racial disorders at the end of the 1960s, Killian projected a future for American race relations that was equally off the mark. In *The Impossible Revolution?* (1968) Killian theorized that no interracial *accommodation** was in the making nor would ever be. While full interracial accommodation is a long way off, racial riots did cease shortly after Killian's book came out; more interracial integration and more upward mobility of blacks in American society occurred in the late 1960s and early 1970s than in the decade before and during the civil rights movement (see: *Almanac*, 1974: 736). Waskow's and Killian's books, which were published just as events were taking new turns, demonstrate the dangers of short-run analysis.

Waskow and Killian failed to account effectively for historical forces and for the fact that people can choose their responses to social issues, thereby influencing their own futures. Both these factors allow hope for tomorrow. In America, there is a tradition of experimentation. The past two centuries have seen thousands of business enterprises established, and towns and cities spring up across the nation. A pervasive sense of hope has characterized American society.

THE POSITIVE CHARACTER OF AMERICAN SOCIETY This positive character of the society is reflected in the eighteenth-century Declaration of Independence, with its emphasis on the individual's right to pursue happiness; in the nineteenth-century observations of Alexis de Tocqueville (1960) on American industry and enthusiasm; and, at the depth of our worst depression, in the nation's rallying behind Franklin Roosevelt, who, in his first inaugural, assured us that "we have nothing to fear but fear itself." The high level of the nation's self-confidence became clear early in its history. In 1801, Thomas Jefferson stated (Bartlett, 1955: 347b):

> If there be any among us who would wish to dissolve this Union or to change its Republican form, let them stand undisturbed as monuments of the safety with which error of opinion may be tolerated where reason is left free to combat it.

There are not many chiefs of state in any society who have encouraged their opposition to speak up undisturbed, not only to challenge policies but to challenge the very political system itself.

This optimistic tradition has periodically had the effect of a self-fulfilling prophecy. American society has always rebounded effectively from traumatic problems such as the economic panics and depressions of 1873, 1893, 1907, and the 1930s, or from such destructive wars as the Revolution and the Civil War. Such past responses encourage hope that we shall be able to weather future economic troubles and military setbacks (such as that in Southeast Asia in the 1970s) — even when those setbacks may result from ineffective government and economic policies.

INCREASINGLY FLEXIBLE AMERICAN ATTITUDES Supreme Court Justice William O. Douglas once asked: "Can we develop a new consciousness that places the individual and humanistic values above the machine?" There are many

HOPES FOR THE FUTURE 465

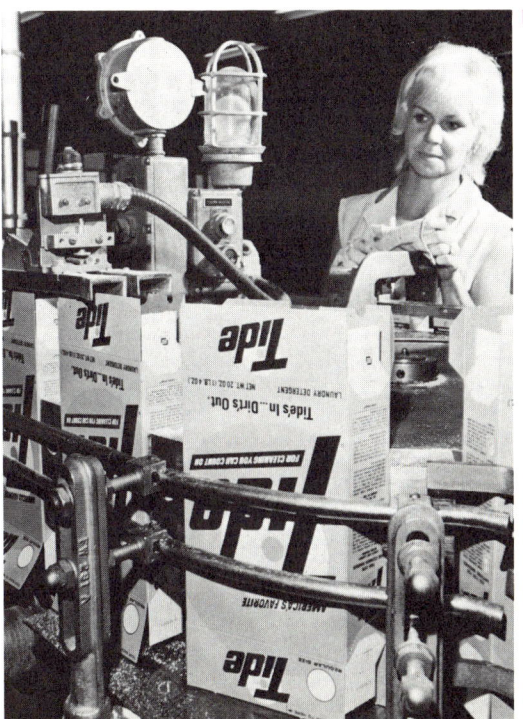

a

b

Scenes like these suggest that American society still exhibits a generally high standard of living and considerable economic, military, and democratic vitality. SOURCE: (a) George Gardner; (b) Courtesy of Procter and Gamble; (c) Joseph Kovacs/Stock Boston; (d) Constantine Manos/Magnum; (e) Bettye Lane; (f) Charles Gatewood; (g) Marc and Evelyne Bernheim/Woodfin Camp and Associates; (h) Norman Hurst/Stock Boston.

c

d

e

HOPES FOR THE FUTURE 467

f

g
h

signs of emerging national attitudes that suggest a renewed flexibility in facing America's problems. Why such flexibility, in the sense of Douglas's "new consciousness," is a prerequisite to constructive change in the future is well put by Erich Fromm, who observes that (1968: 150):

...we must become aware in order to choose the good — but no awareness will help us if we have lost the capacity to be moved by the distress of another human being.... If man becomes indifferent to life there is no longer any hope that he choose the good. Then, indeed, his heart will have so hardened that his "life" will be ended. If this should happen to the entire human race or to its most powerful members, then the life of mankind may be extinguished at the very moment of its greatest promise.

There is evidence that the level of American awareness is increasing on a number of crucial issues.

First, consider our willingness to participate in global affairs. Old-style *isolationism,* in which Americans held to George Washington's policy of avoiding entangling alliances, was strictly followed until World War II. While it was manifestly impossible to be unaffected by international conflicts long before that time, the American electorate punished political leaders such as Woodrow Wilson who, in the 1920s, advocated that the United States join the League of Nations. The national consensus that resulted in American participation in the United Nations after World War II, as well as substantial international involvement through economic and military commitments, particularly to Western Europe, marked a new trend, the rejection of isolationism. The *centralization** of power in the national government, which is characteristic of times of international conflict, does constitute a threat to democratic controls (see Chapter 12). It has become clear to most Americans, however, that *not* facing issues of international conflict in some organized, cohesive manner constitutes an even greater threat with fewer social controls. Even in the aftermath of a national reaction against international involvement following the Vietnam War, there have been no serious public pressures to withdraw from the United Nations or from the North Atlantic Treaty Organization or other alliances.

On the domestic scene, there is also strong evidence of growing awareness which, as Fromm noted, is a precondition to being "moved by the distress of another human being." For example, racism appears to be declining. Racism places one ethnic and cultural group above another — such as whites or white Anglo-Saxon Protestants, above blacks or native American Indians. The reduction of racism is a prerequisite to solving a number of other problems, such as hunger and poverty, in a society where minorities constitute a large part of the hungry and impoverished population. For some measure of the reduction in racism which has occurred, recall the *social distance** findings given in Table 2-1 (page 30). The table presents data from national samples of Americans from all social classes and all walks of life. On the seven-point Bogardus social distance scale, the spread for thirty groups was almost 4 in the 1920s but only 1 to 2.5 by the 1960s.

THE DECLINE IN STEREOTYPES This cultural shift away from racism can be seen in a dramatic way in the decline of racial stereotyping over three generations of college students. Note in Table 15-1 that the pejorative *stereotypes** of blacks and other ethnic groups in American society have significantly faded since the first reported sample in 1933.[1] Since

---

[1] As a sign that Americans are becoming less narrow and more open to objective views of others, the findings relating to Turks, who are not included on Table 15-1, are noteworthy. People of Turkish background represent less than 1 percent of the American population. Consequently, the image of Turks can hardly be based upon extensive experience. Yet, in 1933, 47 percent of the students believed Turks to be cruel and 21 percent thought them to be treacherous. By 1967, these percentages had declined to 9 and 13 percent respectively.

Table 15-1   The Fading of Pejorative Stereotypes in Three Generations of College Students

Trait	1933[a]	1951[b]	1967[c]*	1969[d]*
Blacks				
superstitious	84	41	13	10
lazy	75	31	26	18
Chinese				
superstitious	34	18	8	9
sly	29	4	6	7
Italians				
impulsive	44	19	28	9
revengeful	17	1	1	1
Japanese				
sly	20	21	3	1
treacherous	13	17	1	1
Jews				
grasping	34	17	17	5
sly	20	14	7	8

[a] Princeton University sample. See: D. Katz and K. W. Braly, "Racial Stereotypes of 100 College Students," *Journal of Abnormal and Social Psychology* 28 (1933), pp. 280-290.

[b] Princeton University sample. See: G. M. Gilbert, "Stereotype Persistence and Change Among College Students," *Journal of Abnormal and Social Psychology* 46 (1951), pp. 245-254. Copyright 1951 by the American Psychological Association. Reprinted by permission.

[c] Princeton University sample. See: M. Karlins, T. Coffman, and G. Walter, "On the Fading of Social Stereotypes: Studies in Three Generations of College Students," *Journal of Personality and Social Psychology* 13 (1969), pp. 1-16. Copyright © 1969 by the American Psychological Association. Reprinted by permission.

[d] This table, from "The Fragmentization of Literary Stereotypes of Jews and of Negroes Among College Students," by Leonard Gordon is reprinted from *Pacific Sociological Review*, vol. 16 no. 4 (Oct. 1973) pp. 411-425 by permission of the publisher, Sage Publications, Inc. Arizona State University sample.

* It is noteworthy that the fading effects were found in the late 1960s at both a private university, the 1967 sample at Princeton, and at a public state university, the 1969 sample at Arizona State.

college students represent that stratum of society from which a high proportion of future business, professional, and social leaders are drawn, they are likely to have considerable influence on economic and social conditions in our society.

The emergence of a youth-based counterculture, discussed in Chapter 5, is another sign of growing awareness of the need to change basic American attitudes and institutional processes. *Contraculture* is a term coined by Milton Yinger (1960) to help explain the movement among young people toward cultural values and life styles at variance from the norm.

The emergence of significantly different values and life styles has been part of the American social landscape since the early 1960s. Unlike dissident poor and minority youth, the contraculture youth movement is composed largely of middle- and upper-middle-class young people from their teens to their early thirties, people who, presumably, were socialized to accept the American dream of success. Only a small number — no precise figures are available but the proportion is under 10 percent — of middle-class young people are part of the contraculture. Still, it has social significance in a rapidly changing society. A sign of its influence is the growth in communal *intentional communities,* in which several families live as one household, often *polygamously**. In the early 1960s, only about a hundred such communities existed, founded mostly by religious fundamentalists or utopian socialists. By 1970, there were some 3,000, about a third in rural settings, mostly in California, New Mexico, Oregon, and Vermont *(Time Magazine,* 1970: 36).

The counterculture movement constitutes a revolt against an American future that seems to be heading toward increasing technology, more bureaucracy in the economy and government, and greater isolation of the nuclear family. As an alternative life style, counterculture presents this challenge to the technological–bureaucratic system (Simmons and Winograd, 1967: 12):

Not only are the mainstream institutions and values violated, but their legitimacy is challenged ... what is qualitatively new in this challenge is that the very truth and moral validity of so many notions and practices, long cherished in our country, are being challenged. When caught by parents or authorities, youths are no longer hanging their heads in shame. Instead, they are asserting the rightness, at least for themselves, of what they're doing. And they are asking what right do their elders have to put them down.

Just how open the counterculture is to new, flexible ways of thinking about life is summarized by Charles Reich of the Yale Law School in his best seller *The Greening of America* (1971). Reich summarizes the humanistic, freedom-seeking values of the new system (see the selection from Reich's book).

COUNTERCULTURE VALUES FOR A NEW AMERICA

From *The Greening of America,* by Charles A. Reich. Copyright © 1970 by Charles A. Reich. Reprinted by permission of Random House, Inc. A portion of this book originally appeared in *The New Yorker* in somewhat different form. From pp. 152–154.

Adventure, travel. The Yukon, the Hebrides, a blizzard, fog on the Great Banks, the lost cities of Crete, climbing mountains on rock and ice in elemental cold and wind.

Sex. Experiences with many different people, in different times, circumstances, and localities, in moments of happiness, sorrow, need, and comfortable familiarity, in youth and age.

Nature. The experience of living in harmony with nature, on a farm, or by the sea, or near a lake or meadow, knowing, using, and returning the elements; Thoreau at Walden.

Physical activity. Chopping wood, carrying a boat, running, walking, climbing, experiencing heat and cold, swimming, building a house, paddling a canoe.

Clothes. Clothes to express various moods, and to express the body, its strength, its shape, its sensuality, its harmony with the rest of nature. Clothes for fun, for work, for dignity.

Morality. Having a moral stand with respect to something happening to oneself, to others, or to society; maintaining that stand, and giving it expression.

Creativity. In more primitive cultures, creativity and art are part of everyday life, and each person has an opportunity to exercise his creative side.

Multimedia experiences. Music, light, smell, dance, all together.

Alterations of time. Staying up all night, getting up before dawn, sleeping all day, working three days straight, or being wholly oblivious to measured time.

Seasons. Observing the four changes of season by stopping other activities for a while and going to some place where change is fully visible.

Growth, learning, change. Constantly learning new things, experiencing changes of feelings and personality, continually growing in experience and consciousness.

Harmony. Enough time and reflection to assemble various experiences and changes into a harmony within the individual, relating them to each other and to earlier experiences.

Inner life. Introspection, reflection.

Responding to own needs. Staying in bed when the need is felt, drinking a milk shake on a hot afternoon, or stopping everything to watch a rainstorm.

Own special excellence. Having enough independence to disregard other people's standards of excellence, discover one's own special excellence, and then pursue it.

Wholeness. Being sensually aware of all the stimuli at a given moment; smell, temperature, breeze, noises, the tempo of one's own body.

New feelings. Experiencing feelings or emotions qualitatively different from those previously known.

Expanded consciousness. Experiencing previously unknown kinds of awareness, new values, new understandings.

New environments. Experiencing a new total environment long enough to make adjustments to it and understand its terms (such as six months in the tropics).

Creating an environment. Taking whatever elements are given, natural, human, and social, and making a unique pattern out of them as one's own creation.

MODIFYING BUREAUCRATIC SOCIETY Countercultural values differ so greatly from the values of the traditional American work ethic, and modern technological-bureaucratic-urbanized society, that it is difficult, if not impossible, to practice them completely. The difficulties that the new communities have had in practicing these values as a total life style have been formidable. Most groups have lasted only a few months or a few years. They have faced lack of support from the general society as well as internal strains. Practical problems related to making a living continually arise: how to make enough money to support individuals, the extended family, or the whole communal system. How to accomplish such essential tasks as feeding infants, shopping, cooking, housekeeping. One former member of an urban commune described how greatly his experience differed from the ideal (French, 1971: 26):

Gradually, we began to see a brittleness in the ways Community members dealt with one another, in the set of their faces, in what they said. Compassion was held to be condescending. Favored instead was a sort of brutal honesty that forced distances between people, stressed their apartness.

Given institutional inertia and the continuing effect of traditional values, it is doubtful that the counterculture can take a consistent and effective stand against the predominant technological and bureaucratic trends in modern society. The social significance of the counterculture is that it is an important source of criticism of the dehumanizing qualities in modern society and a source of encouragement for the renewal of humane values.

The trend toward more flexible values that is reflected in the social distance and stereotyping studies gives some hope that Americans are increasingly open to new humanizing ideas; but such new ideas will have to be put into effect in the context of the existing technological, urban society. For instance, dismantling industry and dispersing urban population (if a large enough area could be found) would be drastic social changes to make simply on the vague assumption that they would lead to other beneficial changes. Americans tend to opt for security over what is seen as extreme change. (Recall, for example, the overwhelming defeat of Senator George McGovern by Richard

Nixon in the presidential election of 1972; most voters thought him too radical.) It is not that Americans resist change, but that we approach change with great caution.

A HISTORY OF CULTURAL ADAPTATION In the past, American society has been able to adapt to change. For example, the Constitution does not mention political parties. Yet, the two-party system was created in order to set up a workable, republican government. When nonpropertied citizens, blacks, women, and others were excluded from the political, economic, and social mainstream of the society, *social movements** arose to insist upon equal rights for the excluded groups. Political parties do not always function effectively, of course, and minority groups still have not attained full equality of treatment and opportunity. Yet, past changes in values and institutions suggest that there is real hope for shifts in attitudes, values, and institutions in the future. Great changes are occurring whether we will them or not. The economic historian John Sawyer puts the case for consciously moving to achieve needed social changes (1974: C23):

This task should not be beyond the creative capacities of an enormously resilient culture. It requires realization, however, that new and unaccustomed constraints are henceforth a persistent condition of life on earth. And this in turn requires us to recognize that we are living in an era fundamentally different from the one in which our nation grew and in which we ourselves were formed.

Just what these constraints[2] are, and how they can be managed to enable the individual to maintain her or his uniqueness in modern society, is a growing concern of sociological research.

---

[2] One constraint that may serve as an example is the end of our land frontier. We must now live within relatively fixed boundaries with increasing population and increasing needs for food, lumber, and other resources.

REASONS FOR HOPE Let us summarize here the hopeful evidence for the future. We have selected developments that are discussed more fully elsewhere in the book, particularly in Chapters 5 through 12, as well as in this chapter:

CHANGING VALUES A trend toward more flexible, adaptive, and humanistic values is reflected in the increasing acceptance of different racial and ethnic groups (see Table 2-1 on changes in social distance since the 1920s and Table 15-1 on the fading of pejorative stereotypes since the 1930s). Signs of this trend are suggested as well by more acceptance of different life styles (discussed in Chapter 5) and of different age groups (discussed in Chapters 5 and 7). References in this chapter to the observations of Alvin Toffler and Charles Reich further take up this point.

INCREASING TECHNOLOGICAL CAPABILITY The advanced technology of American society, and increasingly of world society, provides a means of meeting the needs of mass modern society for communication, transportation, products, and so on. The technology of the *cybernetic** age can be used to help end poverty (see Chapter 6) and to redevelop our deteriorating cities (see Chapter 10). Figure 15-1 summarizes some of the rapidly expanding phenomena in modern society (increasing pollution, travel needs) to which advanced technology can usefully be applied.

GREATER PUBLIC INVOLVEMENT IN ISSUES The black, Spanish-American, women's, and other minority *social movements** as well as such citizens' groups as Common Cause, the Sierra Club, and Ralph Nader's consumer-protection organization, give evidence of a high level of informed public opinion on pressing issues facing the society. While public controversy may be the initial result, an informed public opinion has great potential for solving problems (see the section, Beyond Survival, in this chapter).

CORPORATE-UNION RESPONSIBILITY   In response to greater *public** involvement in social issues, corporations and labor unions have begun to take their public responsibilities as seriously as their profit interests. Since the 1960s, prodded by various pressures and resulting legislation such as the Civil Rights Act of 1964 and the Clean Air Act of 1970, corporations and unions have increasingly opened their ranks to minority group members (see Chapter 8), have moved to control industrial pollution, and have begun to adopt energy-conserving processes in the face of declining supplies of fossil fuels.

INCREASING EXPERTISE IN FORECASTING   Our ability to forecast and plan has been growing rapidly. This is most evident in the areas of economic and political forecasting, which have moved far beyond the Gallup and Harris polls or the Census, designed to provide useful information on public attitudes or population characteristics. Now, the work of such survey research centers as those at the University of California at Berkeley, the National Opinion Research Center in Chicago, the University of Michigan, and Columbia University (see Chapter 4) are tools for answering analytical questions about the future of the economy, intergroup relations, the cities, and so on. The discussion at the end of Chapter 10 on urban planning and the discussion in this chapter of George Fairweather's analysis of organizational prerequisites to adaptive change and Willis Harman's analysis of needed *microdecisions** and *macrodecisions** are indications of the implications for policy-making of this increasing ability to forecast and plan.

Since the 1930s, collective bargaining between company and union has become an institutionalized process, replacing the often violent confrontations of the past. SOURCE: Owen Franken/Stock Boston.

SOCIOLOGY AND THE STUDY OF THE FUTURE

The study of the future is a particularly delicate process of sociological analysis. Any projection for the future goes beyond an analysis of the hard, collectible data available for the study of the past or the present. A discipline rooted in empirical research is hesitant to predict what *will* be and certainly to prescribe what *should* be. Yet, much of what happens in the present is based on what people think will happen in the future. We know that people's behavior is influenced by whether or not they expect to go to college, be employed, serve in the armed forces, get married, and so on, and is thus based implicitly on certain assumptions about the future — that there will be colleges to go to, jobs to hold, an army to join, suitable people to marry, and social approval of family life in some form.

Since people base so much of their behavior on such assumptions about the future, sociologists realize that the systematic study of the future is a necessary part of their field. For those who specialize in the sociology of the future, there are several good signs. Two of these relate to social processes. One is the greatly expanded ability that technological innovations, particularly computers, give sociologists to accumulate and analyze large quantities of data, making it possible to construct complex and accurate social models on such basic topics as population, transportation systems, intergroup relations, and community planning (Bell, 1965). Another is that, through sociological analysis, we can formulate social policies to bring about desired results. As two specialists put it (Huber and Bell, 1971: 288):

The sociology of the future is not confined to the study of trends and predictions of the most likely future. It also includes the study of values, so that "wished-for" futures can be distinguished from undesirable futures, and it includes an evaluation of when, where, by whom, how intensely, under what conditions, and with what consequences the values are wished for.

COMMON VALUES The sociology of the future, then, does not depend on the direction taken by wise elders. Rather, the wished-for futures are founded on values that have long been growing in American society and around the world. In his presidential address to the American Sociological Association (ASA) in 1966, Wilbert Moore described some common goals toward which humanity is moving and to which the sociology of the future might address itself. Moore noted these convergent worldwide goals and desires: people everywhere prefer health to sickness, and well-being to poverty; people increasingly recognize, even if they do not yet universally accept, that orderly ways of resolving conflict without violence are prerequisite to survival; and there has been a rapid extension since mid century of the common rights of citizens — in contrast to privilege derived from wealth, power, or birth — that has brought greater access to health services and economic opportunities and more mass influence on politics and governments.

Moore's conclusion is that these common values provide a basis for building realistic models of future social systems that are widely wished for. Another development in modern society generally is the introduction of planning in nearly all aspects of business and government (Huber and Bell, 1971: 287). Planning and the evolution of common goals together encourage the formulation of future possibilities, probabilities, preferences, and policies (Toffler, 1969: 1).

REALITY AND UTOPIA   There are also reasons for caution if not despair. Projections for the future are often utopian, and there are good reasons to be critical of utopias. The most influential utopian concept of the past century has been Karl Marx's classless society. Yet, societies like the Soviet Union and China, which espouse the Marxian utopia, are neither humanitarian nor classless. Furthermore, optimistic sociological projections of the 1920s and 1930s, such as H. G. Wells's novel *The Shape of Things to Come* (1933) and the social-scientific analyses of Nathan Israeli (1930), Hadley Cantril (1938), and Douglas McGregor (1938), were disproved by worldwide depression, war, atomic armament, and continuing tensions from a variety of causes including the *revolution of rising expectations,* the sudden awareness of and demand for items formerly available only to others.

For all these reasons, since the late 1950s, the tone of any sociology of the future has been cautious. Even Wilbert Moore, in his presidential address "The Utility of Utopias," gave reasons why sociologists and other analysts have not been specific about the shape of the future. Moore noted that one basic problem is that most models of the future have been static and functional, ignoring the fact of widely differing cultural values and traditions, the real complexities of social life. John Edwards picked up Moore's point by observing (1967: 168):

The quest for perfection, after all, can be only as successful as the material to be perfected. And men, Tocqueville observed, "are neither very good nor very bad, but mediocre." Before embarking, serious consideration and reconsideration of a sociological venture in utopia seems very much in order.

Even with such cautions, the sociology of the future is developing as an important new aspect of sociological and policy analysis (see the selection on The Future of Optimism). The nature of rapid social change in modern society, and the fact that people's acts in the present are influenced by their assessments of the future, strongly encourage systematic analyses of the future. This is true not only for sociology but for other disciplines. Until recently, *futurology,* for want of a better term, was largely the province of novelists, whether optimists like H. G. Wells or pessimists like Aldous Huxley. The rationale for sociological and other analyses was strongly stated by Frank Hopkins (1967: 149):

... the future is too important to be left to the writers of imaginative fiction, however brilliant and provocative their efforts may be. It needs rather to be studied soberly and systematically by [physical] scientists, engineers, economists, sociologists, political scientists, historians, and others, professionally trained ... who can determine trends and who have the special expertise in each field to foresee the problems which lie ahead, and to prepare for them.

Two additional goals beyond those noted by Wilbert Moore lend weight to this interest in the future: the short-term universal desire to survive and the long-term universal desire that goes beyond survival, for wished-for futures.

SURVIVING THE TWENTIETH CENTURY

Analysis of the future includes both the short term and the long, as Alvin Toffler, the author of *Future Shock* (1970) and *The Eco-Spasm Report* (1975), has noted: "I expect that in the short term there will be some pain and turbulence and in the long term we'll work out of it." Since there can be no long-term future without short-term survival, the first challenge is to get through the last quarter of the twentieth century.

The stakes are high. In nineteenth-century England, already a technological, urban, bureaucratic society, John Stuart Mill addressed himself to the potential dangers to "human freedom and advancement." In his classic *On Liberty,* Mill observed these dangers of modern economic and government processes (1947: 117–118):

... a State which dwarfs its men, in order that they may be more docile instruments in its hands even for beneficial purposes — will find that with small men no great thing can really be accomplished; and that the perfection of machinery to which it has sacrificed everything, will in the end avail it nothing, for want of the vital power which, in order that the machine might work more smoothly, it has preferred to banish.

THE NEED FOR AN INFORMED PUBLIC AND ENLIGHTENED LEADERSHIP As in *The Subjugation of Women* (1869), Mill accurately anticipated a crucial issue of the twentieth century. At the very time when the problems and changes confronting society call for independent and innovative thinking, the impact of large economic, government, and other institutions inhibits independent expression. We have produced many small men. One significant result of this constraint is noted by the American historian Henry Steele Commager, in comparing leadership at the beginning of the republic with that of today (1973: 1-4):

No other generation in our history produced a galaxy of statesmen comparable to that which provided the leadership for revolutionary America. A nation of fewer than 3 million[3] . . . gave us in one generation a Franklin, a Washington, a Jefferson, a Madison, a John Adams, a Hamilton, a George Mason, a John Marshall, a James Wilson, a Tom Paine, and many others of almost equal distinction.

Why is it that the United States today — a vast, modern, urbanized country with over 200 million people — has nothing to show that is remotely comparable to this record?

Part of the answer to Commager's question is that people come to exploit a social system rather than nurture its original purpose. As C. Wright Mills says in *The Power Elite* (1973: 293):

The structural trends of institutions become defined as opportunities by those who occupy their command posts. Once the opportunities are recognized, men avail themselves of them.

---

[3] If black slaves and native American Indians had been included, the figure would be fewer than 4 million.

At this point, individuals tend to serve their own personal interests. It is then — which indeed is *now* — that new ideas become most important to keep the perspective broad and the leadership aware of their responsibilities. Mills, echoing John Stuart Mill, saw the need today for autonomous, independent thinking (1956: 353):

Only when mind has an autonomous basis, independent of power, but powerfully related to it, can mind exert its force in the shaping of human affairs. This is democratically possible only when there exists a free and knowledgeable public, to which [people] of knowledge may address themselves, and to which [people] of power are truly responsible.

In modern society, how possible is it to achieve the informed public and enlightened leadership whose absence Commager laments? One explanation of how they might emerge is given by the early sociologist William Graham Sumner, in observing that people "begin with acts, not with thoughts" (Ross, 1973: 177). Sumner was not denying that thought influences human events. He was saying that change generally stems from changing conditions that directly and clearly affect the interests of people. This is as true of not installing a traffic signal until after a fatal accident as of the acceptance of government controls on the economy only after a great depression. Once change is recognized, conditions exist for a new state of balance — though, as Toffler observed, not without some pain and turbulence.

Conditions are, in fact, changing in so many fundamental ways that Sumner's observation that people begin with acts is being demonstrated before our eyes. Various acts in response to changing conditions have been *ad hoc* and unplanned. Racial rioting in our cities brought a variety of emergency responses, including the expansion of local police forces, the increasing protection of civil rights, and a movement of whites out of the cities and into the suburbs. The international oil cartel's increase in the price of imported oil brought about hurried efforts to speed production of nuclear, solar, and other kinds of energy — with little short-term success. It should be noted, however, that while there have been many examples of inadequate responses to crises, we are more likely to notice failures than unspectacular successes.

OLD AND NEW VALUES The sense of national disorientation appears to be related to the strain and challenge that changing conditions have posed for certain American *value orientations**. Value orientation means that, in spite of all the diversity and change in values, certain commonly held presumptions frame the American outlook (Williams, 1960: 415–470). (See also Chapter 2.) These value orientations have included assumptions about infinite resources, open domestic and international markets, unlimited individual opportunities, an open and effective political process, and faith in human progress (Sawyer, 1974: C23). Changing domestic and international conditions have run counter to these presumptions, so that (Sawyer, 1974: C23)

... we are painfully finding that resources are not infinite, that markets will not necessarily remain open or raw materials available on terms favorable to industry, that technology is not always benign, and that the earth, sea and biosphere cannot absorb the unlimited outpouring of economic growth.

These changing conditions at first affect the task of maintaining and increasing economic abundance. They also affect a wide range of other issues, such as working out accommodations in intergroup relations and halting the deterioration of big cities.

A TIME FOR REASSESSMENT The changing social situation has begun to force new priorities, choices, and directions upon this society. Bertram Gold, executive vice president of the American Jewish Committee's Institute of Human Relations, a research group, observed in his annual report for 1975 entitled "A Time for Reassessment" (1):

Although generally above average in income and education, delegates to the 1976 Democratic National Convention included more blacks and more women than ever before. SOURCE: Joe Di Dio/National Education Association.

We are currently in a watershed period of American history. Not since the American Revolution 200 years ago, has there been such widespread uncertainty about where our nation is heading. . . . Many . . . reassessments are long overdue. Whether we like it or not, the truth is that most of our old ways of doing things — in international relations, in economics, in energy consumption, in health-care delivery, in social welfare and in a host of other areas — have simply not worked out the way we wanted them to. But if our national reassessments are to have any meaning — if they are to result in more than breastbeating over past failures — we need to understand the forces which have led to these failures.

THE FUTURE OF OPTIMISM

From: Andrew A. Spekke, "The Future of Optimism," *Intellect*, May, June, 1976, p. 605.

Spekke brings out the point that situations, when looked at in new ways, may encourage very different possibilities, based on seeing sources of problems as being other than what we had supposed.

Much has been written about the impending global crisis in population, energy, food, and materials. The perception of future peril has fostered a "futurism" concerned most frequently with trying to understand and anticipate scientific and technological developments in order that control may be exercised over their effects.

One's expectations regarding the survival of the human species will determine what action is taken — too much optimism or too great a pessimism lead to inaction. Accordingly, what estimates do people have regarding survival and what estimate serves as a stimulus to action?

The future is likely to be much better than a lot of people now think, say researchers at the Hudson Institute and the Aspen Institute for Humanistic Studies in policy papers exploring state-of-the-world concerns. In a booklet entitled *Human Requirements, Supply Levels and Outer Bounds: A Framework for Thinking about the Planetary Bargain,* they assert that civilization has an excellent chance of meeting all minimum human needs to the year 2000 and beyond. This can be done without transgressing the "outer bounds" of the planet's given natural resources. As *The Times* in London somewhat facetiously remarked in its review of the Institute's work, "... we are not inexorably driving ourselves towards a ravaged earth on which we are doomed to watch each other starving to death on color television sets."

The policy paper intends to promote a just and workable new international economic order — "The Planetary Bargain" — a concept designed for what the Institute perceives as the centerpiece of world politics in the coming decades, the development and distribution of resources to serve the needs of humanity. This new "fairness revolution" is already well under way.

What emerges is an understanding that, as societies change, the manner in which they consume resources changes. "In most affluent societies, people who can afford 'more' are spending not on quantity but on quality, and beyond that on 'symbolic consumption.' It turns out that as people clamber up the income ladder and move into the towns and cities, the status of women changes, the reasons for having large families subtly mutate, the technologies of family planning become more available ... and the fertility rate skids off its exponential trajectory."

It now appears certain that we are not going to breed ourselves into a state of severe overpopulation. The UN has released a forecast which indicates a world population of around 6,000,000,000 in the year 2000. Thus, for the first time in the experience of the UN, estimated population trends had to be revised downwards. This could mean, as the Institute sees it, "if we were to decrease population growth by even a half of one percent a year, this would cut material requirements by a large amount. It has been estimated that reducing the world growth rate from 1.8% to 0.5% would cut the total amount of additional goods and services needed by about 75 to 80%." The central thesis is that, rather than population increase being the controlling determinant of supply levels, the levels of the global material standards are the real control factors of population.

Certain issues concerning living standards, however, are not adequately covered by the proponents of an equitable distribution of the world's resources. If the living standards are raised in India, China, Southeast Asia, and Latin America to American levels, the world as organized today would surely drown in a sea of garbage. As Theodore Roosevelt observed, "optimism is a good characteristic, but if carried to excess, it becomes foolish."

Many point out that it is what we waste, rather than what we use, of energy supplies that gives reason for alarm. "Strictly speaking we do not have an energy crisis but an oil crisis — and then not a crisis in the availability of oil but in money to pay for it." Politics, too, intervene in the supply and demand equation, perhaps even more than the availability of finances. The facts suggest that the people of the biosphere can obtain, process, and utilize enough of the relevant resources to enable the global community to maintain the minimum standards of life, without threatening the "outer limits," if we....

The "if" question remains unanswered, and still has to be treated as an enormous uncertainty. The potential, as well as the dangers, rests with the range of socioeconomic and political policies, and our collective capacity, imagination, and the one key resource — the intellect of man. The intellect of man is not a nonrenewable resource!

Social forces already in operation are forcing this kind of reassessment. (See the selection on the Future of Optimism.) It is increasingly clear that American society, like all societies, cannot continue to develop and prosper if some of its basic value orientations result in the continuation of policies that fail to recognize reality. The conflict between value orientation and social reality has occurred before in the American experience, for example, the clash between interventionism and isolationism in the late 1930s. The old isolationist value orientation was decisively dropped for an interventionist value orientation. Any debate on interventionism after the defeat in South Vietnam in the mid 1970s is simply a matter of *how* the United states should intervene, whether economically, militarily, through an international forum such as the United Nations, or in other ways. Few now advocate a return to an isolationism that worked in the nineteenth century but cannot work today.

FUTURE SHOCK AND PRESENT IMPERATIVES

Alvin Toffler (1970, 1975) cites evidence of changing attitudes and behavior patterns, indicating a new sense of American awareness that planning — in a sense, intervention — is needed at every personal and institutional level of American life. Toffler envisions a new kind of *anticipatory democracy,* restabilizing the social system and avoiding dysfunctional conflicts. He feels that people, through selected interest groups, will influence the social policies of government and industry. He also sees an advanced people-oriented technology emerging that will conserve resources and energy. There will be a trend toward aggregate families, consisting of parents and children with close ties to other families on the basis of previous marriages and multiple marital relations, or more traditional nuclear units in close primary interaction with each other. Toffler summarizes the movements in this direction (1970: 249):

> Minorities experiment; majorities cling to the forms of the past. It is safe to say that large numbers of people will refuse to jettison the conventional idea(s).... They will, no doubt, continue searching for happiness within the orthodox format. Yet, even they will be forced to innovate in the end, for the odds against success may prove overwhelming.

This last comment has many historical antecedents. Descendants of farmers have moved to the cities in this industrial century. The ideal family of five to ten children, dominant for over a century, has been replaced by families of one or two or three children. These are but two of many recent shifts in American value orientation as changing social conditions have caused national reevaluation.

SOCIAL PROGNOSIS A number of social analysts hold that American society is changing enough so that a prognosis of survival is reasonable. As Benjamin DeMott notes in *Surviving the 70's*, "People have come to believe that the character of human experience and human time can be altered: life is ... more pliant than our fathers knew" (1971: 11). Reviewing a number of the issues facing American society, the New York *Times* columnist James Reston observes (1975):

> ... despite the alarming growth of the human race, the shortages of food and fuel and the general derangement of world politics, economics and finances, it is hard to believe that the world is likely to see in these next 25 years anything like the upheavals and disasters of the previous 75.
>
> The things that agitate the United States at present — unemployment, high prices, fuel shortages, inflation, the inequality of women, feeble leadership and a general distrust in its institutions — are all correctable.

This view of a long respected, hard-nosed analytic reporter of world events points up one long-held American value orientation that we shall have to call upon as we face the challenges before us. This is the optimistic belief that human problems can be solved by human effort. As Eleanor Roosevelt said (1964: 19, 129):

> It is my conviction that there is almost no area of life which we cannot transform according to our own desires, if we want something badly enough, if we have faith in it, and if we work for it with all our hearts ... [but] ... before we can meet successfully ... the challenge of tomorrow, we must learn to think freshly, to re-examine our beliefs, to see how many of them are living and real.... *We cannot deny that the choice is to be made. We must not forget that the choice must be made now.* [Italics in original.]

Some newly emerging ideas about social change may help move our society toward a future of stability and ongoing development. Let us consider some of these ideas.

BEYOND SURVIVAL

The problems confronting American and world society are so pervasive and so serious that what Martin Weinberg and Earl Rubington (1973) call *the sociology of solutions* will probably engage the attention of sociologists even more than in the past. This is a venture based on the possible, if not necessarily probable, resolution of society's most pressing problems. The increasing sociological focus on the future makes it necessary for sociological analysts to break away from the habit of perceiving the nature and direction of social change in the context of the present.

Social change is so broad and happens so fast that the existing social context can shift quickly and radically. An American now in her or his seventies (a normal life span) has lived through both a predominantly rural and a predominantly urban society, a nation at peace and at war, economic depression and unprecedented prosperity. Accompanying these extremes have been periods of both weak and intense social *conflict**. Perhaps the emphasis of sociologists in the past on an ahistorical (here and now) point of view has led to too much emphasis on conflict. Weinberg and Rubington point out the implications of this emphasis on what they call order–accommodation theories (1973: 308–309):

As society moves closer to crisis, conflict theory becomes more popular.... Under conditions of decreased social conflict, however, order theory becomes more popular.

(Recall the discussion of conflict in Chapter 8.) Given the recent conflicts in American society, Weinberg and Rubington go on to note (309):

Conflict ideas are close to the ideas of everyday life ... but ... conflict does not provide a basis for cohesive and harmonious relations in a complex, urban–industrial society. Thus, when it comes to establishing routines to cope with social problems on a continuing basis, the conceptions of resocialization and the construction of effective guidelines are more likely to be given attention.

The stress on conflict has been close to the ideas of everyday life. From the mid 1950s to the mid 1970s, such issues as civil rights, war in Southeast Asia, government corruption, urban civil disorders, environmental pollution, vulnerability to international cartels in control of needed raw materials, and economic recession have increased the emphasis upon conflict theory. With this in mind, it is useful to review the opening comment in Alvin Gouldner's influential *The Coming Crisis of Western Sociology* (see Chapter 14), which summarizes the influence of recent conflicts on theories about where the social system is heading (1970: vii):

Social theorists today work within a crumbling social matrix of paralyzed urban centers and battered campuses. Some may put cotton in their ears, but their bodies still feel the shock waves. It is no exaggeration to say that we theorize today within the sound of guns. The old order has the picks of a hundred rebellions thrust into its hide.

RECONCILING CONSENSUS AND CONFLICT THEORIES It is possible to reconcile Weinberg and Rubington's order and consensus theories with Gouldner's conflict theory. Conflict theorists point to the new order that social conflict can engender in modern democratic society. James Vander Zanden argues that (1972: 160)

... a multiplicity of conflicts between large numbers of differing groups within a society (conflicts among racial and ethnic groups, labor vs. business, consumer groups vs. producer groups, business vs. business, etc.) may be conducive to a democratic as opposed to a totalitarian order.

Even conflict, then, can be a part of the move toward a new sense of accommodation. Attaining order in society requires consensus about the need for directed social change.

EXPONENTIAL GROWTH The urgency with which American and world society faces the problem of survival is underscored by the exponential growth of social change induced by technology. *Exponential growth** is the process by which increases proceed at a geometric rather than arithmetic rate (2, 4, 8, 16, 32, rather than 2, 4, 6, 8, 10), much as in Thomas Malthus's projection of population growth (see Chapter 11). Geometric increases are evident in production, pollution, population, scientific findings, energy release, urbanization, and speeds of travel and communication, among other things (see Figure 15-1). The enormous strain on people and institutions to respond effectively to these exponential rates of change is a central influence on the current state of society.

We referred earlier to the growing receptivity to change in such fundamental areas as minority relations, labor–management relations, and government responsibility for health and education. Established political, economic, civil rights, religious, and other organizations will have to bring their influence to bear in order to accomplish planned changes.

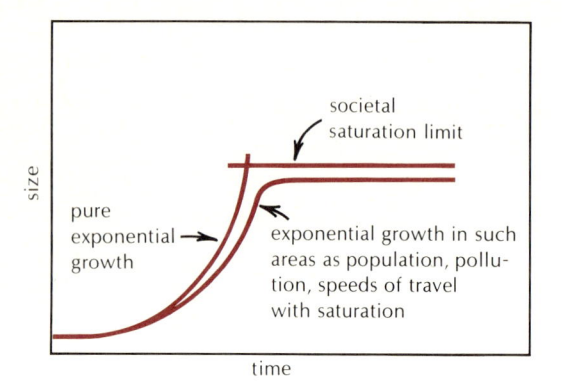

Figure 15-1 An exponential growth curve. SOURCE: Adapted with permission from Derek De Solla Price, *Science Since Babylon* (New Haven, Conn.: Yale University Press, 1961), p. 116.

CHARACTERISTICS OF ADAPTABLE ORGANIZATIONS Once existing and new organizations take up specific issues like air and water pollution or increased job opportunities for hard-pressed groups — or general issues, such as urban renewal or participation in international forums to work out global issues peacefully — they create a social basis for planning based on coordinated activities of informed citizens. Characteristics of organizations in which change can be induced are summarized by George Fairweather.[4]

1. Organizations have varying capacities to adopt new practices. Some organizations are changeable and some are not. Indentification of those organizations that can be changed is the first step in producing the adoption of an innovation.

2. An adopting group that is dissatisfied with current institutional practices and seeks change must be located within a changeable organization. Outsiders probably can rarely produce change without the help of such an inside group.

3. Active, intense efforts to produce adoption will yield higher rates of acceptance than written, verbal, or other inactive techniques.

4. The active effort to achieve adoption must be continuous throughout the adoption process.

5. An outside action consultant, working with the inside group, is usually necessary for adoption. His role involves keeping the group intact and motivated and the members' behavior directed toward adoption.

6. Institutions that involve many persons within organizations in the change process have a higher probability of adopting than those that involve few.

7. The more workers who are involved, the more likely that the adoption will occur.

8. The administrators of an institution usually play the role of gatekeeper, not of change agents. They can deny but they cannot create change. Thus, democratic leaders who encourage the participation of others in the decision-making process help create a social atmosphere that promotes change.

9. As information about the adoption diffuses to other organizations that initially did not adopt the innovation, non-adopters will begin to adopt when the pressure to conform becomes sufficiently strong.

10. Efforts at implementing an innovation should be national or international in scope. Such a broad approach creates a large population of persons or institutions that can adopt new practices and thus creates the possibility of identifying high-probability adopters.

These characteristics of organizations capable of change assume a belief in responsive organizational interaction. For exmple, a civil rights organization such as the NAACP might attempt to pressure a number of large corporations to institute

---

[4] Fairweather, George W., *Social Change: The Challenge to Survival.* © 1972 General Learning Corporation, General Learning Press, Morristown, N.J.

equal employment opportunity for blacks. Some corporations are more receptive than others to minority employment opportunity changes, as well as being strategic targets for civil rights pressures. Once change is instituted successfully within these corporations, pressures are produced both within them and on other corporations to adopt similar changes.

MICRODECISIONS AND MACRODECISIONS

Fairweather is, in effect, showing how microdecisions can affect macrodecisions in society (Harman, 1972: 2). *Microdecisions** are made by individuals, corporations, and government agencies in the normal course of their self-interested activities. *Macrodecisions** can be cumulative decisions, based on those made at micro levels, that influence the overall society, such as the rate of economic expansion or contraction, and the levels of air and water pollution. Both survival and wished-for futures are related, of course, to the ability to control significant problems. We have come to the point in industrial society where pursuit of uncontrolled self-interest at the micro level can produce debilitating social effects such as these listed by the 1972 White House Conference on the Industrial World Ahead (Harman, 1972: 4):

The tragedy of the commons. Microdecisions regarding use of resources (land, air, water, fuels, minerals) are reasonable from the viewpoint of corporate management and stockholders but result in macrodecisions of resource depletion, environmental degradation, urban crowding, which are unsatisfactory to society at large. (See also Chapter 10.)

Unintended technological impact.[5] Even with technology assessment, we do not know how to preserve market macrodecision-making regarding technological innovations and still achieve satisfactory macrodecisions about technological unemployment, quality of the environment, infringements on human rights, interference with natural recycling processes, and resource depletion.

Alienation. Individual, corporate, and government decisions are widely believed to have been guided by such principles as economic growth as a self-justifying end, "the business of business is business," the affluent society, the underdeveloped world as a supplier of raw materials for that affluent society, and the technological imperative that any technology that can be developed and applied should be — and that this fact is leading the world toward an intolerable future. Further, individuals feel themselves forced by pressures of the system to act in ways that they perceive as neither what they want to do nor what would be to the general social good. The result is a serious alienation from the society and its institutions.

COORDINATING INDIVIDUALS AND ORGANIZATION In sum, the conference pointed to the damaging results of the continued normative operation of contemporary American industrial society. The movement toward a post-industrial society (Bell, 1967; Toffler, 1970, 1975) in which the normal operation of the system will enrich life and opportunities for individuals, is perhaps plausible if such a movement follows from the most influential social forces now operating within society. Utopian schemes and isolated individual efforts are unlikely to succeed. What is needed is coordination between the efforts of informed individuals and those of enlightened organizations. It is likely that large, privately owned and managed corporations

---

[5] Recall here the concepts of *manifest aims** and *latent consequences** discussed in Chapter 1.

will continue to be the dominant economic institutions, and they will greatly influence the prospects for and stability of other institutions such as the family and education.

If this proves true, then what are the chances of major changes in corporate values that will provide a stable social base for continuity and innovation in other areas of life? In assessing the possible shift in cultural values to a greater concern for the welfare of individuals, Willis Harman argues the practicality of achieving humanistic capitalism to bring social changes to solve modern dilemmas and give the society a new future in which microdecisions will increasingly benefit macrodecisions (1972: 7):

The public can exert tremendous power through engaging in political buying, stock purchase, and job seeking, favoring those corporations of whose operative values they approve. Thus the balance could easily shift to where it is the corporations that display serious social responsibility, which have the competitive advantage, not the reverse. Requirements for effective functioning of large, complex systems naturally support such values as personal honesty, openness (to ensure accurate information flow); responsibility (hence self-actualization); and cooperative trust. The values required in the team that puts a man on the moon and gets him back are a far cry from those that suffice for operation of a used-car lot. Thus as the production and service tasks of the society become more complex, humane values become not only moral but also functional imperatives. As such institutions as industrial conglomerates, multinational corporations, and international labor unions, not directly accountable to the public, become larger and more powerful relative to representative governments, their operative goals have to become more congruent with those of the overall society — else the goals of the society will become distorted toward those of the dominant institutions. Thus, political pressure will urge corporate goals toward personal fulfillment of participants, public good, and social responsibility.

Can all this be accomplished? Can American society develop the perspective and social mechanisms to rehumanize its institutions, social life, and the basis for a continuing central focus on the individual? Erich Fromm is hopeful (1966: 250):

Prophecies of doom are heard today with increasing frequency. While they have the important function of drawing attention to the dangerous possibilities in our present situation they fail to take into account the promise which is implied in ... human ... achievement in the natural sciences, in psychology, in medicine and in art. Indeed, these achievements portray the presence of strong productive forces which are not compatible with the picture of a decaying culture. Our period is a period of transition ... an end and a beginning, pregnant with possibilities.

We must remember that we decide our future either actively or passively. Both sociologists and lay persons have opportunities not only to see and foresee problems but to see and foresee solutions. The coming years will provide plenty of problems and plenty of discouraging words. Vested interests will frustrate efforts at reform and improvement. The unanticipated consequences of solution-making may beget still other problems. But where people believe there is hope, they act accordingly.

Where there is life, there is hope. It can reasonably be said that after two centuries of independent national existence, American society continues to exhibit a good deal of life. Is it too much to wonder whether there may also be something in the converse proposition: that where hope is vigorous there may also continue to be life?

SUMMARY

Just as fearful assessments of the future call for use of the sociological imagination, so do hopeful assessments. There are good reasons to be hopeful about the future of American society. Our society is by nature flexible. Contemporary evidence of flexibility and adaptability includes our willingness to face domestic and international conflict. The values of the *contraculture** of the 1960s in such areas as new forms of interpersonal and intergroup relations seem less radical in the 1970s.

The sociology of the future as a field of study developed in the 1920s and declined in the crisis years of depression, war, and cold war that followed. The nature of future-oriented studies can be discussed in Alvin Toffler's terms of possibilities, probabilities, preferences, and policies.

In the nineteenth century, John Stuart Mills, in *On Liberty,* explored the need to take into account and harness the impersonal, bureaucratic forces that characterize modern economic and government processes. We reviewed the basic American value orientations, as summarized by Robin Williams, in the context of modern challenges; and we discussed Benjamin DeMott's theme that people have increasingly come to believe that the character of human experience and human time can be altered.

Earl Rubington's and Martin Weinberg's thesis of the sociology of solutions suggests a variety of proposals for stabilizing and further developing democratic American institutional capabilities while meeting and resolving current and emerging problems. In particular, conflict can be part of the process of achieving a new sense of accommodation.

We noted the necessity of coming to terms with *exponential growth**, and we explored the nature of *microdecisions** and *macrodecisions** needed to resolve a variety of social dilemmas and the relationship of individual efforts and enlightened organizational actions.

QUESTIONS FOR DISCUSSION

1. To what extent is the sociology of the future similar to nonsociological considerations about the future — in personal, business, religious, or other terms?

2. Is Charles Reich's list of humanistic values attainable as a new, normative style of American life? Whether attainable or not, do you believe that most people in the society would hold his views to be desirable?

3. In Robin Williams' list of the value orientations in American society, which ones appear most conducive to flexible social change? What contradictions do you find?

4. What implications are there for Americans in the convergent world trends delineated by Wilbert Moore?

5. On what grounds does Willis Harmon argue that no clear distinction can be made between macrodecisions and microdecisions in modern society?

6. Review your understanding of the following terms and concepts:

the sociology of the future

value orientations

exponential growth

microdecisions

macrodecisions

REFERENCES

1970 "The American family: future uncertain." Time (December 28): 34–39.

1976 "Is there any future in futurism?" Time (May 17): 51–52.

Bartlett, John
1955 Bartlett's Familiar Quotations. Boston: Little, Brown.

Bell, Daniel
    1955   "The study of the future." The Public Interest I (Fall): 119–130.
    1967   "Notes on the post-industrial society." The Public Interest (Winter): 24–35, and (Spring): 102–118.

Commager, Henry Steele
    1973   "A bicentennial question: what happened to creativity?" The Arizona Republic (July 15).

Cantril, Hadley
    1938   "The prediction of social events." Journal of Abnormal and Social Psychology 33: 364–389.

DeMott, Benjamin
    1971   Surviving the 70's. New York: Penguin.

Edwards, John
    1967   "The disutility of utopias." The American Sociologist 2: 165–168.

Fairweather, George
    1972   Social Change: The Challenge to Survival. Morristown, N.J.: General Learning Press.

Feinberg, Gerald
    1969   The Prometheus Project. New York: Anchor.

French, David
    1971   "After the fall." The New York Times Magazine (October 3): 20–36.

Fromm, Erich
    1956   Man for Himself. New York: Bantam.
    1968   The Heart of Man. New York: Holt, Rinehart and Winston.

Gilbert, G.M.
    1951   "Stereotype persistence and change among college students." Journal of Abnormal and Social Psychology 28: 245–254.

Gold, Bertram
    1975   A Time for Reassessment: Annual Report of the Executive Vice-President. (May 1). 8 pp. New York. Institute of Human Relations.

Gordon, Leonard
    1973   "The fragmentation of literary stereotypes of Jews and Negroes among college students." Pacific Sociological Review 16: 411–425.

Gouldner, Alvin
    1970   The Coming Crisis of Western Sociology. New York: Equinox.

Harman, Willis
    1972   A Look at Business in 1990: A Summary of the White House Conference on the Industrial World Ahead. Washington, D.C. Government Printing Office. 9 pp.

Hopkins, Frank
    1967   "The United States in the year 2000: a proposal for the study of the future." The American Sociologist 2: 149–150.

Huber, Bettina and Wendell Bell
    1971   "Sociology and the emergent study of the future." The American Sociologist 6: 287–295.

Israeli, Nathan
    1930   "Some aspects of the social psychology of futurism." Journal of Abnormal and Social Psychology 25: 121–132.

Karlins, M., T. Coffman and G. Walters
    1969   "On the fading of social stereotypes." Journal of Personality and Social Psychology 13: 1–16.

Katz, D. and K. W. Broly
    1933   "Racial stereotypes of 100 college students." Journal of Abnormal and Social Psychology 23: 280–290.

Killian Lewis
    1968   The Impossible Revolution? New York: Random House.

Marx, Karl
- 1969 Capital (first edition 1859). New York: International Publishers.

McGregor, Douglas
- 1938 "The major determinants of the prediction of social events." Journal of Abnormal and Social Psychology 33: 179-204.

Mill, John Stuart
- 1947 On Liberty (original 1859). New York: Appleton-Century-Crofts.

Mills, C. Wright
- 1956 The Power Elite. New York: Oxford University Press.

Moore, Wilbert
- 1966 "The utility of utopias." American Sociological Review 31: 765-772.

- 1974 The Official Associated Press Almanac. Maplewood, N.J.: Hammond Almanac, Inc.

Price, Derek De Solla
- 1961 Science Since Babylon. New Haven, Conn.: Yale University Press.

Reich, Charles
- 1971 The Greening of America. New York: Bantam.

Reston, James
- 1975 "Whatever the last quarter century brings, we'll survive it." The New York Times (January 24).

Roosevelt, Eleanor
- 1964 Tomorrow Is Now. New York: Harper and Row.

Ross, H. Lawrence
- 1968 Perspectives on the Social Order. New York: McGraw-Hill.

Sawyer, John
- 1974 "The era now ending can be said to have begun five centuries ago." The New York Times (December 30).

Simmons, J. L. and Barry Winograd
- 1967 It's Happening. North Hollywood, Cal.: Brandon House.

Spekke, Andrew
- 1976 "The future of optimism." Intellect (May/June): 605.

Tocqueville, Alexis de
- 1960 Democracy in American Society. New York: Knopf.

Toffler, Alvin
- 1969 "Value impact forecaster — a profession of the future." K. Baier and N. Rescher (eds.), Values and the Future. New York: The Free Press: 1-30.
- 1970 Future Shock. New York: Bantam.
- 1975 The Eco-Spasm Report. New York: Bantam.

Vander Zanden, James
- 1972 American Minority Relations. New York: The Ronald Press.

Waskow, Arthur
- 1966 From Race Riot to Sit-In. Garden City, N.Y.: Doubleday.

Weinberg, Martin and Earl Rubington
- 1973 The Solution of Social Problems. New York: Oxford University Press.

Wells, H. G.
- 1933 The Shape of Things to Come. New York: Macmillan.

Williams, Robin
- 1970 American Society. New York: Knopf.

Yinger, Milton
- 1960 "Contraculture and subculture." American Sociological Review 25: 625-635.

Appendix A

CAPSULE VIEW OF THE HISTORY OF SOCIOLOGICAL ANALYSIS

Sociological analysis has come from two primary sources: from social philosophers and from applied practitioners interested in the social policy problems of their day.

The discussion in Chapter 1 notes the modern beginning of sociology in the nineteenth century. However, the subject matter of sociology is evident in the earliest of biblical and other historical writings. The desert wanderings of the formerly enslaved Hebrews were predicated upon Moses's awareness that resocialization was needed to develop a new free society. Aristotle's writings take up the issue of equality and inequality in the treatment of citizens and the effects of one or the other upon the stability of ancient Greek society. In more recent history, in America, the delegates to the Constitutional Convention in 1787 debated many sociological issues, such as the effects of centralized or decentralized government authority on society and how various conflicting social movements (such as those for free trade versus those for restricted trade and those in favor of general voting franchise versus those in favor of franchise only for the propertied) could be accommodated within one governing social system. The efforts of researchers to provide insights into these and related questions are part of the ongoing American social experiment. This is the substance of much sociological analysis.

It is this emphasis upon research that brings us back to the nineteenth-century beginnings of the field. Like the early social philosophers, the founders of sociology advanced many propositions about the nature of society, but in doing so, they attempted to research empirically the validity of their theories. This list of sociologists and their theories offers only a thumbnail sketch of the history of the field. It does give some historical perspective on the nature and scope of sociological theory and research.

AUGUSTE COMTE: SOCIAL STATICS AND SOCIAL DYNAMICS

Auguste Comte's *The Positive Philosophy* (written between 1830 and 1840 in six volumes) represents the beginning of modern sociology. Comte (1798–1857) was influenced by such writers of the Enlightenment as Montesquieu, Rousseau, and Voltaire and their emphasis upon rationality and humanism. They, in turn, had been influenced by early Greek Athenian philosophers. Like Plato and Aristotle, Comte perceived of society as having rational and positive potential. He conceived of positivism as the historical process by which society advances beyond a theological stage and a metaphysical stage into a modern, positive, scientific stage in which humans actively control their society and their individual destiny. Comte believed that society consists of statics, which constitute structural organization, and dynamics, which constitute the functional processes of society.

In addition, Comte emphasized the need to evaluate the structures and functions of society on the basis of observation and experience rather than through philosophical speculation. It was this emphasis on research, even more than Comte's theories of society, that gave rise to modern sociology.

GRAND THEORIES: SOCIAL DARWINISM, ECONOMIC DETERMINISM, AND GRAND MODIFICATIONS

The first sociological theories advanced after Comte's day were closer to earlier social philosophical approaches than to those of empirical research, characteristic of a scientific discipline. Two prominent theoretical schools that developed by the mid-nineteenth century were *social Darwinism* and *economic determinism*. Herbert Spencer (1820–1903) was the leading social Darwinist. In his *Principles of Sociology* (three volumes), Spencer applied Charles Darwin's biological thesis of the survival of the fittest to human society. While Spencer emphasized the stability of society, Karl Marx (1818–1883) addressed himself to what he conceived of as the inherent conflict and instability of society, at least until achieving a final synthesis in which society becomes classless. Marx's *Das Kapital* provides an economic interpretation of society predicated on inherent conflict in industrial society between the bourgeois managing class and the proletarian working class.

By the early twentieth century, sociological theorists were still advancing grand theories about society but were beginning to heed Comte's admonition to engage in empirical research to test theories. Two prominent theorists of the day were Max Weber (1864–1920) and Emile Durkheim (1858–1917). Weber's *The Protestant Ethic and the Rise of Capitalism* employed the historical method used by Comte to demonstrate the influence of religious and other institutions on social dynamics in addition to the economic influences highlighted in Marxian theory. Durkheim in *Suicide* and other works used empirical data to test the influence of various forms of collective consciousness on individual behavior. Along with the efforts of George Simmel (1858–1918), Gustave Le Bon (1841–1931), Vilfredo Pareto (1848–1923), and other analysts at the turn of the century, Durkheim's and Weber's works marked a movement toward testing sociological theories.

THE CHICAGO SCHOOL: URBAN ECOLOGY AND GROWING EMPIRICISM

In the early twentieth century, most sociological contributions were made by Americans. The early flowering of American sociology took place at the University of Chicago. The Chicago school has a long and influential history. Beginning with the leadership of Lester Ward (1841–1913) and Albion Small (1854–1926), the Chicago school established the first academic sociology department and, in 1895, began *The American Journal of Sociology*. In the May 1916 issue, Small published a valuable contribution to the history of American sociology, in his article "Fifty Years of Sociology in the United States." Small's *General Sociology* and other works, and Ward's in his *Pure Sociology* and *Applied Sociology* represented the shift of research efforts in sociology away from grand theory (such as Spencer's social Darwinism and Marx's economic determinism) toward more limited testable theoretical approaches and also toward increasing concern with applied research designed to alleviate social problems.

The Chicago school produced substantive contributions to the field, particularly to the analysis of urban life. By the 1920s, the city of Chicago was being used as a social laboratory. Research-based theories developed about the nature of urbanism, minority status, and other concerns of modern society. Robert Park (1864–1944) and Ernest Burgess (1886–1966) developed the specialized field of human ecology. In their book *The City*, Park and Burgess advanced the concentric zone theory of urban development, which, in modified form, is still being tested (see Chapter 10).

A number of Chicago school sociologists became presidents of the American Sociological Association, including Lester Ward (1911), Albion Small (1914), Robert Park (1925), Ernest Burgess (1934), and Louis Wirth (1944). In the process, the Chicago school helped nurture the development of the national association that began *The American Sociological Review* in 1936, the most widely subscribed of the many research journals now in the field.

ADVANCES IN RESEARCH METHODS AND DATA TREATMENT

Sociologists at Chicago and other academic centers of sociological research — notably Michigan, Columbia, and Berkeley — began to devise new methods of gathering data to test theories. Quantitative methods emerged as a way to assess many aspects of a mass urban society. Survey centers were developed by mid century to collect samples about every area of social life (recall here the research specialties in the field noted in Chapter 1). The large amount of data on social attitudes and behavior patterns in society led to advances in the use and employment of statistical techniques and models to assist in interpreting data. Paul Lazarsfeld (1901–1976) was a leading methodologist who brought into focus methodological issues of the field in his *The Language of Social Research* and other works. The development of new statistical procedures and the employment of computer technology in recent years has led to further advances in analyzing complex sets of data. Procedures such as multiple regression and path analysis are now used to analyze limited research questions (such as what combination of factors best explains student achievement) and more comprehensive research questions (such as what combination of factors best explains community conflict or community consensus formation).

The ultimate task of all these methodological research technique advances is to assist in the development of more valid explanatory and predictive sociological theories. It is to the current state of sociological theory that we now turn.

SOCIOLOGY TODAY

The grand theories of the nineteenth century were significant but rudimentary efforts at social analysis. Partly in reaction to this approach, sociologists in the first half of the twentieth century often emphasized data collection and techniques of statistical analysis. This was the case to such an extent that many research efforts of that period did little to advance a basic or an applied theoretical understanding about social behavior. While this is a continuing problem, since about mid century, a group of middle-range theorists began to attempt a synthesis between grand (macro) theory (like Spencer's) and limited (micro) theory (like Burgess's) as well as between basic and applied (often problems-oriented) theory. Perhaps the clearest explanation of this synthesizing approach is given by Robert Merton (1910-   ) in his *Social Theory and Social Structure*.

Past and recent sociological theorizing and research have produced several models of society. Each model is thought by some sociologists to provide more valid insights and knowledge about people and society than others. Three of the most influential models can be categorized as *consensus, conflict,* and *process* models, listed in the order of their emergence since Comte's day. The consensus model emphasizes the persistence of shared values and stable institutionalized processes. Talcott Parson's *The Social System* is the most comprehensive statement of the consensus perspective, which rests upon a structural-functional interpretation along the lines advanced by Durkheim. The conflict model holds that the most consequential aspect of society is the inherent power struggle between dominant and subordinant groups. Ralf Dahrendorf's *Class and Class Conflict in Industrial Society* presents a systematic analysis of the major elements in the conflict model, which draws heavily upon Marxian ideas of economic class conflict. The process model shifts the focus away from structure and group conflict toward the individual and his or her social behavior. The process theorists hold that all social meaning is determined by the symbolic meaning given to any occurrence. A summary analysis of the process model is offered in Herbert Blumer's *Symbolic Interactionism,* which highlights the influence of reference groups upon a person's definition and reaction to a social situation. The differences between the consensus, conflict, and process models can be summarized in the following manner:

CONSENSUS MODEL

1. Society is held together by consensus of values and stable institutionalized forms of social life.

2. The social system is composed of well-integrated and interdependent parts.

3. The actions of individuals and of groups are based upon functional needs to keep the social system in a state of cohesive equilibrium.

4. The institutionalized structures and functional prerequisites of the social system result in pressure upon individuals to adopt and follow a given set of values that are predominant over conflict issues or individual variations.

CONFLICT MODEL

1. Society is characterized by the domination of some groups by others who are in a state of change-producing conflict.

2. Any temporary appearance of consensus is transitory; dissent and conflict will reemerge.

3. The coercion some members of the society experience contributes to the ultimate disintegration of the system as it exists and results in change.

4. By focusing upon conflicting groups rather than allegedly stable social structures or individualized social behavior, it is possible to determine how power shifts in society and the nature of emerging change.

PROCESS MODEL

1. Society is made up of individuals who interact and communicate with each other.

2. Through the process of symbolic interaction, people make sense of social situations.

3. The individual responds to the social world based upon the meaning he or she places upon her or his own acts and on the acts of others.

4. By focusing upon the individual rather than on institutionalized structural forms or conflicting groups, it is possible to determine the ways in which individuals sustain or change their social environment.

The images of society provided by the conflict, consensus, and process models are not mutually exclusive. In fact, all societies are characterized in differing degrees by some form of stable institutionalized structures and integrated functions, by inherent conflicts generated by social and natural environmental phenomena, and by an interaction process whereby individuals modify their social environment. Sociologists employ all three models and variations of them. The particular social situation of a society determines which perspective will provide most insights into the system's social dynamics, which Comte considered the most important part of sociology.[1]

---

[1] One further note: The May 1977 issue of *The American Sociologist* contained an article that rekindles an old "nature-nurture" argument that has been brewing in the field for six or seven years. A few analysts, including Lee Ellis, Arthur Jensen, and the biosociologist E. O. Wilson, are taking the position that most human behavior can be explained on the basis of genetic makeup rather than social and environmental influences. This view is generally rejected by most social scientists. However, given the attention that biosociologists have gained (recall the mass media coverage of Jensen's thesis, published in the Winter 1969 issue of the *Harvard Educational Review*, that blacks and whites score differently on IQ tests because of heredity rather than environment), it is likely that in future textbooks some critical attention will need to be given to them, if only to explain why their theories have not been generally accepted in the social science community.

Appendix B

SOCIOLOGICAL RESEARCH USE OF THE SCIENTIFIC METHOD

Discussing his admiration for Jeremy Bentham's contributions to science, the nineteenth-century English philosopher John Stuart Mill observed that (1952: 487):

If we were asked to say ... what we conceive to be Bentham's place among ... great benefactors of humanity.... It was not his opinions ... but his method.

Mill disagreed with much of what Bentham had to say about human behavior for the same reasons many sociologists disagree with founding father Auguste Comte's positivist philosophy. The ideas of Bentham and Comte about human behavior have proved less important in sociology than their emphasis on verifying the facts on which their ideas and the ideas of others about human behavior are based. Verification — or proof — goes beyond the careful empirical techniques of *observation**, *interviews**, and other forms of data collection discussed in Chapter 4. It involves a method of research that increases the likelihood of accuracy and can be independently checked by other investigators. The procedure for verification is the *scientific method**, which uses *experimentation*.

The scientific method is based on a system of logic that goes back to Aristotle's time. The use of this system to verify facts is merely a systematic extension of the common effort to explain what affects and interests us but also may perplex us. As Stuart Chase put it (1951: 177):

The folkways, of course, provide many explanatory theories to order: "It rained because the moon was full." Individuals, however, gather up stray items of experience and formulate their own theories: "The car is knocking because the last filling-station must have sold us some low-grade, watered gasoline."

ELEMENTS OF THE SCIENTIFIC METHOD

To make these explanatory theories scientific, two additional steps must be taken beyond drawing conclusions based on haphazard observation and experience. First, *concepts**, that is, ideas, generalizations, explanations, or statements of belief which have developed over a period of time, must be precisely rephrased as theories or *hypotheses**. And second, these hypotheses must be tested or verified by *controlled experiments** or *systematic observation** (Goode and Hatt, 1952: 41–73).

The Chase excerpt contains concepts, in this case implied beliefs or explanations, about the nature of precipitation and the operation of gasoline engines. Concepts can be very general, like *institutions* and *progress*. Or they may be more limited and specific, like the political concept *democracy* and the value concept *ethnocentrism*. Goode and Hatt point out that concepts are the foundations of all human communication and thought (1952: 43). They represent accumulations of experience in specific areas of interest, and may be built on many bases. Thus, out of superstition come such concepts as spells, curses, and the evil eye; out of religion such concepts as salvation, original sin, forgiveness, and eternal life; out of politics such concepts as sovereignty, popular government, and the right to vote. In sociology, concepts are statements about or descriptions of observed social phenomena.

In any science, concepts must be carefully defined and restated in the form of hypotheses before they can be tested and either verified or disproved. Whether we want to know more about the consequences of such general concepts as social class and primary group relationships or a more focused concept such as the influence of religious beliefs on economic behavior, we must first formulate them into testable hypotheses. The first step in this process is to be sure that all elements in the concept have *operational definitions** that are precise and observable. If you recall the discussion of occupational status of fathers and sons in Chapter 6, you will see that no meaningful comparisons can be made within or among the three countries under study unless the terms used have the same meaning in all three. Thus, if pharmacists or engineers are listed as managerial occupations in one country and professional in another, meaning is bound to become confused. Similarly, occupations listed as skilled, unskilled, and clerical must all be the same. And unless the range covered by high and low occupational status is the same or very nearly the same, no accurate conclusions can be reached.

Once all terms are clear, it is then possible to formulate a testable hypothesis, that is, a statement about the concept that can be shown to be true or false by the results of an experiment or by systematic observation. Hypotheses have been defined as future-oriented statements about the relationship of two or more social phenomena (Goode and Hatt, 1952: 56). In our example, the two social phenomena are the occupational status of fathers and the occupational status of their sons. The *statement*, which links and expresses a relationship between these two phenomena, is the idea *that they are likely to be the same* — that sons tend to follow in their fathers' footsteps. Thus: "*As adults, sons are likely to* be in the same occupational status as were their fathers." This statement is a sentence, it is future-oriented in that it deals with a prediction, and it expresses a presumed relationship that can be tested and proved true or false.

Once all concepts are stated in a clear operational form and a testable hypothesis has been formulated, the stage is set to add to our store of knowledge about human behavior by testing the hypothesis. It may deal with a very limited question, or it may involve a whole culture over generations, like Max Weber's thesis on the Protestant ethic and Gerhard Lenski's on capitalism in a metropolitan area.

Let us use a limited hypothesis by Max Gunther to illustrate in simple form part of the operation of testing a hypothesis. Gunther proposed this hypothesis to the entrepreneurial readers of *Playboy* (1973: 118):

[It is a] reasonable proposition that people get a lot of headaches when their business affairs, love affairs and other affairs are turning sour. Such a period of failure and sore synapsis would expectably be followed by a market collapse. Therefore . . . you can see the market's future by watching the ups and downs of the aspirin business. . . . When aspirin sales and production rise in a given year, the market will drop the following year.

To test this hypothesis, Gunther gathered data from the U.S. Trade Commission on the stock prices of companies producing aspirin over a series of years. He then checked Standard and Poor's composite stock index to see whether the stock market went up or down in the year after each change in the price of aspirin stocks. Table B-1 is the table he drew up to test his hypothesis.

Once data are collected to test a hypothesis, analysis can begin in earnest. In this case the trend supported the hypothesis in every year except 1967, when the stock market went up after aspirin prices

Table B-1   Upward or Downward Trend of Aspirin Sales and the Standard and Poor's Index, 1964-1972[a]

Aspirin sales		Standard and Poor's Index	
Year		Year	Price trend
1964	down	1965	up
1965	up	1966	down
1966	up	1967	up
1967	down	1968	up
1968	up	1969	down
1969	up	1970	down
1970	down	1971	up
1971	down	1972	up

[a] Originally appeared in *Playboy* Magazine; copyright © 1973 by Playboy. Table from "How to Beat the Stock Market by Watching Girls, Counting Aspirin, Checking Sunspots and Wondering Where the Yellow Went" by Max Gunther, April 1973, p. 118.

had gone up in 1966. This deviation indicates the need for caution in accepting the validity of this alleged causal relationship. Perhaps the 1967 variation was produced by chance. Perhaps the time span is too brief to establish a firm trend. Or perhaps the entire hypothesis is inaccurate. It could reasonably be argued that headaches are more likely *to follow* a decline in the market than to precede it. Indeed, if the data in Table B-1 are considered as the basis for a correlation of yearly prices of aspirin stock and the Standard and Poor's average, this thesis is supported in most years — 1966, 1967, 1969, and 1971 — and there is no price differential in the other years. Any such limited testing of a hypothesis is likely to leave out too many important *variables**, that is, factors influencing the behavior being studied. A good deal more research (perhaps involving *multi-variate analysis**, analysis of a number of variables), would be needed before entering the stock market on the evidence presented, interesting as it is.

Yet, this example contains the logical components of the scientific method. It includes an experimental design which involves attempts to control for and isolate the effects of one or more variables on patterns of behavior. The variable could be the effects of economic or other operationally defined troubles on the price of aspirin stock as per Gunther; the impact of Protestantism and other religious beliefs on economic behavior as per Lenski; or the analysis of any other variable that can always be found in the research literature.

TESTING THE ACCURACY OF HYPOTHESES BY EXPERIMENTAL DESIGN

The basic logic of the scientific method for testing the validity of a hypothesis is contained in the classic *experimental design** outlined by John Stuart Mill (1951). Mill called this design the *method of difference**, and showed how it could be employed in the physical and social sciences.

Mill held that, if the elements of one situation — call it X — are the same as for another — Y — *except* for a particular difference — Z — then any observed differences between X and Y can be attributed to Z. In a controlled experiment, Mill's design would involve the use of at least two matched groups having the same basic characteristics, but only one would be exposed to a variable experimental stimulus to measure its effects. Figure B-1 shows Mill's design in diagram form. This is a simplified statement of a complex method capable of many modifications. Yet, this method and its underlying logic are the pattern for much sociological and other scientific research.

One project that employed the design diagramed in Figure B-1 was Harold Gosnell's voting study. Gosnell (1927) matched different voting districts in the Chicago area before the 1924 presidential election (Goode and Hatt, 1952: 95-96) on the basis of such factors as nationality, sex ratio, economic conditions, and stimulus from the political parties. Then one district was designated a *control group**, in which there was no exposure to an assumed causal, or independent, variable (A in Figure B-1). The other group was designated an *experimental group**, which was exposed to an assumed causal variable (B in Figure B-1). In Gosnell's study, the control group, District A, was not given any special stimulus before the election, whereas the experimental group, District B, received mail and other special stimuli to get out the vote. The measurably higher vote in District B, the experimental group, could reasonably be attributed to the added stimulus. To further verify the influence of the stimulus variables, Gosnell matched sets of control districts and experimental districts, and was able not only to average the differences in voter turnout for the two sets but also to check for variation such as occurred in the case of the experiment on aspirin and the stock market.

Gosnell's project was a clear example of applied logic used to verify hypothesized human behavior. Unfortunately for research workers, life is not often that simple. Unlike experiments in the physical sciences, where inanimate phenomena can be analyzed in a controlled laboratory situation, sociologists are generally engaged in research on thinking and feeling human beings, far removed from any such controls. This fact often affects the experimental design in social science.

Figure B-1	Before		After	Results
Control group	A	stimulus "Z" withheld →	A_1	Difference $A_1 - A$
Experimental group	B	stimulus "Z" added →	B_1	Difference = $B_1 - B$

The dangers inherent in research on human behavior, even using the classic experimental design in a relatively controlled setting, are illustrated by the *Hawthorne effect*. Between 1927 and 1932, F. J. Roethlisberger and W. J. Dickson conducted a classic experiment at the Western Electric Company's Hawthorne plant in Chicago (1939). Matched work units in the plant were selected for experimental analysis. One experiment increased the lighting for the experimental units but kept the lighting unchanged for the control units.

The result of this and other experiments was that *both* the control and the experimental units increased their efficiency and productivity. What had happened was that all the workers in the different units felt themselves part of the experiment. The presumed stimulus of changes in lighting and other working conditions proved less stimulating than the latent variable of merely taking part in the experiment. This Hawthorne effect demonstrates the need for great care in checking the independent stimulus in any given observation of human behavior.

Both the Gosnell and the Hawthorne experiments started appropriately with hypotheses that related to testable concepts and a body of theory. Gosnell empirically tested the hypothesis that mail and other communications will positively influence residents in a political district to vote in elections. The Hawthorne project empirically tested the proposition that improved physical stimuli alone will positively affect productivity. In the Hawthorne study, unlike Gosnell's, the communication within a closed organized structure made the experiment itself a prime source of influence. Indeed, this very discovery was a useful finding by *serendipity**, the finding of something valuable that was not sought.

The flaw in the Hawthorne study was not in the scientific method and its logical constructs but in too simplistic an application and analysis of variables. When well used, the method has often proved a useful diagnostic tool in objectively evaluating behavior, even when all *before* and *after* cells (boxes in which data are placed) are not available.

A variation in the classic design that had to leave out the before cells was Samuel Stouffer's World War II survey of American soldiers. This study included an analysis of white soldiers' attitudes about serving in combat units with blacks (1949). The hypothesis to be tested was that black and white soldiers working toward a common goal would result in a greater acceptance by white soldiers of blacks in their units. Since there were some all-white units and some integrated units, there existed, in effect, the after cells in the design for both control and experimental groups; but, since the white soldiers had not been tested on their attitudes before entering the Army, the before cells were missing. Stouffer and his research team assumed that whites generally resisted racial integration, and independent national studies gave supportive evidence of this. A technique to control for the missing data was that white soldiers had been assigned to all-white or to integrated units at random.

This *randomization* process, discussed in Chapter 4, enabled Stouffer to match the white soldiers in different units and to set up the modified experimental design illustrated in Figure B-2.

In this case, the hypothesis was confirmed, since 62 percent of soldiers in all-white units objected to being placed in a racially integrated combat unit, while only 7 percent of white soldiers who were already in such units objected.

Further variations of the classic design provided additional insights into the question of interracial relationships. Stouffer and his associates also found that when white men were in the same division or regiment as blacks but not in the same company, which is the unit of closest interaction, then 23 percent of the white soldiers objected to being

Figure B-2

	Before (not available)		After	Results (% negative attitudes toward integrated units)
Control group	(A)	stimulus (of black soldiers) withheld	A_1	62%
Experimental group	(B)	stimulus (of black soldiers) added	B_1	7%

placed in a racially mixed unit. Figure B-3 shows how this variation would appear in an experimental design.

It may be that this finding does not ultimately uphold the hypothesis. It may be that war is too special a circumstance to draw general conclusions. Indeed, a good deal of additional research is needed on this point, and some conducted by Muzafer and Carolyn Sherif (1953) and others supports Stouffer's findings in other settings. The method employed by Stouffer and others was sound in that it carefully observed and evaluated empirical evidence.

Here, then, are glimpses of some of the basic elements of the scientific method. As Goode and Hatt caution, these are only the first steps (1952:102). The selection of a method of research, whether the classic experimental design or some variation of it — and there are many which are not touched on here — does not guarantee sound results. What it does do is increase the likelihood of getting valid results. In addition to the basic method, some common cautionary steps in interpreting research results will be useful.

SOME CAUTIONARY NOTES ON DATA INTERPRETATION

The assertion of the great nineteenth-century British prime minister Benjamin Disraeli that "there are lies, big lies, and statistics" sums up a major concern of sociologists. As is evident in all the tables in this text, sociologists often use statistical data to present evidence to substantiate some point

Figure B-3

	Before (not available)			After	Results (% negative attitudes toward integrated units)
Control group A	(A)	Stimulus (of black soldiers) withheld		A_1	62%
Experimental group B	(B)	stimulus intensity x (black soldiers in division or regiment but not in company unit)		B_1	23%
Experimental group C	(C)	stimulus intensity 2x (black soldiers in division or regiment and in company units)		C_1	7%

or other. The question here for sociologist and student alike is: How accurate are the statistical and other data collected in giving us a picture of whatever human behavior is being described?

Some problems of interpretation have already been alluded to in Chapter 4 and in this Appendix, particularly with respect to information from the mass media and other sources that are not meant for technical research. In this section, we shall discuss checking research-based information in relation to these four common problem areas: imprecise data, attitude–behavior correlations, oversimple cause-and-effect correlations, and the need to crosscheck data.

THE PROBLEM OF IMPRECISE DATA Remember that one requirement of the scientific method is precision of meaning in collecting and interpreting data. Even such a sound source as the U.S. Census can present problems in this respect. For example, in the 1940 Census, Mexican–American citizens are categorized as nonwhite, whereas in the 1950 Census, they are not. Given this shift in categories — apart from the accuracy of the information — it is difficult to make a trend analysis regarding whites and nonwhites in a variety of economic, educational, and other areas, since several million Americans were arbitrarily placed in one category in one census year and another in another census year.

Perhaps the best, or worst, example of imprecision in data collection used for research purposes is in the curious world of crime statistics. National crime statistics based on various crimes against persons and property are gathered by the Federal Bureau of Investigation (FBI) and presented in an index called the Uniform Crime Report (UCR). According to the UCR index, crime in the United States in the decade between 1960 and 1970 increased from approximately 2 million to approximately 5.5 million offenses, or by 176 percent (1970 UCR, 1971: Table 2). This reported increase in crime was considerably greater than the increase in population growth. Or was it? In reality, the UCR index is based on statistics that are highly suspect as sound sources of consistent and accurate data.

There has been a basic problem with UCR data that illustrates the weakness of relying on data that are imprecise and not systematically collected at the source. The source of most crime data is the information gathered from local police departments. The FBI's UCR format for reporting specific crimes against persons and property was not adopted by most local departments until the 1960s. Before that, each department used its own system for categorizing crimes. When a number of city departments began to adapt to the UCR, what happened to the crime rate over the next year or two is

Table B-2 Reporting System Changes — Uniform Crime Report Index Figures Not Comparable with Prior Years

Name of city	Years of increase (first year pre-UCR index)	Amount of increase from	to	Index offenses percent increase
Baltimore	1964–1965	18,637	26,193	40.5
Buffalo	1961–1963	4,779	9,305	94.7
Chicago	1959–1960	56,570	97,235	71.9
Cleveland	1963–1964	10,584	17,154	63.0
Indianapolis	1961–1962	7,416	10,926	47.3
Kansas City, Mo.	1959–1961[a]	4,344	13,121	202.0
Memphis	1963–1964	8,781	11,533	31.3
Miami	1963–1964	10,750	13,610	26.6
Nashville	1962–1963	6,595	9,343	41.7
Shreveport	1962–1963	1,898	2,784	46.7
Syracuse	1963–1964	3,365	4,527	34.5

[a] No report was published for Kansas City in 1960.

SOURCE: "Uniform Crime Reports," 1959–1965 in the *Challenge of Crime in a Free Society* (Washington, D.C.: United States Printing Office, 1967), p. 25.

graphically demonstrated in Table B-2. Did the crime rate in Buffalo really go up 94.7 percent between 1961 and 1963? Was there really a 41.7 percent increase in Nashville between 1962 and 1963? Did the citizens of Kansas City face a 202 percent crime increase between 1959 and 1961? One could have reasonable doubts. What happened is that the number of *reported* crimes went up but not necessarily the actual number of crimes.

Consider the kinds of outside factors that could influence the UCR index: the more general use of a systematic reporting form; police personnel better trained in reporting specifically defined crimes; with more reported crime, more political pressure to increase well-trained police forces, who locate more crimes, which then show up in larger figures. The problem of accurate interpretation and reporting of data may relate to specific kinds of crimes as well. When the Los Angeles *Times* reported that rape increased in Los Angeles during the first three months in 1973 in sharp contrast to a dramatic drop in the city's overall crime rate (June 30, 1973), one should ask whether this was a real or a reported increase. With the greater frankness about sex, combined with the stress on female assertiveness by women's liberation groups, it may be that a crime that has generally gone unreported (Clinard, 1963:20) is now more likely to be reported. The old value that the victim is ashamed (Ellis, 1961:171) of being a victim no longer inhibits reporting of this kind of assault.

It is no wonder that the former attorney general Elliot Richardson observed that "we have no mechanism in place for measuring the volume of crime committed" (Associated Press, August 6, 1973). The point here is not to make light of crime, nor is it to dismiss the possibility of getting accurate data. Crime data are one kind of widely used statistic that needs special care in interpretation. This means considering how the data were collected and what outside influences may have affected the reporting process.

There are common problems in the accurate collection of data even when trained researchers are collecting it. Misunderstanding and misinterpretation can occur between researchers and those being investigated. Do the data mean what one thinks they do? To help answer this question, researchers commonly use a *pretest**, a preliminary check of the data to be collected. If the Hawthorne plant researchers had used an effective pretest, they might not have ended up measuring the effects of their own experiment rather than the stimuli they thought they were measuring. In interview research, the pretest is a tryout of the questionnaire to see how it works and whether changes are necessary before the start of the full-scale study (Selltiz, 1963:550).

This investigator and an associate found out how valuable a pretest can be in a study designed to test the images held by college students of various American racial and ethnic groups including Indians (for partial results see: Gordon and Hudson, 1970). In a pretest, it was discovered that most students thought that Indians referred to natives of India. While this was a useful serendipitous finding that would have implications for other research, the questionnaire was revised to specify American Indians. As this case suggests, the pretest also demonstrates why empirical research is necessary. Often it is not possible to figure ahead of time what people will do or say.

THE PROBLEM OF ATTITUDE-BEHAVIOR CORRELATIONS Even when research is reported accurately, there may be a problem in accurate interpretation. Given limited time and resources, researchers rely in part on expressed attitudes of people secured from such techniques as *interview schedules** and *questionnaires**, discussed in Chapter 4. The interpretation problem is to determine how closely people's *expressed attitudes* parallel their *actual behavior*, which is, after all, what counts in the long run.

Some researchers (see Ehrlich, 1969; Westie, 1953) feel that expressed attitudes provide enough insight into the actions people will take to make such research sociologically worthwhile. Others (see Deutscher, 1973; La Pierre, 1934) hold that expressed attitudes are so often not related to the way people actually behave that researchers ought to concentrate only on measurable behavior. Still other researchers (see De Fleur and Westie, 1958; Merton, 1949) have attempted to specify the conditions under which attitude–behavior correlations are positive, or close together, and when they are negative, or far apart.

One check on attitude–behavior correlations can be made in the research process itself. The technique specified by De Fleur and Westie (1958) advocates using questions on both attitudes and behavior. For example, white students in one experiment by Harold Gilliken (De Fleur and Westie, 1958:72) were asked how willing they were to interact with blacks who held similar occupational aspirations and had similar educational backgrounds. Respondents with a high acceptance response were then asked the following questions about behavior:

I will pose for a photograph . . . with a Negro person of the opposite sex with the following restrictions on its use:

I will allow this photograph to be used only in laboratory experiments where it will be seen only by professional sociologists.

   Signed _____

I will allow this photograph to be shown to hundreds of university students as a teaching aid in sociology classes.

   Signed _____

I will allow this photograph to be published in my home town newspaper as part of a publicity report on this research.

   Signed _____

The results confirmed the need to specify the conditions under which attitudes and behavior correlate. On the last question, most students who had said they were willing to interact with blacks were not willing to have a photo of themselves with a black student of the opposite sex published in their hometown newspaper.

This check determines the consistency of the responses. The next question to be investigated is: Why are some people inconsistent in what they say and what they do? De Fleur and Westie point out that intervening social variables affect how willing individuals are likely to be in acting out their personal views. For example, they note the influence of our reference groups, our *significant others** discussed in Chapter 2, on the direction of people's behavior. The students who accepted blacks in their values but rejected overt association were operating under the same kind of influences that worked upon Captain Anson Mills after he killed the mother of a three-year-old Sioux girl in one of the massacres in the Black Hills in 1867. Captain Mills tried to comfort the little girl and told his adjutant, "I intended to adopt this little girl, as I had slain her mother." However, Captain Mills said (Brown, 1972:288):

Before starting, Adjutant Lemly asked me if I really intended to take the little girl. I told him I did, when he remarked, 'Well, how do you think Mrs. Mills will like it?' It was the first time I had given that side of the matter thought, and I decided to leave the child where I found it.

Robert Merton provides us with an *analytical paradigm** on the subject of prejudice and discriminatory behavior that gives some insights. Merton illustrates how such a paradigm, which is a logically constructed syntax of possibilities, does or does not conform to actual behavior (1949). Recall from Chapter 8 that Merton started with the traditional American value that all people are created equal. He then outlined the various attitude-behavior possibilities, all of which are to be found in the research literature (1949: 100–110).

Only Type I, the unprejudiced nondiscriminators, and Type IV, the prejudiced discriminators, are consistent in their expressed attitudes and in their actions. The Type I people are all-weather liberals, many of whom can be found among activists in civil rights movements. The Type IV people are all-weather illiberals, many of whom adhere to the segregationist credo (Vander Zanden, 1966: 141–145) which opposes equal treatment of racial minorities under any circumstances.

Type II and Type III respondents are of particular interest here, since they behave in a manner opposite to their personal attitudes and values. By considering actual examples, it is possible to gain insight into what intervening variables result in such an apparent contradiction. The Type II unprejudiced discriminators are fair-weather liberals who operate expediently to get along or gain profit. This process was seen in a Wayne State University project in Detroit in the early 1960s on assessing white resident attitudes about racially changing neighborhoods. A researcher reported that on one block *everyone* reported that they would be willing to sell their home to a black person or family but would not do so because it would offend their neighbors. Similarly, the unwillingness of corporate managers to hire or promote minority members may stem from fears of negative consequences from their alledgedly more prejudiced associates and organizational superiors (Kahn, 1968).

Similar factors seem to operate in the attitude-behavior discrepancies in those of Type III, the prejudiced nondiscriminators or fair-weather illiberals. As with the Type II responders, expediency is often involved. Many racially prejudiced army officers conformed to President Truman's 1948 order to desegregate the armed forces, and businesspeople and labor leaders operating under lucrative government contracts often desegregate only under the threat of losing these contracts if they do not comply (Merton, 1949: 318).

As De Fleur and Westie (1958) pointed out, it is necessary to take a look at the social pressures affecting a situation before interpreting how literally to take data on expressed attitudes.

THE PROBLEM OF OVER SIMPLE "CAUSE-AND-EFFECT" CORRELATIONS What happens when attitudes are accurately measured and behavior correlates with them? Can we now infer that attitudes and behavior are accurately brought together or, if we are considering behavior only, one set of observed activities and another? Not necessarily. There is a distinction to be made between cause-and-effect relationships and between all kinds of statistical correlations. There may be a strong correlation between prior use of marijuana and the use of hard drugs such as heroin, but there may be an even stronger statistical correlation between prior consumption of milk and the use of hard drugs. On the face of it, the correlations provide possible relationships, but by no means do they give independent proof of the cause of various kinds of behavior.

What often operate in correlations are *spurious relationships** (Goode and Hatt, 1952:354–5, 357), in which observed actions occur together but do not cause each other. The columnist Sidney Harris (1973) explains this interpretive problem in discussing the almost perfect correlation between pollution and the rate of crime in a given area: the more pollution, the more crime; the less pollution, the less crime.

Does this imply, therefore, that pollution is a "cause" of crime, or in any way "creates" crime? Certainly not. All it means is that crime increases in dense, industrialized urban areas; and such areas have more pollution. Country towns have little pollution, and also have low crime rates but one has little to do with the other.

THE NEED TO CROSS-CHECK DATA A common safeguard before interpreting correlations and other forms of data analysis is to use more than one technique of data collection to help verify the meaning of relationships.

An example of crosschecking data by different techniques is provided by Alice Miel's project discussed in Chapter 4 in which white suburban children were examined for racial feelings (1967). Recall that the study showed first-, second-, and third-graders a picture of a black boy and a white boy walking down a city street. Both boys wore shirts and jeans, and the black boy had his arm around the white boy's shoulder. Then the children were asked the question: "Which boy would you choose to play with and why?" Of the 235 children interviewed, 187 (80 percent) chose the white boy.

On the basis of statistical chance variance (see the *normal curve** distribution discussed in Chapter 4), one might expect as many as 130 or so to pick the white boy as a playmate, but not 187. Yet, racial feeling may not have been involved at all. Perhaps the white children, having known only other white children, were simply attracted to the familiarity, thus skewing the results. To check on this, Miel engaged in *projective interviewing** of the children to find out why they chose as they did. Typical responses were (1967:18):

Well, most people don't like colored people, but I like him (pointing to the white boy in the picture) because mostly I see Americans.
He (pointing to the black boy in the picture) is different than an American.
It looks as if the Negro has knocked out the white boy and is dragging him away.
I like the white boy because he didn't carry a knife. (Neither boy carried a knife.)

By gathering both *quantitative**, statistically tabulated, data and *qualitative**, nonquantified, projective interview data, Miel increased the likelihood that her interpretation was accurate, that prejudicial racial feelings were operating in this situation.

SUMMARY

All objective information gathered by various techniques is used to test the accuracy of *concepts** advanced about social behavior. For this purpose, much of the *data** is marshalled for analysis by means of the *scientific method**. The two basic elements in the scientific method are the development of *hypotheses** about *concepts** and the testing of hypotheses. Concepts are ideas about human behavior such as: civilization, the equality of humankind, or socialization into a particular social class will influence the occupational choices and incomes of people. Hypotheses formulate concepts into testable propositions which include *operational definitions** such as: as adults, sons are likely to be in the same occupational status as their fathers. The formulation of hypotheses involves *precision of meaning* in the language used and *a system of logical design*, often using what John Stuart Mill called the *method of difference**. To determine what apparently causes certain behavior, the design includes a *control group** and an *experimental group**, in both of which is analyzed the influence of certain *stimuli**, such as mass-media appeals to voters.

Caution is called for at all points in interpreting research-based and non-research-based sources of information. Even in a project employing scientific method there can be problems, as the Hawthorne effect demonstrated when the respondents reacted to the experiment rather than the test variables of stimuli presumably being tested. Major points of caution in interpretation include the following:

There may be a problem of imprecision, as in crime data for which some local police departments systematically used the FBI's Uniform Crime Reporting system while others did not. A technique often used to avoid problems of imprecise meaning is a *pretest**, in which it can be determined whether the research design will actually collect the information desired.

There may be a problem in determining to what extent expressed attitudes reflect actual behavior. One check on how closely attitudes reflect actual behavior is to ask respondents about a subject and then ask what they would do under certain circumstances. A stronger measure is to evaluate attitudes and then observe behavior in various social situations. It can then be determined what kinds of social factors influence the behavior of individuals whatever their personal views. This was illustrated by Robert Merton's paradigm of prejudicial attitudes and discriminatory behavior.

There may also be a problem of too simple cause-and-effect correlations. The fact that two or more developments occur together, such as pollution and high crime rates, does not prove that one causes the other. There may be a spurious relationship. Checking the research literature on each development such as pollution and crime is one way of avoiding unwarranted causal correlations. Another is to use more than one research technique, such as self-administered *questionnaires**, *projective interviews** and *observation** of behavior to analyze the same situation.

The purpose of all research techniques, of the scientific method of analysis, and of all precautionary steps in interpretation is to increase the likelihood that our knowledge of social behavior has a basis in objective reality.

QUESTIONS FOR DISCUSSION

1. Why are concepts necessary as a starting point in physical or in social scientific research?

2. Explain why it is necessary to check the research literature before beginning a research project.

3. State a concept and develop a hypothesis that could test its accuracy.

4. What is the difference between a testable concept and an empirical test of verification?

5. Develop operational definitions of what you mean by the terms uneducated, moderately educated, and highly educated.

6. To test John Stuart Mill's method of difference, how could you match two groups of students, treating one as a control group and, by changing one characteristic, using another as an experimental group?

7. Check some statistics noted in the daily newspaper that could be misleading without further interpretation.

8. Make up a question about a political viewpoint. Guess the answers of ten respondents in advance, then ask each of them his opinion. Check to see how accurate or inaccurate were your prior guesses.

9. Try to think of some expressed attitudes of people that did not agree with their behavior. Why do you think the two disagree?

10. Review your understanding of the following terms and concepts:

pre-tests

concepts

testable hypotheses

operational definitions

experimental design

Hawthorne effect

control group

experimental group

method of difference

analytical paradigm

spurious relationships

attitude–behavior correlations

REFERENCES

Bloom, Leonard and Ruth Riemer
    1949   Removal and Return. Berkeley: University of California Press.

Bright, George and Carol-Ann Jones
    1973   "Teaching children to think metric." Today's Education (April). Washington, D.C.: National Education Association: 16–17.

Brown, Dee
    1972   Bury My Heart at Wounded Knee: An Indian History of the American West. New York: Bantam.

Chaiklin, Harris and Verl S. Lewis
    1964   A Census Tract Analysis of Crime in Baltimore City. Baltimore, Maryland: University of Maryland School of Social Work.

Chase, Stuart
    1951   "The scientific method in action." G. Leary and J. Steel Smith (eds.), Think Before You Write. New York: Harcourt, Brace: 173–177.

Clinard, Marshall B.
    1963   Sociology of Deviant Behavior. New York: Holt, Rinehart and Winston.

De Fleur, Melvin L. and Frank R. Westie
    1958   "Verbal attitudes and overt acts." American Sociological Review 23: 667–673.

Deutscher, Irwin
    1973   What We Say/What We Do. Glenview, Illinois: Scott, Foresman Company.

Ehrlich, Howard J.
    1969   "Attitudes, behavior, and the intervening variables." American Sociologist 4:29–33.

Ellis, Albert
    1961   The Folklore of Sex. New York: Grove Press.

Gallin, Bernard
    1961   Hsin Hsing: A Taiwanese Agricultural Village. Unpublished dissertation, Cornell University.

Goode, William J. and Paul K. Hatt
    1952   Methods in Social Research. New York: McGraw-Hill.

Gosnell, Harold
    1927   Getting Out the Vote. Chicago: University of Chicago Press.

Gordon, Leonard and John W. Hudson
    1970   "Emergent white Protestant student perception of Jews." Journal for the Scientific Study of Religion 9:235–238.

Gunther, Max
    1973   "How to beat the stock market by watching girls, counting aspirin, checking sunspots and wondering where the yellow went." Playboy (April): 117–118.

Harris, Sidney
    1973   "Cause and effect and correlation are not the same." Arizona Republic (July 29).

Kahn, Robert et al.
    1968   Discrimination Without Prejudice. Ann Arbor: University of Michigan Press.

Kahn, Robert L. and Charles F. Cannell
　1961　The Dynamics of Interviewing. New York: John Wiley and Sons.

La Pierre, Richard T.
　1934　"Attitudes vs. actions." Social Forces 13:230-237.

Leary, William G. and James Steele Smith
　1951　Think Before You Write. New York: Harcourt, Brace.

Lenski, Gerhard
　1963　The Religious Factor. New York: Anchor.

Liebow, Elliott
　1967　Tally's Corner: A Study of Negro Streetcorner Men. Boston: Little, Brown.

Mayer, Milton
　1949　"How to read the Chicago Tribune." Harper's Magazine (April): 24-35.

Merton, Robert K.
　1949　"Discrimination and the American creed." R. M. MacIver (ed.), Discrimination and National Welfare. New York: Harper & Row: 100-110.
　1959　Social Theory and Social Structure. Glencoe, Illinois: The Free Press.

Miel, Alice
　1967　The Shortchanged Children of Suburbia. New York: Institute of Human Relations.

Mill, John Stuart
　1951　Bentham (based upon an 1859 article). Franklin Le Van Baumer (ed.), Main Currents of Western Thought. New York: Knopf: 486-488.

Roethlisberger, F. J. and W. J. Dickson
　1939　Management and the Worker. Cambridge, Mass.: Harvard University Press.

Selltiz, Claire, Marie Jahoda, Morton Deutsch, and Stuart Cook
　1962　Research Methods in Social Relations. New York: Holt, Rinehart and Winston.

Sherif, Muzafer and Carolyn Sherif
　1953　Groups in Harmony and Tension. New York: Harper & Row.

Stouffer, Samuel
　1949　The American Soldier (2 vols.). Princeton, New Jersey: Princeton University Press.

Stouffer, Samuel and Eugene Hartley
　1952　"Opinions about Negro infantry platoons in white companies of seven divisions." T. M. Newcomb and E. L. Hartley (eds.), Readings in Social Psychology. New York: Holt, Rinehart and Winston: 502-506.

Thomas, William I.
　1931　"The relation of research to the social process." Essays on Research in the Social Sciences. Washington, D.C.: The Brookings Institute: 189.

Vander Zanden, James
　1966　American Minority Relations. New York: Ronald Press.

Wallis, W. Allen and Harry Roberts
　1959　Statistics: A New Approach. Glencoe, Illinois: The Free Press.

Wattenberg, Ben and Richard Scammon
　1973　"Black progress and liberal rhetoric." Commentary 51 (April): 34-44.

Weber, Max
　1930　The Protestant Ethic and the Rise of Capitalism. New York: Charles Scribner's Sons.

Westie, Frank
　1953　"A technique for the measurement of race attitudes." American Sociological Review 18: 73-78.

Whyte, William Foote
    1943   Streetcorner Society. Chicago: University of Chicago Press.
    1962   "Unstructured observation." C. Selltiz, Research Methods in Social Relations. New York: Holt, Rinehart and Winston: 107–221.

GLOSSARY

Accommodation A temporary or long-term process in which individuals or groups modify their behavior to terminate conflict and reach an adjustment.

Achieved status A social position an individual attains on the basis of ability and personal effort.

Ageism The process of singling out the elderly for discriminatory treatment by other members of the society.

Analytic research Research designed to test hypotheses and theories that attempt to explain or predict social phenomena.

Anomie A condition of normlessness in society, in which some individuals' or groups' sense of social cohesion is broken or severely weakened.

Applied research Research designed to assist in the formation and implementation of policies to achieve specific desired social change.

Ascribed status The placement of an individual into a status based upon the individual's group qualities, rather than his or her personal efforts or performance.

Assimilation The absorption of one culture by another, although in the process, behavior patterns of the two (or more) interacting cultures become meshed.

Authority Legitimized power accepted by others that accompanies a prestigious office or position of status.

Basic research Research designed to test theories of social behavior and add to the existing body of theoretical knowledge, which becomes subject to further research and modification.

Bureaucratization The subdivisions of large, complex organizations, in which each division has separate functions designed for maximum efficiency in accomplishing particular tasks.

Caste system Social stratification based on the ascribed status of individuals in differentiated, socially ranked groups. Members are encouraged to marry among themselves.

Census The total enumeration of a population according to such demographic characteristics as age, sex, and marital status.

Centralization 1. The concentration of formal authority and power. 2. An ecological process involving the concentration, often by zoning, of particular types of houses or business or other services in given locales.

Charismatic authority Power as an outgrowth of exceptional qualities of grace and sanctity attributed to a leader by a group.

Circular reaction The process by which unified crowd action develops when members of a crowd influence each other to act alike.

Churches Formal religious organizations, usually with professional clergy, members who congregate for the manifest purpose of expressing religious beliefs they hold in common.

Cohort Any particular group of people who experienced the same event at the same time, such as being born in a given year or entering a particular graduating class.

Collective behavior Relatively spontaneous mass behavior that may be unstructured as in the case of situational crowds or highly structured as in the case of social movements.

Community disorganization (see: social disorganization)

Community organization (see: social organization)

Community power The concentration or diffusion among groups and individuals of political and economic decision-making influence within a community.

Concentric zone theory The thesis developed in the 1920s, now modified, that large urban communities are structured spatially around the downtown business district and proceed outward into a zone of transition, a working residential zone, and a commuting zone.

Conflict A regulated or unregulated form of intense competition in which rival individuals and groups try to attain their goals by overpowering (sometimes physically) the opposition.

Constant A property that does not vary from one member of a group to another or within a particular set of defined conditions.

Content analysis A form of quantitative coding of qualitative data as found in fictional or nonfictional narrative material.

Contraculture (or counterculture) The normative value system of a group that is contrary to the values and way of life prevailing in the larger society.

Control group In experimental research, a group that is studied to determine the difference between it and an experimental group after the latter alone has been exposed to an independent variable.

Crowd A temporary grouping of people in physical proximity who are engaged in some form of collective behavior.

Cults A loosely structured and often transitory voluntary religious association.

Cultural diffusion The social change process by which elements spread from one culture to another.

Cultural evolution theory The thesis that three revolutionary global cultural changes have occurred, each of which sparked major population growth: 1. revolution caused by the advent of tools a million or more years ago; 2. the agricultural revolution some ten thousand years ago; and 3. the modern industrial technological revolution.

Cultural lag The tendency of some aspects of a culture (usually the material culture) to change more rapidly than others, causing periodic strain.

Cultural pluralism (see: pluralism) In a heterogeneous society, the peaceful and coequal maintenance of unique cultural identities by different ethnic groups.

Cultural relativism The doctrine that holds that values are not necessarily absolute but vary according to a given culture's norms.

Culture All patterns of behavior and shared customs, beliefs, values, and norms that are transmitted by the process of symbolic interaction among members of a cultural group.

Culture of poverty The way of life among the very poor, characterized by high unemployment, low education, a present-time orientation, and an anomic sense of hopelessness.

Customs Regularity of social behavior, often supported by informal group pressure.

Cybernetic revolution An advanced form of automation involving computer control and analysis in mass production; it has major consequences for the nature of the work force.

Data Any set of phenomena that are the subject of study in quantitative form.

Decentralization The diffusion of political power or economic functions beyond any dominant center.

Demographic characteristics Population characteristics, such as age, race, sex, income, and education, that are collected and reported by a census bureau or other demographic source.

Demographic transition theory The theory that all societies eventually pass through three periods as they evolve from rural agrarian to urban industrial society: 1. a high birth rate, high death rate period; 2. a high birth rate, low death rate period; and 3. a stabilizing low birth rate, low death rate period.

Demography The statistical study of population, with particular emphasis on the analysis of birth, death, and migration rates.

Denominations A formal religious association of members organized into a church group: a denomination is larger than a sect and smaller than an ecclesia.

Descriptive research Research designed to collect and report data about given social phenomena.

Developmental tasks Tasks that arise for people at different stages of the life cycle, the successful achievement of which leads to healthy psychological and social adjustment.

Deviance The violation of group norms that generally brings informal or formal sanctions. In pluralistic societies, toleration of some types of deviance is common.

Deviant means The thesis that when institutionalized routes to achieve cultural goals are blocked, people will engage in individualized or organized deviant behavior to achieve their goals.

Differential association The thesis that the degree to which an individual associates intimately with a group determines the socialization process that results in various types of noncriminal or criminal behavior.

Discrimination Unequal negative treatment of members of minority groups forced upon them by dominant members of society.

Disorganization (see: social disorganization) The process whereby the social structure is in a state of disarray and group norms are neither clear nor followed.

Division of labor The formal or informal allocation of tasks to achieve group goals. Division of labor is particularly evident in complex industrial production processes.

Dysfunction A phenomenon that undermines the stability of all or part of a social system.

Ecclesia The largest and most formal of religious associations, often transcending national boundaries.

Ecological city The urban complex of central city and surrounding suburbs within any Standard Metropolitan Statistical Area (SMSA) as established by the U.S. Census Bureau.

Emigration The geographic movement of people from their nation of origin into one or more other nations.

Ecology (see: human ecology)

Empirical research Research based upon observation and experimentation that is designed to test the validity of theories.

Empiricism (see: empirical research)

Endogamy A cultural norm that prescribes marriage within an individual's in-group.

Ethnocentrism The tendency to view one's own group as superior to other groups.

Experimental group In experimental research, a group that is studied to determine the difference between it and a control group after it alone has been exposed to an independent variable.

Experimental research Systematic observation of phenomena in a laboratory or natural setting, in which researchers are able to accurately assess the apparent relationship between independent experimental and dependent control variables.

Exponential growth Technologically induced social changes that occur at geometric rates of growth in such areas as population, production, pollution, and urbanization.

Extended kinship family A family system in which there is an active primary group kinship network based upon marital and blood relationships.

Factor (see: variable)

Family The primary group-based social institution, found in some form in every society, whose primary functions include reproduction, elements of social control over members, and a major share of the socialization of children into the larger society.

Family life cycle Stages of family life, including marriage (inception of a nuclear family), childbearing, childrearing, and retirement.

Fecundity The total capacity to reproduce in a society, based on the total number of women between the ages of fifteen and forty-four.

Fertility The reproduction rate in a society, measured on the basis of births per thousand women between the ages of fifteen and forty-four.

Folkways Customs of a people that are based upon weak sentiment and are backed by few sanctions.

Functional analysis The theoretical approach to the operation of society that emphasizes the interdependence of institutionalized elements to the stability and maintenance of society.

Functional imperatives In functional action theory, the universal organizational needs of society, including adaptation, goal attainment, integration, and latency.

Functions Any consequence that a social unit has for the social system as a whole or for some component within the system, usually considered in terms of contributing to successful adaptation and adjustment of the system.

Gemeinschaft Intimate, personal, primary relations that tend to be found in small communities.

Gerontology The study of the social and psychological effects of the aging process.

Gesellschaft Limited, impersonal, secondary relations that characterize much social interaction in large urban communities.

Ghettos A region or neighborhood of a city in which the predominant population is composed of an ethnic group whose members may encounter resistance if they attempt to move elsewhere.

Group marriage (see: polygamy)

Groups People who share common values and who engage in regular social interaction.

Human ecology The research specialty dealing with the way people relate and adjust to their physical environment.

Hypothesis A proposition that can be empirically tested by analyzing the relationship between two or more variables.

Ideal types Abstract concepts used to describe, in exaggerated form, those characteristics typical of a given phenomenon.

Ideology Any philosophy that provides the justification for a set of norms.

Immigration The movement of natives of one nation into another nation.

In-group A group in which an individual feels that he belongs and is accepted.

Inner-directed Behavior based upon a person's internalized set of values and goals rather than the values and goals of others.

Institutionalization The process by which a social pattern becomes a widely accepted and implemented set of norms and values that meet basic needs of a society.

Institutions Stable beliefs and practices organized around familial, religious, educational, economic, political, and other basic needs of a society.

Interview schedule A written questionnaire that is administered verbally and that usually includes both precoded questions and open-ended questions.

Labeling The perspective that deviance is not a quality of the act committed but rather the consequence of the definition of rules and sanctions.

Latent consequences (see: latent functions or dysfunctions)

Latent function or dysfunction Social phenomena whose negative or positive consequences are neither intended nor immediately recognized by the participants in a social system.

Life cycle The view that stages of life from childhood to old age involve developmental tasks, the successful completion of which enables each stage to be lived in a satisfying manner and permits adjustment at succeeding stages.

Looking-glass self The social self in which judgments about oneself are based upon the perceived attitudes of others toward oneself.

Macrodecisions Social policy decisions that affect the entire social system or major aspects of the system.

Manifest function A social phenomenon that makes an intended and recognized contribution to the functioning of the social system.

Megalopolis Highly urbanized tracts of interconnected cities and suburbs in a particular geographic area; the northeastern seaboard of the United States is the prototype.

Method of difference (see: scientific method)

Microdecisions Social policy decisions that affect limited segments of the social system.

Machismo An exaggerated form of masculinity characterized by aggressive virility and an exploitive attitude toward women.

Migration The movement of groups of people from one place to another, either within the boundaries of a nation or from one nation to another.

Minority Any social or ethnic group within a given population that is discriminated against by other members of the society.

Monogamy A form of marriage which legally sanctions only one mate at a time.

Mores Norms and rules backed by strong community pressure and severe sanctions if transgressed.

Mortality The total number of deaths in a society, measured in terms of annual deaths per thousand population.

Multiple nuclei theory A theory of urban ecological development that holds that a city and its suburbs develop in a series of nuclei, each having specialized activities.

Normal curve A bell-shaped mathematical model designed to predict some body of empirical data.

Norms Standards by which social behavior is approved or disapproved.

Nuclear family The basic family unit, composed of father, mother, and children, with few ties to the extended network of relatives.

Other-directed Behavior based upon the values and expectations of others rather than upon a person's own values and goals.

Out-group A group that experiences from others a lack of acceptance or of belonging.

Organization (see: social organization)

Parkinson's law The satirical theory that bureaucratic organizations tend to devise ways of expanding their activities and work processes at the expense of efficiency.

Participant observation A research method in which the investigator participates in the situation being studied.

Peer group A group composed of status equals who interact with and identify with each other.

Pluralism A social condition in which people from differing cultural backgrounds live together in harmony.

Polyandry (see: polygamy)

Polygamy A form of plural marriage most commonly composed of one husband and two wives *(polygyny)* and sometimes one wife and two or more husbands *(polyandry)* or two or more husbands and two or more wives *(group marriage)*.

Polygyny (see: polygamy)

Prejudice Negative opinions of persons or groups based upon perceptions rather than facts.

Primary groups Small groups characterized by members who maintain intimate, empathetic, relationships.

Public A large aggregation of people who share certain common interests.

Public opinion The process by which members of a public express by voting or other means their opinions on issues of common interest.

Questionnaires Forms designed to elicit information from written answers to written questions.

Racial distance quotient (see: social distance quotient)

Racism The doctrine that genetic inheritance of a designated group determines human capabilities, generally in reference to race but often applied to ethnic origin, religion, sex, and other group categories.

Random sample A sample in which every member of the population being studied has an equal chance for selection so that reasonable inferences may be drawn about the total population.

Rational-legal authority A form of authority attached to appointment or election to a particular position.

Reference group A group with which an individual identifies in terms of values and norms of behavior.

Relative deprivation The condition in which individuals of similar status feel deprived in comparison to others whose social situation they perceive to be better.

Religion One of the basic institutions in society in which doctrines, beliefs, and practices are developed to advance values about aspects of life considered sacred.

Role The expected behavior pattern attached to a particular status position.

Role conflict A situation that arises when an individual attempts to fulfill the demands of competing or contradictory roles.

Role set The multiple roles associated with a given status.

Role strain A situation in which individuals experience difficulty in meeting their role obligations.

Sampling (see: random sample)

Sanctions Informal or formal punishment designed to maintain conformity to norms of accepted behavior.

Scaling A process of quantifying data along a continuum for purposes of analysis.

The scientific method The logic and techniques behind experimental research designs involving control and experimental variables.

Secondary groups Groups characterized by limited, impersonal, and task-oriented relationships.

Sector theory A theory of city development in which sectors extend from a central downtown business district along transportation routes to the suburbs.

Sect A small religious group that maintains strong adherence to particular religious beliefs that tend to set them apart from the larger society.

Segregation Social and/or physical separation of minority group members from others in the society who wish to avoid social contact with them.

Serendipity The discovery through research of valuable findings not anticipated in the original research design.

Sexism Prejudicial attitudes and discriminatory behavior directed toward someone because of their sex.

Significant others Those who are socially important to oneself and from whom one internalizes role behavior.

Social area analysis A comparative model of urban growth and development that uses three major indexes based upon measures of social rank, urbanization, and segregation.

Social change Alterations in customary social patterns or relationships.

Social class A stratification system in which people are socially distinguished by income, education, occupational rank, family prestige, and related factors.

Social cohesion A high degree of integration and resistance to disintegration within a group, a community, or an entire society.

Social conflict (see: conflict)

Social disorganization The condition in which the social structure weakens to the point where the institutions of a society lose their cohesiveness.

Social distance The limits placed by individuals and by group norms upon social interaction with individuals and groups of different statuses.

Social distance quotient (or scale) (formerly called "racial distance quotient") A seven-point scale designed to measure, by means of survey samples, the degree to which most people in the society would be willing to interact socially with members of designated ethnic groups.

Social gerontology (see: gerontology) The study of the social and psychological aspects of the aging process.

Social groups (see: groups)

Social institutions (see: institutions)

Social Interaction A process of interaction in which symbolic verbal or nonverbal communication takes place between individuals.

Social mobility The movement of people up or down the social class stratification system.

Social movement A process for seeking social change through the organized efforts of a group.

Social organization The system of norms and values prevailing in formal and informal groups of society.

Social pathology Individual or group manifestation of unacceptable deviant behavior that undermines societal stability.

Social status (see: status)

Social structure The patterned set of relationships among the organized components of a social system, including familial, religious, educational, governmental, and economic institutions.

Socialization The learning process by which an individual acquires the values and norms of social behavior.

Society A structured social system of an integrated and organized group of people who have their own territory.

Standard deviation A measurement used in the analysis of sampling data to determine the probability that two or more samples are alike or significantly different.

Standard Metropolitan Statistical Area or SMSA The U.S. Census Bureau's definition of an urban area, consisting of a central city of at least 50,000 inhabitants together with contiguous populated communities.

Status A person's relative position within a group; it includes a set of rights and obligations and may involve either high or low rank.

Status conflict Two or more concurrently held status positions in which an individual's role expectations are in conflict with each other.

Stereotypes Preconceived, often negative perceptions of members of ethnic or other groups.

Stratification (see: social class)

Structural-functionalism (see: functional analysis)

Structured observations A common research technique that focuses on predetermined aspects of behavior in order to provide systematic description of social phenomena or to test causal hypotheses.

Subculture A group that lives by a set of norms different from those of the larger society.

Suburbanism The expansion of a large city's population base beyond city limits into outlying areas, which then become separate governing communities.

Symbolic interactionism A theoretical perspective that holds that the development of an individual into a social being is the consequence of symbolic communication between the person and others.

Synergy A group-oriented concept that holds that the sum of individual efforts within a coordinated group is greater than that of the same number of people functioning in social isolation.

Thomas theorem The proposition that, if people believe something to be true, then real consequences will follow, often as a self-fulfilling prophecy.

Traditional authority A form of authority based upon custom or inherited status.

Unstructured observations A research procedure used as an exploratory technique and often involving participant observation in which data are collected without a complete predetermined set of questions.

Urbanism The way of life in large cities, characterized by cultural heterogeneity, social and residential mobility, a predominance of secular values, and rapid social change.

Urbanization Concentrated population growth that results in the development and growth of large cities and suburbs.

Utopia An abstract conception of a perfect society; utopias are sometimes influential in determining the course of contemporary social action.

Value conflict Basic disagreement between groups within a society about what are desirable and acceptable forms of behavior and social policy for the society.

Values Accepted standards about what is good, right, and desirable.

Variable A research value that can be designated a cause or effect of a given phenomenon.

Voluntary associations Organizations people join to facilitate the pursuit of values and interests common to group members.

NAME INDEX

Abrams, Charles, 244, 249, 262
Adams, Robert Lynn, 72, 93
Albrecht, Ruth, 216, 225
Albrecht, Stan, 243, 262
Alisky, Marvin, 363, 370
Allport, Gordon, 241, 262
Altheide, David, 420, 434
Alvarez, Rudolfo, 179, 199
Anderson, Nels, 408, 434
Anderson, William, 270, 288, 292, 321, 331
Aristotle, 80, 93
Aron, Marcia, 114, 128
Aronson, Harvey, 182
Atchley, Robert, 205, 210, 217–218, 223
Aveni, Adrian, 163–166, 199
Axelrod, Morris, 310, 331

Baldwin, James, 452, 460
Ball, Samuel, 79, 93
Banfield, Edward, 316, 332
Barnes, Clive, 424
Barron, Milton, 321, 332
Bartlett, John, 464, 485
Barton, Allen, 269–270, 275, 277, 279, 288, 292
Bates, Frederick, 270, 292, 294
Bates, Marston, 19
Bealer, Robert, 141, 156
Beard, Charles, 29, 54

NAME INDEX

Beard, Mary, 29, 54
Beard, William, 29, 54
Beaumont, Charles, 452, 460
Becker, Howard, 147, 156, 408, 416–417, 434
Beckerman, Wilfred, 366, 370
Bell, Daniel, 432, 434, 474, 483, 486
Bell, Inge Powell, 149, 157, 246, 262
Bell, Wendell, 310, 315–316, 332, 474, 486
Bendix, Reinhard, 84, 173, 201
Benedict, Ruth, 49, 54, 71, 93
Bennis, Warren, 50, 54
Bensman, Joseph, 308–309, 334
Bent, Dale, 115, 127
Berelson, Bernard, 351, 371
Berger, Bennett, 140, 157
Berger, Peter, 406–407, 409–411, 433–434, 445
Bernard, Jesse, 136, 157
Bernard, Viola, 388, 390, 399, 413
Bernard, William, 28, 54, 238, 262
Berry, Brewton, 242, 244, 262
Berry, Mary, 245, 263
Bierstedt, Robert, 57, 93
Birren, James, 214, 223
Blalock, Hubert, Jr., 112, 126
Blanchard, Eric, 192, 199
Blau, Peter, 50, 54, 211, 432, 434
Blau, Zena, 211–212, 215–216, 218, 224
Blauner, Robert, 238, 263
Bloom, Leonard, 28, 54, 390, 399, 506
Bloomberg, Warner, 306, 332
Blum, Lucille, 428–429
Blumer, Herbert, 99, 127, 246, 249, 256, 263, 492
Boat, Marion, 310, 332
Bogardus, Emory, 29–30, 54, 212, 224, 263
Bogatz, Gerry Ann, 79, 93
Boler, Deetje, 215–216, 225
Bommarito, Barbara, 195, 199
Bonjean, Charles, 318, 332–333
Borah, William E., 219

Borlaug, Norman, 368, 370
Bowers, William, 151–152, 158
Boyd-Orr, Lord, 343, 371
Bradbury, Ray, 449, 460
Bradlee, Benjamin, 388, 399
Braly, K. W., 213, 225, 469, 486
Branch, Taylor, 318, 332
Branscombe, Art, 75, 93
Braungart, Richard, 149, 154, 157
Bright, George, 127, 506
Brookover, Wilbur, 195, 199
Broom, Leonard, 44, 54
Brothers, Ann Janice, 447
Brown, Claude, 186, 199
Brown, Dee, 502, 506
Brown, Harrison, 457, 460
Brown, Lester, 369
Brown, Michael, 269, 292
Broyles, J. Allen, 456, 460
Bruner, Jerome, 7, 17
Buckley, Walter, 431, 434
Burgess, Anthony, 449, 459–460
Burgess, Ernest W., 9–10, 211, 213, 216, 224, 310, 312–314, 316, 332, 491

Cabot, Natalie, 214, 224
Caldwell, Robert, 80, 94
Calley, William, 390, 399
Camargo, Alberto Llaras, 366
Campbell, Arthur, 358
Cannell, Charles F., 108, 127, 507
Cantril, Hadley, 290, 292, 474, 486
Carman, Harry, 88, 94, 199, 239, 263, 363, 371, 374, 399
Carmichael, Stokely, 251, 260, 263, 322, 332, 416, 434
Carnegie, Andrew, 87, 94
Carp, Frances, 218, 224
Carr-Sanders, A. M., 339, 347, 371
Carter, Jimmy, 102
Cavan, Ruth, 216, 224
Cavan, Sherri, 409, 414, 435

Centers, Richard, 163, 199
Chaiklin, Harris, 109, 127, 263, 506
Channing, Edward, 234, 263
Chase, Stuart, 495, 506
Chiazze, Leonard, 179, 203
Chisholm, Shirley, 256, 358
Chown, Sheila, 210, 224
Clausewitz, Karl Von, 375, 395, 399
Cleaver, Eldridge, 259, 263
Cleland, John, 422
Clemens, Samuel, (Mark Twain), 103–104, 127
Cleveland, Harland, 387, 397, 399
Clinard, Marshall B., 501, 506
Coffman, Thomas, 225, 260, 264, 469, 486
Cohen, Albert, 148–149, 157, 292
Coleman, James, 78, 94, 140, 157, 195, 199, 248, 263, 272, 292
Commager, Henry Steele, 476, 486
Commoner, Barry, 364, 371
Comte, Auguste, 8–9, 17, 99, 405–406, 413, 418, 433, 435, 490
Conot, Robert, 277–278, 292
Constantine, Joan, 65, 94
Constantine, Larry, 65, 94
Cook, Edwin, 437
Cook, Fred, 382, 399
Cook, Stuart, 507
Cooley, Charles Horton, 33, 54, 224
Cooper, David, 442, 460
Coser, Lewis, 233, 263, 396, 399, 445, 460
Cottle, Thomas, 141, 157
Cowgill, Donald, 207, 217, 224
Cox, Harvey, 311, 332
Creedon, Carol, 185, 200
Cressey, Donald, 148, 157, 159
Cuber, John, 66, 94, 442, 460
Cumming, Elaine, 211, 215–217, 224
cummings, e. e., 41, 54
Currie, Elliott, 442, 462

Dacy, Douglas, 286, 292
Dahrendorf, Ralf, 492
Danzig, Elliott, 292

Darwin, Charles, 87, 413, 435, 490
Davies, James, 345, 371
Davis, Allison, 40, 54, 180, 199
Davis, Kingsley, 47, 54, 134, 157, 301, 306, 332, 338, 352, 359, 366–367, 369, 371
Dean, Lois, 216–217, 224
DeFleur, Melvin L., 243, 262, 502–503, 506
de Gre, Gerard, 82–83, 94
Demerath, III, N. J., 69, 94
DeMott, Benjamin, 480, 485–486
Denney, Reuel, 461
Deutsch, Martin, 193, 199, 507
Deutscher, Irwin, 502, 506
Deutscher, Linda, 437
Deward, Robert, 237, 263
Dewey, John, 73, 94
Dick, Everett, 308
Dickenson, Emily, 454
Dickson, W. J. 426, 436, 498, 507
Dixon, Mort, 267
Downey, Fred, 272, 293
Doxiadis, C. A., 330, 332
Drachler, Norman, 196
Dragastin, Sigmund E., 136, 141
Duncan, Otis Dudley, 172, 199
Durkheim, Emile, 9, 17, 48, 54, 67–68, 80, 94, 121–122, 127, 206, 224, 490
Dynes, Russell, 270, 272, 283–284, 293–294, 321, 331

Eakin, Beth, 453, 460
Eames, Edwin, 190, 192, 200
Edwards, John, 475, 486
Edwards, Newton, 72, 94
Ehrlich, Anne, 371
Ehrlich, Howard, 501, 506
Ehrlich, Paul, 343–344, 364, 371
Eifler, Deborah, 34, 56
Eisenhauer, Ward, 334
Eisenhower, Dwight, 360, 381, 399

Eisenstadt, S. N., 135, 157
Elder, Jr., Glen, 136, 141, 157
Elkin, Frederick, 141, 157
Elliot, Delbert, 147, 157
Ellis, Albert, 123, 127, 501, 506
Ellis, Lee, 493
Ellis, Robert, 168, 200
Ellison, Ralph, 263
Endres, Michael, 343, 369, 371
Eng, Evelyn, 269, 293
Engels, Frederich, 162
Epstein, Benjamin, 456, 460
Etzioni, Amitai, 50, 54, 364, 371, 391, 399

Fairchild, Henry, 347, 371
Fairweather, George, 458–460, 473, 482–483, 486
Farber, Bernard, 66, 94, 209, 224
Farley, Reynolds, 12, 17, 220, 224, 248, 263
Farrell, Kenneth, 337, 364, 371
Fava, Sylvia, 314, 332
Feilitzen, Cecilia, 33, 54
Feinberg, Gerald, 486
Feldman, Saul, 151
Fellows, Donald, 240, 263
Felton, Gary, 426, 435
Fendrich, James, 151, 158
Ferman, Louis, 179, 200
Fidell, Linda, 252, 263
Field, Edward, 45
Fiore, Quentin, 139, 159
Fitzgerald, F. Scott, 445, 460
Flacks, Richard, 139–140, 149, 158
Flowerman, Samuel, 226
Flowers, Brian, 457, 460
Fogelman, C. W., 292
Fogelson, Robert, 251, 263, 321, 332
Ford, Gerald, 193
Ford, II, Henry, 195
Form, William, 273, 276, 280, 283–284, 293

Forrest, Thomas, 276–277, 293
Forrester, Jay, 365
Forster, Arnold, 456, 460
Fowler, John, 376, 399
Fox, Robert John, 72, 93
Fox, Robin, 61, 94
Franck, Thomas, 454, 462
Frazier, E. Franklin, 263, 408, 435
Freedman, Ronald, 351, 358, 371
Frejka, Thomas, 365
French, David, 471, 486
Friedenberg, Edgar, 146, 150, 158, 217, 224
Friedman, Lawrence, 244, 263
Fritz, Charles, 268, 272, 275, 278–279, 281, 284, 289–290, 293–294
Frolkis, V. V., 210, 224
Froman, Robert, 231, 234, 245, 263
Fromm, Erich, 414, 435, 468, 484, 486
Fuller, Richard, 152, 158, 414, 435
Fullerton, Gail Putney, 65, 94

Galbraith, John Kenneth, 86, 90–91, 94, 171, 178, 384, 399, 432, 435
Gallin, Bernard, 107, 127, 506
Gans, Herbert, 302–303, 330, 332
Garb, Solomon, 269, 293
Gardner, Burleigh, 40, 54, 199
Gardner, Mary, 40, 54, 199
Gazell, James, 140, 147–148, 158
Gerver, Israel, 439, 462
Gibben, Kathy, 214, 223
Gibbons, Don, 158
Gilbert, George, 213, 224, 469, 486
Gilliken, Harold, 502
Ginsberg, Eli, 179, 200
Gist, Noel, 314, 332
Gitchoff, G. Thomas, 140, 147–148, 158
Gittlin, Todd, 409, 435
Gladwin, Thomas, 184, 190, 200
Glazer, Nathan, 90–91, 94, 261, 264, 461
Glazer, Nona, 185, 200
Glenn, Norval, 200
Goffman, Erving, 417, 435, 460

Gold, Bertram, 477, 486
Goldhamer, H., 216, 224
Goldin, Amy, 269, 292
Goode, Judith Granich, 190, 192, 200
Goode, William, 495, 497, 499, 503, 506
Goodman, Leon, 172, 200
Gordon, David, 178, 200, 220, 224
Gordon, Leonard, 72, 94, 242, 264, 276, 278, 293, 326, 332, 469, 486, 501, 506
Gordon, Milton, 233, 264
Gosnell, Harold, 497-498, 506
Gottlieb, David, 136, 141, 158, 195, 199
Gottmann, Jean, 324-325, 332
Gouldner, Alvin, 4, 17, 58, 95, 411, 433, 435, 443, 461, 481, 486
Graham, Fred, 245, 264
Graham, Hugh Davis, 421
Green, Christopher, 192, 200
Greene, Wade, 365, 371
Greer, Ann, 408, 435
Greer, Scott, 304, 323, 332, 408, 435
Griffin, C. W., Jr., 308-309, 333
Grimes, Michael, 318, 333
Gross, B., 201
Gross, Neil, 40, 54, 76, 95
Gubrium, Jaber, 221, 224
Gunther, Max, 496, 506
Gurdon, J. B., 447
Gurr, Ted Robert, 421
Gusfield, Joseph, 83, 95
Gussow, Joan Dye, 62, 95
Gutmann, David, 210-211, 225

Haas, J. Eugene, 284, 293
Hachiya, Michihiko, 270, 293
Haeckel, Ernst, 311
Haenszel, William, 179, 203
Hage, Dean, 158
Halberstam, David, 380, 392, 393, 399
Hamilton, Charles, 251, 263, 322, 332, 416, 434
Handler, Joel, 184, 200

Handlin, Oscar, 347, 371
Hankins, F. H., 242
Hardin, Garrett, 309, 365
Hargrove, Stephen, 437
Harman, Willis, 473, 483-484, 486
Harrington, Michael, 152, 158, 186, 200, 298, 432, 435
Harris, Chauncey, 315-316, 333
Harris, Marvin, 231, 265
Harris, Sidney, 503, 506
Harrison, Bennett, 298, 328-329, 333
Harroff, Peggy, 66, 94, 442, 460
Hartley, Eugene, 507
Harvey, Patricia, 109, 127
Hastings, Philip, 144, 158
Hatt, Paul, 495, 497, 499, 503, 506
Havighurst, Robert, 136, 141, 158, 216, 224-225
Hayden, Thomas, 400
Heer, David, 270, 293
Henderson, Charles, 413, 435
Henry, Jules, 221, 225
Henry, William, 215-216, 224
Henze, Lura, 139, 158
Herbers, John, 422
Hermalin, Albert, 12, 17, 220, 224
Herman, Judy, 182, 201
Hersh, Seymour, 390, 399
Hershey, John, 270, 293
Hesburgh, Theodore, 358
Higham, John, 240, 264
Hill, Gladwin, 368, 371
Hill, Richard, 132, 158
Hill, Robert, 321, 332
Hilmer, Herman, 21, 55
Hockett, Homer, 87, 95
Hockschild, Arlee, 221, 225
Hodge, Robert, 163, 170-171, 200
Hodges, Harold, 47, 54

Hoge, Dean, 144
Hokada, Elizabeth, 34, 56
Hollander, Nanci, 409, 435
Holmes, Lowell, 207, 224
Homans, George, 55, 57, 95, 453, 461
Honigman, John J., 49, 55, 71, 95
Hopkins, Frank, 475, 486
Hoult, Thomas Ford, 37, 55, 58, 67, 72, 95, 211, 225, 317, 333, 425, 435
Hourwich, Isaac, 88, 95, 175, 200
Howard, John Robert, 141, 143, 158, 257, 264
Howe, Florence, 152, 158
Howe, Irving, 152, 158
Howton, F. William, 439, 462
Hoyt, Homer, 306, 314, 316, 323, 333
Huber, Bettina, 474, 486
Hudson, John, 139, 158, 501, 506
Hughes, Helen MacGill, 254, 264
Hull, C. Hadlai, 115, 127
Humphrey, Hubert H., 184, 200
Hunt, Morton, 62, 95, 148, 158, 214, 225
Hunter, Floyd, 317–318, 333
Hutchings, Edward, 457, 460
Huxley, Aldous, 445–446, 448–449, 459, 461

Iklé, Fred Charles, 380, 399
Illich, Ivan, 79, 95
Inglehart, Babette, 180, 200
Israeli, Nathan, 474, 486
Ivy, James, 245, 264

Jackson, Jesse, 358
Jackson, Robert, 390
Jacobs, Jane, 329, 333
Jacobs, Paul, 320, 333
Jacobs, Robert, 186
Jacobson, Lenore, 33, 55
Jaffe, Frederick, 361, 371
Jahoda, Marie, 507

Janis, Irving, 454, 461
Jefferson, Thomas, 306, 464
Jenkins, Jean, 115, 127
Jensen, Arthur, 493
Johnson, John, 108, 127
Johnson, Lyndon, 192, 362, 420
Johnson, Rudy, 279, 293
Johnson, Virginia, 214, 225
Jones, Carol-Ann, 127, 506
Joyce, James, 371
Jungk, Robert, 270, 275, 293

Kahn, Herman, 377, 399
Kahn, Robert, 108, 127, 243, 264, 503, 506–507
Kahn, Roger, 151–152, 158
Kalichman, Betty, 277, 293
Kanter, Rosabeth Moss, 65, 95
Karlins, Marvin, 213, 225, 260, 264, 469, 486
Katz, David, 213, 225, 469, 486
Katz, Judith, 66, 95
Katz, Michael, 72, 95
Keene, Donald, 293
Keith-Spiegel, Patricia, 179, 202, 252, 256, 263, 265
Kelly, George, 357, 371
Kennan, George, 375, 399
Kennedy, John F., 25, 55, 362
Kenniston, Kenneth, 456, 461
Kephart, William, 65, 95, 236, 264
Kerber, August, 195, 199
Kerr, Clark, 454
Kesey, Ken, 450, 461
Keutfield, Calvin, 267, 272, 280, 293
Key, William, 281, 294
Killian, Lewis, 230, 265, 267, 294, 391, 401, 453, 457, 461–462, 464, 486
King, Martin Luther, Jr., 246, 250, 264, 329, 333, 393, 399, 456, 461
Kirchner, Walter, 201
Kissinger, Henry, 379, 400
Kluckhohn, Clyde, 19, 20, 21, 31, 55
Koestler, Arthur, 449, 461

Komarovsky, Mirra, 442, 461
Kornhauser, William, 84, 95, 163, 201
Kroeber, Theodora, 389, 400
Kuhn, Maggie, 220
Kunreuther, Howard, 286, 292
Kvaraceus, William, 148, 158

Lalli, Frank, 322, 333
Landecker, Werner, 173-174, 201
Lane, W. Clayton, 168, 200
Lang, Gladys Engel, 278, 294
Lang, Kurt, 278, 294
La Pierre, Richard T., 502, 507
Lauer, Robert, 430, 435
Laurenti, Luigi, 244, 264
Layman, Marvin, 294
Lazarsfeld, Paul, 7, 18, 491
Leary, William G., 127, 507
Le Bon, Gustave, 491
Lee, Shu-Ching, 65
Leighninger, Robert, 445, 461
Leighton, Isabel, 461
Lekachman, Robert, 385, 400
Lemert, Edwin, 417, 435
Lenski, Gerhard, 69, 72, 95, 127, 162, 201, 496, 507
Leopold, Richard, 234, 264
Levine, Irving, 182, 201
Levinson, Andrew, 150-151, 158
Levy, Marion, 65
Lewin, Kurt, 259, 264
Lewin, Leonard, 385, 400
Lewis, Oscar, 188, 201
Lewis, Sinclair, 55, 309, 333, 448, 461
Lewis, Verl, 109, 127, 263, 506
Liebow, Elliot, 107-108, 127, 191, 201, 409, 414, 435, 507
Lineberry, Robert, 318, 333
Link, Arthur, 234, 264, 375, 378, 392-394, 400
Linne, Olga, 33, 54
Linton, Ralph, 23, 231, 410, 435
Lippmann, Walter, 27, 55, 212, 225, 374, 400
Lipset, Seymour, 82-84, 95, 149, 151-152, 158, 173, 201, 219, 225
Locke, Harvey, 314

Loether, Herman, 127
Lofland, John, 146, 159, 416-417, 435
Logan, Rayford, 244, 264
Loomis, Charles, 283, 293
Lopata, Helena, 218, 225
Lord, Walter, 268, 289, 294
Low, J. O., 237, 265
Lowenthal, Marjorie, 215-216, 225
Lucas, Robert, 179-180, 203
Lunt, Paul, 166-167, 176, 183, 203
Lyman, Stanford, 443, 459, 461
Lynd, Helen, 306, 318, 333, 409, 435
Lynd, Robert, 14, 18, 306, 318, 333, 409, 435
Lyon, J. Larry, 318, 333

Mace, David, 60, 95
MacIver, Robert, 243, 386, 400
Madge, John, 9, 18
Maida, Peter, 156
Makielsky, S. J., 190, 195, 201
Malcolm X, 250, 264
Malthus, Thomas, 339, 345, 362-363, 371, 481
Mangione, Anthony, 180, 200
Mann, Horace, 76
Manning, Peter, 147, 149, 159
Marks, Edward, 284, 294
Marston, William Moulton, 36
Martindale, Don, 85, 95
Marwell, Gerald, 7, 18
Marx, Karl, 162, 165, 201, 474, 487, 490
Maslow, Abraham, 49, 55, 71, 95
Mason, Ward, 54
Masters, William, 214, 225
Matras, Judah, 166-175, 201
Matteson, David, 140-141, 159
Matthews, Tom, 379, 400
Matza, David, 192, 201
Maxwell, Richard, 421
Mayer, Albert J., 69, 95, 317, 333
Mayer, J. P., 55, 388, 400

NAME INDEX

Mayer, Milton, 101–102, 127, 507
Mayhew, Rev. Jonathan, 234
McCaffrey, Isabel, 216–217, 224
McCary, James, 96
McEachern, Alexander, 54
McGregor, Douglas, 474, 487
McKee, Alice, 265
McKenzie, R. D., 314, 333
McLuhan, Marshall, 139, 159, 445, 461
Mctavish, Donald, 127
Mead, George Herbert, 33, 55, 225
Mead, Margaret, 37, 55, 86, 96, 139–140, 159, 442
Medicine, Beatrice, 179, 201
Melman, Seymour, 374, 380–382, 388, 400
Melville, Herman, 422
Mendelson, Mary Adelaide, 225
Merrill, Judith, 445, 461
Merton, Robert K., 5–6, 14–16, 18, 37, 43, 49, 55, 60, 96, 124, 127, 149, 159, 185, 192, 201, 243, 261, 265, 273, 278, 294, 317, 333, 338, 416–417, 429, 435, 492, 502–503, 505, 507
Michael, Donald, 176, 201
Michels, Robert, 83, 96
Michenor, James, 159
Midlarsky, Manus, 400
Miel, Alice, 118, 127, 504, 507
Miles, Rufus, 144, 159
Milgram, Stanley, 452, 461
Mill, John Stuart, 359, 371, 475–476, 485, 487, 494, 497, 504, 507
Miller, Henry, 422
Miller, Herman, 265
Miller, S. M., 180, 192, 195, 201–202
Mills, Anson, 502
Mills, C. Wright, 83–84, 96, 381–382, 384, 400, 405–406, 412, 424–426, 429, 433, 436, 476, 487
Moore, Dumas, 400
Moore, Harry, 278, 284, 286, 294
Moore, Wilbert, 75, 96, 430, 436, 474–475, 487
Moraes, Dom, 367, 372

Morgan, James, 202, 225
Morris, Terrance, 148, 159
Mothner, Ira, 298, 333
Moyers, William, 202
Moynihan, Daniel, 5, 18, 190, 202
Murdock, George, 65, 80, 96
Myers, Richard, 152, 158, 414, 435
Myrdal, Gunnar, 197, 202, 240, 242, 252, 261, 265, 415, 436

Neal, Fred, 385, 400
Nelson, Keith, 391–392, 400
Neugarten, Bernice, 159, 211, 225
Newell, David, 216–217, 224
Nie, Norman, 115, 127
Nimkoff, Meyer, 219, 225
Nisbet, Robert, 47, 55, 338
Nixon, Richard, 192–193
Norman, Lloyd, 379, 400
Northcutt, Norvell, 75
Nosow, Sigmond, 273, 276, 280, 284, 293
Noyes, John Humphrey, 65

O'Donnell, James, 151, 159
Ogburn, William F., 76, 96, 219, 225, 349–350, 372, 414, 436
Olesen, Virginia, 168, 200
Olmstead, Alan, 299, 304, 333
Olson, David, 318, 332
O'Neill, Eugene, 183
O'Neill, George, 65, 96
O'Neill, Nena, 65, 96
Oromoner, Mark, 410, 436
Orwell, George, 448–449, 453, 459, 461
Ottenberg, Perry, 388, 390, 399, 414
Owen, Wilfred, 326, 333

Paddock, Paul, 364–365, 372
Paddock, William, 364–365, 372
Page, Charles, 170, 202
Panati, Charles, 369, 372
Parenton, Vernon, 292, 294
Pareto, Vilfredo, 491

NAME INDEX

Park, Robert E., 9-10, 18, 310-311, 313, 333, 491
Parker, Richard, 184, 202
Parkinson, C. Northcote, 382, 400
Parsons, Talcott, 44, 55, 65, 80, 96, 416, 436, 492
Passow, A. Harry, 202
Pepys, Samuel, 351, 372
Perrucci, Robert, 259, 265
Peterson, Richard, 58, 95
Peterson, William, 339, 343, 372
Piao, Lin, 306
Pilisuk, Marc, 259, 265, 400
Pinckney, Alphonso, 249, 265
Pittman, R. H., 292
Polsby, Nelson, 318, 334
Polsky, Ned, 392, 400
Pope, Liston, 69, 96
Power, Jonathan, 352, 372
Price, Derek De Solla, 482, 487
Pryor, David, 220, 226

Quarantelli, Enrico, 272, 284, 293-294, 321, 331

Rainwater, Lee, 5, 18
Ramsey, Charles, 133, 135, 147-148, 155, 159
Rapaport, Anatol, 387, 400
Rauch, Basil, 400
Ravitz, Mel, 432, 436
Redl, Fritz, 388, 390, 399, 414
Reich, Charles, 470, 472, 487
Rein, Martin, 180, 192, 201-202
Reisman, David, 90, 96, 443, 453, 461
Reston, James, 60, 96, 430-431, 436, 480, 487
Reston, Jr., James, 390, 400
Richey, Herman, 72, 94
Riemer, Ruth, 28, 54, 390, 399, 506
Rist, Ray, 202, 426, 436
Rivers, Caryl, 446, 461
Roberts, Harry, 124, 128, 507
Roberts, John, 22, 23, 56
Robertson, Morgan, 267-268
Robinson, Edwin Arlington, 186, 202
Roby, P., 201

Rockefeller, Nelson, 193
Rodman, Hyman, 190, 202
Roethlisberger, F. J., 426, 436, 498, 507
Rogers, William, 310, 334
Roosevelt, Eleanor, 480, 487
Roosevelt, Franklin Delano, 184, 448, 464
Roosevelt, Theodore, 479
Rosenberg, Bernard, 439, 442, 462
Rosenthal, Robert, 33, 55
Ross, Catherine, 34, 56
Ross, H. Lawrence, 476, 487
Rossi, Peter, 170-171, 200
Rubington, Earl, 413-418, 436, 480-481, 485, 487
Rustin, Bayard, 197, 202, 322, 334, 393, 400

Saenger, Gerhart, 226
Safilios-Rothschild, Constantina, 14, 18, 256, 265
Saint-Exupery, Antoine de, 462
Samuel, Edwin, 61, 96
Samuelson, Paul, 84-87, 91, 96, 176, 185, 195, 202
Sanford, Nevitt, 389, 401
Sawyer, John, 472, 477, 487
Seammon, Richard, 257, 266, 507
Schlesinger, Arthur, Jr., 176, 196, 202, 219, 226, 247, 265, 375, 393, 401
Schmidhauser, J. R., 219, 226
Schrag, Peter, 442, 462
Schur, Edwin, 96, 148, 159, 417, 436
Schwartz, Barry, 429
Scott, Marvin, 443, 461
Scranton, (report), 154, 159
Sebald, Hans, 147, 159
Selltiz, Claire, 101, 108, 123, 127, 407, 436, 501, 507
Selznick, Philip, 44, 54
Semenoick, Alexander, 340
Serrin, William, 85, 96
Sexton, Patricia, 76, 78, 96
Shanas, Ethel, 218, 226
Shank, Alan, 329, 334
Shanley, Fred, 148, 159
Sharp, Harry, 69, 95
Shaw, George Bernard, 184

Sheldon, Henry, 205, 207, 226
Sheldon, J. H., 210, 226
Sherif, Carolyn, 499, 507
Sherif, Muzafer, 499, 507
Shevky, Eshref, 315-316, 334
Shirer, William, 47, 55
Short, James F., 421
Siegel, Alberta, 32, 55
Siegel, Paul, 170-171, 200
Silberman, Charles, 33, 55, 76, 78, 96
Sills, David, 283, 294
Simmons, J. L., 470, 487
Simpson, George, 121, 127, 206
Sinclair, Upton, 408, 436
Sisson, George, 294
Skinner, B. F., 449, 462
Skolnick, Jerome, 442, 462
Smith, Adam, 87
Smith, James Steepe, 127, 507
Smith, Robert, 394-395, 401
Smith, Samuel, 413, 437
Smolensky, Eugene, 299, 304, 333
Solzhenitsyn, Alexander, 449, 462
Sontag, Susan, 214, 226
Sorokin, Pitrium, 170, 202
Sowell, Thomas, 236, 249, 265
Spaulding, John, 206
Spekke, Andrew, 478, 487
Spencer, Herbert, 87, 96, 490
Spiegel, David, 179, 202
Spiegel, Don, 256, 265
Spitz, David, 386
Sprehe, J. Timothy, 4, 17
Stanton, Esther, 253, 265
Steele, C. Roy, 266
Steinbeck, John, 57
Steinbrenner, Karin, 115, 127
Steinem, Gloria, 36, 55, 367
Stern, Richard, 294

Stevenson, Adlai, 373, 375, 501
Stewart, Maxwell, 326, 328, 334
Stocker, Terrance, 427-428, 437
Stockwell, Edward, 359, 372
Stoddard, Ellwyn, 18
Storer, Norman, 38, 56
Stouffer, Samuel, 7, 15, 18, 185, 202, 498, 507
Strehler, Bernard, 211, 226
Sumner, William Graham, 87, 96, 476
Suter, Larry, 265
Sutherland, Edwin, 148, 159
Swift, Jonathan, 365-366, 372
Syrett, Harold, 88, 94, 199, 239, 263, 363, 371, 374, 399

Taeuber, Karl, 179, 203, 245, 265
Tautfest, Claudia, 257, 265
Taylor, Gus, 152, 160
Taylor, James B., 277, 281, 294
ten Broek, Jacobus, 12, 18
Terkel, Studs, 78, 96
Thielbar, Gerald, 151
Thomas, W. I., 33, 56, 128, 244, 265, 418, 437, 507
Thomlinson, Ralph, 105, 128, 342-343, 346, 348, 351-352, 357, 359, 367, 372
Thompson, C., 249
Thompson, Warren, 352, 372
Thoreau, Henry David, 306
Thrasher, Edwin, 148, 160
Thrasher, Frederick, 265, 408, 414, 437
Thurow, Lester, 178-180, 203
Tibbits, Clark, 206-207, 226
Tocqueville, Alexis de, 464, 487
Toffler, Alvin, 442, 472, 474-475, 479, 483, 485, 487
Tolkien, J. R. R., 462
Tönnies, Ferdinand, 45, 56, 299, 334
Trieman, D. J., 163, 200
Troeltsch, Ernst, 69, 97
Trumbell, Robert, 270, 294
Truzzi, Marcello, 147, 149, 159, 426, 437

Tumin, Melvin, 75, 96
Turner, Frederick Jackson, 176
Turner, Ralph, 230, 265, 267, 294, 391, 401, 453, 462
Tylor, Edward B., 20, 56

Udall, Morris, K., 379, 401
Ullman, Edward, 315-316, 333
Urofsky, Melvin, 319, 334

Valentine, Charles, 197, 203
Vander Zanden, James, 56, 74, 97, 212, 226, 232, 236, 265, 389, 401, 456, 462, 481, 487, 503, 507
van Gennep, Arnold, 132, 160
Vatter, Harold, 178, 184, 203
Veblen, Thorstein, 85, 97, 408, 437, 445, 462
Venetoulis, Ted, 334
Vidich, Arthur, 308-309, 334
Vogt, Evon, 22, 23, 56

Wagley, Charles, 231, 265
Waldheim, Kurt, 369
Walker, Daniel, 154, 160
Wallingford, Daniel, 26-27
Wallis, W. Allen, 124, 128, 507
Walters, Gary, 225, 260, 264, 469, 486
Ward, Barbara, 345, 372, 396-397, 401
Ward, Lester, 99, 491
Warner, Lyle, 243, 262
Warner, W. Lloyd, 166-168, 171, 176, 183, 203, 237, 265
Warren, Donald, 321, 334
Waskow, Arthur, 246-247, 265, 464, 487
Wattenberg, Ben, 203, 257, 266, 507
Weber, Max, 9, 18, 45, 50, 56, 68-69, 81, 83, 86, 97, 162, 165, 203, 386, 388, 401, 407, 433, 490, 496, 507
Weinberg, Martin, 413-418, 436, 480-481, 485, 487
Weisband, Edward, 454, 462
Weitzman, Lenore, 34, 56
Welch, Robert, 456
Welford, A. T., 210, 226

Wells, H. G., 474, 487
Westie, Frank, 242-243, 266, 501-503, 506-507
Westley, William, 141, 157
Whelpton, Pascal, 358
Whyte, William Foote, 107-108, 128, 414, 437, 508
Whyte, William H., Jr., 51, 56, 444, 453, 458, 462
Wilber, George, 190, 203
Wilensky, Harold, 150, 160
Wilkens, Roy, 259-260, 266, 358
Will, Robert, 178, 184, 203
Willhelm, Sidney, 179, 203
Williams, E. I. F., 76, 97
Williams, Harry, 287-288, 295
Williams, Marilyn, 315-316, 334
Williams, Robin, 20, 56, 85, 97, 403, 477, 485, 487
Williams, William, 375, 401
Willits, Fern, 156
Wilson, E. O., 493
Winch, Robert, 59, 62, 65, 97
Winograd, Barry, 470, 487
Wirth, Louis, 231-232, 266, 301-303, 310, 312, 314, 330, 334
Wiseman, Jacqueline, 114, 128
Wish, Harvey, 176, 203
Wogaman, Philip, 194, 203
Wolfgang, Marvin, 148, 160, 421
Woods, Harry, 267
Woolf, Virginia, 254
Woytinsky, Emma, 346, 372
Woytinsky, Vladimir, 346, 372
Wright, Carrol, 97
Wright, Nathan, Jr., 334
Wright, Quincy, 396, 401

Yancy, William, 5, 18
Yankelovich, Daniel, 144-145, 152, 160
Yetman, Norman, 266
Yinger, J. Milton, 58, 97, 140, 160, 469, 487

Zorbaugh, Harvey, 24, 25, 56, 408, 437
Zurcher, Louis, 281, 294

SUBJECT INDEX

Abolitionists, 236
Abortion, views on, 349, 360, 362, 368
Accommodation
    defined, 219, 233, 257
    and intergroup conflict patterns, 234–238
    in minority relations, 257–261, 464
    to problems of adolescence, 154–155
    to problems of the elderly, 219–220
Acculturation. *See* Assimilation; Pluralism
Adolescence, 131–155
    accommodation toward, 154–155
    adult attitudes toward, 139–144
    and apprenticeship era, 135
    and collective behavior, 149–154
    college vs. noncollege, 144–145
    and deviant behavior, 148–150
    and disaster situations, 280–281
    as a problem period, 133–134
    as a status position, 131, 136, 147, 256
    as a subculture, 140–143
    as a transitional stage, 140–141
Adult Performance Levels, (APL), 75
Affluence, and influence, 317–318
Audubon Society, 359
Affirmative action, and discrimination, 260–261
Age
    composition of U.S. population, 355, 360
    and sex population pyramids, 354–355
Ageism, and the elderly, 212
Age of Reason, 351

Aging. *See* Social gerontology
Agricultural Adjustment Administration (AAA), 196
Agriculture
   and cultural evolution, 341-342
   and megalopolis concentrations, 325, 338-339
   and technical innovation, 299, 301, 363
Aid to Dependent Children (ADC), 320
Alienation
   in American society, 47, 425, 443-445, 483
   and lack of political power, 322
American Association of Retired Persons, 431
American Association of University Women, 254
American Automobile Association, 430-431
American Civil Liberties Union, 243, 420
An American Dilemma (Myrdal)
   and prejudice-discrimination paradigm, 243-244
   thesis, 240, 415-416
American Farm Bureau Federation, 430-431
American Federation of Labor-Congress of Industrial Organization (AFL-CIO), 52, 88, 176, 246, 430
   early policy toward blacks, 240
   early policy toward women, 240
   and ethnic upward mobility, 237-238
American Indian Movement (AIM), 259
American Jewish Committee, 246, 420
American Red Cross, 51-52, 277, 283-284
American society
   creed and dilemma of, 240, 246, 416, 419-420
   demographic transition of, 354
   value orientations, 20-21, 72, 323, 464, 472, 477, 479-480
   and vigilante tradition, 421
American Sociological Association, 253-254
Analytic paradigm, 502
Anomie, 414, 442
   in cities, 25, 310, 408
   defined, 206
   and disasters, 283

and the elderly, 206, 209, 217-218
   in literature, 445
   and suicide, 24-25, 122, 206
Anthropology, as related discipline, 12
Anti-Defamation League of B'nai B'rith, 246
Anxiety, and modern society, 47
Apartheid, in South Africa, 232
Apathy, to disaster warnings, 289-290
Applied research, 5, 14, 407
   see also Basic research
Arabs
   and oil cartel, 396, 442, 476-477
   and the Palestinian cause, 279
Arapesh, cooperative temperament of, 37
Army and Air Force, in disasters, 284
Art
   and cities, 298, 304, 306
   and science, 405
Ascription-achievement
   and class, 174
   and minority status, 230
Assimilation, 230, 314
Assassinations, 442
Associations
   and disasters, 283-284
   and goal attainment, 43-44
   with limited purpose, 51
   membership in, U.S. 51-52, 431
   as organized interest groups, 83
   in urban communities, 299
   voluntary, 268, 283, 299, 303
Attitude-behavior correlations, 501-502
Authority
   breakdown in disasters, 272
   centralized and decentralized, 385-386, 397
   charismatic type, 81, 386
   delegitimation during limited warfare, 394
   and obedience, 452-453
   rational-legal type, 81, 386
   in small groups, 453
   traditional type, 81, 386
   in war decisions, 386-388

Automation
    defined, 175
    and disaster warning, 286–287
    effects on class system, 175–178

Bakke case, 261
Basic research, 4, 407
    See also Applied research
Beat generation, 392
Biological inheritance, 22
    and cloning (eugenic control), 407, 446–448
    and the elderly, 209–211
    and social Darwinism thesis, 87, 413, 490, 491
    and sociobiology, 493
Birth control
    feminist perspective on, 367–368
    public opinion on, 361
    and race, 358
    and religion, 357–358
Birth cycle interval, 134
Birth rate
    in American society, 61, 348
    crude (CBR), 348
    and income, 105
    and social norms, 348–350
    see also Fertility
Black Muslims, 259
Black Panther Party, 252, 259
Black power, 251–252, 416
Blacks
    compared with whites on income, 258
    and civil rights movement, 245–252
    identification with African societies, 239, 279
    and migration to cities, 12–13, 316
    and Moynihan (family) Report, 190–191
    percent of in ten largest cities, 259
    poverty among, 178–180, 183
    and power, 322
    self images, 259
    stereotypes of, 260, 469
    in U.S. population, 232

Blue-collar workers
    and the Lordstown Plant protest, 150
    and the mass assembly line, 85–86
B'nai B'rith, 431
    Anti-Defamation League, 246
Bourgeousie, in Marxist theory, 162
Brown decision, 15, 68, 245
Bureaucracy
    and democracy, 83
    in denominations, 71
    and mass education, 72–73, 75
    and modern society, 81, 397, 471–472
    and modification of, 471–472
    and Parkinson's Law, 382–384, 388
    re-assertion after disasters, 282

California Water Plan, 339
Caste
    racial, 40, 179–180
    in traditional India, 40–172
    See also Social class, Social stratification
Catholics
    and birth control, 357–358
    and cultural pluralism, 26
    economic status of, 69
    and overcategorization of, 241
    and parochial schools, 76
    and religious liberty, 236
    in U.S. population, 71
Census, United States, 109–111, 299, 337, 343, 363
    5 and 15 percent sample excerpt, 120
    questionnaire form excerpt, 110–111
    and racial classification, 260, 500
    rural and urban definitions of, 304
Center for the Study of Democratic Institutions, 385
Central Intelligence Agency (CIA), 385
Centralization vs. decentralization, 385–386, 468, 489
Charisma
    and authority, 81
    and leadership, 81, 250
    and social mobility, 174

Chicago School of urban sociology, 9-10, 491
Chicanos (Spanish, Hispanic or Mexican Americans), 22-23, 45, 47, 174, 230, 249, 259-260, 316, 322, 500
   and minority status, 230, 256-257
   and poverty, 179-180
   in U.S. population, 232
Children
   and color (race) consciousness, 119, 504
   as disaster victims, 279
   and family position, 61
   sex-role socialization, 34-37
China, 373, 379, 448, 474
Chinese
   in ethnic urban enclave, 25, 237
   hostility toward, 237
   stereotypes of, 469
   traditional family structure, 62-64
   in U.S. population, 232
Christianity
   and the American dilemma, 240
   and economic values, 68-69
   and the poor, 194
   see also particular denominations
Church, 69
   See also Denomination
Church-state separation, 71
Cities
   anomie in, 25, 310, 408
   and civil disorders, 184
   and cosmopolitanism, 410
   daytime and residential populations, 326
   defined, 302
   images of, 304-311
   Model, 184
   and the modern urban condition, 297-298
   and suburbs, 298-299, 407
   and urban planning, 324-328
   and urban renewal, 324

Civil Defense, 288
Civil disorders
   as collective protest, 250
   and counterrioters, 321
   and disaster research, 276-277
   perceived causes of, 321
   racial, 229, 250-251, 419-420, 464, 476
   and the urban poor, 184
Civil liberties, 448
Civilian Conservation Corps (CCC), 196
Civil Rights Act of 1964, 246, 319, 473
Civil Rights Movement. *See* Social movements
Class. *See* Social class
Clean Air Act of 1970, 473
Collective bargaining, 237-238, 409, 426, 473
Collective behavior, 44, 230
   in crowds, 149-150, 246
   defined, 230
   and deviance, 149-150
   and directed change, 430
   in disasters, 267, 281-282
   and social movements, 150-154, 230, 246
   See also Public opinion; Publics; Social movements
Collective morale, in disasters, 273
Colleges
   in hierarchy of American education, 77
   and job prospects, 194
   and student attitudes, 241, 469
Commission on Population Growth and the American Future, 356, 359-362
Common Cause, 430, 472
Common sense and nonsense, 7-8
Communes, 143, 306
Communism
   Marxist concept of, 162
   reaction against, 237
Community
   cohesion, 281
   defined, 50
   disorganization, 268, 272
   in ecological analysis, 311
   organization, in disasters, 267, 272-290
   power, 317-319

Competition
    as an ecological process, 311, 314
    as an economic process, 87–88
Compromise of 1877, 244, 249
Comstock Laws, on obscenity, 356–357, 422
Concentric zone theory of urban organization, 312–314
Concepts, in research, 495
Conflict
    defined, 233
    and democracy, 481
    and intergroup accommodation patterns, 232–238
    international, 373, 396
    nonviolent, 246
    resolution, 396–397
    and social meaning, 443
    violent, 250–251
Conflict theory
    compared to functional and process theory, 481, 492–493
    and Marxian class analysis, 162, 492
    and social instability, 44, 481
Congress, U.S., on housing, 323
Congress of Racial Equality (CORE), 246, 250
Consensus model, 492
    See also Functional theory
Consumer Price Index (CPI), 178
Cooperation
    and conflict resolution, 396
    as an ecological process, 311
Corporations
    and the industrial revolution, 87–88, 425
    and labor unions, 426, 473
    and the military, 380–386
    and social change, 483–484
    special treatment of, 192
Correlations, interpretation of, 501–504

Counterculture. *See* Subculture
Cox Commission, on student protest, 152
Crime, 148
    in deteriorated city sections, 312, 320
    and punishment, 80
    and Uniform Crime Report index, 500–501
    victimless, 80, 154, 417–418
Crowds
    and circular reaction, 453
    and civil disorders, 250–251
    and collective behavior, 149–150, 230, 246
    lonely, 443–444
    publics and, 149–150
Crude rate of natural increase (CRNI), 351
Cuban missile crisis, 380
Cults, 69
    See also Sects
Cultural diffusion, 410–411
Cultural evolution, 341–342
Cultural lag thesis, 341, 349–350, 414
    and medical lag, 351
    and population control, 366
    and schools, 76
Cultural pluralism. *See* Pluralism
Cultural relativism, 31, 409, 416
Culture, 19–31
    American, 20–21
    and biological inheritance, 22
    concept of, 19–20
    defined, 20
    diversity, 22–25
    norms, 20
    and personality, 34
    and physical setting, 22
    of poverty, 188–191
    types of, 46
    values, 20
Customs, 27, 81, 209, 312
Cybernation, 175–178
    defined, 176
    effects on class system, 86, 175–178, 184, 186, 188, 191, 193
    and social change, 353, 374, 432, 472

Data
   defined, 105
   cautions on interpretation of, 499-504
   qualitative and quantitative, 504
Death rate
   crude (CDR), 350-351
   effects of, 351
Declaration of Independence, 246
De Funis decision, 261
Dehumanization, and modern warfare, 386-391, 414
Delinquency
   and crime rate, 48, 312
   differential association and, 148-149
   and ethnic discrimination, 237
   and public concern, 221
Democracy
   and American Revolution, 234
   anticipatory, 479
   and bureaucracy, 81, 83
   as governmental system, 81-82
   and organized interest groups, 83
   and sociological research, 409
   and social stability, 82, 84, 326, 481
Demographic analysis (Demography), 337-369
   and class position, 166
   and controlling triad, 346
   defined, 337
   and demographic transition theory, 352-353
   and Malthusian thesis, 362-364
   and triage thesis, 365-366
   and policy proposals (global), 364-369
   see also Population
Demographic transition theory, 341, 347, 352-354, 364, 366
Demonstration Cities Act, 327-328
Denomination, 69-70
   See also Church, Ecclesia; Sects
Deterrence strategy, 378-380
Developmental tasks, 136

Deviance
   and adolescents, 148-150
   and collective behavior, 149-150
   defined, 147
   and functional theory, 149, 416-417
   and labeling theory, 416-418
   and minority relations, 244
   as normative, 149
   from norms, 407
Differential association, 148
Diffusion, 23
Disaster
   and anomie, 283
   class and race factors in, 278
   collective behavior in, 267, 281-282
   defined, 268-269
   general frequency of, by type, 269
   hypersensitivity to, 289-290
   and the military, 284
   sequential effects, 288-289
   stages of response to, 275-283
   and society, 267
   syndrome, 272-273
   utopian mood following, 281-283
   warning systems, 286-290
Discovery, 23
Discrimination
   and affirmative action, 260-261
   defined, 242
   toward the elderly, 211-215
   ethnic, 237
   toward minorities, 243-244
   and prejudice paradigm, 243
   see also Prejudice
Dissent, groupthink and, 454-455
Division of labor, 40, 58, 386
   in disasters, 267, 279-281, 284
   in modern economy, 87, 303, 312
Divorce
   rate, 66, 442
   as variance in family cycle, 132

Dysfunctions, 3, 5-6, 57-58, 447
    of established welfare system, 190
    of hypersensitivity in disasters, 89-290
    of status inconsistency, 194
    see also Functions

Earth Day demonstrations, 359
Ecclesia, 71
    See also Denomination; Religion
Ecological city, 304, 314
Ecology. See Human ecology
Economic Opportunity Act (EOA), 196-197, 247
Economics, as related discipline, 12
Economy, 84-91
    and barter system, 87
    and conspicuous consumption, 85
    current economic mix, 88
    and cybernetic effects, 175-178
    and economic determinism thesis, 87, 162, 490
    and the economically active, 177
    and depression effects, 13
    functions of, 59, 85-86
    and global interdependence, 196
    and laissez faire system, 87
    and mercantilism, 87
    and monopolies, 87-88
    politics of, 88-90
    and population growth, 362
    social change and, 90-91, 442
    and structural exclusion of the poor, 190
    structural forms of, 86-90
    and unequal employment opportunity, 247
Education, 72-79
    as a class factor, 162, 168-170
    and Coleman Report, 78, 195, 248
    and credentials-oriented society, 195
    and functional incompetence, U.S., 75
    financial support of, 74
    functions of, 59, 73-75
    historical impetus toward mass public education, 72-73
    latent consequences, 6, 74-75
    and poverty programs, 195-196
    social change and, 76-79
    structural forms of, 75-77
Elderly, 206
    and ageism, 212
    and anomie, 206, 209, 217-218
    in disasters, 281
    prejudice against, 211-215
Elementary and Secondary Education Act (ESEA), 195-197, 247
Elites
    and community power, 318-320
    and national power, 381-382
Emigration, 346
Eminent domain, right of, 324
Emotional disorders, among elderly, 206, 214
Empiricism, 9, 99
Employment
    of males and females, 183
    of minority groups and Anglos, 181
    See also Unemployment
Endogamy, 149
Enlightenment, The, 490
Environment
    and American value orientations, 458, 472
    and energy resources, 310, 457, 477
    and population growth, 338, 359
Environmental Protection Agency (EPA), 359
Epidemics
    on the frontier, 308
    and medical cultural lag, 351
Episcopalians, 31, 234, 236
Equal Rights Amendment (ERA), 253, 255, 259
Ethnic groups
    conflict and accommodation patterns, 236-238
    general characteristics of, 27
    and the near poor, 180-182
    and restrictive immigration acts, 28, 175, 237
    and social distance, 30

Ethnocentrism, 27-31
Ethnomethodology. *See* Labeling theory
Experimental research. *See* Research method
Exponential growth, 481-482

Family, 60-67
   adjustment strains in modern society, 61, 131
   and class placement, 172, 174
   contrasts in functions, 62-64
   cycle, 132-133
   decline thesis, 442
   extended, 61
   functions of, 59-64
   in *gemeinschaft* and in *gesellschaft* settings, 299
   life cycle, 132-134
   natural system, 209
   nuclear, 60-61
   and paterfamilias values, 252
   social change and, 66-67, 478-479
   structural forms of, 65
   variation in American society, 65
   See also Divorce; Marriage; Sex
Famine, 364-365, 368
Fecundity, 348
Federal Bureau of Investigation (FBI)
   and Uniform Crime Report index, 500-501
   and Watergate break-in, 385
Federal Housing Administration (FHA), 196, 219, 244, 247
Females. *See* Women
Fertility, 346
   trends, 348-351
   U.S. compared with Indonesia, 348
Firemen, in disaster situations, 276, 283
Folkways, 27, 495
France
   and demographic transition, 352
   and the Maginot Line, 454
   as nuclear power, 375

Freedom
   and American values, 47
   constitutional guarantees of, 71, 83, 236, 238-239
   and environment, 359, 458
   in rural and urban areas, 306
Freedom House, 250
Frontier
   myth and reality of, 308-310, 472
   nostalgia for, 306
   and open class system, 175-176
Functional theory
   compared to conflict and process theory, 481, 492-493
   criticism of, 58
   and deviance, 149, 416-417
   and division of labor, 47
   and functional imperatives, 44
   and institutional analysis, 57-58, 413
   and interdependence, 48-49
   manifest and latency concepts of, 5-6
Functions
   and alternative life styles, 143
   of culture of poverty, 191
   defined, 49, 57
   economic, 59, 85-86
   educational, 73-75
   familial, 59-64
   governmental, 59, 80
   latent, 5-6, 374, 380-381, 407, 447, 483
   manifest, 5-6, 407, 483
   religious, 59, 67-69
   See also Functional theory

Gangs
   and differential association, 148
   and group goals, 149
Gemeinschaft, 45-47
   contrasted to *gesellschaft*, 46, 299
   and education, 195
   values, 46, 51, 281, 306
   See also Gesellschaft

General Motors, 51
Genocide, 358
Geography, and ecology, 311
Gerontology. *See* Social gerontology
Gesellschaft, 45-47
   contrasted to *gemeinschaft*, 46, 299
   and education, 195
   values, 46, 51, 306
   See also gemeinschaft
Ghettos, 250, 277, 312-314, 320-323, 326
Goals
   and deviant means to achieve, 416-417
   in disaster situations, 277
   and organized groups, 458-459
Government, 80-84
   authority, 81, 386
   bureaucracy and democracy, 83
   democratic and totalitarian prototypes, 81-82
   functions of, 59, 80
   and military-industrial complex, 380-386
   multipartite, 82
   municipal and state, in disasters, 284, 289
   pluralist, 82
   social change and, 83-84
   structural forms of, 80-83
   See also Laws
Gray Panthers, 212, 220
Great Britain
   and intergenerational occupational changes, 172
   as nuclear power, 375
Great Society programs, 393
Greco-Roman culture, 351
Greeks, 12
Groups, 44-52
   formal, 51
   with a purpose, 51-52
   and pressures to conform, 453
   primary, 46
   secondary, 46
   territorially based (friendship), 50-51
   types, 45, 227
   See also Associations; Primary groups;
     Secondary groups
Groupthink, 453-455

"Hawthorne effect," in research design, 498, 501
Health, Education and Welfare (HEW),
   Department of, 193, 219
Hippie contraculture, 141-143, 306, 392, 448
Hiroshima, atomic bombing of, 375
Historical intergroup conflict, 232-240
History, as related discipline, 12
Homosexuality, 256, 417, 427
Housing, 323
Housing Act, 323
Human ecology, 297-330, 491
   and biological concepts, 311
   defined, 50, 311-312
   urban theories of, 311-316
Human Relations Area File, 58, 60, 65
Humanism, 414, 425
Ideal types
   of cultures, 46
   defined, 45
   of groups, 46
   and open or closed societies, 175
   and patterns of intergroup change, 234
Immigration
   automation effects on, 175
   and ethnic pluralism, 25
   illegal, 238, 348
   and population growth, 346, 354
   and U.S. restriction of, 28, 175, 237-238, 347-348
Index of aging, 207
Index of Status Characteristics (ISC), 166, 183
India
   and famine in, 351
   and former caste system, 40, 172
Indians. *See* Native American Indians
Individual vs. social interests, 310
Individuality, and pressures to conform, 349-451
Indonesia, population rates, 348, 351
Industrial Revolution, 87

Industrialization
    and cultural evolution, 341-342
    decentralization of, 303
    economic consequences of, 299, 301
    and pollution, 309
    and specialized technology, 301
Influentials
    and functional method of study, 318
    local and cosmopolitan, 317
    and positional method of study, 318
    and reputational method of study, 317-318
    See also Power elite thesis
In-groups, 28, 192, 213, 273, 391
    See also Out-groups
Inner-directedness, 443
    See also Other-directedness
Innovation, 23
Institutions (and institutionalization), 57-91
    and cultural imperative for effectiveness, 269
    defined, 44
Intential communities, 470-471
Interfaith Emergency Center, in Detroit riots, 277, 280
Intergroup relations. *See* Minorities
"Invasion from Mars" broadcast, 290
Inventions
    material, 363
    social, 425
Irish, 236-238, 249-250, 279, 347, 366
Isolationism, 468, 479
Israel
    immigration to, 346
    and kibbutz system, 61-64
Italians, 12, 236-238, 249, 260, 469

Japanese, 28
    in internment camps during World War II, 390
    stereotypes of, 469
    in U.S. population, 232
Jews, 12, 231
    and Bar Mitzvah rite, 135
    and cultural pluralism, 31
    discrimination toward in social clubs, 68
    economic status of, 69
    and ghetto experience, 312-314
    and Israeli security, 279
    and Nazi holocaust, 389, 414
    and religious liberty, 236
    stereotypes of, 237, 260
    in U.S. population, 71
John Birch Society, 455-456
Judeo-Christian ethic, 195

Kent State killings, 389
Kibbutz, Israeli, 61-64
Kinship, 60-61
    in American society, 65
    in Chinese tradition, 62-64
Ku Klux Klan, 237, 244, 415, 421, 456

la raza movement, 259
Labeling theory, 147-148, 406
    and deviance, 416-418
Labor force
    black-white, 181, 258
    male-female, 181, 183
    and production line work, 85-86
Labor unions
    American Federation of Labor (AFL), 52, 88
    as interest groups, 83
    and management, 83, 422, 425-426, 429, 473
    membership in, 178
    and National Labor Relations Act, 88
    United Auto Workers (UAW), 51
    and upward mobility, 176
Language
    role in socialization, 31-32
    in symbolic interactionist theory, 493
Latent consequences. *See* Functions
Law
    and civil rights legislation, 246
    deviant behavior and, 416-417
    international law and American ideals, 390-391
    and normative boundaries, 80
    and paternalistic values, 252
    See also Government *and* Supreme Court

Leadership
　　charismatic, 81, 386
　　community types of, 316–318
　　in times of stress, 476
Legitimacy
　　and dehumanizing processes, 389
　　and tradition, 27
Leisure, and alternative stratification, 163–166
Life cycle
　　adolescents in the, 132–134
　　defined, 132
　　and the elderly, 207
　　and families, 132–134
　　and social class effects on, 161
Literary Digest sample, 116
Looking glass self, 33
　　See also Significant others; Socialization
London plague of 1665, 351
Looting, in disasters, 272–273, 275, 320–321

Macho syndrome, 34, 349
Macrodecisions, and social policy, 473, 483–484
Males
　　and affirmative action issue, 260–261
　　in course text material, 254
　　income distribution of, 258
　　occupational pattern, 183, 254
Management
　　and labor, 83, 422, 425–426, 429
　　and occupational status, 166–167
　　and office status, 444
Manifest functions. See Functions
Marriage
　　in American society, 31, 65–66
　　classification of, 65
　　and family cycle, 132
　　open, 65
　　and romantic love ideal, 66
Marshall Plan, 378

Mass media
　　and charismatic leadership, 81
　　and disaster coverage, 273–275, 287, 420
　　as educational tool, 79
　　and effects on cultural isolation, 139, 409
　　and political behavior, 497
　　as source of research data, 122–124
　　as a source of social information, 101–102
　　and urbanism, 303
Mass society
　　and conformity, 453
　　and mass movements, 303
　　and totalitarianism, 448
Mate-selection, 64
McCarthyism, 392
Medical care
　　and cultural lag, 351
　　and the elderly, 220
　　and disasters, 275
　　on the frontier, 308
　　and high status of physicians noted, 169
　　and low-income family expenses, 182
　　and Population Commission report, 360
　　in warfare, 365
Medicare, 220
Medieval period, and science, 351
Megalopolis, 324–325
Memberships, and class, 170
Method. See Research method
Methodist Church's Board of Christian Concerns, 420
Metropolitan urban areas, 298
Mexico, population growth in, 363
Mexican Americans. See Chicanos
Microdecisions, and social policy, 473, 483–484
Migration, 346
　　and declining available space, 347–348
　　and the industrial revolution, 175, 347, 349
Military
　　balance of terror, 375–378
　　and black-white relations in, 393, 498–499
　　draft, 374
　　and industrial complex, 84, 380–381, 407, 412

Minorities, 229-266
   and affirmative action, 260-261
   characteristics of, 231
   defined, 211, 231
   discrimination toward, 243-244
   and employment patterns, 181, 258
   and low-income levels, 247, 258
   and name symbolism, 245-256
   and social movements, 245-256
   social status of, 230, 232, 238
   See also Race; Segregation
Mobility. See Social mobility
Model Cities Plan, 184, 326-328, 432
Modes of individual adaptation (Merton's typology), 417
Monogamy, 31, 65
Mores, 20, 26-27, 209, 362
Mormons, 22-23, 65, 71, 236
Mortality, 346
   trends, 347, 350-353
   U.S. compared with Indonesia, 351
Multiple nuclei theory of urban organization, 315
Music, and cities, 298
My Lai massacre, 390, 414

National Association for the Advancement of Colored People (NAACP), 51, 243, 245, 248, 250, 259, 329, 358, 430-431, 482
National Advisory Commission on Civil Disorders, 15-16, 418-420
National Catholic Conference for Interracial Justice, 420
National Commission on the Causes and Prevention of Violence, 418, 421-422
National Commission on Obscenity and Pornography, 15, 418, 422-424
National Conference of Commissions on the Status of Women, 252-253
National Council of Churches, 246
National Education Association (NEA), 52, 431
National Grange, 52, 431

National Guard, 284
National Labor Relations Act (NLRA), 188, 237-238, 426
National Labor Relations Board (NLRB), 196, 237
National Organization of Women (NOW), 253
National Rifle Association, 430-431
National Severe Storms Forecast Center, 286
National Weather Service, 286
National Women's Political Caucas, 367
Nationalism, and utopian moods, 282
Native American Indians, 22-23, 29, 45, 47, 229-230, 236, 256-257, 259, 322, 389
   in U.S. constitution, 238
   and expanding frontier, 176, 347, 422
   and poverty, 179-180
   in U.S. population, 232
Natural area concept, 314
Navajos, 22-23, 210
Nazi Germany, 82, 281, 389-390, 409, 414, 449-450, 454
Negative income tax proposal, 192
Negroes. See Blacks
New Deal programs, 323
New Frontier programs, 298
New York as every city, 322
Non-violent direct action, by blacks, 246
Norms
   conflicting, 25, 80
   and deviance, 147
   in disaster situations, 277
   industrializing effects on, 363
   and inevitable family situations, 133
   legal enforcement of, 80
   and schools, 73
North Atlantic Treaty Organization (NATO), 374, 379, 387, 468
Nuclear family, 60-61
Nursing homes, 220-222

Obscenity, 356-357, 422
Occupational status
   and prestige ratings, 169-170
   in Warner's classification, 167-168

Occupations
   and class status, 167
   differences by race and sex, 181, 183
   and effects of cybernation, 175–178
   and generational differences, 133–134
Older Americans Act, 219
Organization. *See* Social organization
Other-directedness, 443–444, 453
   See also Inner-directedness
Out-groups, 28, 68, 192, 273, 391
   minorities as, 213–214
   in small towns, 309
   See also In-groups

Panic, in disasters, 275, 290
Parkinson's Law of bureaucracy, 382–384
Participant observation, 276
   See also Research method
Pearl Harbor, attack on, 289–290
Peer groups
   and adolescents, 135
   influence on self-perceptions, 33
Planned Parenthood Federation, 362
Plessy decision, 244–245
Pluralism
   in American society, 31
   cultural, 26, 31
   ethnic, 13, 31
   religious, 236
Poles, 238, 309
Police
   and crime, 500–501
   in disaster situations, 276, 283–284
   and low-income blacks and whites, 182, 476
Political behavior
   and political machines, 5–6
   and white backlash, 260
   See also Power; Public opinion

Policy making. *See* Social policy
Political parties, 472
Political power. *See* Power
Pollution
   and population growth, 359
   and urbanization, 309–310, 337–339
Polygamy, 31, 65, 236, 470
Polygyny, 31
Poor People's March on Washington, 197
Population, 337–369
   and the American future, 353–356
   composition, 343–344
   distribution, 343
   explosion, global, 339–344
   and longevity, U.S., 205
   and Malthusian theory of, 339–341
   pressures to control, 358–359, 364–369
   projections, 339–340, 343, 356, 364–365, 478
   pyramids, 354–355
   U.S., by age and sex, 355
   world, 344
   See also Birth rate; Death rate; Fertility; Migration; Mortality
Positivism and Comte, 8–9
Post-industrial society, 89, 432–433
Potlatch celebration, 84
Poverty
   among blacks, 178–180, 183
   criteria used to measure, 183–184
   culture of, 166, 188
   cycle of, 190–191
   and effects of cybernation, 178, 472
   as a global issue, 353
   insular, 86
   and low income whites, 180–182
   and powerlessness, 196–197
   proposals to end, 187–197
   war on, 184
   and welfare recipient characteristics, 193

Power
    and authority, 81
    and centralized authority, 84, 89, 384–386
    in communities, 316–322, 328–329
    and decentralized authority, 385–386
    and democracy, 82, 373
    and deviancy, 416–418
    military, 373–382
    and pluralism, 84
    political, 162–163, 237, 258–259, 318–319, 322
    and public opinion, 83
    and social class, 162–163
    in totalitarian systems, 82
    and urban renewal, 329–330
Power elite thesis, 84, 382
    applied to communities, 318–320
    applied to national power, 381–382
Powerlessness
    in modern society, 439
    among poor, 186, 196–197, 220, 321
Pragmatist school, 73
Prejudice
    toward adolescents, 139–144
    defined, 242
    and discrimination, 243–244
    toward the elderly, 211–215
    toward minorities, 243–244
    See also Discrimination
Presidential study commissions, 418
    on civil disorders, 15–16, 419–420
    on obscenity and pornography, 15, 422–424
    and social policy, 14–16
    on violence, 421–422
Primary groups, 45–46
    See also Secondary groups
Privacy, and role release, 429
Process theory, compared to conflict and functional theory, 492–493
    See also Symbolic interactionism
Professions
    and class status, 167–169
    earnings in, 258
Prohibition, failure, of, 154, 417

Proletariat
    in American society, 171
    in Marxist theory, 162
Protest movements. *See* Social movements
Protestants
    as homesteaders, 22–23
    and religious liberty, 234
    in U.S. population, 71
    and work ethic, 68–69, 186, 218
    See also Christianity; specific denominations
Psychology, as related discipline, 12
Public opinion
    on birth control, 361
    on cities and small towns, 308–309
    and collective behavior, 230, 472–473
    about the elderly, 217
    and groupthink, 455–456
    polling for, 116–121
    and power of state, 83
    in warfare, 394–395
    See also Collective behavior
Publics
    and collective behavior, 230, 246, 472–473
    and the law, 133
    organized, 430–431
    and social issues, 426, 473, 476–477
    See also Collective behavior; Public opinion
Puerto Ricans, 179, 249, 257, 259
Puerto Rican Independence Movement, 259
Puritans, 31, 236

Quakers, 31, 236, 281, 351

Race
    and the American dilemma, 240–245
    and caste criteria, 40
    and changing attitudes about, 30
    and minority status, 230
    and property values, 244
    and U.S. constitution, 28–29, 238
Race riots. *See* Civil disorders

Racial Distance Quotient (RDQ). *See* Social Distance Quotient (SDQ)
Racism
   on the decline, 468
   and discrimination, 212, 420
   institutional, 245
Randomization, in research, 116–117, 498
Reconstruction Finance Corporation (RFC), 196
Reference groups
   in disasters, 278–279
   and relative deprivation, 185
   and significant others, 33
Reflexive sociology, 411–412
Reform movements. *See* Social movements
Relative deprivation
   defined, 185
   in disasters, 279
   among the elderly, 217
   nonmaterial, 185–186
   and poverty, 184–187
   in the urban setting, 184–185
Religion, 67–72
   and church-state separation, 71, 83, 236
   cohesive and divisive tendencies, 67–68
   changing influence of, 72, 143–145
   and economic values, 68–69
   and fertility norms, 348–349, 356–358
   functions of, 62–63, 67–69
   and intergroup conflict, 72, 234–236, 277
   lowered religious service attendance, 72
   social change and, 72
   structural forms of, 69–71
   U.S. composition, 71
Report from Iron Mountain, warfare satire, 384–385, 395
Research and Development Corporation (RAND), 101, 377–378
Research method
   and analytic research, 105
   and cautions on data interpretation, 101–104
   and content analysis, 122–124
   and descriptive research, 105
   empirical emphasis, 9, 99–100, 494
   experimental design, 105–107, 495–499
   hypotheses, 105–107, 495, 497–499
   interviews, 108–109, 504
   and method of difference, 497
   and multivariate analysis, 491, 497
   observations, structured and unstructured, 107–108
   and operational definitions, 495
   and questionnaires, 108
   and reading tables, 124–125
   reliability, 116, 500–501
   sampling, 116–121
   scaling techniques, 112–116
   scientific, 494–499
   and survey research, 121, 491
   validity, 116
   variables, dependent and independent, 350, 496–499, 502
Restrictive covenants, in housing, 244
Retirement communities, 217
Revolution
   American, 72, 81, 234, 306, 422, 464, 477
   Cuban, 347–348
   cybernetic, 176, 184, 188, 452
   French, 81, 281
   industrial and post-industrial, 432
   Lin Piao view of, 306
   Russian, 81
   technological (industrial), 342, 347, 363
   the triple, 374
Revolution of rising expectations, 345, 475
Riots
   commodity type, 320–321
   damage in urban race riots, 250–251
   of whites in black communities, 244
   See also Civil disorders
Rites of passage, 63, 135–136
Role, 40–43
   conflict in disasters, 273, 276
   emergent in disasters, 277

Role (cont.)
  exit, and elderly, 212, 215-216
  as an interaction concept, 40
  playing, 40
  set, 43
  and sex-role socialization, 34-37
  strain, 42-43, 139, 207
  See also Status
"Roots," slavery dramatization, 239
Royal Commission on Environmental Pollution, 457
Rural community idealization, 306-309
Rural-urban migration, 12-13
Rural and urban population, U.S., 13

Salem witch trials, 415
Salvation Army, 284
Sampling, 116-121
  nonprobability, 117
  probability, 117-121
  in U.S. census, 119-120
  See also Research method
Sanctions, 41, 66, 80
Scales, 112-116
  Guttman, 115
  interval, 113
  Likert, 113
  nominal, 112
  ordinal, 112
  ratio, 113
  social distance, 29, 115
  Thurstone, 114-115
Schools
  and Coleman Report, 78, 195
  organized pressures on, 76
  and poor children, 195
  public and private, 75-76
  sources of support, 74
  and suburban values, 118-119
  See also Education
Science, 405
Scientific method. See Research method

Scranton Report, on Kent and Jackson State shootings, 154
Secondary groups, 45-46
  See also Primary groups
Sector theory of urban organization, 314-315
Sects, 69
  See also Cults
Segregation
  de facto, 245, 249
  defined, 230, 244
  de jure, 244-245
  and ghettos, 313-314, 328-329
  and minorities, 244-245
  in social area analysis, 316
Self-fulfilling prophecy, in classroom, 33
  See also Thomas Theorem
Self-help doctrines, and the poor, 188
Self identity, 138
Seneca Falls Convention, on women's rights, 252
Serendipity, in research, 498, 501
Sesame Street, 79
Sex
  and changing sexual ethic, 61-62
  and the elderly, 214
  and exclusive ideal, 65
  in open marriage, 65
  role socialization, 34-37
Sexual attitudes, 123-124, 361
Sicilians, 26-27
Sierra Club, 359, 473
Significant others, 33, 185, 211, 502
  See also Looking glass self; Reference groups; Socialization
Slavery, 234, 238, 240, 252, 347, 389
Slum
  clearance, 323-324, 329-330
  as an ecological zone, 312
Social area analysis, 315-316
Social bonds, and social class, 170-171

Social boundaries, change in, 154
Social change
   adjusting to, 426–429
   and the economy, 90–91
   and education, 76–79
   and the family, 66–67, 478
   and government, 83–84
   collective behavior and, 150–154, 245–252
   and fears for the future, 439–459
   and hopes for the future, 463–484
   and religion, 72
Social class
   changing structure of, 166–168
   closed system of, 172–175
   and cybernetic effects, 176–178
   defined, 161, 170–171
   and disaster situations, 278–279
   Marxist model of, 162
   multiple criteria for, 162–163, 168–171
   objective criteria for, 168
   and occupational status, 167, 169–170
   open system of, 172–175, 178–180
   and the racial factor, 178–180
   and social opportunity, 161
   subjective criteria for, 168
   See also Social stratification
Social cohesion
   in cold and hot wars, 391–395
   and collective beliefs, 67
   in disasters, 281–283
Social Darwinism theory, 87, 490–491
Social disorganization theory, 414
Social distance, 29–31
   decline in, 30, 242, 260, 469
   quotient (SDQ), 29
Social dynamics, 99
Social equilibrium, 80
Social experimentation, 458

Social gerontology, 206–211
   and activity theory, 216
   defined, 207
   and disengagement theory, 215–216
   and female and male elderly, 214, 217–218
   and index of aging, 207
   and minority status of elderly, 211–218, 256
   and the physiological factor, 209–211
   and roleless image of elderly, 211
   and sexuality, 214
   and work stability of elderly, 214
Social institutions. *See* Institutions
Social mobility, 171–175
   among ethnic groups, 180–182
   defined, 166
   factors influencing, 173
   and hierarchical class structure, 173–174
   horizontal, 170–171, 174
   individual or group, 174
   intergenerational, 172–173
   and occupational competency, 195
   upward and downward, 171–175
   vertical, 170–171, 174–175
   See also Social class
Social movements
   abolitionist, 149, 252
   and adolescents, 150–154
   anti-war, 149, 151, 394
   Berkeley Free Speech, 149
   and blacks, 245–252
   and civil rights, 151, 185, 392, 472
   defined, 246
   and the elderly, 212, 219
   environmental, 359
   feminist, 252–253
   and minorities, 245–256, 374, 443
   and students, 151–152
   and utopian moods, 282
   for welfare, 194
   and women, 152, 252–256
Social organization, 43–52
   and adaptation, 482–483

Social organization (cont.)
   and bureaucracy, 49–50
   community, 50–51
   defined, 44, 275
   and division of labor, 47
   and functional interdependence, 48–49
   group structure of society, 44–45
   types of, 44–47
Social pathology theory, 413–414, 463
Social policy
   and American society, 429–433, 483–484
   private and public, 14–15
   and sociology, 14–16, 100
Social problems
   criteria for, 152
   and sociology, 4–5
   theories, 414–418
Social role. *See* Role
Social Security Act, 219, 409
Social statics, 99
Social status. *See* Status
Social stratification
   among autocrossers, 163–164
   and caste, 40
   and Warner's classification system, 166–167
   See also Social class; Status
Social structure
   and consequences of conflict, 233
   institutions as, 58
Socialization, 31–43
   and cultural personality, 34
   and cultural values, 37, 489
   defined, 31
   and development of the social self, 32–33
   and distortion of social reality, 418
   and educational functions, 59, 73
   and family functions, 61–62, 132
   and language role, 31–33
   and looking glass self, 33
   and nonverbal communication, 32
   in poor urban areas, 186–187
   and role sets, 43
   and role strain, 42–43
   sex-role, 34–37, 236
   and significant others, 33
   and social mobility, 175
   and social policy options, 14, 481
   and status conflict, 42–43
   and status sets, 43
Society, defined, 19
Society for the Suppression of Vice, 356
Sociobiology, 493
Sociological analysis. *See* Research method *and* Sociological inquiry
Sociological inquiry
   and social problems issues, 4–5
   and the sociological imagination, 405
   and the scientific orientation, 8–9
   and theorizing, 413–418, 492–493
   See also Research method
Sociology
   of the absurd, 443–445
   employment opportunities in, 11–12
   as a form of consciousness, 407–410
   and government, 15–16
   humanistic strain in, 405
   and major theoretical orientations, 492–493
   nature of, 8–11
   and objective analysis, 16
   and other research disciplines, 8, 12
   and social policy, 14–16, 474–475
   and the sociological imagination, 405–433
   and study of the future, 473–475
   specialization in, 10
   See also Research method; Sociological inquiry
Southern Christian Leadership Conference (SCLC), 245–246, 250
Soviet Union, 82, 373–375, 389, 396, 409, 414, 448, 474
Spanish Americans. *See* Chicanos
Specialization
   as an economic process, 87
   in modern society, 48, 299, 301
   in sociology, 10

Sports, and American values, 38
Standard Metropolitan Statistical Area (SMSA), 302, 304–305, 324
Standard and Poor's stock index, 496
Statue of Liberty, 362
Statistics
    available, 121–122
    types of measures, 118–121
    See also Research method
Status, 37–40
    achieved, 40–42, 174, 299, 317
    ascribed, 40–42, 174, 230, 299
    and authority positions, 81
    and class position, 162–163, 167–168
    conflict, 42–43
    defined, 37, 230
    and income, 85
    inconsistency, 194
    minority, 230, 232, 238
    in the office, 444
    set, 43
    See also Social class; Social stratification
Stereotypes
    of adolescents, 133
    of Americans, generally, 213
    of blacks, 242, 469
    of Chinese, 469
    of city life, 310
    cross cultural, 27
    decline in, 260, 468–469
    defined, 206, 212
    of the elderly, 212–214
    and groupthink, 454
    of Japanese, 469
    of Jews, 469
Strategic Arms Limitation Treaty (SALT), 380, 396
Stress management, 426
Structural-functionalism. See Functional theory
Student Non-Violent Coordinating Committee (SNCC), 151, 246, 250–251, 259, 421, 456
Students for a Democratic Society (SDS), 421, 455–456
Subcultures
    and adolescents, 140–143, 469
    and contraculture values, 470–471
    and pluralism, 24–27, 409
    defined, 31
    and ethnic groups, 24–27
    and poverty, 188
Suburbanism, as a way of life, 303
Suburbs
    and city ties, 258, 298–299, 322
    movement from cities to, 303, 316–317
Succession, as an ecological process, 314
Suicide
    altruistic, 121
    and anomie, 24–25, 122, 206
    egoistic, 121
    and social factors, 24, 121–122, 206
Supreme Court, U.S.
    on abortion, 362
    altered position on segregation, 245
    on miscegenation laws, 245
    on obscenity, 16, 422
    on restrictive covenants, 244
    See also specific decisions
Survey research. See Research method
Swedes, 25
Symbolic interactionism
    and early socialization, 32
    as a theoretical orientation, 492–493
    See also Process theory
Synergy, 49
Systems theory, and the cities, 431–432

Technology
    assembly-line, 85–86
    and automation, 175
    cybernetic, 175–178
    and the modern military, 374–375, 380
    and specialization, 299, 301
    and urbanization, 338–339
Technostructure, 384
Tension management theory, 430–431

SUBJECT INDEX

Terrorism, 457
Theater, and cities, 298
Theories, sociological,
 general, 492-493
 of social problems, 413-418
 and the study of social problems, 4, 406-407, 412-418
Theory of deviant means, 149, 406, 416
Titanic, sinking of and human disasters, 268
Thomas Theorem, on beliefs and consequences, 33, 244, 418
Totalitarianism
 control techniques, 448-451
 as government system, 81-82
 in Nazi Germany, 82
 in Soviet Russia, 82
Townsend Plan, 219
Trade unions, *See* Labor unions
Tradition
 toward cities, 304
 and human ecological analysis, 312
Tragedy of the Commons thesis, 309-310
Transportation, and urban living, 325, 338
Triple revolution, 374
Tunisia, and demographic transition, 352
Turks, images of, 468

Unemployment
 adolescent rate of, 146
 general rate of, 194
 and social movements, 150
Uniform Crime Reporting index (UCR), 500-501
Unions, *See* Labor unions
United Auto Workers (UAW), 51, 150-151, 246
United Nations, 468
United States, *See* American society
Untouchable caste, 40
Urban and rural population, U.S., 13
Urban Coalition, 329
Urban League, 245, 250, 329
Urban models, 311-316
Urban planning, 322-330

Urban renewal
 disruptive aspects, 182, 249, 323-324
 stabalizing aspects, 326-330
 See also Model Cities Plan
Urban Renewal Agency (URA), 323-324
Urbanism
 adjustment to, 310-311
 and ethnic pluralism, 24-25
 and relative deprivation, 184-185
 spread of, 302-303
 and voluntary associations, 299-303
 as a way of life, 301-302
 see also Suburbanism
Urbanization, 297-304
 and early medical care problems, 351
 and growth of cities of over one million, 356
 and industrialization push-pull complex, 299-301
 and nuclear warfare vulnerability, 376
 and recognition of poverty, 184
 social effects of, 358, 409
 spread of, 13, 297-304
 as used in social area analysis, 316
 as a worldwide trend, 306
Urbanized areas, 304
Utopianism
 and disaster aftermath, 281-283
 and social change, 456, 459, 474-475

Validity. *See* Research method
Value conflict theory, 414-416
Values
 American, 20-21
 college and noncollege, 144-145, 470-471
 contracultural, 141-145, 470-471
 diversity of, 31
 and inevitable situations, 133
 and labeling theory, 416-418
 and schools, 73
 universal, 31, 474

Variables. *See* Research method
Vested interests, 388, 403, 409, 484
Veteran's of Foreign Wars of the U.S., 431
Victims, social response to, 278-279
Vietnamese refugees, into U.S., 348
Violence
   against contracultural advocates, 143
   in poor urban areas, 186-187
   presidential commission on, 421-422
   and racial conflict, 250-251
Voters
   and political machines, 6
   and polling techniques, 116

Walker Report, on 1968 Democratic Convention, 154
War
   Civil, 247, 250, 374, 389-390, 422, 464
   Clausewitz on, 375
   games analysis, 376-378, 387-388
   in Korea, 373, 392-395
   limited, public reaction to, 394-395
   nuclear, 229, 269-270, 375-379, 390
   protest and, 143
   theories on, 396
   total, public reaction to, 394-395
   in Vietnam, 259, 373, 379-380, 389, 417, 479
   world, 269-270, 281, 289, 365, 373-374, 386, 391, 394-395
Watergate break-in, 385, 442, 448
Welfare state, 412
White House Conference on the Industrial World Ahead, 483
Whites
   and opposition to desegregated busing, 248-249
   and political backlash, 260
   and poverty, 179-182
Wolfenden Report, on homosexuality, 417

Women
   and aging, 210-211
   and biblical status, 252
   and minority status, 230-232
   and positions of influence, 253-254
   and sex-role socialization, 34-37
   and social stratification, 174, 182-183
   and social protest, 152, 252-256
Wonder Woman, 36-37
Woodstock rock festival, 281
Work
   on the assembly line, 85-86
   ethic, 68-69, 86, 192, 218
   and occupational status, 167
   and racial inequality, 183, 254
   and sexual inequality, 183, 254
   and specialization, 299, 301
World Food Conference, 364, 368
World Population Conference, 367-369
Worldwide Institute, 369

Yankee City study, 166

Zero Population Growth (ZPG), 349, 354, 359
Zuni Indians, 22-23, 45, 47